THE BOOK OF THE
AMERICAN WEST

THE BOOK OF THE

AMERICAN WEST

JAY MONAGHAN *Editor-In-Chief*

CLARENCE P. HORNUNG *Art Director*

Authors

RAMON F. ADAMS	B. A. BOTKIN
NATT N. DODGE	ROBERT EASTON
WAYNE GARD	OSCAR LEWIS
DALE MORGAN	DON RUSSELL

OSCAR OSBURN WINTHER

Simon and Schuster
New York

Illustration on title page and those on binding are pen and inks by
Ed Borein and are reproduced through the courtesy of the Edward
Borein Memorial, Santa Barbara, California. Photographs of sculpture on part title pages are reproduced by permission of Kennedy Galleries, New York.

CONTENTS

INTRODUCTION by Jay Monaghan

INTRODUCTION

When the last crusader returned from the East, hung up his helmet and stood his lance in the corner, men who craved opportunity and adventure knew the time had come to turn their eyes and ambitions elsewhere. There was a New World to be found and conquered, a mythical Atlantis, perhaps, out beyond the watery horizon or perhaps a dreamed-of island like the one called Utopia. But whatever and wherever this fabled new world, there was one certainty: it lay to the West.

For almost five centuries, the spell of the West was magic, its lure and riches something that dominated men's imaginations. What they found there and what they did there is a story as spectacular as any that has come out of the great ages of history.

Many who went West—and some who did not—have tried to capture that story in words. Books in Spanish, English, French and German described each new West as it was opened and often described it falsely (a practice that unfortunately persists to the present day). Explorers, travelers, gold seekers, even fur traders and adventurers committed themselves to paper and published what they saw—or liked to think they saw—in the West. And there was always a large and hungry public ready to devour each new account.

Some of these publications were what librarians classify as "Description and Travel," the most enduring of which were books such as Francis Parkman's *Oregon Trail,* Washington Irving's *Astoria* and Josiah Gregg's *Commerce of the Prairies.*

Unfortunately, for every account like these, there were dozens that distorted and misrepresented. Witness, for example, the sixteenth-century accounts of the fabulous jewel-studded Seven Cities of Cíbola and the fraudulent publications that preceded Lewis and Clark's meticulous account of their expedition.

But the worst bane of western literature has been the accumulation of exaggerated fiction written to attract attention rather than tell the truth. Early writers of pulp fiction never failed to assure their readers of the truth of their melodramatic extravaganzas. Late in the nineteenth century, a new breed of writers, like Alfred Henry Lewis and Emerson Hough, peopled their books with hugely personable and attractive ranchers and cowboys who differed from the artificial characters of melodrama and fixed a new image. This new image reached its ultimate with the publication of Owen Wister's *The Virginian* which set the pattern for the next half century.

The plethora of romanticism, however, was not without its opponents. A few writers tried to discredit the aura of glamor surrounding the Old West. They complained about the stark monotony of western life, the harshness of the weather, even the unpleasant smell of sagebrush, and said that pioneers were people unable to cope with the problems back home. These writers exaggerated as much in reverse as the gaudiest romantic ever did, but their efforts failed—perhaps because there was something about the Old West that every emigrant who followed the Oregon trail never forgot, something cherished in the memory of every cowboy who helped move big herds across the unfenced and unmapped ranges.

In a field so boundless, so full of excitement and so popular in literature, this book offers something new, something different from the legions preceding it. It tells the facts—not literary imaginings—about the Old West without totally debunking the accepted pattern (for there is much truth in the old image). It casts the picture in perspective, establishes a balance between the two extremes of exaggerated romance and exaggerated drabness.

The West is, of course, a tremendous subject—geographically, historically, sociologically. It has many facets, many phases, so many, in fact, that no one man could possibly be expert in all of them. This fact was recognized from the very beginning in the conception and organization of our book. So that the subject could be covered fully, with the depth and accuracy it deserves, ten distinguished western authorities were invited to participate in its preparation, not as advisers or editors, but as *writers,* each on his own specialty.

In determining the scope of our book, the first task was to establish the geographical boundaries of the West, a difficult decision because the transition from Middle West to West is gradual. However, a definite change begins with the short-grass country of the Great Plains, not far beyond the eastern borders of Texas, Oklahoma, Kansas, Nebraska and the Dakotas. These state lines have therefore been selected as the eastern boundary of this book's West. To the north and south our area ends at the Canadian and Mexican borders.

Defining the time span for our book presented a second organizational problem. Because the first Europeans to enter this vast region were Spanish and because they established a way of life there that still persists in many parts of the West, it seemed logical to begin with them. Nevertheless, since the Indians were there first, some attention is given to them in the book's opening section. The closing date for our American West is more difficult to fix. That great historian, Frederick Jackson Turner—whose theories have been reflected in all American history texts since his death—assumed that the frontier had disappeared by 1890. (His critics, however, have pointed out that more settlers made "final" filings on free homesteads in 1916 than during any previous year.) For this book, we have assumed that the Old West vanished in 1912 when Arizona and New Mexico—the last of the western territories—attained statehood.

As the writing of our book progressed, it was found that limitations of space necessitated several omissions. It was decided, for example, that the slavery troubles in Kansas and the military campaign against Confederates in New Mexico and Arizona belong more properly to Civil War history than to the West. With much regret, it has been necessary to omit the Oklahoma "runs"—those spectacular races for choice homesteads when Indian territories were opened to settlement. The experiences of men who purchased fast horses in order to be first to claim a previously selected homestead are typical of western initiative. Equally important to an understanding of sardonic western humor is the oft-repeated story that these same men sometimes galloped up to the chosen site to find a "Sooner" already there with a team of oxen.

The Book of the American West is a truly remarkable undertaking, bringing together a magnificent array of material, much of it previously available only in dozens of scattered books and in the special collections of widely separated libraries. Some information—that concerning the Rocky Mountain fur trade, for example—appears here for the first time. Some of the opinions and interpretations expressed may startle or disconcert readers, but I can assure them that every word in this book is based upon painstaking research and scholarship. Its authors are all men who go straight to the sources for their facts, not to the writings of others.

The Book of the American West offers a richly diverse and illuminating experience in reading. I hope that in these pages readers will come to know our American West as it really was, and I know many will become aware, perhaps for the first time, that the West was a region infinitely vaster and more thrilling than the never-never land of the "Western."

Jay Monaghan

Santa Barbara, California
June, 1963

PART ONE

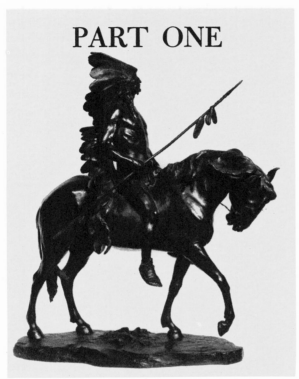

"Indian Warrior" by Charles M. Humphriss

Opening of the West: Explorers and Mountain Men

by Dale Morgan

Indian war dance by Minataree warrior. Engraving, after painting by Carl Bodmer.

1. *First There Were Indians*

WESTERN HISTORY HAS been written by the white man, mainly in celebration of himself, but the Indians have refused to fade into the landscape as so much vegetation or a part of the wild life. Had the Indians not dwelt there, white men might not have established themselves in the West yet: no Coronado, no Vérendrye, no Lewis and Clark, no Jedediah Smith, none to answer the great roll call all the way down through time. When white men entered the West to stay, for a long time they maintained themselves there only by becoming Indians of a sort themselves.

But who then were the western Indians? Our ideas about them are colored by the sunset light in which the tribes were viewed through most of the last century. Go back three hundred years and you may search the West in vain for many of the tribes that seem most characteristically western. They hadn't got there yet, or they had not acquired the traits that set them apart from other Indians. Rare are the exceptions, like the village dwellers of the sun-drenched Southwest, with a culture so tightly knit and so rooted in the earth as to have held at bay all finally destructive change.

Where the American Indians came from has been a topic of speculation since Columbus returned from the Indies in 1493. Indian accounts of their origin are fascinating without being wholly informative. Lewis and Clark were told in 1804 that all the Mandan had once resided in a single large village underground, near a subterranean lake. A grapevine having extended its roots down to their home and admitted the golden light, a few of the Mandan climbed up the vine to discover the earth, black with buffalo and rich with fruit. Seduced by the taste of the grapes, the Mandan resolved to abandon their dull residence for the region above. Men, women and children began ascending the vine, but when half the nation had reached the surface, the vine broke under the weight of a fat woman, condemning the rest of the people to remain in their sunless home below. The Mandan believed that when they died they would return to the subterranean home of their forefathers.

Another, and now more general, view respecting the origin of the Indians is that over a period of not less than 20,000 years—perhaps twice as long as that—various migrations found their way from Asia across the intermittent Bering land bridge, each migration moving imperceptibly down through the corridors of the Rocky and Andean mountains to spread out into the vast reaches of the Americas. Ethnologists classify the various modern Indian tribes which descended from these inconceivably ancient migrations according to the language they speak. Culturally, linguistic cousins may differ widely, and live on terms no more cordial than do members of ordinary families; the language may also have undergone vast

YAKIMA

SALISH

GROS V

CAYUSE

PIEGAN

NEZ PERCÉS

BLACKFEET

SHOSHONI

SHEEPEATER

CRO

KLAMATH

COMAN

MODOC

BANNOCK

SHOSHONI

YO-SEMITES

U T E

PAIUTE

MARIPOSA

NAVAJO

ZUÑI

MOHAVE

HOPI

YUMA

PIMA

A P A C H E

Indian Tribes of the
AMERICAN WEST

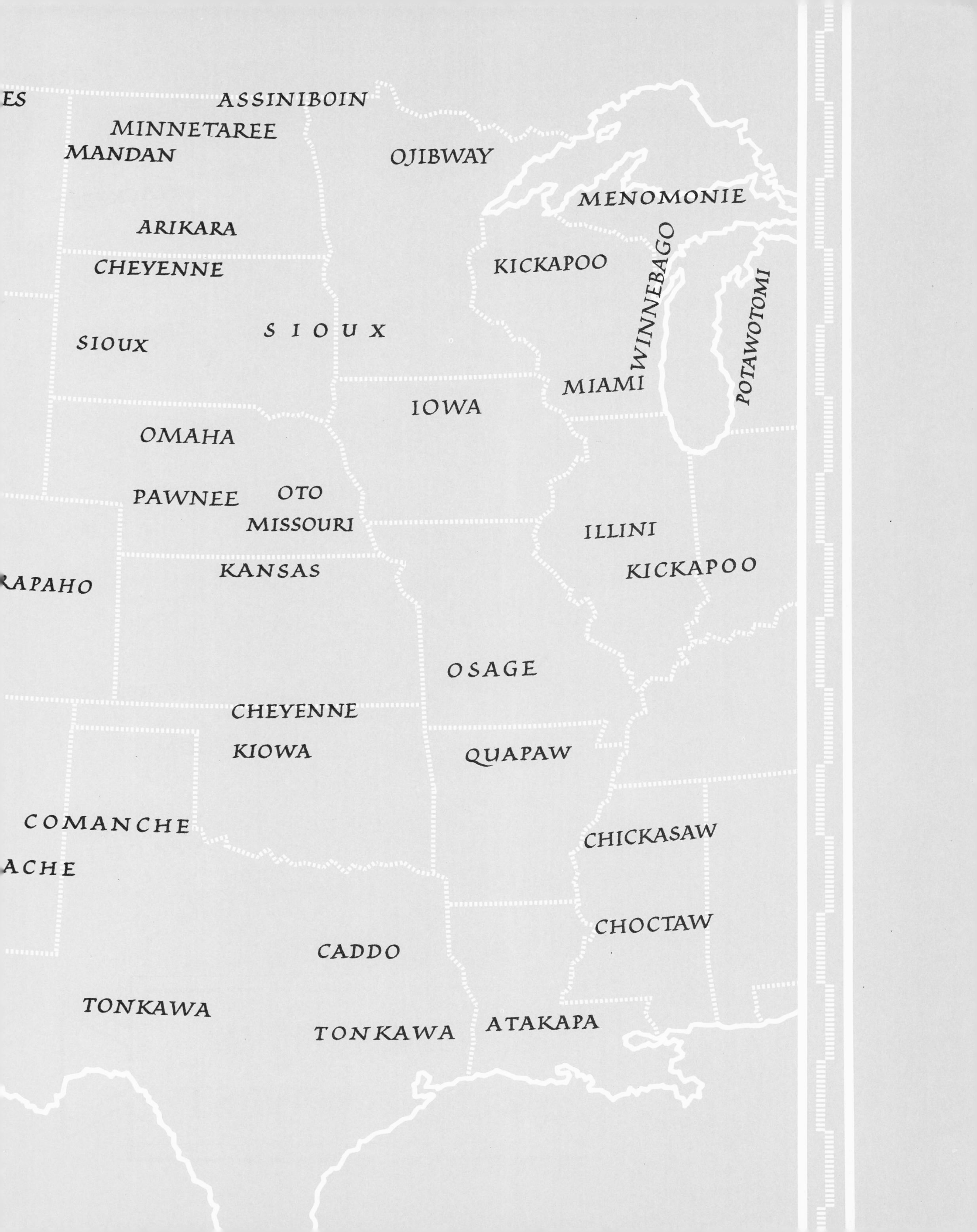

ES

ASSINIBOIN

MINNETAREE

MANDAN

OJIBWAY

MENOMONIE

ARIKARA

KICKAPOO

WINNEBAGO

CHEYENNE

S I O U X

SIOUX

POTAWOTOMI

MIAMI

IOWA

OMAHA

PAWNEE   OTO

MISSOURI

ILLINI

KICKAPOO

KANSAS

RAPAHO

OSAGE

CHEYENNE

KIOWA

QUAPAW

COMANCHE

CHICKASAW

ACHE

CHOCTAW

CADDO

TONKAWA

TONKAWA   ATAKAPA

change, so that an Osage finds an Assiniboin no more comprehensible than a Portuguese finds a Romanian. But so stubborn is the substructure of language that careful study of it can establish ancient kinships and vaguely make out the lineaments of an unwritten history beyond the ken of even the mistiest tradition.

Indian Linguistic Groups

The Indians north of Mexico have been divided into the following main linguistic stocks: Algonquian, Iroquoian, Siouan, Muskhogean, Caddoan, Shoshonean, Athapascan, Salishan and other small groups in high mountains of the Northwest, and Yuman and Piman in the deserts of the extreme Southwest. A clutter of smaller groups lived down the Northwest Coast and in California, around the Gulf of Mexico, and up the Rio Grande. In general the Algonquians occupied the forested country from the Mississippi to the Atlantic, with vast islands of Iroquoian peoples around the lower Great Lakes and down the Appalachians. The Siouan peoples, apart from a detached branch in Virginia and the Carolinas, lived primarily in the western reaches of the Mississippi Valley above the mouth of the Arkansas. As late as 1800, most of the Siouans still resided east of the Missouri River, and none very far from it. The Muskhogean peoples of the southeastern United States became associated with the West only after Indian removal began in 1831, when such so-called civilized tribes as the Creeks and Choctaw despairingly followed the "trail of tears" to new homes in what became Oklahoma.

West of the original homeland of the Muskhogeans, the Caddoans occupied much of Louisiana, eastern Texas and southwestern Arkansas, with a few, like the Pawnee and Arikara, living along the edge of the Plains farther north. West of these families dwelt the Shoshonean peoples, who took for their home the central Rockies and the high desert plateaus beyond.

The Athapascans, probably the last great linguistic stock to enter North America, though no one is certain of the time, were divided into two main groups. The Northern Athapascans, before 1800 as since, made their homes in Alaska and northwestern Canada; there were also many small enclaves of them down the Northwest Coast as far as California. The Southern Athapascans once occupied most of the Great Plains, as well as much of the Southwest, but in the period of recorded history became concentrated mainly in New Mexico, Arizona and northern Mexico, where they were called Apache and Navajo.

The Old Oregon country, embracing Oregon, Washington, British Columbia and parts of Idaho and Montana, was principally occupied by Salishan and other small groups of people, while in western Arizona, southeastern California and northwestern Mexico the Yuman and Piman peoples held sway.

These various groups seem mere abstractions until they are broken down into specific tribes, using the names by which we chiefly know the Indians of the American West. In most instances, these names have never been used by the tribes among themselves. In their own languages, the Navajo are the Diné, the People; the Arapaho are the Inuñaina, the People; the Mandan are the Numakiki, the People. Most tribes have always thought of themselves as the People, the Folks, Us. Coming from outside, whites usually learned of a new people through a neighboring tribe and fixed an alien name upon that people before encountering them. The name Sioux, for example, is an abbreviation of Nadowessioux, a

French corruption of a name applied to an enemy tribe by the Ojibway and signifying (not cordially) snake or adder. Still, the names fixed upon the tribes, whether native or alien, have served their purpose, for names are simply convenient handles for things.

The Blackfeet, or Siksika, along with two subtribes called Piegan and Bloods, speak an archaic form of Algonquian and presumably are the oldest members of their family in the West, having come out of the eastern woodlands many generations before any of their kinsmen. They have preserved a tribal memory of a remote time when they lived in the Red River country, from which they advanced into the Canadian and American West, driving other Indians before them. They were followed out of the woodlands by another Algonquian people, who became the Plains Cree; and farther to the south, yet other Algonquians advanced to and beyond the Missouri, becoming known as Cheyenne and Arapaho. An offshoot of the latter, the Gros Ventres of the Prairies, eventually took up residence among the Blackfeet.

The Siouans would be notable if only because an extraordinary number of states have taken their names from particular tribes. Arkansas, the Dakotas, Iowa, Kansas and Missouri all bear Siouan names. Some branches of this family early established homes on or near the Missouri, including the Mandan, Ponca, Omaha, Oto, Iowa, Missouri, Kansa and Osage—

"Crow Chief." Painting by W. H. D. Koerner.

COURTESY OF RUTH-ANN OLIVER

farming peoples who at the eastern margin of the Plains also did some hunting. Though not the less western for that, they are better thought of as river-and-prairie than as Plains Indians.

Sioux Indians Move West

The earliest of the Siouan peoples to migrate out into the Plains, north of the Missouri, may have been the Assiniboin, recorded as a separate tribe as early as 1604. From a homeland in the lake and canoe country around the heads of the Mississippi, they drifted west and north, reaching Lake Winnipeg by 1690. They then moved on to the Plains of Canada and the upper Missouri. It is possible that they were preceded into the farther West by that Siouan tribe now termed the Crows. The Crows, or Absaroka, came originally to the banks of the Missouri as one people with the Gros Ventres of the Missouri (not to be confused with the Gros Ventres of the Prairies). These Gros Ventres, also known as Hidatsa or Minnetaree, settled in permanent villages near their remote cousins, the Mandan. For some reason the Crows split off and moved on into the valley of the Yellowstone, which they made into a famous homeland, tenaciously defended, first against the Blackfeet, later against the main body of Sioux. The separation from the Hidatsa may have occurred before 1700, but the Crows preserved a sense of kinship, and over the next century and a half made periodic pilgrimages back to the Missouri to visit and trade with their only near relatives.

Much later came the peoples we know collectively as the Sioux. Most of the Sioux proper, who called themselves Dakota (allies), were driven out of Minnesota at the end of a centuries-long conflict with the Ojibway (Chippewa); some were forced out of Iowa by the Sauk and Foxes. (These peoples had been pushed west by yet more easterly tribes, and this continual pressure and displacement was a fact of life for all the Plains tribes through most of the nineteenth century; an Indian homeland was one of the most unstable entities imaginable.) The Sioux were moving up to and crossing the Missouri, their culture and character changing all the while, throughout the half-century after the Declaration of Independence. They consisted of three principal subtribes, the Santee, Yankton and Teton. The last-named, comprising more than half of all the Sioux, made the adaptation to Plains life which, together with their numbers, predestined them as the ultimate defenders of an Indian way of life on the Plains against the unappeasable whites.

Prey of the Siouan peoples through most of recorded history were those Caddoan cousins, the Pawnee and Arikara. The latter settled on the Missouri near its Great Bend (but under Siouan attack later moved up closer to the Mandan), while the Pawnee established their home villages on the Platte and its branches.

The Earliest Plains Indians

In striking contrast to the foregoing tribes, the Kiowa did not enter the Plains from the east. They were long an ethnological mystery, their language thought to be unrelated to any other. Patient analysis has finally shown that Kiowan is related to one of the two principal tongues spoken by the Pueblo Indians of the Rio Grande Valley. Either the Kiowa are one of the very oldest of Plains peoples, having remained there after their kinsmen settled on the Rio Grande as farmers, or at some remote time the village people who became the Kiowa separated from their sedentary kinsmen, moved out into the Plains and became so attached to that expanse of earth and sky as to lose all memory of any other home. During the nineteenth century they migrated from the northern to the southern Plains and brought with them the conviction that their original homeland was the upper Yellowstone and the Missouri.

The Kiowa were so closely affiliated with one Apache group as to be called Kiowa Apache; they were the last of the Athapascan peoples who had ruled most of the Great Plains for several hundred years. Coronado's army on its great *entrada* of 1540–41 marched out into the Plains to encounter Indians who were surely Apache, and in describing them one of the Spanish chroniclers gave a memorable picture of the buffalo-hunting Plains Indian as he was during the age-long time before he acquired the horse:

> These Indians live or sustain themselves entirely from the cattle, for they neither grow nor harvest maize. With the skins they build their houses; with the skins they clothe and shoe themselves; from the skins they make ropes and also obtain wool. With the sinews they make thread, with which they sew their clothes and also their tents. From the bones they shape awls. The dung they use for firewood, since there is no other fuel in that land. The bladders they use as jugs and drinking containers. They sustain themselves on their meat, eating it slightly roasted and heated over the dung. Some they eat raw; taking it in their teeth, they pull with one hand, and in the other they hold a large flint knife and cut off mouthfuls. Thus they swallow it, half chewed, like birds. They eat raw fat without warming it. They drink the blood just as it comes out of the cattle. Sometimes they drink it later, raw and cold. They have no other food.
>
> These people have dogs similar to those of this land [Mexico], except that they are somewhat larger. They load these dogs like beasts of burden and make light pack-saddles for them like our pack-saddles, cinching them with leather straps. The dogs go about with sores on their backs like pack animals. When the Indians go hunting they load them with provisions. When these Indians move—for they have no permanent residence anywhere, since they follow the cattle to find food—these dogs carry their homes for them. In addition to what they carry on their backs, they carry the poles for the tents, dragging them fastened to their saddles. The load may be from thirty-five to fifty pounds, depending on the dog.

Besides the Apache associated with the Kiowa, others, including the Lipan, Jicarilla, Mescalero and Chiricahua, ranged through western Texas and New Mexico, southern Arizona and northern Mexico, proving themselves in a harsh desert environment one of the toughest, most resistant peoples who ever lived. North of these Apache, in northwestern New Mexico and northeastern Arizona, dwelt their remarkable cousins, the Navajo, who found ways to wring a living from a country little richer than so much blue sky. On the basis of recent tree-ring evidence, the Navajo were already in their present homeland in Coronado's day; in all likelihood, they had settled there many centuries before the first Spaniards arrived.

North of the Navajo dwelt the numerous Shoshonean peoples—"tribes" is for most of them too cohesive a term—who made the Rocky Mountains and the intermontane basins to the west yield them a reluctant living. Many existed in so barren an environment as to be reduced to eating anything and everything that ran or hopped or crawled upon the ground. They also gathered seeds and dug for edible roots—hence the term "Diggers" applied later by contemptuous whites (who were sometimes more than glad to partake of the same fare, not excepting grasshoppers and crickets).

A detached branch of this Shoshonean linguistic stock were the patient, peaceful, incredibly enduring Hopi, who are known to have lived in the vicinity of their present mesas in northern Arizona for seven hundred years or more. They resembled the Pueblo Indians of the Rio Grande and Gila valleys in everything but language.

Some small groups of the Shoshonean family lived in southern California. The Chemehuevi made their homes on the lower Colorado River, the Southern Paiute on both sides of that river and well up into Nevada and Utah. These two peoples, with the Hopi and a few Ute, were the only Shoshonean growers of maize, beans and pumpkins. North of the Southern Paiute, in the western and northern reaches of the Great Basin, lived a diversity of peoples: the Ute, Northern Paiute, Bannock, Western Shoshoni and Eastern Shoshoni, with the Comanche an offshoot of the latter. The dark mountain-people called Ute ranged between

"Shoshone." Painting by W. H. D. Koerner.

northern New Mexico and the Great Salt Lake. Familiar to the Spaniards in New Mexico early in the seventeenth century, they were renowned from the beginning for their valor. It was the Ute who first brought the Comanche to the New Mexican settlements, soon after 1700. The Comanche were just then cutting loose from their old homes in southern Wyoming. Having acquired horses, their life and character were being revolutionized.

In the far Northwest were those Salishan tribes who have their own distinctive place in the history of the West, including such inland peoples as the Flatheads (whose heads were no flatter than yours or mine) and their close cousins. These interior tribes made the most of the salmon runs, but after the coming of the horse they hunted extensively, often crossing the Continental Divide in present Montana seeking buffalo.

Much like the Flatheads were the Nez Percés and Kutenai. All three were of different linguistic stock, but in a similar environment developed similar cultures. They were further united by a common enmity toward the Blackfeet, who held sway on the buffalo ranges. These three tribes are among the most remarkable of all Indian groups, morally superior to most of the early whites who entered their country. Their conquest has given to western history a peculiarly somber note.

Too diverse for comment are the many peoples living intermixed down through Oregon and California, though some, like the Modoc, have their own place in the history of the West. California, islanded in time almost since time itself began, presents a singular contrast to the unceasing cultural ebb and flow of Indian life elsewhere on the continent; until the white man arrived, nothing ever seemed to happen in California, societies remaining stable from one millennium to the next.

On the lower Colorado and in the country adjacent lived peoples of the ancient Piman stock, like the Pima and Papago, who have tilled the soil under the blazing Arizona sun for nine thousand years or more. Their immediate neighbors were also farmers, tall red men of Yuman stock, including the Maricopa, Yuma, Cocopa, Mohave, Walapai, Yavapai and—highest up the Colorado, dwelling in the depths of the Grand Canyon—the Havasupai.

Immense as the American West is, few of its tribes lived in a stage of savage innocence when Lewis and Clark set out up the Missouri in the spring of 1804. Many of the tribes had been in contact with whites for two and a half centuries, their life already greatly changed by the fact that white men existed on the same continent. Europeans sailed to the widely separated ocean shores of America with various trade goods (above all, iron and the gun), while at the same time they journeyed up out of Mexico bringing grains, fruit trees, sheep, cattle, asses and horses. Over immemorially ancient intertribal trade routes, along which for thousands of years had passed such things as sea shells and copper, the astonishing new goods brought by the white men were carried into the interior, stimulating a return flow of beaver and otter pelts, deerskins, elk and buffalo hides—and slaves, usually redskinned, occasionally white. Some tribes became prime suppliers, others carriers. New forms and accumulations of wealth made warfare more worthwhile, and trade itself became a fighting matter. Particularly in the case of guns and ammunition, it was important to be able to control the trade and to cut it off altogether when self-interest required. Lewis and Clark found that this was exactly the position of the Teton Sioux in 1804; they themselves meant to conduct any trade with their enemies, not neglecting their middleman's profit.

"Indian Camp Near Yellowstone, 1860." Painting by Eliphalet Terry.

Indians Get the Horse

The gun and the horse were the two prime factors that shaped the history of the West after the coming of the white man. Outside the West itself, the gun counted most, enabling more easterly tribes to overpower their neighbors and hustle them along toward the sunset, even as they themselves were being pushed westward by the whites. In the West the horse had a yet more revolutionary impact. Although the horse had flourished in North America during past geological time, it died out along with the mammoth and the giant sloth. When Cortez and his conquistadors brought the horse back to the New World, the Indians of Mexico beheld it as a god, and the horse inspired much the same awe throughout the first era of the Spanish advance into the interior of the continent.

But mastery of the horse has always enlarged men's ideas of themselves; they, not the horse, become the true god. In the presence of the horse, Indians quickly grew in stature. Between the time of Coronado's *entrada* and Oñate's colonization of New Mexico at the end of the sixteenth century, Indians on the advancing Spanish frontier began to steal from the ranchos or capture mounts from the multiplying wild herds. Indians in southern Texas may have begun to master the use of the horse before Oñate reached the Rio Grande, but the real impact of the horse upon the American West followed the establishment of a Spanish crown colony in New Mexico. When, about 1693, the first Frenchmen ventured up the Missouri, one piece of news brought back was that the Pawnee were trading for horses in the Spanish Southwest. By the close of the century, the horse had spread up through the Rockies as far as the basin of the Columbia. By 1730 the Snakes (or Shoshoni) were using the horse in warfare against the Blackfeet on the Saskatchewan plains; coincidentally, at just this time the Blackfeet had acquired their first guns and iron points for their arrows. The Big Dogs (a name given horses by most Plains Indians) were as terrifying to the Blackfeet as the death-dealing guns were to the Snakes, but the Blackfeet were quick to learn. They could keep the Snakes from getting guns, and they were able to steal horses. Soon the Snake lands were infested with Blackfoot horsethieves, and by 1754 the Blackfeet had become superb horsemen, evolving a nomadic Plains culture of tepees, war bonnets, baskets, skin receptacles instead of breakable pottery, and all the accouterments that went with a life dependent on chasing buffalo. By the time Lewis and Clark reached the Rockies, the Blackfeet had fastened their grip on the country as far south as the Missouri.

One tribe utterly transformed by the acquisition of the horse, rendered into something new and terrible, were the Comanche. As early as 1706 they had begun to harry the Apache from the Plains, and they soon extended their raids to the Spanish settlements. By 1739 the Comanche were masters of the central and southern Plains, and fell heir to the French gun trade based on the Missouri and Red rivers. The Comanche kept the Spanish settlements bleeding all through the 1740's, and despite peaceful interludes were a fearful fact of life on the frontier until Spanish dominion in North America ended in 1821.

Fugitive glimpses of the coming of the horse to the Blackfeet and the Comanche give us an insight into the revolutionary change that worked upon Indian life in the West throughout the eighteenth century. The impact and meaning of the change can again be seen in the case of the Cheyenne. These valiant Algonquians once lived in Minnesota, but were pushed westward by enemy tribes. Reaching the Missouri about 1678, they became farmers like the Arikara, but unlike their neighbors, when goaded by the ever-advancing Sioux, the Cheyenne became nomadic too. Feasting on the limitless buffalo herds they wandered as far south as the Spanish settlements. Trading peltries at Santa Fe and San Antonio for horses, they would steal a few for good measure before riding north. The Cheyenne retained a hankering for the corn of their agricultural days, and each summer at harvest time they appeared over the skyline southwest of the Arikara villages eager to trade horses for the ripe grain.

In the 1830's, influenced by the establishment of Bent's Fort on the Arkansas (near the present La Junta), the Cheyenne made the southern Plains their permanent home. But their earlier seasonal movements to the last settled place they had ever called home proved to be of incalculable importance to white traders attempting to establish themselves in the West after 1800. The Cheyenne, as the main source of horseflesh, gave the Arikara villages strategic importance in the evolution of Western history. It was at the Arikara villages in the summer of 1811 that John Jacob Astor's associate in the fur business, Wilson Price Hunt, abandoned his intention of following Lewis and Clark's water route across the continent and traded for horses to take a more southerly course, the first land crossing of the American West. William H. Ashley and many another fur trader similarly supplied themselves at the Arikara villages in later years.

Not all western Indians became horse Indians. In many parts of the West, the country was too poor to support a horse culture, and the best use to which the Indians could put a horse was to eat him. (The taste was one easily acquired, and in California a whole class of Indians became known as Horse-Eaters.) The settled Indians of the Southwest did not take enthusiastically to the horse, burros being better suited to their needs; and much of the Pacific littoral simply wasn't horse country. In the Southwest the Spanish colonists, superimposing their own culture upon that of the Pueblo Indians, were transformed into a kind of Pueblo Indian themselves, though addicted to the horse and the raising of livestock—an addiction enthusiastically acquired by the Navajo. Still and all, it was the horse Indian who became the primary barrier to any further white advance, and in the end he became the mentor of the white man who must adapt himself to life in the West.

Indians chasing wild horses. Painting by Charles Abel Corwin.

KENNEDY GALLERIES, NEW YORK

2. *The Race for Empire*

Imperial Spain Enters the West

IN THIS BOOK we are above all concerned with the nineteenth-century West, but we must go back in time to note some of the antecedents of the remarkable things that began to happen after the year 1800. Some events we have glimpsed already, as factors precipitating crucial change among the Indians. As early as 1536, word reached Mexico City from adventurers who had been shipwrecked on the coast of Texas that fabulous cities, having streets paved with gold and walls studded with precious jewels, stood somewhere in the vast deserts to the north. A Franciscan friar, Marcos de Niza, made an unsuccessful search for the so-called Seven Cities of Cíbola, but was driven back by Indians at the Zuñi pueblos. In 1540 Francisco Vásquez de Coronado with an army of horse and foot defeated these Indians and marched on across eastern New Mexico and the Texas Panhandle to the heart of the continent in present Kansas, but he found no fabulous cities. Coronado wrote his king that he had found a wonderfully fair land, and later his men lamented the opportunity missed, "the good country they had in their hands" and might have possessed. But Coronado's search had been for another Aztec or Inca kingdom, ripe for looting. No such realm had been found, only the poor adobe empire of the Rio Grande and the limitless plains to the east, black with wild cattle.

Time passed, half a century nearly, and the memory of Coronado's quest vanished like a stone dropped in still waters. The line of settlement moved north in Mexico, and eventually rumor revived at fresh word of the pueblos of the Rio Grande. The mirage of distant, wealthy kingdoms shimmered anew, and between 1581 and 1593 no less than five expeditions, all unauthorized, ventured into the north, exploring much of New Mexico and Arizona. If the kingdoms did not exist, rich mines might; to this extent had the Spaniards grown more sophisticated. In 1598, after interminable official delays, Don Juan de Oñate led a formal colonizing expedition up into New Mexico, afterward exploring the country, in vain pursuit of quick wealth, from Kansas to the Gulf of California. Recalled in disgrace, he left on the Rio Grande a precariously situated community that was allowed to remain only for the sake of the Indians who had been brought to the door of salvation and could not be abandoned.

In 1610, Oñate's successor, Pedro de Peralta, founded the city ever since known as Santa Fe—except for St. Augustine in Florida, the oldest surviving European community in the present United States. In 1680 the Indians drove out the Spaniards in what is known as the Pueblo Rebellion. Nowhere in the West did Indians ever come so close to ridding themselves of white masters, but Spanish rule was re-established in the 1690's, and henceforth these Indians, settled as they were in pueblos, unable to shake off their overlords, could only endure.

The Spaniards, for their part, had reached the limit of possible expansion. The horses which Plains Indians had received from them almost outweighed Spanish armament. Not until the invention of repeating arms in the nineteenth century was there a significant shift in the balance of force. Spanish troops made forays and demonstrations but failed to advance the New Mexican frontier.

In Arizona the Spanish advance was also slow. Jesuit missionaries, with great energy and devotion, labored with the Indians in Sonora and pushed constantly northward. By 1692, the year the reconquest of New Mexico was launched, Padre Eusebio Francisco Kino founded a mission eight miles north of Nogales, followed it with others and explored the valley of the Gila. The Jesuits continued to work in southern Arizona and Mexico until expelled in 1767—not for any misconduct in North America but for political considerations in Europe, where the King of Spain feared the Order's rising power.

The Franciscans remained in New Mexico, the territory allotted to them, but had no community of interest with the Arizona settlers except that both had roots in Mexico, Spain and Rome. Both also had to cope with an ever-worsening Apache problem. To the west and north of the Colorado River everything remained a terra incognita until the latter part of the century.

France and England: Three Generations Struggle for the West

In the Spanish Southwest while time slowed, seeming almost to have ceased, in the remote lands to the north and east it quickened and pulsed. During the first quarter of the sixteenth century mariners from England, Holland and France drove their vessels along the eastern coast, and Jacques Cartier sailed his ship up the St. Lawrence as early as 1535.

That river and the Great Lakes afforded a natural means of access to the heart of North America, and the interior was rich in furs to finance the advance. The first English adventurer did not cross the Alleghenies until 1671, and by that time the French had moved into the west. Adopting the birchbark canoe, they developed a new breed of men, the *coureurs de bois,* or woods runners.

To withstand the furious cold of the northern latitudes, these men possessed "Blood compos'd of Brandy, . . . Body of Brass, and . . . eyes of Glass," to say nothing of the superb, complex skills basic to survival on white-water rivers, amid the endless dark forests and the muskeg. The *coureurs de bois* went out among the tribes armed chiefly with their own spiritual toughness. In morals they were frequently inferior to the Indians among whom they passed their days; they drank mightily, whored, wived and fathered children with abandon, debauched and cheated the tribes and, except in relation to one another, scarcely knew the name of responsibility. Usually they were outlaws, for French authority attempted to carry on the fur trade (the basis of the colonial economy) as a monopoly—preferably by requiring the Indians to bring in their furs from the far lands to the comfortable settlements where the favored merchants lived. In presuming to trade for furs beyond the frontiers, the *coureurs de bois* gave the backs of their hands to authority at the outset. Their only market was corrupt, with no merchant in it averse to double-dealing that would outwit a rival, and all determined to punish, by imprisonment, fines and confiscation of furs, *coureurs de bois* who ignored the authorized monopolies.

Facing these obstacles, men who grew up at the edge of the wilderness, who had the wilderness in their hearts, and who knew that the hazards of the wilderness must be accepted as the only gamble for a better life, slipped into that wilderness and made it their home. Harassed and exploited as they were, their supreme mastery of the wilderness enabled France to maintain her empire in America for a century and a half against the overwhelming military and economic force England brought to bear. The French fur trade took its direction and character from the *coureurs de bois,* and sooner rather than later, the merchants had to send their own authorized agents into the interior. Fur trading establishments began to dot the remote waterways, and the chain of posts eventually extended as far as the Saskatchewan and the Missouri.

All this took time. Meanwhile two French adventurers, the Sieur de Grosseilliers and his brother-in-law, Pierre Radisson, had returned from an expedition with a fortune in fur and a report that an arm of the sea (Hudson Bay) reached deep into that fabulous country. Deprived of their profits by the licensed traders, they went to England and in 1670 induced capitalists there to form the Hudson's Bay Company, which from new bases closer to the furs could challenge the French monopolists.

The Englishmen were not interested in exploring southward and westward so long as the Indians floated their furs down to their trading posts. One of them, a servant named Henry Kelsey, did venture inland in 1690, the first non-Spanish white man to see the Great Plains and hunt buffalo. He wandered with friendly Cree or Assiniboin Indians for two years, but whether he got as far south as the future United States cannot be determined. The Company was indifferent to his efforts.

France extended her empire by discoveries down the Mississippi, claiming the valley as Louisiana, building in 1720 a great stone fort on the river east of the future St. Louis and importing French *habitans* to farm the land. From these villages Frenchmen began to trade with Indians on the edge of the Great Plains. It was not long before these traders learned from the Pawnee that horses were being driven north from the Spanish colonies. The French began to think of raiding these colonies in the name of France and of appropriating the silver mines reported to be there.

Rumors of this French interest filtered into New Mexico through the Plains Indians. Spanish officials listened with an apprehensive ear, disquieted especially by evidence that guns —which they had always refused to trade—might be coming to the Indians from the French. Particularly alarming were the reports, magnified and distorted as they were, of the activities of Étienne Véniard de Bourgmond, the first great figure in the history of the Missouri River.

Of old Norman descent, commandant for some years at Fort Detroit, veteran of the bloody Fox wars, Bourgmond was a *coureur de bois* of the old breed, with an appreciative eye for women white or red and a superb flair for wilderness life. About 1712 he left the service, married a "sauvagesse," doubtless very beautiful, and went off to live among the Missouri Indians. The Jesuit fathers took exception to this "scandalous and criminal" life of Bourgmond and his fellow *coureurs de bois,* but others found him a useful man. In the spring of 1714 he paddled up the Missouri at least as far at the Niobrara (just below the South Dakota border), the highest point any Frenchman had yet attained. The next year, it may be, he established

Trappers on a swift stream. Engraving, after drawing by Frederic Remington.

on the east bank of the Missouri, at some point between the mouth of the Platte and that of the Nemaha, a stockaded post called Fort du Missouri, the remotest trading post ever established on the rolling brown river by the French.

Spanish officials decided to send a military expedition to investigate the rumored French military establishments over the horizon to the northeast. With a force of nearly 110 men, including 70 Pueblo Indians, Pedro de Villasur rode out from Santa Fe in June, 1720. He crossed the Plains to the Platte, the farthest journey yet attempted from the Spanish settlements on the Rio Grande.

Early in August, at some point on the Platte, Villasur's little army was cut to pieces by Pawnee aided by a few Oto. No disaster of comparable proportions occurred to white arms in the West until the Fetterman defeat by the Sioux in 1866; forty-five men were slain, including Villasur himself. The return of the frightened survivors occasioned the wildest alarm in New Mexico, for it was supposed that the French had been involved in the onslaught.

Bourgmond was not on the Missouri at this time but he returned later, and in the fall of 1724 traveled far up the valley of the "Cansez" River, perhaps as far as present-day Salina, to a vast camp of Plains Apache. Always superbly skilled with Indians, he distributed the French largesse, feasted with the chiefs on buffalo meat and dried plums, joined in the spacious oratory, and came back with a present of seven horses and the conviction that he had opened the road to New Mexico.

France failed to profit by Bourgmond's exploits, but among his worthy heirs were the brothers Pierre and Paul Mallet, who in 1739 crossed the Plains from the vicinity of the Niobrara to Santa Fe—first of their kind to see the Rocky Mountains, a blue edging on the horizon. During the next decade other French traders straggled across the Plains, usually to be thrown in jail and have their goods confiscated. Thus the first hesitant Santa Fe trade guttered out. However, about 1743 an Indian trading store and military post known as "Fort Cavagnolle" was begun in present Kansas, a little above the site of Fort Leavenworth. Never much more than a circular palisade enclosing a few poor cabins in which lived an officer, seven or eight soldiers and some traders, this was the ultimate extension of French military power in Louisiana. The post was abandoned in the spring of 1764, incident to the French withdrawal at the conclusion of the Seven Years War with England, after which all of Canada fell into British hands. Its remains were still to be seen when Lewis and Clark ascended the Missouri in 1804.

The Vérendryes on the Upper Missouri

In Canada, during the same period, France had made a far deeper penetration of the West, an advance necessary to compete with the English after the Treaty of Utrecht in 1713 forced France to yield Hudson Bay to Britain. The very existence of New France depended on maintaining at a high level its commerce in furs, so in 1728, one of the great figures in the annals of American fur trade and exploration, Pierre Gaultier de Varennes, Sieur de la Vérendrye, took the field.

Vérendrye understood that the superior strategic position of the British could be countered only by establishing posts on the northward running rivers to intercept the flow of furs to

Hudson Bay. The first of these on the Plains was built in 1734 west of Lake Winnipeg. For years he had been hearing Indian tales about the Mandan, a distant people with white skins who lived in fortified towns on a great river. In September, 1738, he set off to investigate, and on December 3 reached one of the villages on Heart River (near Bismarck, North Dakota). Disappointingly, the great river flowed east, not into the Sea of the West he had hoped to find. Leaving two men here, Vérendrye returned to his Canadian posts. The two came out in September, 1739, telling the same story that had interested Frenchmen on the Mississippi: Nomadic Plains Indians were bringing horses every summer from the Spanish colonies to trade with the agricultural Indians for corn and beans. The distance was only a summer's drive, but "Snakes"—probably Comanche—made it dangerous.

In May, 1742, Vérendrye's sons, Louis-Joseph and François, like their father hoping to find the Sea of the West, visited the Mandan villages and waited until late July for the Horse People to arrive. Then with friendly Indians they journeyed into the Plains as far as the Black Hills. From those highlands they had hoped to sight the Sea of the West, but their companions feared the Snakes too much to venture to the crest.

In February, 1743, the Vérendryes returned to the Missouri at present-day Pierre, South Dakota, and buried a lead plate which a fourteen-year-old schoolgirl kicked out of the earth in 1913.

Anthony Henday Counters French Advance

The diminishing supply of fur spurred the Hudson's Bay Company to send Anthony Henday inland in 1754 to persuade the Indians to patronize them rather than the French. He was an outlawed smuggler from the Isle of Wight capable of matching wits and stamina with the *coureurs de bois*. With friendly Indians and a dusky sleeping partner, whom his London superiors would have disapproved, Henday reached the Blackfoot country and from the neighborhood of present Calgary glimpsed the Rockies. He was the first Englishman to lay eyes on the spine of the continent unless, improbably, Kelsey had done so sixty years before. Henday's report of Indians using horses instead of canoes heralded a change in the fur business, for horse Indians would not float their furs to the Bay. Henceforth it became an almost annual custom to thwart the French by sending buyers to the back country.

France Loses a Continent

The English and the French had both penetrated now to the horse country. It was obvious that new trading methods would be required. However, before the two nations adjusted to the change, England defeated France in the Seven Years War. All of Canada fell into her hands, as did the Mississippi Valley east of the river. The valley west of the Mississippi, together with New Orleans, France ceded to Spain, thus consolidating her western empire. To establish a base in the upper country on the Spanish side of the Mississippi, Pierre Laclede ascended the Mississippi in the fall of 1763 and founded St. Louis near the site of an old mission. In his party was his stepson, Réné Auguste Chouteau, then an active boy of fourteen who was destined to become the progenitor of a fur trading dynasty. Most of the population of the new town came from the French settlements on what had become the English side of the Mississippi.

Despite the fact of Spanish sovereignty, it was the old French residents of Louisiana and Canada who maintained, and by degrees extended, the fur trade of the Missouri during the next three decades. But progress was slow. The Kansas Indians and the Osage objected to traders bypassing them to serve their enemies.

Out on the Plains the Comanche were an almost insuperable barrier to direct communication between St. Louis and Santa Fe. In 1759, with the help of allies, they even decimated an army of more than five hundred men Spain had mustered to crush them. In 1779 Juan Bautista de Anza campaigned successfully against them, but the fitful peace that followed was not one of subjugation. Rather it was an alliance to hold back the hated Apache, then gnawing at the vitals of the Spanish frontier far to the west and south. This strange arrangement may have been influenced by the dreadful smallpox epidemic of 1780-81 which ravaged all the tribes of the western half of the continent, from Texas to the Arctic.

During this period of catastrophic adjustment another effort was made to open the Santa Fe Trail, this time from the west. A French wanderer, Pierre (Pedro) Vial, with a few companions, crossed the Plains from Santa Fe to St. Louis in 1792 and returned the next year. However traders were reluctant to hazard any large quantity of merchandise in country subject to the whim of so many unruly and powerful tribes. No true Santa Fe trade developed until Mexico won her independence from Spain in 1821, and by that time the trail had to be pioneered all over again.

Spain and Russia Meet in the Pacific

On the far Pacific Coast, where the Indians were docile, Spain had a different problem in establishing her empire. In 1540 an expedition associated with Coronado's explored the Gulf of Mexico and mouth of the Colorado River. In the years that followed, Spanish mariners explored the California coast but Spain resolutely refused to entrench herself until threatened by Russians from the north.

As the eighteenth century wore on Muscovite fur traders, as tough a breed as any the Canadian North or the American West ever knew, reached Alaska and swarmed down the coast hunting sea otter and fur seals and driving their frail bidarkas and kayaks into every inlet and tidal estuary.

Spanish alarm over this penetration coincided with a brief and brilliant colonial renaissance. A chain of missions and presidios, begun at San Diego in 1769 was extended northward to San Francisco. However, these settlements failed to keep away the Russians who in 1812 established, only sixty miles north of San Francisco, an agricultural colony called Fort Ross to support bases in Alaska. Despite rumblings of Spanish (and later Mexican) discontent, the Russians stayed on until they sold Fort Ross to John A. Sutter in 1841.

The founding of the Spanish missions in California led to the last great Spanish exploration of the interior West. In order to find a direct route between New Mexico and the new missions, two Franciscan padres, Silvestre Vélez de Escalante and Francisco Atanasio Domínguez, set out from Santa Fe in 1776 with a small military escort. Their route led them through western Colorado, then west through northern Utah to the wonderfully fertile valley of Utah Lake. Dazzling vision came upon them: Here Spain would establish a mission to serve the Ute Indians, thereby changing all the history of the interior West. The Indians told the Spaniards of Great Salt Lake, a few miles to the north, but they did not pause to investigate this marvel. Still hoping to reach Monterey, they turned southward. When no likely route through the western deserts appeared, the Spanish friars at last made for Santa Fe, crossing the Colorado at the ford known ever since as the Crossing of the Fathers to return home via the Hopi villages. (There they crossed the trail of a fellow Franciscan, Francisco Garcés, who had pioneered a way from the coast of California down the Mohave River, thence to the Colorado, and east across Arizona south of the Grand Canyon to the Hopi towns. Only their trails crossed; the far-wandering Franciscans did not meet.) Domínguez and Escalante came home with a vision, but the dream was in vain; imperial Spain would never find the resources to raise her red and gold banner among the distant Ute. Only poor traders for skins and slaves, operating illegally and not eager to publicize their travels, would follow the path of the fathers and beat out dimly known trails; real discovery of the interior must wait upon the coming of British and American fur hunters.

The North West Fur Company Is Born

While these events transpired in far corners of the continent, developments basic to the history of the West occurred in Canada. As a result of her victory in 1763 in the Seven Years War, England fell heir to the St. Lawrence fur trade which had fought the Hudson's Bay Company since its inception. The business rivalry continued, in fact became worse, because, under British rule, the various St. Lawrence concerns united as the North West Company, a famous outfit worthy of the French traditions it inherited.

Both companies continued to send emissaries to the Mandan villages, but both realized that the greatest source of prime fur was the vast forested wilderness of western Canada. To scout this area for the North West Company, Alexander Mackenzie explored much of Canada, and in 1793 became the first man to cross the continent north of Mexico.

While the Hudson's Bay people and the Nor' Westers competed along the northern border of the American West, Spain issued licenses to upper Louisiana traders who boated up the Missouri River as far as the Mandan villages—now on Spanish soil—where they found British competitors. To add to Spanish difficulties, the Arikara and the Sioux decided to put an embargo on upriver traffic. A fort was built at the Omaha village but that was as far as traders with Spanish licenses could safely go. However, in the spring of 1796, a young Welsh-man named John Evans started for the Mandan villages with trade goods. He had come to America seeking to establish the existence of the long-rumored Welsh Indians, thought to live somewhere in the interior of the continent as descendants of an eleventh-century Welsh prince, Madoc. He hoped also to find the western ocean.

Evans never got farther than the Mandan villages; the wonder is that he got so far. Finding British traders among the Mandan, he ordered them off Spanish territory. The Indians compared his sparse merchandise with the English goods and soon drove him back down the river.

Evans' expedition was almost a complete failure. He had not even found any Mandan able to speak Welsh, and he returned to St. Louis with the conviction that no Indians anywhere were Welsh. (This would not deter men from hunting for white or Welsh Indians in the fastnesses of the West for another half-century; as late as the 1850's Brigham Young was sending Welsh converts to the Hopi, seeking to establish their identity as these fabled Indians.)

The last effort of the French and Spanish to cross the continent by way of the Missouri had fizzled out. Yet much had been learned about the upper country. Therefore Lewis and Clark had serviceable maps as far as the Mandan villages when they ascended the Missouri. They even knew that a river existed called the Rochejaune or Yellowstone.

3. *Americans Enter the Fur Trade*

Lewis and Clark

MERIWETHER LEWIS AND William Clark entered the Missouri River in the spring of 1804 to explore for the United States the land that had just become its property by the Louisiana Purchase. Their voyage of discovery was a culmination of nearly two decades of exploration by fur traders. The Big Muddy was known to be a rough and tough river in which only durable craft could survive. Lewis and Clark started with a twenty-two-oar bateau and a large and a small pirogue. Their first crisis came late in September—not from the turbulent waters but from equally turbulent Indians.

Above Bad River (in central South Dakota) they encountered the Teton Sioux, who were bound to take from the expedition such tribute as they had been exacting from the traders. They seized the tow ropes of the small pirogue, and a match flared above the open powder barrel, Americans tensing with rifles cocked, the vastly more numerous Sioux flexing their bows. Then the Sioux backed away; there was hospitality, oratory and feasting. Before the Americans went on, the Sioux made another try. Armed with muskets, bows, spears and what Clark calls "cutlashes," some two hundred braves gathered on the banks to hear the chiefs

"Lewis and Clark Meeting the Flathead Indians." Painting by Charles M. Russell.

announce that the river must remain closed. "They Sayed we might return with what we had or remain with them, but we could not go up the Missouri any further." Lewis ordered his boatmen to their oars and the rest of his force to battle stations; Clark was prepared to fire a swivel gun loaded with scrap iron point-blank into the crowd. And all at once the Sioux had had enough. The head chief, Black Buffalo, announced that the expedition could go on if he were paid a carrot (twist) of tobacco. Clark flung the tobacco into his face, an insult rather than a payment of tribute. The boats got under way, and the Sioux were reduced to the status of beggars, following along the river bank and whining for presents. News of what had happened traveled up the river ahead of the boats, and there was no more trouble; the Arikara, for one, would be sized up by Clark not as the bullies and extortionists traders had known, but a people "Durtey, Kind, pore & extravigent."

Not that these Indians, or any Indians, lacked courage. But they had their own way of doing things, their own notions of war. The unexpected they were not prepared to cope with, and they were inclined to play the percentages. Lewis and Clark established in the West the moral ascendancy over the Indian the French *coureurs de bois* had once enjoyed, and though this ascendancy would have periods of ebb and flux, depending on the character of the white men who went among the Indians, those who entered the West from this time on, down to and including the mountain men, could maintain themselves there and travel with immunity among the tribes to the extent that they shared the willingness of Lewis and Clark in the ultimate emergency to shoot the works whatever the cost.

The explorers went on up the Missouri to reach the Mandan villages the last week of October, 1804. Here they built a triangular stockade, Fort Mandan, in which they wintered while gathering information about the country west to the Rockies and even beyond. Next April, while some men set out downstream with collections made thus far, the permanent party started on. They numbered thirty in all—the two captains, the hunter and interpreter George Drouillard (a man of the same temper as the *coureurs de bois* of the past), the querulous French Canadian interpreter Toussaint Charbonneau, who had been taken into service during the winter, Charbonneau's young Snake squaw Sacagaweah and their infant son Baptiste, Clark's stalwart Negro slave York. And with all the rest, Lewis' Newfoundland dog Scammon.

They went up the Missouri past the Yellowstone, past the Marias, past the Great Falls and the Three Forks, the landscape becoming permanently known and named with their passage. They continued up the Jefferson and across Lemhi Pass to the waters of the Salmon, where they fell in with Snakes who shook and trembled lest these strangers be predatory Blackfeet. The Snakes said, and Lewis and Clark soon found their information correct, that it was impossible to descend the Salmon. It was necessary to cross another divide to the Bitterroot and starve their way across the Lolo Trail to the Nez Percé country. Having reached the Forks of the Clearwater by this hard route, the expedition built canoes and early in October floated down to the Snake and the Columbia, so at last reaching the sea. On a big pine William Clark carved his name and a date, December 3, 1805. Also: "By land from the U. States in 1804 & 1805."

After a miserable winter in the sluicing rains at the mouth of the Columbia, the expedition turned homeward, taking their outbound trail as far as the Bitterroot River in western Montana. Here the two leaders separated, to find a better route across the Continental Divide. Clark made his way south and then east to the Yellowstone (which in the meantime had been visited by François Antoine Larocque, one of the British traders encountered at the Mandan village in the winter of 1804-5). Lewis took a more northerly route to fall upon Sun River beyond Lewis and Clark Pass. He went on to reconnoiter the Marias River, and there he ran into a small party of Piegan, accompanied perhaps by a few Gros Ventres. Small though this party was, it outnumbered that of Lewis two to one. Red men and white treated cautiously, each apprehensive the other might have large reinforcements at hand. That night the Blackfeet attempted to steal the rifles and horses of the whites; in the melee one of the red men was stabbed to death, and Lewis shot another through the belly. The two parties fled in opposite directions, and afterward there would exist a mortal enmity between Blackfeet and Americans in the high country.

The two captains got together again below the mouth of the Yellowstone. By that time Lewis had been shot through the buttocks by one of his men, who in the underbrush had mistaken him for an elk. (Thus commenced still another chapter in western history, enthusiastically continued to the present day and going stronger every year.) Yet another precedent had been set, in that all of Clark's horses had been run off by those artful thieves, the Crows. Most meaningful of all, just below the mouth of the Yellowstone, Clark spied a canoe. Two trappers, Joseph Dickson and Forrest Hancock from Illinois, were coming upriver. They had spent last winter among the Sioux. The two turned back, with the expedition, to the Mandan villages. Here John Colter asked to be discharged so that he might become a trapper, too. Lewis and Clark let him go.

Observe that these men, hard on the heels of the explorers, were trappers, not Indian traders, a change important in the history of the West. We shall return to Colter, who not only has a large symbolic significance but also, in his subsequent adventures, stands forth as the prototype of that storied breed, the mountain men. Save for the Charbonneau family, who had reached home at the Mandan villages, the other members of the expedition floated on down the rolling brown tide of the Missouri. Bernard DeVoto, who like so many in our day would have given much to have lived in the age of Lewis and Clark and to have shared in the great adventure, has understood how it was with the company by now, the kind of men they had become:

> Their shirts and breeches of buckskin or elkskin had many patches sewed on with sinew, were worn thin between patches, were black from many campfires and greasy from many meals. They were threadbare and filthy, they smelled bad, and any Mandan had a lighter skin. They gulped rather than ate the tripes of buffalo. They had forgotten the use of chairs. Words and phrases, mostly obscene, of Nez Percé, Clatsop, Mandan, Chinook came naturally to their tongues. . . .
>
> And still, men who by guts and skill had mastered the farthest wilderness, they must have had a way of standing and a look in their eyes. . . . [Even in searching men's faces] their glance took in the movement of river and willows, of background and distance. . . . their minds watched a scroll of forever-changing images. What they had done, what they had seen, heard, felt, feared—the places, the sounds, the colors, the cold, the darkness, the emptiness, the bleakness, the beauty. Till they died this stream of memory would set them apart, if imperceptibly to anyone but themselves, from everyone else. For they had crossed the continent and come back, the first of all.

On September 23, 1806, the Corps of Discovery reached St. Louis: "the people gathered on the Shore and Hizzared three cheers," Sergeant Ordway says. Except for paying off the men, writing reports and more reports, everlastingly signing vouchers and receipts—the paper trail that any government expedition must scatter behind it, then, now and forever—the great venture was ended, and the American people had become incomparably richer. Rich in pride for what these men had done at such small cost in human life—only Sergeant Charles Floyd had died, of a "Biliose Chorlick," during the ascent of the Missouri in 1804. Rich in information about the great West and what was to be found there—information which to this day we are assessing, the whole sum not yet toted up. And rich in economic and political potential, for in the end the Republic's claim to Oregon would rest in large measure upon this journey to the Columbia and back.

The majority of the men scattered to the quiet life of farm and homestead, but some had been born to the wilderness life and must return to it and die of that compulsion. Others would live close to the frontier all their days, including William Clark, who as Territorial Governor and Superintendent of Indian Affairs over a period of nearly three decades would make St. Louis known to Indians everywhere as Red Head's Town.

In the summer of 1806, a few months before Lewis and Clark returned, Zebulon Montgomery Pike launched upon the famous expedition to the upper Arkansas and New Mexico, which ended in his arrest by Spanish soldiers. When he returned east across Texas from the Rio Grande, American knowledge of that area was considerably enlarged. But it was Lewis and Clark's journey to and from the far edge of the continent that revived the centuries-long dream of a route to the Orient. The imagery persisted over another half-century, coloring even the emotions men brought to the building of a Pacific Railroad; Thomas Benton envisioned a statue of Columbus on the tallest peak of the Rockies standing with outflung arm: "There lies the road to India." Even so, Lewis and Clark had carried west no court dress in which to greet the Chinese emperor, and they came home with a half-understanding that they had found the greatest wealth of all, the American West. In the end, all the wealth of the Indies could not have compared with that the West itself would shower upon the Republic.

Manuel Lisa

In the beginning, the West's wealth was furs. We have seen Dickson and Hancock pushing up the Missouri hard on the heels of Lewis and Clark, ready to pursue the quest for furs to the Yellowstone. Not much is known about the fall and spring hunt they and Colter made, but there is reason to suppose it was not very successful. In the early summer of 1807 Colter fashioned a dugout and started down the Missouri for home, alone: that is the measure of the man, and the kind of thing the West would see continuously from now on.

In coming downriver, Colter was bucking the tide of western history, for this year, in numbers far greater than historians have yet appreciated, trappers and traders were thronging to the Rockies. Least-known has been a body of fur hunters who penetrated to the Three Forks of the Missouri as early as July, 1807, possibly built a stockade there, and for two and a half years trapped and traded in the country, until driven out by the deftly murderous Blackfeet. They are the first Americans known to have trapped west of the Continental Divide, and we hope some day to know more about them.

Harper's Weekly, 1900

A white trapper. Engraving, after drawing by Frederic Remington.

Best known among those who penetrated to the high country this year is the company headed by Manuel Lisa, out of which evolved, with the participation of the Chouteaus and others, that famous concern the Missouri Fur Company. Few had neutral feelings about Lisa, a turbulent fellow of Spanish descent. A contemporary described him as a man with a dark-complexioned Mexican face in which rascality was seated in every feature, gleaming from his black Spanish eyes and "enthroned in a forehead 'villainous low.'" Another viewed him as "a man of a bold and daring character, with an energy and spirit of enterprise like that of Cortez or Pizarro," none better acquainted with the Indian character and trade, and few his equals in persevering indefatigable industry. Meeting Colter somewhere above the mouth of the Platte, Lisa urged him to turn back. And though John Colter had now been three years from home, he let himself be persuaded.

Down to this time, Lisa had been known primarily as a trader on the lower Missouri, but from 1807 until his death in 1820 he was the dominant figure in the fur trade of the upper Missouri, the man with the most drive, the highest skill with Indians, the indispensable knack of finding backers when he needed them. His competitors cordially detested him, and his men did not like him very much.

Lisa's first mountain venture forced its way up the Missouri past the Mandan villages, and on up the Yellowstone to the mouth of the Big Horn, where in the fall of 1807 he erected the first post on Yellowstone waters, named in honor of his young son, Fort Raymond, but best remembered as Manuel's Fort. From this base of operations his men spread out, some trapping on their own account, others sent to seek out the Indians and persuade them to enter into trade relations.

Colter's Hell

The most famous mission was performed by John Colter, who was sent to seek the Crows and perhaps the Snakes. Supposedly alone, but possibly with some companions, including an Indian guide, Colter journeyed far to the south, up the Big Horn and Wind River, west to Snake waters, from Jackson Hole again west to Pierres Hole by Teton Pass, then back to the Yellowstone by a route that took him past the west shore of Yellowstone Lake. His route is shown on William Clark's famous map, attributed to 1807, but unless that was an incredibly open winter, so long a journey through such high country is more likely to have been performed in the spring of 1808. The most pleasant heritage to have come down to us from this wilderness foray is that sulphurous hot springs in the vicinity of the present Cody, Wyoming, became known as Colter's Hell and contributed their part to the legendry of the West. The thermal phenomena in Yellowstone Park itself, more spectacular today, Colter seems not to have seen.

This was only the first of a series of famous exploits. In the summer of 1808, after Lisa started down the Yellowstone to make arrangements for the next year's outfit, Colter set off on a new mission, to find the Flatheads who regularly crossed the Rockies to hunt buffalo on the plains of the upper Missouri and Yellowstone and to induce them also to open a trade at the fort on the Big Horn. Colter was in company with the Flatheads and some Crows when the Blackfeet attacked. In a valiant fight, the outnumbered Flatheads and Crows stood off the foe. Colter was in the thick of the battle; a wound in the leg did not prevent his firing away from a small thicket while seated on the ground. It is said, as though the Blackfeet required any additional fuel to fire their enmity toward the Americans, that the sight of Colter engaged against them in this battle set a final seal upon their mortal hatred for the Long Knives.

After this came the famous adventure involving Colter and his old companion of the Lewis and Clark expedition, John Potts. They went trapping in the Three Forks country and were taken unawares by Blackfeet. Potts picked up his rifle and killed one of the enemy on the spot. "This conduct, situated as he was, may appear to have been an act of madness," the contemporary account of the English naturalist, John Bradbury, observes, "but it was doubtless the effect of sudden, but sound reasoning; for if taken alive, he must have expected to be tortured to death, according to their custom. He was instantly pierced with arrows so numerous, that, to use the language of Colter, 'he was made a riddle of.'" Colter was seized, stripped naked, and the manner of his death debated. Instead of using him for a mark to shoot at, the Blackfeet elected to run him. He was given a head start of three or four hundred yards, then the pack pelted after him. In the most celebrated of all races for life in the West, Colter ran mile upon heart-bursting mile to outdistance every brave except one. Unarmed and despairing, he turned upon his pursuer. When the half-exhausted Blackfoot fell in trying to hurl his spear, Colter snatched it up and ran his enemy through, then again took to his heels. Even when he had won free of the Blackfeet, as Bradbury wrote after getting his story at first hand, Colter's situation "was still dreadful: he was completely naked, under a burning sun; the soles of his feet were entirely filled with the thorns of the prickly pear; he was hungry, and had no means of killing game, although he saw abundance around him, and was at least seven

"Raiding Party" (Blackfeet). Painting by W. H. D. Koerner.

days journey from Lisa's Fort.... These were circumstances under which almost any man but an American hunter would have despaired. He arrived at the fort in seven days, having subsisted on a root much esteemed by the Indians of the Missouri," commonly known as breadroot.

After another brush with the Blackfeet, next year Colter set out for home. He got as far as the Mandan villages when he met Lisa coming upriver. He turned back for yet another year in the mountains, chilling the blood of his fellows with the tale of his adventures. He had used up more than his share of good luck, and in the spring of 1810, with other men he embarked for St. Louis in a dugout. A voyage of thirty days brought them safely home in May, 1810. Ironically, he died in Missouri three years later, yellowed by jaundice. John Colter bequeathed the West a larger-than-life-size legend, yet the legend is no taller than the facts. That was the sort of thing that would characterize the West.

First American Trading Post on the Pacific Slope

Lisa's men made a determined effort to extend their fur-gathering to the vicinity of the Three Forks. In the spring of 1810 they erected a stout stockade near the confluence of the Jefferson and the Madison. The stockade served no purpose, for the Blackfeet cut and hacked at the scattered parties of trappers; the redoubtable George Drouillard was among those hewed down. This murderous clime must be abandoned, but reluctant to admit defeat, urgently appreciating the necessity to open new trapping grounds, Andrew Henry took a party across the Continental Divide at the head of the Madison—a locality known for a time thereafter as the Southern Pass, to distinguish it from the northern passes Lewis and Clark had used. Beyond the divide, on what has ever since been called Henrys Fork of the Snake, Andrew Henry built the first American fur trading post known to have been erected on Pacific waters, certainly the first in the vast basin of the Snake. (The North West Company had established a post on the Columbia waters in 1808.)

Henry and his men had a starving time, having to subsist on their horses, nor did they make out too well in their trapping. In the spring of 1811 the party scattered; some found their way south to Santa Fe; others crossed the Tetons into Jackson Hole, then climbed over the Wind River Mountains to the waters of the Big Horn. Henry himself returned home as he had come, via the Yellowstone and the Missouri. He may have had a half-expectation of returning in force, but miscellaneous disasters including the destruction by fire of a Sioux post with total loss of stored furs and trading goods, prevented any immediate step of the kind; and soon afterward the outbreak of the War of 1812 made it hazardous to seek furs above the Sioux. From the time Henry descended the Missouri in the summer of 1811, for ten full years, the high country was left to the Crows and the Blackfeet.

John Jacob Astor's American Fur Company

Meanwhile, in New York, John Jacob Astor had set about pre-empting the empire of fur centering upon the Columbia Lewis and Clark had opened to the sight of all. Astor, a modern biographer says, had very strong views about reserving the fur trade of the West to American citizens; in fact, it was his purpose "to concentrate the Western fur trade in the hands of only such American citizens as had been born in Waldorf, Germany, in 1763 and had arrived in the United States from London in the spring of 1784." By the time of the Louisiana Purchase he was the leading fur merchant of the United States, a shrewd, hardfisted, thoroughly acquisitive master of the business. Having obtained a charter for his American Fur Company, and with the sanction of the United States government, Astor conceived a grandiose project. He would establish a principal base on the Columbia, with dependent inland posts, from which he would ship furs directly to the prime market afforded by China—a market closed to his British rivals by reason of the monopoly enjoyed by the East India Company. Further, he would arrange to supply the Russian posts in Alaska. Astor organized a subsidiary, the Pacific Fur Company, reserving fifty shares for himself and dividing fifty among various men who would be acting partners. (In an effort to keep the North West Company within bounds, Astor offered that concern a one-third interest in the business, but the Canadians declined, having ideas of their own.) Astor himself provided the capital—no inconsiderable sum.

Astor's first ship, the *Tonquin,* sailed from New York in September, 1810, bound for the Columbia by way of Cape Horn and certain to get there ahead of the large overland party led by Wilson Price Hunt. After a rough voyage, she bumped her way across the dangerous bar at the Columbia's mouth in March, 1811, having eight men drowned before winning through to safe anchorage. On April 12 the construction of Astoria was commenced, an affirmative act of settlement held to have great diplomatic importance when the United States and Great Britain began arguing out the thorny question of title to the Oregon country.

Lisa Races the Astorians up the Missouri

While these things were happening west of the Rockies, the overland Astorians led by Wilson Price Hunt were struggling across the immensities of the West to the Columbia. Principal lieutenants of Hunt were Donald Mackenzie and Ramsay Crooks, both former Nor' Westers. Having hired men at Montreal and Mackinac, early in September, 1810, Hunt reached St. Louis where he was viewed with jealous suspicion by the Missouri Fur Company. Astor thus far had been kept out of the Missouri trade, and the Chouteaus and their associates wanted that to continue; they took no comfort from the assertions of Astor's men that the Pacific Fur Company would limit operations to the Columbia. That was their own sphere of expansion, with Andrew Henry already beyond the divide. In any event, no trader trusted another much farther than he could throw a buffalo by the tail. Anyone who went up the Missouri was suspected with good reason of bland willingness to hatch out trouble for those behind. Usually the first to meet obstructive Indians made extravagant promises of presents to be delivered by the next in line, promises which the latecomers would be called upon to make good. Finally, there was competition for hired men, of whom there were never enough, and this bid up the cost of wages.

Hunt had started much too late to cross the mountains this year. To save the expense of wintering in the settlements, he took his party up the Missouri as far as the Nodaway (just north of present St. Joseph, Missouri), where they could subsist by hunting. In the course of the ensuing winter he himself returned to St. Louis to complete his preparations. There he got into a row with Lisa by hiring as his interpreter the half-breed Pierre Dorion, who had signed on with Lisa earlier. At that, Dorion only agreed to make the journey when Hunt stipulated that his squaw and two children might come along. (Up to this time it was chiefly the French Canadians who had taken Indian wives; the Americans in an otherwise womanless West would come to it, but not until they had evolved as mountain men.) Thus the Iowa girl, Marie Dorion, became the first woman after Sacagaweah to cross the plains and mountains of the West to the Pacific.

In a boat of ten oars, Hunt set out from St. Louis in mid-March, 1811. With him traveled John Bradbury, an English naturalist, eager to examine plants of the upper Missouri and, therefore, considered by the Canadians to be out of his mind.

Lisa could not complete his own preparations until three weeks after Hunt's departure, but he set out with every determination to overtake the Astorian before the latter should reach the Sioux. Henry Brackenridge, one of the young pleasure seekers occasionally seen in

"Tomahawk and Long Rifle." Painting by W. H. D. Koerner.

the West now, says their barge was the best that had ever ascended the river, manned with twenty stout oarsmen, Lisa having taken "much pains in rigging his boat with a good mast, and main and top-sail; these being great helps in the navigation of this river." Brackenridge adds:

> Our equipage is chiefly composed of young men, though several have already made a voyage to the upper Missouri, of which they are exceedingly proud, and on that account claim a kind of precedence over the rest of the crew. We are in all, twenty-five men, and completely prepared for defence. There is, besides, a swivel on the bow of the boat, which, in case of attack, would make a formidable appearance; we have also two brass blunderbusses in the cabin, one over my birth [*sic!*] and the other over that of Mr. Lisa. These precautions were absolutely necessary from the hostility of the Sioux bands, who, of late had committed several murders and robberies on the whites, and manifested such a disposition that it was believed impossible for us to pass through their country. The greater part of the merchandise, which consisted of strouding, blankets, lead, tobacco, knifes,

guns, beads, &c., was concealed in a false cabin, ingeniously contrived for the purpose; in this way presenting as little as possible to tempt the savages.

In a few words, Brackenridge has said much about the conditions under which life in the West might be possible. Beyond the Spanish rimlands, white penetration of the American West in this decade was more or less limited to the pulsing artery of the Missouri, and men survived there on such terms as these. Moreover, men who had ascended the river past the mouth of the Platte considered themselves a race apart, to which new initiates were admitted only after such ceremonies as are seen on shipboard on the crossing of the equator: "All those who had not passed it before, were required to be shaved, unless they could compromise the matter by a treat."

Nearly always the rivermen were of the old French blood. They did not take to the rifle, did not like to hunt and had no stomach whatever for fighting. There were exceptions, like the now-dead George Drouillard, the brothers Robidoux, and the later-to-be-heard-from Étienne Provost, but Kentuckians and Virginians were becoming the backbone of any trapping and trading operations—in particular, any that strayed far from the banks of the Missouri. Yet in their own milieu these "Canadians and Creoles" were a marvel. Brackenridge comments:

> I believe an American could not be brought to support with patience the fatiguing labors and submission which these men endure. At this season, when the water is exceedingly cold, they leap in without a moment's hesitation. Their food consists of lied corn homony for breakfast, a slice of fat pork and biscuit for dinner, and a pot of mush, with a pound of tallow in it, for supper. Yet this is better than the common fare; but we were about to make an extraordinary voyage, and the additional expense was not regarded.

These details are essential to an understanding of the West over the next three decades; all that was done there depended upon the character of the men. The individualistic Americans with their long rifles and marksman's eye had an essential role, but so did the mercurial, gregarious French Canadians who were the working hands of the fur trade and made all of the rest possible.

Lisa made frantic efforts to overtake the Astorians by hoisting sail at every opportunity. In one twenty-four-hour period he navigated seventy-five miles. Through such tireless efforts he managed to catch up, but not until both he and Hunt, with presents and threats of war, had passed the Sioux. Afterward they traveled more or less together in a friendly state of mutual distrust. Lisa could outpace the Astorians, and they feared he would pull ahead and hatch out trouble for them at the Arikara villages.

Three Important Strangers

For all these doubts and fears, the two parties reached the Arikara together, and Hunt ended by selling two of his boats to Lisa. While Hunt was ascending the river, soon after passing the Niobrara, Hunt had met three men descending the Missouri in two canoes. Their names were John Hoback, Jacob Reznor and Edward Robinson; they had wintered with

Andrew Henry beyond the Continental Divide and started home by a new route. "They had been several years hunting on and beyond the Rocky Mountains," says Bradbury, "until they *imagined* they were tired of the hunting life; and having families and good plantations in Kentucky, were returning to them; but on seeing us, families, plantations, and all vanished; they agreed to join us, and turned their canoes adrift." Robinson was sixty-six years old, one of the first settlers in Kentucky, and had actually been scalped in a fight with the Indians there, so that he had to wear a handkerchief on his head to protect the exposed part; but none of this counted with men born for the wilderness life (Bradbury had observed earlier, when talking to John Colter, that Colter was almost irresistibly impelled to join the expedition, despite the experiences he had survived and despite having recently been married; the charms of the wife barely outweighed those of the wilderness.) More immediately important, these leathery recruits convinced Hunt that the route of Lewis and Clark he had intended taking was not the best, that they had discovered a better route to the south. Hunt decided to leave the Missouri at the Arikara villages and find his way overland.

The First Overland Travelers to the Pacific

So, having reached the Arikara on June 12, Hunt delayed among them until July 18, trading for horses with the Indians and with Lisa's people and waiting impatiently for the Cheyenne to ride in from the Plains on their annual trading visit. The Cheyenne did not appear, and Hunt launched out upon his journey anyhow, though the eighty-two horses he had acquired were sufficient only to transport his goods, besides one for Dorion's belongings and children and one each for the Astorian partners. Fortunately, on August 5, Hunt fell in with the Cheyenne. From them he was able to buy another thirty-five horses, and this made it possible for his party, now consisting of fifty-six men, one woman and two children, to get along a little less laboriously, one animal being allotted to each of the six prime hunters, the others distributed among the voyageurs, so that with a horse for every two, the men could ride and walk alternately. This expedition was going to be characteristic of travel in the West; in all ages there was much more of hoofing it than of galloping along on horseback. Packs always came first; men rode only if there were horses and mules to spare.

The westward march of the Astorians has been described by Washington Irving, and nobody has improved upon his account. The adventures of these wayfarers are important to us above all because they traveled through new parts of the West and opened up fresh chapters in its history. By a route generally southwest, some of the time following a trail the Crows had beaten out on their periodic visits to the Mandan and their Hidatsa cousins, the Astorians reached a Crow camp at the foot of the Big Horn Mountains. After trading for more horses, they went on to Wind River, already so called by Lisa's men. With Hoback, Reznor and Robinson for guides, Hunt journeyed up Wind River for seven days, traveling a broadly beaten Indian trail. On September 15, as Hunt says in his diary, "One of our hunters, who had been on the shores of the Columbia, showed us three immensely high and snow-covered peaks which, he said, were situated on the banks of a tributary of that river"—and thus the magnificent Tetons, called by Hunt "the Pilot Knobs," rose up on history's skyline.

Scarcity of game would not allow Hunt to make direct for Jackson Hole via Togwotee Pass, the route Henry's men had taken in coming east; instead he took his men across Union

Pass and down to what the fur hunters called Spanish River (the Green), correctly conceiving it to be a source of the Colorado of the West. From the upper Green, taking the trail via the Hoback River, Jackson Hole and Teton Pass which the mountain men would make so much their own in time to come, the Astorians found their way to Pierres Hole, on October 8 reaching what Hunt calls "the fort of Mr. Andrew Henry . . . several small buildings which he had erected so as to spend last winter there. . . ."

Hunt built dugouts from cottonwood logs, and after leaving a small party to trap the Snake country (five men who have come down in history as the Detached Astorians), entrusted his horse herd to some Snakes and set out for the Pacific by water. That was a mistake, soon repented: Hunt would better have kept on by horseback, for in adversity, as men were about to learn, you could eat your horses—which were more than could be said of a dugout canoe. By the time Hunt reached the vicinity of Twin Falls (Idaho), he had lost several canoes and one man. In truth the rivers of the mountain-desert West could not be subdued to the service of water transport. In this high country one must foot it if he could not ride a horse or a mule. Hunt cached most of his goods and in the shadow of starvation began the long hike to the Columbia.

He and his men had a terrible journey. A few, led by Donald Mackenzie, an enormously corpulent fellow whose fat served him now as a source of energy, succeeded in finding a way through or past that awesome gorge known today as Hell's Canyon of the Snake. The rest, including Hunt himself, had to leave the river and follow Indian trails across the Blue Mountains, a route eventually to be known as the Oregon Trail.

Having reached the Columbia near the mouth of the Umatilla, Hunt made his way down the river through frequent rain and fog. In mid-February, 1812, he arrived at palisaded Astoria. Mackenzie and his detachment had got there a month earlier, but other news was not so good: Astor's ship *Tonquin* had been blown up by its crew on the Northwest Coast during an Indian attack. The company might have survived this and various other disasters, but presently war broke out with Britain, and word reached Astoria that a British naval vessel was en route to the Columbia to make a prize of the post. In October, 1813, the partners decided—Astor never forgave them for it—to sell Astoria to the North West Company, which had established itself under the very noses of the Americans. Thus, for perhaps a third of its value, Astor's property passed into British hands. Late in November the naval vessel arrived and her commander took formal possession of the Oregon country. That elevation of a commercial transaction to a matter of state was a mistake. When peace came, Astoria was handed back to the United States. Under other circumstances, the North West Company, as purchasers of Astoria, might have remained in full possession of the property and the country: On so fine a legal point hung much of the eventual American claim to Oregon.

Discovery of the Oregon Trail Route

A little company of Astorians left for a return trip to the States in 1812. Headed by Robert Stuart, they were the first fur hunters to traverse South Pass and the first to mark out the long road down the valley of the Platte which became the primary artery of travel to and from the northern Rockies, as later between the States and the settlements of Oregon, California and Utah.

Carrying dispatches for Astor, and with five companions, all of whom had accompanied Hunt west, Robert Stuart set out for home late in June, at a time when Astoria's prospects seemed encouraging. One of the party, half-insane, had to be sent back, but the rest went on, retracing Hunt's route as far as the Snake River. There Stuart fell in with a Snake Indian who had guided Henry across the Tetons the previous autumn. From this much-traveled Indian, white men first heard of South Pass: "There is a shorter trace to the South than that by which Mr. Hunt had traversed the R Mountains." This Indian being "perfectly acquainted with the route," Stuart offered him "a Pistol a Blanket of Blue Cloth—an Axe—a Knife—an awl—a Fathom of blue Beads a looking Glass and a little Powder & Ball if he would guide us from this to the other side, which he immediately accepted, saying that the Salmon were not as good as *La Vache* (which signifies Buffaloes)." Alas, two days later the Snake vanished from camp, taking Stuart's horse as well as his own. Stuart set a night guard thereafter, but he did not forget what he had heard about a southern pass.

Soon after, near the mouth of the Bruneau River, Stuart ran into four of last year's Detached Astorians; one of their number had deserted, and they had been twice plundered by the Indians, so that they were fishing to keep their bones inside their skin. These men had wandered widely, evidently so far south as to become the discoverers of the Bear River. One of them joined Stuart, having had enough of wilderness life, but Hoback, Reznor and Robinson, after being reoutfitted from Hunt's cached goods chose to stay in the country and trap its wealth of beaver. (They stayed forever, being killed by the Snakes near the mouth of the Boise

"An Indian Stampede." Painting by F. O. C. Darley.

River in January, 1814.) The rest of the Astorians, now again totaling six men, made their way south to the Bear River only to fall in with a party of Crow Indians, ranging farther to the southwest than could have been expected. "Knowing the adroitness of these fellows in stealing Horses we doubled our Watches," Stuart remarked. In the hope of evading these unwelcome visitors, next day the Astorians turned north toward the Snake, up Thomas Fork. This availed nothing; six days later, two yelling Crows stampeded the horses, leaving the Astorians afoot, a thousand miles from anywhere. Resolutely they kept on: "We have just food enough for one meal, and rely with confidence on the inscrutable ways of Providence to send in our road wherewith to subsist on. . . ."

Taking the route Hunt had used westbound, Stuart and his men crossed the Tetons to Jackson Hole and went on to the upper Green, starving along from day to day. So hard was the going that one of the Canadians proposed lots be cast for one to die that the rest might live. When the man would not yield to reason, Stuart says, "I snatched up my Rifle cocked and leveled it at him with the firm resolution to fire if he persisted," which so terrified the man that he fell on his knees and asked the whole party's pardon. Somehow food was always found, something killed or a beaver caught in the only trap they had.

Seeing to the southeast "the point of a mountain" beyond which they expected to fall upon Missouri waters, the Astorians slogged along in that direction. In this way, on October 22, 1812, the little band of ragged adventurers, almost but not quite lost in the heart of the West, made their way across that broad upland plateau which history would know as South Pass. Continuing east, they came upon the North Platte sunk in deep red canyons which Stuart called "the Fiery Narrows."

Winter was breathing cold upon their necks, and they resolved to establish a winter camp. Near the mouth of Poison Spider Creek, slightly southwest of present Casper, Wyoming, they built a cabin eight by eighteen feet. A thaw materialized, the frozen river began to run, and along came twenty-three Arapaho on a foray against the Crows. The neighborhood was suddenly much too populous; with past experience giving wings to their imaginations, the six Astorians concluded that their retreat was less than snug, after all.

So they resumed their journey down the stream they soon decided was the North Platte. On December 31, the river running thick with ice, the little band made a new winter camp not far west of the future Wyoming-Nebraska line. Here they remained until the second week of March, laboring on two dugout canoes.

These craft, however, proved of small utility when floated out upon the Platte, that shallow stream so little disposed to work for men. The Astorians had to foot it again, making their slow way down the broad Platte until April 13, when they reached the Oto village, some thirty-six miles above the river's mouth. Among these Indians they found two traders just arrived from St. Louis, who confirmed "the disagreeable intelligence of a war between America and Great Britain." Obtaining a small supply of provisions, they had an easy passage the rest of the way to St. Louis, and on April 30, as Stuart says, a little before sunset they reached that town "all in the most perfect health after a voyage of ten months from Astoria during which time we had the peculiar good fortune to have suffered in one instance only by want of provisions—"

Their arrival created a sensation, no news of Hunt's party having yet got back to the

States. The *Missouri Gazette* printed a long account of the far-traveled Astorians. And also: "By information received from these gentlemen, it appears that a journey across the continent of North America might be performed with a waggon, there being no obstruction in the whole route that any person would dare to call a mountain."

So was announced the key fact of South Pass and the ultimate accessibility of the West. Beyond all else, that was the news brought home by the returning Astorians.

British Ascendancy in the West

The acquisition of Astoria marks a high point in the history of the North West Company. That concern was now locked in a mortal struggle with the mighty Hudson's Bay Company, a struggle which as the decade wore on became so murderous that the British government had to intervene, leading to the merging of the two companies in 1821 and the extension of Hudson's Bay Company operations to the Pacific (previously its charter limited the English firm to waters draining into Hudson Bay). While the issue was being fought out east of the Rockies, the North West Company had a season of greatness farther west.

Donald Mackenzie, who had returned home in 1814 only to be hired by the North West Company and sent back to the Columbia to bring a much-needed vigor to the fur-hunting there, accomplished all that had been asked of him and a good deal more. The Company had various posts on the upper Columbia but none were very productive. He founded a new base, Fort Nez Percé or Walla Walla in the Nez Percé country, and from it took a trapping brigade southeast into the Snake lands. Such a brigade, big enough to protect itself from the Indians, would trap furs on its own account instead of trying to trade them from Indians, and would stay in the field indefinitely. Mackenzie thus trapped almost continuously from the fall of 1818 to the spring of 1821, giving to most of the tributaries of the Snake the names they have borne ever since, while ranging as far south as Bear River and as far east as the Green.

Sending out white (or near-white) men to trap instead of trade was new to the British. Both Manuel Lisa and Wilson Price Hunt had done this in a small way, but it was possible only where the Indians were at least benevolently neutral. White men made better trappers than most red men, who valued scalps and horses above European goods and disliked sustained work. A Shoshoni in this era might even prefer to burn the hair off a beaver he had caught to save the trouble of skinning it. Thus the Snakes did not object, as the Blackfeet and some other tribes did, to white men trapping in their country.

During the period of British ascendancy in the West, during and immediately after the War of 1812-1815, Americans were slow to challenge their powerful rivals, confining their operations to the lower country. Lisa established two bases on the Missouri, one in 1812 just south of the future boundary between North and South Dakota, and a more long-lived post called Fort Lisa among the Omaha in 1814. It was at the former base, Fort Manuel, that the celebrated Sacagaweah died of "putrid fever" on December 20, 1812; as Lisa's clerk regretfully observed, "she was a good and the best Woman in the fort, aged abt 25 years."

Lisa sent traders as far west as the Crow country and south to Santa Fe. He tried unsuccessfully to maintain trade with the Mandan villages but found that the British concerns had influenced all the tribes north of the Sioux against Americans. Several of his men were killed, and he could only bide his time. Lisa's great service during the war was to win over the Teton Sioux, never again a serious problem to Missouri fur traders.

Under one firm name or another, and with various partners, Lisa kept up the Missouri trade, and for a time in 1818-1819 it seemed possible he might again get a grip upon the Mandan trade. The U. S. government conceived a "Yellowstone Expedition" which would found a military post at the mouth of that river, both to assert American sovereignty and to keep British traders from tampering with the Indians. The Yellowstone Expedition was altogether too grandiose; plagued by overambition and mismanagement, it got little higher than Fort Lisa, in the vicinity of which that capable soldier Henry Atkinson founded a military post named for him. From 1819 to 1827, when it was abandoned in favor of Cantonment (Fort) Leavenworth, Fort Atkinson was the remotest United States military establishment in all the great basin of the Missouri. Undoubtedly it had a tranquilizing effect upon the tribes of the middle river—the Kansa, Iowa, Oto and Pawnee—if not upon the tribes beyond the Sioux.

A new era in the Missouri fur trade began in 1820 but it was not to be a Lisa era; the turbulent Spaniard died in June of that year—died in bed in St. Louis, after voyages up and down the Missouri which over the years had become equivalent in mileage to a voyage by pirogue around the world.

Prior to this revival of the Missouri trade, an abortive effort had been made to trade and trap on the upper Arkansas. After two years of trapping, one such party was arrested by Spanish soldiers.

A member of that party, having become familiar with the country on this trapping expedition, served as guide when Major Stephen H. Long of the Corps of Topographical Engineers set out for the Rockies at the head of a small scientific party in the summer of 1820, seeking to salvage something from the debacle of the Yellowstone Expedition. Long rode up the Platte and the South Platte to the Front Range of the Rockies, then south to the Arkansas. He clarified some geographical details concerning that stream's tributaries and fastened on the Great Plains one of the most enduring of names, the "Great American Desert."

Reopening of the Santa Fe Trail

The boundary between Spain and the United States in the West was diplomatically defined in 1819, but the opening of the southwestern fur trade and commercial traffic between New Mexico and Missouri had to wait upon the attainment of Mexican independence in 1821.

The notable figure in the reopening of the Santa Fe Trail is William Becknell, who conceived a trading venture to New Mexico. Only four men volunteered to share the risks, but in late August, 1821, they set out from Franklin, Missouri, a new river town almost a hundred and fifty miles west of St. Louis. Becknell carried his trade goods on pack animals and reached Santa Fe in mid-December. Successful in selling out at a profit, he promptly returned home in January with news of the marvelously changed attitude of the authorities in New Mexico. Several other parties of Americans were in Santa Fe at the same time as Becknell, having found their way to the mountains from Arkansas, and one of these groups built wintering

On the Santa Fe Trail.　　　　

houses on the Arkansas between present Pueblo and the mountains—the first substantial structures built by Americans in this area. (These other ventures, in contrast to Becknell's, were anything but financial successes.) Encouraged by Becknell's reports, several expeditions left Missouri for Santa Fe in the spring of 1822. Becknell himself went along, taking three wagons—the first ever hauled to Santa Fe and back—thus dramatically establishing the Sante Fe Trail as a road. The "commerce of the prairies" would have to contend with the wild tribes of the Southwest, burdensome duties, wagon tolls and official graft, to say nothing of the normal vicissitudes of trade; but from 1822 a Santa Fe trade existed to change the history of the Southwest. And from New Mexican bases—Santa Fe, Taos and Abiquiu—beaver hunters could now get their teeth into the southern Rockies.

Four Big Competitors

It was the Missouri with its great tributaries the Kansas, the Platte and the Yellowstone which afforded the primary avenues for a full-scale advance by American traders upon the Rocky Mountain West. Some fur hunters, individuals of whom almost nothing is known, akin to Joseph Dickson and Forrest Hancock in the era of Lewis and Clark, made for the mountains on their own hook; a "free man" named Jacques Laramie was killed about 1821 on the sparkling mountain river that has borne his name ever since. But in the main, the invasion of the Rockies was by organized companies.

There were four principal claimants to the wealth of the Missouri. The lead was taken by the Missouri Fur Company, reorganized in 1820 after Manuel Lisa's death; in this firm such notable traders as Joshua Pilcher, Charles Bent, Lucien Fontenelle, Andrew Drips and William Henry Vanderburgh first rose to prominence. A lower post was opened just above the mouth of the Kansas River in support of Fort Lisa, and in the summer of 1821 Pilcher sent a party under Michael E. Immell and Robert Jones to reoccupy the old ground at the mouth of the Big Horn. This post, Fort Benton, was intended to re-establish the trade in Crow beaver (the finest known on the Missouri, far superior to the river beaver, since it came from a higher and colder country), and at the same time provide an advance base for operations beyond the Continental Divide. Pilcher also proposed to re-establish his company at the Mandan villages and even to locate a post in the Blackfoot country, near the mouth of the Marias. In 1822 the Missouri Fur Company looked like the most solid bet to dominate the American fur trade in the Far West.

An active competitor was the Columbia Fur Company, founded by Nor' Westers at loose ends after the merger with the Hudson's Bay Company. These experienced men took out naturalization papers, rounded up American partners and began to operate on both the upper Mississippi and the Red River of the North, tapping the Mandan trade as well.

The third big firm, termed by its rivals the "French Company," was made up of the closely intermarried French traders of St. Louis whom for convenience we call the Chouteaus. In 1822 they clearly bulked largest in Pilcher's calculations. These Creoles had long traded on the lower Missouri but in 1822 moved upstream, establishing posts in opposition to Pilcher's as far north as the Sioux country.

In a hotly competitive business, as the North West and Hudson's Bay companies had learned in Canada, it was essential to oppose a rival at every point; otherwise he could build up resources that would enable him to undercut prices. When two concerns were everywhere competitive, so that no advantage could be gained by either, the usual result was an "accommodation"—the two would divide up the trade or merge, the Indians not likely to benefit in either case.

The French Company was slow to lift its sights beyond the Mandan villages, not getting even that high until the summer of 1825, but no fur traders ever showed themselves so well adapted to the Missouri trade, and from 1822 the Chouteaus were in that trade to a finish.

Radically different from the first three, a maverick destined to revolutionize the whole fur trade of the Far West, was a concern organized in St. Louis in the late summer of 1821 by the then lieutenant governor of Missouri, William H. Ashley, in association with Andrew Henry. Ashley & Henry began buying goods, mainly from St. Louis firms and on credit, in September, 1821, about the time Immell and Jones reached the Big Horn for the Missouri Fur Company, and in February, 1822, made public announcement of their plans in the most famous want ad ever printed:

To Enterprising Young Men:

The subscriber wishes to engage ONE HUNDRED MEN, to ascend the river Missouri to its source, there to be employed for one, two or three years.—For particulars enquire of Major Andrew Henry, near the Lead Mines, in the County of Washington, (who will ascend with, and command the party) or to the subscriber at St. Louis.

Wm. H. Ashley

Most of the men selected from those who responded to this advertisement were not hired at a fixed wage. Instead, they were to be "free trappers"—the first of the mountain men, a remarkable breed, for there would never be a time when a free trapper did not consider himself the peer of any man alive, and ultimately the nobility of the mountain fur trade.

4. *The Mountain Men*

PRIOR to ASHLEY'S innovation the fur trading companies had always conducted their operations with hired servants, *engagés*. Men were paid so much a month for a period of a year or so; and usually an advance was given them before leaving St. Louis or nearby St. Charles, money on which wives and families could get along until the men returned. Now Ashley was proposing to change all this. He would take to the mountains men free of any obligation to him, intending to buy their furs in the mountains at fixed prices, roughly half their value in St. Louis. These purchases he would make in goods, a great deal more useful to the trappers in the mountains than hard money. In effect, Ashley was gambling that he could begin storekeeping on the sources of the Missouri, making more money by trading furs from men spurred by the profit incentive than he could hope to make by hiring men to trap for him. It may be that Ashley's revolutionary conception originated as much in his own lack of funds, and need to cut down his overhead, as in the original bent of his mind and his understanding of the American character. Later he saw the need for *engagés* himself, and hired his full share of them. But the class of men brought into being must henceforth exist for all to reckon with.

Those who laid claim to the West as Ashley men, that year and the next, stand tall in history, their caliber a sufficient comment on Ashley's sagacity. Among them is the intelligent, mule-tough, religiously inclined Jedediah Smith. The lank, Jackson-faced, durable, consistently fortunate William L. Sublette. The ruddy-featured Thomas Fitzpatrick, with his iron control over a volcanic nature. The quiet, ever-dependable David E. Jackson. The stripling Jim Bridger, destined to become a supreme master of the wilderness. The swarthy-featured, irascible, self-sufficient, yarn-spinning Moses "Black" Harris. And countless others whose names evoke spectacular events or exploits—Hugh Glass, he of the misadventure with the grizzly; Mike Fink, king of the keelboatmen, the ring-tailed screamer who could outrun, outjump, outshoot, outdrink, outfight "ary" man on the western rivers, and who was in no way behindhand with the "wimming" either. Add to the list vaguely aristocratic Louis Vasquez, wrytongued James Clyman, and a great many more like John H. Weber, Ephraim Logan and

James Kirker. They seem now like a race of giants in a golden age, though no one of them was exempt from having to earn a living.

The first contingent left St. Louis at the beginning of April, 1822, commanded by Andrew Henry. They had to "gant up" their belts for long stretches of the voyage when game could not be found, and their horses were run off by the Assiniboin beyond the Mandan villages, but late in the summer they reached the mouth of the Yellowstone to begin building the stockaded post called Fort Henry. Ashley's second boat, the *Enterprize,* left St. Louis in May, carrying that most brilliant of his recruits, Jedediah Smith, raised on New York and Ohio farms, but with a marksman's eye for all that and initially engaged as a hunter, roaming along the river banks in search of game while others profanely forced the boat upstream. The *Enterprize,* was unlucky; some thirty or forty miles below the mouth of the Kansas River, while she was turning a point hazardous with sawyers (trees washed into the river, and bobbing up and down in the current), the top of the mast struck an overhanging tree. The *Enterprize* swung around broadside to the current and instantly was swept under, spilling men and $10,000 cargo together into the Missouri.

Like so many half-drowned dogs, the men swam to safety, but boat and goods alike were gone. The crew could only set up a makeshift camp on the river bank and send word down to St. Louis. Ashley never showed himself in a better light than when called upon to cope with such an emergency. With never a whimper over losses, which might have sunk the Ashley-Henry business before it was well-launched, he found another boat, replaced his lost goods, and within eighteen days was off for the mountains, this time going himself. Ashley showed imagination and willingness to spend money intelligently, for he laid in a supply of provisions, especially sea bread and bacon, so that he need not depend on the success of his hunters. He made good time up the river to Fort Atkinson, and again to the Arikara villages. There he traded for horses, as the Astorians had done, and with a few of his party, including Jedediah Smith, set out for the Yellowstone in advance of his keelboat, stopping off at the Mandan villages to distribute presents. He reached the Yellowstone on October 1 to find Fort Henry brought into existence; a cannon boomed a welcome to the post. After conferring with Henry and taking in charge such furs and robes as they had been able to trade, Ashley returned to St. Louis in a pirogue, promising to come back next summer.

Ashley's men set about making themselves at home in the high country. They had plenty of company, for in the early fall Immell and Jones returned to the Big Horn to make a second year's hunt; Pilcher himself had come up the river as high as the Mandan villages, establishing there a post with Vanderburgh in charge.

The Ashley-Henry men wintered in various parts, some at their fort, some up the Yellowstone and some, including Jedediah Smith, on the Missouri at the mouth of the Musselshell. Of this winter Jedediah recalled later that he and some of the best hunters laid in a supply of deer and antelope meat while others built cabins. When the weather became cold enough to freeze the Missouri they were astonished to see buffalo, which they thought had left the country, come pouring from all sides into the valley and cross the ice to the south. The men, snug in their encampment and now with a limitless supply, of choice meat, spent their time hunting buffalo and indulging in other winter sports.

This was life falling into the pattern mountain men would know. Beaver were sought primarily in the spring and the fall. Summer furs were poor in quality, so that over the years there was ever less incentive to seek them in that season: summer became the time for trading, the time for the annual Rocky Mountain gathering or rendezvous, as it was called. For fifteen years this institution would dominate mountain life. But in the depths of a frozen winter, mountain men found it expedient to hole up where there was feed for their animals and game for themselves. Thus the trapping season ended and began with the freezing and "discharging" of the streams. The expedients and the techniques of this kind of life—including the discovery that horses could be wintered on the bark of the sweet or round-leaf cottonwood, the habits of buffalo and the likelihood of finding various kinds of game in various parts of the West—all had to be learned.

Mike Fink was originally one of the party at the Musselshell, but sometime in the late fall or winter he returned to Fort Henry. Mike had two bosom friends, Carpenter and Talbot, whose pleasure it was to fill tin cups with whiskey and shoot them from one another's heads at seventy paces. In the course of the winter, Fink and Carpenter fell out, an example of what the West would come to know as "cabin fever." The quarrel was patched up, and Mike proposed that he and Carpenter perform their accustomed rite with rifle and whiskey cup. Carpenter expressed misgivings, but pride would not let him show the white feather. He set the tin cup atop his head and waited. Mike marched off the seventy paces, raised his rifle, and said pleasantly, "Hold your noddle steady, Carpenter, and don't spill the whiskey, as I shall want some presently." Thereupon he shot Carpenter squarely through the center of his forehead. "Carpenter," he said then, "you have spilled the whiskey!"

"Trek of the Mountain Men." Painting by W. H. D. Koerner.

An early account says: "Talbot, who was Carpenter's fast friend, was convinced of Mike's treacherous intent, and resolved upon revenge whenever an opportunity should offer. Some months afterward, Mike, in a fit of gasconading, declared that he had killed Carpenter and was glad of it. Talbot instantly drew his pistol, the same which Carpenter had bequeathed to him, and shot Mike through the heart. Mike fell and expired without a word." Sometime afterward, Talbot was drowned, attempting to swim a river in the Sioux country, and thus the story of the three friends passed immortally into the legendry of the West.

The Arikara Defeat

The party on the Musselshell stayed holed up over the winter while the Missouri froze four feet deep. When the ice went out in April, they embarked in canoes for the Judith River to open the spring hunt. One man, accidentally shot through the knees, had to be taken down to Fort Henry by Jedediah Smith. On arrival, Jedediah was given by Andrew Henry the further mission of descending the Missouri to request Ashley to trade for more horses. Henry himself with a small party set out to join the trappers on the upper Missouri.

Going down the Missouri by canoe was comparatively easy, and Jedediah Smith had no problem reaching Ashley before his arrival at the Arikara villages toward the end of May. There had been trouble between the Arikara and the Missouri Fur Company during the winter, so Ashley approached the stockaded villages with caution, anchoring his two keelboats well out in the river.

The Rees dissembled well and eventually traded nineteen horses for a supply of ammunition and the light guns called "fusees" (fusils). But in the wake of a violent storm, and before Ashley could move his horses from the exposed sand bar where he had received them, the Rees opened fire. The shore party seems to have been commanded by Jedediah Smith, and included William L. Sublette, David E. Jackson and James Clyman. In vain Ashley sought to swing his keelboats inshore to aid his men; the panic-stricken boat hands could not be made to expose themselves to the Ree fire. Nor in its pride would the shore party at first give way.

Well sheltered behind their stockade, the Indians shot down most of the horses in a few moments, while the Ashley men crouched behind the bleeding bodies. Several men were wounded and a skiff carried them to the boat. The rest plunged into the river and swam. The boat hands chopped through the anchoring cables and from hell let loose the brown Missouri swept all to a haven below.

Ashley lost fifteen men in this affray, shot down on the beach, drowned or killed in the water, or shot in the boats; nine more were wounded but survived. In all the annals of the western fur trade, no disaster had ever compared with this. At the first timber Ashley sought to place men and boats in a better state of defense. He had conceived a plan for getting past the Ree villages, but the backbones of his boatmen had dissolved into quivering jelly. Nothing would induce them to face the Arikara again. Ashley then asked how many would stick with him until reinforcements could be summoned from the Yellowstone. Only thirty spoke up, of whom half a dozen were wounded. Plainly the boatmen would desert overnight if Ashley did not send them down the river under orders.

The beleaguered fur trader asked for a volunteer to carry word to Henry. Jedediah Smith stepped forward, a fateful act of courage and resolution. A French Canadian of the valiant breed known in other days agreed to accompany him, and the two set off overland for the Yellowstone. Ashley packed some of his cargo and all of his dangerously wounded men on one of his keelboats and started it down the Missouri to Fort Atkinson. With the rest of his shrunken force he put a little more distance between himself and the Rees, setting up a camp near the mouth of the Cheyenne where he could wait, week on weary week, for Henry to arrive.

The disaster at the Arikara villages was only one among several that gave the spring of 1823 bloody distinction. Henry's party up the river had been attacked by Blackfeet above the Great Falls. Four were killed; the others abandoned their traps in the water. Pilcher's party led by Immell and Jones was ambushed near the Yellowstone by Bloods. Seven were killed including the two leaders. The loss in equipage, horses, traps and beaver amounted to upwards of $13,000 and virtually bankrupted the Missouri Fur Company. Fort Benton and the Mandan post had to be abandoned; and the deaths of Immell and Jones deprived Pilcher of the leaders he needed for expansion beyond the Continental Divide.

These events—especially the Arikara defeat—led the army to take a hand. Colonel Henry Leavenworth moved out of Fort Atkinson with six companies of the 6th Infantry, supported by fur men and Sioux allies. He bombarded the Arikara villages in August. The embattled Indians asked for a truce, but instead of surrendering, men, women and children, with horses and all movables evacuated during the night without Leavenworth's sentinels being any the wiser.

The army called this a victory and returned down the river, but there was no reason to believe that the Arikara had been chastened, and with that cloud darkening the whole landscape, fur men knew it would be foolhardy to transport trade goods upriver to the high country. Ashley and Henry's only recourse was to revise their plan of operation.

Henry must return to his fort overland, with such supplies as he could transport on what horses could be obtained from the Sioux. He would abandon trapping on the Missouri and advance up the Yellowstone to trade and trap in the vicinity of the mountains, where the friendly Crows would provide a certain security. But also a small party with Jedediah Smith in charge would be started directly west for the Crow country, across the Black Hills. These were major decisions: Ashley and Henry were cutting loose from the river transport on which Missouri traders had always depended; they would commit their fortunes to land transport, employing pack horses and mules.

Hugh Glass

Henry's return to the Yellowstone is famous, not for these ultimately significant reasons but because in the course of his journey one of his men, the reckless and insubordinate Hugh Glass, was set upon by a grizzly. So ripped and torn was Glass that it seemed impossible for him to live. Yet Henry could not wait upon his death, with the whole party and the vital goods for operations on the Yellowstone exposed to marauding Arikara. He offered to reward any two men who would agree to stay with Glass until he died. One John Fitzgerald spoke up, and so did the youthful Jim Bridger. The sequel is one of the West's enduring epics of fortitude, good fortune and the will to live.

Thinking Glass dead, or overcome by their fears when he clung to life, Fitzgerald and Bridger abandoned their helpless companion, as a matter of course carrying off his rifle. But in Glass the flame of life burned beyond extinguishing. A spring was close enough for him to reach. Above it branches of wild cherry hung low with their burden of ripe fruit, while in the nearby thicket tart buffalo berries grew in profusion. In his wallet Glass found his razor, which could serve as both knife and fire steel. Yet he was scarcely able to crawl, ravaged by wounds he could not dress and distant half the length and width of South Dakota from Fort Kiowa (near the present Chamberlain), the nearest place he could hope to find help.

For ten days Glass remained beside the spring, then staggered off in the direction of the Missouri. He was lucky, as men in the West who survived beyond final extremity had to be, for he came upon a buffalo calf just as it was brought down by wolves. He drove the snarling pack from their prey by setting fire to the grass; and afterward, for days, stayed beside the carcass, gorging upon the buffalo flesh as his wounds began to heal. Just strength enough he gained; when Glass started on again, he could make a mile or so a day, then two miles, five, ten, living on rose haws, roots, decaying buffalo carcasses, anything that came to hand. Eventually, it is said, he fell in with some Sioux who had come up the Missouri to glean in the abandoned Arikara cornfields; it is also said that these Sioux took him back to Fort Kiowa. The facts are not fully known; perhaps after reaching the Missouri and before descending to the fort he fell in with a small party the French Company had dared to send up to the Mandan villages. Wherever he joined it, Glass started up the Missouri with this party. Before they reached the villages, Rees attacked the traders and killed all except Toussaint Charbonneau and Glass, the latter saved by the whim of a Mandan horseman who happened along at the critical instant and swung him up to bear him off to safety.

The unresting Glass, determined to settle accounts with the men who had abandoned him and taken his rifle, continued his solitary journey up the Missouri to the Yellowstone. A note scrawled on the gate of Fort Henry said that the trader had left to establish a new fort at the mouth of the Big Horn. Glass kept on and near the end of 1823 reached his destination.

A tale beloved of western chroniclers says that Fitzgerald had long since gone down the Missouri but that the young Bridger, still there, was terrified by this apparent resurrection of the dead. According to this story, Glass forgave the youth, and perhaps there were extenuating circumstances, for Bridger had a blameless reputation in the West afterward. His fault—if a fault—was not held against him by either Glass or his contemporaries. But Fitzgerald's case was different. Toward the end of February, 1824, Hugh Glass made one of an express which Henry started off to the States with dispatches for Ashley. The Missouri was frozen over, so the five men went south via the head of Powder River, then down the North Platte. In the vicinity of the Laramie River, they fell afoul of a band of Rees who had strayed inland, and who killed two of Glass's companions. Two others reached Fort Atkinson to report Glass among the slain, but this inconceivably indestructible old man had again eluded the Arikara. He made his way to one of the fur trading establishments in the Sioux country, and descended the Missouri to Fort Atkinson sometime late in the spring.

At the United States post Glass found the faithless Fitzgerald, who had enlisted in the army after descending the Missouri the previous fall. One of the early chroniclers winds up the tale in this fashion:

Glass found the recreant individual who had so cruelly deserted him, when he lay helpless & torn so shockingly by the Grizzly Bear—He also there recovered his favorite Rifle—To the man he only addressed himself as he did to the boy—"Go false man & answer to your own conscience & to your God;—I have suffered enough in all reason by your perfidy—You was well paid to have remained with me until I should be able to walk—You promised to do so—or to wait my death & decently bury my remains—I heard the bargain—Your shameful perfidy & heartless cruelty—but enough—Again I say, settle the matter with your own conscience & your God."

Glass rode off to the Southwest and other incredible adventures. Eventually he returned to the Yellowstone. That was a mistake, for in the winter of 1832–33 his old enemies the Rees caught up with him, killing and scalping Glass and two companions as they were crossing the frozen river. But by then Glass had created something greater than himself, his own immortal legend, to be cherished in the West as long as mountain men are remembered.

Jedediah Smith

Through the months and years in which Glass was shaping his legend, Jedediah Smith was making history of another kind. In the fall of 1823, as he was crossing the Black Hills, a bear mauled him—all over the West men were learning about the gentle ways of grizzlies now—tearing an ear almost from his head and ripping away an eyebrow. Jedediah would carry the scars to the end of his brief life, but the wounds healed fast. He was soon able to go on to the Crow encampment on Wind River, where he wintered with other Henry men.

The weeks Jedediah and his companions remained among the Crows seem like the crossing of a great divide in history. The men who reached the Crow lands this winter arrived as river men or farm boys a long way from home, comparative innocents in the country. They went on as novice mountain men, wiser in the ways of survival, more at ease under the great sky and the far sun, beginning to be knowledgeable about horses, Indians, buffalo, the weather, the country, beaver and themselves. They had learned much in coming this distance from the Missouri, and much more they learned from the Crows. After the winter of 1824, as never before, we recognize in the western scene that new breed, the mountain man.

Late in February, Jedediah and his men rode south to the Sweetwater. In March they crossed wind-swept South Pass, the first white men to use the pass since Robert Stuart, twelve years before. Smith's passage has been called the effective discovery of the pass, for history was now prepared to exploit such a discovery to the full.

British and American Rivalry in Utah

In the spring of 1825 Peter Skene Ogden led a Hudson's Bay brigade from Flathead Post through the Snake country, down Bear River and through Cache Valley east of Great Salt Lake. His expedition was a model for future fur brigades, for it included thirty Indian women and a still larger number of half-breed children; and its fifty-nine men were a wonderfully mixed lot consisting of French Canadians, some few of Anglo-Saxon descent (Ogden himself was born of Loyalist American parents), a goodly number of half-breeds and a number of Iroquois and Abenaki Indians who had followed the fur trade and its way of life the whole width of Canada.

To Ogden's surprise he met two trapping parties in this wild country. One led by Étienne Provost had outfitted in New Mexico, traveled across Colorado, trapped the Uinta basin in northeast Utah, and crossed the Wasatch Mountains to discover the Provo River. These trappers may have been the first white men to lay eyes on Great Salt Lake.

The other party were Henry men who had crossed South Pass after Jedediah Smith. Virtually "free trappers," they were led by John H. Weber. Jim Bridger was in this party and possibly sighted the Great Salt Lake ahead of Provost. Learning of Ogden's presence, some of Weber's men attempted to bluff him out of the country, asserting that joint occupation of Oregon as provided in a treaty of 1818 had ended. As a matter of fact, all the trappers were now south of 42° latitude and therefore on Mexican soil, as conceded by the United States. Ogden had more right to be where he was than the Americans, since Great Britain had not agreed upon a boundary with either Spain or Mexico. But these niceties of international relations mattered little in the mountains. Ogden showed his teeth, saying that when his government ordered him to leave, that would be time enough to do so. But the ground broke up under his feet, for his party, the strongest ever to set out for the Snake country, fell apart in the face of the enemy. Grasping for profit, the British companies had kept the price for beaver far too low. In 1822 a considerable number of Hudson's Bay men had deserted, crossing the Rockies to the American posts in search of better prices. Now twenty-three of Ogden's men repudiated their debts, and with their furs joined the Americans. Six more soon followed. Ogden had to abandon the country to his rivals and flee north to the Snake, convinced for a time (until his superiors revised their price structure) that the Hudson's Bay Company could not maintain a brigade anywhere the Americans opposed them. A squabble between fur traders during the spring of 1825 had become the opening skirmish in the struggle for Oregon.

5. *Rendezvous—New Marketplace of the West*

THE SPRING OF 1825 is memorable for another reason. The necessities of the developing commerce in furs led to the first annual rendezvous, an institution which beyond any other has come to symbolize the era of the mountain man.

The initial rendezvous was William H. Ashley's doing. Ironically, Ashley was not a mountain man—not then, not ever. He had entered the fur trade to make his fortune, but his primary objectives were political: he wished to live as a wealthy man in a civilized community, wielding influence of a kind political power alone conferred. Since coming to Missouri in 1802, Ashley had risen steadily into prominence, becoming the state's first lieutenant governor and a general in the militia. In the summer of 1824, while Andrew Henry was trying to work out the destinies of the partnership in the high country, Ashley was unsuccessfully running for governor. At the end of August, a few weeks after the election, Henry reached St. Louis with the firm's meager returns, having brought them down the Yellowstone and the Missouri. The partners were bankrupt to all intents and purposes. What saved them was that they owed so much money their creditors could not afford to have them fail. But by now Henry had had more than enough of the fur trade. It had never brought him any luck, and the future seemed of a piece with the past.

Ashley was not the man to watch passively while his life went to ruin. If Henry would not return to the mountains, he himself must go, for they had absolutely no claim on the trappers. Beaver that might be taken would not come to him automatically. Unless he got goods to the mountains to exchange for those furs, the whole flimsy edifice he and Henry had erected would come tumbling down.

Getting together a supply of merchandise Ashley set out from Fort Atkinson early in November, with twenty-five men, fifty pack horses, "a wagon & team, &c." Ashley's is the first mention of a wagon on the northern Plains, doubtless soon abandoned in heavy snow. He had a cold and stormy winter to contend with, but with the help of horses traded from the Pawnee was able to make his way up the Platte and South Platte to camp within sight of Longs Peak. In February, 1825, though the world around seemed "one mass of snow and ice," Ashley rode into the Front Range of the Rockies via the Cache la Poudre. Three days of difficult and dangerous travel brought him to the comparative security of the Laramie Plains, but he kept on to the North Platte, then again west, crossing the Continental Divide in the barrens south of South Pass. He reached the Green River in April, not without paying a midnight tribute to Crow horsethieves. On the banks of the Green Ashley divided his comparatively small party into four detachments and sent three to trap in different directions. The fourth he took with him in a voyage of exploration down the Green in bullboats, those superbly useful contrivances fashioned from buffalo hides stretched over a wooden framework.

All this provides a fascinating chapter in the West's record of discovery, but more significant is the arrangement Ashley made before separating from his men. He told them he would transport his goods and extra baggage down the Green toward the distantly visible

"Green River Encampment." Painting by Alfred Jacob Miller.

Uinta Mountains, at the base of which he suspected a river must enter the Green. There he would cache the goods. "The place of deposite," as Ashley's diary records, was to be

> The place of rendavoze for all our parties on or before the 10th July next & that the places may be known—Trees will be pealed standing the most conspicuous near the Junction of the rivers or above the mountains as the case may be—. Should such point be without timber I will raise a mound of Earth five feet high or set up rocks the top of which will be made red with vermillion thirty feet distant from the same—and one foot below the surface of the earth a northwest direction will be deposited a letter communicating to the party any thing that I may deem necessary.

So were plans made for the first rendezvous. It is interesting that from the beginning Ashley used the term; we may regret that the name "Randavouze Creek" he applied a few days later to the stream now called Henrys Fork of the Green did not stick. Ashley's men fanned out in various directions, and one of his parties made contact with Jedediah Smith and John Weber, as also the Hudson's Bay Company deserters, to apprise them of the arrangements made.

Ashley himself went on down the frightful canyons the Green has slashed through the Uintas, a waterway such as his men had never seen. To enter those dark chasms and float in a frail skin-boat down the turbulent river, never knowing whether the next bend would disclose a waterfall over which they might be swept, was a strenuous pastime for Ashley, who could not swim, and who a year earlier had contemplated a way of life no more demanding than governing the state of Missouri. The men pushing into the West were finding how foreign to previous American experience this high country was, how continuously hazardous; new skills and adaptability required of all. Ashley continued down the river, and, where it emerged from the canyons, came with no evident surprise upon men of Provost's party, who told him that "the country below for a great distance is Entirely destitute of game."

Ashley explored a little farther but found it expedient to buy horses from Provost's people and from a band of Ute Indians who seemed perfectly familiar with Americans; they even carried guns, which showed how rapidly trade was advancing in the Rockies. The general then set out for rendezvous by a circuitous course around the high Uintas.

Ashley reached the appointed place on July 1, finding all his men, except one who had been killed, camped within twenty miles. Twenty-nine deserters from the Hudson's Bay Company had also come, making a total of 120. A lively trade of beaver pelts for merchandise began at once.

Rendezvous has come to be viewed as a kind of annual convention at which all mountain men in the West were obliged to show themselves, a convention that was also a sort of saturnalia. More recently scholars have suggested that the rendezvous of the American fur traders and hunters was no more than a white institution superimposed upon Indian trading fairs already general in the West. Neither of these ideas accords with the facts; rendezvous initially was a business convenience directly occasioned by problems of supply and distribution in a country too thinly peopled, too isolated and perhaps too poor to justify maintenance of a permanent post. For several years rendezvous continued more or less on the happenstance basis of its origin. At this first rendezvous it is doubtful that Ashley had any liquor to sell, though he saw at once the demand that had arisen for that article and would undertake to supply it hereafter. As for the Indians, it seems more than doubtful that any were present at this first rendezvous, and save for the Crows and a Snake or a Ute or two, most of the white men present, Ashley in particular, had scarcely seen an Indian in the Far West as yet. If as the years went by the character of rendezvous underwent some change, that change reflected the changing fur trade itself. Undoubtedly in 1825 there was reunion and rejoicing as friends long separated laid eyes upon one another again, all come safely through the vicissitudes of a mountain year or two; there may also have been gambling and horse racing, as usual in the West when red men or white get together. But mostly rendezvous in 1825 was a business proceeding; Ashley bought beaver, sold goods, and took orders for goods that men wanted sent up from the States. Until conditions should change, he was the only supplier for men who had learned the charm of mountain life and were beginning to find that they might want to remain in the mountains forever.

His business done, Ashley set out for home. Knowing that General Atkinson and Major Benjamin O'Fallon, the Indian agent on the Missouri, were ascending the Missouri this summer to negotiate treaties with the tribes, Ashley could expect safe passage home by a water route. Accordingly, instead of packing his furs down the Platte, which would have been expensive both in men and in horses (the latter high-priced and hard to acquire in the mountains just then), Ashley made for the Big Horn River. Below the Big Horn Mountains he built bullboats, and bounced down with his furs to the mouth of the Yellowstone where, as expected, he found the Atkinson-O'Fallon expedition encamped. (Not for three decades would the army again be seen on the upper Missouri in force.)

Atkinson gave Ashley a warm welcome and offered to transport his furs down the river. There were some anxious moments along the way, but Ashley and his furs reached St. Louis together early in October.

Ashley's mountain foray had enabled him to recoup past losses but he had not yet made his fortune. He had realized at rendezvous that he would need a new partner in Henry's place unless he was prepared to remain indefinitely in the wilds. Accordingly he had proposed to Jedediah Smith, who in the space of three years had risen meteorically into prominence, that they organize a firm, Ashley & Smith, in which Ashley would provide most of the capital, Smith the wilderness service.

Late in October, Jedediah set off for the Rockies with some seventy men and an outfit valued at $20,000. In this company, among others, traveled Robert Campbell, a young Scotch-Irishman who had begun to cough out his lungs in St. Louis and, like so many "lungers" of later decades, thought to regain his health by a sojourn in the mountains.

The Rocky Mountain fur traders still had lessons to learn. One was that late-autumn expeditions up from the States were ill-advised. Jedediah Smith got no farther than the Republican River in northwestern Kansas before being stopped by a series of blizzards. He lost many of his horses and had to hole up in a Pawnee village. During the winter he sent word of his predicament back to Ashley. With characteristic energy the general prepared a new outfit and met Jedediah in the spring near Grand Island, then led the combined party up the Platte and on to Cache Valley for the rendezvous of 1826.

Indians at Rendezvous.

Ballou's, 1856

At this meeting or shortly thereafter Ashley sold out to Smith, David E. Jackson and William L. Sublette with the understanding he would supply them in 1827. Ashley then returned to the States, going all the way by land. If he had not yet made his fortune, he had taken a long stride in that direction. He had also immensely impressed his St. Louis competitors; Ashley was the first man ever to demonstrate that a successful fur-trading business could be carried on in the Rocky Mountains.

During the winter of 1826-7 Ashley tried to persuade the Chouteaus to take a half-interest in his next year's supply party. They finally agreed, meanwhile entering into "arrangements" with John Jacob Astor. In the summer of 1827 the Columbia Fur Company also joined Astor's firm as its Upper Missouri Outfit. This gigantic concern, the American Fur Company, so powerful as to dwarf all rivals on the Missouri, would in due course expand into the Rockies.

The Discovery of Yellowstone Park

Following the rendezvous of 1826, Smith, Jackson & Sublette divided their forces. One party was led by Jackson and Sublette to the Snake country; the other, termed "The South

West Expedition," was taken by Jedediah Smith to explore the unknown country southwest of Great Salt Lake, with the objective of falling upon one or another of the legendary rivers thought to rise in those parts and empty into the Pacific at or near San Francisco Bay. Smith's primary purpose was exploration—but exploration with a practical end in view, the finding of new trapping grounds.

Both parties made major contributions to the exploration of the West. Sublette and Jackson went north, so as to reach the western shore of Yellowstone Lake, known for some years thereafter as Sublette Lake. John Colter had been through this country eighteen years earlier but, unlike Colter, Sublette discovered the spectacular geysers and colorful hotpots. One of his men, Daniel T. Potts, wrote home to a Philadelphia newspaper in the summer of 1827 the first description of the extraordinary thermal phenomena of the Yellowstone region.

Sublette and Jackson returned to Cache Valley to set up a winter encampment. Having been successful enough to justify the commitment, on New Year's Day, 1827, Sublette set out for St. Louis with Black Harris on snowshoes, their provisions packed on a dog, to confirm with Ashley the order for a new outfit. It was to be brought in the summer of 1827 to Bear Lake, on the present Utah-Idaho line.

Jedediah Smith Goes to California

While Sublette and Jackson were gathering in beaver, their partner, Jedediah Smith, was having a belt-tightening time. He had ridden south from the valley of the Great Salt Lake, crossing mountains and sandy deserts until he came to the Colorado River, which he crossed at the mouth of the Virgin, near the southern tip of Nevada. Passing down the great brown river's eastern bank thereafter cost him three weeks of hard travel and half of his horses.

Above the present town of Needles, he came to the villages of the Mohave Indians. These tall, powerfully built men seemed affluent with their patches of corn, beans, pumpkins and melons. One of them could speak a little Spanish, and one of Jedediah's men had a sketchy command of that tongue. Thus during fifteen days spent recuperating among the Indians, Jedediah learned about the California missions and determined to go there. On November 10 he set out into the deserts west of the Colorado, and by way of the Mohave River—which he called the Inconstant owing to its tendency to flow beneath the ground. In sixteen days Jedediah reached and crossed the San Bernardino Mountains. Beyond, Jedediah entered another world. In the San Bernardino Valley, greening from the first winter rains, he found abundance after the starving times—cattle by thousands, horses, sheep. An Indian herdsman killed a fine young cow for the Americans to feast upon, and provided corn meal besides. And soon came two Franciscan friars in their gray habits, who escorted Jedediah on to Mission San Gabriel—in a suburb of present Los Angeles. Giving up his arms, the young American wrote the California governor, describing his distressed situation and requesting horses and permission to pass through the country, north to the Bay of San Francisco.

In San Diego Jedediah's letter was received with alarm. Jedediah had accomplished a historic feat; he was the first ever to cross the western half of the continent from the Missouri River to California. But the feat was not one to be acclaimed by Mexican officials. California had always been exposed on its seaward frontiers, but on the east had been shielded from the incursions of outlanders by the continental distances and deserts. Jedediah's arrival in California announced the destruction of barriers which had walled out all interlopers for more than seven decades; his exploit, in the Mexican view, might better have waited till the end of time.

The governor summoned Jedediah to San Diego to question and cross-question him at length. "Much of a Gentleman but very Suspicious" was Jedediah's impression of his host. The quest after beaver was scarcely comprehensible to the Spanish mind, so that the Mexican officials tended to call beaver hunters *pescadors,* fishermen; it seemed incredible that Jedediah should have crossed a continent seeking these animals. More probably he had a military purpose in entering California, and who should say what force he had left in the unknown country to the east?

Like most provincial officials, the California governor was disposed to pass the buck. He would have preferred to leave matters as they were for three or four months while getting instructions from Mexico or, better yet, send Jedediah himself to Mexico City to be dealt with. Such a prospect scarcely appealed to the American, for most of his men were *engagés,* requiring to be paid whether they earned their keep or not; and any delay would entail the loss of the spring hunt. Since the fall hunt through the barren Southwest had produced only a wretched forty beaver skins, it was all the more imperative to recoup.

A solution was found when American shipmasters then in San Diego signed a document vouching for Jedediah's probity. The governor gave sanction for Jedediah to depart as he had come—back across the mountains—but not to go up the coast toward the Russian establishment, Fort Ross. Accordingly, resupplied and with fresh horses, Jedediah recrossed the San Bernardino Mountains. To his mind that fulfilled the governor's requirement. He had no intention of retracing his difficult and profitless outbound trail from the Great Salt Lake. Instead, he skirted the western reaches of the Mohave Desert and crossed the Tehachapi Mountains to the San Joaquin Valley. Finding the beaver he had been seeking, he trapped his way north as far as the American River. At the beginning of May, feeling the pressure of rendezvous, Jedediah attempted to cross the Sierra Nevada. The snow in the rugged canyon of the American River was too deep; his horses floundered and died to the number of five before Jedediah retreated to the flower-bright lowlands. He turned back on his trail some seventy-five miles to the Stanislaus River and, after a period spent in recruiting, left most of his party there while with two men and seven animals he undertook to force a passage of the mighty Sierra. In eight days Jedediah got across, though he lost two horses and one mule: this was the first crossing, by any white man, of California's tremendous barrier range. Jedediah and his men came down out of the Sierra south of Walker Lake, then launched out into the totally unknown country that separated them from the Great Salt Lake. His brief account of that hard journey says that he traveled over a country completely barren and destitute of game, sometimes without water for two days at a time; and Jedediah adds, "when we found water in some of the rocky hills, we most generally found some Indians who appeared the most miserable of the human race having nothing to subsist on, (nor any clothing) except grass seed, grasshoppers, &c."

Jedediah and his companions, the first men to cross central Nevada and west central Utah, made their way through by the thinnest of margins, having to live on the flesh of their starved horses; one of the men nearly died of thirst almost in sight of Great Salt Lake. Worn down to skin and bones, the three desert wayfarers reached the rendezvous at the south end of Bear Lake on July 3, 1827. They had been given up for dead by their friends, who enthusiastically saluted their arrival by firing the cannon that had been hauled out to the mountains that spring.

The rendezvous at Bear Lake, in late June and early July, had attracted all the trappers, some Snakes and Ute, and a sizable party of Blackfeet who slaughtered a couple of Snakes and were besieged by Snakes, Ute, and trappers who killed six of the Blackfeet before they made off. William Sublette had taken a valiant part in this affray, further contributing to the reputation he was making for himself.

Altogether, the foregathering of 1827 may have been the first rendezvous worthy of the name. With everybody returned from the back parts of everywhere, plenty of rum on hand for the one big blowout the mountain men could expect all year, friendly Indians present to give the scene color and dash, this assemblage in the open meadows at the upper end of one of the West's most beautiful bodies of water was an occasion to remember; and there would be none to compare with it for another five years.

Smith, Jackson & Sublette were now dominant in the mountain trade, but still in debt to Ashley. Except for the successful hunt made last fall and again this spring by Jackson, they might have been out of business. Jedediah Smith had taken 1,500 pounds of beaver on the

"Blackfeet — The Captive." Painting by W. H. D. Koerner.

San Joaquin—roughly 900 skins—but these furs were in far-off California where they could not be applied on the partnership debts. Obviously it was necessary for Jedediah to return to his men and bring in his furs.

Jedediah set off with eighteen men by much the same route taken in 1826, losing little time along the way and reaching the Mohave villages early in August. New Mexico trappers had visited the Mohave in the spring, killing a few of them and leaving the others with a hatred of all white men. Not knowing this, Jedediah divided his party to cross the Colorado. The watchful Indians chose that moment to attack, killing ten and capturing two women (probably squaws of the French-Canadians). Nine survivors, including Jedediah, crossed the deserts to the San Bernardino Valley carrying what trade goods they could on their backs, then having jerked some beef made their way north to the encampment on the Stanislaus. Jedediah had to go to Monterey and spent some time in the *calabozo* but was finally allowed to sell his beaver and resupply himself. After trading for a herd of horses which were cheap in California and dear at the rendezvous, Jedediah started on by way of Oregon. On the Umpqua, Indians surprised his men, killing all but Jedediah and three others, who managed to reach Fort Vancouver, the principal Hudson's Bay Company post. No rendezvous for Jedediah at Bear Lake in 1828; but he succeeded in getting back to rendezvous in Pierres Hole in 1829.

Smith, Jackson & Sublette had done fairly well during Jedediah's absence, but he brought bad news. In addition to the loss of most of his property (the Hudson's Bay Company had purchased what furs and horses could be retrieved from the Umpqua Indians) Jedediah had to report that the vast spaces which he and his associates had counted on for expanding their business were mostly desert, barren of fur.

Indeed the fur supply everywhere was rapidly diminishing. Even the highest and roughest Rockies and the desert basins to the west were being trapped by men from New Mexico, men like Ewing Young, Michel Robidoux, Thomas L. ("Pegleg") Smith, and a young greenhorn, Kit Carson. At last year's rendezvous Joshua Pilcher had come with goods to trade. His supply was scanty and much of it damaged, but that he had come at all boded no good for Smith, Jackson & Sublette. In their first year they had not had much room to maneuver, being bound to furnish beaver to Ashley at $3.00 per pound, or $5.00 per skin, the same price they paid the free trappers. They had had to boost prices on merchandise, which had naturally enraged the free trappers, who sent emissaries to the Yellowstone asking for competitive trading by other companies.

These free trappers by now were making all the companies fretful, Americans and British alike. In small parties they roamed recklessly about the country, stirring up the Indians, getting themselves killed, and sowing dissension among *engagés*. Mountain men had become a breed to be reckoned with. They were taking squaws from among the tribes, adopting Indian ways and increasingly cutting themselves off from the life they had known below—except that they had to have powder and ball, "foofarraw" for their women, traps and trappings for themselves, and occasionally the makings for monumental drunks to demonstrate that they were white men after all.

Confronted with these conditions, the three partners, reunited in the summer of 1829, elected to gamble. Jackson would attempt to wring further returns from the ever-more-impoverished Snake country. Smith and Sublette would take a powerful brigade north to the Blackfeet lands, hoping for rewards to justify the risks. The gamble paid off. Smith and Sublette had done so well by the time they met Jackson on Wind River at Christmas that the partners concluded to send Sublette on a midwinter journey to St. Louis to arrange for yet another outfit in the spring.

6. *The First Wagons West*

SUBLETTE CAME BACK to the Wind River rendezvous of 1830 with goods in ten wagons, each hauled by five mules, and two dearborns drawn by one mule each—the first wheels to the Rockies since Ashley's cannon in 1827. This innovation in Plains travel was so impressive that the partners reported it to the Secretary of War, saying that wagons could cross the Continental Divide by way of South Pass thus demonstrating "the facility of communicating over land with the Pacific Ocean."

The nation had not yet reached the point of thinking about the West in these terms, but a long stride had been taken toward opening the Oregon Trail. The route Sublette took with his wagons left the Missouri near the mouth of the Kansas, and after ascending that river some miles, turned northwest to the Little Blue and the Platte, reaching the latter river near the head of Grand Island. Thence Sublette's route continued via the North Platte and the Sweetwater to the junction of Wind River with the Popo Agie. If there were no wheel tracks across South Pass yet, other than those made by Ashley's cannon in 1827, they would be seen in that region soon enough. "Sublette's Trace" marked the beginning of a new National Road.

This road-making was tremendously important in the history of the West, but to Smith, Jackson & Sublette the wagonloads of trade goods brought to the mountains and the packs of beaver ready to go out on them meant financial independence. A climactic season had brought them enough to quit the mountains. Knowing when they were well off, they sold out to a group of practical trappers at the rendezvous. (Better for Jedediah had he remained in the mountains. In the spring of 1831, he engaged in a trading venture to Santa Fe. Scouting ahead of the caravan for water, he was killed by Comanche who were lying in wait for buffalo.)

The men who bought out Smith, Jackson & Sublette—Fitzpatrick, Bridger, Milton Sublette, Henry Fraeb and Jean Baptiste Gervais—all knew the business but had gone deeply in debt to organize their Rocky Mountain Fur Company and from the beginning were faced with stiff new competition. The American Fur Company had sent two trapping brigades to the mountains, one led by W. H. Vanderburgh, the other by Andrew Drips and Lucien Fontenelle. All appreciated that new hunting grounds must be found, but almost the only areas not heavily overtrapped seemed to be the Blackfoot country.

Both concerns did fairly well in 1830-31, though they lost men to the Blackfeet. In the course of his hunt, Fontenelle met a mixed village of Flatheads, Nez Percés and Pend d'Oreilles (Kalispel), who bore an English flag but were characteristically friendly. These Indians had picked up some idea of Christianity and several of them wanted to go to the States to seek out this "medicine."

On such small foundations large historic consequences may build. Fontenelle took the Indians to St. Louis, but only one lived to return to his people. He succeeded in getting back to a hunting party of his kin on the upper Missouri but was killed by Blackfeet before they got home. However, history in its inscrutable way was shaped by his wanderings and the tales the hunting party carried across the mountains to the tribe.

In the East church groups, hearing about the four Indian "wise men," interpreted it as a request from out of the wilderness for "the Book of Heaven." Thus the celebrated Oregon Crusade of the 1830's began. In the Far West the Nez Percés and Flatheads, for their part, began to look toward the East for a white "medicine man."

The Remarkable Rendezvous of 1832

There was no true rendezvous in 1831, though Provost brought supplies to Green River for Vanderburgh. The price of beaver in world markets was still high, as it had been for several years, and various parties of independent trappers prowled the Rockies, while sizable new outfits entered the field. The most notable of these was headed by Captain Benjamin L. E. Bonneville, who had obtained a leave of absence from the army and in 1832 came west with twenty wagons—the first ever to cross South Pass. Bonneville was slow in reaching the mountains that summer and so was Lucien Fontenelle, neither being in time for rendezvous. Nevertheless the rendezvous of 1832 was the most remarkable yet. In Pierres Hole gathered the parties of the Rocky Mountain Fur Company, Vanderburgh and Drips, and any number of free trappers. A New England ice merchant, Nathaniel Wyeth, headed a band of the rankest greenhorns who ever entered the West. They had accompanied William Sublette's supply train up from the States. Perhaps 350 white men and as many Indians gathered to trade and carouse.

Rendezvous was on the verge of breaking up when a dramatic event flared up at the south end of Pierres Hole. Milton Sublette, Fraeb and Gervais had been detailed to take a brigade to the headwaters of the southern tributaries of the Snake. A few free trappers were going along, and also Nathaniel Wyeth, with the ten men who stayed on after his party broke up at rendezvous. As John Ball, a member of Wyeth's party, tells the tale, on the morning of July 17

> just as we had packed, ready for march, we saw a band of Indians in the direction in which we were to go. Mr. Frap sent an Indian and a half-breed named Antoine to meet them. As they approached, they discovered the Indians were Blackfeet [really Gros Ventres]. The chief left the party and came out in a friendly way to meet Antoine and his [Flathead] Indian companion. But Antoine's father [the Hudson's Bay Company deserter of 1825, Thyery Goddin] had been killed by the Blackfeet; he was going to have his revenge then and there. So he said to the Indian "I'll appear friendly when we meet, but you watch your chance and shoot him." This he did. Antoine caught his robe or blanket of blue or red, turned and fled to camp. The Blackfeet fired after him, and as he rode into camp he said: "They were Blackfeet. We killed their chief. Here is

"Arapahoe Attack." Painting by W. H. D. Koerner.

his robe." We, to our dismay, expected a battle, which we did not like. An express was sent back to Captain Sublette's camp to tell the state of affairs and ask assistance.

The whites made a breastwork of their saddles, while the Indians, with their women and horses, retreated into a beaver swamp to prepare for a stand. Shooting began at once. Ball says the Indians considered the leaden bullet "a sort of thunder and lightening death," but adds dryly, "the whites did not think the barbed arrows any better." John Wyeth, Nathaniel's young cousin, agreed. "There was something terrific to our men in their arrows. The idea of a barbed arrow sticking in a man's body, as we had observed it in the deer and other animals, was appalling to us all, and it is no wonder that some of our men recoiled at it."

Meanwhile the express had reached William Sublette's camp, six or eight miles to the north. All the whites on hand, and a good many Nez Percés and Flatheads, rode under Sublette to the assistance of those engaged. The Gros Ventres were outmatched, but stubbornly defended their position against all attacks, shrieking their defiance. An Indian with the trappers understood them to be saying that six or eight hundred of their tribesmen were attacking the distant white camp. Pell-mell, off to the rescue galloped the whites, and the Gros Ventres improved the opportunity to make tracks from the valley. That was the Battle of Pierres Hole, the most famous incident of the decade.

In the fight two white men and six Nez Percés were killed. Among the wounded was William Sublette, shot in the shoulder and borne away to safety by Robert Campbell; several of the wounded died afterward from gangrene. The Gros Ventres fared no better. Nine men and two women were thought to have been killed on the spot. Though all escaped from Pierres Hole, their further march took them through the Crow country, and the Crows gleefully fell upon these old enemies. "Forty of them were killed," Washington Irving says on Bonneville's authority, "many of their women and children captured, and the scattered fugitives hunted like wild beasts until they were completely chased out of the Crow country."

Antoine Goddin (or Godin), who precipitated this affray, reaped his reward a few years later, after the founding of Fort Hall. A party of Blackfeet headed by a Canadian enticed him across the Portneuf River to trade for their beaver. While smoking the pipe of peace, they shot him in the back, tore off his scalp, and carved Wyeth's initials, "N J W," on his forehead. That was life in the mountains in the 1830's, treachery for treachery, murder for murder, and never an end to the savage interplay.

At the Pierres Hole rendezvous, the whites waited uncertainly for ten days lest the main body of Gros Ventres show up, then the parties began to make off in various directions. Both American and Rocky Mountain companies ventured again into the dangerous Blackfoot country. Bridger was shot in two places with arrows, while Vanderburgh, whose brigade had now been combined with that of Drips, was killed. As a way of life and as a business, the fur trade had its drawbacks.

Down in the States, meanwhile, William Sublette joined with Robert Campbell in a new partnership to challenge the American Fur Company frontally. It was decided that in the spring of 1833 Sublette would ascend the Missouri, establishing posts to oppose the giant combine at every point, and as a speculation, Campbell would take an outfit to rendezvous to trade for the furs of the free trappers and the Rocky Mountain Fur Company. Campbell was to transport his furs down the Big Horn, meeting Sublette at the mouth of the Yellowstone to help build a post in opposition to Fort Union which had been founded in 1828–29 and was now the most powerful of the northern posts.

Campbell took along a few pleasure-seekers, notably including the half-pay British army officer, Captain William Drummond Stewart, who would leave his own mark on the West over the next five years. This rendezvous of 1833 was the first ever held in the valley of the Green, the sparkling Siskadee, and Stewart, for one, thought its like was never seen again.

The various camps were several miles apart, for the better control and sustenance of horses and mules, but there was much visiting back and forth, much roistering, with the best animals of each camp (man or beast) pitted against those of the others, and any amount of frolicking and chaffering. Still the dust of the racing horses could not obscure the economic realities—less fur, ever more competition—which made the heads of the several companies ponder the possibilities of survival.

When the rendezvous broke up, those headed for the States started, as planned, for the Big Horn. Wyeth, on his way back from the Columbia, accompanied them. Along the way

"War Council on the Plains." Painting by Charles M. Russell.

he concluded a deal with Fitzpatrick and Milton Sublette by which he would furnish them merchandise next year at a cheaper figure than William Sublette and Campbell offered. He agreed to forfeit $1,000 if he failed to deliver the goods, and the R. M. F. Company would forfeit the same amount if they refused to accept delivery. At the head of navigation, north of the Big Horn Mountains, the men built bullboats, and away went the fur-bearing community. Robert Campbell's bullboat upset on the way down; he lost his gun but salvaged most of his beaver.

7. *The Era of Rival Forts*

AT THE MOUTH of the Yellowstone, Campbell met Sublette, as agreed, and they erected a stockade called Fort William three miles below Fort Union. The fort-building era had come to the West. Only last year the Chouteaus had established Fort Cass near the mouth of the Big Horn, the better to prosecute the Crow trade. Still more important, they had opened a trade with the Blackfeet, and now had an establishment near the mouth of the Marias. The trade was a prickly one, but it survived—perhaps because the Blackfeet found the post a convenient source of supply for the guns and ammunition they turned against trappers, traders and other Indians in the hinterland.

All these posts were river-supplied, in the tradition of the past, but as a really major development during the 1830's and early 1840's any number of interior trading posts sprang up. Those were usually small, often located close together, the better to keep an eye on the competition, and all fighting over the bedraggled remnants of the fur trade. Dozens of them appeared on the North and South Platte, the small tributaries of the Missouri and the Yellowstone, in the forbidding Uinta basin of Utah. On the upper Arkansas (in future Colorado), John Gantt built another Fort Cass near the mouth of Fountain Creek, primarily to trade with Cheyenne and Arapaho. Bent & St. Vrain established a log fort nearby, which they called Fort William, and farther down the Arkansas they began to erect that famous adobe citadel named Bent's Fort. The forts of the high Plains depended upon increasingly valuable trade in buffalo robes, which could not be economically packed from beyond the mountains—where, in any event, buffalo were vanishing—but could be hauled to the States in the Santa Fe wagons at a cost competitive with the steamboat transportation available to Missouri River posts. Increasingly, as beaver declined, buffalo robes would become the mainstay of the fur trade. This trade in robes would corrupt the relationship of the white traders with the tribes. Previously many of the Indians had been unfamiliar with the evils and blessings of firewater. The liquor problem had not hitherto existed in the American West. Now it sprang into full-blown life, the Plains Indians being primarily victimized.

Astor Bows Out With the Silk Hat

Down in the States the winter of 1833–34 was a momentous one for the fur trade. John Jacob Astor, making a visit to Europe, noted a new phenomenon: For more than four centuries the finest of all hats had been made from felted beaver fur, which was the reason beaver had been the mainstay of the fur trade in America throughout its history. Now, Astor observed, hatters were beginning to fashion hats from silk. Astor had already made up his mind to retire from the American Fur Company, but this development doubtless gave point to his decision to break up his giant concern. Before this came about, a striking negotiation was carried through by William L. Sublette. Having built competing trading posts along the Missouri, he entered an "arrangement" with his rivals. By this agreement the two firms divided the West, Astor's people to monopolize the river trade, Sublette & Campbell to have the mountain trade. Bringing the American Fur Company to terms was gratifying and served the important purpose of extricating Sublette and his partner from an unpromising Missouri River venture. But the mountain trade was worth only what they could make of it, if indeed anything could be made of it. In the first year, at least, Sublette could not expect to gather in any fruits of the treaty-making in New York, for Drips & Fontenelle (now, in effect, independent operators marketing their furs under agreement with the American Fur Company) must be supplied by Chouteau, an 1834 outfit for which they had contracted earlier. It would be another year before Sublette & Campbell could hope to get a secure grip on the mountain supply business.

Consequently it mattered greatly who got to rendezvous ahead of all others in 1834. There were others aplenty. A new outfit was being taken to Bonneville, besides that Étienne Provost was packing up to Drips & Fontenelle; and Wyeth, who had secured backing in the East, was returning to meet his engagement with the Rocky Mountain Fur Company, Sublette's main source of beaver in the past.

Wyeth knew as well as anyone the importance of being at rendezvous with goods ahead of the competition. Come spring, he was first to get away from the States. He traveled with a remarkable cavalcade which included the well-known naturalist, Thomas Nuttall, the promising ornithologist, John Townsend, and most extraordinary of all, the Methodist missionaries Jason and Daniel Lee, Cyrus Shepard, and several lay helpers. The Flatheads' well-publicized plea for a Book of Heaven was being answered with glowing zeal.

Milton Sublette started for the mountains with Wyeth, but had to give up the journey after a few days; his left leg simply would not bear traveling (and ultimately had to be amputated). He turned back toward the settlements, and the very next day met William's party. Milton spent some hours in his brother's company, and no one has ever been quite sure what transpired, whether Milton gave William a power of attorney to aid in resolving the tangled affairs of the Rocky Mountain Fur Company. William drove on, passed Wyeth's party east of the Big Blue, and was never overtaken afterward. On May 30 he reached the Laramie River, where he paused for a day or so to open another era in the history of the West, founding Fort Laramie. The foundation logs were laid on May 31, 1834, suitably baptized with champagne brought along for the purpose. Then, leaving fifteen of his men to complete the

"Laramie's Fort." Water color by Alfred Jacob Miller.

THE WALTERS ART GALLERY, BALTIMORE

post that must become the new mountain base of Sublette & Campbell, the lanky and forever energetic William hastened on to the mountains.

The Rendezvous of 1834

Fitzpatrick had tentatively named the banks of the Green, somewhere near the mouth of the Sandy, as this year's place of rendezvous for the R. M. F. Company. (In other years the Green River rendezvous was held farther north, near Horse Creek.) Sublette arrived about the middle of June, and there was a joyful reunion of old comrades, business rivalries aside. Wyeth came up on June 18, just as it was being decided to move over to Hams Fork. Soon encampments were scattered along the creek for six or eight miles.

In all probability, this was the unhappiest rendezvous yet. In the collection of furs, none had done well, Drips and Fontenelle better than most. The various small traders hanging on at the fringe almost universally had lost their shirts. Off to the west, Bonneville had experienced a similarly disastrous year. He had gathered in few beaver himself, and the party Joe Walker had led to California for him gained little but knowledge of the country. They had been the first after Jedediah Smith to cross the High Sierra and first to glimpse the awesome chasm of Yosemite. Walker returned by a new and more southerly route across Walker Pass, thereby opening the way for a company of emigrants he would lead to California in 1843, but he came back with few furs.

The Rocky Mountain Fur Company shared in the general humbling. One party had gone to the Columbia and come back to the rendezvous as empty-handed as Joe Walker. Another had hunted the Utah country without success. Jim Bridger brought in the best returns, from the three "Parks" of the Rockies and the Laramie Plains. Fitzpatrick had been robbed of most of his horses by the Crows and had lost his fall hunt. After four always precarious years the day of reckoning had come.

On June 20, 1834, Sublette sat down to tot up accounts with Fitzpatrick. One thing was clear. Fitz did not have resources enough to settle with Wyeth for the goods brought up. The R. M. F. Company would have to hand over the forfeit. Fitzpatrick would also have to dissolve the company. He posted notice in camp to that effect. Business in the future would be conducted by a new partnership—Fitzpatrick, (Milton) Sublette and Bridger—presumably supplied by William.

Bitterly disappointed, Wyeth found himself in the middle of the wilderness with a year's supply of goods and no market. All around him men were quarreling. To his brother he wrote: "Murder is rife and distrust among themselves makes the whites an easy prey to Indians." Also, surveying the scene with pardonable jaundice: "There is here a great collection of scoundrels."

The Establishment of Fort Hall

Wyeth was not a man to sink easily under misfortune, and before leaving Boston he had fully worked out in his mind what he proposed to do. He would establish a permanent base somewhere in the Snake country, with various subsidiary posts to be built later—some, perhaps so far south as the Great Salt Lake. So, now, with all his goods he went on another 150 miles and built Fort Hall near the confluence of the Snake and the Portneuf. As he wrote to his brother:

> We manufactured a magnificent flag from some unbleached sheeting, a little red flannel and a few blue patches, saluted it with damaged powder and wet it in vilanous alcohol, and after all [the fort] makes, I do assure you, a very respectable appearance amid the dry and desolate regions of central America. Its Bastions stand a terror to the sculking Indian and a beacon of safety to the fugitive hunter. It is maned by 12 men and has constantly loade in the Bastions 100 guns and rifles. These bastions command both the inside and the outside of the fort.

Later in the summer of 1834 Wyeth went on to the Columbia to find that the supply ship he had sent around the Horn had been struck by lightning. Although a congenital optimist, Wyeth was at bottom a realist. Eventually he admitted defeat. In 1836, he returned home via the Green River rendezvous and Santa Fe. Next year Fort Hall, which had been rebuilt as an adobe structure, was sold by his agent to the Hudson's Bay Company. The post was maintained by the British company until the 1850's, through all that time draining off its share of the beaver (and later dressed deerskins), a constant thorn in the flesh of its American rivals.

Missionaries Open the Oregon Trail

Much more is notable about the rendezvous of 1834. Jason Lee met the Flathead Indians he had come so far to serve and realized that he had no business accompanying them to their homeland. What Lee perceived, without question or discussion, was that he could have no truck with Indians as Indians. He must make white men of them, after which they might be capable of accepting the white man's religion. He must go on to the Columbia and with his brethren take up farms, begin a long labor of colonization. So the Methodist missionaries, guided by parties of fur hunters, traveled to the Columbia, following in reverse Robert Stuart's eastbound path of 1812, treading what must now become the Oregon Trail.

Sublette & Campbell Are Bought Out

Soon after Wyeth and the missionaries left rendezvous, William L. Sublette set out for home, pausing only briefly along the way to observe the progress made in building his post on the Laramie. Apparently he had accomplished all he had hoped for. But back on Hams Fork both Fitzpatrick, Sublette & Bridger and Drips & Fontenelle were chewing the bitter cud of reflection. Had the two firms no recourse but to accept the suzerainty of Sublette & Campbell? They decided otherwise, and as August came in decided upon a merger, organizing a new firm named Fontenelle, Fitzpatrick & Co. Bridger took a brigade in one direction, Drips in another, and the other two partners set off for the States to see if they could make different arrangements for supplies.

The upshot was that Fontenelle, Fitzpatrick & Co. purchased the mountain interests of

Sublette & Campbell. Nominally what they purchased was the post on the Laramie; in actual fact they bought the right to deal with the Chouteaus, who were now carrying on the Western business of the American Fur Company in their own name, following the breakup of Astor's concern. Campbell went up to the Laramie in the spring of 1835 to transfer the property to the new firm, and for the next year, while Sublette & Campbell settled down as St. Louis merchants, Fontenelle, Fitzpatrick & Co. carried on the mountain business. This did not work out to the satisfaction of Pierre Chouteau, so in the summer of 1836 he sent Joshua Pilcher to buy out the mountain partners. For three years after that, Chouteau conducted the mountain business through his "Rocky Mountain Outfit," Bridger, Drips, and Fontenelle being hired from year to year to conduct the brigades.

Fitzpatrick dropped out in 1837, moving over to the South Platte in the service of Vasquez & (Andrew) Sublette, who in the summer of 1835 had organized a partnership and a few months later founded Fort Vasquez, the first post on the South Platte (a few miles north of the site of Denver). Despite savage competition from Bent & St. Vrain on one side and Chouteau's people on the other, to say nothing of a variety of independents, Vasquez & Sublette managed to keep their heads above water until 1840. Two years after that, Vasquez became Jim Bridger's partner in the post Bridger commenced on Blacks Fork of the Green.

During these years missionaries accompanied the fur traders west almost every summer. In 1835 Dr. Marcus Whitman and the elderly Samuel Parker rode with the caravan to Green River, where Whitman carved out of Jim Bridger's back a three-inch Blackfoot arrowhead which "Old Gabe" had been carrying since the fall of 1832. Looking on, Parker commented, "The Doctor pursued the operation with great self-possession and perseverance." Bridger, though operated on without anesthetic, showed to equal advantage. The surgery gained for Whitman the mountain men's abiding respect. Some later sent their half-breed children to be educated at the mission he founded at Waiilatpu, near present Wallula, Washington.

Kit Carson Gains Renown

It was at this same rendezvous that Kit Carson took his place in the first rank of the mountain men. He had gone to California and back with Ewing Young in 1829–31, then had roamed widely as a free trapper. With Taos, New Mexico, as a home port, he had ranged the Great Plains, the Colorado Rockies and the Uinta basin. With a Bridger party, in the fall of 1834 he had gone into the Blackfoot country, where trappers could hardly go a mile from camp without being fired upon, but he made a fairly good hunt and came to rendezvous to await, with his restless mountain companions, the arrival of the caravan from the States.

Here Carson had his famous duel. On hand, Carsons says, was a large Frenchman, an overbearing kind of man, and very strong. He made a practice of whipping every man that he was displeased with—and that was nearly all. One day, after he had beaten two or three men, he said he had no trouble to flog Frenchmen, and

Kit Carson.

as for Americans, he would take a switch and switch them. I did not like such talk from any man, so I told him that I was the worst American in camp. There were many who could thrash him but for the fact that they were afraid, and that if he used such expressions any more, I would rip his guts.

He said nothing but started for his rifle, mounted his horse, and made his appearance in front of the camp. As soon as I saw this, I mounted my horse also, seized the first weapon I could get hold of, which was a pistol, and galloped up to him and demanded if I was the one he intended to shoot. Our horses were touching. He said no, drawing his gun at the same time so he could have a fair shot at me. I was prepared and allowed him to draw his gun. We both fired at the same time, and all present said that but one report was heard. I shot him through the arm and his ball passed my head, cutting my hair and the powder burning my eye, the muzzle of his gun being near my head when he fired. During the remainder of our stay in camp we had no more bother with this French bully.

Samuel Parker appears to have witnessed this duel with Shunar, "the great bully of the mountains," and his description of the affair made Carson famous before he gained reputation through his association with Frémont in the 1840's. "C's ball," Parker observed, "entered S's hand, came out at the wrist, and passed through the arm above the elbow. S's ball passed over the head of C; and while he went for another pistol, Shunar begged that his life might be spared."

8. *Some Mountain Men as Contemporaries Saw Them*

As a RELIGIOUS man, Parker was moved to meditate upon this singular breed, the mountain men.

Such scenes, sometimes from passion, and sometimes for amusement, make the pastime of their wild and wandering life. They appear to have sought for a place where, as they would say, human nature is not oppressed by the tyranny of religion, and pleasure is not awed by the frown of virtue. . . . Their toils and privations are so great, that they more readily compensate themselves by plunging into such excesses, as in their mistaken judgment of things, seem most adapted to give them pleasure. They disdain the commonplace phrases of profanity which prevail among the impious vulgar in civilized countries, and have many set phrases, which they appear to have manufactured among themselves, and which, in their imprecations, they bring into almost every sentence and on all occasions. By varying the tones of their voices, they make them expressive of joy, hope, grief, and anger. In their broils among themselves, which do not happen every day, they would not be ungenerous. They would see "fair play," and would "spare the last eye"; and would not tolerate murder, unless drunkenness or great provocation could be pleaded in extenuation.

Trappers of the Northwest. Engraving, after drawing by H. P. Sharp.

Jim Bridger

But let us look at two of the most famous of the mountain men through the eyes of David L. Brown, who joined their ranks in 1837. Here is a close-up of the matured Jim Bridger. Brown found him a leader not only thoroughly acquainted with the most inaccessible streams of the mountains but having

a complete and absolute understanding of Indian character, in all its different phases, and a firm, though by no means over cautious, distrust with regard to these savages, based upon his own large experience of their general perfidy, cunning and atrocity. To sum up, his bravery was unquestionable, his horsemanship equally so, and as to his skill with the rifle . . . he had been known to kill twenty buffaloes by the same number of consecutive shots. The physical conformation of this man was in admirable keeping with his character. Tall—six feet at least—muscular, without an ounce of superfluous flesh . . . he might have served as a model for a sculptor or painter, by which to express the perfection of graceful strength and easy activity. One remarkable feature of this man I had almost omitted, and that was his neck, which rivalled his head in size and thickness, and which gave to the upper portion of his otherwise well-formed person a somewhat *outre* and unpleasant appearance. [Bridger had developed a goitre.] His cheek bones were high, his nose hooked or aqueline, the expression of his eye mild and thoughtful, and that of his face grave almost to solemnity. To complete the picture, he was perfectly ignorant of all knowledge contained in books, not even knowing the letters of the alphabet; put perfect faith in dreams and omens, and was unutterably scandalized if even the most childish of the superstitions of the Indians were treated with anything like contempt or disrespect; for in all these he was a firm and devout believer.

Brown turned to look at the still more remarkable Old Bill Williams, an ex-circuit-riding Methodist who had given up the Bible for beaver, and was regarded as an eccentric even by the mountain men:

A more heterogeneous compound than this man, it has never been my fortune to meet withal. He was confessedly the best trapper in the mountains: could catch more beaver, and kill more horses, by hard riding, in so doing, than any that had ever set a trap in these waters. He could likewise drink more liquor, venture farther alone in the eager pursuit of game into the neighborhood of dangerous and hostile Indians, spend more money, and spend it quicker than any other man. He could likewise swear harder and longer, and coin more queer and awful oaths than any pirate that ever blasphemed under a black flag, over a black ship, and from a blacker heart—He could shoot (so *he* said) higher and deeper, wider and closer, straighter and crookeder, and more rounding, and more every way, than "ever a son of a —— of them all," as I had the ineffable pleasure of hearing him say . . . in daring the whole camp, the world included, to a proof of skill with him in shooting at a mark.

This astonishing personage, said Brown (exaggerating somewhat, for Old Bill had been born in 1787), "was near seventy years of age." Old Bill's brag, typical of some mountain men, foreshadows the tall tales for which his kind became famous.

Squaw Men

The mountain man who had not taken an Indian wife was rare indeed. One squaw at a time was usually more than enough, for although he ordinarily had to buy her by paying a bridal price to her father (horses, guns or other valuable consideration), he married her entire family, and could expect to support them for the rest of their lives. It was a man's pride to deck out his wife in the finery the French called *fanfaron,* "foofarraw" in the mountains—the bright-colored clothes, the sleigh-bells, bangles, looking glasses, and all else that might make her "shine" brighter than the wives of others. One such was described by a mountain visitor of the 1840's: "Saw a fat squaw with a broad, glazed leather St. Louis fireman's belt around her waist, marked 'Central' in large gold letters!"

Wives were selected from nearly all the tribes. At different times Bridger had Flathead, Ute and Snake squaws. Carson married an Arapaho girl; and many were taken from among the Nez Percés and Flatheads. Andrew Drips married an Oto girl from the farming Indians on the lower Missouri. He took her to the upper country, and at the Pierres Hole rendezvous of 1832 she had a baby daughter. Moccasins fashioned for the little girl, which she wore when brought down from the Rockies in 1837, are still preserved. The Crow women initiated many of the mountain men to high life in the high country, but they were not notable for personal beauty and few were taken to wife.

At the 1834 rendezvous Robert Newell married a girl variously described as a Nez Percé and a Flathead, whom William Marshall Anderson thought the only pretty Indian woman he saw in the mountains that summer. Although she bore him a child next year, Newell left her among her tribesmen when he revisited the States in the fall of 1835. He came back to her only at the rendezvous of 1837. One of the Oregon missionaries commented at that time:

> A man by the name of Dr. Newell . . . won a woman on a wager. On hearing that his old Flat Head wife was coming with McLeod's [Hudson's Bay Company] party, he said he must get rid of the woman. Accordingly, he went and sold her to her previous owner for One Hundred Dollars. A second individual, they tell me, lost his wife on a wager. A few days after, he won a horse, and bought his wife back again. The buying and selling of Indian women is a common occurrence at this Rendezvous, especially among those having a white face. The principal White trader from the East of the Mountains, I am told [probably Fontenelle], has taken three wives. He tells the Indians to take as many as they can—thus setting at defiance every principle of right, justice, and humanity, and law of God and man.

Few of the missionaries, Samuel Parker excepted, had anything good to say of the mountain men, particularly because those who came west, as the thirties drew on, were a pretty self-righteous lot, smug to the point of being sanctimonious. Many of the settlers in the West in later years were a mirror-image of these missionary forerunners, regarding the mountain men as "old liers," little better than the Indians, and men who had demeaned themselves by taking Indian wives they would not put away for the sake of acceptance into white communities. There is still an edge of contempt to the term "squaw man" which has come down in western annals.

Many squaw men showed themselves possessed of more character than their neighbors who sat in judgment upon them. A notable example is Joe Meek, whose Nez Percé wife, conscious of his near-ostracism by the settlers of the Willamette Valley in the 1840's, urged him to put her away and take a white wife. Loving her and their children, dark skin or no, he refused to listen to any such talk. Little wonder that in later years, blind, she thought back over the past to tell a visitor, "No man can run like Joe; no man can fight like Joe; no man like Joe."

Nor were the mountain men quite the unlettered lot tradition implies. The long winter nights were put to good use through what was facetiously called the "Rocky Mountain College." Many learned to read and write in the winter lodges, wearing to tatters the few books that found their way west in this age—the Bible, Shakespeare and others. Joe Meek named one of his daughters for that Scottish heroine Helen Mar, as one reflection of this cultural flowering.

Even the mountain men who did not learn to read were like Indians in their power to absorb anything spoken; they could recite whole chapters and scenes of books, merely from hearing them read aloud. Some of the mountain men were rough-souled characters, to be sure; but they delighted in shocking genteel sensibilities, and some of the more extravagant tales that have come down are mere theatrics, shows put on for the benefit of the genteel and the gullible. The mountain men were amazingly varied, from the quietly devout Jedediah Smith ("a mild man and a Christian, and there were few enough of them in the mountains") to the one-time divine, Old Bill Williams, muttering and gobbling to himself with the spectacular and highly original profanity that made such an impression on David L. Brown.

Mountain men were much given to foot racing and horse racing as well as to wrestling, in which they were like the farm boys back home; they loved to dance around campfires to the monotonous thump of an Indian drum, and equally they loved a spree, the leaders with their men. Few remained in the mountains who did not love to hunt. Running buffalo on horseback was the supreme sport, but "old Ephraim," the grizzly, was always worth a man's time and attention. If the majority of the mountain men were rather simple men with simple values, so were most of the American people during their time.

9. *The End of an Era*

THERE WERE FIVE more rendezvous after 1835, each aglitter with its own spectacle. The spectacle must not be forgotten, but what was happening in the hinterland, the way the ground was being cut from beneath the fur brigades, must also be remembered.

The rendezvous of 1836 was notable because Marcus Whitman returned that year to the mountains with his wife, the immortal blonde, Narcissa. Whitman's fellow missionary, Henry Harmon Spalding, also brought his wife, Eliza. The two women were the first white women ever to cross South Pass, their passage commemorated by a monument there today. Whitman was a practical man, not much given to the torture of doubt or oppressed by his awful unworthiness. He tried to take a wagon all the way to Oregon in 1836 but failed, as explained in a later chapter. He did serve faithfully the cause of Oregon and the red men for eleven heartbreaking years until disaffected Cayuse Indians murdered him, his wife and their children. Whitman's thwarted ambition to haul the first wagon to the Columbia was accomplished in 1840 by Robert Newell, a trapper turned settler. Thereafter, it was just a question of time until there should be a well-beaten Oregon Trail, as obvious to the eye as any turnpike of the Atlantic shore, marvelous to the Sioux as the Great Medicine Road of the whites.

The Green River rendezvous of 1837 differed from all others because the British sports-

"Bull Boating on the Platte River." Painting by Alfred Jacob Miller.

JOSLYN ART MUSEUM, OMAHA

man, William Drummond Stewart, brought to it an artist, having employed the young painter Alfred Jacob Miller to record scenes along the trail—the great landmarks, the Indians and their ways and the rendezvous. Other painters had entered the West before Miller, including Samuel Seymour, George Catlin and Carl Bodmer, but Miller alone recorded the interior West in the age of rendezvous. The record is a priceless one, for which we shall ever be indebted to him and to Stewart.

The imaginative Stewart also seems to have brought to the mountains a gift to Jim Bridger, what is described as a suit of armor, but what from Miller's sketches would appear to have been cuirass and greaves. It is a pleasant thought, Jim Bridger riding off to the Blackfoot wars in armor, but the equipment was scarcely practical; the metal would have roasted Old Gabe in summer and stripped the skin from him in winter, and at that would not have turned a Blackfoot musket ball. Perhaps the armor was left in the mountains to be thrown away or used when the mountain men needed a strip of iron for a piece of blacksmithing. Possibly Stewart took the rejected gift back to the States; no one knows. But it is agreeable to think that some one may yet dig Bridger's armor from a long-forgotten hiding place.

More distant events also make the year 1837 memorable. On the Missouri the annual steamboat sent upriver by the Chouteaus carried with it the seeds of a terrible smallpox epidemic. Some tribes, like the Arikara and Mandan, were all but wiped out, and there were frightful ravages among the Blackfeet, humbling that tribe as nothing had done since the dreadful epidemic of the 1780's; for several years the mountain men could pursue the vanishing beaver in all parts of the Blackfoot country, almost undisturbed. More remote from the mountains, the panic of '37 brought on hard times and "the pressure." Finance capital could scarcely be found, and the falling price of beaver only reflected general economic desolation.

In any event, during the flush years the price of beaver in the mountains had been bid up beyond all reason under the stress of competition, and an adjustment was overdue. The Chouteaus necessarily adopted a tough line with the trappers, boosting prices and clamping down on credit. Understanding little of conditions in the States, the trappers bawled their fury, feeling themselves mercilessly exploited. Some, seeing the writing on the wall, departed the mountains, while others entered into service with the new forts being built. That proud breed, the mountain man, was descending the road to extinction.

Those who attended the rendezvous of 1838, which was held at the confluence of Wind River and the Popo Agie, eyed more missionaries heading for Oregon, and as one sign of the times, a Swiss of imposing presence named John A. Sutter, making for California by the roundabout Oregon route. There was talk at this rendezvous that the company would send no more goods to the mountains, and it was not at first certain that Bridger and Drips would take the field at the head of another brigade. The two able partisans made a hunt, but for the last time in the old tradition of the fur brigade. At the Green River rendezvous of 1839 even the unworldly Oregon missionary, Asahel Munger, could see that the end was at hand: "The men are most of them out of business and know not what to do." Drips announced that the last rendezvous had been held, that no more caravans would be sent to the mountains. He and Bridger departed for the States—Old Gabe making his first visit home in seventeen years, since he had left St. Louis as an Ashley man in 1822. In all that time he had not tasted bread.

The mountain men scattered over the country—some to Fort Hall, some to Fort Davy Crockett in Brown's Hole. Through the ensuing winter, scenes of criminal violence followed one another, inconceivable to self-respecting mountain men like Robert Newell. Fort Hall was raided, and so were friendly Indians. With nothing better to do, in the early winter of 1840 a band of mountain men, including Pegleg Smith, Old Bill Williams and others of note, rode south to raid the southern California ranchos. They were chased into the deserts, so that the bones of many stolen horses were left to bleach north of the Mohave. Yet some were driven to the Colorado Rockies and disposed of there.

Others of the mountain men could not countenance such actions even in these starving times, and there was, after all, a rendezvous of sorts in 1840. Drips led a caravan to the old Green River site. With this party came from St. Louis the Belgian Jesuit, Pierre-Jean De Smet, who had labored for several years among the Indians of the Missouri Valley, and was now answering the call of Flatheads and Christianized Iroquois for black robes. De Smet entered upon this labor gladly, celebrating the first mass in what is now Wyoming. He left a permanent impress upon the Indians of the Northwest, helped to shape both their history and the world's knowledge of their country. But he appears in this narrative only as he helps to ring down the curtain on an era.

After all, perhaps the symbols of greater import were the men with whom De Smet traveled to the mountains. One of them, Joel Walker, the brother of Joe, was bound for Oregon as a homeseeker, and next year would make his way down the interior trail to California, his wife the first white woman to enter California overland.

10. *The Spanish Trail*

THE NORTHERN FUR TRADE and northern overland trails have attracted more attention from western historians than the little-publicized Spanish Trail from Santa Fe to Pueblo de los Angeles, but that trail must not be overlooked. During the five or six years beginning in 1827, several parties worked out this important thoroughfare. The trail was one of many variants, but in essence it followed the old Escalante path of 1776 north to the vicinity of the Grand (or Colorado) River, swung northwesterly to ford the Green near the present town of Green River, Utah, then after crossing the Wasatch Mountains to the Little Salt Lake country descended the Virgin River for many miles, struck out into the desert to the springs at Las Vegas, crossed more deserts (roughly U. S. Highway 91) to the Mohave River, and went on to Los Angeles near the shore of the Pacific.

This was essentially a mule path, though it is said an effort was made in 1837 to take a wagon the full length of the trail—whether successfully the record sayeth not. Manufactured goods taken from New Mexico were traded for mules and horses, the only California product that could profitably be moved overland in that age, beaver excepted. The hides that were traded by shipmasters along the California coast were far too bulky and low in value, especially in New Mexico, to admit of land transport.

Many place names in the West survive from the era of the Spanish Trail and the fur trade, our heritage from the men who opened the West. These first comers tucked away in their collective memory a far-ranging knowledge—how the land lay, the lift of the mountains and the way the rivers flowed. In due course this knowledge would be tapped by army officers heading formal expeditions of discovery, by emigrants seeking homes on the Pacific and in interior valleys, and by many others. The mountain men made an unknown land their home and left their impress upon it.

After 1840, when this section ends, memories of the glorious days died slowly. Some of the mountain men continued to lead small companies of trappers with ever poorer returns. Some settled in remote corners of the West they knew so well. Some took up farms in Oregon or Missouri, or served emigrants as guides and interpreters. Some were swept along to California by the gold rush, or operated ferries for overland travelers. Jim Bridger built the fort which became famous as a stopping place for emigrants though he himself was often away on trapping expeditions. In the sunset of life Bridger and other mountain men guided army columns in action against the Indians in country they had known in its morning splendor. Kit Carson became a colonel commanding New Mexican cavalry; he, Fitzpatrick, and others also served as Indian agents. Yet others re-entered the society they had been born into; Robert Campbell, for one, died a millionaire, one of the wealthiest citizens of Missouri. They had all lived through a strange and wonderful era. No man who entered the West during that epoch was quite the same again, and the American West itself was changed because they had claimed it as their own.

"Westward Ho!" Painting by William R. Leigh.

WOOLAROC MUSEUM, BARTLESVILLE, OKLA.

PART TWO

"White Man's Burden" by Charles M. Russell

Transportation in the American West

by Oscar Osburn Winther

Zuñi cart and burros.

11. *Beasts of Burden — from Squaw to Horse*

IT WAS LESS than fifty years from Columbus' landing to the day when a dying De Soto explored the Mississippi River. Yet, in this short span of time, the world began to move. There were uncharted seas for a Vespucius and a Magellan to sail and lands unknown to white men for Ponce de Leon, Cartier and Cortez to see. Whether these ambitious expeditions were the result of material greed or just plain curiosity is not the point. What is important is that wherever there is a frontier there will be men, even if they have to walk to get there. And many of them did.

Álvar Núñez Cabeza de Vaca was one. With three other survivors of an ill-fated Spanish expedition to Florida in 1528, he managed to escape across the Gulf of Mexico and for eight years wandered among the tribes of what later became New Mexico and Arizona. Pack on back, he walked the great grasslands, came to the desert escarpments, looked down on butte and mesa, waterless seas of cacti and brittle brush. Wherever he went he found that red men had walked before him. And on the high plains of Texas he must have noticed that buffalo had walked before them.

It was the buffalo that were the real road engineers of the Great Plains. Centuries before the first Spaniard set foot in America buffalo had marked their routes from watercourse to watercourse across a world of grass as flat as the ocean. They had established for themselves, and those who followed, the "superhighways" of their day. Secondary roads and detours were designed by deer and antelope. Indians made good use of all these pathways in their constant search for game.

Though these trails were ideal for the hunt, the Indian soon needed others. So it was that for purposes of peaceful trade with friends, and war with enemies, and for just plain visiting—the American Indian became a road builder in his own right. The trails that converged at The Dalles trading center on the Columbia River, the Olachen Trail over which candlefish oil was moved from the Pacific coast, and the network of paths from California to the Rio Grande were by-products of the red traders.

All the native tribes of North America, except the Eskimos, engaged in some form of inter-group trade. And most of these tribes had to wander far and wide just in their normal food-gathering activities. Transportation, then, was a necessity of Indian life long before Cabeza de Vaca walked the West—and long before the three tiny ships captained by Columbus touched the coast of San Salvador.

SMITHSONIAN INSTITUTION

One of the earliest American pack trains.

Although the pre-Columbian Indian had trails, he also had major handicaps: He had no horse, nor had he invented the wheel. But despite these shortcomings, he made excellent use of what he did have—his head. Or, for the sake of accuracy, *her* head, for it was the squaws who carried the loads by means of "burden straps," or tumplines, across their foreheads. The male of the species had to remain alert, ready for instant combat, the hunt—and sometimes just plain loafing.

Human portering was not the only means by which Indians moved things from place to place. They had tamed the dog into a hunting companion, a pack and draft animal. When an encampment was to be broken up, so that the tribe could move on to greener pastures, two poles were lashed far enough apart to allow room for a dog between the ends. The other ends were allowed to drag. On this affair would be bundled the covering of the small shelter tent and the rest of the family possessions. A big dog could drag as much as fifty pounds.

This type of rig, known as the travois, was commonly used by the migratory Plains Indians even after the arrival of the horse and the Spaniards' introduction of the wheel. Travois trails were still common sights in the nineteenth century when George Catlin, the noted artist, traveled to the upper Missouri River in order to see and draw horse Indians in their natural haunts. One of Catlin's canvases offers a vivid picture of a band of Comanche on the move; it demonstrates as no words possibly could the effectiveness of the crude travois system. In fact in later years this same device, used on horses, proved useful and efficient to American frontiersmen and army units in the West.

Neither the travois nor human portering, however, could solve the problem of water transport. Few of the Indian tribes were completely landlocked, and they were often forced to cross streams and rivers. Dugouts, balsa and dry-grass rafts as well as the sleek bark canoe can all be credited to Indian inventiveness. Once the stream was crossed, the contrivance might be cast aside and forgotten or perhaps it would be used by the next traveler going the other way. But the old slogan, "Waterways in the East; wagon ways in the West," pretty much tells the story of pre-twentieth century transportation in this part of America.

The beginning of the seventeenth century was the beginning of a new era for both the Indian and the white man, for this date marked the introduction of the horse into the Indian culture. Though it was Columbus who had first brought horses to the New World on his second voyage in 1493, it was Coronado, in 1540, who brought them into the American West. The introduction of the horse had an immediate and profound effect on the Indian. During his early and ill-tempered contacts with the white invader, the aborigine had been treated to many painful demonstrations of the worth of the horse—in the open a moccasined brave was no match for a rider (though in the skulking, tree-to-tree type of warfare a horse was not as useful). Before long the horse became possibly the most cherished, and consequently the most stolen, beast in the West.

It put a culture on the move. It also was used for food among the Digger Indians, for it beat, as one old-timer put it, "snakes and snails and the like." Above all though, it was a beast of burden that had replaced the dog but, much to her sorrow, not the squaw.

In the first hundred years after the introduction of the horse, the total horse population among such nations as the Comanche, Crow, Sioux and Blackfoot had grown to number scores of thousands. The horse had become a measure of personal wealth, a medium of exchange, a class symbol, a means of hunting buffalo, a tactical instrument in war.

And with it had come the development of one of the most skilled horsemen the West has ever known. Riding at full gallop with nothing but a pelt cinched to the horse's back and belly, the Indian put to shame the generation of "leather pullers" that was to come. In battle or in play the Indian and the horse were one, and out of that association something new was born to him: a deep sense of friendship with an animal. In later years when the sunshine of his day had become the sunset of his memories and the red man was pacified and "civilized" or restricted to reservations, his mustang was still his inseparable companion.

"Going to the Dance," in a travois rig. Engraving, after drawing by Frederic Remington, Century *Magazine, 1888.*

Fort Clatsop
Fort Vancouver
Lewis
Clark
Clark
Smith Spring of 1828
Fremont 1843-44
Oregon Trail
Fremont 1843-44
California Trail
Fremont 1843-44
Oregon Trail
California Trail
Pony Express Route
Pony Express Route
Smith Spring of 1827
Winter 1827-28
San Francisco
Monterey
John Fremont
Smith Winter Summer 1826-27
Old Spanish Trail
Smith Summer 1827
Summer 1826
Smith Summer 1827
Old Spanish Trail
Smith Winter 1826-27
Fall of 1826
Los Angeles
San Diego
Gila River Trail
Pike 1806
Butterfield Overland Stage 1858-61

Routes and Trails of the
AMERICAN WEST

Carreta *drawn by two oxen.*

12. *Conquistadores to Carretas*

WHEN, IN 1540, Francisco de Coronado set out with his entourage from Compostela, a town some hundred and fifty miles south of the later-day Mexican resort city of Mazatlán, his purpose was twofold: to find wealth in the fabled "Seven Cities of Cíbola" and to impress his religion on the aborigines. To hasten the former and to add a powerful persuasion to the latter he was accompanied by a magnificent military array of foot and horse, as well as a multitude of friendly Indians. According to the records which have been preserved 559 horses were listed as being part of his parade of officers and lancemen, while upwards of a thousand horses and mules were catalogued as beasts of burden. Although Coronado captured the seven Zuñi pueblos of New Mexico in midsummer of that year, he found no fabled wealth. Hoping that other cities whose wealth had been mistakenly attributed to these might lie ahead, he plodded eastward across the Rio Grande and then northward into the plains of Kansas only to be disappointed again.

For the next half-century New Mexico and Arizona simmered in the desert sun, undisturbed by conquistadores. A few priests eager to save the souls of red-skinned pagans disappeared forever in the desolate country, and at least five feeble expeditions ventured unsuccessfully northward, but it was not until 1598 that Don Juan de Oñate established a permanent Spanish foothold in what would be the southwestern United States.

Oñate was very different from the earlier conquistadores. Unlike Cortez, Cabeza de Vaca and Coronado he was not Spanish-born, nor did he need to look to Spain to finance his projects. A true Mexican "señor," or lord, his wife was a granddaughter of Cortez, and his father had founded the prosperous city of Guadalajara. Inheriting great wealth Don Juan de Oñate also inherited his people's spirit of conquest, as well as the persistent idea that perhaps the real "Seven Cities of Cíbola" did stand somewhere in the unexplored north.

So it was that this Mexican grandee and 400 soldiers, 130 of them with their families, set off from Zacatecas for the 700-mile march across roadless deserts to the Rio Grande (at

El Paso). The column drove 7,000 head of livestock. Horses, mules and burros served as mounts and pack animals. In addition baggage was transported on eighty-three crude two-wheeled carts called *carretas.*

In all probability Juan de Oñate left his *carretas* near the future site of El Paso, for the way ahead along the river was rough and he traveled another 300 miles into the heart of the pueblo country before settling at two adjoining Indian villages, which would be pointed out to tourists 350 years later as the quaint and devout mission of San Juan. From here Oñate made expeditions east and west seeking the "Seven Cities" but all to no avail. The date and manner of his death remain a mystery. His immigrants soon moved to the site of another Indian pueblo which became known as Santa Fe, capital for other Spanish settlers who followed.

The Spaniards brought many things to these Indians besides Christianity. Among them was the wheel and the know-how for building *carretas* so important to later generations of Pueblo Indians. The *carreta* was a simple vehicle, not too difficult to make. At rest it resembled a woodpile and in motion it sounded much like a pig caught by the ear. Sometimes lubricants were used to eliminate the howling of the wooden axles, but, in the main, the nerve-shattering sound would precede the vehicle, serving as both a warning and identification. The *carreta* rolled on rimless wheels made from a slice cut from an oak log, through which an eight-inch hole for the axle was chiseled at a reasonable approximation of the center. Sometimes the wheels were made of sections crisscrossed in a rather helter-skelter fashion and secured by pegs. The crate or box that formed the body was usually held together by pegs and thongs.

The design doubtless came from the Old World, and its appearance in the American West can be traced back to at least the 1600's. The California pioneer, John Bidwell, in his reminiscences of the days before the gold rush, wrote, "I have seen the families of the wealthiest people go long distances in such carts." By this he meant thirty miles in one day.

However, the backs of sturdy horses and tough burros and mules continued to provide the mainstay of travel and transportation in the West with the establishment of the *presidio,* or garrison, and mission and rancho life.

The routes over which most traffic moved were called *caminos reales,* which could be interpreted literally as royal roads but which were actually nothing more than crude bridle trails. One such casually defined path, *El Camino Real* in California, later called U. S. Highway 101, formed links in the chain of Spanish coastal missions and garrisons. Over this historic trail traveled the padres and rancheros, traders, adventurers, soldiers and officials most of whose names are forgotten. Remembered would be Father Junípero Serra and Captain Gaspar de Portolá, who were the founders of Alta California in 1769, and Father Eusebio Kino, the "Padre on Horseback."

Another royal road, the Chihuahua–Santa Fe Trail, emerged as an important trader's route as did the so-called Old Spanish Trail which connected Santa Fe with California.

Civilization moved along these trails, although the trickle was not yet a torrent. That would come later when the covered wagon and the iron horse found their way westward. Nevertheless, whether on horseback, by burro or mule or riding shank's mare, men were marching toward the Pacific and the race for the West was on.

13. *The Pack Train*

AT THE CONCLUSION of the War with Mexico in 1848, the bell tolled for the end of dominant Spanish influence in the American West. Gradually the glamour of the *conquistadores* was dissipated by the new Anglo-Saxon settlers from the East.

To these strangers, the *carreta,* although useful for hauling produce to and from local markets, failed when called upon to satisfy the requirements of heavier commerce. By and large commercial operators moved their goods from place to place by pack train.

Although horses, llamas, burros, dogs and even camels served as pack animals in the New World, the outstanding favorite was the mule. During the period of Spanish influence in the Southwest, the Mexican mule was used, but later this breed was largely replaced by the American variety, most of which seemed to come from Missouri. Though a mule's disposition was uncertain, he was sure-footed, tough and, next to his cousin the "mountain canary," or burro, was best equipped to exist on scant desert forage.

Choosing a mule was a procedure something like the one described in the old Etruscan proverb about selecting a wife: "Close your eyes and put your trust in God." But there were rules of thumb—the mule should be sturdy-legged, sure-footed, muscular and bright-eyed. It should have sharp teeth, a swishy tail and sound skin; in short, it should be tough, strong, healthy and spirited. Many a muleteer learned to his dismay, and relatively temporary discomfort, that these very same qualities could also make the beast a formidable adversary. It was better, mule drivers generally agreed, if a sort of rapport could be established between man and animal. An American mountaineer once wrote that to do this one had to "live on the intimate terms of brother-explorer with your mule" and be thoughtful of his welfare. This meant feed the animal well, keep it properly shod, prevent galling and stay away from behind him.

The success of the mule as a beast of burden depended as much on the skill of the *arriero,* or muleteer, as it did on the animal himself. Mexicans made better muleteers. They understood their beast and he understood them. And Mexicans knew the art of packing and unpacking. One British observer said they were the best muleteers in the world.

In loading a mule the first step was to blindfold the animal. Like belling the cat, this was the major part of the battle. Afterward, a broad, thick pad across the animal's back served as a cushion for a "saw-buck" or "cross-buck" saddle. Some packers preferred an *aparajo,* which was two rectangular leather bags stuffed with straw and lashed together. This arrangement, similar to outsized saddlebags, was contoured to fit the mule's back. After being properly placed and cinched, the load could be lashed on top of either the "saw-buck" or *aparajo.* A breeching or crupper and a breast strap prevented longitudinal movement.

Behind the white bell mare, the endless train.

Loads were carefully balanced and articles of heaviest weight were placed nearest the animal's side while the lighter items rode on top. As protection a tarpaulin was sometimes wrapped around the finished load and held in place by a diamond hitch. Thus arranged a mule could carry up to two hundred pounds, although packers were inclined to exaggerate their figures. But, whatever the load it usually included about fifty pounds of fodder.

If loaded properly, the mule generally made no protest, but if he felt that he had been mistreated, he registered resentment in one of several ways. He could lie down in passive resistance, or he could take to his heels, jolting his load across the wild and rocky hillsides.

In the hands of experts such antics were rare, and once packed with blinds removed the mule would take his place in line behind the bell mare. Mules were trained to follow this white or gray mare that was chosen to be their leader; they would graze with her and in general respond to her wishes.

The number of mules in a "string" varied from five to seventy-five, but the manner of operation would be generally the same. An average string might be managed by five or six *arrieros* one of whom would be the *cargador,* or boss.

In good weather mule-train driving involved arising before dawn, eating breakfast, and then watering and packing the mules. As the first daylight broke, the bell mare would be off down the trail, and one by one the mules would fall in behind her, the pace seldom exceeding a walk. At midday there would be a break for feeding and watering the train, and nightfall would find the bell mare stopped and the mules circled awaiting their unloading. The men ate their supper in the crisp starlight, their chatter punctuated by the tinkling of the mare's bell as she grazed down the slope.

And in neat stacks, ready for the next morning's reloading, were the trade goods, cloth and clothing from eastern mills, sugar, flour and spices, hides and even, on occasion, pieces of furniture or a sheet iron stove. And atop it all might be a *caballero's* guitar.

14. *California's Pack-Mule Express*

WHEN IN THE late 1830's the Swiss adventurer, John Augustus Sutter established the estate he called New Helvetia at the confluence of the American and Sacramento rivers he had no way of knowing what was to follow. The land grant of eleven square leagues he had obtained from the Mexican authorities at Monterey soon grew into a sort of empire supported by the traders, ranchers and farmers who came that way. But gold? A little of that precious metal had been found far to the south near Los Angeles, but not enough to excite anyone.

In 1847 Sutter, with the sole idea of expanding his operations, ordered James Marshall, one of his employees, to locate a site for a mill and to oversee its construction. Then one day (January 24, 1848) Marshall discovered gold in the tailrace of his mill. In spite of Sutter's desperate efforts to keep the discovery secret, the great news eventually leaked out. As the months passed, countless thousands of Argonauts invaded New Helvetia, trampled Sutter's crops, slaughtered his cattle, and left the once proud Swiss embittered, disillusioned and financially ruined.

From the Sacramento and the American, the gold seekers spread out over much of California and with the bustling exploitation came demands for more efficient transportation. The *carreta* was disappearing with the waning of Spanish influence and was being replaced by the four-wheeled wagon. Clumsy sailing ships soon made way for sleek Yankee clippers on the hazardous trip around South America, and inland the stagecoach offered a new form of passenger service. But with all the change that came out of the building of a new civilization in the West, two of the most ancient methods of transport still survived: the horse and the pack animal.

The persistence of a rancho economy in much of the Southwest made the riding pony virtually a necessity. It was astride a wiry mustang that the rancher made his visits to town and cared for his herds.

Pack trains also remained indispensable. The miners who had overrun California's gold-bearing hills depended on packers for food and supplies. The mining camp soon became a home away from home, and accordingly, supplies had to be brought in regularly—food and clothing, medicines and tools. But many other less pressing necessities of life made their precarious way up the valleys and along the ledges: mirrors for saloons, pianos and even billiard tables. Gold diggers had huge appetites and the money to satisfy them.

Most goods needed by the miners had to be imported from the "States," with San Francisco the chief port of entry. Crescent City and Eureka were also important ports, while Sacramento, Marysville, Stockton and other river ports that could be reached by steamboat grew into advanced transfer points. It was from these places that the packers would set out for the isolated mining camps in the foothills of the Sierra Nevada. And packing became big business, so big in fact that American capitalists soon relieved the Mexican of the work and worry of the pack trains. The hardy *arriero,* however, was retained to handle the mule trains, the philosophy being that, "if you want a thing done well, hire someone who knows how to do it."

By 1852, two years after California's admission to the union as a state, California had more than sixteen thousand mules valued at more than eight hundred thousand dollars, according to Governor John Bigler's reports on the census of that year, and these were concentrated in the mountain counties. Twenty-five hundred mules, for example, were required to handle the Marysville-Downieville freight; eighteen hundred mules operated out of Shasta and hundreds more trudged the trails of the Mariposa area. The high point in mule population of California came in 1855 when the total swelled to over thirty-one thousand.

Although packing in California retained much of the flavor of Old Mexico, some changes were inevitable under the new management. The Yankee insisted that casualness be replaced by precision and, in turn, an increase in freight volume. Staple food and clothing items were soon augmented by other types of freight and services. In one instance, a printing press weighing nearly four hundred pounds was carried into one of the mountain settlements. Before long, enterprising "pack-mule express" men began carrying special delivery mail and transporting gold from mine to city bank, thus assuming the functions of the conventional express companies which soon flourished in California and gained national importance. But until the construction of adequate roads made wagon-freighting and coaching possible between isolated mining communities, the packing business remained king in California.

"Mule-Skinners" of the Santa Fe Trail.

15. *Eastward, Ho!*

LIKE A MIGHTY tide the treasure hunters flowed over California. The gold camps were born boisterous and lusty. Less than one man in ten found enough gold to become rich but many were infected with a disease called "gold fever"—an ailment they never outgrew. When the favored few acquired title to all the good claims in what was known as the Mother Lode, the fabulous Comstock was discovered in Nevada. Farther east Pikes Peak gold and Leadville silver made Colorado. Gold mines flourished in Montana during the Civil War, and in 1875 the Black Hills became still another great bonanza.

During all of these rushes many changes occurred, but one thing remained pretty much the same: the pack-mule trains. Operations in the Pacific Northwest followed the pattern set in the Southwest, operating regularly between Humboldt Bay and southern Oregon, between Portland and points in both the upper Willamette and Columbia River valleys, between Fort Langley and the Frazier River diggings and eastward to Fort Benton, the head of navigation on the Missouri.

But now pack trains were not the only way to move freight: supplies for the miners could be carried by wagon and even by boat as far as the advanced transshipment points, from where they were forwarded by mule. Freight rates were high and returns to the packers highly satisfactory. Some indication of how satisfactory is clear in a memorial to Congress forwarded by the Washington Territorial Legislature in 1866.

This document stated, among other things, that "no less than six thousand mules have left Walla Walla and the Columbia River loaded with freight for Montana." Moreover, the *Montana Post* estimated that during the spring and summer of the same year there were between eight thousand and ten thousand pack animals operating in the Montana freight trade.

Besides the commercial operators there were, throughout the West, individuals or small groups who used pack animals as means of transport. The gold seekers themselves, often traveling over trails, were forced to make use of pack mules and horses. Guide books of the period, such as Captain John Mullan's *Miners' and Travelers' Guide* published in New York in 1865, advised the use of pack mules to reach mining camps in the Pacific Northwest.

The biggest user of pack mules in the West, however, was the United States Army. During the last half of the nineteenth century there were about a hundred army posts scattered throughout the West, many of which were in fairly inaccessible places that could be supplied only by pack animals. Great quantities of freight that eventually arrived at the army posts were first moved by steamer to Missouri River ports such as Atchison, Leavenworth and Nebraska City, from where they continued by wagon freight and then by pack mule.

The keeping of the peace often called for military operations over rough and unmarked land; mules loaded with supplies could go wherever the "yellow legs" went. Some of the largest pack trains of those days were used in General George A. Custer's campaign against the Sioux and in General George Crook's attempts to rid the world of Geronimo and his Apache followers.

Even though the West was fast being tamed and changed, and the tide ebbing where before it had moved in a freshet, the pack animal lived on—at least in the form of the small, tough, long-eared burro. Not as antisocial as the mule, the burro possessed the same ability to exist where little or nothing grew. The coarsest of desert plants would do for a meal, and the burro could sustain himself on the water from a mirage. The few solitary prospectors left, who searched for the "Lost Dutchman" or looked for "color" in the mountain recesses, preferred a burro as their companion. The animal served as confidential adviser and friend as well as beast of burden. Loaded to virtual invisibility with pick, shovel, blanket, rifle, canned goods, flour and other *accoutrements* of the desert rat, the docile burro was there.

16. *Uncle Sam's Camels*

ONE DAY IN early summer of 1856, the town of Indianola, Texas, was treated to a sight that made even the more hardened citizenry shudder and take the pledge. Up to this day, the clean air from the Gulf had been a decided advantage; now it suddenly became a detriment because the very chinks of the houses were filled with the nostril-pinching odor of a shipment of very seasick but still bellicose camels. In all, seventy-five were imported into the United States; according to the Texans, one would have been more than plenty. So bad was the smell that some Abolitionists in the North proclaimed the shipment a screen to cover up the stench of an illicit landing of African slaves.

The record shows that Colonial Virginia had carried on unsuccessful experimentation with camel transport during the eighteenth century. Among the first to advocate the importation of dromedaries from Africa or Asia Minor were George L. Glidden, a man who had had experience with the camel in the Near East, and John R. Bartlett, who, as chief of the Mexican boundary survey, was convinced that the camel could be used effectively. The idea had gained high official backing with the approval of Secretary of War Jefferson Davis. As an indication of his own interest in the proposal, Davis made repeated pleas that the War Department be granted funds for the experiment. Finally the objections were overcome and Davis' proposals were carried out by Congress in 1855.

An amendment to an army bill appropriated about thirty thousand dollars for the project, and in due time Army and Navy personnel were dispatched to the Mediterranean on a procurement mission. These officers not only were to buy camels but were to arrange for the hiring of experienced camel drivers as well. The mission was successful, and in a short time the first shipment of thirty-three dromedaries crossed the Atlantic to be unloaded near Indianola. A second government purchase arrived in 1857. The experiment interested several civilians who began importing camels.

The government camels were penned in what were officially designated as caravansaries— established for the purpose northwest of San Antonio and named Camp Verde. The entire operation there was under the direction of Major Henry C. Wayne.

In a test operation during the spring of 1857, Lieutenant Edward Fitzgerald Beale, a naval officer, directed a twenty-five-camel caravan from Camp Verde to California. The caravan, with professionally trained Turkish, Greek and Armenian drivers, was to supplement a mule-drawn wagon train serving a party of army engineers.

In about four months, despite a rather disorganized start, the camels reached Los Angeles, and Lieutenant Beale's praise of the experiment was forwarded to Secretary of War John D. Floyd, who had succeeded Davis. Floyd, however, did not share his predecessor's enthusiasm for the humpbacked beasts and refused to approve the experiment. Without his endorsement Congress decided to deny additional appropriations, and a request for the purchase of a thousand more camels was promptly rejected.

The camels were used, in one way and another, until the Civil War, but the outbreak of hostilities does not bring an end of the story. What happened to some of them we know; the rest has become part of the legend of the West.

The record shows that Lieutenant Beale's camels were not returned to Camp Verde but instead were taken to Fort Tejon, an Army post north of Los Angeles. Some of the animals remained at Tejon for several years and were used in the provisioning of the fort, while a few of the beasts were placed in a camp at San Pedro, where they wound up their days hauling freight between that point and Los Angeles. Others were used by army engineers in further explorations of the Southwest.

Twenty-two of the camels were sold at San Francisco in 1862, destined to be shipped to Victoria, British Columbia, and from there to the mainland for use in building the Cariboo

The 1857 camel express, a noble experiment.

U. S. BUREAU OF PUBLIC ROADS

Wagon Road. Eventually they graduated to service between Douglas and Lillooet where they "frightened horses and mules and caused several accidents."

In the spring of 1864, just eight years after the memorable landing at Indianola, the government auctioned a batch of camels to the highest bidder. A man named Samuel McLeneghan bought some of them. He planned to use the dromedaries for moving freight between California and the Comstock mines. But McLeneghan evidently had a change of heart, for part of his camels eventually went to a circus, while others were allowed to graze at peace on his ranch. Some even turned up later in remote areas of the West.

Camels were allowed to roam at will in the far Northwest, and stories of their appearances continued to circulate for many years. Some, it is said, were killed and eaten by Indians, who reported the steaks appetizing when fried. Others were seen in Idaho and western Montana where they reportedly caused a freighting team to stampede. Of the six camels that served on the Mullan Road linking Fort Benton with the upper Columbia River, one was mistaken for a moose and shot, and another drowned.

In spite of Jefferson Davis' partiality for the camel there is no evidence that the Confederates made any especial use of them, and in 1865 when Camp Verde was once again in Union hands, the camels there were either auctioned off or abandoned in the desert.

But the legends live. There were those who reported a half-century later that they still saw the strange configurations of camels silhouetted against a starlit sky and moving across the lonely desert wastes.

One such, known as the "Red Ghost," was "seen" in a farm yard in broad daylight where it reportedly trampled a woman to death, and it was likewise seen in various mining camps where it turned things topsy-turvy. So it is that, in the realm of fancy if not in fact, "Uncle Sam's camels" continued for another half-century to roam the parched land of the yucca, the mesquite and the Joshua tree.

17. *Transportation and the Fur Trade*

WHEN, DURING THE summer and fall of 1804, Lewis and Clark ascended the Missouri in a "22-oar bateau" and two *pirogues,* they wintered in the Mandan villages at the river's great bend. Here they set their men to work cutting down trees for the construction of six canoes. With these and the two *pirogues* the expedition continued upriver in the spring, for the big bateau had been sent back to the States with specimens and reports.

A detailed description of these boats has not been preserved, but in all probability the bateau was a keelboat of the type in common use on the Mississippi and Ohio. These craft were even suitable for moving freight on the "Harlot" herself, the turbulent and muddy Missouri. Literally a flatboat with a keel to increase stability, it was about fifty-five feet long,

"The Jolly Flatboatmen," 1844. Painting by George Caleb Bingham.

decked over fore and aft with walkways along each side. Midships was a cabin and, in the Lewis and Clark version at least, the boat was rigged with a square sail.

The crew would walk the length of the boat thrusting long poles against the bottom of the river to propel the craft. As an alternative, long ropes were available, and in places where the nature of the river banks permitted it, either man or horse power could be used. At rare intervals, perhaps, the wind would be favorable and the sail could take over the work.

Whatever the motive power, however, upstream progress was slow; a good day might log eighteen miles while the average was closer to twelve or fifteen. The swift and treacherous Missouri had shoals and sand bars to trap the unwary boatman, and, in addition, the river bed was ever changing. At the best, keelboating the Missouri was a task that separated the men from the boys, and it was probably with no regrets that the river men said good-by to the keelboat when steam power arrived in the West. Until that day, however, the scowlike craft provided the chief means of transportation between St. Louis and the trading posts of the upper Missouri and its tributaries.

Keelboats, however, were not the only form of river transport. Some traders used the Mackinaw, a flat-bottomed boat with pointed bow and square stern that could carry about fifteen tons. The Mackinaw had decided advantages over the keelboat in that, being propelled by oarsmen and guided by a steersman, it could move more swiftly and be controlled more easily in the shifting currents of the Missouri River.

The *pirogue,* still another type of river boat made by fastening two canoes together with top flooring, found widespread use by the fur traders. While the Lewis and Clark records do not describe their *pirogues* as this particular type, the chances are that they were the same light vessels. They were usually about thirty feet long and from six to twelve feet wide with pointed bows and square sterns. (However, the term *pirogue* was used rather loosely and is known to have been applied to what were simply extra large canoes; this may have been the case with Lewis and Clark.) Oars were generally used as motive power, making them useful and high maneuverable.

In the Southwest, where smallish navigable streams were rare, it was the prevailing practice for the fur traders to pack their catch as far as the nearest protecting "fort," which was usually located on a large navigable river, and transship it from that point by boat.

One of the more grotesque, and widely used, contraptions for moving cargo downstream was the bullboat. Known in Europe as the Welsh *corwgl,* or carcass boat, it was also used by Tibetans in Asia. Whatever the name, it was about the same and about as predictable as a tub in a whirlpool. The bullboat was simply a round dome-shaped framework made of willow or cottonwood shoots or anything else that was pliable and handy. These ribs were arranged in a spokelike fashion, all crossing at the center, then bowed into a cup shape and secured with a circular wooden ring. Over this basket-like framework, freshly skinned and sewn buffalo hides were placed and secured. Then the whole contraption was inverted over a slow-burning fire to be cooked until done. The heat would shrink and harden the green hide until it fit tightly and was almost inflexible. During the process, melted buffalo tallow was applied to the seams as caulking.

If all the work was done properly, the bullboat was ready for its two or two and a half tons of freight and, so loaded, had a draft of only a few inches when dry. There was one disadvantage. During the course of a day the bullboat became increasing waterlogged and consequently less maneuverable. It was therefore necessary to drag the craft from the water at night, unload it, and redry it over the campfire. But there was an advantage to offset this problem. The bullboat was easily made.

Another form of transportation used by fur traders in the north woods was the birch-bark canoe employed extensively by the Hudson's Bay and North West companies. These graceful craft with their elliptical upturned ends were so efficient that the design is still used for canoes made of modern materials. Eight or nine skilled *voyageurs* could carry three or more tons in their canoes and do it swiftly. It was in this way that Canadian traders carried goods and supplies across the wide stretches of Canada to exchange them for furs in the Oregon country.

The total distance from Montreal to the mouth of the Columbia River was about forty-eight hundred miles; the trip was made in a little over three months. When the difficulty of the trip is considered, with its maze of rivers and network of portages, it is no wonder that the movement of goods over this route was referred to, in a complimentary way, as "The Hundred Day Express."

18. *The Pembina Buggy*

THE DISTANCE FROM Pembina, on the American side of the Canadian border, to the Mississippi headwater port of St. Paul was about four hundred and fifty miles. For the fur man, the trip was worth every step of the way, since prices paid for pelts in the major markets were, in many instances, double what the traders would pay in the field. And thrown into the bargain were the gaslights and companionship St. Paul offered after a hard and lonely winter on the Plains.

But the trip was a difficult one, because of both the nature of the country through which the route passed and the prohibitive cost of owning pack animals. Trappers and traders were compelled, therefore, to turn to the wheel for relief.

The carts they used, although similar to the Spanish *carreta,* were more likely of French European (Normandy) design and were probably introduced into the area by the Nor' Westers.

Yoked oxen draw this Pembina buggy.

Perhaps the most extensive use of the two-wheeled carts was made by the mixbloods of the Red River Valley of the North, the *Bois Brûlés*. With their pelts, the smoke-dried skins of beaver, muskrat, mink and even fox, these "wood burners" found two roads that led them to market—the East Road and the West Road that soon became the trade routes from Pembina to St. Paul.

The big difference between the Pembina buggy and the *carreta* lay in the wheels. They were spoked rather than solid, which made the vehicle lighter and more maneuverable. But, otherwise it was the same rickety contraption as the *carreta*—a box pinned to cross members and an axle. The cost to make one of these carts was about fifteen dollars, and usually it was good for about three round trips to St. Paul. If horse-drawn, the animals were customarily hitched tandem—one in front of the other—whereas if oxen were used they were yoked side by side. In many cases only one horse would be available to draw the load, so the driver would have to walk either alongside or behind the cart.

About thirty or forty ear-splitting days were spent en route from Pembina to St. Paul—noisy because the Pembina cart was as unlubricated as the *carreta*.

"Hellish, horrifying and nerve-wracking," wrote one traveler who had been privileged to hear the Pembina buggy. Another writer of the time amplified by saying: "The creaking of the wheels is indescribable. It can be heard six miles away. It is like no other sound you ever heard in all your life and it makes your blood run cold."

Despite the racket, however, the cart would get to St. Paul, and on the Mississippi levee the huge loads of hides and pelts were exchanged for supplies needed back north in the Red River Valley. Beaver and fox fur were traded for guns and gunpowder, new traps, tobacco, salt and flour. If the trapper or trader had female companionship back in Pembina, there would also be part of a bolt of cloth on the return trip. Fortunately, however, for the nerves of all concerned, the "iron horse" and the steamboat came along in the 1870's to quiet the Pembina buggy forever and consecrate it to history.

19. *Steamboat 'Round the Bend*

IT WOULD BE impossible to name the one man who was responsible for introducing the steamboat to America, for there were many. History, however, does record that steam navigation was successful in France twenty-four years before the August day in 1807 when Robert Fulton's *Clermont* made her much-heralded trip from New York to Albany. (The Marquis de Jouffroy is the true inventor due to his having built a steamboat which operated on the River Saône for sixteen months during 1783–84.)

While several Americans had built steamboats before Fulton, he was a competent engineer, and he had the good fortune to be backed by Robert Livingston, late minister to France, who in turn had secured from the New York state legislature exclusive rights to navigate the Hudson with a vessel propelled by steam. The success of this monopoly immortalized

Fulton and resulted in the use of steamboats for general commercial traffic. Even fur companies in the far West began to use them.

The British North West and Hudson's Bay companies and the American Pacific Fur Company operators in the Oregon country needed access to the sea. Large quantities of supplies were imported in ocean-going ships, and in turn much of the annual fur catch was taken aboard windjammers for delivery to London, Canton, New York and other ports. The steamboat promised a faster, more dependable way of handling this commerce.

As early as 1817, St. Louis was visited by the *Pike*—the first steamboat to moor at the levee, and two years later another steamer, the *Independence,* became the first vessel of its kind to make the trip from St. Louis up the river to Franklin, Missouri, the starting place where wagons were loaded for the Santa Fe Trail.

By 1818, the *Western Engineer* had reached Council Bluffs, and it was not long before Kenneth McKenzie of the American Fur Company adopted the steamboat for upriver fur trade. This became practical in 1831 when the Louisville-built steamer *Yellowstone* reached Fort Tecumseh. A year later this same steamer reached Fort Union, three miles above the mouth of the Yellowstone River and 1,760 miles above St. Louis. The pattern was then established, and trips were made regularly between St. Louis and Fort Union.

In 1859 an old stern-wheeler reached the head of navigation on the Missouri River at Fort Benton, putting the steamboat within reach of the Continental Divide. But by this time the fur trade had passed its zenith and had no need of such expansion.

By this time, too, other tributaries of the Mississippi had long since been opened to navigation. As early as 1814 a steamboat ventured into the Red River, and six years later another reached Fort Smith, on the Arkansas, an outfitting point for the West. Eventually the Mississippi boasted 16,000 miles of navigable waterways.

Two types of river steamboats were in use: side-wheelers and stern-wheelers, both of which permitted the use of a hull with very shallow draft. Side-wheelers were generally preferred by operators on the lower Missouri and Mississippi rivers, while stern-wheelers were favored in more shallow waters. The boat with the paddle wheel at the rear, however, had the advantage of being more maneuverable in landings at the river bank or at jerry-built wharves.

Although St. Louis remained the great center of western steamboating during the big rush of settlers to Oregon and miners to California, other river towns were also coming into their own as important ports. On the Missouri River, Atchison, St. Joseph, Independence, Fort Leavenworth, Nebraska City and Council Bluffs were all developing as outfitting places from which emigrants, miners and teamsters made their treks to Oregon, California and the Rocky Mountain region. At the beginning of the Civil War, about sixty steamers were making some three hundred calls a year to outfitting points, and, after the war, a fleet of stern-wheelers

Steamboat model of the "Ben Johnson."
CITY ART MUSEUM OF ST. LOUIS

Steamboat model of the "Tennessee Belle."
LOUISIANA STATE MUSEUM

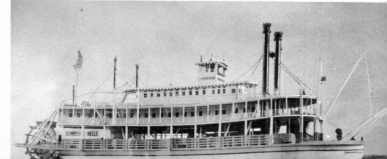

was used by the army to carry men and supplies to Fort Benton during the high-water season.

The Missouri River, however, had no monopoly on steamboats. The first such craft to sail Pacific waters was the Hudson's Bay Company's SS *Beaver*. Built by Blackwall on the Thames, this sturdy 109-ton steamer was taken to the Columbia District in 1836, and for several years after that she was used in the conduct of the Honourable Company's coastal trade. Since she was armed with four brass cannon, she aided in the defense of the company posts against Indian attacks, at the same time facilitating the movement of men and goods.

The story of the *Beaver* is important because it marks the beginning of steamboat transportation in the Oregon country. Fifteen years after the *Beaver's* trip up the Columbia, steamboats were common on such rivers as the Sacramento, San Joaquin and Colorado in California; on portions of the Columbia and its tributaries as well as Puget Sound in the Pacific Northwest; and in and out of Pacific coastal waters. By 1880, more than three hundred steamboats served the Pacific watershed and were the chief means of transportation.

Except for differences in roominess and luxuriousness, all river steamboats, generally speaking, followed the same pattern. They had shallow hulls and were wider than ocean going vessels. They usually had three decks, with the freight deck nearest the water.

Next would come the passenger deck, a light hurricane deck and a pilot house, above all of which would tower the belching stacks. Most river boats were about one hundred feet in length, while the luxury boats had a two-hundred-foot expanse. The river boats were designated for profitable freight hauling rather than for the less rewarding passenger service, and for this reason their accommodations were something less than plushy.

Steamboaters had their problems. There were always collisions with other boats, the danger of crushing winter ice, the constant battle with shifting sand bars, hidden rocks and logs to make the life of a river pilot interesting, and sometimes short. Add to these perils the ever-present danger of a boiler explosion and fire, and the total was an uncertain future. Despite these things, the steamboat won public approval and patronage and so contributed to the great movement West.

20. *Wagons . . . Roll!*

As EARLY AS 1830 William Sublette, the St. Louis trader, experimented with wagons. Being a businessman, he realized that a horse could haul much more trade goods than could be carried on its back. However, in roadless country, wagons caused endless problems, and experienced fur traders were slow to make a change. The first to put a wagon train across the Continental Divide was a beginner in the business. Captain Benjamin L. Bonneville possessed considerable ability and liked to show off. He got a leave from the army and with the financial backing of eastern financiers—including John Jacob Astor—he loaded Indian trade goods on twenty wagons and started west in 1832. Crossing the Rockies by South Pass he reached Green River. Another 800 miles separated him from the Pacific, but he had opened the way. More than a decade went by, however, before wagons began to roll Westward, Ho! By the time of the "Great Migration" in 1843 the "prairie schooner," as the covered wagons soon came to be called, was playing a major role in the march of American empire.

Perhaps it all started when the eighteenth-century Dutch settlers in the Conestoga Valley of Pennsylvania cast aside their traditional Palatinate carts and replaced them with a four-wheeled wagon of their own design. This "Conestoga" wagon served as a model for various makes that were to see service in the West.

The most distinctive features of the Conestoga wagons were their sturdy, out-turned, saucer-shaped wheels. For ease in steering and to compensate for rough and often slanting mountain roads, the front wheels were commonly made some two feet smaller in diameter than the rear. In addition, the wagon's boat-shaped body caused the load to hold toward the center rather than the ends or sides, preventing too great a shift in the center of gravity. For protection from the sun and rain, there was a canvas top on a framework of sturdy ribs or bows. As it moved along the ridges, silhouetted against the sky, its boatlike appearance was emphasized, and perhaps it was then that some New Englander, homesick for the white-sailed ships that beat in and out of East Coast harbors, dubbed the Conestoga a "prairie schooner."

The prairie schooner was the dominant vehicle in the Santa Fe trade in the period between 1820 and 1840 and was used by the thousands of migrants who traveled west over the Oregon-California Trail. Because it could carry more freight than pack animals and was easier to defend against Indians and outlaws, it soon became the favorite of the commercial freighters.

The first overland emigrants to start for Oregon with wheeled vehicles were Dr. Marcus Whitman and Henry Harman Spalding and their wives. This missionary party left Leavenworth in 1836 bound for Cayuse Indian country, near where Walla Walla, Washington, would be built. It was natural, then, that for mutual protection and companionship they should join the Rocky Mountain-bound fur traders.

On this particular trip, which followed the Platte River, the Whitman party managed to drive their wagons as far west as Fort William, more popularly known as Fort Laramie. Here Whitman's companions complained about the hard work they had experienced with the wagons, which had sometimes upset two or three times a day. The men also objected to the time lost digging a rut on sidehill slopes to prevent the wheels from skidding to the bottom of a gulch, and the necessity of cutting down trees to let the wagons through woodlands. They urged Whitman to go no farther with the abominable wheels.

Whitman had hoped to be the first to drive wagons across the continent, but he consented reluctantly to leave one of his vehicles at the fort. With the other he struggled on to Bear River where the front axle broke, forcing him to improvise a cart on the rear wheels. With this makeshift arrangement, Whitman reached Old Fort Boisé, near Snake River, one day to be the site of Nampa, Idaho. Steep mountains loomed ahead. His companions again balked at the idea of wasting more time building roads, and the cart was left behind, but Whitman was still determined to be the first to take wheels to Oregon. He therefore removed the iron tires, flattened them and packed them the rest of the way on a horse.

In the next few years, more and more emigrants ventured west, but few were able to take their wagons all the way. In 1840, a man named Robert Newell succeeded in hauling a

The Conestoga wagon or "prairie schooner."

wagon's running gear as far as the Columbia River. West of Snake River, however, his chief difficulty was the sagebrush that grew so high the axles could not pass over it. A year later, the Bidwell-Bartleson party of sixty men, women and children in thirteen wagons set out from Sapling, Missouri. They crossed the Continental Divide and separated before reaching Snake River. One party, bound for the Willamette Valley, continued along the Oregon Trail as far as Fort Hall, where it became clear to them that they had best abandon the notion of following Newell's wagon tracks—and their wagons as well.

The second party groped their way across the salt deserts of Utah and Nevada. No one knew the country. The distance between water holes was great and feed for the stock hard to find. In desperation they abandoned their cumbersome wagons and pushed as fast as they could toward the mountain wall of the Sierras which separated them from California.

It was another year or so before all the problems of wagon transportation were ironed out. When difficulties were met, ingenious migrants worked out solutions and passed the word back by eastbound guides or by letters. One by one, at the cost of tremendous effort, frequent bloodshed and even lives, the problems were solved, and the year 1843 witnessed the beginning of the floodtide of westward pioneers.

Jumping-off places for this wave of settlers were the Missouri River ports that were served by steamboat transportation. Wagon roads and trails led out from these supply towns and converged at Fort Kearny on the Platte River.

From there the Oregon Trail followed the old trapper route up the south side of the Platte, crossing to the north bank west of Fort Laramie, then following the North Platte to the Sweetwater, up it to South Pass and across Green River to the Bear in southeast Idaho, and along it to the river's U-turn where the soda springs gurgled from the ground. At this point the Trail, still running north, crossed a low ridge and dropped down to Fort Hall on Snake River, then curvey away, crossing the Snake to Fort Boisé. From here the Snake had to be crossed once more, and beyond it the Trail traversed the Blue Mountains and came down to the Columbia River near the mouth of the Umatilla. This at first was called the end of the Oregon Trail because most of the wagons were loaded here onto rafts or barges to be floated down to the Willamette Valley opposite Fort Vancouver. Later, however, when a road was extended another hundred miles to permit loading below the rapids there, the Oregon Trail was said to end at The Dalles.

The trek to California was about twenty-two hundred miles, with Soda Springs and Fort Hall the main turnoffs. These branches led in a southwesterly direction passing north of the Great Salt Lake and following the Humboldt River to the site of future Carson City, Nevada, and on across the Sierra Nevada by Routes either north or south of Lake Tahoe down into the Sacramento Valley. It was because of these southwestern forks that this route eventually became known as the Oregon-California Trail. It was only one of the major trails, of course, and many more equally well-known come to mind.

21. *The Endless Stream*

B Y 1843 THE METHOD of organizing a wagon train for the long haul West had settled into a definite routine. Some promoters even advertised in newspapers inviting prospective emigrants to meet and organize at certain outfitting towns on the western bank of the Missouri. Many experienced guides, some of them mountain men, could be hired at these hamlets. The month of May, when grass was well grown, was the usual starting date. Families making the trip would come to the rendezvous fully equipped.

Each group had to have a sturdy covered wagon, usually drawn by oxen although horses and mules were also used. There had to be an adequate supply of flour, bacon, coffee, salt, tobacco and similar necessities. At least a barrel of flour would be needed, perhaps two hundred pounds of bacon, twenty-five of coffee and twice that amount of dried fruit and molasses. Also needed were cooking utensils, other tools and equipment as well as firearms, gunpowder and lead. Whatever else was carried depended upon personal preference: a farmer, for example, would carry his plow while a miner would pack his pick and shovel. The weight of the loads varied, but most fully packed wagons could safely handle from two to three thousand pounds. Beef stock and extra draft animals were brought along on the hoof.

At the rendezvous amidst the bawling of animals, the excited clamor of children and the dust churned up by the wheels of the wagons, the wagon master or captain would be given his authority, sometimes in a formal constitution and as frequently by informal arrangement. At this time, too, the choice of route was made and a guide who had firsthand knowledge of the trail would be hired. Although companies varied considerably in size, a workable unit usually consisted of about twenty-five to thirty wagons.

Then, in late May when most of the spring freshets were over, when the grass was green and the ground firm, the wagon train would line up and the call of the wagon master would sound down the ranks. Once on the move, a more or less fixed routine would be followed.

The story of everyday life on the trail—the trials and privations, gaiety and adventure—has been told in hundreds of overland diaries, journals and reminiscences written by those who took part in the great experience. At dawn, a bugle call would signal breakfast. Then the animals were rounded up and hitched to the wagons. At seven o'clock the day's trek began.

On the trail, it was customary for the wagons to move in single file, with the women and children riding while the men walked or rode horseback. Those who were mounted often acted as outriders, hunters and scouts or took care of the loose livestock. A four-to-five hour "nooning period" would divide the day. This would allow time for watering and grazing the animals, the noon meal and a chance to rest during the hottest part of the day. About midafternoon the trek was resumed and continued until dusk. At night the wagons would be circled and the animals herded or tethered close by. Inside the firelit circle the migrants would have their evening meal, some talk, songs or other amusement, and, at last, they would sleep either in or under the wagons or in tents.

The rate of travel varied with the season and the terrain. About fourteen miles a day was the usual distance covered; about five months was required for the entire two-thousand-mile trip. Schedules had to be kept too, as far as was possible, since it was imperative that the wagon train pass the Sierras before the heavy snows of late October began to fall.

Delays were as frequent as they were unscheduled. Tired or footsore animals had to be

Wagon train in camp formation on Denver Street, 1866.

given time to recuperate. Some caravans remained in camp on the Sabbath. When passing through buffalo country there were stops to replenish the supply of meat. In general, though, time was of the essence, for winter would be along.

Perhaps the most serious problems of all for these caravans were river crossings. Though toll-ferries and bridges were eventually provided, the first wagon trains to make their way over the Oregon-California Trail had to rely on makeshift substitutes. Some built rafts to float the wagons across a stream; others simply tied logs to the sides of the vehicle and trusted to luck. These systems worked, but not without loss of human lives, wagons and animals.

Disease, too, took its toll. Cholera was a constant threat. There were deaths from drowning, from gun wounds, from falling beneath the wheels of the wagons and from Indian attacks. Elderly people who could not withstand the rigors of the trip were buried en route, and crudely marked graves along the way became the road signs of the trail west.

But in the memories of those who lived through the trip, hardship was erased by the recollection of interesting, exciting and enjoyable experiences. These included everything from romance and marriage and companionship around the evening campfire to participation in buffalo hunts.

Rafting down the Columbia River, 1843.

U. S. BUREAU OF PUBLIC ROADS

Ironically, the most trying part of the trip came when the goal was in sight. The western extremities of the trail to Oregon meant that the balance of the journey must be made rafting down the Columbia.

Jesse A. Applegate, nephew of the Oregon trail blazer, Jesse Applegate, whose party he accompanied, told in *Recollections of My Boyhood* how many of their boats came to grief at a place northeast of Mount Hood. "The boat we were watching," he wrote, "disappeared and we saw the men and boys struggling in the water." Three of them drowned.

By 1845 the settlers in the Willamette Valley had provided the answer to the dangers of rafting down the Columbia by beginning to build the Barlow Road. When completed over a course south of Mount Hood, it permitted wagon trains to reach the valley without "taking to water."

The California-bound emigrants found their journey at its toughest after crossing the Continental Divide. One of their ordeals was the crossing of the alkali flats of Carson Sink; another was the perilous passage over the Sierra Nevada. Traveling in the parched Humboldt Valley, one narrator, J. Goldsborough Bruff, wrote: "Fatigue and heat cause the train to move slowly . . . road-powder blinding and choking one." He continued: "I found, near an orange colored clay spur, a well, or tank, of water, and a crowd of thirsty men and animals surrounding it. A few yards to the left of this another similar hole, filled up with a dead ox, his hind quarters and legs still sticking out above ground." By way of color, Bruff added: "Dead oxen thick about here and stench suffocating. The road here sweeps round westerly."

The ascent of the Sierras was, of course, slow and hazardous, but, as we have said before, the real danger in this last lap of the journey to California lay in being caught, as was the Donner party in 1846, by heavy snows.

Despite the multiple tribulations of wagon travel, several thousand American families reached the Willamette Valley during the 1840's, and it is estimated that twenty or thirty thousand Argonauts traveled to California during 1849 in covered wagons. Scores of thousands followed them in the 1850's, and for more than three decades long caravans of prairie schooners continued to stream westward. One would think that the completion of the transcontinental railroad in 1869 would have sounded the knell for the covered wagon, but it did not. A man who went by train left his team and wagon behind and both were necessary for him to make a living wherever he decided to stop. Moreover, since time had little value, an emigrant could move his family and their household belongings in a wagon much cheaper than on the railroad cars.

James H. Kyner, who was active in railroad construction work during the 1880's, recalled in his book, *End Of Track,* that on one of his trips into western Nebraska he had seen an endless procession of humanity headed West: "I could see an almost unbroken stream of emigrants from horizon to horizon—a distance of not less than eight miles or ten. Teams and covered wagons, some drawn by cows, horsemen, little bunches of cows, men walking, women and children riding—an endless stream of hardy, optimistic folk going west to seek their fortunes and to settle an empire."

Furthermore, arrival at the end of the trail did not mean the end of a covered wagon's life. On the contrary, it continued in service, hauling crops and supplies. And, until the day when the family could afford a surrey "with fringe around the top," the prairie schooner carried pioneers to and from church, picnics and the nearest town.

Pushing and pulling to Zion, 1856.

22. *Handcarts to Zion*

"THEY WILL BECOME a mighty people in the midst of the Rocky Mountains." But when that prophecy was made by Joseph Smith he could not have foreseen the long, hard trail that lay ahead. For the Mormons and their Church of Jesus Christ of Latter-day Saints there seemed to be no easy way. From the very beginning, theirs was a history of hardship.

Perhaps the second chapter of the Mormon story begins with their expulsion, by neighbors of different faiths, from Nauvoo—their City Beautiful—on the east bank of the Mississippi. Guided by the practical common sense of Brigham Young, they reached a decision to settle in the valley of the Great Salt Lake. During the winter of 1846–47, the Saints traveled across Iowa to the Omaha–Council Bluffs area where they established a settlement they called Winter Quarters. It was from here that the major western emigration began.

In the years that followed the Saints's first trying winter in the territory later known as Utah, emigrant Mormons continued to assemble at Winter Quarters and from there begin the great trek over the "Mormon Trail" to their Rocky Mountain Zion. Each party of ten needed one wagon with one yoke of oxen, two milk cows and a tent. With this equipment, and under the direction of their bishops, it was possible for Mormons to move in trains of several hundred wagons toward the "Gathering Place."

For the more destitute Saints, however, such comfort and convenience were almost unattainable. So, beginning in the year 1856, new plans had to be devised. Wagons would continue to be used for the movement of the heavier items, but handcarts would be pressed into service to carry food and personal baggage.

Iowa City, then the terminal of the Chicago, Rock Island & Pacific Railroad, was to be the departure point for these "handcarts to Zion."

The carts themselves varied in size and quality of construction, but each consisted of two wheels, some with iron tires, an axle, a shaft and a wooden box. These vehicles usually weighed about sixty pounds and, when drawn by two people, could carry a five-hundred-pound load.

By the time the 1856 season ended, five handcart companies had left Iowa City for the Great Salt Valley—nearly two thousand people made the trip, with a cart to each four or five along with about five ox-drawn supply wagons. Individual members of the companies took turns pulling the carts, and, under normal conditions, fifteen miles could be covered in a day.

The first three companies, having left Iowa City in June, reached the valley without serious mishap in about nine weeks' time. The fourth and fifth companies met with disaster. They had left Iowa City in July, and could not reach the Rocky Mountains before the onset of heavy winter snows. The weather, as well as starvation, accounted for more than two hundred deaths out of the one thousand who started the trip.

Despite the grim beginning, however, handcarts to Zion continued to move. In the years 1857 and 1860, five other companies made the hazardous trip across the Plains. Nearly 3,000 people were members of handcart companies employing 653 carts and 50 supply wagons. The total loss of life was about 250.

23. *The "Windwagon"*

"HARNESS THE WIND and reap the whirlwind" is an apt proverb to state the principle and the epitaph for one of the most bizarre means of transportation in the history of the West. Impatient in the desire to reach the Rockies and Denver as quickly as possible, many a traveler or gold seeker fumed at the plodding movement of the covered wagon trains. One novel answer to the problem, and one that turned out to be the butt of comment and ridicule was the sail-equipped, wind-powered wagon. The name of the genius who developed the "windwagon" is lost, but some of the comic results are not.

As early as 1853, a man named Henry Sager had built a huge twelve-by-twenty-five-foot wagon with a pilot deck and a twenty-foot sail. His idea was to take advantage of the reasonably constant winds that favor the Great Plains. On the day of its maiden voyage out of Westport, Missouri, this ungainly contraption was pulled into the open by a yoke of oxen and, from that point on, nature took its course. At first the windwagon managed "to take the bone in its teeth and show trim heels to a fresh breeze." Fired with optimism at this initial success, the pilot then tried a tacking, or zig-zag, course. It was at this point that some of the vital members of the steering mechanism parted company, and the wagon took off for uncharted realms. The fate of the pilot remains unrecorded, but one can only hope that he had the good judgment to part with the wagon at the first opportunity.

All windwagons, however, did not meet with the same fate. By 1860 several of them had traveled the Smoky Hill Road leading to Denver, and some of them were relatively successful. A wagon owned by Samuel Peppard of Oskaloosa, Kansas Territory, covered fifty miles in one day and is reported to have passed 625 teams along the way.

But having successfully come to within fifty miles of Denver, the Peppard wagon then showed its true nature by first listing badly and finally going over with a thud, at which point it was abandoned.

In May, 1860, a Colorado correspondent reported the actual arrival of a windwagon in Denver. "Everyone," he wrote, "crossed the street to get a sight of this new-fangled frigate."

It would appear that most of the onlookers were unimpressed with what they saw—at any rate, the windwagon never emerged from the trial stage. And as a means of hauling freight it was obviously impractical.

24. *The Santa Fe Wagon*

THE TRADE ROUTE between St. Louis and Santa Fe, which merchants failed to open in the 1790's, was finally established in 1821 by William Becknell, "Father of the Santa Fe Trail." Two routes were commonly used. Both crossed the Plains to the Big Bend of the Arkansas. From there, the safer route led up that stream to Bent's Fort at the mouth of the Purgatory (mispronounced "Picket Wire"), up this tributary to Raton Pass and across into New Mexico.

The other—much shorter and more dangerous—route left the Arkansas River near the western border of present Kansas and struck southwest across the Cimarron Desert. Even though wagons often had to go sixty miles without water, this cutoff proved more practical than the old one, and other freighters soon began assembling at Franklin. Later, Independence became a favored starting place and, still later, Council Grove, a hundred miles west. The freight was moved in huge Conestoga-type vehicles, pulled by three or more yokes of oxen or teams of mules and carrying upward of five thousand pounds of merchandise. It was these vehicles of the early freighting trade that came to be known as "Santa Fe wains."

When Indian raids threatened along the trail, teamsters would travel closely together, driving several wagons abreast. The caravans varied in size from year to year, but usually consisted of up to fifty wagons. At night they would corral, or circle, and guards would be stationed.

The rate of travel over the Santa Fe Trail averaged about fifteen miles a day and the time required for the round trip would be between two and three months.

Once in Santa Fe, the cargoes of textiles, lead, hardware, cutlery, glassware and many other such items were traded with the Mexicans for silver, mules, pelts and hides, blankets and other things in demand back East.

In 1848, when New Mexico became an American territory, traffic and trade over the Santa Fe Trail underwent many changes. For example, during the Mexican regime the caravans made only one round trip each spring and summer, but now with United States soldiers, civil servants, and settlers to be served, teaming operations to Santa Fe were modified to allow regular year-round schedules.

One of the largest wagon-freighting firms ever to emerge on the Great Plains was headed by three men who were veterans of the Santa Fe trade. This was the firm of Russell, Majors and Waddell. The first member of the firm, William E. Russell, was born in Vermont but came West as a child. As a young man, he operated a store in Missouri and during the Mexican War shipped goods—much of it military supplies—to Santa Fe. The trade proved profitable, and Russell formed a merchandising firm with William B. Waddell as a partner. Then, after some business shifts the firm was expanded to include Alexander Majors.

These three had one thing in common: They were aggressive and enterprising frontier businessmen. But there the similarity ended. Russell was a tense, nervously energetic New Englander with a gentlemanly background and manner, while Waddell was a slow-moving, introspective and sometimes quarrelsome Virginian. Majors came from Kentucky. In his autobiography, *Seventy Years On The Frontier,* he said simply, "I was brought up to handle animals." It is not surprising, then, that this practical and devoutly religious man became indispensable to the successful operations of the business.

Prominence, success and wealth came to Russell, Majors and Waddell as a result of war rumors. Brigham Young, in Salt Lake City, had been appointed governor there, but inept officials were sent from Washington to help him administer the territory. Friction soon de-

An army train crossing the Plains.

CLARENCE P. HORNUNG COLLECTION

veloped into what seemed like a threat of rebellion. At this point, President Buchanan decided to send an army and a new governor to replace Young.

Fifteen hundred troops were ordered from Fort Leavenworth to the Great Salt Lake Valley, and the contract to move the three million pounds of supplies they would require went to the firm of Russell, Majors and Waddell.

For movement of the freight over the 1,161-mile trail that lay between the Missouri River and the Mormon headquarters, the War Department contracted to pay rates varying from $1.80 to $4.50 per hundred pounds per hundred miles. A project as enormous as this had never before been witnessed on the Plains, and called for the innovation of a system that was to serve as a pattern for the future.

Alexander Majors worked out a plan for the movement of the vast array of men, animals and vehicles. Eventually he formulated his method in a manual for his men, entitled *Rules and Regulations for Governing of Russell, Majors & Waddell's Outfit* (Nebraska, 1859). The manual went into great detail specifying the most suitable number of wagons in a train, the animals needed, and the duties of the wagon master and his assistants. It also prescribed the daily routine of travel, the distances to be covered and the stops for grazing the animals and serving meals to the men. This manual was, in short, the teamster's bible.

Although the firm grew financially through its military contracts, much of its profits were plowed back into other transportation schemes that were considerably less successful and resulted in bankruptcy for the firm.

But the financial ruin of Russell, Majors and Waddell did not lessen the march of wagon freight across the Plains. In fact, except for temporary fluctuations, the freighting volume increased steadily until the completion of the various transcontinental railroads.

25. *The Overland Coach*

As SUCCESSFUL AS the wagons were for the movement of freight, they were not the total answer for a new demand from the growing West: the more comfortable and convenient transportation of passengers. Heavy migrations to the Oregon country during the 1840's and the great influx of Argonauts into California during and after 1849 had created a need for overland passenger service. Ultimately, of course, the West would be satisfied with nothing less than transcontinental railroads. But until the rails could be laid, stagecoach passenger service was a necessity to the Pacific Coast population.

The "coach and four" had emerged in England during the reign of Queen Elizabeth I and had come to the American colonies late in the seventeenth century. By the end of the colonial period, all thirteen colonies were enjoying a measure of coaching service, and this service began to move westward with the advancing frontier.

By 1820 the stagecoach had made its appearance west of the Mississippi River and offered regular passenger service both to and from St. Louis, Missouri. In less than twenty years, similar operations were established in Iowa and, by mid-century, monthly service was ex-

Concord was synonymous with stagecoach.

tended from Independence to Santa Fe, New Mexico. By then, the coach was serving the Willamette Valley of Oregon and the bustling state of California; even Texas boasted a number of independent stage lines.

As a vehicle, the stagecoach had been nearly perfected in its two centuries of use in America. There were many types: the Troy coach, the mud wagon, various coaches of local manufacture and the Concord coach. The last was the most famous of all such vehicles in commercial use.

The Concord, of course, received its name from its place of manufacture—Concord, New Hampshire. It was produced by Abbot-Downing and Company of that New England town, who took pains throughout, from running gear of the sturdiest of woods to the finishing coat of paint. It was designed with two thoughts in mind: to provide comfort for the passenger and to withstand the abuse it had to take on the rough western roads. Thoroughbraces—two thick, strong leather straps, one on each side—held the graceful, egg-shaped body slung between the axles. Thus suspended the sturdy body had a rolling motion far more pleasant to its occupants than the jolting of a wagon. Besides front, rear and middle drop seats inside, there was a driver's seat protruding in the front, a baggage boot extending from the rear, and a strong roof where excess passengers and baggage could be carried. The coach was usually painted to suit the purchaser, and as its crowning glory, portraits, usually of beautiful women,

A "shotgun messenger" often sat next to the driver.

were painted on the door panels. It weighed approximately a ton and was pulled by four, and sometimes as many as six, horses.

So widely used was the Concord that in the West its name became almost synonymous with the word stagecoach.

The key figure in stagecoach transportation was the driver. Although variously characterized in the literature of the day as taciturn, loquacious, sober, dependable and all the rest, he had to be, first of all, a master at the reins. His fingers controlled the activities of spirited mustangs that usually took the road at a goodly gallop. He was responsible as well for the comfort and safety of his passengers and had to be able to drive over roads so convulsed with curves that, as was said, "the horses could eat from the baggage boot." In addition it was up to the driver to collect the passenger tickets and try to hold, insofar as possible, to a fixed schedule from one station to the next, usually a distance of ten to twenty miles.

A home station was usually located in a town's leading hotel. Travel schedules called for early-morning departures, and passengers had to be awakened in time for breakfast before boarding the coach. The most distinguished passenger was usually given a place of honor on the driver's seat unless the nature of the load required the services of a "shotgun messenger," or guard, in which event the important personage was given his choice of inside seats.

Out on the road the pace was customarily a moderate gallop except where hills and curves might slow the pace to a walk or a gentle trot. The average speed was about five miles an hour.

Passengers on long runs, such as the cross-country trek from the Missouri River to the Pacific Coast, tried to save time by traveling day and night. There were many stops, of course, because teams had to be changed at every station and drivers relieved at the end of the day. The journey was a tiring one for many passengers, and those who wished to break up the trip could find lodgings of a sort at some of the wayside stations. It was quite common for passengers reaching their destinations to take a good bath, get a full night's sleep and have nothing more to do with stagecoaches—at least for a while.

Regular and commonplace as stagecoach travel grew to be, it was neither free from accident nor devoid of adventure. Runaway teams caused upsets or breakdowns. When a coach got stuck in the mud, the passengers were expected to get out to lighten the load and often lend a push through the boggy spot. Many western drivers on the central route reported Indian attacks during the mid-1860's. Stagecoach holdups were most frequent in the Rocky Mountain, Black Hills, and Pacific Coast areas; these were the regions where the mines were located and where passengers usually carried large sums of money. Rough hills or thick timber enabled highwaymen to surprise a coach and concealed their escape.

Each stagecoach line of importance, was plagued by "road agents" who worked singly or in gangs. Most of them wore masks, and their standard procedure was to appear suddenly from the wayside brush before an oncoming coach, command the driver to halt, throw down the treasure box which rode beneath his seat and, if there were reasons for believing that the passengers were well laden with cash, to have everyone step out and "reach for the sky." The most famous of these outlaws were C. E. Bolton, alias "Black Bart," in California and Henry Plummer in Montana, whose careers are described elsewhere in this book. In New Mexico, on the Alamoso-Del Norte Stage Line, Henry W. White demonstrated his ingenuity by rigging white dummies in the roadside bush which helped convey the impression of a gang. As the stage approached his "set," White gave the customary command, ordered the frightened driver to get down, blindfolded him, and ordered his "dummies" to cover him. He repeated this act with each passenger and, having done this, relieved them of all their money and made his getaway. As a career, however, the evidence shows that stagecoach robbery did not pay. Sooner or later the culprits were caught and either landed in jail or swung into eternity at the end of a rope.

26. *The Transcontinental Mail*

J UST AS THE movement of U.S. military goods brought wealth to Russell, Majors and Waddell in the wagon-freighting business, it was the government that contributed to the success of the overland stagecoach. For several years mail contracts had been let to various carriers who used the so-called trans-Isthmian route. Pacific Coast mail—and many passengers—would travel by ship from the East Coast to Panama where overland transportation had been arranged. Once on the Pacific side of the isthmus, coastal ships were again employed for the balance of the trip to San Francisco.

The route was long, the service costly, and the people of the West impatient. Finally an appeal was addressed, not to private business, but to the federal government. Congress was petitioned to terminate the old land and water contract and establish an all-American overland mail and passenger stagecoach service.

There was no argument about the validity of such requests, but red tape being then what it is now, Washington was slow and niggardly in its response. The first answer to these requests came in the spring of 1851 when a contract was let to two enterprising, but somewhat indigent, individuals named Absalom Woodward and George Chorpenning. The terms of the franchise called for the carrying of mail on a thirty-day schedule between Sacramento and Salt Lake City. This service was coordinated with a like contract issued to one Samuel H. Woodson for a similar schedule between the Mormon capital and Independence, Missouri. Thus, a letter mailed at Independence would be delivered at Sacramento two months later. The best that could be said of this "service" was that it was an exhibition of the courage of those holding the contracts.

Unfortunately, however, some areas of the West were without even this cumbersome service. New Mexico, with a population of over sixty thousand people, had no regular mail service with the rest of the country and southern California, too, was isolated. It was 1857 before the pleadings of these out-of-the-way sections fell on attentive ears. In that year a contract was let to a well-known stagecoach operator named James Birch for the establishment of service twice a month between San Antonio, Texas, and San Diego, California. As on the northern routes, Birch was allowed thirty days to put each coach through, and because he used mules to pull his mail wagons, his enterprise was soon dubbed the "Jackass Mail."

At about this time other factors intensified the need for reliable mail service in the Far West. Acting under the authority of Congress, the War Department had conducted extensive railroad surveys throughout this area, and it was established that lack of capital and local political disagreements would indefinitely hamper the construction of a transcontinental rail line. In the meantime, the population of California was growing by giant leaps and becoming daily more dissatisfied with its monthly mail service. Finally, after considerable and typical debate between southern and northern politicians, Congress, on March 3, 1857, approved a post office measure.

One section of an amendment to the measure stated that "the Postmaster-General be, and he is hereby, authorized to contract for the conveyance of the entire letter mail from such point on the Mississippi River, as the contractors may select, to San Francisco, in the State of California, for six years. . . ." The act further stated "that the contract shall require the service to be performed in good four-horse coaches, and spring wagons, suitable for the conveyance of passengers, as well as the safety and security of the mails." And finally, it provided that "said service shall be performed within twenty-five days for each trip" and that the service must "commence within twelve months after the signing of the contract."

The postmaster general in 1857 was Aaron Venable Brown, a Tennessean of Virginia birth, and his selection of a route for this new and faster service is said to have been politically motivated. Or perhaps he became confused trying to read the entire post office measure. At any rate, Brown established the service over the 2,795-mile Ox Bow Route. Rather than following a straight line as far as practical, this route described an arclike dip into the South. The Ox Bow Route really had two official jumping-off places: one at St. Louis and the other at Memphis, Brown's home town. These two lines of travel converged at Fort Smith, Arkansas, and from there followed a southwesterly course to El Paso, Texas.

From El Paso the coaches were to follow a westward course across New Mexico, to Tucson, Arizona, on to the Gila River and along this watercourse to Fort Yuma. At this point

Harper's Weekly, 1866

Butterfield's Overland Mail Coach starting out from Atchison, Kansas.

the Colorado was crossed, and the route arced northwestward through the Imperial Valley of California and into Los Angeles. Leaving the City of the Angels the mail traveled north through the San Joaquin Valley following the route of what is now U. S. Highway 99 and finally across Pacheco Pass and through the Santa Clara Valley to San Francisco.

The successful bidder for this contract was a group who become known as the Overland Mail Company. John Butterfield, a stagecoach operator from Utica, New York, was its president, and other associates were William B. Dinsmore, a New York financier, and William G. Fargo, the well-known co-founder of Wells, Fargo and Company.

Before the new service could begin, a hard twelve months lay ahead. The company divided its operations into two major sections and set about the task. Old roads were used where possible, but over many parts of the southwest desert, new routes had to be staked out. Although the road standards of the day were not demanding, still a considerable amount of grading and removal of rocks and desert growth was necessary. There were bridges to be built, wells to be dug and water to be hauled to where otherwise there would be none. Stations had to be built every nineteen miles or so, and corrals constructed.

It was, for its era, a tremendous organizational and operational problem. Before the first stage ever moved, over one million dollars had been spent. Scores of men were put to work, and hundreds of animals and wagons were used. Troy wagons and the stagecoaches had to be ordered and no less than eight hundred men hired to operate the line when completed. Thousands of major and minor details and problems had to be worked out and solved.

The target date was September 16, 1858, and thanks to the able and efficient management of John Butterfield, the date was met. Service began out of St. Louis, Memphis and San Francisco simultaneously. The major eastern terminal was the St. Louis post office, from

which point the mail was carried by train to the western end of the Pacific Railroad at Tipton, Missouri. President Butterfield of the Overland Mail Company and Waterman L. Ormsby,
a correspondent for the *New York Herald,* went along on the initial trip. It is to Ormsby's
dispatches to his newspaper that we are indebted for the details of the long journey over the
Ox Bow Route to San Francisco.

The train trip from St. Louis to Tipton took about ten hours, and after this hundred-
plus mile run the transfer of mail to stagecoach was accomplished in nine minutes.

The stage route followed a southwesterly course from Tipton and passed through the
Ozark Mountains, on what Ormsby described as the "wildest" of mountain roads. At first
Ormsby seemed to suffer from a case of nerves, for he imagined what he called "lurking
foes," namely Indians, behind every rock and bush. But by the time he had reached the area
that might be actually dangerous, he seemed to be more indifferent; he no longer mentioned
attacks by the savages. Ormsby was not impressed by the road taken across the "wilds of
Texas," and his description of the accommodations at one Texas station makes it quite plain
that there was a great deal to be desired. The chairs, Ormsby wrote, were inverted pails or
stumps; tin cups served as plates, and food consisted mainly of hardtack, baked over hot
coals, and unsweetened black coffee. He described breakfast at another station as hardly
better—coffee, tough beef and butterless shortcake. It was prepared, he said, by a Negro
woman "who, if cleanliness is next to Godliness, would stand little chance of Heaven."

Even the mules used to pull the coaches over the southwest desert needed considerable
coaxing in order to hold to the schedule. And yet, despite the difficulties, the Butterfield stage

The overland mail eastbound from San Francisco.

Harper's Weekly, 1858

reached San Francisco twenty-three days, twenty-three hours and thirty minutes after leaving Tipton.

By the time he had arrived at his destination, however, Ormsby viewed the operation in a more kindly light:

> Safe and sound from all the threatened dangers of Indians, tropic suns, rattlesnakes, grizzly bears, stubborn mules, mustang horses, jerked beef, terrific mountain passes, fording rivers, and all the concomitants which envy, pedantry and ignorance had predicted for all passengers by the overland mail route over which I have just passed, here I am in San Francisco. . . . The journey has been by no means as fatiguing to me as might be expected by the continuous ride of such duration, for I feel almost fresh enough to undertake it again.

The eastbound coach likewise made it on scheduled time, and the success of the Butterfield operation was transmitted to Postmaster General Brown and eventually to President James Buchanan. Service thus begun over the Ox Bow Route continued until political eruptions and the outbreak of the Civil War brought this amazing transportation venture to a halt. Perhaps no greater tribute could be paid this effort than a statement in the Los Angeles *Star*:

> The arrival of the stages of the Overland Mail had been heretofore as regular as the index on the clock points to the hour, as true as the dial to the sun. During all seasons, in cold and heat, in winter and summer, the overland stage has kept its time. . . .

27. *The Express Companies*

THE INADEQUACIES OF the United States postal service in California had led to the development of the transcontinental stagecoach mail service, and it was this same inadequacy that was responsible for another unique American enterprise, namely express. As far back as 1839 New York and Boston banks were using an express messenger service for the special handling of lightweight, valuable parcels in the West that accompanied the California gold rush.

The father of the California express was Alexander A. Todd who, in 1849, saw the necessity of providing the miners in the Mother Lode country with a special delivery letter service. This received instant and warm response from the news-hungry miners, and before long Todd was engaged in extended services which included the movement of gold dust from individual miners at the diggings to San Francisco banks or shipping lines.

Soon, there were other enterprising expressmen operating in and out of the sprawling mining regions of California, and in time the area became literally saturated by this kind of business. The number of individual operators grew to exceed three hundred, and each expressman had his own distinctive frank, or postage mark, and his own special group of clients.

Harper's Weekly, 1866

On the overland route—a "council of war" on the Plains.

In the transportation business, as in any other, a monopoly was convenient to say the least and consolidation the shortest way to liquidate the competition. Since antitrust laws were not yet in existence, the way was clear for a larger operator, well supplied with capital, to gather in the smaller companies. The first attempt to consolidate a number of smaller outfits in California and elsewhere in the Pacific Coast area was made by the Adams and Company Express.

Founded in the East by Alvin Adams in 1840, this thriving concern was quick to sense new business in the California gold rush boom. Before the end of 1849, Adams had a resident-partner in San Francisco, and by 1852 the Adams company had formed connections that gave it state-wide coverage. The method was simple: Adams offered a service that small individual operators could not duplicate—both local and nation-wide forwarding and the issuance of bills of exchange negotiable in all leading banks in the country. So, the Adams concern thrived.

Also in 1852 another joint-stock company was formed for the purpose of doing business in California. Now, latecomer Wells, Fargo and Company began to challenge the Adams empire. Because of the past experience of Henry Wells and William G. Fargo, their performance in California proved so successful that when in 1855 a financial panic hit the banking houses of San Francisco, the California branch of Adams and Company failed and Wells, Fargo and Company weathered the storm. This was just two years before William Fargo began his financial participation in the Overland Mail Company.

From this time on Wells, Fargo and Company was the unchallenged "big wheel" in both banking and forwarding concerns in the West. There were Wells Fargo offices in practically every mining town in California, in Oregon, Victoria (British Columbia), Virginia City (Nevada), and in all leading mining towns in the Rocky Mountain area, as well as in

New York City and Philadelphia. By then, the banking business had been separated from the express operations, but one branch continued to serve well the interests of the other.

It was as forwarder of gold dust, letters, special valuables, perishable items and the like that Wells, Fargo and Company first operated in close association with established stagecoach lines. Later the company changed its policy and began operating its own stage lines. Its entrance into the stagecoach field was the result of a struggle with Ben Holladay who, having bought the Russell, Majors and Waddell interests when they went bankrupt, had become the greatest stagecoach operator in the West. Holladay, with all his wealth and power, had shown great reluctance to handle Wells Fargo express. Perhaps he was unwilling to assume a new risk, for the Wells Fargo box—commonly called the "express box"—had become synonymous with ready and easy cash to the stage robber, but possibly Holladay had other motives.

An aggressive businessman, Holladay may have been reluctant to deal with Wells, Fargo and Company because of a desire to thwart a competitor's growing strength. Indeed, by 1862 he was openly struggling with Wells Fargo for control of the Central Overland Mail route— a struggle which lasted until Holladay, knowing that the completion of the Pacific Railroad would undermine his staging operations, wisely sold all his holdings to the rival company. After that time (at least until the transferral of express to railroad baggage cars), Wells, Fargo and Company controlled both the major stagecoach *and* express business in the trans-Missouri West.

28. *The Pony Express*

MAN HAS ALWAYS been in a hurry to get where he wants to go and, once there, is often in just as big a rush to get the news from the place he left. This demand for speed has always been the whip of progress, and in the western part of our country it was no different. The settlers had traveled, as fast as they were able, to the free land and new homes. The gold seekers had come and rapidly spread across the hills and valleys. Merchants, lumbermen, stockmen—all followed, and no sooner had they reached their destination than they became hungry for word and goods from home.

The accent on speed and on uniting East with West had brought the stagecoachers and the expressmen onto the scene in the first place and started the nation stringing telegraph wires and driving railroad spikes. It is ironic, therefore, that the Pony Express, the synonym for haste, was not the product of the speed merchants. Rather, it was the slower-paced freight firm of Russell, Majors and Waddell that gave untimely birth to the Pony Express—untimely because the service was doomed from the beginning.

The imaginative undertaking appears to have been conceived by California Senator William H. Gwin. At a time when critical need for speed existed, Gwin visualized a pony relay line, a weekly, ten-day service between the Missouri River and Sacramento. It is likely that the senator made such a proposal to William H. Russell when the latter was at the na-

"Coming and Going of the Pony Express," 1860-61.
After a drawing by Frederic Remington.

tion's capital and that the freighting magnate consented on the condition that government subsidies would follow.

The firm of Russell, Majors and Waddell underwrote the ambitious project. Stations were to be established about ten miles apart over the planned 1,966-mile course. There were 190 way stations to be built, although at first many of them were tents, and the hiring of the same number of station tenders. All in all, before these things could be done, five hundred fast horses and equipment for them procured and at least eighty young and courageous riders obtained, one hundred thousand dollars in cash was spent.

By April 3, 1860, the job was done. Pony Express riders set out from St. Joseph, Missouri, the eastern end of the line, and from San Francisco, by boat, for Sacramento, the western terminus. Riding in relays, changing horses in each way station and carrying only their locked leather pouches, or *mochilas,* these superb horsemen made their first scheduled crossing in ten and one-half days. To properly appreciate this remarkable record it should be remembered that the trip by fast stagecoach took twenty-two-or-three days and mail delivery to the West Coast prior to that time had taken about a month.

The Pony Express, however, expected and received much from both riders and animals. Fast galloping for sustained periods exhausted the ponies, and the pounding absorbed by the riders was more than most men could long endure. But the Pony Express had other problems as well. Attacks by marauding Indians disrupted service, bad weather on sections of the route often slowed the riders down, and payments by subscribers to the service fell far below maintenance costs. Furthermore, the government subsidies were not forthcoming.

These things were not the end, but they foreshadowed the death of the Pony Express. On October 22, 1861, the knell was sounded. It was the singing of the wind in the first transcontinental telegraph line. Just two days after the beginning of regular telegraph service, the Pony Express came to an end as a glorious financial failure. It had been a daring, imaginative and exciting experiment, an unforgettable and magnificent part of the American experience. And though the riders, their horses, the mail pouches and most of the way stations are gone now, they have become an integral part of the deathless legend.

29. *The Railroads*

THE END OF the beginning came on a peninsula in Great Salt Lake called Promontory Point, Utah, on May 10, 1869, with the driving of a golden spike into a railroad crosstie. When the first white man had walked the hills and plains of the American West, the story had begun. Throughout the years humanity had dug, cleared and built during a time crowded with adventure, change and growth.

By that October day in 1861 when the Pony Express ceased to operate, the events that led to Promontory Point and beyond were already in focus. Acts dated July 1, 1862, and July 2, 1864, and signed by President Abraham Lincoln provided legislation that would assure the building of a rail line to the Pacific. It was planned that two railroad companies, the California-chartered Central Pacific and the federally chartered Union Pacific would, with generous government aid, build a railroad from Omaha to Sacramento. And on July 2, 1864, the federal government also brought into being the Northern Pacific Railroad and authorized it to build a second line to the Pacific—from Lake Superior to Puget Sound.

Thus began the era of massive, feverish railroad construction west of the Missouri. As early as 1857 it was possible, by making five changes, crossing rivers by ferry, and taking two short steamboat rides, to travel by rail from the Atlantic Ocean to St. Louis. Rail service spanned Missouri by 1865 from St. Louis to Independence, and in 1866 Irish laborers and Chinese coolies were rhythmically driving spikes into ties on the Union Pacific and Central Pacific railroads that would, within three years, join the two great oceans.

By 1865 railroad-building had taken hold in most of the western states and territories. Iowa was second only to Missouri in linking the Mississippi and Missouri rivers; Texas was next, with no less than eight different rail enterprises connecting the hinterland with the Gulf and Houston with New Orleans. Minnesota was trying to overcome its isolation with the building of railroads toward the South, and Kansas—the recent scene of so many fights between proslavery and free-state settlers—had within its borders 122 miles of track by the end of the Civil War.

There was always the sense of greatness in western railroad projects both in blueprint and in reality, because nearly all of them aspired to rapid growth and about half of them were headed for the Pacific. They were inspired by professional promoters and by the local citizenry who firmly believed that their own success as well as that of the West depended upon rail outlets to markets.

States made their most significant contributions to railroad building by granting charters and authorizing and underwriting the sale of bonds that could be exchanged for cash. In turn, the federal government sometimes cooperated in the generous dispensation of public lands to railroad companies. In the case of the Union Pacific, as an example, a two-hundred-

European and Chinese laborers at work on the last mile of Pacific Railroad.

foot right of way and ten alternate sections of land on each side of the road were provided For the Northern Pacific Railroad the gift was even more generous: a four-hundred-foot right of way and twenty alternate sections of land on either side of the track. The first project also received generous second mortgage loans, but the northern road was allowed no such money grants.

Other Pacific railroad projects also received huge gifts of public lands, among them the Kansas Pacific; the Atchison, Topeka and Santa Fe; the Southern Pacific; and the Texas Pacific. The Illinois Central, in 1850, had been the first to receive federal land grants; the Texas Pacific, in 1871, was the last. During these two decades more than one hundred and fifty million acres of public land were given to western railroads.

However, these companies did more than build ribbons of steel across the nation; they met and conquered problems of a magnitude never seen before. The Union Pacific–Central Pacific laid 1,775 miles of main line track. The Union Pacific track began at Omaha and led west; the Central Pacific track led east from Sacramento.

Construction and transportation problems for the Union Pacific were met, in the main, by General Grenville M. Dodge, who had campaigned against Indians on the Plains, knew the country well, and got leave of absence from the army to become the railroad's chief engineer. When construction began at Omaha there was as yet no rail connection to Council Bluffs, the neighboring city on the east bank of the Missouri River, nor was this city connected by rail with the East. This meant that supplies had to be hauled overland (although steamboats were used a great deal in the movement of the heavier freight). At the height of the construction work across the almost treeless Plains, ten thousand men and as many animals worked for the Union Pacific.

Still more stupendous was the task before the builders of the Central Pacific. All equipment and nearly all the supplies had to be shipped several thousand miles by sea and river before they reached the construction camps. In addition, the western section of the railroad had to climb the Sierra Nevada, tunnel through granite mountain peaks and battle the heavy snow. To further plague the Central Pacific there was a man-power shortage which was later solved by the importation of Chinese coolies, ten thousand of them.

As the two lines approached a possible meeting point, the rivalry between the companies became fierce. Each was to get large blocks of land as well as a cash subsidy from the government for every mile built. When the advance survey crews met they refused to recognize each other. For miles past the meeting point parallel cuts and fills were graded so close together that the blasting by one crew showered the other with rocks and dirt. The Union Pacific's Irish workers, the "paddies," boasted about the number of miles of track they could lay in a day while the Chinese laborers on the Central Pacific were no less determined to beat them. Fantastic were the feats and even greater the boasts, until one day in April, 1869, Charles Crocker's (Central Pacific) "Pets" laid 10.6 miles of track between dawn and dusk. On that day 31,000 ties were laid under 4,037 rails and secured by the driving of over 120,000 spikes. And this was not on the straightaway but around curves. If the line had been straight, boasted one reporter, the crew could have done half again as much.

The race and the rivalry ended in compromise. The two companies agreed to designate Promontory, a point north of the Great Salt Lake, as the official meeting place of the two

Railroad building on the Great Plains.

Harper's Weekly, 1875

Harper's Weekly, 1869

*Locomotive engineers of the Union and Central Pacific shake hands at Promontory, Utah,
May 10, 1869.*

lines. Here history was made on May 10, 1869, when Leland Stanford, president of the Central Pacific, and Thomas C. Durant, vice-president of the Union Pacific, tooks turns driving the famous golden spike which connected the rails of the two companies. As their blows fell the word went out by telegraph to all parts of the nation that the great job was done.

Completion of other rail lines came soon afterward. In a year the Kansas Pacific Railroad reached Denver from Kansas City, and the Denver and Pacific line established a connection between the Kansas Pacific and the Union Pacific at Cheyenne. The Kansas Pacific—a choice property—soon became a part of the Union Pacific system. The Northern Pacific Company, chartered in 1864, moved too slowly and the Panic of '73 halted its construction at Bismarck, North Dakota. Ten years later, however, it became the second transcontinental railroad to reach the Pacific coast when its rails were laid into Puget Sound.

By 1893 the "Great Empire Builder," James J. Hill, had completed his privately constructed (i.e., without federal subsidy) Great Northern Railroad to Seattle, and before the great age of railroad building was over, the Pacific Northwest could be reached not only by the Oregon Short Line, which was an extension of the Union Pacific from its main line to Portland, but also via the Chicago, Milwaukee, St. Paul and Pacific Railroad, which finally reached its goal in 1909 at Tacoma, Washington.

The Southwest, too, had its share in the new transportation empires. From a twenty-nine-mile nucleus the Atchison, Topeka and Santa Fe Railroad began, in 1873, to push toward New Mexico. The line reached Albuquerque by 1882 and there connected with the Atlantic and Pacific on to Needles, California, where connections with other lines were made.

In these pioneering days, railroads often gained their rights of way by brute force, sometimes arming track-laying crews to discourage rivals. There was almost a pitched battle before the Atchison, Topeka and Santa Fe beat the enterprising Denver & Rio Grande through to Albuquerque by way of the Raton Pass. At another point of conflict farther north, in the narrow Royal Gorge on the Arkansas River, blockhouses were built and shots exchanged for the privilege of suspending a single line in the chasm. The combination of court action, restraint on the part of officials and a temporary lease extended by the Denver & Rio Grande to its hated rival forestalled what might have been a long, bloody private war whose prize was a bleak and awesome canyon.

Not all the rail building in this area was westward, however. The Southern Pacific Railroad (a company controlled by Leland Stanford, Collis Huntington, Mark Hopkins, and Charles Crocker, the "Big Four" builders of the Central Pacific) moved southeastward from San Francisco toward New Orleans. In 1883, through-service began over its Sunset Route between California and the "Crescent City." Other important lines that blanketed the West were the Frisco Line, a sprawling network of rails known as the Missouri Pacific in the Great Plains region, and the Western Pacific which, like the Central Pacific, connected Salt Lake City with San Francisco.

But trunk lines were not all it took to make a railroad system. Branch or feeder lines

Unreserved coach accommodations on the "modern ship of the Plains."

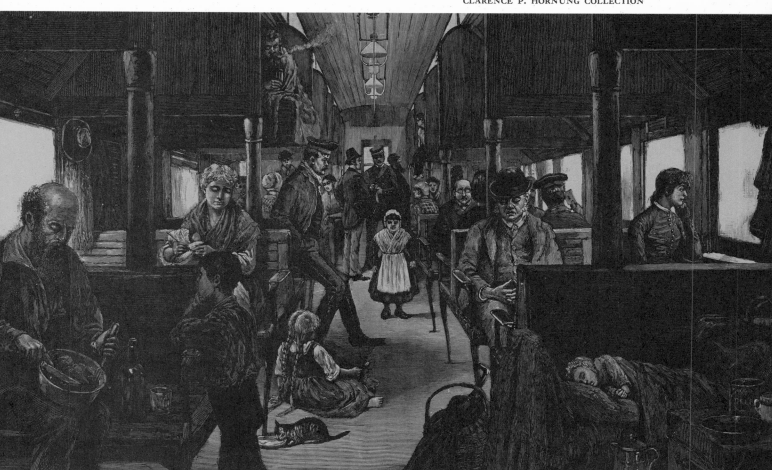

were also necessary. At first, stagecoaches and wagon-freighting firms served as feeders for the main railroads. Due in part to the efforts of Jay Gould, a railroad financier, literally thousands of branch-line miles were constructed to form a vast network across the West. When the great boom in railroads began at the close of the Civil War there were 3,272 miles of track west of the Mississippi River. By 1890, when the railroad building race began to lag (but had by no means stopped), the total mileage was a staggering 72,473.

The impact of the railroads on traveling conditions in the West was equally fantastic. Where the traveler had once had to be content with a thorough jolting in a Concord coach and indifferent fare at rough, untidy stage stations, now, in 1869, he was catapulted to luxury. There were the newly invented sleeping coaches called "Pullmans" and "Silver Palace Cars" which lived up to the name. They were richly appointed, had private toilet facilities and were equipped with individual brass spittoons. If such elegance was beyond a man's pocketbook, there were the unreserved coach accommodations which, as one traveler pointed out, allowed for great freedom of movement. And as a special inducement to attract the patronage of recently arrived emigrants from Europe, there was the emigrant car—plain, but equipped with a toilet, a coal-burning pot-bellied stove, hard seats and bunks with straw-filled bags for mattresses. Dining cars were available to all, as were trackside eating places; both offered foods of a standard never before known in the West.

Whatever the class of service, the impression left by this new mode of travel was profound. Passengers could go faster and see more in greater safety. Guidebooks, providing information about the route, towns and countryside, were available to make the trip more interesting. It is no wonder that the transcontinental railroads became the new tourist attraction.

Plush service in dining car, 1890.

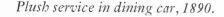

Building a new road.

Harper's Weekly, 1890

30. *Cycling Faddists and Automobiles*

BEFORE THE RAILROADS had entered their golden age, both the American people and their government had evinced great interest in roads. As early as 1802 Congress provided that public lands be sold for the purpose of constructing a highway to the West. A National Road from the head of navigation on the Potomac all the way to St. Louis, Missouri, was planned and partially built. For years it served as a hot political issue and was finally abandoned—too much government spending. However, the need for this artery of travel persisted and when the railroad did come, it was felt that here was the final answer to man's transportation needs. Why build roads when steel rails could carry more people and heavier weight farther and faster? With this neglect of roads, the post–Civil War years saw most of them disintegrate into mere rights of way or almost bottomless quagmires. West of the Missouri River the situation was no better. The frontier states had left the building of roads

133

either to the stagecoach companies or to county agencies. The road work that was done was based on an antiquated system whereby each citizen was required to contribute a couple of day's labor each year to the task. Farmers took a more or less fatalistic view, getting their products to market the best way possible. By 1870 the condition of the roads of the nation was such that they became a national blight.

Revival of interest in road improvement came, strangely enough, not from those who stood to gain economically, but from a small, somewhat esoteric group of faddists known as wheelmen. The wheel or cycle had been a long time in evolving from the clumsy velocipede through the high-wheeled "boneshaker" to the lighter, more maneuverable "safety bicycle." The national bicycle craze took fire with the mass-production of Colonel Albert Pope's "Columbia" safety bicycle in Boston in 1877, and by the end of the century the census reported about thirty million of these vehicles of all kinds in the United States.

But the cycle faddists had their problems. Without good roads they were limited in their travels, and they refused to accept this condition without protest. They organized into what became a very effective pressure group—the League of American Wheelmen—that met in local and national congresses, issued road maps and handbooks and organized tours. Most important of all, they continually prodded both local and national governments to do something about the roads.

From this came the National League for Good Roads which was founded in 1892 for the purpose of bringing about federal action. The following year Congress established an Office of Road Enquiry charged with the duty of collecting data on the condition of the roads and of making its findings public. As the years went by the responsibilities of this office

Third annual meet of League of American Wheelmen.

CLARENCE P. HORNUNG COLLECTION

Sunday cycling party.   CLARENCE P. HORNUNG COLLECTION

broadened until they included the building of sample roads and cooperation with local agencies in road-improvement programs. As the century came to an end, the West—and for that matter the entire nation—stood on the threshold of a new road-building era.

By 1900 a new and still greater force in behalf of better roads came to the fore. Busily and somewhat secretly, inventors had been experimenting with the internal combustion engine and, rather suddenly, they were successful. With the gasoline-fueled engine came the means whereby such ingenious men as Charles B. Duryea, Elwood Haynes, Henry Ford and many others could produce the "horseless carriage." The triumph of the automobile, as it soon came to be called, augmented interest in good roads, and soon crude overland trails were being replaced by smooth roads and highways.

The railroad trains continued to roll as before, but the Concord coaches and the Conestogas soon passed forever from the scene. In 1903 a Winton was the first automobile to cross the continent from San Francisco to New York, arriving on July 26. With two drivers working alternately, it passed through Sacramento, Marysville, and Alturas in California; Lakeview, Oregon; Caldwell, Idaho; Grange and Cheyenne, Wyoming; North Platte and Omaha, Nebraska; also Chicago, Cleveland and New York. The trip took sixty-three days—forty-five of actual travel—averaging 175 miles per day. On the way the odometer broke, but the distance covered was estimated at 6,000 miles.

Less than five months later (December 17, 1903), on the sandy beach of Kitty Hawk, North Carolina, Orville Wright made man's first sustained flight through the air. In 1911, one year before the end of the period described in this book, the first transcontinental flight was made from Sheepshead Bay, New York, to Long Beach, California, in eighty-four hours.

Together the automobile and the airplane transformed America. Together they fulfilled, as the Pony Express riders had failed to do, Senator Gwin's dream—the bringing of the great West into a closer union with the rest of the nation.

First transcontinental automobile trip, 1903.

U. S. BUREAU OF PUBLIC ROADS

PART THREE

"Mountain Sheep" by Charles M. Russell

Treasures of the American West

by Oscar Lewis

John L. Routt.

John F. Jones.

James G. Fair.

Horace A. W. Tabor.

Jerome B. Chaffee.

Nath'l P. Hill.

J. F. Matthews.

Mining kings.

31. *Gold*

Spanish Dreams of Gold

SINCE MAN FIRST emerged from savagery, the one thing above all others that has caused him to push back the frontiers of the known world has been his search for treasure. And it is one of history's ironies that while he rarely found the gold, jewels and other riches he sought, the result of his quest has made known to his fellow men new sources of wealth of a value far beyond his wildest hopes.

The story of the opening of the American West follows that familiar pattern. It was in the year 1539—less than a half-century after the discovery of the New World, and a full eight decades before the landing of the Pilgrims—that the first treasure hunt on this continent got under way.

In the summer of 1536, four ragged, travel-worn strangers—three Spaniards and an African called Estavanico, probably a slave—arrived at Mexico City, the ancient Aztec capital which Cortez had captured and plundered fifteen years earlier. They were the sole survivors of a Spanish expedition of three hundred men who had landed on the Florida coast in 1528, the others having been lost to disease, shipwreck and hostile Indians.

The four had crossed the Gulf of Mexico by means of a crudely constructed craft and had landed on the Texas side, from where they wandered westward through the deserts and mountains of the area now a part of New Mexico and Arizona. Eight years passed before they found their way south to Mexico City.

In telling of the adventures that had befallen them the party's leader, Alvar Núñez Cabeza de Vaca, mentioned some "large and powerful villages, four or five stories high" which they had heard spoken of, but had not seen, in the country to the north. This news deeply interested Don Antonio de Mendoza, the Viceroy of New Spain, for it appeared to confirm other reports which had already reached him: that a group of fabulously rich cities lay somewhere in the region which Cabeza de Vaca and his companions had passed.

By all accounts these mythical settlements, known to the Spaniards as the Seven Cities of Cíbola, were a prize worth striving for. The streets were said to be paved with gold and the walls of the houses adorned with rubies, sapphires and other precious jewels. Mendoza, who was eager to claim this treasure in the name of his king, prepared at once to organize an expedition and dispatch it northward. Cabeza de Vaca and his Spanish companions, however, preferred to return to Spain rather than to the region where they had suffered so many hard-ships, but Estavanico remained. Perhaps Don Antonio bought him to guide the treasure-hunting expedition he planned to send northward in 1539. The records are vague.

To head the expedition Mendoza selected Marcos de Niza, a Franciscan friar born in Nice, France. Another priest, Fray Onorato, was second in command. Soon after the start Onorato became ill and had to return to Mexico City. Estavanico, with several companions, traveled far ahead of the rest under instructions to send an Indian messenger back to the main party from time to time to report on the progress of the advance group. The messenger was to carry a cross, the size of which would indicate the value of what Estavanico had found. If the discovery was of only moderate importance, he was to send a cross one span in length; if it was more important, two spans; and if it was more important than any other in New Spain, he was to send a much larger cross.

Records tell us that Estavanico dressed fantastically with plumes, bells and rattles on his legs and arms—medicine men's rattles no doubt. The natives in their far-flung desert *rancherias* looked on him as a sort of deity, while he in turn accepted their adoration, their supplies and their young women, whom he carried triumphantly with him. En route he sent back progressively encouraging reports. Finally, having come in sight of the fabled cities (in reality the villages of the Pueblo Indians of New Mexico), he dispatched a messenger bear-ing a cross "as tall as a man."

On the messenger's arrival at the main camp, Marcos de Niza, after having, in his own words, "given thanks to our Lord," pushed forward at top speed. Natives along the way supplied further details as to the size and magnificence of the settlements. Cíbola, the largest of the Seven Cities, he was told, was "a place of many people, streets and squares, and in some parts there were houses eleven stories high . . . the entrances and fronts of the principal buildings were of turquoises. . . ."

But as he drew near his destination Fray Marcos learned that disaster had befallen the advance party. Though Estavanico had learned about Indian witchcraft during the eight years he wandered with Cabeza de Vaca among the tribesmen, he had not learned enough to save himself from tragedy. It seems that when Estavanico and his group entered Cíbola they had been attacked by the inhabitants; a few escaped but the African and several of his companions were killed. Accounts of exactly what happened vary greatly. Some say that Estavanico's vaunted magic caused his downfall, that the amulets which he sent ahead to impress the natives of Cíbola were recognized as the "medicine" of a tribe with whom they were at war. Perhaps this is so. On the other hand, it may be that powerful witch doctors resented the encroachment of Estavanico. There is also the story that Estavanico, drunk with power, his conscience calloused by success, began killing the maidens in his entourage as he tired of them. Whatever the truth was, there is no question about his death or about the fact that because of it Fray Marcos decided against approaching any of the hostile Cities of Cíbola.

Before turning south, however, Fray Marcos did go close enough to see the first of these pueblos. "It had," he wrote later, "a very fine appearance for a village, the best that I have seen in these parts. The houses, as the Indians had told me, are all of stone, built in stories, and with flat roofs. Judging by what I could see . . . , the settlement is larger than the City of Mexico. I was somewhat tempted to go thither, but . . . if I should die, there would be no knowledge of this land, which in my estimation is the largest and best of all discovered. . . ."

Fray Marcos turned about and began the long return journey. On reaching Mexico City, he described the cities in such glowing terms that, according to one account, "nothing else was talked about . . . everybody was for going there and leaving Mexico depopulated." Fired by Marcos' account, Don Antonio set about assembling a strong force of cavalry and foot soldiers with Francisco Vásquez de Coronado in command and Fray Marcos as guide. The column set off in 1540, its proud leader arrayed in magnificent gilded armor and plumed helmet, his charger draped in brilliant trappings. The procession contained more than a thousand horses and countless mules. Men in armor and coats of mail rode under lustrous banners. They carried lances, swords and metal shields. Companies of footmen bore crossbows and harquebuses, while light artillery added an invincible martial touch. A thousand servants and camp followers, Indian and white, led spare horses and drove pack animals, oxen, herds of beef cattle, sheep and perhaps even swine for food.

In midsummer, when the first of the Seven Cities appeared over the horizon, Coronado ordered an attack at once, and after a brief fight he and his men entered the town. What he found there fell far short of what he had been led to expect. Gold-paved streets and jewel-encrusted houses were nowhere in evidence, and in his report to the viceroy the disillusioned leader wrote: "The Seven Cities are seven little villages." He added that Fray Marcos had grossly exaggerated what he had seen the previous year. "Everything is the reverse of what he said, except the name of the city and the large stone houses."

But even though faced with disappointment, Coronado persisted in his belief that there were fabulously rich cities somewhere in the region. For two full years he continued the search and not until 1542 did he finally lead the remnants of his army back to Mexico City. They returned empty-handed, and the expedition was counted a failure. Yet in those two years of exploration Coronado had established for Spain a claim to an expanse of territory far larger than the homeland—a region whose potential richness was a thousandfold greater than that of the mythical Seven Cities.

The California Discovery

More than three centuries passed after the failure of Coronado's expedition before the next concerted search for gold and other treasure got under way. This time word of the existence of another fabulously rich store of precious metals, in the California foothills, set off a second and far-greater treasure hunt.

To be sure, the presence of gold in California had been known for several decades before the discovery that brought on the world-wide rush of 1849. But when traces of it were first found, the region was still a sparsely settled Mexican province; the needs of the indolent, easygoing residents were few, and the sale of hides and tallow to the Boston trading ships enabled them to buy whatever they fancied. They saw little point in exerting themselves to dig gold from the ground.

The only early-day strike that attracted anything more than passing attention was in the southern part of the province, near the sleepy pueblo of Los Angeles. There, in the spring of 1842, Francisco López washed out a few flakes of gold in San Feliciano Canyon, on land that had once belonged to the San Fernando Mission. Others learned of López's find; a few joined him, and for several weeks the placers were worked in a dilatory fashion. But a shortage of water hampered operations and, the yield being small (averaging less than two dollars per day), the amateur miners quickly lost interest. The diggings were abandoned. But the first shipment of California gold to reach the East Coast came from these San Feliciano Canyon diggings. Early in 1843 Abel Stearns, a Los Angeles merchant, forwarded some twenty ounces of it to the Philadelphia mint.

Not only gold but a number of other metals were found and in some instances mined in various parts of the West prior to January 24, 1848. That date, however, marked the true beginning of western mining. Ironically enough, neither of the two men who were responsible for making known to the world the extraordinary richness of the California gold fields profited by the discovery.

One of this ill-starred pair was a Swiss-born adventurer, John Augustus Sutter. After some fifteen years of wandering on the western frontier, Sutter had reached California in the late 1830's and had at once begun laying plans for a project that had long been in his mind. This was the founding of an estate—protected by his private fort—that would be self-sustaining in all things and over which he would rule with the stern but benevolent authority of a feudal lord.

As the site of his experiment, Sutter chose an area of fertile land in the middle of the Sacramento Valley, a region that was uninhabited except for roving bands of docile Indians. Having first secured from the Mexican authorities at Monterey a grant to many thousands of acres, he established headquarters near the confluence of the Sacramento and American rivers. There he built workshops, storehouses and living quarters, raised a wall to surround the establishment, mounted cannon at strategic points on the wall, and began his ten-year reign as the Lord of New Helvetia.

By the mid-1840's Sutter's Fort was a flourishing center of industry and trade. A labor force of Indians, under the supervision of a few white overseers, planted the nearby fields to wheat. Herds of cattle and sheep grazed on the ranges beyond and, in and about the fort, Sutter established a gristmill, tannery, distillery, carpenter and blacksmith shops, and a primitive loom for the weaving of cloth. It wasn't long before his active building program pointed up the need for still another facility: a sawmill to furnish lumber both for his own needs and for sale to ranchers who, by then, had begun to settle in Sacramento Valley.

The valley itself being for the most part treeless, the thick stands of pine and oak on the Sierra foothills to the east provided the nearest source of lumber. Early in 1847, Sutter dispatched one of his helpers into that area to choose a site for his mill.

The man he sent was thirty-three-year-old James Wilson Marshall, a native of New Jersey, who two years earlier had reached California via Oregon. The spot Marshall selected lay in a little valley on the South Fork of the American River, forty miles northwest of the fort; the place was called Culloma (later changed to Coloma) after a nearby Indian village. When Sutter had approved Marshall's choice, the two entered into a pact whereby Sutter agreed to finance the project and Marshall undertook to oversee the building of the mill and to operate it after it was completed.

Toward the end of August, 1847, Marshall and a party of workmen set out from the fort

Gleason's, 1852

Sutter's mill, with view of Coloma, California.

carrying their tools and supplies in oxcarts and driving a herd of sheep to serve as food. On reaching the spot they built a log shelter, then began the mill itself. By the end of the year its framework had been finished, the dam upstream that was to divert the water from the river was in, and the digging of the tailrace had begun. In order to widen and deepen the tailrace, Marshall each night left the sluice gate open so that the water would flow down the ditch and wash away the sand and gravel.

On the afternoon of January 24, 1848, while walking down the length of the tailrace, Marshall noticed some flakes of yellow metal at the edge of the channel. At first, as he reported later, he was only mildly interested, but a closer look revealed other particles. Now his curiosity was aroused, and he sent an Indian to the cabin for a pan, then scooped up a few handfuls of sand and gravel and washed it out. At the end of the process there remained in the bottom of the pan a small amount of the yellow metal, "about as much . . . as a ten-cent piece would hold." That evening he half-jokingly announced to his companions, "Boys, I think I've found a gold mine!" The others greeted the remark with derision.

Next morning Marshall resumed the search. After closing the gate and diverting the water from the tailrace, he again walked along the bank, peering down into its bed. This time he saw something new: a bright yellow pellet "about half the size of a pea." From all accounts, Marshall was phlegmatic by nature, little given to any show of emotion. This time, however, he could not conceal his excitement. He called the others to the spot and, while they looked on, tested the weight of the little pellet by hefting it in his hand, then pounded it between two stones to see if it was malleable.

Four days later Marshall rode up to the fort, soaked to the skin from his long ride in a driving rain, sought out Sutter and briskly demanded to see him alone. Sutter led him to his office, closed the door and asked the purpose of his unexpected visit. For answer, Marshall produced a leather pouch, poured several ounces of the yellow metal into the palm of his hand and, holding it before his companion, announced that he believed it to be gold. Sutter carefully examined the samples, then nodded slowly. It might well be gold, he admitted, but first he must submit it to two simple tests. From the fort's apothecary shop he brought in a pair of scales and carefully weighed the particles, placing three silver dollars on one pan and pouring the metal on the other pan until the two sides balanced. He then immersed the whole in water, whereupon the pan containing the silver rose toward the surface and the other descended. He next applied aqua fortis, or nitric acid, to some of the samples; the powerful acid had no effect on them. Finally, Sutter took down his copy of Francis Lieber's *Encyclopaedia Americana,* a standard reference work of the time, and read with care the article on gold. When he closed the book there was no longer any doubt. Gold had been found on the American River.

News of The Gold Discovery Spreads

Marshall, by then highly excited, insisted on returning at once to the foothills; ignoring the storm, he remounted his horse and rode off through the rain. Sutter followed two days later. He arrived at the mill in a thoughtful mood, for in the interval he had had time to reflect on what effect this discovery was likely to have on his thriving empire. On reaching the spot he first satisfied himself that gold in considerable quantities existed there; he then exacted from the workmen a promise to stay on the job until the mill was completed and in operation.

But the shrewd enterpriser had a further plan in mind, one that he hoped would give him control of the new gold field. He negotiated a treaty with the local Indians by which in exchange for "a few shirts, hats, handkerchiefs, and other articles of trifling value" he was given a three-year lease on "ten or twelve leagues" of land surrounding the mill. That accomplished, he dispatched a message to Monterey, asking that the lease be validated by Colonel R. B. Mason, the military governor of newly conquered California.

Although an attempt was made to keep news of the strike from reaching the public, it was a badly kept secret. On his way to Monterey Sutter's messenger showed a sample of the "dust" to an acquaintance he met en route. And in a letter to his friend General Mariano Vallejo at Sonoma, Sutter himself could not refrain from boasting that an "extraordinarily rich" gold mine had been found on land he controlled in the Sierra foothills.

But although the fact that gold had been found on the American River soon became known throughout northern California—and indeed was being exchanged for goods over the counters of stores in Sacramento and San Francisco—the residents as a whole were only mildly interested. When, in its issue of March 15, San Francisco's pioneer newspaper, the *Californian,* first reported the discovery, the news was relegated to a few lines on the little weekly's back page. Ten days later the second San Francisco paper, the *California Star,* was equally noncommittal, confining itself to the announcement that gold dust had become a medium of trade at Sutter's Fort.

It was Sam Brannan, the bombastic Mormon elder and early-day promoter, who awakened his fellows to a belated realization of the importance of the discovery. According to H. H. Bancroft's monumental history of California, Brannan returned to San Francisco early in May from a visit to the diggings, passed through the streets holding aloft a quinine bottle full of nuggets and shouted, at the top of his lungs, "Gold! Gold! Gold on the American River!"

These words have been repeated in many other histories, yet they may not be entirely accurate. The great scholar of the gold rush, Ralph Bieber, has pointed out that three eye-witnesses of the event reported only that Brannan displayed the bottle, waved his hat and shouted in the streets. Regardless of what he may actually have said, his dramatics triggered the excitement, and the next few days saw the beginning of a rush to the new El Dorado.

So rapidly did the "yellow fever" spread that within a week or two San Francisco and Monterey were all but deserted. Merchants closed their shops, workmen left their benches, and professional men abandoned their offices as everyone joined the exodus. Crews of ships in the harbors left en masse, and the garrisons at military posts were depleted by wholesale desertions. In mid-June Walter Colton, *alcalde,* or mayor, at Monterey, the capital of the territory, reported to Washington that there remained there only the women, an occasional soldier and a squad of prisoners. Sacramento, San Jose, Benicia and other northern settlements were likewise emptied of virtually every adult male, and even the communities in the south, including Los Angeles, lost so many residents that they took on the appearance of ghost towns. This surging mass of gold-crazed men showed no respect for Sutter's land, appropriated it without leave and, outnumbering him thousands to one, made their claims stick. Jim Marshall also lost out in the scramble.

Sailing ship card shows typical dock scene—loading in New York for San Francisco.

STATE STREET BANK & TRUST CO., BOSTON.

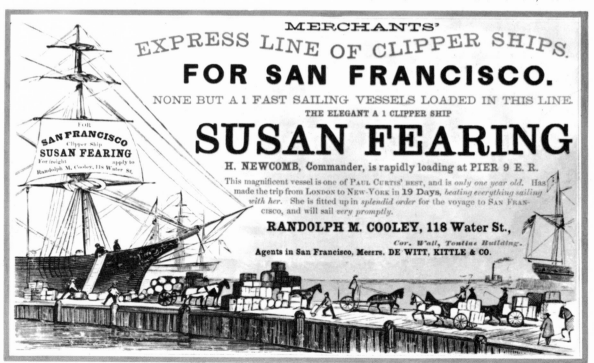

The sudden abandonment of San Francisco and other northern towns was followed almost immediately by a revival in their trade and a period of unprecedented prosperity. The demand for tools, provisions and supplies of many sorts caused prices to shoot skyward. Every ship for which a crew could be found was pressed into service to carry the miners upstream on the first leg of their trek to the diggings. Soon, too, a number of the prospectors, disappointed at having failed to make quick and easy fortunes, drifted back to the towns, where jobs were plentiful and wages high.

This first wave of prosperity was only a prelude to what was to come. As the news spread, first throughout California, then to Oregon, Washington and the Sandwich Islands, it was greeted with intense excitement and caused hundreds to join the stampede. By late summer of 1848, an estimated ten thousand were washing gold from the foothill streams, with others arriving daily.

Meanwhile, references to California's gold had begun to appear in print on the East Coast, often in letters from former residents to the editors of their hometown newspapers. There, too, the first reports were greeted with skepticism. It was not until late that year, when Colonel Mason's report confirming the discovery reached Washington and was officially announced by President Polk in his message to Congress on December 5, that the last doubts vanished and the massive, world-wide movement got under way.

The Forty-Niners

The story of that mighty trek is one of the most colorful chapters in the annals of the West. The stream of prospectors from both hemispheres who poured into California during the next two years transformed what had been a sparsely settled frontier land into something the likes of which the world had never seen. Changes that in the ordinary course of events would have taken decades were accomplished virtually overnight. San Francisco Bay, which but a short time earlier had been deserted except for an occasional whaler or trading ship, became crowded with hundreds of vessels, all abandoned by their passengers and crews. The sleepy village of San Francisco changed into a confused, hustling metropolis, with substantial business houses surrounding its old Spanish plaza and acres of tents and brush shelters covering the nearby sand hills.

It was a city unlike all others; few of the rules that governed the conduct of business elsewhere were observed here. Not only bars and gaming rooms, but restaurants, shops, shipping offices and even banking houses remained open twenty-four hours a day. Merchants

San Francisco in 1850. Lithograph by Currier & Ives.

Ballou's, 1856.

A scene from actual life at the mines.

who could not find store space from which to sell their goods—or who refused to pay the exorbitant rents—dumped their stock in the nearest open space, put up handmade signs, and were soon doing a flourishing business. Prices were determined by the law of supply and demand, and the cost of goods and services soon rose to dizzy heights. By the summer of 1849, new arrivals found eggs selling at anywhere from 75¢ to $1.00 each; a small potato brought 25¢, and quail or duck cost from $2.00 to $5.00 each. Lodginghouses, mostly barracks-like rooms, each fitted with from ten to fifty bunks, charged $20.00 per week, and the customer was expected to furnish his own blankets.

Everything else rose in proportion. Unskilled laborers—who had formerly earned a maximum of $2.00 a day—demanded, and received, from $10.00 to $12.00, while the going rate for carpenters, blacksmiths and other skilled artisans was $20.00 and more. The town's merchants and landowners could well afford to pay such wages, for their own profits were astronomical. Real estate prices kept pace with the city's inflated economy. A lot facing the plaza, which a year earlier had cost its owner $16.50, was sold in the spring of 1849 for $6,000, and later that year for $45,000. A second lot that had cost $15.00 brought $40,000, and a third, which two years earlier had been exchanged for a barrel of whiskey, changed hands for $18,000. Rentals followed the same trend. For a lot at the corner of Kearny and Washington streets a banker paid $6,000 a month; a one-room office cost $1,000 monthly, and a twelve-foot-square basement room was offered a newly arrived attorney for $250. A tent on a lot facing the plaza was rented as a gaming house for $180 a day, and single faro tables brought $30.00 for each twelve-hour shift.

Other towns through which the miners passed on their way to or from the gold fields likewise prospered mightily, while in the diggings themselves scores of camps sprang up, some destined to become permanent settlements, others to disappear once the placers were exhausted. Following the discovery on the American River, prospectors had ranged far to the north and south. With a flat metal dish, or gold pan, the miners scooped sand and water from stream banks and swirled the muddy mixture. The lighter minerals were slopped over the pan's edges. The heavier gold and black sand—really iron particles—settled to the bottom. The yellow specks of gold which sparkled in this black sand were called "colors," and the richness of the bar was reckoned by the number of colors per pan. When these played out, the miners attacked the solid rock veins on the hills, crushing the quartz to extract the imbedded treasure. Nearly all of the foothill streams in this area showed traces of "color," while many proved extremely rich. On the Feather River, fifty miles northwest of Sutter's mill, seven newly arrived miners panned out 275 pounds of gold in two weeks, while a claim on the nearby Yuba yielded its owners $75,000 in three months. One of the richest strikes was at Dry Diggings (later known as Hangtown and later still as Placerville), only a few miles from the mill. There, in the summer and fall of '48, the daily yield ranged from a few ounces to five pounds per man.

California emigrants' last day on the Plains.

The success of those who headed south was no less sensational. On the Stanislaus, Calaveras and Tuolumne, earnings averaged an ounce a day, while many did better. On the last-named stream one newcomer panned out forty-five ounces on his first day; another gathered fifty-two pounds in eight days; and a third struck a pocket so rich that after he had scooped out the gold and piled it in his pan he was barely able to carry it back to his tent.

Such finds were, of course, well above the average, yet as dozens of stream beds and hundreds of bars were worked over, it grew clear that quantities of gold existed all along the western slope of the mountains from Downieville to Mariposa, a distance of more than a hundred miles. Later a number of other lucrative fields were opened up—in the Mount Shasta area, at Weaverville in the Coast Range and at the far southern end of the Sierra.

These first waves of miners merely scratched the surface. Using shovels and pans or rockers, they sifted the gravel from the creeks or, in the so-called dry diggings, patiently spooned out the metal from crevices in the rock. A bit later, more formal equipment came into use: long toms replaced the rockers, and flumes were built to carry water to the dry diggings. Dams were built and canals dug to divert the streams and permit working their beds.

Ballou's, 1856.

Later still, as the placer claims began to run out, quartz mining was introduced. This was a much more complicated and expensive process, and before discussing it the reason for gold's presence in quartz should be explained. Gold, unlike most metallic elements, makes few chemical compounds and therefore occurs in the earth in a pure state. During the dim ages when the world was soft and hot, melted gold became integrated physically, not chemically, in minerals that later hardened into quartz veins. As the world cooled and buckled, these veins were elevated by the great upheavals which formed mountain ranges. Through the geological ages that followed, wind and water broke down the exposed edges of the quartz veins. Streams and rivers carried the released gold and sand down their courses. The gold, being heavy, settled in sand bars along the upper reaches of the streams while lighter soil flowed on as muddy water. These sand bars where nature had let the gold collect were the

"Cradle-rocking."

first and easiest places for prospectors to find gold. As the supply of this "placer gold" diminished, Argonauts sought gold in the upstream quartz veins which had not yet eroded away.

Extracting gold from a quartz vein was much more complicated than washing it out of the sand. First, the solid rock had to be mined, crushed in a stamping mill and then washed. This cost money, and to prevent losing any of the gold that often washed away by crude panning, the crushed ore was passed over shelves of mercury, or quicksilver, which amalgamated with the gold and let the crushed rocks pass on. The process was the same which dentists use to prepare gold fillings, but miners, having captured the gold in the amalgam, released it again by distilling off the mercury. The process required elaborate machinery, as well as men with both skill and capital.

To complicate the entire situation and vindicate the old prospectors' belief that gold is where you find it, gold does occur sometimes in loose sand and gravel high on hillsides and mountain slopes. In these cases the sand was probably once the bottom of an ancient river before the upheaval created the country in its present form.

The gold-bearing gravel high on hillsides of California's upper Mother Lode country is said to have been the bottom of the prehistoric Columbia River which flowed into San Francisco Bay until it broke the escarpment at the Dalles in Oregon and found a new outlet to the Pacific. However this may be, the presence of gold in loose dirt on mountainsides far from water presented a third mining problem which was often solved by what is known as hydraulic mining. By this method water was pumped from the nearest source and squirted by powerful engines against the "pay dirt," washing it down into gulleys where it could be worked for gold. Again the expense was great—sometimes greater than the returns—but rich companies could balance failures against successes, and hydraulic mining flourished until the late 1870's. At that time the process was discontinued because farmers in the valleys vigorously objected to the debris-clogged streams. Quartz mining, however, continued; some of the properties operated with hardly an interruption for more than a century.

Life on the Mother Lode during the heyday of the gold rush had few counterparts elsewhere. With adventurers of every race and creed, and of every degree of virtue or rascality, engaged in an uninhibited scramble for wealth, it was inevitable that the conventions of older-established communities should go by the boards. The history and folklore of the forty-niners are replete with stories of crime and violence, of claim jumping, murder, robbery, swindles, gaming, prostitution, bad liquor and general hell-raising. Since the days of Bret Harte and Mark Twain the era of the

gold rush has been much written about, but it has lost none of its fascination.

Gold in Montana, Washington, Idaho, Utah and Colorado: Denver and Cripple Creek

One result of the California gold rush was to set in motion an intensive hunt for the metal in other parts of the West. Fired by news of fortunes being made on the Mother Lode, men in many places, from Canada to the Mexican border and from the Pacific to the Rockies, took up pick an pan or rocker and hopefully set off on prospecting trips into the mountains, valleys or deserts of their own localities.

Flutter-wheel on the Tuolumne River.

Not all of this was wasted effort. In the early 1850's, while the California excitement was at its height and thousands were still streaming into that state, came word of other strikes: in Arizona, Utah, Colorado and neighboring territories and, farther north, in Montana and Idaho. Each set off a rush of its own. Some attracted only a few, while others drew hundreds. The gold in some deposits was quickly exhausted. In others it lasted for years.

Among the many camps that sprang up during this period, prospered briefly and then sank into obscurity were, to name but a few, those along the Fraser River in British Columbia, Bannack and Last Chance in what is now Idaho, Arizona's Gila City, Utah's Gold Hill, and Conconully and Ruby in Washington Territory.

Among the gold towns that were destined for longer life, those in Colorado may be regarded as typical. Although traces of color had previously been found at a number of places there, the first strike to attract widespread attention occurred in 1858. In the fall of that year, Green Russell, an experienced southern gold miner and veteran of California, came to Cherry Creek. He was a picturesque hillbilly who wore his full beard in braids, had married a Cherokee, and brought with him a party of Georgia whites and Indians. Russell located a claim near the future site of Denver, and greatly exaggerated reports of his discovery quickly spread. By the end of the year several hundred miners had assembled there. Operations had to be suspended during the winter months, but with the coming of spring a new and greater rush got under way. However, the excitement was short-lived, for the expected fortunes failed to materialize, and by the spring of 1859 the disillusioned prospectors were leaving in even greater haste than they had arrived. Then, while that mass exodus was still under way, came word of a sensational new strike some forty miles farther west. Within a few weeks a new boom town, Central City, had sprung up. The place was soon attracting national attention. Horace Greeley, the *New York Tribune's* famous editor, stopped off there in the summer of 1859, and described the scene:

Helvetia quartz mill.

As yet the entire population of the valley—which cannot number less than four thousand, including five white women and seven squaws living with white men—sleep in tents, or under booths of pine boughs, cooking and eating in the open air. I doubt that there is as yet a table or chair in these diggings. . . . The food, like that of the plains, is restricted to a few staples—pork, hot bread, beans and coffee forming the almost exclusive diet of the mountains; but a meat shop has just been established, on whose altar are offered up the ill-fed and well-whipped oxen who are just in from a fifty days' journey across the plains. . . .

Greeley added that the rush was in full tide with upward of five hundred arriving daily.

The story is told that when word reached the miners that the New York editor was about to arrive, they salted a claim by shooting gold dust into the ground with a shotgun; then they took Greeley to the spot and invited him to wash out a few panfuls. Greeley was taken in by the hoax, and his description of the richness of the diggings helped further increase the flow of newcomers.

The mines in and about Central City were profitably worked until the mid-1860's. Then, when the placers and quartz veins had been exhausted, most of the claims were abandoned. A few years later, with the introduction of more efficient methods of treating the ore, operations were resumed and the area enjoyed a second boom. This one lasted until the early 1870's, when all but a few of the mines shut down permanently. In all, Central City produced about sixty-five million dollars in gold.

Cripple Creek, Colorado's most renowned gold-mining district, was opened in 1891. The story of that "300-million-dollar cow pasture" illustrates once again how large a part luck played in such discoveries. The man responsible for the find was a cowhand named Robert Womack. While riding range for his employers, Womack was in the habit of doing a bit of prospecting on the side. One day at a spot misnamed Poverty Gulch he came upon an outcrop of rock that looked promising. He staked out a claim, named it El Paso and sent some samples to an assayer at nearby Colorado Springs. When the report came back stating that the ore assayed $250 a ton, the jubilant cowhand "unloaded" his claim for $500 and, according to one account, "headed for the nearest bar to celebrate his good fortune." During the next few years the claim yielded more than five million dollars in gold. (As so often happened, its discoverer died penniless.)

A few were attracted to the scene during the first weeks, but no immediate rush followed. However, further strikes in the area soon made it clear that Womack's find had been no flash in the pan. By the end of 1891 thousands were streaming into the region, and by 1896 the population of the district stood at 25,000; the yield that year reached eight and a half million dollars. Five years later the population had doubled, and production had soared to twenty-five million dollars, making Cripple Creek the world's second largest producer of gold, topped only by the Witwatersrand field in the Transvaal, South Africa.

Cripple Creek was so named because in the early days many cattle were injured while crossing the rocky stream. Its elevation ranges from 9,500 to more than 11,000 feet. The country is volcanic in origin; its ore had been spewed from deep in the earth by ancient eruptions. The field, covering an area only six miles square, has been extensively explored and worked. More than five thousand shafts were sunk during the first twenty years, and at one

THE DISCOVERY.

"WHISKY GOES"

FREIGHT FOR THE DIGGINGS.

JUMPIN CLAIMS, IS YER?

THE MILL.

MAIN STREET.

THE PACK-MULES.

"JOHN"

SUNDAY AMUSEMENTS.

Harper's Weekly, 1869.

Scenes in typical mining district.

time no less than eleven towns occupied the site, each with its mines, stores and clusters of miners' cabins.

In its heyday, Cripple Creek, the chief settlement on the site, had a population of 20,000. It was a typical wide-open mining town, complete with bars, dance halls, gambling casinos, theaters, shops, hotels, restaurants, and an extensive and well-patronized "line." The last-named consisted of a row of bawdyhouses on both sides of Myers Avenue at the lower edge of the town. Early in this century a well-known journalist visited the place and wrote an article describing its wonders. When the magazine containing his impressions reached Cripple Creek the citizens were incensed; he had, they felt, devoted too much space to Myers Avenue and ignored many of the more commendable aspects of their community life. By way of retribution, the town council at its next meeting voted to rename Myers Avenue, and conferred on it that of the offending writer, whose name was Julian Street.

In 1906 two major fires within a period of three days virtually wiped out the jerry-built town, whereupon it was rebuilt, this time with brick and stone. During the period of its greatest activity, Cripple Creek had, according to one authority, 41 assay offices, 91 lawyers, 46 brokerage houses, 88 doctors and dentists, 14 newspapers, 70 saloons and 1 coroner, who, according to the same authority, "was usually very busy."

Gold in Gila City, Wickenburg and Tombstone

Arizona, too, had its share of gold rushes. One of the first was to a spot in the southwest corner of the territory, close to the Colorado River. There, in 1858, placers were discovered that showed enough promise to attract a considerable number of miners from California and elsewhere. Here sprang up, on the banks of the normally dry Gila River, Gila City, which by the mid-1860's boasted some twelve hundred residents. But the richer placers were presently worked out, and reports of new strikes farther east caused all but a few to hit the trail again. In the early 1870's a visitor to Gila City summed up the whole town in five words: "three chimneys and a coyote."

The lives of several other Arizona gold towns were equally brief. These included Rich Hill and Lynx Creek near the center of the territory, and Hassayampa in the Bradshaw Mountains north of Phoenix. Destined to last longer was Wickenburg, northwest of Phoenix, which grew up around a well-known quartz mine, the Vulture. The mine received its unusual name because a prospector, Henry Wickenburg, chanced to see an outcrop of quartz when he stooped to pick up a vulture he had shot. During the fifteen years the mine was operated, from 1863 to 1878, it yielded handsomely. By 1865 forty *arrastras* (primitive drag-stone mills for pulverizing the ore) were in use there. These were later replaced by power-driven stamp mills operated by water from the Hassayampa River.

During its active period Wickenburg was one of the liveliest towns in the West, with nightly shootings in the saloons and frequent lynchings. Stealing, or high-grading as it was called among the miners, became so widespread that eventually the mine owners were forced into bankruptcy. Gold and silver coins were rarely seen there. The men were paid off with locally minted gold slugs, each with its weight stamped on its surface, and these were practically the only medium of exchange.

In addition to lawlessness, high-grading and isolation from the rest of the world, Wickenburg faced a number of other problems. One was the warlike Apache bands which are said to have waylaid and slain a total of four hundred white men during the first decade and a half of the town's existence. A few miles from Wickenburg stands a monument that marks the site of one such tragedy. This was the so-called Wickenburg Massacre, during which a stagecoach was set on by a gang of Apache, and six of its eight occupants slain.

Transporting the gold was another problem, one that involved serious hazards, for during the long haul to Phoenix the bullion wagons were frequently ambushed by bandits who killed drivers and guards and made off with the treasure.

The Vulture mine has been abandoned for many years, and little stands as a reminder of its former operations. One of the few surviving relics is a large rectangular building once used as an assay office; its three-foot-thick masonry walls are said to contain some three thousand dollars in gold. This estimate is based on the fact that when several similar structures were demolished and their walls run through a mill, their yield in gold averaged twenty dollars a ton.

Another of Arizona's picturesque gold towns was Tombstone, in the southeast corner of the present state. That name was originated by Ed Schieffelin, a soldier stationed at a nearby army post, Fort Huachuca. According to the story, when Schieffelin set out from the fort on a prospecting trip into the Apache-infested back country, he was told by a fellow soldier, "Instead of a mine, you'll find a tombstone." Schieffelin kept the warning in mind, and when he happened on a promising outcrop of rock and staked out a claim, he called it Tombstone.

Later, in 1878, he, his brother Al, an assayer named Gird and several others returned and filed a number of additional claims, to which they gave such names as Lucky Cuss, Tough-Nut, Goodenough and East Side. Some development work was done, but the yield was so meager that most of the original group gave up in disgust. On leaving they suggested that Tombstone be rechristened Graveyard because, they said, it was the spot where they had "buried their hopes." Those who remained were themselves on the point of leaving when Ed Schieffelin struck a ledge so rich as to set off a concerted rush into the district. By the end of 1879 Tombstone had forty houses, several hundred tents, and a population of one thousand; two years later that number had increased sevenfold.

During its first decade Tombstone was, by all accounts, as high-rolling a town as any ever dreamed up by writers of wild West fiction. It was the boast of its residents that the place had more saloons and gambling houses, a larger and better patronized red-light district, and a graveyard containing more men who had died "with their boots on" than any town of its size in the country.

Tombstone remained a large producer of gold and silver for more than ten years. But in the early 1880's, a decline set in—largely because the amount of water flowing into the mine shafts made it unprofitable to operate below the 500-foot level—and by 1890 its population had shrunk to less than two thousand. However, its mines continued to be worked intermittently for many years longer. During the first sixty years they added an estimated eighty million dollars to the world's supply of gold and silver.

Many reminders of Tombstone's flush period remain to this day: rows of two-story brick buildings dating from the 1870's and 1880's, some standing vacant, others occupied by bars or hotels or rooming houses, their original furnishings and ornate decorations still intact; the cemetery on Boot Hill; a huge cavern at the southern end of the town from which so much wealth had been extracted that it was called the "Million Dollar Stope"; and, on a nearby hillside, immense mounds where the worked-over ore was dumped.

Glittering Gold in the Dreary Black Hills

No account of gold mining in the West, however brief, could fail to make mention of South Dakota's Black Hills and world-famous mine, the Homestake. In 1963, after more than eighty years of continuous operation, the Homestake was still going strong. The largest gold producer in the United States it has yielded more than half a billion dollars, making it by far the country's largest producer of gold.

Of all the West's major gold fields, the Black Hills district was the last to be developed. Although traces of the metal were found there as early as 1870, the return from the early placers was small, averaging only from eight to ten cents per pan. It was not until mining experts with the Custer expedition of 1874 reported gold that settlers swarmed into the country in spite of the army's efforts to keep them out. On August 10, 1875, the town of Custer, in the southern Black Hills, was laid out regardless of threatening Indians and severe winter weather. By October 1 the town of Custer boasted one thousand inhabitants and by mid-December ten thousand. That same fall a prospector, who had evaded the soldiers, found unbelievably rich "great free-gold placers" sixty miles to the north in Deadwood Gulch. This started a stampede in 1876 which brought hordes of miners into the Black Hills.

Once the extent and richness of the strike had been established, three San Francisco capitalists, George Hearst (father of William Randolph Hearst), Lloyd Tevis and J. B. Haggin, acquired five square miles in the center of the field, organized the Homestake Mining

Gold prospectors building a dam.

Company and laid the foundations of great fortunes.

Long known as the most lucrative mining property on the continent, the Homestake's profits have come largely from the working of huge quantities of low-grade ore. Between 1877 and 1901 the quartz, originally removed from underground and later from an immense open pit, yielded in excess of a hundred million dollars in gold, plus some four million dollars in silver. That, however, was only the beginning. As improved methods of handling the ore were introduced and the capacity of the mills increased, profits soared. Well over half a century later the fabulous mine was still annually producing fifteen million dollars in gold.

32. *Silver*

Discovery of the Comstock Silver

FROM 1849 ON, it was common for parties of miners bound for California to stop for a few days beside the Carson River, near the base of the Sierra range, to rest from their long overland trek before beginning the ascent of the mountains ahead. Some occupied their time by washing a pan or two of gravel from the edges of the stream. A few found traces of gold in the bottom of the pan, but the amount was small, and most of them pressed on to the far side of the mountains.

Among those who remained to investigate further were two Mormons, John Orr and Nick Kelly, who had arrived in the spring of 1850. After the rest of their party had left, they followed the course of a small stream, a tributary of the Carson, that wound down from the hills to the west. At first they found little "color"; however, the prospect grew brighter as they continued up the canyon, and when word reached the outside that they were averaging $5.00 a day, others joined them. By 1853 Gold Canyon, as it had come to be called, had a population of about one hundred. But the surface diggings presently began to diminish, earnings dropped to below $2.00 a day, and in 1858 news of a new strike at Mono Lake drew all but a few to that area. That ended Gold Canyon's far-from-spectacular first boom.

Those who stayed pushed farther up the canyon, hoping to find something better than the worked-out claims below. Their success, though moderate, was enough to cause others to join them. Some of the newcomers, finding the ground at the canyon's head all staked out, passed over the shoulder of Sun Mountain to the headwaters of a second small stream, Six Mile Creek.

Again the district prospered moderately, with the placers on both sides of the ridge averaging 15¢ a pan. The population soon increased to the point where the district's first town, Gold Hill, was founded. Meanwhile the yield of the claims in Six Mile Canyon continued to rise, and by the fall of 1858 their owners were taking out a total of between $500 and $1,000 daily. When word of this new strike spread, scores of others descended on the spot.

One of the newcomers who arrived early in 1859 was J. F. Stone, a veteran of the California quartz mines. When he found the miners cursing a troublesome blue sand that clogged their rockers and had to be tossed aside, he sent a sample across the mountains to an assayer at Nevada City, California. The assayer made a routine test and the startling result convinced him that a mistake had been made. He ran through a second specimen. The result was the same. The supposedly worthless "blue stuff" was an extraordinarily rich silver sulfide; it would, he estimated, run about $4,700 a ton, one-quarter gold and three-quarters silver.

The assayer's report was so startling that on its receipt Stone hurried to Nevada City, still only half-convinced of its truth. In the meantime the assayer had shared news of his findings with a friend, Judge James Walsh, a millowner in nearby Grass Valley. When Stone arrived, he reported to the assayer and his friend that the miners in Six Mile Canyon were tossing aside tons of the material every day. That same night the excited trio—Stone, Walsh and the assayer—mounted mules and set off posthaste across the mountains. They carried with them the secret of Nevada's famous Comstock Lode.

Although it was the Nevada City assay that first revealed the surpassing richness of the lode, the presence of silver in the area had been known for some time. The question of who was the actual discoverer has long been debated. Some have accorded the honor to the Grosch brothers, Allen and Hosea, California placer miners, who found traces of silver while working a claim in Gold Canyon in 1857. Others have named a pair of Irish prospectors, Peter O'Reilly and Patrick McLaughlin, and still others credit the discovery to James "Old Virginny" Fennimore, the first to work a claim in Six Mile Canyon and for whom the area's chief town, Virginia City, was named.

However, the man who conferred his name on the lode—and thereby won a cheap but lasting fame—was a picturesque character named Henry T. P. Comstock. Comstock, so the story goes, came riding up Six Mile Canyon one day in 1859, astride a borrowed pony, "his long legs dragging in the sagebrush," and met O'Reilly and McLaughlin, who were digging out a little spring to increase the flow of water. The pair had just washed a pan of dirt, and Comstock, seeing gold in the bottom of the pan, proceeded to order the two off "his" claim, insisting that the spring was on property he had located earlier and that he and a partner, "Manny" Penrod, had been working there. So long and vehemently did he argue that at length the two Irishmen agreed to take him and Penrod in as partners. Thereupon the four dug a trench up the hill from the spring, following a six-inch-wide vein that for the next week yielded them "hundreds of dollars a day" in gold.

Although word of this sensational strike quickly spread through the California mines, it set off no immediate rush. There had been a number of such reports during the previous year, none of which had lived up to expectations, and news of this latest bonanza was greeted with skepticism. In its issue for July 2, 1859, a Nevada City paper, the *Journal,* having reported the assay, added this warning: "Of course, the discoverers of this vein may have struck a good thing, but the odds are about ten to one that instead of opening up their quartz vein they intend to open a provision store." It was not until late that year, when the first shipments of the rich ore reached San Francisco, that the last doubts vanished and a belated rush got under way.

None of the group that had uncovered the lode and made its riches known to the world benefited materially by the discovery. Like so many prospectors everywhere, they sold their holdings for next to nothing, then proceeded to blow that and start over again. The amounts received by three of the group for their claims are revealing. McLaughlin parted with his for $3,500; Penrod got $8,500. Comstock who considered himself a shrewd bargainer, sold out for $11,500. Comstock's property alone soon had a market value of $80,000,000.

At Comstock Lode, as elsewhere, the real rewards were reaped by those who came later: the bankers, mineowners and millowners, stockjobbers and merchants, plus the gamblers, barkeeps and camp followers of many sorts. Lawyers profited mightily by litigation over land titles. The original claims had been filed in a "record book" kept beneath the bar of a Gold Hill saloon. They consisted of only a few scrawled lines applying for so many feet to the right or left of other claims—vague descriptions which caused boundary disputes that clogged the courts for years.

A number of obstacles had to be overcome before large-scale operations could begin at Comstock. The spot, high on the sterile side of Sun Mountain (later called Mt. Davidson), was remote and difficult to reach. Everything—food, fuel, lumber and the complex machinery of quartz mining—had to be brought up from below, first in great freight wagons drawn by six- and eight-horse teams and, after 1869, over the corkscrew roadbed of the Virginia & Truckee Railroad. But the richness of the mines more than compensated for these inconveniences.

Horrors of Work in the Comstock

During the first several years the mining and milling of the ore was a routine operation, but as the surface deposits were worked out and the shafts were sunk deeper, new problems arose. The ore was a black sulfide that crumbled easily and tended to cave. This characteristic, plus the fact that the veins widened steadily as they slanted into the mountainside, made the usual methods of timbering useless. The question of how to remove the ore from these underground caverns—some of which measured a hundred feet or more from floor to ceiling—and at the same time prevent the cavern roof from falling in and trapping the workmen, for some time defeated the best efforts of the owners and threatened to bring operations to a halt.

At length, a young engineer, Philip Diedesheimer, was brought up from the quartz mines of California and asked to devise some means of coping with the problem. After several weeks of study, he hit on a solution. A series of interlocking frames, built of twelve-inch-

The Gould and Curry Mill, Virginia City, Nevada Territory.

square timbers, was placed in tiers, one above the other, so as to fill the stopes from floor to roof. The "Diedesheimer square sets," as they were called, remained in use throughout the life of the Comstock.

But other problems remained, chief of which was the supplying of air to workmen on the lower levels. As the shafts were deepened and the lateral drifts grew longer, the atmosphere at the faces of the cuts became so foul that the miners often could work no more than fifteen minutes at a time. To correct this condition, a number of expedients were tried. Great funnel-like "air traps" were rigged up at the mine heads, designed to catch whatever wind was blowing and force it underground through canvas pipes. This procedure sufficed for a time, but as the shafts descended to a depth of a half-mile and more, powerful air pumps and intricate ventilating systems had to be installed. Even these did not fully solve the problem. In 1878 a visitor to the lower level of one mine found the air so thin and impure that candles inside the miners' lanterns "flickered and burned with a faint blue flame."

These difficulties were bad enough, but the owners were presently faced by even more serious trouble. As the miners probed deeper, the temperature on the lower levels rose steadily, reaching 120 degrees at 2,300 feet, and continued to rise with each additional foot. In one property, the Crown Point, it eventually reached a fantastic 150 degrees—a circumstance that prompted a Virginia City editor to boast that the Comstock mines were not only the world's richest, but were also incomparably the hottest.

Working in such temperatures was an ordeal only the hardiest could endure, and then for only brief periods. Yet somehow the ore was got out. Miners wearing nothing but breech-cloths and shoes pecked away at the faces of the stopes, their pick bundles and drills wrapped in cloth that every few minutes had to be dipped in ice water. Huge quantities of ice were lowered down the shafts. In the summer of 1878 the daily allotment was ninety-five pounds per man; a total of more than two million pounds were used that year. One account tells of "half-fainting men" who chewed bits of ice to cool their throats, and "carried lumps in their clenched hands." Only the introduction of power-operated Burleigh drills permitted the work to continue; to swing a pick or use a hand drill would have been impossible. Even with such tools, production fell off to the point where it took four men to accomplish what ordinarily would have been done by one.

Exposed to such temperatures [wrote one visitor], and breathing the stagnant air, the men spent forty-five minutes of each hour beneath the nearest air-vent, going forward to their stations for successive brief periods and returning bathed in sweat and often bent over with cramps. The pain of these "stomach knots" was intense; workmen so stricken were hurried to the surface and given rigorous massage treatment until the perspiration began to flow, whereupon they returned to their posts, seemingly as well as ever. There were occasional deaths, but on the whole the miners—picked men all—came through the ordeal well. Usually they spent no more than a week in the deepest parts of the mines; they were then transferred to workings nearer the surface, whereupon they rapidly put on the weight they had sweated off in the inferno-like areas below.

In addition to the extreme heat at the lower levels, hot springs were tapped and scalding water flooded the tunnels adding still another complication to a situation that had already taxed the ingenuity of the country's ablest mining engineers. To prevent the flooding of the lower levels, ever more powerful pumps had to be installed. By the end of the 1870's engines developing as much as 600 horsepower were in continuous operation at the mine heads, lifting 10,000 gallons an hour for distances of 3,000 feet and more. Even such massive equipment sometimes proved inadequate, and in several mines the water level continued to rise, driving the workmen from the lower levls.

Sutro's Tunnel

The problem of ventilating the stiflingly hot lower workings, of pumping out the water and of lifting the ore from the bottoms of the shafts eventually grew so complex—and expensive—as to threaten to bring operations to a halt. At that juncture a plan was proposed that gave promise of solving all three difficulties: the digging of a five-mile-long tunnel, beginning at the base of the mountain and striking the lode at a point low enough to drain off the water and permit the ore to be carried by gravity into the valley below.

That ambitious project was conceived by a shrewd and able entrepreneur named Adolph Sutro, a German-born immigrant who had reached the lode in the early 1860's, opened a cigar store at Virginia City and, a year or two later, took over the management of a quartz mill at nearby Dayton. When he organized his tunnel company in 1865 it had the enthusiastic backing of mineowners whose tunnels were being flooded. Nineteen of them signed contracts by which they agreed to pay Sutro's company a royalty of two dollars a ton on all ore passing through the tunnel. That backing enabled Sutro to raise funds to start construction, and work began in the fall of 1869. However, strong opposition presently developed. The mineowners withdrew their support, mainly because they foresaw that the two-dollar royalty would cut sharply into their profits, particularly in the handling of low-grade ore. Merchants and property owners at Virginia City, Gold Hill and other lode towns were even more violently opposed, for they realized that the mills would be moved to the tunnel's outlet in the valley, thus taking from them many of their free-spending customers.

Against this powerful opposition Sutro fought back with vigor. Deprived of support both locally and in San Francisco (where all the leading mines were owned), he ranged far afield.

He succeeded in having bills introduced at several sessions of Congress, authorizing the granting of government funds to complete his project. Unsuccessful there, he carried his campaign to England, where a group of London bankers eventually agreed to make him a loan of $2,500,000. This eased the financial situation, but a variety of other obstacles arose, including labor troubles and a succession of difficult technical problems. Somehow, though, the work continued, and at last, on July 8, 1878, the tunnel was broken through to the main shaft of the Savage Mine.

To the story of the Sutro Tunnel must be added this ironical footnote: During the thirteen years required to build it, all but a fraction of the richest ore was mined. By 1878 the Comstock had passed its crest; some of the mines had shut down entirely, and others were operating with sharply reduced staffs, working low-grade surface deposits that had been ignored earlier. During the first five years after the tunnel was opened, royalties for its use averaged only $44,000 annually—far short of Sutro's original estimate. Later, earnings picked up somewhat with the increased milling of the lode's less valuable ore, but its promoter's dream of large profits went unrealized. In 1889 the company went into bankruptcy and the mortgage holders took over.

The profits from the mines built three populous, though short-lived, communities on the lode itself, but the permanent beneficiary was San Francisco. Its capitalists financed the development of the most valuable properties, and a major share of the profits went to enrich them, making great fortunes for only half a dozen. These silver kings, in turn, transformed San Francisco. They built the multiple-story hotels, stores and office buildings in the downtown district, and caused a cluster of ornate wooden "mansions" to rise on the heights above.

Nevada Ghost Towns

As was the case with virtually all the West's bonanzas, the Comstock mines were eventually worked out. One by one the mills closed down, and the shafts were boarded over. As jobs grew scarce and the miners drifted away, the lode's once-booming towns began a slow, steady decline. Well before the turn of the century they were already half-deserted, with rows of brick and stone buildings standing vacant and hundreds of back-street wooden cottages falling to ruin. The exception was Virginia City, which continued to maintain a precarious existence as a tourist center.

But in the first twenty years after the discovery, the Comstock produced an amount in excess of three hundred million dollars and strongly influenced the economy of the entire West. Not only did its discovery intensify the search for precious metals and thereby lead to the discovery of many new fields, but its operation meant that other business could thrive: immense quantities of machinery, tools, fuel and timber were purchased for mines and mills; transportation facilities for men and materials prospered.

The mining fever, raised to a high pitch by the Comstock, focused national attention on Nevada's sage-covered plains and waterless mountains. During the first two decades after the Civil War there was no lack of men willing to grubstake prospectors on trips into the back country in return for a half-interest in whatever of value they might find. The result was a long series of "discoveries," nearly all of which were accepted at face value by the credulous, who scrambled to buy shares in the newly organized companies on the floor of the San Francisco and other exchanges.

Few of these supposedly rich finds materialized; almost invariably the stockholders lost their entire investments, and only the promoters profited. But there were exceptions. One was the White Pine Mountains in the east central part of the territory. Silver-bearing ore was first found in that area (its altitude 11,000 feet) in 1865. At once a company was organized, stock was sold, and with the proceeds a shaft was sunk, a mill built, and operations begun. But the returns were so small during the first two years that the White Pine district seemed headed for oblivion. The owners were on the point of suspending operations when an Indian appeared one day bearing a piece of ore that, on being assayed, proved to be a rich silver chloride. The Indian led a group of miners to the spot where he had found the ore, and they staked out a claim, naming it the Hidden Treasure.

News of this strike spread far, losing nothing in the telling, and the usual rush ensued. The following is typical of the wildly exaggerated reports that circulated concerning the richness of the field: A party of prospectors who on first arriving had built a small cabin for protection against the icy winds, later demolished its rock walls and, having run them through the mill, recovered $75,000 in silver. Tales of that sort had the hoped-for result, and before the year ended the White Pine district was one of the most active in the West. At the height of the excitement an estimated 25,000 were swarming over the mountainsides, and the number of filed claims reached a staggering 13,000. Towns were hopefully laid out, scores of mining companies were organized, mills were built, and speculation in stocks and town lots sent prices skyrocketing.

By 1870 Hamilton, the district's chief settlement, had a population of more than 10,000. Among its attractions were—besides the usual quota of saloons, shops and gambling houses— an iron-shuttered Wells Fargo office, a commodious hotel built of native sandstone and, on an adjacent hillside, a well-populated cemetery that covered several acres. Descriptions of the place during the years it was riding high tell of bars and restaurants and gaming rooms filled to capacity twenty-four hours a day, of frequent shootings and occasional lynchings, and of a narrow main street so crowded day and night that drivers of stages and freight wagons had trouble forcing their way through.

Soon, however, Hamilton's bright hopes began to fade, for although the surface ledges were extremely rich—during 1870 the monthly yield averaged $350,000—as the miners probed deeper they found only barren rock. But realization that the town was not sitting on a bonanza came slowly, and for several years more the hunt went on; meanwhile, merchants and other property owners continued putting up buildings designed to last a century. By 1877 the continuing decline in the yield of the mines had convinced even the die-hards that the boom was over. People began drifting away, their exodus hastened by a destructive fire that year, which reportedly was set by a merchant who hoped to collect enough insurance to finance his removal to a nearby camp that was on the upswing.

Operations continued on a steadily diminishing scale for ten years longer, until the day in 1887 when the last mill was permanently shut down. During its twenty years of activity the district produced twenty-two million dollars in silver and gold.

The story of the rise and fall of the White Pine mines was repeated, with variations, in a number of other parts of Nevada: at Austin, on the Reese River near the center of the territory, in 1861; at Pioche, close to the Utah border, two years later; at Eureka in 1864; and at Belmont and Ely.

Puritanic Tonopah

From the beginning, silver and gold had been the territory's chief, in fact almost its only, source of wealth. And as its mines shut down, one by one, and the bulk of the population moved to more promising fields elsewhere, a spirit of pessimism settled over the land. By the end of the century Nevada's forty-year-long mining boom had, to all appearances, come to an end. But not for long.

In the spring of 1900 an itinerant hunter, farmer and part-time prospector named Jim Butler camped overnight at a spring called Tonopah (Indian for "Little Water") on the semi-arid plains in the southwestern part of the state, about fifty miles from the California border. As was his custom, Butler turned his burro loose to feed during the night on the sparse grass. Next morning he set out to retrieve the beast, and having found him, sat down for a few moments before returning to pick up his kit. While he rested he noticed an outcrop of rock nearby and, by force of habit, chipped off a few specimens. Later that day he came on several men who were working an unpromising claim called the Little Klondike. Butler took the samples from his poke and asked one of the group, Frank Hicks—who had a crude assaying kit with him—to see if they showed color, offering a share in his claim as payment.

Hicks, who was "tired of doing free assays," refused. So Butler carried his samples forty-seven miles up the dusty desert road to his home in Belmont, and later showed them to an acquaintance, a young attorney named Tasker L. Oddie. Oddie, fresh from the East, knew nothing of mining; however, Butler's rock fragments aroused his interest, and he forwarded them to a friend in Austin, a schoolteacher named Gayhart, who did occasional assays as a side line.

Gayhart ran his tests; the ore was so rich in silver that he repeated the process several times. Half-believing someone had played a joke on the greenhorn lawyer, he reported his findings to Oddie. Oddie in turn forwarded them to Butler, who was at work on his farm. Butler was busy harvesting hay; it was not until several weeks later that, prodded by his wife, he returned to the scene of his discovery.

Meantime, news of the find had leaked out, and when Butler and his wife arrived they found a number of prospectors in the vicinity diligently hunting for the outcrop. The couple proceeded to stake out six additional claims, two of which were entered in Oddie's name. Their next step was to raise funds to pay for tools and buy food to sustain them until the first ore could be mined and sent to the smelter at Austin. To solve the transportation problem, a miner named Wilson Brougher—who owned a wagon and team of mules—was taken into partnership. Oddie, meanwhile, had abandoned his unflourishing law practice and joined the little group. With $25.00 worth of provisions on hand, they set to work; Oddie and Brougher did the digging, Mrs. Butler served as cook, and Butler oversaw the operation. Several weeks passed, and when their supplies were nearly exhausted, the group was about to give up and return to town. It was at this point that they received payment for their first wagonload of ore from the smelter. The amount was $800.

Among the many people who soon converged on the spot was Walter Gayhart himself. Another of Gayhart's talents was a knowledge of surveying, and this he put to use by laying out the town of Tonopah.

During its early period Tonopah was an unprepossessing-looking settlement. Of the miners, only a few had tents; the others slept in dugouts or sagebrush shelters, or under their wagons; all cooking was done above open fires. However, that phase quickly passed. Once the extent and richness of the field had been demonstrated, a familiar process began: Agents for established mining concerns appeared, negotiated leases with the owners of the more promising claims and prepared to begin large-scale developments. Under the terms of the leases, the owners received 25 per cent of the profits, a percentage that eventually totaled more than four million dollars.

During its first years Tonopah shared the inconveniences common to many other western mining towns, namely, an acute shortage of water and a high cost of freighting in supplies. The nearest spring was four miles distant, and when the tank wagon made its daily visit the water was doled out to customers for 25¢ a bucket. For a time the town's only bathtub was in the back room of a saloon; over its door was a sign reading: "First chance $1, second chance 50¢, all others 25¢." But that period of austerity soon passed. As the place grew, water was piped from the spring, regular freight and passenger service was established between Tonopah and the railhead at Sodaville, fifty miles to the northwest, and by the summer of 1902 crews were laying tracks connecting the two towns.

By the time the railroad arrived, Tonopah was a city of more than ten thousand, its streets lined with stone buildings housing banks, brokerage offices, stores and hotels, plus a liberal sprinkling of bars, gaming rooms and combination dance halls and bawdyhouses. But for all its high-stake poker games, prodigious consumption of hard liquor and the other divertissements of its free-spending residents, Tonopah, for some reason hard to explain, never became the hell-raising mining town of tradition. Times were changing. The wild West was disappearing. Prosperous people at the turn of the century, even in remote towns, were copying the new pattern of respectability. Visitors to Tonopah who arrived expecting to hear the frequent sound of gunfire and see the vice-ridden dens to which the miners retired in their off hours were shown instead the town's new opera house, the luxurious headquarters of the volunteer fire department, or taken to dine at the Tonopah Club, the spacious, elegantly furnished rooms of which were the center of its social life.

Gorgeous Goldfield, Nevada

The strike at Tonopah raised hopes that other rich finds might be made in the same area, and an intensive search got under way. It was not until late in 1902, however, that anything turned up. This was high on a ridge in the barren country to the south; there a Shoshone Indian, Tom Fisherman, one day came on a ledge of decomposed rock that seemed to show some promise. The Indian's discovery aroused mild interest, but when the first ore was taken out, it assayed only $12.50 per ton. Most of the $12.50 was in gold. The novelty of finding gold in what was predominantly a silver state stirred the curiosity of those who first arrived, and a number of claims were staked out. Tonopah then had a surplus of laborers, and some of the jobless drifted south to look over the new field. Other claims were located and some development work began, but it was a lackadaisical movement at best, for later assays were no more encouraging than the first.

Then—the month was December, 1903—came news that electrified not only Tonopah but the entire West: the discovery of surpassingly rich ore in one of the mines, the Jumbo. This triggered a rush that drew hundreds, then thousands, to the spot. A town was laid out on the crest of the ridge, its sponsors prophesying that Goldfield, as it was called, would one day surpass Tonopah, its neighbor to the north.

This, as events were to prove, was no idle boast, for it soon became clear that an abundance of gold existed in the area. Competition for control of the new field grew so keen that most of the original owners sold out, several receiving $25,000 or more for their claims. Some properties changed hands half-a-dozen times in the course of a month, always at a substantial

No. I.

No. II.

No. VII.

THE MINERS' TEN COMMANDMENTS.

A man spake these words, and said: I am a miner, who wandered "from a way down east," and came to sojourn in a strange land, and "see the elephant." And behold! I saw him, and bear witness, that from the key of his trunk to the end of his tail, his whole body has passed before me; and I followed him until his huge feet stood still before a clapboard shanty; then with his trunk extended, he pointed to a candle card tacked upon a shingle, as though he would say Read, and I read the

MINERS' TEN COMMANDMENTS.

I.

Thou shalt have no other claim than one.

II.

Thou shalt not make unto thyself any false claim, nor any likeness to a mean man, by jumping one; whatever thou findest on the top above or on the rock beneath, or in a crevice underneath the rock;—or I will visit the miners around to invite them on my side; and when they decide against thee, thou shalt take thy pick and thy pan, thy shovel and thy blankets, with all that thou hast, and "go prospecting" to seek good diggings; but thou shalt find none. Then, when thou hast returned, in sorrow shalt thou find that thine old claim is worked out, and yet no pile made thee to hide in the ground, or in an old boot beneath thy bunk, or in buckskin or bottle underneath thy cabin; but hast paid all that was in thy purse away, worn out thy boots and thy garments, so that there is nothing good about them but the pockets, and thy patience is likened unto thy garments; and at last thou shalt hire thy body out to make thy board and save thy bacon.

III.

Thou shalt not go prospecting before thy claim gives out. Neither shalt thou take thy money, nor thy gold dust, nor thy good name, to the gaming table in vain; for monte, twenty-one, roulette, faro, lansquenet and poker, will prove to thee that the more thou puttest down the less thou shalt take up; and when thou thinkest of thy wife and children, thou shalt not hold thyself guiltless—but insane.

IV.

Thou shalt not remember what thy friends do at home on the Sabbath day, lest the remembrance may not compare favorably with what thou doest here.—Six days thou mayest dig or pick all that thy body can stand under; but the other day is sunday; yet thou washest all thy dirty shirts, darnest all thy stockings, tap thy boots, mend thy clothing, chop thy whole week's firewood, make up and bake thy bread, and boil thy pork and beans, that thou wait not when thou returnest from thy long tom weary. For in six days' labor only thou canst not work enough to wear out thy body in two years; but if thou workest hard on Sunday also, thou canst do it in six months; and thou, and thy son, and thy daughter, thy male friend and thy female friend, thy morals and thy conscience, be none the better for it; but reproach thee, shouldst thou ever return with thy worn out body to thy mother's fireside;

and thou shalt not strive to justify thyself, because the trader and the blacksmith, the carpenter and the merchant, the tailors, Jews, and buccaneers, defy God and civilization, by keeping not the Sabbath day, nor wish for a day of rest, such as memory, youth and home, made hallowed.

V.

Thou shalt not think more of all thy gold, and how thou canst make it fastest, than how thou wilt enjoy it, after thou hast ridden rough-shod over thy good old parents' precepts and examples, that thou mayest have nothing to reproach and stir thee, when thou art left ALONE in the land where thy father's blessing and thy mother's love hath sent thee.

VI.

Thou shalt not kill thy body by working in the rain, even though thou shalt make enough to buy physic and attendance with. Neither shalt thou kill thy neighbor's body in a duel; for by "keeping cool," thou canst save his life and thy conscience. Neither shalt thou destroy thyself by getting "tight," nor "slewed," nor "high," nor "corned," nor "half-seas over," nor "three sheets in the wind," by drinking smoothly down—"brandy slings," "gin-cocktails," "whisky punches," "rum-toddies," nor "egg nogs." Neither shalt thou suck "mint-julips," nor "sherry-cobblers," through a straw, nor gurgle from a bottle the "raw material," nor "take it neat" from a decanter; for, while thou art swallowing down thy purse, and thy coat from off thy back, thou art burning the coat from off thy stomach; and, if thou couldst see the houses and lands, and gold dust, and home comforts already lying there—"a huge pile"—thou shouldst feel a choking in thy throat; and when to that thou addest thy crooked walkings and hiccuping talkings, of lodgings in the gutter, of brollings in the sun, of prospect-holes half full of water, and of shafts and ditches, from which thou hast emerged like a drowning rat, thou wilt feel disgusted with thyself, and inquire, "Is thy servant a dog that he doeth these things?" verily I will say, Farewell, old bottle, I will kiss thy gurgling lips no more. And thou, slings, cocktails, punches, smashes, cobblers, nogs, toddies, sangarees, and julips, forever farewell. Thy remembrance shames me; henceforth, "I cut thy acquaintance," and headaches, tremblings, heart burnings, blue devils, and all the unholy catalogue of evils that follow in thy train. My wife's smiles and my children's merry-hearted laugh, shall charm and reward me for having the manly firmness and courage to say No. I wish thee an eternal farewell.

VII.

Thou shalt not grow discouraged, nor think of going home before thou hast made thy "pile," because thou hast not "struck a lead," nor found a "rich crevice," nor sunk a hole upon a "pocket," lest in going home thou shalt leave four dollars a day, and go to work, ashamed, at fifty cents, and serve thee right; for thou knowest by staying here, thou mightst strike a lead and fifty dollars a day, and keep thy manly self respect,

and then go home with enough to make thyself and others happy.

VIII.

Thou shalt not steal a pick, or a shovel, or a pan from thy fellow miner; nor take away his tools without his leave; nor borrow those he cannot spare; nor return them broken, nor trouble him to fetch them back again, nor talk with him while his water rent is running on, nor remove his stake to enlarge thy claim, nor undermine his bank in following a lead, nor pan out gold from his "riffle box," nor wash the "tailings" from his sluice's mouth. Neither shalt thou pick out specimens from the company's pan to put them in thy mouth, or in thy purse; nor cheat thy partner of his share; nor steal from thy cabin mate his gold dust, to add to thine, for he will be sure to discover what thou hast done, and will straightway call his fellow miners together, and if the law hinder them not, they will hang thee, or give thee fifty lashes, or shave thy head and brand thee, like a horse thief, with "R" upon thy cheek, to be known and read of all men, Californians in particular.

IX.

Thou shalt not tell any false tales about "good diggings in the mountains," to thy neighbor, that thou mayest benefit a friend who hath mules, and provisions, and tools and blankets, he cannot sell,—lest in deceiving thy neighbor, when he returneth through the snow, with naught save his rifle, he present thee with the contents thereof, and like a dog, thou shalt lie down and die.

X.

Thou shalt not commit unsuitable matrimony, nor covet "single blessedness;" nor forget absent maidens; nor neglect thy "first love;"—but thou shalt consider how faithfully and patiently she awaiteth thy return; yea, and covereth each epistle that thou sendest with kisses of kindly welcome—until she hath thyself. Neither shalt thou covet thy neighbor's wife, nor trifle with the affections of his daughter; yet, if thy heart be free, and thou dost love and covet each other, thou shalt "pop the question" like a man, lest another, more manly than thou art, should step in before thee, and thou love her in vain, and in the anguish of thy heart's disappointment, thou shalt quote the language of the great, and say, "sich is life;" and thy future lot be that of a poor, lonely, despised and comfortless bachelor.

A new Commandment give I unto thee—if thou hast a wife and little ones, that thou lovest dearer than thy life,—that thou keep them continually before thee, to cheer and urge thee onward until thou canst say, "I have enough—God bless them—I will return." Then as thou journiest towards thy much loved home, with open arms shall they come forth to welcome thee, and falling upon thy neck weep tears of unutterable joy that thou art come; then in the fullness of thy heart's gratitude, thou shalt kneel together before thy Heavenly Father, to thank Him for thy safe return. AMEN —So mote it be.

FORTY-NINE.

No. III.

No. VIII.

No. IV.

HANNA & CO., PRINTERS.   No. VI.

No. IX.

No. X.

profit. Real estate prices in the newly laid-out town followed the same trend. One corner lot in the center of the embryo business district brought $45,000.

Goldfield's spectacular strike stirred even greater interest than had the one at Tonopah three years earlier. Speculators all over the country, fired by reports of tremendous profits made by a fortunate few, were anxious to share in the new bonanza, and there was no lack of promoters willing to accommodate the credulous. A score of mining companies were organized under impressive-sounding names, and their worthless stock was eagerly snapped up by the public.

But Goldfield also had its bona fide mines, and these were among the richest in the country. Their output increased from year to year, reaching the high point in 1910, when production topped eleven million dollars. Thereafter the yield fell off rapidly; a decade later it had dwindled to $150,000 a year. During the years it was riding high, however, Goldfield was one of the nation's best-publicized towns. Many were the attractions it offered. One was the ornate Goldfield Hotel with its mahogany-paneled lobby and lush thirty-dollar-a-day suites. Another was Tex Rickard's Northern House, where on occasion as many as eighty barkeeps were needed to serve its thirsty clientele. Rickard achieved considerable fame in the fall of 1906 when he staged his widely ballyhooed "Battle of the Century," a forty-two-round fight between Battling Nelson and Joe Gans for the lightweight championship of the world.

A number of incidents helped keep Goldfield in the public eye. One that made headlines all over the nation took place in the fall of 1907 when, on President Theodore Roosevelt's orders, federal troops were sent into the area to prevent open warfare between the mineowners and their employees. The trouble began when the owners, concerned over the amount of high-grading going on, took drastic steps to stop the practice. Until then, high-grading had been virtually unknown in Nevada. In the few gold mines that existed there was too little to attract the free-loaders. Silver in most mines occurred in compounds, like silver sulfide or silver chloride, and therefore required chemical processing at a mill, so chiselers had little chance to pocket anything of value. But the Goldfield workings were so rich in "jewelry gold" that it was sometimes possible for a miner to make off with several hundred dollars' worth during a single shift. The practice became so widespread that a number of "fences" went into the business of buying the stolen metal and smuggling it out of town.

When the situation threatened to get out of hand, the owners set up "change rooms" where employees were required to change their clothes on entering and leaving the mines. This caused sweeping indignation, both among the high-graders themselves and among the honest miners as well. An already tense situation was made worse by agents of the powerful Industrial Workers of the World—popularly called the "I.W.W.'s." They gained adherents to their union by denouncing not only the "change rooms" but other allegedly unfair practices, including the reported gouging of workmen at company-operated stores.

At the height of the excitement several companies of United States infantry, commanded by General Frederick Funston, arrived and set up camp on a hillside above the mines. They remained for many months while, in an atmosphere of mutual hostility, negotiations between operators and striking miners continued. Finally concessions on both sides brought about an uneasy peace and, on March 7, 1908, the federal troops were withdrawn and replaced by the Nevada state police.

This was Goldfield's final item of national attention. The mines continued to yield large profits for three years longer. Then, as the richer ore bodies were exhausted, production dropped sharply, and a decline set in that during the course of the next two decades turned Goldfield into a ghost town.

Leadville, Colorado

Among the West's more rambunctious mining towns was Leadville, Colorado. It had all the qualities that made such spots memorable: surpassingly rich mines, easily made—and lost—fortunes, a wide-open code whereby every man was a law unto himself, and as large a collection of picturesque characters as any the country has ever seen.

Situated some seventy-five miles southwest of Denver, the two-mile-high town had its beginning in the spring of 1860 when a prospector named Abe Lee washed a few pans of gravel from the bottom of California Gulch. So rich was his strike that before the year was out the Gulch had a population of five thousand. However, its decline was almost as rapid as its rise, for the placers were soon washed out, and by 1863 Oro City, as it was then called, was all but deserted. It remained so until 1875. In that year two prospectors who had been rewashing the abandoned tailings, worked-over gravel left by earlier miners, became curious about the reddish-colored sand they had been shoveling aside and—as had happened earlier with the troublesome "blue stuff" on Nevada's Comstock Lode—had a sample assayed. It proved to

Miners bringing gold dust to the banking house in Denver City, Colorado.

Harper's Weekly, 1866.

be "a virtually pure carbonate of lead, with a high silver content."

This started a second and far more spectacular boom, one that lasted well over a decade, transformed the camp into a city of thirty thousand and produced a bumper crop of millionaires.

One of this group was a former Vermont stonecutter named H. A. W. Tabor. Tabor had spent fifteen unproductive years in the Colorado mine fields, and by 1875 was making a meager living as postmaster and storekeeper in decaying Oro City. One day two German prospectors entered his shop and asked him to grubstake them on a trip into the back country. More to get rid of them than with any hope of profit, Tabor gave them seventeen dollars' worth of provisions and sent them on their way. The pair, so the story goes, had helped themselves to a jug of whiskey while their benefactor's back was turned and, having sampled it liberally, they stopped beneath a tree only a mile from camp and started to dig. As it happened, they had picked out the only point on the entire mountainside where a deposit of rich silver quartz lay just beneath the surface. They had gone down only a foot or two when they struck what became known as the Little Pittsburg, one of the most valuable mines in the state.

This was the first of a long series of lucky breaks for Oro City's postmaster. Over the next several years his share in the Little Pittsburg netted him $500,000. He then sold his interest for a round million dollars and bought a number of other properties, all of which turned out equally well. One was the Matchless Mine on Fryer Hill, for which he paid $117,000, and which returned him an estimated eleven million dollars. By then Tabor's phenomenal luck had become a byword all over the West. Once he was tricked into buying a salted mine; while those who believed they had "taken him in" gathered about to enjoy their joke, he sent workmen below to deepen the shaft—and promptly struck still another bonanza, the Chrysolite Lode.

Tabor put his newfound wealth to a variety of uses. He developed political ambitions, served a term as mayor of the town—which had meanwhile been renamed Leadville—and, as a reward for his liberal contributions to the Republican campaign chest, was nominated and elected lieutenant governor of the state. He served in this office from 1878 to 1883.

These days of prosperity proved too much for Tabor's wife, Augusta. Having been a boardinghouse keeper for many years, she continued to worry about expenses, chided her husband for his extravagances, nagged him for assurances that they would never be poor again. Harassed by these annoyances, expansive Tabor found a young and comely divorcée, Elizabeth McCourt ("Baby") Doe. She had the ripe-peach complexion of a young woman who is inclined to be plump, relished spending his millions and had no fear of future poverty. With due legal formality, Tabor shunted off Augusta, married Baby Doe and enjoyed buying her carriages with upholstery to match her every dress. To make the ensemble perfect when she went for a drive the horses, too, were selected for colors to suit her mood and costumes—sometimes bays, sometimes sorrels, blacks with gold harness or red trimmings, whites with plumes of green.

In 1883 Tabor received an interim appointment as United States senator to finish the term of H. M. Teller, who had been named Secretary of the Interior in President Arthur's cabinet. In Washington, Tabor remarried Baby Doe and followed the ceremony with an elegant reception at Willard's Hotel. The President of the United States was among the distinguished guests.

Tabor's benefactions included two sumptuous opera houses, one in Leadville and the other in Denver, to which city he moved after his Leadville properties passed their crest. Both structures remained in use for well over three-quarters of a century. Denver's "Tabor Grand" has been described as belonging to the "modified Egyptian Moresque" school of architecture. It stood five stories high with an ornate interior finished in cherry wood and embellished with a profusion of "marble, tapestries and silk." Reputed to have cost a million dollars, it was hailed as the most elaborately appointed playhouse in America.

On the opening night in 1881, Tabor is said to have noticed a large painting of Shakespeare in the foyer.

"Who is that?" he asked. When told, he replied, "William Shakespeare! William Shakespeare!! What in hell did he ever do for Denver? Take down his pitcher and put mine there."

Whether or not this story is true, certainly a large portrait of Tabor, wearing the pompous handle-bar mustache of his era, greeted patrons as they entered "The Grand's" door even after it became a movie theater.

Tabor's flamboyant career ended as modestly as it had begun. A sharp drop in the price of silver, plus the depression of 1893, swept away his fortune, leaving him all but penniless. Through the influence of old-time political friends he was appointed postmaster at Denver, which office he held until his death in 1899. During the years of his reverses he retained ownership of one of his favorite mines, the Matchless, and on his deathbed his advice to Baby Doe was to "hold on to the Matchless." This she faithfully did, living in poverty for more than thirty-five years, in a one-room wooden shack on the property. In ragged clothes, burlap on one foot and an old arctic on the other, she trudged down through the dumps and tipples of deserted mines to Leadville—no sign of plumpness or ruddy health in her drawn cheeks now. At the store she would stuff a few groceries in a paper bag and tell the clerk to "Charge it, please." (The account was duly paid from the city's charity fund.)

Plodding back through mud and snow Baby Doe would huddle again by her little stove, sipping hot tea from a chipped china cup. On the shack's board walls she had pasted newspaper clippings which described the grandeur of her past social triumphs, but they were brittle and yellow with age. Icy, timber-line winds whistled through the cracks, and she died there alone with her memories on March 7, 1935, in her seventy-third year. The newspapers reported that she had frozen to death.

33. *Copper*

The Clifton-Morenci Copper Field, Arizona

FOR MORE THAN three decades after the momentous discovery in the Sutter's Coloma millrace, two metals—gold and silver—were the cornerstones of the mining industry in the West. By the beginning of the 1880's, however, all but a few of the richest fields had been stripped of their treasure, and the value of their yield had fallen to a point where they no longer constituted the region's chief source of wealth.

But, as events were to prove, western mining was not suffering a permanent decline; it was merely entering a new phase. During the latter part of the nineteenth century certain changes were taking place, the effect of which was felt in greater or lesser degree by millions of people all over the globe. This was the advent of what has been called the "age of electricity"—a period when that new source of energy was being put to a widening variety of uses: the illumination of homes, a source of heat, light and power in industry and in many other fields, including transportation and communication. This in turn created an insistent demand for a metal that had long been known to the miners of the West, but for which there was so little market that it had been left virtually untouched. As a conductor of electricity, copper was second only to silver, and by 1880 exploitation of the West's vast deposits of copper ore had begun.

To be sure, small amounts of copper had been mined in the area long before the coming of the electrical age. One of the first to enter the field was the Ajo Copper Company, which in what is now southern Arizona was active as early as 1854. The operation was carried on in the face of all but insuperable difficulties, for to transport their product to the market was an involved and costly process. The ore had to be carried on the backs of burros to the Colorado River, a distance of more than a hundred miles over a barren, waterless countryside. There it was loaded on barges and floated downstream to deep water, then transferred to the holds of sailing ships and sent around the Horn to a smelter at Swansea, Wales. That months-long journey was evidently too severe a handicap, for after only a year or two the Ajo Copper Company passed out of existence.

More than twenty years elapsed before development of the region's vast copper resources was resumed and Arizona began its rise as one of the nation's leading producers of that metal. A number of rich fields were opened. Two were at Clifton and Morenci, close to the New Mexico border; two others were at Clarkdale and Jerome, near the center of the territory, and another centered about Bisbee in the extreme southeast corner.

The discoverer of the Clifton-Morenci field, which was to become one of the world's largest sources of copper, was a prospector named Clifton, after whom the town of Clifton was named; that was in the late 1850's. Then, in 1864, a number of Union soldiers came on the spot while pursuing a band of Apache. After the war, one of them, a scout named Robert Metcalf, returned and staked out a claim, which he called the Longfellow. A growing recognition of the value of copper ore attracted others to the spot, and in 1875 a group of Michigan copper magnates appeared, bought the Longfellow and a number of other claims and organized the Detroit Copper Company. The owners named the field Morenci after a copper town in their home state, and large-scale operations began.

During the first several years the operators of the Morenci field faced difficulties only slightly less severe than those at Ajo two decades earlier. The ore was chipped from the ledges by hand, brought to the surface in wheelbarrows and carried to the mill on the backs of burros. The reduction plant itself was a crude affair, water power being used to pulverize the ore and charcoal for fuel in the furnace. Transporting the copper to the outside was likewise a slow and tedious process. The nearest railroad was eight hundred miles away, and during the weeks-long journey over primitive roads the ox-drawn wagons were frequently attacked by hostile Indians.

But despite these handicaps the mines returned a profit, and gradually more efficient methods were introduced. Ore cars supplanted the wheelbarrows, and, to carry the ore to the mill, a wagon road replaced the burro trail. Then, in 1880, a railroad was built between the Longfellow mine and the mill. To draw the cars over this short line, a small wood-burning locomotive was bought in Pittsburgh, shipped around the Horn to San Francisco and trans-shipped by rail to Yuma. Finally, it was hauled by ox team to Clifton, a distance of more than four hundred miles over "abominable roads." During the years that followed, the mechaniza-tion of the operation continued, with the output mounting steadily. Two generations later, the immense open-pit Morenci mine, a mile wide and several thousand feet deep, together with the group of huge smelters and other works had, in the words of one observer, "a vastness too awe-inspiring to be thought the handiwork of man."

Most of the copper towns closely resembled the earlier gold- and silver-mining com-munities, and Clifton was no exception. One of its widely celebrated features was an impreg-nable "Cliff Jail," blasted out of the solid rock of the mountainside, from which no prisoner ever escaped. When the Mexican who built the jail was paid off, he invested his earnings in a strong local liquor called mescal. He then proceeded to celebrate his handiwork by shooting up a nearby dance hall—and ended as the jail's first inmate.

Arizona's Bisbee Copper

The story of the Morenci mines was duplicated elsewhere in the West. One such field was at Bisbee, two hundred miles farther south. It, too, was discovered by a detachment of United States soldiers while tracking down a band of Apache. They saw an outcrop of copper-bearing ore, and staked out a claim on the floor of the canyon. However, they were too occupied fighting the Indians to do the required development work, and their title to the property lapsed.

Next to appear on the scene was a group of prospectors headed by George Warren. They filed a new claim and began taking out the ore. Then followed an incident typical of many others in the history of western mining. One day during a drinking bout, Warren boasted to a companion that he could run to a spot a hundred yards distant and return to the starting place faster than the other could cover the same distance on horseback. A bet was duly made, Warren wagering his one-ninth interest in the group's claim, the Copper Queen, on the out-come. With other members of the party looking on and cheering their favorites, the race was run. Warren came in second, whereupon he signed over his interest in the property to the victor. It was one of the costliest wagers in history, for had the loser retained his share in the mine, it would ultimately have paid him close to twenty million dollars.

The Copper Queen was the first of many mines that during the next decade were to make the area one of the country's leading producers of copper, a place it still held in 1962. Bisbee, its chief town (named for one of the original owners of the Copper Queen), was built on the floor and sides of two narrow defiles called, respectively, Mule Pass Gulch and Brewery Gulch. So steep were the canyon walls that in many places the foundations of the houses were on a level with the roofs of those immediately below, and it was the boast of their occupants that they could sit on their porches and "spit down the chimneys" of their neighbors.

Bisbee had another distinction. For many years it was the only town of its size in the

"Sunday Morning in the Mines." Painting by Charles Nahl.

West without house-to-house mail delivery, the streets being too steep for postmen to make daily rounds. These streets and surrounding mines and landmarks were given such picturesque names as Jiggerville, Tintown, O.K. Street, Tombstone Canyon, Bucky O'Neil Hill, Brockerville and the Irish Mag mine.

Like other copper towns of the nation, Bisbee's prosperity—or lack of it—depended on the price of that metal. When the demand was heavy and prices up, jobs were plentiful, wages high, and Bisbee's economy flourished. Falling prices had the opposite effect; the mines curtailed their output or shut down completely; unemployment soared, and everyone—merchants, tavern owners, businessmen of all sorts—tightened their belts while they rode out the storm. But although Bisbee's history was one of "boom and bust," the richness and extent of its ore bodies have assured its permanence, and over the years have transformed it from a cluster of rude shacks into a substantial and prosperous town.

Utah's "Jackling Wildcat": Largest of All Copper Mines

Soldiers of the United States Army were responsible for the discovery of still another of the West's great copper mining centers, that at Bingham Canyon, Utah. In 1862 the Third

Infantry of California Volunteers was dispatched to Fort Douglas on the outskirts of Salt Lake City, charged with keeping the Indians under control and the lines of communication open. At Fort Douglas, as at most other frontier army posts, there were long periods of inactivity, and the Californians—many of whom were experienced miners—relieved the tedium of barracks life by doing a bit of prospecting during their spare time. In this they were encouraged by their commander, Colonel Patrick E. Connor. One day in 1863 some of Connor's men brought in a sample of bluish gray rock and asked his permission to have it assayed. The result was highly encouraging; not only was the ore rich in lead, but it also contained measurable amounts of gold and silver.

Bingham Canyon, where the find was made, lay a day's travel to the southwest of Salt Lake City. The place had been named for two brothers who, at the behest of Brigham Young, had settled there in 1848 and engaged in farming and cattle raising. Although the Bingham brothers had done some prospecting there and found what seemed a promising lead, Brigham Young's order prohibiting his followers from mining for gold had discouraged further exploration. Connor and his men, however, were under no such prohibition, and when the colonel learned the result of the assay, he made the news public, promising military protection to all who wished to stake out claims in the canyon.

Several hundred miners responded during the next few months, and toward the end of 1863 the town of Bingham Canyon was laid out. But the early workings yielded only small amounts of gold and silver, and that, plus a lack of roads and the high cost of getting in supplies, caused the camp to languish. A year or two later, however, a second strike was made farther up the canyon, and the area enjoyed a second brief boom. Some two million dollars in gold were mined before the new placers became exhausted, and a second decline followed.

Up to that time Bingham Canyon had been almost exclusively a placer camp. Not until a railroad was built into the area in 1870 did quartz mining begin. Thereupon, a number of shafts were sunk, a smelter was built, and the town entered yet another period of prosperity. During the next fifteen years the chief products of the mines were silver and lead. Although gold was known to be present, it was so combined with other metals that it could not be recovered in profitable quantities by the methods then in use. To overcome that difficulty, the owners of one mine, the Highland Boy, began building a plant designed to treat the ore by a new chemical process.

Before the new mill was completed, however, an event took place that was to have a profound effect on Bingham Canyon's future. As the shaft of the Highland Boy was sunk deeper, a vein of copper ore was struck, one of such extraordinary richness as to attract investors from other copper mining districts and send the prices of the properties soaring. In 1899 a half-interest in the Highland Boy was sold to a New York corporation for twelve million dollars. A second heavy investor was Enos A. Wall, who with a partner, Joseph De Lamar, bought two hundred acres at the upper edge of the field. At the time this seemed a dubious gamble, for while the property contained an abundance of copper ore, it was of such low quality that few believed it could be profitably worked.

Undeterred by the gloomy predictions of the experts, Wall and De Lamar hired two young mining engineers to look over the field and suggest means of developing it. At the end of their survey the pair, Robert Gemmell and Daniel C. Jackling, rendered a report that, in the words of one commentator, "changed the history of copper mining."

This, "the first comprehensive analysis of a mining enterprise based on the treatment of low-grade ores," was rendered late in 1899. One of the engineers, Jackling, backed his faith in the enterprise by buying a share in the property, and prepared to put his theory—which included mass-production methods in handling the ore, plus new milling techniques—to the test. The next task was to raise capital to finance the experiment, and here the sponsors—Wall, De Lamar, Jackling and others—met opposition not only within the industry but in financial circles as well. Few could be induced to invest in what was termed "Jackling's wildcat."

However, one of the nation's largest operators, the United States Reduction and Refining Company, at length agreed to back the venture. By a complex series of deals, the company acquired a controlling interest from De Lamar and Wall. A new corporation, the Utah Copper Company, was organized in 1903, and a pilot plant was built. Seven years later a merger with two other concerns, the Boston Consolidated and the Nevada Consolidated, made it the nation's largest copper company, with a capitalization of one hundred million dollars. Incidentally, the man who brought about that merger, New York attorney Samuel Untermeyer, received a legal fee of a million dollars, said to have been the largest ever paid up to that time.

During the first several years, the Utah Copper Company's ore came from underground workings; then in 1907 surface mining began, steam shovels scooping up the earth and dumping it into ore cars that carried it off to the reduction plant. So vast was the quantity of ore thus removed that after more than half a century the Bingham Canyon pit looked like an immense stadium, hundreds of acres in length and close to two thousand feet deep. Around its sides were a series of terraces where electrically operated shovels loaded the ore onto lines of cars that from the distant rim of the pit resembled toy trains. The copper content of the ore averaged only one per cent—a mere twenty pounds to the ton—yet Bingham Canyon continued to produce approximately 10 per cent of the world's supply. Although during the first fifty years more than two hundred million tons of the metal were mined and milled, it was said that enough remained to last until the year 2000.

Montana Copper Mines and Miners

Another of the West's great copper-producing states is Montana, and as in Arizona and Utah, the fields there were first discovered by miners looking for gold and silver.

The finders of the renowned Butte mine fields—a five-mile-square area that embraces one of the world's greatest concentrations of mineral wealth—were two prospectors, G. O. Humphrey and William Allison, who in the summer of 1864 washed a few pans of gravel from a stream called Silver Bow Creek, near the western boundary of the territory. Encouraged by traces of gold in the bottoms of their pans, they filed their claims—and when news of their modest strike got about, others joined them. By 1867 some four hundred miners were at work on the creek. For several years more the little community prospered moderately; then as the placers were worked out most of the miners left; by 1870 only a few remained.

Another four years passed; then, in 1874, a recent arrival, William Farlin, chipped off a few fragments of a black rock that was abundant in the area and had them assayed. The rock proved to be silver ore of considerable richness. This find brought new life to the declining camp, and Silver Bow Creek entered its second phase, which turned out to be a short-lived silver boom. Two years later the town of Butte was founded, and development of the new field, financed by outside capital, began.

One of those who arrived on the crest of this new boom was Marcus Daly, a veteran of the Nevada silver mines. Acting as agent for a group of Salt Lake City bankers, Daly bought a number of properties and for the next several years oversaw their development. Then he resigned and began working a claim of his own. At first his venture showed little promise, for as the shaft was deepened it was found to contain progressively less silver and more low-grade copper ore. It is said that Daly was on the point of giving up when, at the 400-foot level, the miners' picks unearthed a copper vein of almost unprecedented richness. That find had two results: It marked the beginning of Butte's rise as an important copper town, and it made Daly one of the first of the copper kings.

Many are the stories told of Daly's colorful personality, of his shrewdness in business matters and his unorthodox (and frequently highhanded) behavior. When, in the early 1880's, sulfur-laden fumes from his smelter in Butte grew so dense that gardens withered and died and street lamps had to be kept burning day and night, he abruptly ordered that the plant be moved elsewhere. The spot he chose was a little valley twenty miles farther west, where an abundance of water and limestone—two elements useful in the smelting process—was to be found. While he and a surveyor were inspecting the site and planning the future town, Daly pointed to a herd of cattle grazing nearby and said: "Put the main street there; run it north and south through that nearest cow." His original intention was to call his new settlement Copperopolis, but on learning that a village of that name already existed in the territory, he named it Anaconda in honor of one of his Butte mines.

Anaconda was a "company town," which meant that it was Daly's town, and Daly ruled it with an iron hand. One of the enthusiasms of his later years was horse racing, and Anaconda had a track second to none in the West, where he trained and raced his thoroughbreds. In 1888 he ordered the building of a hotel, one that would be in keeping with the town's importance. He then left with his string of horses for a season of racing at the eastern tracks, and on his return he went to inspect the partially completed hotel. "Doesn't look big enough," he announced. "Add another story." This was done, and his Montana Hotel was long regarded as the most elegant mining town hostelry in the West, its closest rival being the International at Virginia City, Nevada. One of its most celebrated features was the bar; this was patterned after the Hoffman House in New York, and had a representation of Daly's favorite race horse fashioned in mosaic on the marble floor.

Daly's wealth was so great at the time Montana was admitted to statehood in 1889 that he believed he could establish the capital in Anaconda despite its scanty population of only three thousand. To further his ambition he founded a newspaper, the *Anaconda Standard,* which assumed the size and most of the features of a metropolitan journal. Daly outbid the *New York Herald* for artists who gave his paper the dubious distinction of being the first news sheet west of New York to print a Sunday comic section.

Several towns sought the honor of becoming the state capital, and Helena, which had been the territorial capital in 1875, became Anaconda's greatest rival. Helena, located sixty miles northwest across the mountains from Anaconda, had started in 1864 as a gold-mining town. Later, when that metal became exhausted, silver took its place. Helena's gold and silver are said to have produced more than fifty millionaires. In the period immediately before Montana became a state, the town was indulging in an orgy of prosperous display. The "best people" built cupola-crested mansions, decorated their lawns with marble statues, iron dogs and bronze stags. Liveried servants and fine carriages spun up and down Last Chance Gulch —the main street in a hollow that opened on the wide plain called Prickly Pear Valley. Even a man as rich as Marcus Daly should have known that he had only a slim chance to win a contest for the capital against such a town, but he made a good fight and might have won had it not been for the energetic opposition led by a neighbor of his in Butte. William Andrews Clark was a business rival, wealthy, ambitious and fully as capable as Daly.

The two men, Daly and Clark, were as different as two men could be. Daly had been a poor Irish boy with little education who worked his way up from a pick and shovel to managerial status before investing on his own account. A self-effacing man, almost timid in a crowd, he had no desire for political office, but among friends in a smoke-filled room he expressed himself boldly and was willing to back his opinions with his wealth. Clark, on the other hand, was an office seeker, a man always eager to make a speech. A native of Pennsylvania, he was well educated, spoke French, appreciated good art and had traveled extensively in Europe.

Both Daly and Clark had conflicting mining interests in Butte and in several other towns. Both held interests in rival banks and rival stores throughout western Montana. The fact that Daly wanted to make Anaconda the state capital was enough to make Clark insist that it be elsewhere.

Clark, with his wealth and his oratory, beat Daly and his newspaper's well-planned campaign. Helena got the capital, but Daly determined to get revenge. His first chance came in 1894, when Clark sought a seat in the United States Senate. In those days senators were elected by state legislatures. Daly and Clark were both Democrats, and during the infighting to gain control of the legislature no holds were barred. Bribes, threats and promises were lavished by both sides. Butte, the largest city in the state, became the focal point of the battle.

On election day supporters of both men stormed the polling places in such numbers that the result was utter confusion. Each faction accused the other of having stuffed the ballot boxes, and each sent its slate of delegates to Helena. This deadlocked the legislature which, after weeks of wrangling, solved its problem by naming four senators-elect—two Republicans and two Democrats, one of the latter being Clark.

Daly appeared to have been defeated in the second round, but appearances are sometimes deceptive. The fight continued in Washington. After a long and stormy debate in Congress the Republican-controlled Senate voted to seat the two members of its own party.

Thus Clark lost and Daly won the second round—but that was not the end of it. Clark bided his time, and in 1899 when the Democrats got control of the Montana legislature he managed to beat the Daly forces again and was elected senator. This time he was seated, but trouble still pursued him. His enemies in Montana complained that he had been fraudulently elected, and when a Senate committee was appointed to investigate, Clark resigned. Thereupon, in the absence of the Republican governor who was temporarily out of the state, the lieutenant governor, a Democrat, appointed Clark to fill the seat he had just vacated. The governor returned and further complicated the situation by rescinding Clark's appointment

Harper's Weekly, 1888.

Rival hotels in a mining town.

and naming a Republican, Martin Maginnis, in his place. The Senate refused to accept Maginnis, and for the next two years Montana had to be content with only one United States senator. Finally, in 1901, Clark achieved his ambition. Daly had died in 1900, and the legislature once again elected Clark. This time he was seated, served one term and then retired from public life. Thereafter he devoted himself to managing his extensive mining properties, while Montana politics, after more than a decade of bitter wrangling, returned to something approaching normal.

34. *Quicksilver*

IN THE EARLY SPANISH days Mexican *rancheros* noticed that some Indians south of the San Francisco area painted their faces and bodies a brilliant red. They did not know that this pigment had any value, that the lucky man who laid claim to its source would become a rival of the Rothschilds—wealthiest of Europe's capitalists—and that the struggle for its title would leave a blemish on the record of Abraham Lincoln. Indeed the contest for title to California's cinnabar mines might possibly have changed the final outcome of the Civil War.

Twenty years before the war, while California was still a Mexican province, Secundino

Robles and his brother Leodero, with José Castro, took some of the red pigment to a nearby cavalry post. The commander, Andrés Castillero, recognized it as cinnabar—the source of mercury. He organized a stock company of thirty-two shares. The Robles brothers held four shares, Castro four and Castillero the balance. The firm was named the New Almadén Company after the famous Almadén mercury mines of Spain, the largest in the world. Those mines were controlled by the Rothschilds who held a monopoly of the mercury market and thus dictated the price.

The Mexicans placed an American, William G. Chard, in charge of a reduction mill. This was a difficult assignment, for formal equipment of all sorts was lacking, and Chard was forced to make ingenious use of whatever was at hand.

> Taking several gun-barrels [wrote the California historian, Hubert H. Bancroft], he filled them with bits of the broken ore, stopped the vents with clay, placed the muzzles in a vessel of water, and built a fire around the other end. The heat vaporized the mercury, which, passing into the water, was condensed, and precipitated in the form of metal. Chard next tried a furnace, which proved a failure. His third experiment was with six try-pots used by whalers, capable of holding 3 or 4 tons of ore. By inverting one over the other he formed a furnace, and by the application of heat, and conducting the vapor into water, succeeded in saving about 2,000 pounds of quicksilver.

However, California was then too remote from the world's markets to make the operation profitable, much less pose any competition for the Rothschild interests. That would come later. In August, 1846, Chard and his Indian helpers were discharged and the primitive plant shut down.

But not for long. The transfer of California from Mexico to the United States in 1848, and the discovery of gold there the same year caused an urgent demand for mercury from miners in the nearby Mother Lode. Mercury's ability to amalgamate with gold made it extremely valuable for recovering the very fine particles of that metal. Castillero, back in Mexico after the transfer of sovereignty, sold part of his interest in the abandoned cinnabar mine to the British firm of Barron, Forbes and Company, which managed mines south of the United States border. This company renewed the California operations on a large scale, shipping machinery and other equipment from England. An experienced engineer was put in charge, and New Almadén became, and long remained, America's largest source of mercury.

By 1852 six big furnaces were in use. The product, packed in iron canisters weighing seventy-six pounds each, was sent by oxcart to Alviso at the southern end of San Francisco Bay. There it was loaded on light-draft boats and carried to Stockton, Sacramento and other valley towns, from which it was forwarded to the diggings. During the next few years the New Almadén owners found a ready market, at sixty cents a pound, for all the mercury they could produce. Toward the end of the 1850's, however, placer mining slackened off. Fewer and bigger operations required less quicksilver, and the demand became less urgent. But the decline was only temporary. When Nevada's rich Comstock Lode was opened in 1859, a new and even greater market opened. Since mercury amalgamated with silver as readily as it did with gold, the New Almadén entered a second period of prosperity. By the mid-1860's five hundred men were at work in the mines and mill, and on the floor of the valley the town of

New Almadén developed, complete with shops, bars and restaurants. On the hillside above, rows of quaint wooden cottages housed the workmen.

During this period, the Rothschilds realized that a real competitor had broken their monopoly and might force down the price of mercury. Thus the New Almadén Company became tremendously important, not alone to California but to European financiers, and a group of American speculators—probably backed by Rothschild interests—schemed to get control of the mines. The transfer of California's sovereignty from Mexico to the United States gave such manipulators a splendid opportunity to question the validity of the title, and President Lincoln's most intimate friends seem to have been in this scheme. Among them was Leonard Swett who had done so much to nominate Lincoln for the Presidency; Ward Hill Lamon, a former law partner; and at least three members of the President's cabinet. A decision on the title was pending before the Supreme Court, and Lincoln, harassed by the uncertainties of the war and prospects of Lee's invasion of Pennsylvania (which was stopped at Gettysburg), failed to investigate the entire situation. Taking his friends' recommendations, he signed with undue haste an order which deprived the New Almadén operators of their property.

The legal principle which Lincoln cited to justify his order, if applied to other California titles, might invalidate most of them. Naturally this possibility caused wide protest. California's entire economy was threatened.

Frederick Low, a Lincoln man, was a candidate for governor in the fall of 1863. Should he be defeated at the polls, a man opposed to Lincoln's administration would assume the office.

California contained many Confederate sympathizers, as well as those who wanted to set up an independent Republic of the Pacific. These groups were part of the anti-Lincoln faction. Had they obtained control and deprived the North of California's gold, diverting it to the South, the outcome of the Civil War as well as the future development of the United States might have been altogether different. Lincoln saw this danger and canceled his order—a humiliating but wise act.

New Almadén's period of activity lasted more than twenty years, until in the late 1880's a decline in the price of mercury, plus the approaching exhaustion of the deposits of cinnabar, sharply reduced production. Small-scale operations continued, nevertheless, until after the turn of the century. The mill was then dismantled, the workmen and others departed, and New Almadén joined the ranks of the ghost towns. More than fifty years later one of the few surviving relics of the old days was the Casa Grande, the ornate twenty-room home of the mine superintendent, which stood at the head of the town's main street.

The coastal area of central California has many deposits of cinnabar, and a number of these were worked during the silver mining boom. All have long since been abandoned, and all but one were soon forgotten. The single exception was the Silverado Mine on the slope of Mount St. Helena at the head of the Napa Valley—and it is remembered only because of its literary associations. A young Scot, Robert Louis Stevenson, and his bride spent several weeks there in the summer of 1880; later he wrote engagingly of their stay in a little book called *Silverado Squatters*.

California's contribution to the world's mercury production of that time is impressive. In 1881 the output of the world's mines totaled 115,600 seventy-six-pound flasks, of which, 60,851 flasks were from California (26,000 flasks were from New Almadén).

35. *Black Diamonds*

AT THE CLOSE of the period covered by this book, beds of coal still lay under large areas on both sides of the Rockies in quantities sufficient to supply the world's needs for centuries to come. The Colorado coal fields alone still occupy 20,000 square miles and, according to an estimate of the U.S. Geological Survey in 1959, contain upward of 500 billion tons. In neighboring Utah, deposits from eight to seventeen feet thick underlie one-sixth of the state's area. Other huge fields, most of them still untouched, exist at many other places from Arizona and New Mexico to the Canadian border.

Coal mining in the West was for many years a comparatively small operation. Until the coming of the railroads and the building of factories, smelters and other industrial plants, coal was chiefly used for fuel by ranchmen and in nearby communities. In general, the mines were worked only until timbering became necessary to prevent cave-ins; they were then abandoned and new shafts sunk elsewhere.

The presence of coal was known in Utah at least as early as 1847. The first Mormons arrived that year and Indians showed a party of them pieces of a mysterious "rock that burns." However, few of the deposits were worked during the next decade, and then only in dilatory fashion.

One of the earliest fields to be extensively developed lay east of San Francisco at the base of Mount Diablo where, in the mid-1850's, prospectors seeking gold found large quantities of coal. Presumably it was low-grade, though after a hundred years the exact quality is difficult to determine. Records describe it as "of half-bituminous character"—an uncertain analysis, surely. Coal is composed of the element carbon. In crystallized forms, carbon may be either a diamond or the graphite used in pencils, depending on the nature of the crystals. Neither form is combustible. Strangely enough, when this same carbon appears in noncrystallized form, as coal, it burns readily and the higher the percentage of pure carbon in the coal the more readily it burns. Coal that is almost pure carbon is called "hard coal," or anthracite. Soft, or bituminous, coal has many impurities mixed in the carbon. It burns, but the impurities make a heavy, foul-smelling smoke. If Mount Diablo coal was "half-bituminous," as records indicate, it was probably even more impure than standard bituminous coal, and this might account for the pall of dense black smoke which hung continuously over early-day San Francisco when Mount Diablo coal was used as a fuel for homes and factories.

In 1861, 23,000 tons of Mount Diablo coal were mined, and the output continued to increase annually. As usual in most coal regions, whether in Pennsylvania or in Australia, Welshmen came to the pits like flies to a honey jar. Having mined coal for generations in the old country, they felt at home and met their own kind of people at the Diablo mines. Two towns,

181

Nortonville and Somersville, mushroomed there, and by 1874 production reached a peak of 206,000 tons. Thereafter, the depletion of the field, plus the competition of better grade, and less smoky, coal imported cheaply on ships from England and Australia, brought a sharp decline. The region's last mine closed in the early 1880's. The miners and merchants drifted away. Nortonville and its neighbor, Somersville, fell to ruins. By 1963 the only reminders of the Mount Diablo coal industry were great heaps of waste rocks below the abandoned tunnels and a group of moss-covered gravestones, many bearing Welsh names, in the cemetery on the ridge between the two dead settlements.

Typical of the evolution of the coal industry in other parts of the West was the development of the fields in and about the town of Helper, Utah. The first settler in that region of canyons and high desert plateaus was a Mormon named Teancum Pratt who, with his two wives and two children, arrived in 1870. Finding an abundance of coal in the vicinity, Pratt pre-empted other land and hopefully laid out a town, but as there was no profit in coal when there was no railroad for shipping it, he had to support himself and family by farming, while he waited for the day when the exploitation of his coal fields could begin. He had a long wait. It was not until the tracks of the narrow-gauge Rio Grande Railroad reached the valley in the early 1880's that the town of Pratt became a reality. Ironically, it did not retain its founder's name for long. The railroad made the place a division point, built a roundhouse and living quarters for the crews, and—because the "helper engines" needed to push trains up the grade to nearby Soldier Summit were stationed there—the spot was rechristened Helper.

During the next few years Helper, and the several other coal towns that grew up in the area, differed little from other western mining towns. Their streets were thronged with miners from many parts of the world, who lived in rough board cabins or rooming houses and spent their earnings in the stores, bars, cardrooms, pool halls and other places of entertainment thoughtfully provided by the companies. As time passed, some of the original villages were abandoned while others became well-ordered towns, the workers' houses clinging in picturesque fashion to the steep canyonsides and substantial buildings of brick and stone lining the streets below.

In the Helper mines, as in those of other coal-mining districts, the possibility of explosion was an ever-present hazard. Gases and inflammable coal dust filled the stopes, calling for constant vigilance to protect the workmen below. And despite elaborate ventilating systems and other safety measures accidents were frequent, sometimes with heavy loss of life.

One of the area's major disasters took place in the Winterquarters Mine near the town of Scofield, Utah. On the morning of May 1, 1900, the thud of an underground explosion shook the town, and the inhabitants, well aware of what the sound meant, hurried to the mine head. Their worst fears were realized, for the tremendous explosion, which presumably had been set off by a blast of dynamite, had ignited the coal dust and sent the lethal fumes into every part of the mine. Of the 310 men below, only 105 escaped. A Salt Lake City newspaper, the *Daily Tribune,* reported:

> The bodies as they were brought out were placed in company buildings, boarding houses, the Mormon church, the schoolhouse, and all available buildings. . . . Coffins came to Scofield by the carloads, and as the supply in Utah ran short, some were sent from Denver. At nearly every home caskets could be seen, either on the porch or through

the open door, sometimes one, sometimes several. . . . President McKinley expressed his condolence, and President Loubet of France sent a message of sympathy.

When an underground vein would begin to burn, it had to be extinguished at once or not at all. Once out of control, there was nothing to do but to seal off the buring area or else abandon the mine entirely. Some underground fires continued to smolder for years, eating their way along the entire length of the veins. Finally some years later one effectual means was found for coping with the problem. Miners made wide cuts through the veins well beyond the burning area and filled the space with earth. Thus contained, a fire would burn itself out.

By the twentieth century, the bulk of the West's coal was being mined by mass-production methods which included power-operated drills that broke out the coal from the underground deposits, or steam shovels that scooped it from surface pits to dump it into strings of coal cars. Most of this coal came from the fields at Colstrip, Montana, the Carbon-Emery field in Utah, and Colorado's Moffat County and San Juan Basin.

36. *Precious Stones*

The Great Diamond Hoax

PERHAPS THE LEAST known of all phases of the western treasure hunt was the search for precious stones; yet it had been carried on since the first white men put foot in the territory. More than four centuries ago, when Coronado set off in search of the Seven Cities of Cíbola, the lure that drew him into the wilderness was his belief that the buildings of the Seven Cities were adorned with rubies and sapphires.

The search has gone on ever since, and although no treasure-trove such as Coronado sought has come to light, the list of the region's precious and semiprecious stones is a long and varied one. Among those that have been found, and at one time or another mined in commercial quantities, are the following: agates, turquoises, jaspers, opals, sapphires, rubies, garnets, onyxes, amethysts and topazes. As early as 1865 opals were being mined at Mokelumne Hill in California's Mother Lode—and finding a ready market among the gem merchants of Europe. Idaho, which is sometimes called the Gem State, has long been noted both for its opals and its "flawless blood-red rubies," while neighboring Montana is the nation's main source of gem sapphires, which are used chiefly in the making of watches and other precious instruments. And, of course, the Indians of the Southwest have been fashioning jewelry from silver and turquoise since long before the coming of the white men.

But although the hunt for precious stones had been going on for centuries before the California gold rush, it attracted so little attention that for more than three decades after '49 the general public, absorbed in the riches of the region's gold and silver mines, hardly knew it existed. Then, in the early 1870's, came startling news: the announcement of the discovery of a field of gems that promised to exceed in value the combined output of all the West's other mines.

The story of that sensational strike—and of its no-less-sensational aftermath—began prosaically enough. In the summer of 1871 two strangers appeared at the office of the Bank of California in San Francisco. They identified themselves as miners just back from a prospecting trip and made known their wish to deposit in the bank's vault a canvas bag, the contents of which, they hinted, were of great value. This, naturally enough, aroused the curiosity of the bank officials, for the Nevada silver mines were then producing heavily, and the speculative fever was high among all classes.

When the pair, Philip Arnold and John Slack, were asked to say what the bag contained, they refused; however, on further urging, they agreed to open it for the inspection of several local citizens, including the bank's president, William C. Ralston, after first swearing them to secrecy. A handful of stones of various sizes and shapes were poured out onto Ralston's desk, and Arnold, spokesman for the pair, explained that they were uncut diamonds, part of a great store he and his partner had come upon during their recent trip. When pressed for further details, they again refused; they had, said Arnold, made a surpassingly rich discovery and had no intention of sharing it with others. But when Ralston suggested that the stones be examined by an expert to determine if they were really diamonds, they readily agreed. This was done. The stones were submitted to a leading San Francisco jeweler; he unhesitatingly pronounced them genuine.

Among the little group who shared the secret, excitement was intense. Western mining appeared to be on the verge of a new phase, one that promised fantastic returns to those who controlled the new field. So much pressure was brought to bear on the discoverers that at length, with apparent reluctance, they agreed to permit two men selected by Ralston to visit the spot and make a personal examination. Arnold and Slack insisted, however, that the visitors be blindfolded while approaching and leaving the field.

This proposal was agreed to and duly carried out. The pair, one of whom was David D. Colton, a well-known San Francisco attorney, went by train to a small station on the Union Pacific—probably Table Rock west of Rawlins, Wyoming—and were met by Arnold, who drove them many miles into the sage-covered countryside. Finally they donned the blindfolds, and having reached the field, removed them and made their inspection. They returned to San Francisco and reported their findings: The richness of the field, they asserted, far exceeded their expectations; it was literally strewn with diamonds.

Plans to exploit the find got promptly under way. A ten-million-dollar corporation was proposed, with half the stock to be given Arnold and Slack, and the remainder divided among Ralston and his friends, a group of San Francisco capitalists. There being no further need for secrecy, some of the diamonds were put on display in the window of a Market Street jeweler. News of the discovery made the expected sensation, though some were skeptical. Several local editors advised caution, pointing out that investors had often been duped by wildcat mining schemes, and urging the public to await further proof before risking its savings.

To allay such fears and prove beyond doubt the authenticity of the find, the company officials sent the stones to Tiffany and Company in New York and had them examined and appraised by that firm's diamond expert. The Tiffany expert, too, pronounced them genuine, fixing their value at about $150,000. That appeared to remove the last doubts. The San Francisco and New York Mining and Commercial Company was duly incorporated, and an eminent mining engineer, Henry Janin, was engaged to make a thorough survey of the property. Janin spent some time at the field. His report was quoted as saying that twenty-five miners could wash out a million dollars' worth of stones in a month. This boosted the excitement still higher, starting dozens of men to prospecting for jewels throughout the West—men who did not know the difference between a diamond and a piece of glass and thought a carat was a vegetable.

During this excitement the directors of the new company abandoned their plan of offering stock to the public; instead, it was closely held by the original group, all of whom were confident they would soon become multimillionaires. Meanwhile, Arnold and Slack had been persuaded to sell their interest, and the San Francisco group became sole owners. The precise amount paid the pair was never made public. One version placed the sum at $300,000 each; others had it higher. Whatever the amount, the buyers were convinced they had driven a hard bargain.

They were presently not so sure. In the fall of 1872 a telegram reached the company office at San Francisco. Its sender was Clarence King, a well-known geologist and writer, who was then engaged in a government survey of the 40th parallel. King's wire stated bluntly that the diamond field was a fraud and that he could prove the so-called mines had been salted. On its receipt several company officials were dispatched to the scene where the geologist met them and proceeded to make good his promise.

King explained that he and several companions had visited the spot some days earlier and had located a number of stones, one of which on being examined showed unmistakable evidence of having been partially cut and polished. This, naturally enough, had aroused his suspicion, and further investigation had turned up added evidences of chicanery. Among them were holes that had been made in the ground by a sharp instrument, each with a diamond at its bottom; also several stones were found in mock crevices, where they had been pressed during the salting process.

The party returned to San Francisco, their dreams of fortune shattered, and set about the melancholy task of winding up the company's affairs. Details of the clever swindle soon came to light. The gems were "niggerheads"—stones of little value used chiefly for industrial purposes—that had come from the diamond fields of South Africa. Arnold and Slack had bought them several years earlier for $15,000 from dealers in Amsterdam and London.

For some time efforts to find the guilty pair, who had disappeared in the meantime, were unavailing. Arnold was eventually located at his former home in Kentucky, and when threatened with criminal prosecution is said to have paid back $150,000 of the money he had received from Ralston and his associates. Slack was never apprehended.

The San Franciscans absorbed their losses and the Great Diamond Hoax passed into history. However, two events kept its memory alive for a few years longer. Ralston had one of the defunct company's stock certificates framed and hung on a wall of his office as a warning against further rash investments, and Asbury Harpending, who was also duped, wrote a book about the hoax. Other writers enlarged on the story placing the "field" in Colorado, Utah and even Arizona. The best evidence, however, indicates that it was located in Wyoming as described above.

Giant redwood trees of California. Painting by Albert Bierstadt.

37. *Timber*

NEARLY ALL THE letters, diaries, journals and other memorabilia left behind by the first white men to visit the western third of the nation have one thing in common. Whether their writers came by land or sea, as trappers, traders, members of exploring parties, or in the ships of early navigators, few failed to mention the great forests that covered huge areas from the Rockies to the Pacific.

Although some visitors, more farseeing than the others, realized how important these vast stands of timber would be to the future economy of the region, others took a contrary view, pointing out that in much of the country the trees would have to be cleared away before the land could be put under cultivation and made productive.

It was those who came by sea who first put the western forests to practical use. Initially the trees they cut were used to replace masts, spars, yards or other gear that had been damaged during long voyages. Later, though, supplies of timber were taken aboard, to be sold or traded for other goods at later ports of call.

One of the earliest to enter the timber trade was Captain John Meares, who sailed from Puget Sound in 1788 with a cargo of ship spars lashed to the deck of his vessel, the barkentine *Felice*. The *Felice* met with such severe storms en route to its destination—the Portuguese colony of Macao on the coast of China—that the deck cargo had to be jettisoned. Nonetheless, Captain Meares must be credited with laying the foundation of what was to become an important export trade.

It is interesting to see how closely the early West's two basic industries—mining and lumbering—were allied, and to what extent the fortunes of the one were bound up with those of the other. It was because of Sutter's need for lumber that he built the sawmill at Coloma in the first place; the gold found in the mill's tailrace spurred the great rush of 1849–50; and the desperate need for lumber in the fast-growing mining towns and camps of California gave the industry its first real impetus.

One region whose economy was enormously stimulated by these events was the heavily forested Pacific Northwest. Although logging and processing of the area's timber had been carried on to some extent since the establishment of fur-trading outposts on Puget Sound and at the mouth of the Columbia River in the early 1800's, the operation remained a small one until the California gold rush started almost half a century later. That event, however, completely changed the picture, for not only did residents of the new mining settlements to the south have pressing need for lumber, but they were seemingly able and willing to pay whatever might be asked for it. The prospect of an assured market, at high prices, for whatever they could produce caused hundreds of northerners to enter the lumber business. By the early 1850's, at a dozen bays and inlets on the Oregon and Washington coasts, the edges of the forests were resounding with the sound of woodmen's axes and the screech of early-day sawmills.

By today's standards the methods then used seem crude in the extreme. In the woods,

the "fallers" passed up the larger trees—some of which were twelve feet or more in diameter
—as too cumbersome to handle, and chose instead those of from three to four feet. Once a
tree had been "felled," the "buckers" sawed it into twenty-four- or thirty-foot lengths.

The next step was to move the logs to mills, and for that purpose "skid roads" were built.
That is, small trees were laid crosswise on the ground and greased with tallow or shark oil,
so that logs could be drawn over them by multiple teams of oxen. These roads were abandoned
when "big-wheel rigs"—curious-looking carts that carried the logs suspended beneath their
fifteen-foot-high wheels—came into use. Later still, the logs were snaked out of the woods at
the end of long lines, with wood-burning donkey engines supplying the power. Meanwhile,
the output of the mills was stepped up by the introduction of improved methods and machinery. Steam engines supplanted the earlier water wheels as a source of power, and other
more-efficient equipment, including high-speed circular saws, came into use.

During the quarter-century after the first mill was built in 1847, lumbering in the Northwest was largely confined to the area fronting on Puget Sound. There the forests grew down
to the shore, and the finished product could be loaded directly from the mills to the decks
of ships that carried it to markets in California and, later, in South America and China. The
wood products manufactured there, both for domestic use and for export, were from the stands
of Douglas fir, cedar, hemlock, spruce and other trees native to that area.

At the same time, the great forests of white and yellow pine, cottonwood and aspen east
of the Cascades stood almost untouched, awaiting the settlement of the "inland empire" and
the opening of other markets by the building of railroads. The completion of the Northern
Pacific Railroad in the early 1880's marked the beginning of a new era in that region, for by
the act of Congress that chartered the road in 1864 the company was granted alternate sections
of land for twenty miles on both sides of the tracks over the entire distance. Much of this was
through dense forests, and the company, finding itself in possession of millions of acres of
choice timberland, offered it for sale at bargain prices, often as low as two dollars an acre.
This was to hasten logging and milling operations in the region the railroad served, and so
increase its own revenues by hauling the product to eastern markets.

It was at about this time that a process long familiar in the richer mining districts of the
West was repeated in the northern woods. That is, a group of large, well-financed companies
entered the field, bought up many of the more desirable properties, and by mergers and con-
solidations assumed control of large segments of the industry. One of the most powerful of
these newcomers was the far-flung Weyerhaeuser empire. Its founder, a German emigrant
named Frederick Weyerhaeuser, was long the industry's dominant figure. Beginning in the
early 1860's with a single Wisconsin sawmill, he increased his holdings at such speed that
less than a decade later he was credited with heading "the largest lumber syndicate of the
time." By 1890 numerous Weyerhaeuser mills and logging crews were active in the forests
of Wisconsin, Minnesota, Michigan and other states on both sides of the Mississippi; then, as
the forests there were depleted, he turned to the practically untouched timberlands of the
Northwest. His purchases there were on a prodigious scale. To cite one example: In 1890, by
a single transaction, he acquired title to one million acres of railroad land in Washington and
Oregon.

During that same period several other concerns were also buying with a lavish hand.
Throughout the final decades of the century, as the forests elsewhere were logged over,

Hauling logs.

Sawing off logs.

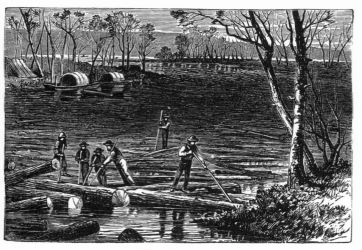

Floating logs.

The log jam.

Loading the ship.

Lumberman's cabin.

lumberjacks and mill hands moved westward by the thousands, setting up camps in the woods of half-a-dozen states and mills beside their rivers or bays. The newcomers were a varied and picturesque crew: Swedes from Minnesota and Michigan, Yankees from Maine, and veterans of the yellow pine forests of the Southeast. But whatever their background or training, all had one quality in common: a thorough knowledge of their trade learned in the hard school of experience. The woodsman of the early West was a skilled and resourceful craftsman, and he had need of both qualities.

Not only was the work hard and often dangerous, but living conditions were anything but luxurious. The usual loggers' camp—whether in the pine, fir or spruce forests of the Northwest, in the California redwood district or in any of a dozen other lumbering regions— was no more than a crude cookshack plus a bunkhouse or two, all hastily thrown up and designed to serve only until the nearby woods were logged over. Nor was the nearest town— which might be several days' travel distant—likely to offer anything more in the way of entertainment than the bars, pool halls and poker tables common to all frontier settlements of the period.

By all accounts, the lumber-milling towns of the West saw little of the violence, gunfire and general hell-raising that distinguished the early-day mining camps. That is not to imply that the average lumberjack was a particularly well-behaved individual, or that, in town on a Saturday night, he conducted himself in an always orderly fashion. On such occasions the per capita consumption of hard liquor was said to have been high, the arguments long and noisy and the resulting brawls both frequent and bloody. But knives, clubs and shooting irons were seldom brought forth during such encounters, and the loggers straggled back to camp next day nursing nothing more serious than aching heads and skinned knuckles.

38. *Black Gold*

ONE OF THE West's long-neglected natural resources was gas. The following excerpt from Bancroft's *History of California,* published in 1890, will make clear how lightly this immensely valuable product was once regarded. Having stated that bitumen and tar were "very plentiful" in some localities and that they "were used, mixed with sand, in making asphalt pavements in San Francisco," he added: "As might be expected, from the presence of the substances named above, natural gas is sometimes discovered in boring artesian wells, but has not yet been much used for lighting or heating purposes." This of a product that only seven decades later was being produced and consumed at the rate of more than five hundred billion cubic feet annually in the state of California alone!

Closely allied to natural gas was another product—one that later formed the basis of a great industry in the West—namely, oil. To be sure, the "oil trade" played an important part in the economy of the Pacific Coast as early as the first half of the nineteenth century; however, the source of supply lay not under the earth, but in the once-numerous schools of whales in the waters of the north Pacific. From the 1820's until the Civil War time, fleets of whalers provided a supply of oil ample for the needs of the day—that is, for use in lamps, as lubricants and in the making of soap, leather dressing and similar products.

Oddly enough, although the presence of petroleum, in the form of a viscous black substance that exuded from the ground, had been known since Spanish-Mexican days—and had been used as a roofing material on the early adobes—its true value long went unrecognized. It was the development of the Pennsylvania oil fields in the early 1860's that belatedly drew attention to the western "tar pits." The new industry got off to a slow start. Technical problems hampered the refinement of western oil for, unlike that of the Pennsylvania fields, it had an asphaltum rather than a paraffin base. Until the development of new methods of treating the crude oil, only two products were produced in quantity: namely, coal oil and axle grease.

The building in the mid-1870's of California Star Oil Company's refinery near the present town of Newhall may be marked the real beginning of the oil industry in the West, for it antedated by a number of years similar developments in the fields of Texas, Oklahoma, Montana and elsewhere. The pilot plant at Newhall drew attention to the many uses to which these underground reservoirs of "black gold" might be put, and public indifference to the struggling industry was replaced by a wave of speculation in oil stocks that, like so many of these ventures, impoverished many while enriching a few. Not all the newly formed companies, however, were of the wildcat variety. With some of the capital raised by the sale of shares, new wells were sunk and new refineries built, and by 1885 California's annual output of crude oil had reached 500,000 barrels, with production elsewhere also increasing steadily.

Even so, the operation was still in its primitive stages. The oil was drawn from the shallow wells by pumps operated by horse or mule power, and in some cases by windmills; it was transported to the refineries in pipes two inches or less in diameter, and the finished product was delivered to the public in tanks mounted on horse-drawn wagons.

By the beginning of the 1890's, petroleum was being put to so many new uses that the supply failed to fill the demand. Production had to be stepped up in existing fields and a number of new ones opened. Among the largest of these new fields—to name but a few—were the Spindletop, near Beaumont, Texas; the Salt Creek fields of Wyoming (later the scene of the famous Teapot Dome Scandals); those centering about Tulsa and Oklahoma City, Oklahoma; and Signal Hill, Santa Fe Springs and others in California. At the turn of the century the industry was well launched on a course that would ultimately add many billions to the nation's wealth.

This was the period, too, when many of the future oil barons laid the foundations of their great fortunes. Among them was Edward L. Doheny, destined to become nationally known as one of the corrupt figures who helped discredit President Harding's administration. Born in Wisconsin, Doheny might have been reckoned a failure until he was thirty-seven years old. Apparently an impractical dreamer, like the gold prospectors of old, he was a drifter looking for the main chance. Then, in 1893, with C. A. Canfield as partner, he sank a shaft on a plot of land near the future center of Los Angeles, the two men's only tools being a pick, shovel and hand-operated windlass. They had gone down but a short distance when a quantity of heavy black oil started oozing from the walls of the shaft—the first of many millions of barrels that were to be pumped from that area during the next several decades.

Now, Doheny displayed great business ability and a genius for organization. He took a leading part in the exploitation of this field and of a number of others in California and elsewhere in the West, as well as in Mexico. His greatest contribution to the industry, however, lay in another direction; that was in opening up a vast new market for the product. Urged by Doheny in the late 1890's, the Santa Fe Railroad began experiments to determine the feasibility of using crude oil as a substitute for wood or coal in its locomotives. The success of the experiments led to the widespread use of petroleum not only by railroads and steamship lines but as a source of heat or power in numberless factories and homes all over the nation.

Until well after the turn of the century the industry's chief function was the production and processing of crude oil. Then came a development that, although few could have realized it at the time, was to have a profound effect not only on the oil business but on the country as a whole—the invention of the internal combustion engine and its use as a means of propelling the odd-looking vehicles that in the earliest days were known as horseless carriages and which within a generation would revolutionize American life. As the automobile industry grew, Doheny, with all his oil interests, became fabulously wealthy—so rich he could financially afford to offer the Secretary of State, Albert Fall, $100,000 for an oil concession, and see him jailed for accepting it.

39. *Other Treasures Without End*

IN ADDITION TO the treasures we have covered, several more should be briefly noted—briefly because while their presence had long been known, few were mined to any extent until well after the turn of the century.

Much of the mineral wealth of the West—the great stores of iron, lead, zinc, manganese, tungsten, molybdenum, uranium and a number of others—was untouched until the industrialization of the nation, plus scientific advances in many fields, made their mining and processing possible, from both the technical and economic standpoints.

The mercury mines at New Almadén and the lead which was mined in small quantities long before that date were exceptions. For years hunters and trappers had melted down bits of lead-bearing ore and cast the metal into bullets. However, it was not until the twentieth century was well advanced that most such metals were produced in commercial quantities. Among these were molybdenum and manganese (both widely used in the hardening of steel) and uranium. The first became Colorado's most valuable mineral product, while manganese would be extensively mined in New Mexico, Arkansas and Montana. Uranium would come mainly from Colorado and Utah.

A lack of markets close at hand long prevented development of the West's vast deposits of iron ore, and only after the rapid rise in population in the early 1900's and the subsequent industrial development of the region did it become possible for western steel to compete with that from the eastern centers. Hence, the group of "Little Pittsburghs" found in many parts of the West by the middle of the twentieth century were all of comparatively recent origin.

PART FOUR

"End of the Trail" by James Earle Fraser

Indians and Soldiers of the American West

by Don Russell

"Indian Scouts." Engraving, after drawing by Frederic Remington.

40. *The Indians*

THE INDIAN WARS of the United States were not a ruthless conquest of an inferior people. The wars were not inevitable because of the savagery of the Indians, who, indeed, chalked up a grisly record of slaughter, torture and rapine. The wars were not an epic and heroic struggle of the Indians for home and country. The Indian was neither the bloody villain of motion picture and television screenplays, nor the injured innocent of some social historians.

The Indian was not pushed relentlessly westward until he reached "The End of the Trail" as in James Earle Fraser's statue facing the Pacific Ocean. The Indian wars were none of these things—yet all of these ideas entered into some or all of them. The Indian wars were primarily a conflict between ways of life that were wholly incompatible.

A half million, three-quarters of a million or a million Indians—all population estimates are wild guesses—lived within the boundaries of what became forty-eight states of the United States of America. When? The date may be 1492 or 1789 or any other, for the Indians, in their natural state, increased very slowly, if at all. There may have been an actual decrease sometime during the nineteenth century, for white men's diseases killed more Indians than were slain in all the wars they ever fought, but it is generally conceded that their descendants today number as many as there ever were. Again an exact figure is impossible because there is no agreement on who is Indian, and few do not have some admixture of white blood.

The Indians inhabited this country, but they did not occupy it. They wandered over it. In 1841, the opening date of this section, most of the Indians in the West still lived precariously by hunting, supplemented by a primitive agriculture. Only a few supported themselves entirely by farming, and many of these—notably the Pueblo peoples of the Southwest—are still to be found, more than a hundred years later, where they have been for centuries. But the nomadic Indians, dependent on the chase, soon killed or frightened off all the game in a considerable area. They were forced to keep moving. Such Indians had no more idea of owning land than they did of owning the waters they traversed in their canoes or the air over their heads. It is said that the Indians who disposed of Manhattan for twenty-four dollars were somewhat in the same position as the man who sold the Brooklyn Bridge for ten dollars; they didn't own it, just chanced to be on the island for a week-end fishing trip.

From the beginning, the United States government's policy favored fair dealing with the Indians. But in making treaties white men always assumed that the red men had unenlightened imitations of their own institutions. The government wanted title to land which the Indians were hunting on, took it for granted that the Indians owned it, even convinced them that this was so and they could therefore transfer title. For white men to realize that Indians might have entirely different ideas, ideals, motives and ways of life was inconceivable.

Indian councils were assumed to be representative legislatures. Americans generally, and even officially, supposed that each tribe had an elected chief executive. Government agents sent to deal with Indian tribes frequently had difficulty in identifying the "chief," but that problem was not insoluble as no Indian would admit that he was not a chief.

No word has been more abused in writing about Indians than "chief." It is often pointed out, for example, that Roman Nose and Geronimo were not technically chiefs of their tribes. They were, however, leaders of war parties, and "chief" means that, if it means anything. Similarly it is often said that Sitting Bull was not a chief, but a "medicine man"—which means, in this sense, a spiritual leader in recognition of many years of successful leadership of war parties. For a time, certainly, he was the most influential man among several tribes of Sioux and their allies, but he was not their commander-in-chief, and he did not direct the strategy that resulted in the defeat of General Custer. There was no such strategy.

Despite the many army officers who set forth in their memoirs opinions that their slippery opponents were led by a strategic genius, a "Red Napoleon," Indians had no strategy and were strangers to tactics for the convincing reason that they had no discipline.

Chiefs never issued specific orders and were unable to exact unquestioning obedience. Their followers, each a rugged individualist, might, and likely would, take the advice of a trusted leader, but if he decided that his "medicine" dictated it was time to quit, he quit.

Among Plains Indians any ambitious young warrior could, at a proper time, proclaim his intention of leading a war party or a horse-stealing expedition, which amounted to much the same thing. To those who joined him, he became "chief" of that particular foray. If successful, he could reasonably expect a larger following next time, but if he had lost one man, killed or missing, the raid was counted a failure, no matter how many horses had been stolen. Continued success might encourage all warriors of the village or tribe to join him. Thus Indians developed leadership through a process of natural selection—they followed the most able. But the "chief" could not command his band to "charge," "right wheel" or "left by twos, march." All he could say was, "Follow me!"

The high honor of counting coup as a motive for valor was seldom understood by the white man. Among most of the Plains tribes a youth did not become a man, could not even take a wife, until he had counted coup. Coup—French for blow or stroke—was counted by striking an enemy with a coup stick, not a weapon but an ordinary stick, perhaps bearing

Left to Right: *Dakota chief; self-portrait of the artist with four chiefs; half-breed. Paintings by Henry Cross.*

KENNEDY GALLERIES, NEW YORK

"medicine" symbols. The highest coup was counted by touching an armed, active enemy in battle. A warrior who shot down an enemy with firearm or arrow could only count coup by physically striking the body of his victim. A coup could also be counted by the first warrior to reach the body of a dead enemy even though he was not the killer.

There were other degrees of coups, varying from tribe to tribe, and the system became quite technical. Once a coup was claimed by a brave who lowered a rock on a string over a bluff until it touched an enemy. The validity of this coup caused grave argument around the council fire. Such academic debate may seem both trivial and amusing, but not to a warrior whose feathered headdress was the record of his coups, with each eagle feather notched or tasseled to show the degree of coup it commemorated.

To count coup in battle young warriors would fight with daring disregard for their own lives, but normally the Indian was a firm believer in the adage: "He who fights and runs away may live to fight another day." Except when cornered, or in defense of family, he seldom fought unless the advantages were great and the risk slight, as many a weary trooper, pounding in pursuit under a blazing sun, could testify.

PHOTO BY HUGO P. COOK

Sioux Chief "Iron Tail," a survivor of the Little Big Horn.

On the other hand, fighting, to the Indian, was as much a natural function as eating; conflict was ingrained in his nature. All strangers were enemies; the Indian had no concept of permanent peace. Even the term "peace pipe" is a misnomer, for the pipe ceremony signified alliance as well as friendship. The white man rarely understood this.

Fighting between tribes that were traditional enemies was often as cruel and vengeful as any recorded between red man and white, and quite as marked by slaughter of women and children and other atrocities. On the other hand, an intertribal fight with casual strangers might be carried on for an entire day of prudent and cautious skirmishing with no one seriously hurt.

Fighting was generally a leisure-time recreation, scheduled after the fall buffalo hunt and before holing up for winter's hardships. Many Indians took no pride in fighting white men because the white men would not play the game according to Indian rules. Soldiers frequently made the same complaint against the Indians.

Few Indians saw any real threat to their way of life from white invaders. Normally Indians saw so few, either soldiers or settlers, that many regarded the white men as a very minor tribe—to be chased off, of course, as they would any other strangers. Fighting against soldiers was usually only a temporary interruption of the customary intertribal warfare. There never was a time when all Indians were united against white invaders; indeed it was rare in

Indian wars for an entire tribe to be hostile. Many tribes, such as the Pawnee and the Crows, did most of their fighting as allies of the whites.

Few Indians were good marksmen, either with bow and arrow or with firearms. In hunting, their objective was food, and to make a sure shot at close range they became experts at stalking game. When these talents were turned to man-hunting, the Indian became an elusive and deadly foe. He was master of the surprise attack and in the use of decoy and ambush.

It was an old army saying that Plains Indians were the "best light cavalry in the world." That was true, but with limitations. Indians would have been quite incapable of the charge of the Light Brigade at Balaclava. They never failed to "reason why," and if reason told them that the chance of dying was greater than that of doing, they promptly whirled their wiry cayuses and headed for the far horizon. As individual fighters, as hit-and-run guerrillas, as raiders and as scouts, they were superb.

Even in defense of their homes and families, however, their lack of discipline often brought disaster. The annals of the West are full of stories of villages surprised at dawn, or even in broad day, by soldiers or enemy tribes who slaughtered ill-prepared warriors, captured women and children, stampeded horses and burned tepees. Chiefs had no authority to post guards or send out scouts. Tribes of Plains Indians were highly organized for buffalo hunts, because failure meant starvation, but were unorganized for warfare, which was mainly an avocation.

Yet few primitive peoples were as good at fighting as the American Indians, or won as many battles against highly trained professional soldiers. But the Indians won no wars.

41. *The Soldiers*

THE MOST HEROIC figure in the unending Indian wars along the frontier was an individual who would have been startled had he been informed that he qualified for a pedestal—the hard-swearing, hard-drinking, "kinder rough and may be tough Reg'lar Army man."

To the cavalry trooper was assigned the thankless task of riding herd upon an audacious foe as elusive as a prairie antelope, wily as a coyote and fierce as a cornered panther. To the infantry soldier was assigned, theoretically, the less arduous chore of guarding some isolated, sun-blasted outpost—theoretically because to each post was assigned a contingent of infantry as garrison and cavalry as a mobile task force. Actually the infantryman usually found himself walking alongside his mounted comrade, sometimes outwalking the horses when the route was long and forage poor. A grudging tribute was paid in an Indian name for infantrymen— "walk-a-heaps."

If he performed some particularly heroic action he might be awarded the Medal of Honor, but it was not practical to send him to Washington to receive it at the hands of the President. It might be presented by his commanding officer with formal ceremonial at dress parade. After 1888 the Regular Army man, if given a choice, might prefer the Certificate of Merit, which he could stow away in the bottom of his trunk locker. At that time it bore no medal, but it did get the soldier two dollars extra pay a month, which the Medal of Honor did not. If the veteran survived until 1905 he might wear the red, later red and black, Indian campaign badge. No campaign badges were authorized prior to 1905.

The Indian-fighting soldier got little honor and less pay. When the Regiment of Dragoons was raised in 1833—to become the first mounted troops to serve against Plains Indians and, three years later, the crack regiment of the army under Colonel Stephen Watts Kearny—the going rate for a private was six dollars a month. Five years later it went up to eight dollars, and by the beginning of the Civil War a private was getting eleven. Wartime inflation boomed the entering recruit's pay to sixteen dollars by the close of the war—a rate not exceeded until 1917. It reverted to thirteen dollars for most of the period of the Indian wars. Even this was not all take-home pay, for "one bit" each month went to the Soldiers' Home—to be practical about it, the paymaster took out "two bits" (twenty-five cents) every two months—and one dollar of each month's pay was withheld until the end of the soldier's enlistment.

What kind of man would be attracted by this governmental largess to sweat out his days in a desert waste, enduring iron discipline, primitive living and frequent threat of death? Opinions differ among those in a position to know—officers and enlisted men who recorded their impressions in letters and diaries. Obviously few were educated men of good families. But it was a period of frequent economic depressions, then called panics, and many a jobless laborer took to the army in desperation. The pay scale should not be judged in the light of a century-of-inflation later. The $11.87½ a month the private got at the pay table was all spending money. He was fed, housed, and he received a clothing allowance on which he could save even when it was at only $3.50 a month. This was a time when "another day, another dollar" meant just that for many a laboring man keeping a family on six dollars a week.

The great cities contributed their quota to Regular Army ranks. Officers have said that a majority of enlisted men were recent immigrants, mainly Irish and Germans. During the period of large and unrestricted immigration, many a youngster fleeing conscription in Europe found the United States Army a refuge when penniless in a strange land. It mattered not if he knew only a word or two of English; he could learn.

Not unexpectedly, desertion was heavy, for many joined to get free transportation west during a gold rush or silver strike. And, despite army protests, the ranks included young toughs and bums, who had been given a choice of going to jail or enlisting. Debtors, too, helped fill the ranks; no creditors and few sheriffs would trace them to a post on the Indian frontier.

Yet these men often became good soldiers. So, of course, did the lads who discovered too late that the monotony of farm life was preferable to the utter boredom of a winter in an army post on the Plains. Many of these adventurous youngsters were attracted by the glamour that even then enveloped the West—and Indian fighting—as a result of dime novels, stage melodramas, Buffalo Bill's Wild West and the military novels of Captain Charles King.

During the entire period of the Indian wars it was almost impossible for an enlisted man to be commissioned from the ranks, yet there were a few who made it, which speaks well for the Indian-fighting soldier. It was almost impossible because nearly every year West Point graduated more officers than there were vacancies. Surplus graduates were commissioned brevet second lieutenants and were allowed to serve until a vacancy occurred. Promotion was slow. An officer could be given a brevet in the next highest rank after ten years' faithful service in the same grade, and it frequently happened. These brevet commissions, usually bestowed as battle honors, carried pay when an officer was called to duty in his higher rank.

The army officer on the frontier, and his wife, suffered isolation, boredom and hardship

FT. COLVILLE ■

X Seattle 1856

Four Lakes 1858 X

X Connell's Prairie 1856

Clearwater 1877

Bear Pau~ X

FT. SHAW ■

Haller's Defeat 1854 X

FT. CLATSOP ■

Cascades 1856 X

FT. WALLA WALLA ■ ■

FT. LAPWAI ■

FT. MISSOULA ■

FT. VANCOUVER ■

X Grande Ronde 1856

Umatilla 1848

White Bird Canyon 1877

Big Hole 1877 X

FT. ELLIS

X L

Grave Creek 1855 X

Galice Creek 1855 X

The Meadows 1856 X

Rogue River 1851

X X

Evans Creek 1853 X

■ FT. KLAMATH

Owyhee Forks 1866

X Lake Albert 1866

Camas Meadows 1878 X

Haufield Fight 1867 X X ■

FT. C. F. SMITH

X Lava Beds 1873

Pit River 1867

FT. READING ■

Bear River 1863 X

FT.

X Pyramid Lake 1860

X Truckee 1860

FT. CHURCHILL ■

FT. BRIDGER ■

FT. DOUGLAS ■

Milk C

X

■

PRESIDIO ■

X Mountain Meadows

■ FT. MOHAVE

■ CAMP VERDE

FT. WHIPPLE ■

FT. YUMA ■

CAMP GRANT ■

CAMP BOWIE ■

FT. CRAIG ■

Skeleton Canyon X

Indian Warfare in the
AMERICAN WEST

X **Battles and Skirmishes**   ■ **Army Posts and Forts**

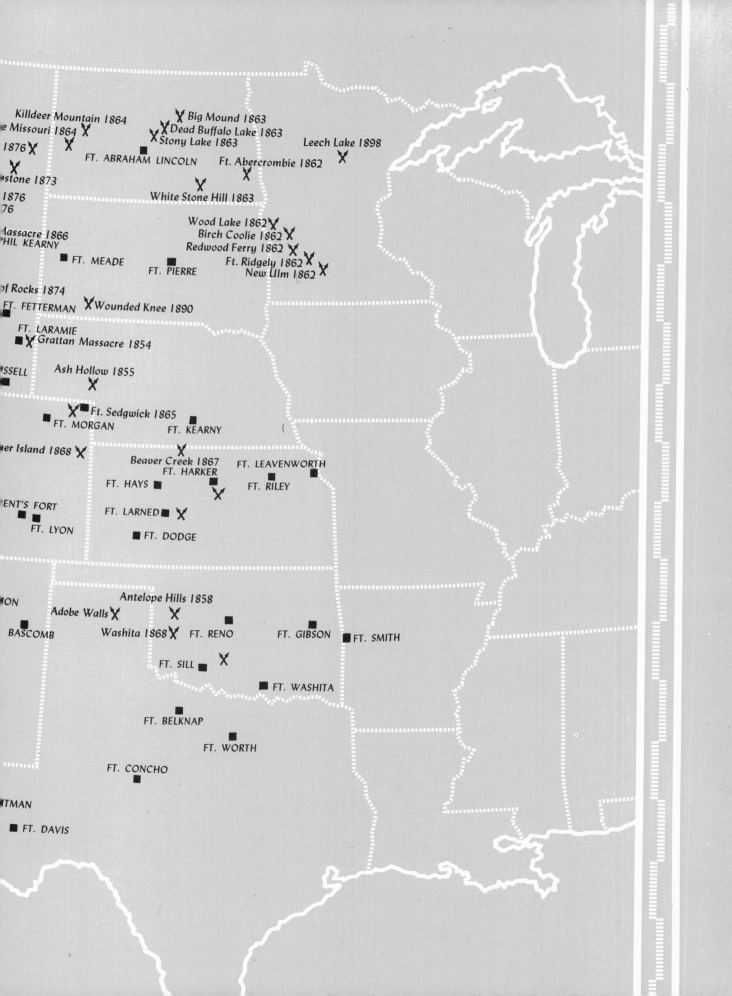

*"U.S. Dragoon, '47." Wash drawing
by Frederic Remington.*

that are almost inconceivable to a later generation. Pay was no great inducement, for as late as 1878 an entering second lieutenant got only $1,400 a year. Yet few resigned, and the great majority were able, dedicated men who served their country well.

Despite the long service of officers and the five-year enlistments of men in the ranks, few had opportunity to become experienced in Indian fighting. This fact, of course, is directly contrary to the impression created by television programs, motion pictures and novels about the Indian wars. It can be readily proved, however, by statistics. From the beginning of the republic in 1789 to the Mexican War the Regular Army recorded 96 Indian fights in which there were casualties, excluding those fought during the War of 1812. That averages less than two fights a year. From the Mexican War to the Civil War there were 206 Indian fights. The number during the rebellion is difficult to determine because Indians fought in both armies as well as independently, so the statistics are uncertain. However, from the end of the Civil War to the last fight between soldiers and Indians at Leech Lake, Minnesota, in 1898, there were 938 fights, an average of more than 27 fights a year for the two periods after the Mexican War. This appears to be like almost constant warfare, but most of the fights were very small affairs involving a few men or a company or two, and it seems to work out that a soldier might expect to be in one fight during a five-year enlistment.

Before rating the soldier as a good insurance risk, let us take a look at casualty figures. In these 1,240 Indian fights, 1,105 officers and enlisted men were killed, and 1,391 wounded. The casualties, then, average less than one killed and a little more than one wounded for each fight. Some authorities estimate that casualties among Indians were even fewer.

All of this bears small resemblance to what we see in wide-screen spectaculars, where soldiers and Indians are shot down by dozens.

It was, however, a small-scale army that fought these battles—always too small for its task. Had it not been for the Indian wars there might not have been a Regular Army, for the Fathers of the Republic were much opposed to the idea of permanent military forces. But even as the Constitution was adopted, a regiment of infantry and a battalion of artillery were in the field against Indians of the Old Northwest, and this force was accepted reluctantly into the service of the United States, with the hope that it might be discharged when the Indian troubles were over.

Instead they grew worse, with only intermittent periods of peace until after the War of 1812 in which Britain encouraged Indians to fight white settlers. After that there were high hopes of a permanent solution of the Indian problem, for the frontier line was marked by a chain of posts stretching from Fort Snelling, Minnesota, to Fort Gibson, Arkansas Territory (now Oklahoma).

President Andrew Jackson proposed to move all of the eastern tribes west of this frontier into an Indian paradise where the buffalo roamed and the antelope played. In actual practice, though, his Indian removal policy was less successful than is commonly assumed. Many Indians were driven ruthlessly along a "Trail of Tears" to territories that became Kansas and Oklahoma, but many stayed behind—in Wisconsin, Michigan, Indiana, Mississippi and North Carolina, to mention only a few.

The Seminole in Florida who refused to go kept soldiers busy for eight years and still remained in their swamps. A powwow in Tallahassee in 1957 announced, somewhat face-tiously, the end of the Seminole War, 122 years

"U.S. Cavalry Officer on Campaign." Wash drawing by Frederic Remington.

after it began. The Black Hawk War of 1832 in Illinois and Wisconsin was the only other important Indian war prior to the Mexican War. During most of this period the Regular Army consisted of seven or eight regiments of infantry, each of ten companies scattered in small garrisons among the frontier forts, and four regiments of artillery, also of ten companies each, mainly employed in seacoast defense.

The artillery had small part in the Indian wars. After the Mexican War the regiments were increased to twelve companies, of which two were light, or field, batteries. The remaining companies manned the heavy guns of coastal forts. During the Mexican War most of these companies were sent to the front to fight as infantry, and in occasional emergencies during the Indian wars artillery companies served as infantry. Artillery stationed in Pacific Coast forts got into a number of Indian fights, and on rare occasions artillerymen manned forts as far from the seacoast as Fort Leavenworth, Kansas; Fort Ridgely, Minnesota; or Fort Randall, Nebraska (later Dakota) Territory, as was the case in 1861. But more commonly, even when artillery weapons were used against Indians, the guns were manned by infantry or cavalry detachments.

From the end of the War of 1812 until the Black Hawk War in 1832 there were no mounted troops in the Regular Army, but that year Congress authorized a battalion of mounted rangers of six companies to serve for one year. It was organized too late to fight Black Hawk and is remembered principally because Washington Irving, in *A Tour of the Prairies,* described one of its companies which guarded his expedition into Indian country. Another ranger company escorted the annual caravan of traders along the Santa Fe Trail to guard it from the Pawnee and Comanche. As early as 1829 soldiers had accompanied traders on this trail, but these were infantry under Brevet Major Bennett Riley, and they proved ineffective.

The rangers were replaced in 1833 by the Regiment of Dragoons of ten companies. Three years later Colonel Kearny took command and started the cavalry custom of an annual expedition into Indian country. To the Indians, Kearny's dragoons looked tough, and there was no fighting, but the troops got good training and some new country was explored.

The marches of the dragoons were long and arduous. In one of them five companies rode from Fort Leavenworth, Kansas, over the Oregon Trail to South Pass, swung cross-country

"The Map in the Sand." Painting by Frederick Remington.

to Bent's Fort, and returned by the Santa Fe Trail—covering 2,200 miles in ninety-nine days.

Policing the Santa Fe Trail and the Oregon Trail after it opened in the early 1840's, as well as the country between them, was plainly beyond the capacity of a single mounted regiment. In 1836 the 2nd Regiment of Dragoons was formed but was of little help because it was diverted almost immediately to Florida to take part in the Seminole War.

By 1846 many immigrants were rolling over the Oregon Trail, and Congress provided the Regiment of Mounted Riflemen for their protection. By the time it was organized, however, the Mexican War had begun, and the regiment was sent to General Scott's army. Thus the 1st Dragoons was the only mounted force available for Kearny's Army of the West and formed the backbone of the volunteer army that took Santa Fe and marched on to California.

The end of the Mexican War, the annexation of Texas and the settlement with Great Britain of the Oregon boundary, all occurred between 1845 and 1848. The old frontier line running a few miles west of the Mississippi River was no more. One million, two hundred thousand square miles were now added to a nation that had previously occupied less than 1,800,000 square miles. Throughout this new country were numerous tribes of Indians, about which the people and their government knew little or nothing. Many were to prove hostile for a long time to come.

Scarcely had the ink dried on the treaty with Mexico than gold was discovered in California, and a new wave of covered wagons began rolling west. Yet the army that was to protect the immigrants and fight Indians scattered over more than a million square miles of the West was reduced from an authorized strength of 12,539 to an aggregate of 10,317. Now available for the purpose were two regiments of dragoons, one of mounted riflemen and eight of infantry, with some possible aid from the four regiments of artillery. Only two other branches of service had any enlisted men: A company of sappers, miners and pontoniers that had served in the Mexican War and was retained in service as a demonstration company of engineers at West Point, and the Ordnance Department, which employed 500 enlisted men in arsenals and maintained a sergeant at each important army post.

Fiction writers have sometimes employed quartermaster regiments or units from other staff departments in their Indian fights, but there were no such units. The Quartermaster Department employed wagoners and master wagoners during the Civil and Indian wars, but had no enlisted men until 1898. The Medical Department had hospital stewards but no privates until 1889, the same year the Signal Corps got its first enlisted men.

The small army of 1848 had forty-one fights with Indians in the six years before it was reinforced by two regiments of infantry and two regiments officially designated as cavalry. This gave the army three branches of mounted service—dragoons, mounted riflemen and cavalry—with separate promotion lists for officers in each service. Early in the Civil War they were consolidated as cavalry and the regiments renumbered, the 1st Dragoons becoming 1st Cavalry; the 2nd Dragoons, the 2nd Cavalry; the Mounted Riflemen, the 3rd Cavalry; the 1st Cavalry of 1855 the 4th Cavalry, and the 2nd the 5th. A new regiment, the 6th Cavalry, was added.

42. *Early Day Wars in the New Territories*

FROM ALMOST ANY reasonable point of view, the Indian wars of the last half of the nineteenth century were more spectacular than important. Never did they halt, or threaten to halt, westward expansion. Indian fights were numerous, small scale, sporadic and widely scattered over the West. Some tribes fought and quit, some rebelled frequently, but none carried on warfare continuously. Yet each year had its quota of fighting.

The Pueblo Rebellion

In 1847, during the war between the United States and Mexico, an insurrection broke out among the usually peaceful Pueblo Indians of Taos, during which William Bent, newly appointed military governor of the New Mexico Territory, was killed.

Colonel Sterling Price—later a Confederate major general—attacked Taos with Missouri volunteers and mountain men, and when artillery failed against the adobe walls, volunteers stormed the pueblo, killing 150. Captured ringleaders were hanged.

Two years later the newly organized Department of the Interior sent its first Indian agent, the able and realistic James S. Calhoun, to New Mexico. Calhoun, who later became territorial governor, negotiated permanent peace with the Pueblo Indians, an act of the territorial legislature making each pueblo a corporate body with perpetual title to its lands.

Navajo Raiders

The Navajo, known primarily as silversmiths, sheep raisers and rug weavers, nevertheless had an unsavory record under the Mexican regime as persistent plunderers of peaceful New

Mexican villages and Indian pueblos. In 1849 Brevet Lieutenant Colonel John M. Washington, major of the 3rd Artillery, escorted agent Calhoun on a peacemaking expedition into Navajo land. But although a treaty was signed, the raids continued.

In 1851 Calhoun tried again, this time with a strong expedition under the command of Brevet Colonel Edwin V. Sumner of the 1st Dragoons. Once more, a treaty was signed, reinforced this time by Fort Defiance, which was established by Colonel Sumner in the heart of Navajo country (the extreme northeast corner of present Arizona). Still the Navajo continued their plundering.

Six years later Lieutenant Colonel D. S. Miles and Major Electus Backus, both of the 3rd Infantry, led columns in an effort to overawe the hostiles. But in 1860 a Navajo band attacked Fort Defiance. They quit after killing one man of the garrison, and though the damage was not too serious, the incident provoked the army into decisive action.

Brevet Lieutenant Colonel Edward Richard Sprigg Canby, major of the 10th Infantry, assembled fifteen companies at Fort Defiance. Moving out on October 11, 1860, he attacked Navajo village after village in a month of continuous action. A total of thirty-four were killed and hundreds of horses and thousands of sheep captured. Survivors scampered into the desert hills. By March, 1861, Canby had induced some chiefs to sue for peace. But the Navajo had many chiefs and many braves who would follow only those chiefs who took the warpath.

A month later, however, the Civil War began, and Canby, promoted to colonel of the new 19th Infantry, had to turn his attention to a Confederate invasion of New Mexico. After repulsing it, he was called east as brigadier general of volunteers, leaving the Navajo problem to Brigadier General James Henry Carleton, who had force-marched his California column across mountains and deserts to aid Canby.

Carleton's first act was to send Colonel Christopher (Kit) Carson, with the 1st New Mexico Volunteer Infantry, 736 strong, into Navajo country with clear-cut orders: kill all hostiles and move all prisoners to Bosque Redondo (the circular forest) on the Pecos River. Here Carson established Fort Sumner, New Mexico, with a garrison to police the Indians.

Carson's regiment killed only 50 Navajo, but by the end of 1863 had rounded up 8,500, most of the tribe. For five years they were held at Bosque Redondo before being allowed to return home to the reservation they have since occupied. They never again took the warpath, and within a century their number increased tenfold.

The Dreaded Apache

There never was a time when all Apache, or even any considerable number, acted together against U.S. troops, for Apache included a varying number of tribes, commonly, but perhaps inaccurately, called subtribes—Mescalero, Jicarilla, Mimbreño, Lipan, Chiricahua, Coyotero, Tonto, Pinal, Arivaipa—who fought everyone and occasionally each other. Like their relatives, the Navajo, they were mainly raiders for pleasure.

As a warrior the Apache was treacherous and guilty of some of the most sadistic tortures ever devised. Warfare was the principal Apache vocation and they gloried in it, but not for them the dashing attack to count a coup or take a scalp. They were more apt to eat their horses than ride them, and never fought on horseback. They wore no war bonnets to record their deeds. They fought from behind rocks and were adept at concealing themselves in almost any kind of terrain. Many a soldier fought Apache all day without seeing one. When pressed hard, the Apache vanished; he could usually outrun a horse, as many a trooper learned in a chase through the mountains.

On March 30, 1854, Jicarilla Apache attacked a mail coach and its escort of sixty troopers of Companies F and I, 1st Dragoons, at Cienequilla, twenty-five miles southeast of Taos. In a bitter three-hour fight twenty-three soldiers were killed. Lieutenant Colonel Philip St. George Cooke pursued with a mixed command from the 2nd Artillery and 2nd Dragoons, Taos Pueblo Indian scouts and Kit Carson as guide. Brought to bay in a deep canyon of the Ojo Caliente (hot hole), the Jicarilla were held down by the rifle fire of the scouts and artillery acting as infantry, while mounted dragoons charged through the skirmish line and routed them. Four or five Jicarilla were killed and their camp destroyed. One trooper was killed.

The Mescalero Apache, occasional allies of the Jicarilla, ambushed Company B, 1st Dragoons, on the Penasco River, New Mexico, on January 19, 1855, killing Captain Henry Whiting Stanton and two privates. In reprisal Captain Richard S. Ewell (later a Confederate lieutenant general) was sent with Company G to punish the hostiles. On February 24, he destroyed a Mescalero village near the White Mountains.

Ewell and others after him continued to harry the Mescalero until they agreed to settle on a reservation between the White Mountains and the Pecos River. Fort Stanton, named for the slain captain, was established nearby.

During the Civil War the fort was occupied by Confederates. The Mescalero made a treaty of friendship with them, then ambushed and killed to the last man a Confederate party of sixteen. When they demonstrated their neutrality by slaughtering forty men and six children of a loyal Union settlement, General Carleton sent Colonel Kit Carson against them. Carson rounded up the Mescalero at Bosque Redondo (prior to his bringing the Navajo there).

"The War Trail." Engraving, after drawing by Felix O. C. Darley,
Harper's Weekly, 1858.

Mescalero and Navajo quarreled continuously—until the night of November 3, 1865, when the Mescalero disappeared into the darkness and scattered. No definite trace of them was found for seven years.

The most widely known Apache in the 1850's was Mangas Coloradas of the Mimbreño who lived and raided in the Gila River country. During the Mexican War he rode to meet General Kearny on his march to California and expressed friendship for Americans. But Mangas Coloradas proved a difficult ally. When the United States signed its treaty of peace with Mexico, Mangas Coloradas refused to recognize it or to free his Mexican prisoners or even to promise an end to his raiding in Mexico.

Now Mangas Coloradas turned against the Americans and for a decade or more led hornet bands to raid and pillage on both sides of the border. Finally in January, 1863, he came to Brigadier General of Volunteers Joseph R. West, commander of the column sent against him, and offered to negotiate a treaty. General West, however, did not negotiate. Instead he ordered Mangas Coloradas held as a hostage. That night he was killed by guards who reported that he had attempted to escape. According to a fairly well substantiated story, however, the guards had goaded him with red-hot bayonets until he tried to break loose.

The Unconquerable Comanche

In its years as an independent republic, Texas sought to drive all Indians from its borders but failed to stop raids by Lipan Apache from Mexico and Comanche from the Plains, who had been the scourge of Texas while it was still a Mexican province. Comanche loot was so considerable that unscrupulous white men, called Comancheros, set up trading posts to deal in Comanche plunder and arrange for the ransom of captives—or their sale as slaves.

Under pressure from Texans, the federal government in 1855 sent its new 2nd Cavalry to take the offensive against the Comanche. This regiment, renumbered 5th Cavalry in 1861, continued in service and saw action both in World War II and in the Korean conflict. When first organized it had a notable group of officers: Colonel Albert Sidney Johnston, Lieutenant Colonel Robert E. Lee, Major William J. Hardee, Captain Earl Van Dorn and Second Lieutenant John B. Hood, all of whom became Confederate generals; and Major George H. Thomas, Captain Innis N. Palmer and Captain George Stoneman, Jr., all of whom served as Union generals.

During its first two years in Texas, the 2nd Cavalry fought twenty-five engagements with Indians. One of these involved some unusual features that illustrate the character of Comanche warfare.

At the headwaters of Devil's River on July 20, 1857, Lieutenant Hood with twenty-five troopers of Company G and an Indian guide saw red men waving a white cloth. Hood had been told that friendly Tonkawa would use such a signal. However, he was cautious and advanced in line of battle, leaving behind eight men whose horses were in need of rest.

The Indians moved forward as if to parley, then suddenly dropped their white cloth and began shooting. At the same instant concealed redskins fired heaps of dry grass and charged, some on horseback with fluttering lances. In the frenzied melee, each trooper fired his single-shot carbine, then drew his Colt navy revolver. The fighting was at such close quarters that an Indian stole a carbine from a trooper's saddle hook while the trooper was busy with his six-gun. Though only a few of the troopers had sabers, they used them so effectively that there-after Hood never allowed his troopers to leave that arm behind.

Before the revolvers were empty, Hood ordered a charge, followed by a quick withdrawal to dismount and reload. This pause gave the Indians a chance to count their dead; of a hundred Comanche and Lipan Apache, nineteen were killed. Howls of grief convinced Hood that the attack would not be renewed. The cavalry loss was two killed and five wounded, including the lieutenant, whose hand was pinned to his bridle by an arrow. He broke off the point and jerked out the shaft.

Pacific Coast Wars

Along the Pacific numerous tribes and bands of Indians, speaking a wide variety of languages and generally not warlike, lived in isolated communities.

Commissioners negotiated eighteen treaties with 139 tribes or bands of California Indians during 1851–52, every single one of which was rejected by the United States Senate. These Indians were left with no rights that could be enforced against lawless gold seekers who swarmed over the region staking claims.

Lieutenant George Crook, later a major general, stated the situation simply: "When they [the Indians] were pushed beyond endurance and would go on the war path we had to fight when our sympathies were with the Indians."

In one such small-scale war, James D. Savage, a trader called the Blond King of the Tulareños because of his influence with that tribe, led a battalion of volunteers against the Yosemites. The pursuit led Savage's force into Yosemite Valley, on March 25, 1851, and their accounts of its grandeur resulted in further exploration, which ultimately made the valley one of California's show places.

For the most part, California's Indian wars were a dismal series of minor skirmishes, with an occasional bloody encounter. These included the Klamath War of 1854-55; the Kern River War of 1856; the war against the Wintoons, 1858–59; the Pit River War of 1859; the Indian Island massacre of 1860; the Hupa War of 1863–65; and expeditions against Shoshoni. By 1865 most Pacific Coast Indians were living on reservations.

Oregon Territory was the scene of a brief uprising in 1847. Dr. Marcus Whitman, famed for his winter overland ride to save his mission at Waiilatpu, near Walla Walla, was killed there with his wife Narcissa by Cayuse Indians on November 29, 1847. Although the territory had only a provisional government, a volunteer regiment was raised. Colonel Cornelius Gilliam, Lieutenant Colonel James Waters and Major H. A. G. Lee showed rare leadership by confining the outbreak to the one tribe. The Cayuse surrendered the five slayers, who were hanged on June 3, 1849.

The Yakima Wars

With the creation of the Washington Territory in 1853, Isaac Ingalls Stevens was appointed governor and superintendant of Indian affairs (Stevens later became a major general in the Civil War and was killed in the Battle of Chantilly).

Stevens held a series of councils with the territory's Indians and was successful in negotiating treaties of peace with many. One, however, a Yakima named Kamiakin, objected to the terms and persuaded several bands to join in what was called the Yakima War.

Major Granville O. Haller, stationed at The Dalles, marched north with a hundred-man detachment from the 4th Infantry to round up the dissidents, but they rounded him up in the evergreen forest along Toppenish Creek, a tributary of the Yakima River. The date was October 6, 1854. After a three-day fight, with five men killed and seventeen wounded, the major and his men slipped away.

With the victorious Indians on the warpath, all settlements were in danger. Volunteer companies were hastily organized, but Kamiakin eluded them all, and on March 26, 1856, he attacked a village located at the Cascades of the Columbia River and defended by only nine men in a blockhouse, who nevertheless held the Indian force at bay.

To the rescue came Second Lieutenant Philip H. Sheridan—who rose to Civil War fame—with forty dragoons and a borrowed saluting gun mounted on a Hudson's Bay Company bateau. Brevet Lieutenant Colonel Edward J. Steptoe arrived with a larger force, and between them they drove off the attackers, killing three. Nine Cascade Indians who had been friendly with the hostiles were captured and hanged for the murders of settlers.

But the war dragged on, and trouble lay ahead for Steptoe. Two years later he was sent to investigate a report that two men had been killed by Indians who stole thirteen head of cattle. He marched from Fort Walla Walla with 158 men—three companies of the 1st Dragoons and one of the 9th Infantry—and two mountain howitzers. At the village of To-ho-to-nim-me (near present Rosalia, south of Spokane) Steptoe tried to question some Indians. They showed signs of hostility, and on May 17, 1858, when he ordered a withdrawal, he was attacked by 1,200 Palouse, Spokane and Coeur d'Alène Indians. Steptoe had no advantage in arms to overcome the great disadvantage in numbers: Two of his dragoon companies had smoothbore musketoons, the original arm of that branch of service, and the third had Mississippi Yager rifles, too long to be muzzle-loaded while in the saddle. In the fight eight of Steptoe's men were killed and three wounded; several Indians, including three chiefs, were killed. When the troops took up a defensive position on a hill—still called Steptoe's Butte—the Indians showed no inclination to close in, and after dark the troops stole away, abandoning the howitzers and pack train.

The army command had not pushed any vigorous campaign, hoping the desultory raiding would cease if the Indians were not provoked; but their attack on Steptoe showed they regarded forbearance as weakness, and decisive action was now necessary. At Fort Walla Walla Colonel George Wright, commanding the 9th Infantry, assembled two companies of his regiment, five of the 1st Dragoons and five of the 3rd Artillery. Except for one section which manned two howitzers, the artillerymen were armed to fight as infantry.

Meanwhile First Lieutenant John Mullan of the 3rd Artillery interrupted his work on the

"A Crow Scout." Wash drawing
by Frederic Remington

laying out of the route which, as the Mullan Road, was to become one of the most famous trails in the Northwest, and took command of thirty Nez Percé allies, uniformed to distinguish them from hostiles.

Wright's troops were armed with the new model 1855 rifle-musket that proved a decisive factor in outshooting the Hudson's Bay guns used by the Indians. Left behind were the uniform coats and "flowerpot" hats prescribed for the well-dressed soldier of the period. These troops wore the blue-flannel shirts and slouch felt hats that became the familiar garb of the Indian fighters painted by Frederic Remington.

On September 1, 1858, at Four Lakes, thirteen miles from present downtown Spokane, hostile Indians attempted an ambush. Colonel Wright pretended to be falling into the trap, but instead sent a company of dragoons to ambush the ambushers. Captain Edward Ortho Cresap Ord—who became a Civil War major general—led Companies E and M of the dragoons in a saber charge that drove the Indians into a wood where they were shelled by the howitzers. The infantry and the artillery acting as infantry, commanded by Captain Erasmus Darwin Keyes—who also became a Civil War general—routed the Indians out of the wood to a plain where they were ambushed by the dragoons. The infantry and howitzers then joined in a final drive that forced the Indians to flee.

Four days later Wright struck again at Spokane Plains. Again Indians took cover in a wood, setting grass afire in front of it. Howitzers routed them from the wood, while the troops charged through the flames. The Indians retreated, hoping to catch the soldiers as they scattered in the chase, but Colonel Wright alternated his infantry and dragoons in a disciplined pursuit of twenty-five miles, fourteen miles of which were a running fight.

On September 8 the dragoons captured 800 of the Indians' horses, which Wright ordered shot. This took the heart out of the Indians. They sued for peace. The terms were severe: those found guilty of murders were hanged and hostages taken to ensure future good conduct.

Through the entire campaign only one man was wounded. Two died of eating poisonous roots.

During the Civil War, Colonel Wright and the 9th Infantry remained on the Pacific Coast, policing minor Indian disturbances. (Wright became brigadier general of volunteers and brevet brigadier general, but was drowned on July 30, 1865, in the wreck of the coastal steamer *Brother Jonathan* near Crescent City, California).

Wars in the Great Basin

The *Book of Mormon* taught that the Indians were descendants of the Lost Tribes of Israel, and Brigham Young decreed that they be treated fairly. Consequently there was no Indian trouble in Utah until 1853, when Walkara (commonly called Walker) of the Ute objected to Mormon interference with his customary slave trading and horse stealing. From behind defensive walls at Manti, Springville, Pleasant Creek and Nephi, alert Mormon militia drove off his raiders. His war a failure, Walkara reluctantly made peace.

"Nez Percé Indian." Wash drawing by Frederic Remington.

During the "Walker War," however, a party of immigrants had fired into a band of previously peaceful Pahvants, killing their chief. Retaliation came when the Pahvants ambushed and killed Captain John W. Gunnison of the Corps of Topographical Engineers and seven of his party surveying one of the possible routes for a Pacific railroad.

Although along the Oregon Trail attacks on wagon trains were not as common as motion pictures and television would lead one to think, still they did occur from time to time. One of the bloodiest took place on September 13, 1860, when Bannock or Shoshoni attacked the Otter train of forty-four persons west of Fort Hall (in present Idaho). After a two-day fight only fifteen escaped, and they suffered such privation that some resorted to cannibalism before being rescued.

Nevada also had its share of Indian troubles. Discovery of the Comstock Lode in 1859 had caused a stampede which resulted, within four years, in the creation of that state. The arrival of these miners of the Washoe stirred up the Paiute—normally peaceful desert dwellers who dug roots and trapped small animals for a scanty living.

Probably in retaliation for their upheaval, the Paiute disrupted the short-lived Pony Express. A hastily organized and undisciplined company of volunteers, enlisted to protect the Pony Express, was ambushed at Pyramid Lake. Forty-six of its total 105 were killed; the rest ran.

To retaliate, Colonel Jack Hays took the field with a regiment of volunteers, reinforced by two companies of the 6th Infantry, parts of two companies of the 1st Dragoons and a detachment of the 3rd Artillery manning howitzers they never had a chance to use. Hays was an experienced fighter, one of the heroes of the Texas Rangers. Using mounted troopers as decoys, he routed the Paiute on June 2, 1860, on the Truckee, near the site of the Pyramid Lake massacre.

A result of the Paiute War was the establishment of Fort Churchill, a story-and-a-half

Mounted messengers attacked by Indians on the Plains. Engraving, after sketch by S. B. Enderton.

Harper's Weekly, 1866

adobe structure, east of Lake Tahoe, which during the Civil War became headquarters for the Military District of Utah. Colonel Patrick Edward Connor, 3rd California Infantry, assumed command there on August 6, 1862. His special charge was to defend the Overland Trail, frequently raided by Shoshoni and Bannock. On January 29, 1863, in a winter campaign, Connor surprised their camp on Bear River and in a four-hour fight killed 224 of them. He lost 14 killed and 53 wounded, but 79 were disabled by the bitter cold.

43. *Horsemen of the Plains*

MUCH HAS BEEN written to explain how the Plains Indians acquired horses, but very little to explain why some groups adopted the horse so eagerly as to change their entire way of life, while others were comparatively indifferent to it. Eastern Algonquian, Iroquoian and Muskhogean peoples undoubtedly stole horses from English and French settlers, but made little use of them, yet Delawares, Kickapoo, Choctaw, and Sauk and Foxes became horsemen after they crossed the Mississippi. Horses came to the Indians almost entirely from Mexico through the Southwest, spreading northward and eastward during the seventeenth and eighteenth centuries. Why, then, did such tough, fighting men as the Apache, living closest to the source of supply, make so little use of the horse in warfare? Why did the Sioux, who were farthest away, take immediate advantage of the horse to become conquerors of the northern Plains?

The Sioux

The name Sioux is commonly applied to the Teton branch of the Dakota wing of the Siouan language group, as was explained earlier in this book. By 1841, they had become a dominant warrior power and after the Civil War were the principals in the so-called Sioux Wars which plagued the next generation. Comparative newcomers to the Plains in 1800, after centuries of harassment by powerful neighbors and near starvation in the inhospitable north woods country, they changed readily to horse Indians. Abandoning such agriculture as they had ever practiced, they prospered hunting buffalo. The migration from north woods to Plains was led by the Teton in two major divisions, the Brulés, or Burnt Thighs (whose later great chief was Spotted Tail), and the Oglala (whose famous men of the future were Red Cloud and Crazy Horse). They found the White River country of central South Dakota a virtual Indian paradise, teeming with game, but by 1835 they had exhausted it and pushed westward. The Teton were beginning to feel their oats—or more specifically their all-meat diet of buffalo. They battled the Arikara along the upper reaches of White River and chased Kiowa, Prairie Apache and Cheyenne out of the Black Hills. They began slaughtering the Pawnee who lived in permanent villages south of the Platte River, raised crops and were more interested in horse stealing than in other war honors.

Happily for the Sioux, as they pushed westward, white men's illnesses proved effective allies. The sedentary Indians, with their corn patches along the rivers, were peculiarly susceptible to contagious diseases. Arikara power was broken by smallpox. Cholera, measles and other epidemics cut the fighting strength of Assiniboin, Mandan, Hidatsa and Crows. Because the buffalo-chasing Sioux had less contact with white men, their population continued to grow.

The Brulé and Oglala, joined by bands of Saone or Sanona, and perhaps other Siouan groups, expanded into five more tribes—the Hunkpapa (Sitting Bull's people), the Miniconjou, the Sans Arcs, the Two Kettles and the Blackfoot Sioux (not to be confused with the Blackfeet, an Algonquian tribe that fought trappers in the Rocky Mountains).

These five and the original two became the "Seven Council Fires of the Sioux." Their council fires were rarely lighted at the same time for any common purpose, and at no time did all of these people go to war against white men or any other enemy. Nevertheless, the United States government called this loose federation the Sioux Nation.

Grattan Massacre

Seldom does a wagon train get very far in movies or television without being attacked by Indians. In 1849, the first year of an endless procession of wagon trains along the Oregon Trail, not one was attacked by Indians. This same year the Regiment of Mounted Riflemen, which Congress had authorized in 1846 for the trail's protection, began its lawful business, after having fought on foot in Mexico. The Riflemen garrisoned Fort Kearny and took over Fort Laramie and Fort Hall from the fur companies. Even when the Sioux moved into Pawnee hunting grounds south of the Platte and were athwart the Oregon Trail, they stayed out of trouble with immigrants until 1854.

But in midsummer of that year High Forehead, a Miniconjou, took a wanton pot shot at a sore-footed cow belonging to a Mormon immigrant. The Mormon lodged a complaint at Fort Laramie. At that time the army was spread so thin guarding the trail that the commanding officer at Laramie was Second Lieutenant Hugh Brady Fleming of the 6th Infantry, two years out of West Point.

Fleming brushed aside attempts made to settle the dispute by Brave Bear, also called Conquering Bear, a Brulé who had been recognized as chief of all the Sioux by the Horse Creek Treaty of 1851. Fleming's subordinate, Brevet Second Lieutenant James Lawrence Grattan, asked for the assignment to arrest High Forehead.

Grattan on August 19, 1854, marched twenty-nine soldiers into the Sioux camp. Apparently he had no plan of action in case of resistance. It mattered little, as he was among the first killed when the shooting started. The troops fired one volley and got off one shot apiece from a mountain howitzer and a twelve-pounder without effect. The leaderless soldiers panicked at first, then rallied and retreated in good order, holding the Indians at a distance with rifle fire until they reached open ground, where Sioux horsemen rode them down. One wounded man got back to the fort, but died of his injuries two days later. Brave Bear, "chief of all the Sioux," was among the dead.

Now the Sioux were on the "warpath." In November a raiding party led by a brother of Brave Bear killed three men and plundered a mail wagon of $20,000. In the spring there were a number of horse-stealing expeditions. Still, the Sioux were taking their war against the United States no more seriously than their customary desultory fighting with the Pawnee.

The government, however, took the war seriously. Brevet Brigadier General William

Selby Harney, colonel of the 2nd Dragoons, was recalled from leave in Paris to lead an expedition to punish the perpetrators of the Grattan massacre. Indian agent Thomas S. Twiss was sent to warn all friendly bands to move south of the Platte and report to him at Fort Laramie; eventually 400 of the 700 lodges of the Sioux were assembled in that vicinity. General Harney marched out of Fort Kearny up the Platte toward Fort Laramie with 600 soldiers, including two companies of the 2nd Dragoons, one of the 4th Artillery, five of the 6th Infantry and one of the 10th Infantry.

Little Thunder, a chief of the Brulés, in camp at Ash Hollow above the forks of the Platte, was warned by a trader that troops were approaching, but did nothing about it. His camp was surprised by Harney's infantry on the morning of September 3, 1855. Little Thunder, Spotted Tail and Iron Shell rode out for a parley, but Harney's orders stated that all negotiating had been taken care of by agent Twiss, so he kept advancing. The dragoons cut off the retreating Sioux in the rear; Indian losses were eighty-six killed, seventy women and children captured.

When Harney arrived at Fort Laramie, he demanded that the Sioux there surrender Spotted Tail and Red Leaf, the leaders in the attack on Grattan and the raid on the mail wagon. Both had been in the hostile camp at Ash Hollow. They were taken to Fort Leavenworth to be hanged but eventually were pardoned. Meanwhile, Spotted Tail had made friends among the officers; he had seen something of the might of United States forces and was convinced that it was futile to fight them. He later became a powerful chief of the Brulé Sioux and kept his following at peace with the army. But, by masterly diplomacy, during the rest of his life (until 1881) he continued to upset Indian Bureau plans to civilize them.

The Fighting Cheyenne

George Bird Grinnell, who knew Indians intimately in their wild days, wrote that the Cheyenne tribe was "a fighting and a fearless people . . . almost constantly at war with its neighbors, but until 1856 was friendly to the whites."

The break occurred over a minor matter concerning four stolen horses at Upper Platte Bridge (the site of Casper, Wyoming). When a Cheyenne was killed bolting an arrest, his tribesmen took to the warpath, and in five small raids against travelers along the Platte River killed eight men, two women and one child and captured two women and a child, following which they made peace with the Indian Bureau for the winter. In the spring they resumed raiding, and the army took action.

Colonel Edwin Vose Sumner of the 1st Cavalry, with six companies of his regiment, three of the 6th Infantry and two pieces of artillery, marched from Fort Leavenworth. On July 29, 1857, at Solomon's Fork of the Kansas River, he came upon 300 Cheyenne, "drawn up in battle array." Without waiting for infantry or guns, Sumner ordered his six troops to draw saber and charge. As we have seen, Lieutenant Hood and Captain Ord used sabers against the Comanche and Yakima, but such weapons seldom proved effective against Indians. However, when Sumner charged the Cheyenne broke and fled; they were pursued seven miles and nine were killed. The cavalry had two killed and nine wounded; one of the wounded was First Lieutenant J. E. B. Stuart. Sumner's second in command was Major John Sedgwick, a Civil War major general of volunteers who was killed at Spotsylvania.

44. *Wild Indians During the Civil War*

MANY OFFICERS OF the Old Army used to say that the Indian wars really started when regular troops were withdrawn from the western posts for the Civil War. The record offers little to support that point of view. There were no great outbreaks in 1861, when the withdrawal actually was under way. Later on, as Indian warfare resumed in its usual desultory and unpredictable fashion and western states' and territories called out regiments of volunteers, there were more troops guarding against Indian forays than there had been before the war.

The theory that Confederate agents stirred up the Indians, an idea popularized by fiction writers and Hollywood productions, is based on the popular notion that Indians were united in opposing white invasion. The fact is that they never were. True, the Confederates did attempt some small-scale efforts, but without material result. The most ambitious effort was that of Brigadier General Albert Pike, who enrolled volunteers from the Five Civilized Tribes of Indian Territory. In fact the Cherokee chief Stand Watie, commissioned brigadier general, was the last general officer of the Confederates to surrender—on June 23, 1865. But the record shows that the Confederate cause was little aided by the efforts of the civilized tribes.

The Minnesota Massacre

Ironically enough, the most serious Indian outbreak during the Civil War began in the American midlands, not in the West covered by this book, but the fighting soon spread westward. It commenced in Minnesota in 1862 with the Santee Sioux, who had long been exposed to the civilizing influence of the Indian Bureau. The immediate cause of the outbreak was a delay in delivering the rations promised by treaty, chargeable to preoccupation of the governmental agencies with Civil War problems. When hungry Indians stole food and killed settlers, the rest of the dissatisfied Sioux lost no time in joining in the slaughter. An estimated 400 to 800 people were killed. Henry Hastings Sibley, commissioned colonel by Minnesota's governor, soon organized the state's defenses, harried most bands out of the settlements and won a considerable victory at Wood Lake on September 22. Of the captured Indians accused of murders, rapes and torture and tried by a military commission, 100 were condemned to death. President Lincoln reviewed the findings, and reduced the number to 38, who were hanged on December 26, 1862.

Meanwhile many of the hostile Santee had fled westward, seeking refuge among their kinsmen, the Teton Sioux. When Major General John Pope, deprived of his army after his defeat in Virginia at Second Bull Run, came to assume command of the Department of the Northwest in September, 1862, he organized punitive expeditions to pursue the hostiles into Dakota Territory. In the summer of 1863 Sibley, promoted to brigadier general of volunteers, moved up the Minnesota River toward Devil's Lake. A larger column marched up the Missouri under command of Alfred Sully, major of the 8th Infantry who had been commissioned brigadier general of volunteers.

Sibley fought the Sioux at Big Mound on July 24, Dead Buffalo Lake on July 26 and Stony Lake on July 28, while Sully captured a village at White Stone Hill on September 3. In all of these fights the use of artillery proved decisive.

In 1864 General Sully undertook a longer campaign into Dakota. After crossing the Missouri River he traversed the Cannonball and Heart Rivers, defeating Santee and Teton Sioux at Killdeer Mountain on July 8. He pursued these Indians westward through the Bad Lands—not far from where Theodore Roosevelt would one day own a ranch—as far as the Yellowstone in western Montana, then turned back down the Missouri.

Sand Creek

No single event of the Indian wars has been subject to more exaggeration and overemphasis than the November 29, 1864, attack by Colorado Volunteers under the command of Colonel John M. Chivington on a village of Cheyenne and Arapaho at Sand Creek, Colorado Territory. In *A Century of Dishonor,* Helen Hunt Jackson made it Exhibit A in her catalog of wrongs inflicted on the Indians. Most later writers have followed her lead, although the colonel does have a few defenders. He was censured in the findings of three inquiries: those of a Joint Congressional Committee on the Conduct of the War, a Joint Special Committee to Inquire into the Condition of the Indian Tribes, and a military commission. Testimony was highly sensational in its gory details on mutilations of Indian bodies, but a surprising amount of it was prefaced by "they told me," "he said," "I heard" and even "according to representations made in our presence," and not nearly enough of it by, "I saw."

Chivington was a popular and persuasive frontier preacher, the presiding elder of the Methodist Episcopal Church. When the 1st Colorado Cavalry was raised in 1862 he declined an appointment as chaplain and asked for a fighting job. He was made major. At Glorieta he led the surprise attack on the rear guard and supply train that was decisive in repelling the Confederate invasion of New Mexico. He was promoted to colonel and district commander, provoking the jealousies of many volunteer officers. Backed by a party demanding immediate statehood for Colorado, he was a candidate for Congress in a bitter political campaign that had bearings on the congressional inquiries into his conduct at Sand Creek.

The southern Cheyenne had been in eastern Colorado since about 1800, when they came from the north. They became allies of the Arapaho, and by constant warfare with the Ute to the westward and the Pawnee to the eastward maintained hunting grounds sufficient for their needs. Atrocities in these intertribal wars make the worst charges against Chivington seem tame and colorless.

Although this idyllic Indian way of life was disturbed in 1859 by the "Pike's Peak or Bust" gold rush, there was no serious clash until 1863, when a Cheyenne war party moving against the Ute levied forced contributions on settlers along the way. This was followed by reports of horses, mules and cattle stolen, possibly by hungry Indians. Troops were sent to recover the stock, and shooting inevitably followed.

On June 11, 1864, rancher Nathan P. Hungate, his wife and two little girls were slaughtered by Indians. Their mutilated bodies were brought to Denver and placed on public view. The town was thrown into panic. One false alarm sent all women and children to brick business houses that were fortified and guarded. Plains travel slowed to a trickle. The supply of coal oil (kerosene) was exhausted and the settlers had to use candles. The *Rocky Mountain News* was printed on pink tissue paper. Chiselers cornered flour.

A regiment of 100-day volunteers to fight Indians was raised as the 3rd Colorado Cavalry. Its colonel, George L. Shoup, in later years became Idaho's last territorial governor and first

elected governor. Subsequently he served as United States senator and was honored by Idaho in National Statuary Hall.

On August 29, before his regiment saw active service, a letter from Black Kettle of the Cheyenne was received by Samuel G. Colley, Indian agent at Fort Lyon on the Arkansas, 150 miles southeast of Denver, which said the hostiles had met in council and agreed to make peace. They offered to exchange prisoners in their hands for those held in Denver. The letter, however, could hardly be considered a "cease-fire" because it admitted frankly: "There are three [Cheyenne] war parties out yet, and two of the Arapahoes."

Major E. W. Wynkoop of the 1st Colorado at Fort Lyon, eager to recover the captives, marched a small force to the Indian camp. There, convinced of Black Kettle's sincerity, he persuaded a delegation of chiefs to go to Denver.

John Evans, governor of the Colorado Territory (and the founder of both Northwestern University and the University of Denver) meanwhile issued a proclamation stating: "Friendly Arapahoes and Cheyennes belonging to the Arkansas River will go to Major Colley, U. S. Indian Agent at Fort Lyon, who will give them provisions and show them a place of safety. . . . The war on hostile Indians will be continued until they are effectually subdued."

From Fort Leavenworth, Major General Samuel Ryan Curtis, commander of the Department of Kansas, telegraphed Chivington prior to the conference with the chiefs: "I shall require the bad Indians delivered up; restoration of equal numbers of stock; also hostages to secure. I want no peace till the Indians suffer more."

Indian warfare—the attack on the village. Engraving, after drawing by T. de Thulstrup.
Harper's Weekly, 1885

These are the orders under which Colonel Chivington acted when he told the chiefs at Denver: "My rule of fighting white men or Indians is, to fight them until they lay down their arms and submit to military authority. You are nearer Major Wynkoop than anyone else and you can go to him when you are ready to do that."

Black Kettle returned to his village on Sand Creek, thirty-five miles northwest of Fort Lyon. He did not move his band to Fort Lyon, as both Governor Evans and Colonel Chivington had demanded. No arms were surrendered, no hostages given, no bad Indians delivered

up, no stock restored. Major Wynkoop, however, had recovered four prisoners, and reported that he was continuing to negotiate with the Indians. General Curtis considered this a violation of his orders and relieved Wynkoop from command, demanding an investigation of charges that the major had issued supplies to hostile Indians, meaning Black Kettle's band.

At this time, Chivington, having waited two months after his conference with Black Kettle, decided to act before expiration of the 100-day enlistment of the 3rd Colorado Cavalry. Detachments from six companies of the 1st Colorado Cavalry with two howitzers joined the expedition, which marched in bitter cold through snow sometimes two feet deep. Chivington halted all traffic as he marched along the roads to prevent any warning from reaching Black Kettle's band through traders.

The attack at dawn of November 29, 1864, on the Sand Creek camp came as a complete surprise for Black Kettle. This fact in itself does not prove, necessarily, that the Indians were relying on white man's promises, for Cheyenne prowess in the field of security and information was quite as lacking in several subsequent surprise engagements when they were definitely on the warpath.

Despite their unpreparedness, Cheyenne and Arapaho quickly rallied and from cover along the banks of the creek put up a stiff fight that lasted all day until dark, giving the lie to any idea that this was a slaughter of unresisting Indians or that the camp was mainly women and children.

Women and children were killed, although Private William M. Breakenridge (in later years a deputy under Sheriff John H. Behan, Wyatt Earp's rival at Tombstone) said, "I saw very few squaws and no children." And further, "There were a lot of scalps of white men and women, some very fresh, found in the teepees; but so far as scalps went, our boys had the best of it, for every dead Indian was scalped once, and some of them two or three times."

Assistant Surgeon Caleb S. Burdsal reported that a soldier brought five or six white scalps to him, and further stated, "My impression is that one or two of them were not more than ten days off the head." What clearer indication could there be that war parties had been out since the peace talks two months before?

And though it is also clear that Chivington commanded an ill-disciplined body of vengeful frontiersmen who fought well and long, did a lot of scalping and perhaps committed other atrocities, there is no proof that Chivington said or did anything to encourage atrocities—or to stop them.

The Sand Creek Aftermath

The final exaggeration of the Sand Creek fight has been its representation as the direct cause of a great uprising of Plains Indians when the Cheyenne spread word of the white men's perfidy. It would be difficult to prove that any other tribes were influenced by such a plea or that Indian warfare became any more intense than it had been previously. One of the causes of the Sand Creek incident was Governor Evans' fear of an "alliance of Indians on the plains." But there was no such concert of action among Plains tribes before Sand Creek or afterward— or at any other time.

The actual result of Sand Creek was that its survivors fled northward, carrying along with them Sioux and Arapaho bands that had been raiding along the Kansas and Smoky Hill rivers. What the Colorado Volunteers had accomplished, then, was to drive Indians out of their territory—only to dump them across the Oregon Trail.

On January 7, 1865, this concentration of Indians attempted to ambush Iowa Volunteer Cavalry at Camp Rankin, guarding Julesburg, Colorado. But too many, too eager ambushers showed themselves too soon. The cavalry held its camp, where citizens took refuge while Indians looted the town. Subsequent raids on Rock Ridge, Sweetwater, Sage Creek and Bridger's Pass, however, stopped traffic along the trails.

At Fort Laramie 1,500 Brulé Sioux, presumed friendly, had been fed during the winter. It was proposed to send them to Fort Kearny under escort to get them out of the war zone. On the way they killed the escort commander, Captain W. D. Fouts of the 7th Iowa Cavalry, and took to the hills. Colonel Thomas Moonlight of the 11th Kansas Cavalry, a district commander, went in pursuit, but the Sioux stampeded his horses and he returned afoot. This ended the war for a volunteer officer who had made a commendable record fighting Confederates in the Missouri border struggle.

First Lieutenant Caspar Wever Collins of the 11th Ohio Cavalry was killed at Platte Bridge on July 26, 1865, while leading a force to the relief of a wagon train which was overwhelmed at the same time by a large war party of Sioux, Cheyenne and Arapaho. In the two separate fights of the wagon train escort and the relief party twenty-five soldiers were killed and nine wounded. The post at Platte Bridge was renamed Fort Caspar in his honor, using his first name to avoid confusion with his father, the regimental commander Colonel William O. Collins. Somehow the city that grew up there got its vowels mixed and became Casper, not Caspar.

Powder River Expedition, 1865

The Civil War over, General Patrick E. Connor, commanding a new District of the Plains, led the largest expedition of volunteer troops ever sent against Indians. The Powder River Expedition was organized in the summer of 1865 at Fort Laramie in four columns.

The right, under Colonel Nelson Cole of the 2nd Missouri Light Artillery, included eight companies of his regiment equipped as cavalry and a section of three-inch rifled guns, and eight companies of the 13th Missouri Cavalry, totaling 800 men.

The center, under Lieutenant Colonel Samuel Walker of the 16th Kansas Cavalry, consisted of 600 men of that regiment. Walker was a veteran of the Bleeding Kansas troubles and, although slightly crippled by a hip ailment, had won a reputation as a fighting man.

The left was commanded by Colonel J. H. Kidd of the 6th Michigan Cavalry, who with his regiment had served under Major General George A. Custer in the Civil War's eastern campaigns. He had six companies of his regiment totaling 200 men, 90 of the 7th Iowa Cavalry, 90 of the 11th Ohio Cavalry and 95 Pawnee Scouts under Captain Frank North.

The fourth, or west, column was commanded by Captain Albert Brown of the 2nd California Cavalry with two companies, 116 men, of that regiment and a company of Omaha and Winnebago scouts under Captain E. W. Nash.

General Connor himself accompanied the left and west columns, with Jim Bridger, the famous mountain man, as scout. The total force was 3,000 men short of what had been planned, due to the fact that many volunteers had demanded their discharges on the ground that the war was ended; others, in the words of Major General Grenville M. Dodge, commanding the Department of the Missouri, were "mutinous, dissatisfied and inefficient."

On August 19 Captain North's Pawnee Scouts overtook a band of Cheyenne and killed all twenty-four of them. The west column was meanwhile detached at Platte Bridge to scout the Wind River country.

General Connor, with the left column, surprised the Arapaho camp of Black Bear on Tongue River on August 29. Charging cavalry fired a volley from their carbines without halting, and the Arapaho fled. General Connor led the pursuit until he found that he had outdistanced all except fourteen of his command, at which point the Indians turned on him. Fortunately, as he fell back, he was reinforced by the soldiers he had left behind and so was able to renew the running fight until the village was reached. There his troops destroyed 250 lodges and rounded up 500 horses. Connor estimated thirty-five Indians killed; he captured seven women and eleven children and lost one Omaha scout killed and seven men wounded.

Colonel Cole's right column marched 1,200 miles in eighty-two days through the Bad Lands and Black Hills, losing twelve killed and two missing in four fights with Indians. To his misfortune, however, a severe sleet storm resulted in the loss of 414 horses within thirty-six hours. Cole had already lost 225 horses and mules in a previous storm and had to abandon most of his wagons.

When Colonel Walker's center column reached the mouth of Dry Fork of Powder River on September 8, he was attacked by Sioux, Arapaho and Cheyenne. Cole came to his aid and in several fights that followed Cole estimated 200 to 300 Indians killed and wounded. Walker more modestly reported, "As to the number of Indians killed in our long fight with them I cannot say as we killed one. I saw a number fall, but they were at once carried off." Walker's column lost 225 horses and 25 mules in its march of 600 miles in forty-seven days.

Cole and Walker failed to make junction with Connor until their men were exhausted and starving. Forced to exist on the meat of their few surviving horses, they fell back for supplies to a depot established by Connor at the Bozeman Trail crossing of the upper Powder River, at the time called Fort Connor but later renamed Fort Reno for Major General Jesse L. Reno, who had been killed at the battle of South Mountain, Maryland, on September 14, 1862.

45. *The Indian Wars Begin*

THE REGULAR ARMY was as woefully neglected during the Civil War as it had been during the previous periods when there were only the Indians to fight. Its increase was one regiment of artillery of twelve companies, making a total of five regiments; one regiment of cavalry of twelve companies making a total of six regiments; and nine regiments of infantry added to the ten in service. The old infantry regiments had ten companies each, with only 52 enlisted men in a company, a regiment consisting of 582 officers and enlisted men. The

Harper's Weekly, 1885

Indian warfare—discovery of the village. Engraving, after drawing by Rufus F. Zogbaum.

nine new infantry regiments, however, had twenty-four companies, each divided into three eight-company battalions (the companies lettered from A to H in each battalion). The aggregate strength of such a regiment would have been 2,444, but none of them reached it during the war.

The Regular Army got few recruits in competition with the recruiting for state volunteers, and all regiments dropped far under authorized strength. Had they been full, however, there would have been no officers to command them. Nearly all field officers, and many captains and lieutenants, accepted commissions in the volunteers. They retained their Regular Army commissions and assignments, and were duly promoted in their permanent ranks throughout the war. There was no provision for filling vacancies, and captains commonly commanded Regular Army regiments in battle.

Officers were advanced one grade in brevet rank after every battle in which they were recommended "for gallant and meritorious service." Brevet commissions in the volunteers terminated at the end of the war, but a Regular Army brevet was permanent, and had many privileges besides the honor that went with it. By courtesy and custom an officer was addressed in his highest brevet rank, even in official correspondence. He could be called to duty in his brevet rank by special assignment, and he served in his brevet rank when a member of a court-martial or in command of a detachment composed of different corps. In these cases he received the pay and allowances of his brevet rank.

The Regular Army as of 1866 had one general of the army (Ulysses S. Grant), one lieutenant-general (William Tecumseh Sherman), five major generals and nineteen brigadier generals, including nine heading such staff departments as quartermaster, subsistence, pay, ordnance and so on. The country was divided into five military divisions—geographical divisions, not divisions in the sense of army units, active or inactive. Within the divisions were departments, and the departments were subdivided into districts. Thus the Military Division of the Missouri included the Department of Missouri, the Department of Arkansas, the Department of the Platte and the Department of Dakota. The District of the Republican was one of the districts of the Department of the Platte.

Each of the former Confederate States became a department under the congressional plan of Reconstruction. Each division, department and district was the proper command of a general officer; there were only sixteen general officers of the line, so considerable employment was available for the 152 brevet major generals and 187 brevet brigadier generals commissioned during the war. In those days regiments rarely saw their colonels, or even lieutenant colonels, except perhaps as brevet generals commanding expeditions "composed of different corps" sent to chastise Indians.

In 1866, however, it was supposed that the Indian wars were near an end. General Curtis, who had wanted no peace until the Indians suffered more, had made a treaty with the Sioux, signed by the chiefs who customarily pitched their tents within hearing of the reveille gun and mess call at army posts. It was recognized that the treaty, opening the Bozeman Trail —a short cut through Sioux country to the mines in Montana—should be signed also by the chiefs who had been at war, and they were summoned to Fort Laramie, in June, 1866, to meet a new peace commission headed by E. B. Taylor of the Indian Bureau.

Red Cloud.

In May the Second and Third battalions and Company F of the First Battalion, 18th Infantry, were assembled at Fort Kearny, Nebraska, under command of their colonel, Brevet Brigadier General Henry Beebe Carrington. This was the largest gathering of one of the triple-deck regiments ever seen in Indian country, and it was almost immediately dispersed. As Carrington marched westward he sent detachments to garrison Fort Sedgwick at Julesburg, Colorado; Fort Bridger in the southwest corner of Wyoming; Camp Douglas at Salt Lake City; and other posts.

General Carrington himself with the Second Battalion carried orders to march north from the big bend of the Platte to establish three posts along the Bozeman Trail. These orders were based on assurances by the Indian Bureau that the Sioux Nation, meaning the chiefs who had already signed, had consented to the opening of the road, but when Carrington reached Fort Laramie he found the peace commission still negotiating with the chiefs who had been on the warpath. Red Cloud and Man Afraid of His Horses refused to be coerced into signing the treaty and walked out. Indian Bureau officials brushed this protest aside with assurances that the two chiefs were unimportant and uninfluential. The upshot was that some 2,000 Sioux accepted the treaty and remained at peace, while 4,000 or more took part in Red Cloud's War.

Red Cloud's War

General Carrington marched north as ordered, into the country where the much larger Powder River Expedition had accomplished little the previous year. On the upper Powder River, at the site of Fort Connor, Carrington established Fort Reno and manned it with Companies B and F of his Second Battalion. Marching on to the Little Piney, he retained Companies A, C, E and H to build Fort Philip Kearny (usually shortened to Phil and commonly misspelled, even by its commander, as Kearney). Companies D and G were sent on to build Fort C. F. Smith on the Big Horn.

Red Cloud and his following lost no time in making the troops unwelcome. During the last five months of 1866 Indians made fifty-one attacks in the vicinity of Fort Phil Kearny. This has been called a siege, but the garrison was never isolated by an impenetrable line of Indians. A wood train went out every day to get timber for building the fort. Supply trains came and went. The mail went through, carried both ways by soldiers or scouts. An inspector general came by and claimed an escort from the meager garrison—replaced after three months' delay by Company C, 2nd Cavalry.

The Fetterman Massacre

On December 21, 1866, a signalman reported that the wood train was being attacked, not an uncommon occurrence. Brevet Lieutenant Colonel William J. Fetterman led a relief party of eighty-one, including two officers and two civilian scouts. Fetterman is said to have boasted a few days earlier: "Give me eighty men and I'll ride through the whole Sioux nation." If he said it, which somehow seems doubtful, he was actually reflecting the official view that had sent 700 soldiers to fight 4,000 Indians. Carrington officially reported that he had ordered Fetterman "under no circumstances pursue over Lodge Trail Ridge." But Fetterman followed a decoy party across the ridge, and his small force was slaughtered to the last man. Ironically the wood train he had been sent to rescue reached the fort safely.

The Indians made no attempt to follow up their victory, even when the snow piled up to the top of the fort's stockade making it possible for them to walk in on the greatly reduced garrison. It was assumed thereafter that Plains Indians would not attempt to storm a fort, and stockades now fell into disfavor. Many officers held that stockades afforded Indians a hiding place to lurk for scalps; they preferred a clear field of view for rifle fire.

Carrington lacked battle experience in the Civil War and was distrusted by his veteran officers; his cautious tactics in Indian fighting, however, were approved by a court of inquiry that met at his request after his transfer to Fort McPherson to investigate his conduct of his command at Fort Phil Kearny, including the Fetterman disaster. However, he failed to survive the army cutback of 1869.

The Wagon Box Fight

In the spring and summer of 1867 the wood train again made daily trips from Fort Phil Kearny. Where trees were being cut, a corral had been made by forming a circle of the wagon boxes that had been taken off to free the wheels and running gears for the hauling of logs. (These wagon boxes were of wood, not lined with sheet steel or boiler iron, as some accounts state.)

On January 1, 1867, the Second Battalion of the 18th Infantry had become the 27th Infantry. On August 2, Brevet Major James Powell, captain of its Company C, was in command of the escort when the wood party was attacked by an estimated 3,000 Sioux.

Thirty-two men took refuge in and among the wagon boxes. Some 500 overconfident Indians charged on horseback, apparently hoping to draw the fire of the soldiers and then close in while the defenders were reloading. However, the troops were armed with "Allin alteration" Springfield rifles, Civil War muzzle-loaders converted into breechloaders by a method developed by E. A. Allin, master armorer at Springfield Arsenal. They could be reloaded very quickly—so quickly that the wall of fire never stopped and the horsemen of the Plains were turned away with heavy casualties.

The Indians rallied and attacked again, this time on foot and more cautiously. In early afternoon a relief party with a howitzer arrived from the fort and drove them off. Powell reported 40 Indians killed and 120 wounded, but some estimates put the dead at 400, 800 and even the improbable figure of 1,137. Six soldiers were killed and two wounded.

The Hayfield Fight

Unlike Fort Phil Kearny, Fort C. F. Smith, ninety-one miles farther up the Bozeman Trail, was isolated by hostile Indians. No party entered or left it between November 30, 1866, and June 8, 1867.

On August 1—the day before the Wagon Box Fight—a fatigue party cutting hay for the fort was attacked by 800 Cheyenne. The haymakers had built a corral of logs, which the Indians charged again and again, both mounted and on foot. The Allin alteration Springfields again surprised the Indians, and several civilians did even better with repeating rifles.

The troops, commanded by Second Lieutenant Sigismund Sternberg, who was killed, included detachments from Companies C, D, G and H, 27th Infantry, and Company I, one of two new companies added to complete the 27th.

A howitzer firing case shot scattered the Cheyenne. Their known loss was eight killed and thirty wounded. The most optimistic estimate upped this to 150. The defenders had three killed.

After these fights along the Bozeman Trail the peace that followed was of a kind that had become characteristic of United States diplomacy. Red Cloud was allowed to save face by appearing to have won the war—and many have interpreted it that he did. In March, 1868, General Grant ordered abandonment of the Bozeman Trail and its three posts, Forts Phil Kearny, C. F. Smith and Reno. Actually the Bozeman Trail had ceased to be of importance, for the advancing railroad was making other routes to the Montana gold fields more feasible.

After a summer of negotiation, Red Cloud was persuaded to sign a treaty on November 6, 1868. It provided a Sioux reservation that included all of what became South Dakota west of the Missouri River.

Most of the Sioux who had been fighting were on lands they were in the process of taking away from the Crows, a tribe generally friendly to the United States. In fact, *Ab-sa-ra-ka,* meaning "Home of the Crows," was the title of the book about Fort Phil Kearny written by Mrs. Margaret Irvin Carrington, wife of the colonel. It was not Sioux country, but the treaty allowed them hunting rights there, mainly because they were there and there was no practical manner of getting them out—appeasement, if you will, or certainly *status quo ante bellum.*

And if in Red Cloud's own mind he had won, he nevertheless stayed on the reservation and never again dug up the hatchet. He obviously wanted no more of the kind of battles he had won, or lost. Reports of Indian casualities may have been exaggerated, but there had been many more than he wanted.

Congress Makes a Strong Fighting Army

The strange procedure by which, at a stroke of the pen, the troops at Forts Reno, Phil Kearny and C. F. Smith received a new regimental name on New Year's Day, 1867, was, of course, part of a general reorganization under an act of Congress of 1866 providing for a larger Regular Army than had been ever before in service (not until World War I were there a larger number of regiments). Each of the eight-company battalions in infantry regiments numbered from 11th to 19th became a ten-company regiment, bringing the number of infantry regiments to thirty-seven. Added were four regiments of colored troops and four regiments of the Veteran Reserve Corps, made up of wounded men.

Though the army now reached its greatest strength during any period of Indian wars, it was not because of the Indian troubles that it was given the additional strength. Most of the new infantry units went to the unreconstructed South. However, four new cavalry regiments were added, and while cavalry did garrison the former Confederate States, more of it served on the frontier—notably the 7th Cavalry, organized in 1866 with Brevet Major General Andrew Jackson Smith as its colonel and Brevet Major General George Armstrong Custer as its lieutenant colonel. Colonel of the 8th Cavalry was Brevet Brigadier General John Irvin Gregg. The 9th and 10th regiments of cavalry were made up of colored troops, and remained so to the end of both cavalry and segregation in the armed forces.

The Hancock Expedition of 1867

The year 1866 was a comparatively quiet one south of the Platte. The Indians were restive, however, and it was felt that a display of force might awe them, as they had rarely seen soldiers

except in small detachments. Therefore, in March, 1867, Major General Winfield Scott Hancock, commanding the Department of Missouri, assembled at Fort Leavenworth, Kansas, an
expedition of 1,400 men, including eight companies of the new 7th Cavalry under General
Custer, seven of infantry and a battery of light artillery. Indian agents went along to make
peace with any awe-struck tribes that might be encountered.

Though parleys were sought from Fort Larned on the Arkansas River with Cheyenne and
Sioux encamped some thirty miles away, the Indians refused to come toward the troops, and
when the troops moved toward the Indians, they fled, abandoning their village with all its
property. When the scattering fugitives raided stage stations along the Overland Trail, killing
three men at Lookout Station, west of Fort Hays, Hancock ordered the captured village
destroyed.

Custer's 7th Cavalry scouted north and westward. Pawnee Killer's Sioux attacked his camp
at dawn on June 24, but were driven off. Later in the day Captain Louis Hamilton's Company
A fought its way out of a decoy trap. On June 26 Lieutenant S. M. Robbins and the escort
for a wagon train sent to Fort Wallace in western Kansas for supplies fought 500 Indians for
three hours. Also on June 26 Lieutenant Lyman Stockwell Kidder, carrying dispatches to
Custer, and ten men of the 2nd Cavalry and a Sioux guide with him were all slain.

It was at this time, on July 30, that Congress set up a Peace Commission with three objectives: to end the Indian wars by giving the Indians whatever they wanted; to make peaceful
farmers of them; and to get their permission to build railroads across the Plains—three mutually contradictory propositions. By October the commissioners were ready to meet with the
southern tribes—Arapaho, Apache, Cheyenne, Comanche and Kiowa—at Medicine Lodge,
Kansas. The war-party season had ended and the tribes were quite ready for a winter of peace,
especially as there were presents, including arms and ammunition. A treaty was signed, and
although the Senate's failure to ratify it delayed some of the promised presents, the peace was
kept, more or less—mostly less—until August, 1868. (Army records show forty-two fights
with Indians between November 1, 1867, and August 1, 1868, in Kansas, Nebraska, Texas,
New Mexico and Arizona.)

Sheridan Takes the Helm

In March, 1868, Sheridan replaced Hancock as commander of the Department of Missouri.
On August 10 a war party of Cheyenne, Sioux and Arapaho began raids along the Saline and
Solomon valleys, killing fifteen settlers and carrying off two children. Kiowa and Comanche
joined in, and by the end of September the death toll of citizens was seventy-nine.

Sheridan moved his headquarters to Fort Hays, Kansas, in the heart of the Indian country.
Pending arrival of the 5th Cavalry, which was gathered in from posts in the South and sent
west in record time, he authorized Brevet Colonel George Alexander Forsyth, a major on his
staff, to enlist a company of fifty scouts.

The Beecher Island Fight

Near the end of track on the Kansas Pacific Railroad a wagon train had been attacked
and two men killed. Forsyth's scouts followed the trail, and on the morning of September
17, 1868, while encamped on the Arickaree Fork of the Republican River (south of the site

of Wray, Colorado) they were attacked by a large party of Cheyenne, Arapaho and Sioux. "The ground seemed to grow them," said Forsyth; an Indian who fought there told him later that there were 970.

The scouts mounted and crossed to a sand island in the river—called Beecher Island after First Lieutenant Frederick Beecher, killed on the first day. The scouts scooped out shelters in the sand, and used their horses, which were soon killed, to help form a barrier.

The unusual feature of this fight was a massed charge by mounted Indians, with a front of some sixty men, led by Roman Nose of the northern Cheyenne and aided by concealed marksmen. The Indians would not have been so bold had they known the scouts were armed with Spencer repeating rifles—six shots in the magazine and one in the chamber. Seven volleys crashed into the oncoming line before the charge broke and swept around the defenders. Roman Nose was among the killed. A second charge was stopped a hundred yards away.

That night scouts Pierre Trudeau and Jack Stillwell slipped through the surrounding Indians to seek help at Fort Wallace. On their way they hid in a buffalo wallow with Indians close by. When a rattlesnake started toward them, Stillwell, master of an old frontier art, stopped the snake by spitting tobacco juice in the reptile's eye. They got through, as did two scouts sent out two nights later, and a detachment of the 10th Cavalry rode to the rescue. They found Forsyth severely wounded; six more had been killed or died later of wounds, and seventeen others were wounded. Many years later some Cheyenne told George Bird Grinnell that only nine Indians were killed in the fight, and some historians have accepted that figure. Forsyth said, "During the fight I counted thirty-two dead Indians; these I reported officially. My men claimed to have counted far more." Later a Sioux participant told him that seventy-five were killed.

Sheridan's Winter Campaign

On October 1, 1868, seven companies of the 5th Cavalry, only nineteen days after they had been summoned from Virginia, North Carolina, South Carolina and Tennessee on September 12, marched out of Fort Harker, Kansas, seeking hostile Indians—a remarkably rapid troop movement for that time. Guiding the 5th as chief of scouts was William F. Cody, known as Buffalo Bill. The expedition fought several sharp skirmishes against Tall Bull's Dog Soldiers, a warrior society of the Cheyenne.

The mounted Indians broke off these fights whenever they were endangered; most pursuit of them was futile, and they had all the advantage in their hit-and-run raids. General Sheridan decided on a winter campaign to strike them in their villages, although Jim Bridger who knew the power of blizzards that swept the Plains came especially to Fort Hays to advise Sheridan not to attempt it.

"The War Party." Water color drawing by Rufus F. Zogbaum.

KENNEDY GALLERIES, NEW YORK

Sheridan planned to strike the winter camps with converging columns. Brevet Major General Eugene A. Carr, major of the 5th Cavalry, led seven troops of his regiment from Fort Lyon, Colorado Territory, to join Brevet Brigadier General William H. Penrose, captain of the 3rd Infantry, who was already in the field, along the Cimarron. This column marched through deep snow in bitter cold and encountered no Indians, but its objective was to prevent them from drifting westward.

Brevet Lieutenant Colonel Andrew W. Evans, major of the 3rd Cavalry, with six companies of his regiment and two of infantry, moved down the Canadian River. On Christmas Day this column destroyed a Comanche village. Evans got his brevet as colonel for the victory.

The main column included the 19th Kansas Volunteer Cavalry, a regiment raised by Governor Samuel J. Crawford, who took the field as its colonel; five companies of infantry under Brevet Major John H. Page, captain of the 3rd Infantry; and eleven companies of the 7th Cavalry under General Custer. Sheridan accompanied this column, escorted by Forsyth's scouts, now commanded by Lieutenant Silas Pepoon of the 10th Cavalry. A base was established as Camp Supply in western Indian Territory.

Custer at the Washita, 1868

Just before reaching Camp Supply, Pepoon's scouts struck the trail of a war party returning from a raid in Kansas. Sheridan ordered Custer's 7th Cavalry to follow the trail, guided by California Joe (whose name was Moses B. Milner), Jack Corbin and Osage Indian scouts. The regiment started out next morning, despite a heavy fall of snow during the night and a continuing storm.

The trail was followed for three days. Before dawn on November 27 an Indian village was sighted. Custer ordered an attack from four directions. As the signal for the assault the regimental band played *GarryOwen* (the spelling preferred in the 7th Cavalry's regimental history)—until their instruments froze. Cheyenne and Arapaho were completely surprised. Black Kettle, the chief who had escaped at Sand Creek, was killed.

Smarting because his leadership had been so mistrusted that Sheridan had requested Custer's return from a court-martial sentence of suspension (Custer, the preceding fall, had taken off on a visit to his wife at Fort Riley without authority), Major Joel H. Elliott raced after a fleeing group of Indians with a shout, "Here goes for a brevet or a coffin." (Elliott had no brevet rank.) He was followed by Sergeant Major Walter Kennedy and eighteen others.

Black Hills expedition under General Custer on the Plains, 1876.

NATIONAL ARCHIVES

Their bodies were found weeks later, two miles from the main battle site.

Captain Louis McLane Hamilton, grandson of Alexander Hamilton, also was killed; three officers and eleven enlisted men were wounded. The Indians lost 103 killed and 53 women and children captured.

Despite the surprise and capture of the village, Indian warriors fought desperately. Their resistance increased toward noon, and it was discovered that reinforcements were coming from villages of several thousand Kiowa, Comanche, Apache and other bands of Cheyenne and Arapaho strung out along the Washita River.

Custer ordered the captured village burned and eight hundred Indian ponies killed. Meanwhile he ordered a series of limited attacks to hold off the assembling warriors, and after dark retreated quickly to the supply train left behind.

Custer was blamed for not waiting to determine the fate of Elliott. It is probable that Elliott and his party were killed long before they were known to be missing. Custer was also accused of attacking a camp of peaceful Indians. Major Wynkoop continued to insist that Black Kettle was innocent of all wrongdoing. That may be so, although it has been denied, but Custer followed the trail of a raiding party to the village, and during the fight a Mrs. Blinn and a small boy, captives from Kansas, were butchered by Indians before they could be rescued.

Sheridan followed up the Washita victory by marching the entire main column in pursuit of the fleeing tribes. Hemmed in on the other side by the forces of Evans and Carr, the Arapaho, Cheyenne, Kiowa and Comanche agreed during the winter to go on reservations.

Buffalo Bill at Summit Springs, 1869

In May, 1869, General Carr and the 5th Cavalry marched from Fort Lyon to Fort McPherson, Nebraska, again skirmishing with Tall Bull's Cheyenne Dog Soldiers along the way. While the troops were at Fort McPherson the Cheyenne raided settlements along the Solomon, capturing Mrs. Thomas Alderdice, wife of one of Forsyth's scouts of the Beecher Island fight, and Mrs. G. Weichel, after killing Mrs. Alderdice's baby and Mrs. Weichel's husband.

General Carr took to their trail with seven companies of his regiment and three of Pawnee Scouts under Major Frank North. Buffalo Bill Cody, chief of scouts for the 5th Cavalry continuously from 1868 to 1872, is credited with suggesting the maneuver that headed them off at Summit Springs. The Indians were evidently traveling toward the Platte, and Cody's plan, in Carr's words, was "to get around, beyond, and between them and the river" instead of following their trail as the Indians would expect.

At midday on July 11, 1869, Buffalo Bill and the scouts located Tall Bull's camp. Carr charged at once with four mounted companies in line, a bugle sounding the charge. He was joined almost immediately by North's Pawnee Scouts and two more companies under Brevet Colonel William B. Royall.

The attack was a complete surprise—Cheyenne security and information facilities seem never to have reached the standard set for Indians in fiction. Tall Bull and fifty-one of his followers were killed, seventeen women and children were captured, with no loss to the troops. Mrs. Weichel was rescued, wounded; Mrs. Alderdice was tomahawked by a Cheyenne woman just before the troopers could reach her. The victory was a blow from which the Dog Soldiers never recovered.

After the Summit Springs victory there was peace of sorts on the northern Plains. Red Cloud and Spotted Tail, taking seriously the treaties that barred white men from the Sioux Reservation, demanded that the Government's Indian agencies be located beyond the reservation boundaries in Nebraska, and they got what they wanted. Both had had their fill of fighting U.S. soldiers, but Spotted Tail had no idea of giving up warfare against tribal enemies, and it was his Brulé who attacked a hunting party of Pawnee at Massacre Canyon, Nebraska, on August 5, 1873, slaughtering ten men, thirty-nine women and ten children. A troop of cavalry belatedly dashed to the rescue, and the Sioux fled.

Crazy Horse and Sitting Bull of the Hunkpapa had signed no treaties—Sitting Bull once told General Miles, "God made me an Indian, but not an Agency Indian." Far out in the Powder River and Bighorn country they were fighting the Crows—on the Crow Reservation. In 1872 and 1873 they attacked Northern Pacific Railroad surveying parties escorted by troops led by Brevet Major General David S. Stanley, colonel of the 22nd Infantry. Custer's 7th Cavalry, a part of the escort in 1873, was attacked by 300 Sioux on August 4. He drove them off by a vigorous mounted charge, and while following their trail was attacked again on August 11, with a similar result.

Custer in the Black Hills, 1874

Some of Custer's detractors have seen his death on the Little Big Horn as just retribution for his invasion of the Black Hills, the "sacred ground" of the Sioux, two years earlier. The connection as a moral judgment is somewhat remote. Custer's exploration of the Black Hills in 1874 was not his own idea; it was ordered by Sheridan. True, the Black Hills were a part of the Great Sioux Reservation, and the Sioux resented any intrusion in the area guaranteed by treaty, but the Black Hills had no ancestral or traditional significance for the Sioux, who only recently chased Cheyenne and Kiowa out—and Bear Butte, at least, was "sacred ground" to

Colonel William F. Cody's troop being attacked.

the Cheyenne. The Sioux seldom went there, mainly because buffalo did not graze there.

Custer found no Indians in the Black Hills, but the geologists on the expedition verified the presence of gold, and newsmen gave this discovery wide publicity. The government attempted to buy the land from the Sioux, but negotiations broke down when Spotted Tail and Red Cloud upped the price. Meanwhile swarms of prospectors defied the Sioux, the government and the Army by flocking into the Black Hills. Early in 1876 the Gold Rush was in full swing.

46. *The Sioux War of 1876*

T HE ISSUE IN the Sioux War of 1876, in which the most notable event was the Custer disaster, was the demand of the Indian commissioner that the "northern non-treaty Sioux, under the leadership of Sitting Bull . . . and such outlaws from the several agencies as have attached themselves to these same hostiles" be compelled to "cease marauding and settle down" on a reservation.

Much of the marauding he referred to had taken place in Montana Territory on the Crow Reservation. Besides attacking the Crows, the nontreaty Sioux, during 1875, had made seventeen attacks on white men, killing nine, wounding ten and killing or driving off 138 head of horses, mules and oxen.

The Secretary of the Interior on December 3, 1875, ordered Indian agents to notify "certain Sioux Indians residing without the bounds of their reservations" that if they did not go to reservations by January 31, 1876, and remain there, "they shall be deemed hostile and treated accordingly by the military force." The injustice of this midwinter ultimatum has often been denounced, but obviously it was aimed at Sitting Bull and his following, and no one seriously believed that he or his band would report at a reservation, regardless of notice. The real purpose of the ultimatum was to turn over the problem of the nontreaty Sioux from the Indian Bureau to the Army.

Commissioner Edward P. Smith's 1874 report estimated Sitting Bull's "wilder portion of this tribe" at 5,000 to 10,000. The report for 1875 split the difference at 7,000, of which, it was said, 4,000 had come into the agencies, leaving Sitting Bull with only 3,000. The commissioner also stated in 1874, and repeated it in 1875, that "except under extraordinary provocation, or in circumstances not at all to be apprehended, it is not probable that as many as five hundred Indian warriors will ever again be mustered at one point for a fight. . . . Such an event as a general Indian war can never again occur in the United States."

Generals Sherman and Sheridan based their plans for the 1876 campaign on these figures. They should have given more heed to the commissioner's 1874 top estimate of 10,000. The plan was a typical Sheridan containing movement, designed to keep the Indians south of the Yellowstone and away from settlements.

General George A. Custer.

Orders issued make it quite clear that there was no plan for the several columns to converge on a concentration of Indians.

Brigadier General George Crook, commanding the Department of the Platte, marched his column out of Fort Fetterman on March 1. On March 17 his cavalry under Brevet Major General Joseph J. Reynolds, colonel of the 3rd, with five companies of his regiment and five of the 2nd, captured and burned an Indian camp on Little Powder River. Frank Grouard, a scout in whom General Crook placed much confidence, identified it as Crazy Horse's camp, and Grouard certainly should have known, for he had once lived in Crazy Horse's camp. The son of a Mormon missionary and a native of Ana, one of the Friendly Islands, he had passed for an Indian when captured by Sioux and had become a friend, or perhaps an enemy, of Crazy Horse. However, Indians have always maintained that Reynolds captured the camp of Two Moon, the Cheyenne. Whoever the Indians were, they rallied and drove Reynolds' troops out so precipitously that he could not be sure of the fate of one or two men left behind. A court-martial resulted which suspended him from command for a year.

On the same day, March 17, Brevet Major General John Gibbon, colonel of the 7th Infantry, started out from Fort Shaw, Montana Territory, near the Great Falls for which a city would be named. When he reached Fort Ellis (near Bozeman) he learned that Brigadier General Alfred H. Terry had been unable to assemble the 7th Cavalry from its several posts because of snow and cold and that the campaign in the Department of Dakota had been suspended. Moreover, General Custer, who had been scheduled to command it, was in trouble again. He had gone to Washington to testify in a congressional investigation that resulted in the resignation of Secretary of War W. W. Belknap. Custer's testimony contributed nothing to that end, but did anger President Grant, who relieved Custer from command for a technical disobedience of orders. Terry and Sheridan intervened, and Custer was permitted to go on the expedition as a regimental officer only, but not in command of the column.

General Terry, therefore, had assumed personal command, and the expedition left Fort Abraham Lincoln on May 17, 1876. It included the 7th Cavalry complete—twelve companies, headquarters, field staff and band—and a complete regiment was a rare sight in the Indian wars. There were also two companies of the 6th Infantry, one of the 17th Infantry and a detachment of the 20th Infantry, manning Gatling guns.

Meanwhile General Gibbon had resumed his march to meet Terry on the Yellowstone. He had six companies of the 7th Infantry, four of the 2nd Cavalry, a twelve-pound Napoleon gun and two .50-caliber Gatling guns, manned by infantry.

General Crook started his second march from Fort Fetterman on May 29 with ten companies of the 3rd Cavalry, five of the 2nd Cavalry, three of the 9th Infantry and two of the 4th Infantry.

Eight companies of the 5th Cavalry assembled at Fort Laramie in early June to scout between the columns of Crook and Terry.

Crook's Battle of the Rosebud

Crook's immediate objective was a hostile village reported by his Crow scouts, but he failed to surprise it. His Indian allies were not the silent masters of concealment depicted by writers of fiction and television scripts. When they sighted a few buffalo they whooped, yelled and shouted, continuing their noise until the last animal was hunted down. Crook was aware that his presence could no longer be unknown to the foe, and he was right.

On the morning of June 17 his 1,325 soldiers and Crow scouts were attacked by an estimated 1,500 Sioux and Cheyenne who charged in a dazzling succession of hit-and-run blows which had the effect of spreading the troops thinly over a front of some three miles as they repelled the several attacks. Crook sent his reserve down the valley of Rosebud Creek in the hope of reaching and destroying the village, but was forced to recall it to bolster his line. Its return took the Sioux in the rear, and they withdrew after fighting that lasted most of the day.

Crook lost ten killed, including one Crow scout, and twenty-one wounded. He reported finding the bodies of thirteen Sioux and Cheyenne on the field; undoubtedly many were carried off, as was Indian custom. Crook held the ground and claimed victory, a fact generally accepted by his contemporaries. Recent writers, however, regard the Battle of the Rosebud as a defeat, and many ascribe the Indian success to the generalship of Crazy Horse. This view assumes that Crook was halted in a movement toward the spot where Custer was annihilated eight days later. But Crook had started with only four days' rations, and after the fight he was low in ammunition and had wounded to care for, so a withdrawal was necessary.

True, Crazy Horse was a leader who inspired followers to fight with him, but this particular battle shows no tactical plan other than that commonly practiced by Indians in defense of their village. Their sudden withdrawal while they were ahead, leaving some of their dead on the field, shows that Crazy Horse did not control them, or the battle. A Cheyenne, questioned years later, said they quit because they were tired and hungry. This seems likely. Considering their losses, it seems doubtful that they were greatly encouraged by their success in halting the troops short of their village.

Hindsight, of course, provides the view that had Crook destroyed the village and scattered the Indians, preventing them from joining Sitting Bull, the course of the campaign would have been greatly altered, and the Custer disaster might have been averted. However, such information was not in the hands of anyone at the time.

Custer's Last Stand

Contemporary opinion gave Sitting Bull credit for generalship in the United States cavalry's greatest defeat in the Indian wars. It was widely assumed that it was he who mobilized the huge Indian force, estimated at from 1,800 to 9,000 warriors—4,000 seems reasonable—to entrap and ambush Custer.

Indian accounts contradict that view and indicate that the large gathering of warriors was mainly fortuitous. After the Reynolds fight in March the Cheyenne and Oglala had taken refuge in the camp of Sitting Bull, where Lame Deer's Miniconjou joined them. Later came Sans Arc and Blackfoot Sioux to complete the six principal circles of the great encampment. Sitting Bull held to the old ways of life, scorning treaties and reservations, and his influence was great when the hunting was good. Other bands of Cheyenne and small numbers of Wahpeton, Yanktonai, Brulés, Assiniboin and Arapaho joined him, as small groups did every summer. That year of 1876 huge herds of buffalo and antelope made it possible for the unusually large assembly to find food and stay together for at least twenty-six days; perhaps for more than a month.

The columns of Terry and Gibbon met on the Yellowstone on June 21, three days after Crook began the withdrawal to his base. Both had some knowledge of the close presence of a large assembly of Indians, but no sure knowledge of its true size. Gibbon's Crow scouts had located an Indian village which Lieutenant James H. Bradley, in charge of the scouting, estimated at 800 to 1,000 warriors. Brevet Colonel Marcus A. Reno, major of the 7th Cavalry, had scouted southward with half the regiment, striking the trail of a large Sioux camp which was estimated to have 800 warriors. Neither intelligence indicated an overwhelming number of warriors. Neither Gibbon nor Reno had shown any desire to attack. And after the campaign ended General Sherman in his official report stated, "There was nothing official or private to justify an officer to expect that any detachment would encounter more than 500, or at the maximum, 800, hostile warriors."

Terry's plan called for Custer's 7th Cavalry as the main striking force. He had left behind the band, the recruits whose horses were unserviceable and the wagon train. He took only a pack train of mules bearing rations and ammunition. His twelve companies, totaling 660 officers and men, were unquestionably a match for 800 or 1,000 Indians. Greater odds were common. Terry's written order prescribed that Custer should make a wide sweep "to preclude the possibility of the escape of the Indians." Gibbon's column was to cross the Yellowstone and march to the forks of the Big and Little Big Horn, by which move "it is hoped that the Indians, if upon the Little Big Horn, may be so nearly enclosed by the two columns that their escape will be impossible."

Controversy over whether Custer disobeyed this order centers on two phrases: "The Department commander places too much confidence in your zeal, energy and ability to wish to impose upon you precise orders which might hamper your action when nearly in contact with the enemy," but "desires that you conform to them [Terry's views] unless you shall see sufficient reason for departing from them."

Custer did not make the wide sweep prescribed in Terry's order. His detractors maintain that he speeded up his march in the hope of grabbing all the glory of victory before Gibbon could arrive. His defenders point to incidents of the march that indicated Indians had discovered his column and maintain that he moved directly towards them to prevent their escape, so heavily emphasized in the order.

On June 25 Custer found the approximate location of the Indian encampment on the Little Big Horn River, which flows out of sight below the surrounding plains. To surprise the enemy, he divided the regiment into three battalions. Brevet Colonel Frederick W. Benteen, captain of Company H, was sent to the left with three companies. Reno, also with three companies, rode straight ahead and came to the Little Big Horn. To his right, downstream, he saw Indian tepees, forded the river and attacked the upper end of the village. Custer, with companies C, E, F, I and L, remained on the plain above the stream. Leading his men parallel to it and out of sight, he apparently intended to strike the lower end of the village, but it stretched on and on—they never reached its end.

Ironically, Indian accounts generally agree that their scouts had not discovered the soldiers' approach and that the attack came as a surprise. There was panic, but perhaps it was the very

"Custer's Last Fight." Painting by Cassily Adams. Lithograph by Otto Becker.

immensity of the camp that made it impossible for the Indians to run away, forcing them instead to stand and fight.

Reno's charge was stopped, and after a short defensive fight in the woods, he ordered a retreat to the bluffs across the stream. In the disorderly withdrawal, thirty-two men were killed. Benteen, finding his mission pointless, cut back, picked up the pack train guarded by Company B and joined Reno in a defensive hill position.

Custer with his five companies rode on to their last stand. The positions in which the bodies were found indicate that they fought to the end against overwhelming odds. How many they killed is not known. Some Indian accounts say very few, perhaps not as many as died with Custer. Total U.S. casualties of the battle were 263 killed, including 10 civilians and scouts, and 44 wounded. Perhaps 212 of those killed were with Custer, but the exact division of the command is not clear.

Those who saw the Indians moving out say their column was three miles long and a half-mile wide. They were gone by the time Gibbon reached Reno's position on the hill.

Buffalo Bill Takes the First Scalp for Custer

Brevet Major General Wesley Merritt was promoted to colonel of the 5th Cavalry on July 1, 1876, and took command that day on the Mini Pusa, near the Black Hills, where the regiment was scouting. When news of the Custer disaster arrived, Merritt was ordered to join Crook, but at the same time he received a report that some 800 Cheyenne had left Red Cloud Agency, presumably to join the hostiles. A "lightning march" of the 5th Cavalry put the troopers across the route of the Cheyenne at Hat Creek. But the ambush Merritt prepared for them was spoiled by two couriers who appeared inopportunely and were discovered by a small group of scouting Cheyenne. To save the lives of the threatened couriers, Buffalo Bill Cody and seven of eight scouts and soldiers charged to the rescue, and it was Cody who shot down the Indian leader Yellow Hand (Hay-o-wei or Yellow Hair). Cody's exploit was widely publicized as "the first scalp for Custer." An immediate charge by the cavalry sent the main body of the Cheyenne fleeing back to the agency.

Merritt reported to Crook with ten companies of his regiment on August 3, and on August 5 a reorganized expedition set off to overtake the hostile Indians. Terry, encamped on the Yellowstone near the Custer battlefield, was reinforced by six companies of the 22nd Infantry under Brevet Colonel Elwell S. Otis and six companies of the 5th Infantry which had been rushed by train and steamboat from Fort Leavenworth under Brevet Major General Nelson A. Miles. Thus reinforced, Terry marched up the Rosebud on August 6, meeting Crook's column on the tenth, but the Sioux had slipped out from between them.

Incessant rain, mud and shortage of rations delayed pursuit. On August 26 the columns separated, Crook turning back toward his own department by way of the Bad Lands and Black Hills. At Slim Buttes on September 9 his advance guard under Brevet Lieutenant Colonel Anson Mills, captain of the 3rd Cavalry, attacked a camp of thirty-seven Miniconjou lodges. Crazy Horse's Oglala got into the fight, but Crook's main body came up and the Sioux were driven off. The chief, American Horse, was killed and the village destroyed.

Winter Campaigns

Crook's column continued its march through the Black Hills and was disbanded at Camp Robinson, Nebraska, but the general immediately set about organizing a winter expedition from troops that had been in garrison during the winter. Its immediate commander was Brevet Brigadier General Ranald Slidell Mackenzie, colonel of the 4th Cavalry. Its 1,400 men included eleven companies of cavalry from the 2nd, 3rd, 4th and 5th regiments; eleven companies of infantry from the 4th, 9th, 14th and 25th regiments; and four companies of the 4th Artillery, dismounted, that is, without guns. There were also 400 Indian scouts, Pawnee under Major Frank North, Shoshoni, Arapaho and even a few Sioux and Cheyenne.

On November 25 and 26, 1876, Mackenzie's cavalry struck Dull Knife's camp of Cheyenne at the forks of the Powder, killing thirty Indians and destroying 200 lodges. From walls of the surrounding canyon the Cheyenne kept up a dogged fight until they were driven off by dismounted skirmishers.

While this was transpiring south of the Yellowstone River, General Miles prepared for his winter campaign. He mounted a part of his 5th Infantry on captured Indian ponies and took great care in equipping his regiment with warm clothes. Army blankets were cut into underwear and masks to cover the men's faces. Buffalo robes were made into overcoats. On October 17 he set off north of the Yellowstone seeking Sitting Bull. The chieftain came to meet him. They talked under a flag of truce but reached no agreement. Miles attacked and drove the retreating Hunkpapa for forty-two miles. A part of the band agreed to go to the agencies and surrender, but Sitting Bull and a few followers fled north. His camp was struck again on December 18 by a detachment under First Lieutenant Frank D. Baldwin. Early in 1877 Sitting Bull led his band into Canada.

Crazy Horse surrendered on May 6, 1877, and was killed at Fort Robinson on September 5 during an attempt to confine him in the guardhouse.

"Dedication of Custer Monument." Drawing by Frederic Remington.

The great Sioux uprising was over. Never again would as many as five hundred Sioux warriors be mustered at any one place for a fight.

47. *Wars in the Far Northwest*

MOST INDIAN FIGHTING was against small bands, but in many cases it took a considerable proportion of the available Regular Army to run them down. Of course, there was not much Regular Army: in 1869 the infantry had been cut to twenty-five regiments, the cavalry remaining at ten regiments and the artillery at five, an aggregate of 37,313. An act of Congress of June 16, 1874, provided that the number of enlisted men in the Army should not exceed 25,000. There was no further reduction in the number of regiments, and because of the importance of cavalry in Indian fighting, most of the cut in numbers of enlisted men was taken in the infantry. From this time to the end of the Indian wars, there was no material change in the organization of the Army.

The Modoc War

More than a thousand soldiers were needed to fight fifty Modoc in 1872–73. These Indians, one of the Pacific Coast's numerous small tribes, resided in Oregon near the California border.

In the 1850's they had raided a few wagon trains and staged a massacre or two; once they were the victims of a countermassacre by miners led by Ben Wright. In the course of time the Modoc adopted white man's clothes and some white man's vices. Their only linguistic relatives were the Klamath, who lived near them in the Klamath Lake region. The Indian Bureau, in its wisdom, decided that Modoc and Klamath should share a reservation, quite forgetting that family quarrels may be the bitterest, but when the Modoc had had enough of being dominated by their kinfolk they returned to their old homes along Lost River, just north of the California boundary. At the time, this region was being rapidly settled by whites. The Modoc's standing among these settlers is indicated by the names they gave their leaders—Captain Jack, Curley-Headed Doctor, Black Jim, Bogus Charley, Shacknasty Jim, Scarfaced Charley, Hooker Jim.

On November 28, 1872, Brevet Major James Jackson, captain of Company B, 1st Cavalry, came with thirty-eight men to move Captain Jack's band back to the Klamath Reservation. Shooting started; one soldier and two or three Indians were killed. The Modoc fled, killing eighteen settlers on their way, but sparing women and children. The Indians took refuge in the Lava Beds south of Tule Lake in northern California. This "Land of Burnt-out Fires" was a dreary area of volcanic rock broken by a labyrinth of sharp fissures, craters, caves and natural tunnels—nature's version of a World War I trench system.

It was not until January 16, 1873, that Brevet Major General Frank Wheaton, lieutenant colonel of the 21st Infantry, assembled sufficient force, about 400, to attack this stronghold. He had awaited the arrival of a section of mountain howitzers, which, manned by cavalrymen in the fight, proved more dangerous to the attackers than to the Modoc. In two days of fighting, few soldiers ever saw an Indian, and it is doubtful whether any were hit. However, the troops lost sixteen killed and nine officers and forty-four enlisted men wounded—adequate reason for not pushing home a charge in the open.

No worse time could have been chosen for appointing a peace commission to negotiate with the Modoc, but that was the next step. At a meeting on April 11 the Indians turned a peace council into a massacre. Captain Jack killed Brigadier General E. R. S. Canby and Boston Charley killed the Reverend Dr. Eleazer Thomas. A. B. Meacham, a former Indian agent, was shot four times but rescued by a Modoc woman, Winema, called Toby Riddle. The only peace commissioner to escape unhurt was Leroy S. Dyar, an Indian agent armed with a derringer. Canby, a brevet major general and brigadier general in lineal rank, commanding the department, was the highest ranking officer ever killed by Indians.

Troops moved in but were called off by the ranking officer Brevet Major General Alvan C. Gillem, colonel of the 1st Cavalry, until he could bring his full force into action. A valued reinforcement came in the form of Donald McKay's Warm Springs Indian Scouts. Gillem's enlarged force included five companies of the 1st Cavalry, two of the 12th Infantry and six of the 4th Artillery. The artillerymen brought a section of twelve-pound coehorn mortars and took over the howitzers, the rest fighting as infantry.

Gillem's fight of April 15 to 17 was on the same plan as that of Wheaton in January—an attack from opposite sides to squeeze the Modoc out of the Lava Beds. This time the coehorn mortars helped, and the two columns joined at Tule Lake, cutting the Modoc off from their water supply. Nevertheless, the Indians escaped.

Their whereabouts were unknown until April 26, when they successfully ambushed Brevet

Major Evan Thomas, captain of the 4th Artillery, with two companies of his regiment and one of the 12th Infantry. Major Thomas, three lieutenants and eighteen enlisted men were killed; one lieutenant, one surgeon and seventeen enlisted men were wounded. The survivors held off the Indians until next day, when they were rescued.

After this defeat a third commander took over—Brevet Major General Jefferson C. Davis, colonel of the 23rd Infantry (not related to the Confederate President, although the similarity of name has caused much confusion). General Davis reorganized the command, recalled Wheaton to duty in his regiment and inspired a new morale while he sent strong detachments in search of the elusive Modoc.

The last fight was commanded by Captain Henry C. Hasbrouck, whose Company B, 4th Artillery, was equipped as cavalry. Accompanying him was Captain Jackson (who had commanded in the first fight against the Modoc) with two companies of the 1st Cavalry and McKay's Indian scouts. At dawn on May 10, 1873, the Modoc band attacked Hasbrouck's camp at Sorass Lake, or Dry Lake, in an area of volcanic clinkers. The horses were stampeded, and while a few cavalrymen rounded them up, the rest of the force charged on foot, routing the Modoc from surrounding bluffs. With McKay's scouts threatening to cut them off in the rear, the Modoc fled precipitously and were pursued for four miles.

The survivors broke up into small parties which surrendered or were captured. Captain Jack, Schonchin John, Boston Charley and Black Jim were hanged on October 3, 1873, for the murders of General Canby and Dr. Thomas.

The Nez Percés and Chief Joseph

The Nez Percés lived among the tributaries of the Salmon and lower Snake rivers. When Lewis and Clark met them in 1805 they had had horses for a century or so; in fact, they were the developers of the Appaloosa horse. The Reverend Henry H. Spalding opened a mission among the Nez Percés in 1836 and christened one of his first converts Joseph. This Joseph was the father of the Chief Joseph of the Nez Percé War of 1877.

A treaty of 1855 confirmed to the Nez Percés the lands on which they actually lived. A new treaty, negotiated in 1863, reduced the reservation by three-fourths. Chiefs of the bands residing within the new boundaries signed it; chiefs of bands residing outside did not. The government held that the lands had been sold by a "majority" of the tribe, but meanwhile the Senate delayed ratification of the treaty until 1867, leaving the cession in doubt.

The band headed by Old Joseph lived outside the new boundaries in the Wallowa Valley, south of the Grande Ronde. His protests were heeded in 1873 and part of the valley was set aside as a hunting reserve for them. Two years later this concession was canceled when it was pointed out that they did not live there the year round. Like many tribes they were migratory, hunting during the hunting season, moving to the camas meadows for the harvest of that root crop, and so on in a fixed, annual routine.

The younger Joseph appealed the cancellation to the department commander, Brevet Major General Oliver Otis Howard. Howard had won the Medal of Honor and lost his right arm at Fair Oaks during the Civil War; he had been voted the thanks of Congress for valor at Gettysburg and had been brigadier general of the line since 1864. He was religious, conscientious and humanitarian. But in this case he had no authority to negotiate; his orders were to move Joseph's band to the reservation.

Joseph agreed to the inevitable, but his hand was forced by young men, most of them of other nontreaty bands, who began raiding and killing white settlers.

Brevet Colonel David Perry, captain of the 1st Cavalry, was ordered to pursue and punish them. With two companies of his regiment he marched out of Fort Lapwai on the Clearwater (about ten miles above present Lewiston, Idaho). At dawn on June 17, 1877, as he approached a Nez Percé village in White Bird Canyon, his force was attacked on both flanks. The troops had been marching for thirty-six hours, and the thin, tired line was thrown into confusion; thirty-four soldiers were killed and four wounded. Perry escaped with the survivors.

Within a week General Howard moved out from Fort Lapwai with a force of 300, including four companies of the 4th Artillery and a company of the 21st Infantry. He detached Captain Stephen Girard Whipple with two companies of the 1st Cavalry to round up Looking Glass's village on the Clearwater. It is not at all established that Looking Glass's Nez Percé band had intended to join the hostiles, but they fled when Whipple appeared, and eventually joined Joseph's band. Meanwhile, Joseph's band had eluded Howard by twice crossing the Salmon River, and on July 3 annihilated a scouting party of ten under Second Lieutenant Sevier McClellan Rains of the 1st Cavalry at Craig's Mountain, before the main body of troops could reach them.

Up to this point Nez Pércé scouting had forecast every army move, but on July 11 Howard surprised the Indian camp on the Clearwater and opened fire on it with a four-inch howitzer and two Gatling guns. In this fight Howard had five companies of the 1st Cavalry, seven of the 21st Infantry and four of the 4th Artillery, mostly serving as infantry, a total of 400 regulars, and 180 citizen volunteers. Even with the advantage of surprise, Howard was unable to overrun the Indian camp and had to entrench with rifle pits in a defensive position. An attack the following day found the Indians abandoning their camp. In two days of fighting Howard lost thirteen killed and twenty-seven wounded. He reported twenty-three Indians killed and forty-six wounded; some Indian accounts admit only four killed and six wounded.

At this point the Nez Percés had reached their greatest strength in the war. There were five bands, totaling 600 to 700 persons, of whom fewer than 200 were warriors. Chief Joseph of the Wallowa band was the dominant figure, but Indian accounts deny that he exercised any military command. He was not at all the master of strategy imagined by Generals Howard and Miles. Even in his own band Joseph's brother Ollokut was war leader, and each of the four other bands was led by its own chiefs and experienced leaders of war parties. Their tactics were concerted and effective only because they were at all times fighting to protect their families.

After the fight on the Clearwater, General Howard pursued the Indians to the Kamiah crossing, where warriors delayed his troops while the main body of the Nez Percés began a slow retreat along the precipitous Lolo Trail over the Bitterroot Mountains. This move was hailed as a masterpiece of strategy; actually the Indians believed that they had no quarrel with troops or citizens east of the mountains, where they came into the department commanded by General Terry.

At Fort Missoula Captain Charles C. Rawn with only 30 men of Company L, 7th Infantry, raised 300 volunteers and attempted to stop the Nez Percés by constructing a barricade, later appropriately dubbed Fort Fizzle. In a parley with Captain Rawn the Indians promised to march peaceably through Bitterroot Valley. As they had built up good reputations during hunting expeditions of previous years, the volunteers took them at their word and dispersed. The Indians bypassed Fort Fizzle and went on to Stevensville, where they bought flour, sugar, coffee and tobacco from local merchants. In many ways this was the most amazing of Indian wars.

They stopped to rest at an old campsite just east of the Continental Divide on the Big Hole River, and with the usual lack of camp guards were surprised on August 9, 1877, by General Gibbon with 200 men, including six companies of the 7th Infantry, two of the 1st Cavalry and volunteers. Part of the camp was captured, and the troops attempted to burn it, but the Nez Percés rallied and hemmed the soldiers in, shooting from concealed positions. The Indians captured a howitzer and put it out of action. Lieutenant Bradley, first to find the dead on the Custer field, was among twenty-nine killed; General Gibbon was one of forty wounded. Howard's pursuing cavalry came to the rescue, and the Nez Percés moved on, having suffered their heaviest battle loss here with sixty to ninety killed, many of them women and children.

Howard was now close on the heels of the Nez Percés, but in a night raid they stampeded his pack mules, and while he reassembled his supply train, they moved leisurely through Yellowstone Park, capturing a party of tourists, who were released unharmed. Small Nez Percé raiding parties, however, killed two tourists in the park.

Brevet Major General Samuel D. Sturgis, colonel of the 7th Cavalry, took the field with six companies of his regiment, which had been reorganized during the winter after the Little Big Horn defeat. Making several false starts. Sturgis found the Nez Percé trail in the gorge of Canyon Creek, Montana Territory. His soldiers were exhausted after long marching and when dismounted made slow progress against the Indians. Even a mounted charge led by Colonel Benteen failed to cut off the Indians' retreat. After dark on September 13 the Nez Percés escaped. They moved north and ten days later crossed the Missouri east of Fort Benton at Cow Island, low-water mark for steamers. They hoped eventually to reach Canada and join Sitting Bull's Sioux.

It was now up to General Miles to resume the pursuit. From Fort Keogh (Miles City) he quickly marched 150 miles to the Missouri with Cheyenne scouts and 600 men—three companies of the 2nd Cavalry, three of the 7th and six of the 5th Infantry mounted on captured

"The Charge." Wash drawing by Frederic Remington.

Indian ponies and armed with a Gatling gun and a twelve-pound Napoleon. When Miles learned that the Nez Percés had crossed the river he ferried his troops over on the steamer *Benton,* only two days behind them.

Marching north, he struck the Nez Percé camp in the Bear Paw Mountains on September 29. As usual the Indians were surprised, and as usual they rallied and broke the cavalry charge, but troopers of the 2nd Cavalry stampeded the horse herd, leaving the Indians afoot. Miles then settled down to a siege, and General Howard, who had never faltered in his long pursuit, arrived with an advance party on October 4. On October 5 Joseph surrendered his rifle with an eloquent speech concluding, "From where the sun now stands, I will fight no more."

The Bannock War of 1878

After their defeat at Bear River by General Connor in 1863, the Bannock had lived mainly in the vicinity of the Fort Hall Reservation in Idaho, confirmed to them by treaty in 1869. They supplemented the scant government rations by hunting buffalo on the Plains and digging camas roots in annual visits to Big Camas Prairie, north of Snake River. During the Nez Percé War they were confined to their reservation for their own protection, but they soon became hungry and restless. While they had understood Camas Prairie to be a part of the reservation guaranteed to them, a clerk had heard it as "Kansas Prairie," which no one could identify, so it was left out of the final draft of the treaty. In the spring of 1878 when the Bannock made their usual trip to Camas Prairie, they found hogs and cattle feeding there and shot two of the herders.

Brevet Colonel Reuben Frank Bernard, captain of Company G, 1st Cavalry, was ordered to the scene from Boise Barracks, eighty miles away. He arrived two days later, found the wounded herders and followed the Bannock across lava beds and through scenes of their raids at King Hill Station and Glenns Ferry. The Bannock were soon joined by their kinsmen, disaffected Paiute bands led by Oytes and Egan, who dragged with them the less disaffected Paiute band of Chief Winnemucca. Bernard, as he continued the pursuit, was fortunate in being able to employ an Indian "princess" as scout and guide. Sarah Winnemucca, educated daughter of the chief, agreed to enter the hostile camp, and was successful in detaching her father's band from the Indian alliance.

Colonel Bernard had a remarkable military record. Having risen from the ranks in the 1st Cavalry, he already had taken part in 98 of the "103 fights and scrimmages" he was to boast of in the Civil War and Indian wars—a record not challenged by any of his contemporaries. He kept close on the trail of the Indians while General Howard pushed reinforcements after him.

He had four companies of the 1st Cavalry with him when he overtook the Indians on June 23 at Silver Creek, which runs into a dry sink west of Silvies River in the south central Oregon desert. Bernard's four troops charged with revolver and carbine in successive waves, capturing and destroying the camp and driving the Indians into surrounding hills. The Indians lost ten known dead with the estimated killed at fifty; the troops lost four killed and three wounded. The Bannock stole away during the night and the four troops pursued them next day for ten miles. A few shots were exchanged at 7 P.M., but the Indians kept moving.

The Bannock did not stop again to fight for ninety miles. On July 8 they opened fire from a mountain ridge near Pilot Rock on Birch Creek, a branch of the Umatilla River (south of Pendleton). General Howard had joined Bernard, who led a charge of seven companies of the 1st Cavalry. Front and flank, they drove the Indians from the crest, but the red men retreated only to another ridge.

The 1st Cavalry's regimental history claims that part of this fight was the first example of cavalry fighting on foot without separating the men from the horses—each trooper firing his carbine while he led his horse by reins thrown over his forearm. The Indians scattered, some eastward into the Blue Mountains, while others tried to cross the Columbia River but were turned back by gunboats manned by detachments of the Ordnance Department and 21st Infantry.

A final fight on July 20 on the North Fork of John Day River was commanded by Brevet Brigadier General James W. Forsyth, lieutenant colonel of the 1st Cavalry, who had arrived from Chicago to take charge of the battalion. The Indians were flanked out of a strong position in a deep canyon and again, for the last time, broke and scattered. This ended the Bannock War. Bernard, who had a key position in this last charge, was brevetted brigadier general in 1890 for his fights at Silvies River and Birch Creek and for one against Cochise at Chiricahua Pass, Arizona.

Sheepeater Campaign, 1879

The last Indian war in the Far Northwest was a small one against a small band of Indians but one of extreme difficulty for the troops. In February, 1879, five Chinese miners were killed at Oro Grande, Idaho; in May two ranchers were killed on the South Fork of the Salmon. These crimes were charged to the Tukuarika, a Shoshonean band numbering about 300, called Sheepeaters because they lived principally on Rocky Mountain sheep. As the campaign developed, it seemed probable that the Sheepeaters were never near the scenes of the murders.

Again it was a campaign for Colonel Bernard's Company G of the 1st Cavalry. From May 31 to September 8 Bernard's troop toiled through middle Idaho, the country of the Salmon River, called the "River of No Return" because it is barely navigable, and that only downstream. This country is so rough it could be mapped adequately only by airplane. Sheepeaters attacked Bernard's pack train on August 20 at Soldier Bar on Big Creek. The train was defended by Corporal Charles B. Hardin (who was later commissioned from the ranks and rose to the grade of major) with six troopers and the chief packer, Jake Barnes. They drove off the raiding party of ten to fifteen. One private was killed. (As late as 1925 a headstone for his grave had to be transported seventy miles by wagon and forty miles by pack mule from the nearest railroad station.)

A company of twenty Umatilla scouts led by Lieutenants Edward S. Farrow and W. C. Brown completed the campaign by negotiating the surrender of the Sheepeaters in October.

The Ute War of 1879

In the years between the coming of the white man's horse and the coming of the white man, the Ute were a powerful and warlike tribe. Then they took to the mountains of western Colorado and eastern Utah (named for them). Like Spotted Tail of the Brulé Sioux, their wise chief, Ouray, born about 1820, realized the power of the United States, had no desire to tangle with it, made no concessions he could not avoid, did the best he could for his people and kept the peace. However, not all of the Ute bands went along with his pacifism.

Oddly enough, the White River Ute were goaded into war by one of the best and most honest men ever assigned to the Indian Service. Appointed personally by President Rutherford B. Hayes he was a talented writer, friend of Horace Greeley, an idealist sincerely interested in the welfare of the Indians. No man ever deserved the name do-gooder more than did Nathan Cook Meeker. He planned to establish schools, teach agriculture, assign the Ute to family farms and abolish tribal government. Meeker moved the agency to the middle of a favorite hunting ground; he wanted to stop their hunting. He built a school across their horse-racing track; he wanted to end gambling. He plowed up the grass where they had grazed their ponies; he told them they had too many ponies and some should be killed. By this time their anger was so evident that he sent for troops.

Major Thomas Tipton Thornburgh of the 4th Infantry commanded the expedition ordered out from Fort Fred Steele, Wyoming Territory, almost 150 miles away. On September 29, 1879, after crossing Milk Creek, a shallow stream on the northern border of the White River Reservation, his command was ambushed in a narrow, brushy draw. Perhaps to avoid alarming the Indians, Thornburgh had taken no precautions. He was killed by the first fire. Captain John S. Payne's Company F of the 5th Cavalry, and Company E of the 3rd, formed in line but were soon driven back by the concealed Ute. Company D under Second Lieutenant James V. S. Paddock had been left behind to guard the wagons. He immediately corralled them, and the two advance companies fell back on this defensive position.

The Ute tried to drive out the troops by setting fire to the grass and, when this failed, began shooting into the enclosure from surrounding rimrocks. Eleven men were killed and most of the horses were shot down. That night Captain Payne sent four men—two guides and two soldiers—who volunteered to ride to the telegraph station at Rawlins, Wyoming, with reports of the disaster.

"An Episode in the Opening Up of a Cattle Country." Engraving, after drawing by Frederic Remington.

Meanwhile Captain Francis S. Dodge, on patrol to the eastward with Company D, 9th Cavalry, heard about the fight from fleeing settlers and rode to the scene. He arrived at the barricade on October 2, but his forty men were also penned in, and during the next three days all their horses were shot down.

General Wesley Merritt at Fort D. A. Russell, near Cheyenne, 280 miles away, received Payne's message on October 1. Within four hours he entrained Companies A, B, I and M of the 5th Cavalry for Rawlins. There he picked up four comapnies of the 4th Infantry, later adding one more from Thornburgh's supply base, and loaded them into wagons for the "lightning march" cross-country—125 miles from 11 A.M. October 2 to dawn October 5.

As Merritt approached the besieged soldiers in the dark, he ordered his trumpeter to sound *Officer's Call*. He remembered that on the night of July 28, 1876, while the 5th Cavalry was bivouacked on the north fork of the Mini Pusa on its way to join Crook's column in the war against the Sioux, he had heard the distant notes of this same call. At that time Captain Payne with Company F and Captain George E. Price with Company E were making forced marches to join him, and to guide them through the dark to his camp he had ordered the trumpeter to repeat the call.

Now, on October 5, 1879, the situation was reversed. He was coming to the relief of Payne and Company F, instead of Payne coming to him.

Henceforth *Officer's Call* would have a traditional meaning to the 5th Cavalry beyond its utility as a service call.

On arriving at the barricade Merritt deployed his tired troopers and wagonloads of infantrymen in the dark. They occupied the surrounding ridges, found no Indians and fell asleep in line of battle. Next morning a small party of Indians appeared accompanied by an employee from the Los Pinos Agency. They had ridden day and night from far off southern Colorado with a message from Ouray saying that a council of southern bands of the Ute had decided to have no part in the fighting and urging the White River Ute to seek peace.

Perhaps the White River Indians had already quit, half-frightened at what they had done. While some had been fighting the soldiers, others had killed six men at their agency, including Meeker, and all had fled to the mountains, carrying off Mrs. Meeker, their grown daughter Josephine and the post trader's wife, Flora Ellen Price. Ouray aided in getting them released.

48. *Indian Wars in the Southwest*

Kiowa and Comanche

SOME INDIAN TRIBES fought a single campaign; many fought frequent wars; but for the Kiowa and Comanche, warfare was continuous. These two tribes, although not related and speaking different languages, became allies before the beginning of the nineteenth century. The Kiowa gained a reputation for having killed more white men in proportion to their numbers than any other tribe.

Typical of Kiowa leadership was Satanta, who came to prominence shortly after the Civil

War. On October 18, 1865, agent J. H. Leavenworth, son of the general for whom Fort Leavenworth was named, negotiated a treaty by which the Kiowa and Comanche agreed to go on a reservation and cease all depredations. In August, 1866, Satanta led a raid into Texas, killing James Box and two children and capturing Mrs. Box and three children. Satanta took his captives to Fort Larned, Kansas, where he boldly demanded ransom for them from Leavenworth, with whom he had signed the treaty. Denounced by Leavenworth for his bad faith, Satanta took his captives sixty-five miles farther west to Fort Dodge, where he got his ransom. In 1867 Satanta signed the Medicine Lodge Treaty; in 1868 he took the lead in a new outbreak. This time he was captured by Sheridan and Custer, along with Lone Wolf, Kiowa war chief who also had signed the Medicine Lodge treaty; Sheridan proposed to hang them for their many crimes, but was talked out of it, and released them on their promises of better behavior.

Satanta's next encounter was with the general of the army. When Grant became President in 1869, Sherman succeeded to the rank we now call "four-star general"—Grant had worn four stars, but Sherman prescribed insignia consisting of two silver stars with the arms of the United States in gold between them.

With his new rank Sherman made an inspection trip in Texas. One of its objectives was to investigate complaints that Indians from reservations in Indian Territory had been raiding into Texas. On May 18, 1869, Sherman rode from Fort Griffin (north of Albany) to Fort Richardson (Jacksboro) with a small escort. Not far behind came a government-contract wagon train carrying corn. That night a wounded teamster limped into Fort Richardson with a report that the train had been attacked and burned by Indians, and seven teamsters killed. Only five escaped.

General Mackenzie pursued the raiders, while Sherman rode on to Fort Sill, Indian Territory. Four days later a band of Kiowa came in for rations. Satanta and another Indian named Satank were with them. Agent Lawrie Tatum questioned them about the wagon train, and Satanta loudly boasted that he had led the raid, naming also Satank and Big Tree.

Learning about this, Sherman invited the chiefs to a conference on the front porch of the quarters of the post commander, Brevet Major General Benjamin H. Grierson, colonel of the 10th Cavalry. When Satanta again boasted of the killings, Sherman told him he was under arrest for murder. Satanta reached for his revolver, but saw he was covered by armed soldiers, who had been concealed in the house.

Mackenzie handcuffed and chained the three prisoners and put them in a wagon. Satank sang his death song and grappled with a guard for a carbine. He was killed before he could use it. Satanta and Big Tree were indicted, tried and convicted of murder in Texas courts. They were sentenced to be hanged, but the governor commuted their sentences to life imprisonment, and was persuaded to patrole them in 1873.

Battle of Adobe Walls

Satanta was released in ample time to take part in the Battle of Adobe Walls on June 27, 1874. This fight brought to prominence Quanah Parker of the Kwahari Comanche, whose mother was Cynthia Ann Parker, captured as a child by Comanche in an 1836 Texas raid—she barely remembered her name when recaptured and taken back to her Texas home in 1860.

Quanah's father had been a chief, and Quanah became a great leader of the Comanche.

Adobe Walls was the ruin of a Bent trading post, abandoned in 1844 and the scene of Kit Carson's 1864 victory over Kiowa and Comanche, aided by a few Apache and Arapaho. While the Navajo were keeping Carson's volunteers occupied, Kiowa and Comanche had stepped up raiding along the Santa Fe Trail. An attack on a wagon train at Pawnee Rock, Kansas, where five men were killed and five small boys carried off captive, particularly incensed General Carleton, who ordered Carson to pursue and punish the raiders. Carson with 335 New Mexico and California volunteers and seventy-five Ute and Apache allies struck a Kiowa village and drove its warriors four miles to the vicinity of Adobe Walls, which the troops were using as a hospital and corral for their horses during dismounted action. There were several Indian villages in the vicinity, one of them large. As the fight continued Carson estimated one to three thousand Indians took part. The fire of his two twelve-pound mountain howitzers kept the Indians at a distance, but in the face of great odds he ordered a retreat, destroying on his way the Kiowa village he had originally captured with its 176 lodges in which were stored food and clothing for the winter and ammunition.

By 1874, Adobe Walls had weathered into further ruin, but its walls were still four or five feet high and gave protection to a trading post of log cabins and sod huts built by buffalo hunters who were rapidly killing off the last of the southern herd. Twenty-eight men and one woman were there on the night the post was surrounded by 700 Kiowa, Comanche, Cheyenne and Arapaho.

The Comanche had been holding a Sun Dance—a ceremony introduced to them by a prophet, Isa-tai, who urged them to destroy all white men and promised to give them, by his magical powers, immunity from white man's bullets. Quanah Parker carried the war pipe and Isa-tai's message to the Cheyenne, Arapaho and Kiowa, but it was his own people, the Comanche, who suggested he destroy the white buffalo hunters at Adobe Walls before leading the war party against distant Texas settlements.

Two hunters were killed in the dawn attack, but the buffalo guns broke up repeated Indian charges. One of the buffalo guns was fired by Bat (William Barclay) Masterson, later a famous peace officer in Dodge City. With a Sharps .50, Billy Dixon, scout and guide, shot an Indian off his horse at a distance which one of those present said afterward measured at 1,538 yards. That was the last shot of the fight.

Comanche and Kiowa Raids Continue

Because the raiding bands of Comanche and Kiowa were accustomed to drawing rations regularly at the reservation and taking refuge there between murderous forays, Brevet Major General John W. Davidson, colonel of the 10th Cavalry commanding Fort Sill, gave orders on July 26, 1874, that all friendly Indians were to remain in fixed camps at the Wichita agency (Anadarko, Oklahoma) and answer periodic roll calls. The agent protested this interference with his attempts to civilize the Comanche and Kiowa, but the army's case was soon proved. Quanah Parker's Comanche did not come in but on August 22 Red Food's band, which had been in the Adobe Walls fight, and Lone Wolf's Kiowa, who had been raiding in Texas, appeared to draw rations. When Davidson demanded the disarming of Red Food's band, fighting broke out. Friendly Indians fled, and some joined the hostiles, but not all; September roll calls showed 479 Comanche, 585 Kiowa and 305 Kiowa-Apache still at Fort Sill—nearly half the estimated populations of these three tribes. Even these warlike peoples did not make warfare a tribal decision. Those who wanted fighting joined Quanah Parker.

Sheridan planned another containing movement with converging columns similar to that of 1868. Davidson moved west from Fort Sill; Mackenzie north from Fort Concho; between them came Brevet Brigadier General George P. Buell, lieutenant colonel of the 11th Infantry, from Fort Griffin. General Miles marched south from Camp Supply, and Brevet Colonel William R. Price, major of the 8th Cavalry, rode east from Fort Union, New Mexico.

From August through December, 1874, these columns fought more than thirty skirmishes with hostile bands. The most decisive was Mackenzie's capture and destruction of a Kiowa village after a tortuous climb down the sides of Palo Duro Canyon on September 27.

Miles struck the Indians on Mulberry, or Salt, Creek on August 30, and the 6th Cavalry charged, driving the hostiles twenty miles. Brevet Major Adna R. Chaffee was captain of the leading company, and it was on this occasion he joked with his men, promising, "If any man is killed I will make him a corporal." Chaffee was brevetted lieutenant colonel for this fight.

Billy Dixon, the marksman of Adobe Walls, Amos Chapman, another able scout, and four troopers of the 6th Cavalry under Sergeant Z. T. Woodhull stood off Indians for two days, September 11 and 12, in the Buffalo Wallow Fight. One was killed, all the rest wounded, before Colonel Price rescued them.

Lieutenant Baldwin, with Companies D, 5th Infantry, and D, 6th Cavalry was escorting twenty-three empty, six-mule wagons toward the Washita River supply camp on November 8 when his scouts discovered the village of Gray Beard's band of 300 Cheyenne on Mulberry Creek. Baldwin brought his wagons in double column to the front and center of his line, put a mountain howitzer ahead of them and charged with everything he had—horse, foot and wheel. The village was surprised, the Cheyenne fled, and two captive children, Julia and Adelaide German, were rescued. Baldwin put his infantry in the wagons and continued the pursuit for twelve miles. For this exploit he was awarded a second Medal of Honor—he won his first while captain of the 19th Michigan Infantry in the Civil War.

Two older German sisters were surrendered by Stone Calf of the Cheyenne to General Miles. Their father, mother, brother and elder sister had been killed in an attack on their wagon in Kansas.

Comanche hostilities did not last much longer. Satanta surrendered in October, 1874, and was returned to prison for violating his parole. He committed suicide there on October 11, 1878. Quanah Parker surrendered at Fort Sill on June 2, 1875. Thereafter he kept the peace and became a powerful leader of the Comanche in their new way of life.

49. *Wars of the Apache*

APACHE WARFARE never ceased, not because the Apache particularly enjoyed fighting but because they lived mainly by plunder. They counted no coups, celebrated no scalp dances, took no pride in exhibitions of courage. Raiding was their business. The admiration of their women and the praise of their men went to the sly, successful thief who provided for his family, not to the dead hero who left his family to starve.

Apache warfare was not glamorous. These Indians wore no feathered headdress, rode no horses into battle. They valued horses more for food than for transportation. Soldiers who fought Apache rarely saw them, for they were masters of concealment and ambush. They could vanish right into the barren desert or mountains and move faster on foot than the cavalry pursuing them.

Ablest of their leaders was Cochise of the Chiricahua. Reuben F. Bernard, the only officer brevetted a brigadier general for a fight against Cochise, said of him:

This Indian was always at peace with the whites until 1860, when he and his family were invited to dine with an officer of the Army, who had his company ready to arrest him for the purpose of keeping him as a hostage for the return of a boy stolen by the Pinals. Since that time this Indian has burned alive thirteen white men that I know of, besides most cruelly torturing to death, by cutting small pieces out of them, five others; fifteen others I know by putting lariats around their necks, tied their hands behind them, and dragged them to death. All this was done in the spring of 1860, within twenty miles of where Camp Bowie now stands. This Indian was at peace until betrayed and wounded by white men.

Bernard, as sergeant of Company D, 1st Dragoons, had been present in 1860 when Cochise was driven to the warpath by the "betrayal" he described. As a brevet colonel Bernard, captain of Company G, 1st Cavalry (the same regiment, renamed) took command on May 29, 1869, of Camp Bowie (twenty miles south of present Bowie, Arizona). On July 4 he skirmished with Cochise's band in the Burro Mountains. In August he started a series of scouts into the Chiricahua Mountains, Cochise's stronghold.

At Chiricahua Pass on October 20 Cochise's band attempted to ambush Bernard's command of sixty-one men of his troop and of Company G, 8th Cavalry. The troopers took cover behind rocks and began picking off every Indian who showed himself. Drives to the right and then to the left were stopped by Apache fire, but Bernard got fifteen men to a hilltop from which they took the Chiricahua in the rear, and the Indians fled. Bernard had two killed, two injured, and claimed eighteen Indians killed. This was one of three fights mentioned in Bernard's brevet as brigadier general; his two lieutenants were brevetted majors, and thirty-one enlisted men were recommended for the Medal of Honor.

In the Dragoon Mountains on January 27, 1870, Bernard's two troops killed thirteen Chiricahua and the next day destroyed Cochise's camp, but the wily chieftain escaped.

Cochise won a last victory against troops on May 5, 1871, when he ambushed and killed First Lieutenant Howard B. Cushing of the 3rd Cavalry and three others at Bear Springs in the Whetstone Mountains. Two of Lieutenant Cushing's brothers had been Civil War heroes, William B., who sank the Confederate ram *Albemarle* with a spar torpedo, and Alonzo, who was killed while commanding a battery at Gettysburg.

Cochise made peace the following year. By a personal appeal T. J. Jeffords of the stagecoach line had obtained a truce with the Chiricahua covering his own operations. In 1872 Jeffords took General Howard to Cochise's camp where a peace was made that lasted until Cochise died.

Camp Grant Massacre

Many writers have condemned the Camp Grant massacre as an unprovoked atrocity, yet the ascertainable facts are so few as to leave some doubts. Early in 1871 Eskimotzin and 510 Aravaipa Apache appeared at Camp Grant, fifty-five miles northeast of Tucson, professing a desire for peace. First Lieutenant Royal E. Whitman fed them and allowed them to stay. However, while they were encamped there, depredations continued near Tucson and south of it, around San Xavier and Tubac. Civilians led by Jesus M. Elias followed raiders driving away cattle and horses, and killed one of them. The victim was identified as a Camp Grant Aravaipa. Elias was aided by William M. Oury of Tucson in organizing a secret punitive expedition. Their party included ninety-two Papago Indians from San Xavier, forty-eight Tucson citizens of Mexican descent and six Anglo-Americans, a total of 146.

They moved quietly across the desert at night, and at dawn on April 30, 1871, surprised the Indian camp. According to Oury's frank statement, "The attack was so swift and fierce that within a half hour the whole work was ended, and not an adult Indian was left to tell the tale."

There is much discrepancy concerning the number killed. Acting Assistant Surgeon C. B. Briesly, first on the field, reported finding bodies of 21 women and children, and later six more, "an old man, two half-grown boys and three women." Survivors he met told him "some eighty-five had been killed, of whom eight only were men." This hearsay figure 85 is commonly repeated, as is also Lieutenant Whitman's similarly indefinite "killed and missing about 125; eight only were men."

It should be noted that only Whitman and his associates stated that the victims were peaceful, and General Crook, who came to the command later, branded Whitman as one who "had deserted his colors and gone over to the 'Indian Ring' bag and baggage, and had behaved himself in such a manner that I had preferred charges against him." By "Indian Ring" General Crook meant the agents, officials and citizens who had conspired to plunder the Indians financially. This same charge was made against Whitman by Oury, leader of the "massacre."

Crook Takes Command

The Camp Grant massacre caused a shake-up in the handling of Apache affairs, both military and civil. George Crook, then lieutenant colonel of the 23rd Infantry, was ordered to duty as department commander in his brevet rank of major general. Vincent Collyer, secretary of the Board of Indian Commissioners, was sent to make peace with the Apache. When reports came back that he was not doing too well at it, General Howard was sent to try his hand. While all this was going on, Crook was organizing small, mobile columns, supplied by pack train, and employing friendly Apache scouts.

When it became evident that the peace drive had failed, Crook's small columns struck hard, and soon got results. On December 28, 1872, Brevet Major William H. Brown, captain

"Satisfying the Demands of Justice: The Head." Wash drawing by Frederic Remington.

of the 5th Cavalry, with three companies of his regiment surprised a camp of Tonto Apache in a cave in Salt River Canyon. The Indians were pinned down by rifle fire, while rocks were dropped upon them. Twenty made a desperate charge, only to be killed. Eighteen surviving women and children were captured.

Other Tonto bands were hit in quick succession, at Turret Butte on March 27, 1873; at Diamond Butte on April 22; on Tonto Creek on June 16. All these fights earned brevets for the commanders. In addition Captain Thomas McGregor of Company A, 1st Cavalry, received a brevet as major for his defeat of Apache Mohave in the Santa Maria Mountains on May 6. These various bands were brought to the reservation at Camp Verde.

In 1875 Crook was promoted to brigadier general in regular rank and assigned to command the Department of the Platte. No sooner had he gone than much of his work was undone by a shortsighted policy of concentrating Apache bands on a few arid and cheerless reservations, sometimes forcing together groups more hostile to one another than they were to the troops.

When Mimbreño Apache were ordered to San Carlos Agency some thirty warriors fled with their chief Victorio. They were joined by a small band of Mescalero led by Caballero. Between 1877 and 1881 Victorio, with perhaps never more than a hundred fighting men, is credited with killing 100 soldiers, 200 citizens of New Mexico and Texas and 200 Mexicans. He was killed in a fight with Mexican troops.

On August 30, 1881, White Mountain Apache rebelled and a company of Apache scouts mutinied at Cibicu Creek. Captain Edmund C. Hentig of the 6th Cavalry and six privates were killed. Brevet Lieutenant Colonel George B. Sanford, major of the 1st Cavalry, rounded up the White Mountain Apache and brought them to the San Carlos Agency.

This stirred up the Chiricahua led by Juh and Nahche, son of Cochise. They attempted a rescue but were met by two companies of the 1st Cavalry under Colonel Bernard, who had just arrived by train from Nevada, and two troops of the 6th Cavalry. The Indians were driven off after a stand-up fight at close quarters—some got as close as ten feet—unusual in Apache warfare.

The thwarted Chiricahua fled to the Dragoon Mountains, and Colonel Bernard loaded six companies from three regiments—G and I of the 1st Cavalry, A and F of the 6th and F and H of the 9th—on a train, perhaps the only case when a railroad was used in active pursuit of Indians. The Chiricahua were in sight on October 2 as the troops unloaded horses from boxcars, using the doors as ramps. After a sharp fight, the Apache scattered and fled to Mexico. There they were joined by Geronimo, who was to become the most famous of Apache warriors. When Juh was drowned accidentaly, Geronimo took over.

General Crook returned to Arizona in 1882 and organized companies of Apache scouts under Captain Emmet Crawford and Second Lieutenants Britton Davis and Charles B. Gatewood. When Geronimo raided into Arizona from Mexico, Crawford's scouts pursued him back across the international border, capturing his camp in the Sierra Madre on May 15, 1883. The Chiricahua agreed to return to San Carlos, but Geronimo delayed to build up his herd of stolen cattle, and it was not until April, 1884, that he surrendered to Lieutenant Davis at the border.

The continued differences in policy and authority between Army and Indian Bureau did little to pacify the Chiricahua, who soon got out of hand once more. On May 17, 1885, Geronimo bolted again after a tizwin drunk—tizwin was a beer made of corn mash, one of a few fermented drinks concocted by Indians. For the rest of the year his band raided on both sides of the border, dodging United States and Mexican troops.

On January 10, 1886, Crawford's scouts surrounded and destroyed Geronimo's camp at Nacori, near the Aros River in Sonora, but Geronimo and some followers escaped. That night he sent word he was ready to surrender, but at dawn next morning Mexican troops, apparently mistaking the Apache scouts for the Chiricahua, attacked, and Crawford was killed. First Lieutenant Marion P. Maus (later awarded the Medal of Honor for his conduct that day) succeeded in stopping the fight.

Maus resumed negotiations with Geronimo, who agreed to meet General Crook at Canyon de los Embudos in northern Sonora. Here after discussion from March 25 to 27 Geronimo once more agreed to surrender. The scene was photographed by Camillus S. Fly, who had come from his studio in Tucson. That night a smuggler got to Geronimo with liquor, and he bolted again, with about a third of the band, leaving seventy-seven to be taken as prisoners to Fort Bowie.

Crook was criticized for the escape of Geronimo and for his surrender terms. He asked to be relieved.

General Miles Takes Over

Crook was succeeded by General Nelson A. Miles, who was ordered to destroy or capture the hostiles "making active and prominent use of the regular troops." This meant disapproval of Crook's use of Indian scouts, who were believed by some to be in league with the hostiles. To enable Miles to carry out the new order the number of troops in the Department of Arizona was increased from 3,000 to 5,000.

Miles divided his command into "districts of observation," each manned by a highly mobile force. He employed an important innovation, the heliograph—a wireless telegraph based on mirrors reflecting the sun's rays—manned by Signal Corps detachments placed upon the highest peaks and prominent lookouts to discover any movements of Indians and to transmit messages.

However, in four months of vigorous campaigning his 5,000 soldiers failed to kill or capture a single Apache raider.

The most durable of his campaigners was Captain Henry W. Lawton of the 4th Cavalry, whose command included thirty-five picked troopers from his regiment, detachments from Companies D and K, 8th Infantry, twenty Indian scouts and Assistant Surgeon Leonard Wood, who doubled as infantry commander and leader of scouts and trailers. It will be noted that General Miles employed Indian scouts, despite the doubts of high officialdom.

On the strength of a rumor that Geronimo was ready to surrender again, Miles sent Lieutenant Gatewood to investigate. Gatewood took with him two Chiricahua Apache scouts, Kayitah and Martine, and accompanied Lawton's command to the vicinity of Geronimo's camp in Mexico. Leaving all soldiers behind, Gatewood entered Geronimo's camp and persuaded him and Nahche to give themselves up. The formal surrender was made to General Miles at Skeleton Canyon, Arizona Territory, on September 3, 1886.

Geronimo had been at his peak strength when Miles began his campaign; his band contained thirty-five warriors and 109 women and children, including six half-grown boys. During his long wanderings his followers came and went, as they pleased, and when he finally surrendered, his band had dwindled to twenty-four men and fourteen women and children, although only six men and four women and children had been killed. From the time he left San Carlos Agency until his surrender to Miles, his band is credited with killing 2 officers, 8 enlisted men, 12 Indian scouts, 75 American citizens and 100 Mexicans.

The entire Chiricahua tribe was sent to Florida as prisoners of war—including Kayitah and Martine, the scouts who had risked their lives with Gatewood.

50. *Last Stand of the Cheyenne*

After Dull Knife's band of northern Cheyenne was defeated by Mackenzie in late 1876, the scattered fugitives were rounded up or came in and surrendered. In the spring of 1877 they were sent to join their relatives, the southern Cheyenne, in Indian Territory. The Indian Bureau liked to wrap up their charges in neat tribal packages, whether the Indians liked it or not. The northern Cheyenne did not like it. Within two months, two-thirds of them were ill; forty-one died that winter. Medical care was inadequate and rations were short. In the summer of 1878 Little Wolf told the agent that he did not want to fight but that he and his band were going back to their old home in the north. Dull Knife's following accompanied Little Wolf's band.

Troops were sent after them; there were fights, but the Cheyenne kept on going, across Kansas and well into Nebraska. They did some plundering, and a few citizens were killed, but Little Wolf tried to make it a peaceful migration. At the Platte River the bands of Little Wolf and Dull Knife separated. Little Wolf surrendered to First Lieutenant William Philo Clark of the 2nd Cavalry, and was taken to Fort Keogh on the Yellowstone. There General Miles enlisted Little Wolf and his warriors as Indian scouts to help run down Sioux hostiles. Little Wolf's people were allowed to remain in the North.

A more tragic end awaited Dull Knife's band. Not knowing that the Red Cloud Agency had been discontinued, he led his people toward it. Troops surrounded, disarmed and imprisoned his entire band in nearby Fort Robinson. When they refused to agree to return south, an attempt was made to starve them into submission. On January 9, 1879, with a few weapons they had managed to hide, they broke out of their barracks prison. Surrounded by troops, the Cheyenne kept on fighting until sixty-four were killed. Seventy-eight, most of them wounded, were captured. The survivors were sent to Pine Ridge Reservation in South Dakota.

51. *Sitting Bull and the Ghost Dance*

Sitting Bull returned from Canada and surrendered in 1881. From then on the Northern Plains were at peace until disturbed by a religious revival. In 1889 Wovoka, also known as Jack Wilson, a Paiute living near Walker Lake, Nevada, had visions. He preached that the Messiah who had been crucified by the whites was coming back, this time for the Indians. The white man and all his works would be swept away; buffalo would return; dead Indians would live again. To aid in bringing this about the ceremonial of the Ghost Dance was instituted. First Lieutenant Hugh L. Scott of the 7th Cavalry said, "The name of Jesus was on every tongue, and had I been a missionary I could have led every Indian on the Plains into the church."

A new administration in Washington had replaced most of the agents among the Sioux with inexperienced men. A new agent at Pine Ridge was frightened by the Ghost Dance excitement, and called for troops. The experienced James McLaughlin at Standing Rock Agency, near Fort Yates, North Dakota, was an honest and able administrator, but he ardently supported the current Indian Bureau policy of civilizing the Indians by suppressing all vestiges of their culture. For several years he had been attempting to undermine the influence of Sitting Bull—most of the downrating of Sitting Bull derives from McLaughlin. There is doubt whether Sitting Bull took any part in the Ghost Dance movement, but McLaughlin believed he was its leader, and even General Miles became convinced that Sitting Bull was planning a great conspiracy of all Indian tribes.

It is improbable that Sitting Bull had any such idea. He had traveled one season with Buffalo Bill's Wild West and had learned much, saying with questionable grammar, "The white people are so many that if every Indian in the West killed one every step they took, the dead would not be missed among you. I go back and tell my people what I have seen. They will never go on the war-path again."

In the hope of determining Sitting Bull's intentions, General Miles decided to employ the services of Buffalo Bill Cody. He had seen the scout in action, and knew of his friendship with Sitting Bull. This procedure outraged McLaughlin, who apparently expected Cody to perform after the manner of the hero of the Buffalo Bill dime novels. Cody was recalled from his mission, and McLaughlin sent Indian police to arrest Sitting Bull, thereby stirring up a feud that was one of the primary causes of the Sioux disaffection. There was a fight; Sitting Bull and eight of his followers were killed, as well as six of the Indian Police.

Battle of Wounded Knee

Sitting Bull's surviving followers fled to the Bad Lands, where they fell in with a Mini-conjou band led by Big Foot, who had just agreed to come into the agency. Alarmed by the killing of Sitting Bull, Big Foot and his band joined the refugees. They were overtaken a few days later by Major Samuel M. Whitside with Troops A, B, I and K of the 7th Cavalry. Brevet Brigadier General James W. Forsyth, colonel of the 7th, arrived to take command with Troops C, D, E and G. He also had Battery E, 1st Artillery, manning four Hotchkiss rapid-fire guns.

The Indians were encamped on Wounded Knee Creek, South Dakota. On the morning of December 29, 1890, Forsyth attempted to disarm them. A Ghost Dancer started a harangue, some Indian fired a shot, and the result was indiscriminate slaughter. Artillery shells tore through the Sioux camp. In the early confusion it is probable that both sides fired shots that hit their own people. As the Indians fled, the troops kept shooting. One count lists eighty-four Sioux men and boys, forty-four women and eighteen children killed. Of the troops, one officer and twenty-four enlisted men were killed; three officers and thirty-two enlisted men were wounded.

"The Borderland of the Other Tribe." Wash drawing by Frederic Remington.

Harper's Weekly, 1891

"The Last Scene of the Last Act of the Sioux War." Drawing by Henry F. Farny.

General Miles moved promptly to avert further fighting and succeeded in calming the Indians. On January 16, 1891, they formally surrendered. Twenty years later wrote Miles, "I did not even then realize that we had probably reached the close of Indian wars in our country." Nor did anyone else at that time. As late as 1903 General Charles King in such military novels as *A Daughter of the Sioux* wrote of Indian wars as part of the contemporary scene, just as writers about cowboys continued for a half-century to use Owen Wister's *The Virginian* as a model for a contemporary West that no longer existed.

End of Indian Fighting

There were fights of record after Wounded Knee, but none of importance. Along the Texas border detachments of the 3rd Cavalry and Indian scouts clashed with remnants of Geronimo's raiders from Mexico three times in 1891 and four in 1892. The 7th Cavalry had two similar encounters in 1896.

Two individual Apache caused trouble for the 7th Cavalry for years. Massai—also spelled Ma-si, Matse and Masse—was one of the Chiricahua entrained for Florida with Geronimo. He escaped from the cars near Springfield, Missouri, and made his way back to Arizona unseen and unreported—proof of his ability as scout and trailer. After many years of raiding he was killed in Mexico.

Has-kay-bay-nay-ntayl may be the correct name of the Indian known to history as the Apache Kid. He was a scout for the famous Al Sieber until he took part in a shooting that brought him to trial and conviction. On his way to the penitentiary at Yuma, Arizona, he escaped. For years the Apache Kid was the border's most wanted outlaw. He faded from view about 1894, and there are a dozen stories of his death, none of them substantiated. Credulous people like to believe that he is still out on his last, lone war trail. He would be 100 years old in 1969 or thereabout.

The last fight in which soldiers were killed occurred at Leech Lake, Minnesota, on October 5, 1898. The Indians were Chippewa, and the soldiers killed were Brevet Major Melville C. Wilkinson of the 3rd Infantry, veteran of the Civil War and of the Nez Percé War, and five enlisted men of his regiment. After an investigation, charges against the Indians were dropped.

In the fall of 1906 some 400 White River Ute—members of the tribe of the Meeker killing and the Thornburgh fight—became dissatisfied with their reservation in Utah and wandered off across the plains of Wyoming. After Inspector James McLaughlin of the Indian Service failed to persuade them to return, eight troops of the 6th Cavalry and eight of the 10th rounded them up on the Powder River in Montana. After spending some time at Fort Meade and on the Cheyenne River Reservation, they returned to Utah. This affair was bloodless.

Even as late as 1915 a fracas occurred in Utah over the arrest of a Paiute for murder. Indians resisted a United States marshal's posse of seventy-five men, and a tribal uprising was feared. General Hugh L. Scott, then Chief of Staff of the Army, went to the scene of the trouble in February, 1916, and with great good sense settled the affair with no loss of face on either side. The wanted Indian surrendered, was tried and acquitted.

These clashes occurred after the period covered by this book and belong more in the annals of crime than in those of warfare. During this period Congress wavered from session to session on whether Indian fighting was war or police action. It sometimes denied brevets and other honors on the ground that there was no war, yet in 1890 and at other times granted brevets so belatedly in wholesale lots that the recognition was meaningless.

The Indian wars were not all the fault of the Indian; nor were they all the fault of the white intruder. They were perhaps inevitable in the collision of two races whose values were so dissimilar that they could not understand each other—and perhaps do not yet. It is easy to say, "We took the land away from the Indians," but they were taking lands away from each other in wars more brutal and bloody than any waged against them by Americans. It is easy to say they resented destruction of the buffalo and other game by white men, but they did their share of destroying it for furs to trade for white man's goods, and even wantonly. That the Indians felt no great urge to defend their homes and hunting grounds is shown in the rarity of wars in the West that involved entire tribes.

The bands that waged war had grievances; in perhaps most cases they had been treated with rank injustice, often through ignorance. Probably many of the Indian wars, like many other wars, could have been avoided by a wise and consistent policy, based on mutual understanding—but there was no understanding.

As in all generalizations, there are exceptions. One among many may be cited, a strange case of an understanding between an Indian and some white men. At dawn on August 29, 1911, some dogs cornered a strange man in the slaughter yards near Oroville, California. He was an Indian, almost naked, probably in his forties and unable to speak English. During all of his lifetime his people, in ever-dwindling numbers, had hidden like hunted animals in the forests below Lassen Peak. This last man subsisted alone for almost three years in the wilderness before he came to the slaughterhouses, fully expecting to be killed as all his people had been.

The sheriff called off the dogs, but was at a loss to know what to do with the wild man. When newspapers announced the incident, two professors of anthropology at the University of California in Berkeley realized that a rare specimen of Stone Age man had been found. They decided to investigate. Subsequently they got permission from the Department of the Interior to take charge of the lone Indian, and they arranged for him to live the rest of his life in an apartment at the University Museum in San Francisco.

On one occasion the two professors took him on a pack trip back into the mountains where he showed them how his people had lived, how they made flint arrowheads, started fires without matches, speared salmon, snared deer and rabbits.

The savage proved to be a man of great patience, gentleness, bravery and loyalty, with a remarkable control over his temper. He was quick to learn, and he readily adapted himself to a strange civilization. However, he clung to the pagan teachings of his childhood, although he showed tolerance for the religious beliefs of others. Watching people in the bustling city around him, the trolley cars and ferryboats, he pronounced civilized man to be very, very clever, but not very wise.

The two professors became much attached to this Stone Age man. Almost five years after his capture he died of tuberculosis, and some scientists demanded that the "specimen" be dissected. The men who knew him best objected, saying they proposed to stand by their friend. "If there is any talk about the interests of science," said Professor A. L. Kroeber, "say for me that science can go to hell."

So an understanding between red man and white was possible—but too little, or too late.

The Indian village. Engraving, after drawing by Charles Graham.

Harper's Weekly, 1885

PART FIVE

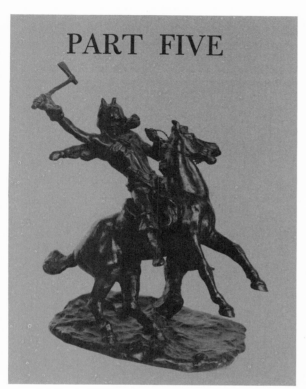

"The Cryer" by Charles M. Russell

The Law of the American West

by Wayne Gard

*Bandit group stages train hold-up. Engraving, after drawing
by Edward Penfield.* Harper's Weekly, *1892.*

52. *Running Wild: Horse and Cow Thieves*

THE HANGMAN'S NOOSE must be included—along with the ax, the plow, the lariat and the miner's pick—as a symbol of the taming of the West. The hardy frontiersmen had to conquer not only the land and the redskins but also disruptive elements in their own number. They could sleep soundly only after they had rid their ranges of the highwayman, the horse thief and the cattle rustler.

The West was pioneered by heroic men and women who braved hardships of every kind to build new homes and communities. They endured blizzards and droughts and risked having their scalps taken by savages. They gave unselfishly of their time to carry to the frontier the banner of civilization. They deserve all the honor that later generations can give them.

Yet to assume that all those who went over the western trails were valiant and honorable would be to distort history. In almost every group of builders was a sprinkling of wreckers. Each area had its quota of those who had gone west to escape jail or to make easy fortunes from the work of others. Nearly every mining camp had its claim jumpers and thugs. Every stagecoach trail attracted highwaymen eager to unload shipments of gold. The entire West was spotted with horse thieves and cattle rustlers.

Many observers of life on the frontier noted the less desirable elements. It was not uncommon to inquire of a man why he had run away from his former home, wrote W. B. Dewees, an early settler. "Few persons feel insulted at such a question. They generally answer for some crime or other which they have committed. If they deny having committed any crime or say they did not run away, they are looked upon suspiciously."

In a similar vein, Frederick Law Olmsted, an eastern visitor to Texas, pointed out that

> . . . in the rapid settlement of the country, many an adventurer crossed the border, spurred by love of liberty, forfeited at home, rather than drawn by a love of adventure or of rich soil. Probably a more reckless and vicious crew was seldom gathered than that which peopled some parts of Eastern Texas at the time of its first resistance to the Mexican government. "G.T.T." (gone to Texas) was the slang appendage . . . to every man's name who had disappeared before the discovery of some rascality. Did a man emigrate thither, everyone was on the watch for the discreditable reason to turn up.

If your life were of the slightest use to anyone, Olmsted added,

. . . you might be sure he would take it. It was safe only as you were in constant readiness to defend it. Horses and wives were of as little account as umbrellas in more advanced states. Everybody appropriated everything that suited him, running his own risk of a penalty. Justice descended into the body of Judge Lynch, sleeping when he slept, and when he awoke hewing down right and left for exercise and pastime.

This was true not only of early Texas but of most of the West. The frontier was settled by a strange mixture of human elements—by the upright and enterprising who sought to improve their condition and by criminals of various types who went West to escape the terrors of the law.

Of all the frontier villains, the horse thief was held in the greatest contempt and was punished the most quickly and severely when caught. In the more sparsely settled areas, any horse thief who was caught could expect to be hanged immediately. The reason for this was plain. Man's dependence on his horse was total and complete. Without it he could be the victim of a sudden storm, have his scalp lifted by Indian raiders or die of thirst or hunger. It is not difficult, then, to see why horse stealing was considered a vicious type of murder. Indeed horse stealing in western Kansas during the 1870's was deemed much more serious than ordinary murder. T. A. McNeal noted in *When Kansas Was Young*:

> A horse was about the only means of conveyance, and in the cattle business it was essential. It was necessary, too, to let the horses run on the range unguarded. The cattlemen reasoned that unless the men who lusted for the possession of good horses were restrained by fear of prompt and violent death, no man would be sure that when he turned his horses out at night he would be able to gather any of them in the morning.

Texans fully shared this view of the horse thief. Early newspapers in that state carried many accounts of losses and bristled with threats to the culprits. The Fort Worth *Democrat* reported on May 2, 1874:

> An unusual amount of horse stealing has been carried on of late in this and adjoining counties. The boldness of some of the thefts has aroused the blood of Texans, and new ropes are being prepared for the benefit of those who love horseflesh not wisely but too well. A few wholesome hangings will soon be in order, and the traffic in horseflesh will be sensibly diminished. We advise these jailbirds to make themselves scarce in this section if they don't want to pull hemp.

Such warnings went unheeded. Early in 1878 a Houston newspaper estimated that 100,000 horses had been stolen in Texas in the preceding three years.

> It is further estimated that 750 men are regularly engaged in this business and that not more than one in ten is ever captured and brought to justice. By common practice in the rural districts, every man caught is either shot on the spot or hanged to the nearest tree. No instance is yet recorded where the law paid the slightest attention to lynchers

Leslie's Weekly, 1877

Horse-stealing raid across the Rio Grande carried out by Mexican outlaws.

of this kind. It is conceded that the man who steals a horse forfeits his life to the owner. It is a game of life and death. Men will pursue these thieves for 500 miles, go any length, spend any amount of money to capture them, and fight them to the death when overtaken. That they will be totally exterminated admits of no doubt. The poor scoundrels cannot last long when the feeling of all civilization is so much aroused against them as it now is in Texas.

Some of the more ingenious thieves disguised themselves as Indians to confuse their pursuers. And since many saddle horses were known by sight and easily recognized in their own communities, thieves would often ride or drive them to distant places for sale. One Montana thief used to drive horses across the border into Canada, sell them there, then steal Canadian horses, and reverse the procedure. Likewise, horse thieves who operated along the upper Brazos River in Texas took their booty to Kansas and drove Kansas horses south to Texas.

But this kind of trickery was soon rooted out. The Wichita *Eagle* complained on July 31, 1873:

> Too many horses are being stolen in southern Kansas this summer. A few gents need catching and elevating in the eyes and estimation of the public. A cheer from the crowd below and a leap from a leafless tree would be good enough, but the hanging should not be interrupted because the tree or limb happened to be leafed out. Summary punishment is the only policy that will dry up horse stealing.

Even more common than the horse thief, though perhaps hated a bit less intensely, was the cattle rustler. Until barbed wire reached across the prairies and plains, almost every range had a few cowmen who were said to swing a wide loop. The meaning was that their ropes caught calves that belonged to others. Neighbors might say of a suspect that he worked ahead of the roundup, that his cows had twins or that his calves didn't suck the right cows. Or someone might remark that "he keeps his branding iron smooth" from overwork.

A man who wanted to enter the cattle business, plainsmen said, needed only a rope, a running iron and the nerve to use them. "Three years ago," wrote Bill Nye in his Laramie *Boomerang* in 1883, "a guileless tenderfoot came to Wyoming, leading a single steer and carrying a branding iron. Now he is the opulent possessor of 600 head of fine cattle—the ostensible progeny of that one steer."

In the era of the open range, the typical rustler was not a man who switched from one type of crime to another. He was a cow hand who had drifted into rustling. He knew the cow country and was adept at riding, roping and branding. After buying a few cows and registering a brand, he had many opportunities to spur the growth of his herd if he were not squeamish about the fine points.

Before barbed wire came to the West the ethics of the cow country actually helped the rustler. After the Civil War the Texas brush country was overrun by half-wild unbranded cattle. Anyone who wanted to could rope and brand them, and many a ranchman established his fortune by gathering, branding and trailing leathery longhorns to market. Those were the days of lax herding and open hospitality when a hungry cowman incurred no ill will by killing a beef which wore his neighbor's brand and when a cow hand whose herd grew too rapidly was regarded tolerantly, especially if his increase came from ranches owned by eastern or foreign capitalists.

Barbed wire, however, brought with it a new point of view. As fencing spread into the Plains in the late 1870's and early 1880's, unbranded range cattle, or mavericks, became fewer. Too, the killing or stealthy branding of strays came to be looked upon as theft. Such animals, it was believed, should be left for the spring or fall roundup, when neighbors joined to gather and divide them.

Now the cowhand with a rapidly growing herd was beginning to be looked upon as an outlaw who deserved to be shot or hanged. In fact, some ranchmen refused, as a matter of policy, to hire any cowboy who had stock of his own.

Rustlers had been busy in the West ever since Spaniards brought in the first cattle, though it was Indians who did most of the early stealing. For obvious reasons the warriors were usually more eager for horses than for cattle, but when their meat supply was low, they drove off beeves, dairy cows and even work oxen. In some sections, repeated forays delayed the development of cattle ranching for years.

Some of the Indian raiders aimed to avenge real or imagined wrongs. Others wanted to keep white settlers out of hunting grounds or reservations and to save the buffaloes from slaughter. In the era of the big cattle drives north from Texas, redskin marauders stampeded many trail herds for fun and for food, and sometimes they killed those animals they could not drive off.

After Texas won its independence, Mexican rustlers became troublesome along the Rio Grande. Claims made against the Mexican government reveal that between 1859 and 1872, Mexican bandits stole 145,298 cattle, along with 4,308 horses, from the vast King and Kenedy ranches near the southern tip of Texas.

For most of the frontier period, however, depredations by Indians and Mexicans fell short of those committed against Mexicans by many Texas stockmen who considered all Mexicans hostile and who had no scruples about appropriating cattle from Mexican-owned ranches even when they were located in the Lone Star State. Some Texans regularly crossed into Mexico and swam large herds north across the Rio Grande by night, trailing this "wet stock" to Kansas markets.

But most rustlers confined their activities to the growing herds of their neighbors. Some stampeded cattle on the northward trails and drove off as many as they could, using six-shooters to defend themselves if necessary. Both before and after the coming of barbed wire, rustling was especially common where canyons and scrub timber offered hiding places for thieves and stolen stock.

Early in 1873 one ranchman, John Hittson, estimated that in the preceding twenty years thieves had driven more than 100,000 cattle from Texas.

During the frontier period, the altering of brands was a common practice among rustlers. Instead of the stamp iron used by most cowmen, the thief used a running iron—a straight rod with a curve at the heated end. With this pencil-like instrument, it was fairly easy to change a 1 into a 7 or an L, a P into a B or an R, an S into an 8, or a C into an O. A Bar T might become a Curry Comb, while a W might be converted into a Flying W, a Box W, a Rafter W, or a Rocking W. Brand burners even changed the XIT brand into a six-pointed star.

IOU · SI- · % · K · B

JD2 · OK · HES · ON · H2

When some states outlawed the use of the running iron, rustlers began to use pieces of heavy wire. They could carry those in their pockets and bend them into any shape desired. To disguise the change made in a brand, they sometimes smeared the marking with axle grease.

Even more common than brand burning was the theft of large unbranded calves, sometimes called mavericking. When a ranchman neglected to brand some of his calves after they were weaned, they became easy prey for the rustler. The thief would cut a pasture fence, drive the calves to his corral and stamp his own brand on them.

Not content with this, some thieves returned for the younger calves, not yet weaned. Stealing these was a more ticklish job, though, because longhorn cows and their calves had a strong instinct for getting back together, even after being separated by miles. If a ranchman found one of his cows nursing a calf with a rustler's brand, the thief might soon have a one-way ticket to the pearly gates.

To prevent detection, the rustler often delayed branding stolen calves until they quit bawling and learned to eat grass. Sometimes, though, he resorted to other means to prevent the calves from returning to their mothers and to hasten weaning. He might cut the muscles supporting the eyelids of the calf, making it temporarily blind. Or he might apply a hot iron between the toes, making the calf's feet too sore for walking. In rare cases, he would even split the calf's tongue to prevent suckling, or "pin crepe on the kid" by killing the mother and making the calf a real orphan.

On occasion, a rustler would mark a suckling calf with some unregistered brand or hieroglyphic that might cause it to be passed over by the owner when branding. Then, after the calf was weaned, the thief would seek it out and stamp it with his own brand.

In many sections weak law enforcement encouraged rustling, and more often than not, stolen cattle were never recovered. County seats were far apart, grand juries were hesitant to indict, and trial juries were reluctant to convict. Many prosecutors were afraid to take vigorous action. Furthermore, frontier jails were notoriously flimsy, so a thief could usually break out easily.

One of the few prosecutors who dedicated himself to the conviction of cattle rustlers was young Jack Garner of Uvalde, Texas, who rose a notch toward the vice-presidency by making his county one of the most dangerous for cattle rustlers and horse thieves. But he was an exception. In most places, cattle rustling went unpunished. In northwestern Texas, for example, the Panhandle Stock Association worked for six years before obtaining its first conviction.

For many early cowmen, the only recourse against thieving seemed to be to take the law into their own hands. To protect their grazing herds, they hired fence riders who were inclined to shoot first and ask questions afterward. The big cattle owners made it amply clear that any man who was careless with his branding iron or whose calves nursed the wrong cows could expect a fatal attack of "hemp fever" or "lead poisoning."

One of the more colorful fence riders was Pink Higgins, who rode for the big Matador Ranch in western Texas. Out on the prairie he came upon a thief starting to skin a cow that he had just killed. Pink shot the rustler, ripped open the cow and pushed the man's body inside. Then he rode into town and casually told the sheriff that if he would ride out to a certain spot he would behold a miracle of nature—a cow giving birth to a man.

Typical Texas cattle brands.

DRAWN BY CLARENCE P. HORNUNG

53. *Outside the Law*

California Outlaws

ALMOST EVERY SPOT in the early West had its hard characters. Even a brief glance at some of them makes very clear the difficulties faced by those who set out to tame the new country.

Many of the boldest of frontier outlaws operated in California. The gold rush brought to the Pacific Coast a vast influx of adventurers and thieves, along with those who wanted to make their living honestly by mining. Soon the ranks of bandits were enlarged by those who had failed at mining and looked at crime as a possible living.

California's Mexicans could rationalize their own lawless activities more easily than others, for early in 1850 the California legislature imposed an outrageous tax system designed to make it almost impossible for foreigners to mine gold. In practice, Germans, Frenchmen, Italians and even those from Australia's convict settlements were counted as native Americans. But the Chinese and the Spanish-speaking Americans had no chance. This unfairness was bitterly resented by the Mexicans, some of whom had spent their entire lives in California, and when one of them turned to crime, he could claim to be righting a wrong.

Joaquin Murieta

Several bands of Mexican outlaws included members who were dispossessed miners. In the two years following the passage of the California tax law, these thieves maintained an intensive program of horse stealing, running off cattle, holding up stagecoaches, robbing saloons and stores. Nobody knew who was in these bands, but when their depredations occurred hundreds of miles apart people came to the conclusion that there were at least five bands. The name of the leader of each was said to be Joaquin—a common Mexican name—and it is noticeable that no surnames were mentioned. In fact, no one knew any of the bandits' names.

Outlawry became so frequent that, in the spring of 1853, a bill was introduced in the California legislature offering a reward for the head of "Joaquin," no last name given. It was pointed out that a law putting a price on the head of a man who was unknown except by the popular sobriquet, "Joaquin," would be unconstitutional, and the bill failed to pass. However, the legislature did authorize a former Texan, Harry Love, to raise a small company of mounted rangers to capture the "robbers commanded by the five Joaquins." Governor John Bigler, on his own authority, offered a reward of $1,500 for any Joaquin killed or captured.

For about two months the rangers did little but chase rumors. Then one day they came on a group of Mexicans sitting around a campfire. After the rangers had asked a few questions, both groups began shooting. The rangers killed two of the band and captured two. One of the dead was identified as Manuel Garcia, a notorious thief and murderer better known as Three-Fingered Jack; the other, though not identified, was said to have referred to himself as the leader.

Since the reward offered had been only for a Joaquin, the rangers quickly decided that the dead leader was a Joaquin. They cut off his head and the hand of Three-Fingered Jack. These mementos were taken to Sacramento. A grateful legislature added $5,000 to the governor's reward and the grisly relics, preserved in jars of alcohol, were exhibited in various California towns. It should be noted that the first reports said only that this head belonged to Joaqüin. No last name was mentioned. Later, however, the rangers obtained affidavits that the head belonged to Joaquin Murieta, a man wanted for murder. Three Mexicans in the party who had escaped said later that the beheaded man was Joaquin Valenzuela. The *Alta California,* a San Francisco newspaper, denounced the entire ranger action as a humbug.

The Joaquin fiasco might have been forgotten except for the appearance in 1854 of a fictional paperback entitled *The Life and Adventures of Joaquin Murieta, the Celebrated California Bandit,* by John Rollin Ridge. This lurid work made Murieta a legendary Robin Hood who suited the romantic tastes of the readers of his time. The work was pirated by many other hack writers until the fictitious and heroic Joaquin Murieta became, in many people's minds, a historic character—so historic that two of California's best early-day historians, H. H. Bancroft and Theodore Hittell, put him in their serious texts as a real person.

Bandit Murieta.

N. Y. PUBLIC LIBRARY

A showman's grisly broadside.

WILL BE
EXHIBITED
FOR ONE DAY ONLY!
AT THE STOCKTON HOUSE!
THIS DAY, AUG. 19. FROM 9 A. M. UNTIL 6 P. M.
THE HEAD
Of the renowned Bandit!
JOAQUIN!
AND THE
HAND OF THREE FINGERED JACK!
THE NOTORIOUS ROBBER AND MURDERER.

"JOAQUIN" and "THREE-FINGERED JACK," were captured by the State Rangers, under the command of Capt. Harry Love, at the Arroyo Cantina, July 24th. No reasonable doubt can be entertained in regard to the identification of the head now on exhibition, as being that of the notorious robber, Joaquin Murietta, as it has been recognized by hundreds of persons who have formerly seen him.

Black Bart.

Black Bart

Although Joaquin Murieta belongs more to folklore than to history, many of his successors were real enough. For thirty years after the gold rush, California's mining camps and mountain trails paid tribute to bandits of every variety. One of the most intriguing was a highwayman known as Black Bart. Between 1875 and 1883, he held up twenty-eight California stagecoaches. He always masked his head in a flour sack pierced with holes and carried a shotgun. In a deep voice he would order the driver:

"Throw down the box!"

After robbing the express box of its treasure, he would slip away, leaving at the scene a few lines of doggerel. His best known effort read:

> I've labored long and hard for bread,
> For honor and for riches,
> But on my *corns* too long you've tred
> *You fine-haired sons of bitches.*
> Black Bart,
the Po 8

Wells, Fargo and Company, whose express shipments had been robbed by Black Bart, offered a reward of $800 for his capture and conviction, but few clues were found. At the time of some of his holdups a few people in the neighborhood reported seeing a stranger who looked more like a preacher than a bandit. Questionable evidence, surely!

However, Bart finally made the mistake of leaving some clues. After a stagecoach robbery late in 1883, officers found a derby hat, a belt, two paper bags containing crackers and sugar, a leather case for binoculars, a magnifying glass, a razor, two flour sacks, three dirty linen cuffs and a handkerchief full of buckshot. Sheriff Ben Thorn noticed on one corner of the handkerchief, in small letters, what appeared to be a laundry mark, F.X.O.7.

The express company's detective, J. B. Hume, who for years had been on Black Bart's trail, now set to work again. He ordered a special operative to investigate San Francisco's ninety-one laundries. After a week's search the mark turned up on a laundry record that linked it with a man known as C. E. Bolton, who lived in a small hotel nearby and was understood to be the owner of a mine.

Soon the detective met Bolton, a straight, broad-shouldered man with a gray mustache and goatee. He was elegantly dressed, with derby hat, diamond pin, heavy gold watch and chain, and small cane. In Bolton's room the detectives found haberdashery bearing the same laundry mark and a half-written letter in the same hand as the verses left at the scenes of the holdups. Bolton was jailed, tried, convicted and sent to San Quentin Prison.

Texas Bad Men—and Women

Like California during its gold rush, Texas in its early years of settlement had a bumper crop of outlaws. The population was thinly spread, and so was the law. Usually a man who ran into serious trouble could get across the Red River or the Rio Grande and lie low until the excitement had subsided.

Things were especially chaotic in Texas during the decade of Reconstruction following the Civil War. The removal of many state and local officials and the imposition of military law had caused deep resentment, and many retaliated by taking the law into their own hands. It was at this time that the state's most notorious gunman, John Wesley Hardin, began his long career in crime.

Wes Hardin

John Wesley Hardin, born in 1853, was named for the founder of the Methodist Church by his father, a circuit-riding preacher who later turned to teaching and the practice of law. Wes differed from most other western gunslingers by remaining more or less religious all his life. He was a brave man, bigoted, quarrelsome and always positive that he was right. He killed more than a score of men and in his memoirs the victims were always the devils incarnate who got their due.

Wes grew up in Texas immediately after the Civil War. Federal soldiers were maintaining order and insisting that the recently freed slaves enjoy all the rights of other citizens. This was distasteful to an unreconstructed Southerner like Wes Hardin. Undoubtedly some Negroes became insolent to their former masters, and in 1868, when Wes was only fifteen years old, he shot one of them with his Colt revolver, claiming that the Negro tried to bully him. Believing that a fair trial for a Southerner was impossible as long as the Yankees held the country, Wes ambushed the three soldiers who came to arrest him and killed them all.

He was now a fugitive from the law in a country where many of the Southerners were willing to shelter him. However, a boy hiding out had to associate with shady characters, and he began drinking and gambling with them. By the time he was seventeen he had killed seven men—some in quarrels over gambling debts, some for trying to arrest him.

In 1871 Wes Hardin hired out as a cowboy to help drive a herd of cattle up the Chisholm Trail—an easy way for a Texan to leave the country without attracting attention. On the trail he killed seven more men—two Indians and five Mexicans, so they didn't count. When the herd reached Abilene, Kansas, the cowboys were paid off. Wes found the town full of cowboys who were drinking, fighting and making merry. He added to the excitement by killing three men.

This extraordinary gunman was an ordinary-looking man with a sun-tanned face and heavy mustache. His eyes were blue, cold and deadly. A cowman once saw him shoot down five men who were firing at him and remarked, "That boy can handle a pistol faster than a frog can lick flies."

Returning from Kansas to Texas, Wes married and tried to settle down to stock farming, but soon he was in trouble again. Still wanted for his old offenses, he had to kill a Negro policeman and a federal officer who tried to arrest him, but—worse for him—he killed a gambling opponent and thus gained the enmity of that man's friends who came to lynch him. Wes held them at bay, was badly wounded himself and, to save his own life, sent for the sheriff to come and get him before his enemies did.

In prison in Gonzales, Hardin's wounds healed and after two months he sawed his way out of jail. During the next two years, a reward still on his head, he lived with relatives while he punched cattle and took part in the range feud between the Sutton and Taylor families. Wes was an in-law of the Taylors. As in most range wars, each party accused the other of stealing their stock. The constant fighting between these armed factions served as a shield to protect a wanted man such as Wes Hardin. In fact, with cousins, uncles and nephews on nearby ranches and in cowcamps, he dared visit small towns to gamble, and he entered a race horse of his own at the track. The sheriff was on Hardin's side in the feud, so Wes ventured into Comanche, the county seat, where his pony was winning big stakes until the deputy sheriff, Charles Webb, from neighboring Brown County heard that he was there and came to arrest him for the reward. Wes put a stop to that and Webb was buried the next day.

Texas, however, was now getting too hot for Wes Hardin. He moved his wife and children to Louisiana. Under the assumed name of Swain, he bought and ran a saloon in Gainesville, Florida, where he helped lynch a Negro, then moved to Alabama where he engaged in the logging business, still as Mr. Swain.

Meanwhile, back in Texas, Lieutenant John B. Armstrong of the Rangers, asked for permission to go after Hardin, who now had a reward of $4,000 over his head. With a little detective work, Armstrong learned the fugitive's whereabouts and, taking along an undercover man from Dallas, followed his trail across Alabama to Pensacola, Florida, where Wes had gone on a drinking and gambling spree.

At Pensacola Junction, eight miles from the city, they finally overtook Hardin on the evening of August 23, 1877, sitting with four companions in a railroad car. A gun battle in true western TV style followed: Armstrong received a bullet through his hat, killed one of Hardin's henchmen, knocked Hardin insensible, and disarmed the other three, sticking their guns in his belt.

Hardin was taken back to Texas to be tried for the murder of Webb. He was convicted, and on September 28, 1878, received a twenty-five year sentence. In the state prison at Huntsville, Texas, he read theological books, became superintendent of the prison Sunday School and president of its debating society. He also studied law. After serving sixteen years he was pardoned by the governor and admitted to the bar. In 1895 he went to El Paso to practice law. Here he began to frequent saloons and gambling dens once more. A policeman arrested his mistress. The policeman's father, John Selman, was something of a gunman himself, having killed a score of men. He heard that Wes Hardin had called his boy, the policeman, a son-of-a-bitch, and went to see him about that insult.

"I am unarmed," Hardin told him.

"Go and get your gun. I am armed," Selman told him.

Wes left and the two men skulked around El Paso's streets, looking for each other.

Between 11 and 12 that night, August 19, 1895, Wes stood at one end of the bar in the Acme Saloon on San Antonio Street. He was shaking dice. Selman came through the swinging doors and killed him with a shot through the back of his head.

Within a year Selman was killed by ex-sheriff George Scarborough. Scarborough, in turn, was killed by Will Carver, who in his time was killed by Elijah Briant—a good enough blood-line, surely, to suit a genealogist, but as an old-time cowman might say, "In them days scratches didn't count in Texas, down by the Rio Grande."

Sam Bass

Texans want to forget Wes Hardin. He was a quarrelsome killer who had a chance to reform and failed. Besides, many descendants of people he killed in the feuds are still living. Texans tell quite a different story about Sam Bass. That renowned train robber of the seventies is something of a hero. Out on the rolling prairies of the cow country, riders still talk about him. He is especially real along Hickory Creek and among the hills and hollows of Clear Creek and Little Elm, forty miles northwest of Dallas. On windy nights folks say they hear the hoof beats of his galloping horse. And, while looking for a stray calf, many a cowboy keeps an eye open for what might be a hiding place for Sam's gold.

Texans have made a legendary figure of Sam Bass, just as Missourians have done with Jesse James. Both robbed trains in a period when the railroads were unpopular, especially with grangers who complained about high freight rates. Both Sam Bass and Jesse James were reputed to be generous with their stolen gold.

The real Sam Bass was neither a hero nor a cold-blooded killer like Wes Hardin, and much of his life did lend itself to the making of folk legend. He never killed anyone except in self-defense during the final battle at Round Rock, in which he was mortally wounded. Many who knew him looked on him as a cowboy who had gone wrong, and they saved their epithets for the pal who betrayed him.

Born on a farm in southern Indiana in 1851, Sam had little schooling. Before he was thirteen, he became an orphan and went to live at the home of an upright but stern uncle. At eighteen, Sam rebelled against hard work and restricted liberty, and he ran off, heading for Texas. On his way, he spent nearly a year working in a Mississippi sawmill and did not arrive at Denton, on the edge of the Texas cow country, until the fall of 1870.

At Bob Carruth's ranch, on Denton Creek, fourteen miles southwest of town, Sam found cowboy life less romantic than he had pictured it in his boyhood dreams. Although he was a good rider and a hard worker, he drifted back to Denton the next year to find a less rigorous job and more sociable surroundings. For a year and a half he worked for the widow, Mrs. S. E. Lacy, tending the horses of travelers who stopped at her Lacy House on the northeast corner of the town square.

Then, after another brief job, Sam began working for Sheriff W. F. ("Dad") Egan, caring for his horses, milking the family cow, hoeing the garden. Sometimes he cut firewood in the creek bottoms south of town or plowed fields or helped build fences on the Egan farm.

Of average height, Sam had black hair, dark eyes and sallow skin. He had acquired a slight stoop and a downcast look. His words were drawled with a high-pitched nasal twang.

Holding up the stage. Painting by Charles M. Russell, 1899.

Since Denton still had no railroad, the enterprising sheriff made some money in freighting. Often he sent Sam to Dallas or Sherman for goods to be sold in Denton, and on these trips Sam acquired a knowledge of the prairies. He became familiar with the winding roads through the cross timbers and learned to know how to guide his team safely past the swamps of Elm Bottom and the tangled brush along Hickory Creek. He visited the frontier towns and made friends.

For recreation, Sam enjoyed the scrub horse races held on a quarter-mile straightaway of prairie turf north of Denton. Here, on Sunday afternoons, cowboys gathered to match their

AMON CARTER MUSEUM OF WESTERN ART, FORT WORTH

ponies, and sometimes sprinters were brought in from nearby counties. In the fall of 1874, Sam bought a race mare of Steel Dust blood. This mount, soon known as the Denton Mare, began winning many races. Sam thought he had "the world by the tail, with a downhill pull."

By the spring of 1875, Sam became so absorbed in horse racing that Sheriff Egan told him he would have to choose between his pony and his job. Sam chose the Denton Mare and raced her from the Red River to the Rio Grande. He won most of the time but usually the stakes were small, earning him only a meager income, until he met Joel Collins. This man "savvied the burro"—horseman's slang meaning "understood fast stock." Together they went to San Antonio, a big town where the big money was. Here Joel took care of the Denton Mare while Sam, pretending that he did not know him, hired out as a trainer for race-horse men until he learned the speed of their animals, then tipped Joel off on how to match the Denton Mare against them.

With their accumulated earnings they decided to speculate, as every one around them was doing, by taking cattle up the Chisholm Trail. They bought as many as they could, borrowed money on them and bought more. To round out the number to the usual two to three thousand head for a trail herd they took additional cattle "on shares" for other cattlemen.

Driving the herd successfully to Dodge City, they found that market glutted so they trailed the herd on to Ogallala, Nebraska, where they sold most of the cattle, but not all. Deadwood, Dakota Territory, was then at the height of its gold-mining boom; they drove the remainder up there and profited handsomely—only to lose it all at the dazzling gambling tables. They were not only broke but deeply in debt for all that money they owed back in Texas. To recoup their loss, they and four other drifters held up several stagecoaches, but the loot was mere chicken feed.

Trying for a bigger haul the six rode down to Big Springs, Nebraska, where on the evening of September 18, 1877, they held up the eastbound Union Pacific express.

"Throw up your props!" Bass ordered the guard at the express car.

That unhappy man may not have known what his props were but with the round muzzle of a six-shooter in his face he understood what was meant and the robbers took $60,000 in twenty-dollar gold pieces from his car. Frightened passengers handed out several thousand more—a great haul. The men then divided the spoils and separated in pairs, some to meet violent deaths while resisting arrest.

Sam returned to Texas, "all right-side-up, with care," according to the folk song about him. Near Denton, in the thickets he knew so well, he formed a new gang which held up two local stagecoaches. Then, in the spring of 1878, he robbed four trains—at Allen, Hutchins, Eagle Ford and Mesquite. Those bold actions, though they brought little gain, put Captain June Peak and a special company of Texas Rangers on Sam Bass's trail.

During most of the summer Bass and his men played hide-and-seek with the Rangers and various local posses. One of the gang was killed. In July, Bass and several others raced south, stopping in Waco to break the last of Sam's gold pieces in the Ranch Saloon. Farther on, they camped on Brushy Creek near Round Rock and planned to rob a small bank there.

The holdup failed. One of the band, a fellow named Jim Murphy, turned against Sam and informed the law of the plan. Rangers and local peace officers surrounded the outlaws at Round Rock. In the ensuing battle, one of the Bass men and a deputy sheriff were killed. Sam escaped, but with a mortal wound. Next morning he was picked up in a woodland pasture and brought back to Round Rock. He died there the following day, July 21, 1878, his twenty-seventh birthday.

In folklore, Sam Bass is the cowboy hero who refused to betray his pals, a Robin Hood who eluded pursuers with ease and shared his stolen gold without stint.

Belle Starr

It was not long after the death of Sam Bass that Texas saw the rise of an outlaw queen. Belle Starr came from a good family, but no one who knew her called her a lady. She had been born Myra or Myra Maebelle or Myra Belle Shirley in Missouri early in 1848, the daughter of John and Elizabeth Shirley. She spent her early childhood on her parents' farm northwest of Carthage. In 1856 her father sold his 800-acre land grant and moved into Carthage, where he operated a hotel.

Most of the town was burned during the Civil War and the discouraged Shirley family moved south. They settled on a farm near Scyene, east of Dallas. The wild life of the frontier appealed to Myra, and in 1872 she eloped with Jim Reed, a hardened young man from Missouri who supported himself by stealing horses and robbing stagecoaches. He was also wanted for several murders. Reed met his death on August 6, 1874, while resisting arrest at a farmhouse northwest of Paris, Texas, near Red River.

In the next few years the young widow roamed the country and, for a short time, ran a livery stable in Dallas. There she was accused of disposing of livestock stolen by her male friends. In 1880 she went north into the Indian Territory and married Sam Starr, a Cherokee. The couple made their home in a cabin on a bluff north of the Canadian River, between Eufaula and Briartown.

Their place, known as Younger's Bend, became the headquarters of a band of outlaws

The stagecoach "Sam Houston" is held up.

who preferred livestock theft and other crime to farming. A striking brunette, Belle usually wore a broad-brimmed hat surmounted by a wide black plush band and trimmed with feathers and ornaments. Sometimes she would ride over the hilly trail to Fort Smith, Arkansas, and find a bit of excitement by playing the piano in a saloon.

Usually Belle stayed in the background, but early in 1883 she and her husband were convicted by the federal court in Fort Smith of having stolen a horse in the Indian Territory. Both were sentenced to a year in the house of correction at Detroit, after which they returned to the Territory. In December, 1886, Sam Starr became involved in fight with a policeman. Both were killed.

Belle survived only three years longer. Early in 1889, while riding between her home and the ferry across the Canadian near Briartown, she was shot from her horse and killed by an unknown assailant. One of her neighbors was suspected but was freed for lack of evidence against him.

New Mexico's Billy The Kid

Of all the famed outlaws of the old West, Billy the Kid remains one of the most legendary and elusive. This may be due to his involvement in New Mexico's controversial and bloody Lincoln County War. That deeply rooted feud arose from cattle rustling, rivalry for choice pastures, competition of country storekeepers, litigation over the settling of an estate, and meddling by unscrupulous politicians who sought to use the Tunstall-McSween-Murphy feud for their own ends.

The first violence came early in 1878, with the killing of an unarmed young English-born ranchman-merchant, John Tunstall, by members of a deputy sheriff's posse. The posse included at least four known outlaws who were more interested in killing their victim than in carrying out the law. One of those with Tunstall when he was slain was Billy the Kid, a buck-toothed boy, slight of build and about eighteen years old. Already a fugitive, Billy had been working for Tunstall only a short time as a range hand. Tunstall had given him a good horse, a saddle and a new gun. Billy was quick to learn and took pride in his work.

Of the early life of the Kid, little is known. The time and place of his birth are uncertain, and no one can be sure of his parents' surnames. Billy's original name appears to have been Henry McCarty. The earliest record of his family is that of the remarriage of his mother, Mrs. Catherine McCarty, to William H. Antrim, of Indiana birth. The wedding took place at Santa Fe on March 1, 1873. Among the five witnesses were Henry McCarty and Joe McCarty, sons of the bride.

The Antrims and the McCarty boys went to live in Silver City, New Mexico, where the boys were known as Henry and Joe Antrim. Mrs. Antrim died on September 16, 1874, from a lung ailment from which she had suffered for four months. After her death, Henry began running wild and became known as the Kid. Within three years he was in serious trouble. On August 17, 1877, near Fort Grant in Pima County, Arizona, he quarreled with Irish-born F. P. Cahill, a man of thirty-two. Name-calling led to shooting, and the Kid put a bullet into Cahill, who died the next day.

A coroner's jury labeled the shooting "criminal and unjustifiable," but by that time the Kid had skipped the county. He went on foot to Georgetown, then a thriving camp of silver miners, twenty miles east of Silver City. After staying in Georgetown for several weeks, the young gunman left for Lincoln County, New Mexico, where he assumed the name of Bonney and went to work for John Tunstall.

Why the Kid chose the name of Bonney is not known. Some think it may have been his mother's maiden name, but that is only speculation. The alias was not a complete disguise. Some in New Mexico still knew him as Antrim, and, on August 3, 1878, the *Grant County Herald* noted that "Kid Antrim's real name is W. H. McCarty."

After the murder of John Tunstall, Billy the Kid set out to take vengeance on the killers who, because they had been in the sheriff's posse, were not prosecuted. On the morning of April 1, 1878, Sheriff William Brady was shot and killed in broad daylight while walking on the main street of Lincoln. Killed with him was a deputy, George Hindman. Witnesses were hard to find, but Billy the Kid was one of several accused. The county commissioners offered a reward of $200 each for the arrest of the slayers.

Three days after the shooting, Andrew L. ("Buckshot") Roberts rode into Lincoln. Roberts had been a member of the posse that killed Tunstall. Hearing confirmation of the reward offer, he set out on a mule, heavily armed. His destination was Blazer's Mill, where he was told that the killers of Brady and Hindman might be. Near the mill he met a party that included Billy the Kid. These men ordered Roberts to surrender and when he refused, one of them, Charles Bowdre, shot him. But before Roberts expired, he shot at three of his assailants, wounding George Coe and John Middleton and killing Richard M. Brewer, the young man who had been foreman on Tunstall's ranch.

On April 18 a grand jury indicted Bowdre, Billy the Kid and several others for the killing of Buckshot Roberts. It also indicted Billy and two others for the slaying of Brady and Hindman. On the following day, the Kid appeared in court and pleaded not guilty. What might be called a minor revolution prevented his being tried until nearly a year later, on April 14, 1879.

This little revolution had been precipitated by the killing of Sheriff Brady who was a member of the Murphy faction. The McSween faction saw their opportunity and immediately held what they called an election and installed a new sheriff sympathetic to their interests. The Murphy faction appealed to the governor of the territory who appointed a Murphy man to the post. Thus reinstated, the Murphy partisans set off to arrest Billy the Kid and subjugate the McSween faction. The Murphy sheriff and his posse, reinforced with hired gunmen brought in from other counties, found Billy in July, 1878, with his McSween friends in Lincoln. Everybody knew that the final showdown had come for the Murphy and the Tunstall-McSween groups, now led by McSween since Tunstall's death.

"Billy the Kid."

After two days of desultory shooting in town, Billy and his friends were finally concentrated and besieged in the McSween residence. Here in the late afternoon of July 19, the third day, the Murphy posse set fire to one wing of the adobe house. With the fire creeping toward them, the inmates defended themselves while Mrs. McSween played the piano. During the fight, Deputy Sheriff Robert Beckworth of the Murphy clan, and four of the embattled partisans, including McSween, were killed. As darkness settled over Lincoln, Billy the Kid emerged from the burning building, dashed across the zone illuminated by the flames and escaped in the darkness. Later that night the posse, and the mob which usually gathers after such an affray, broke into the Tunstall-McSween store and robbed it of about six thousand dollars worth of goods.

With both Tunstall and McSween dead the Murphy faction was victorious and Billy the Kid, their chief gunman, became an outlaw wanted on several murder charges. However, he was popular with many people, and McSween partisans, though they had no organization now, sympathized with him. Grudge killings promised to continue.

News of the bloody vendetta reached Washington, and in August President Rutherford B. Hayes appointed General Lew Wallace Acting Governor of New Mexico Territory with instructions to bring peace between the factions. On arrival Wallace issued an amnesty proclamation, and Billy, gun in hand, met the general alone in a designated house. A reconciliation might have been achieved but two of Billy's deadly enemies escaped from jail, probably released by Murphy sympathizers. To protect himself, Billy retreated to his hideout near San Patricio.

Supporting himself now by stealing horses and cattle, he and his thieving associates fought with a White Oaks posse at Coyote Springs in November, 1880. In that skirmish the Kid and one of his companions had their horses shot from under them, but all escaped. At the Greathouse ranch and roadhouse, on December 1, 1880, another posse from White Oaks tried to capture Billy and two of his fellow outlaws. But the trio got away after killing the leader of the posse. On December 15, Governor Wallace offered a reward of $500 for Billy's delivery to the sheriff of Lincoln County.

Later that month, Pat Garrett, who had just been elected sheriff of Lincoln County but had not yet taken office, set out to capture Billy. With a posse, he besieged the Kid and four of his companions in a stone hut that sheepherders had abandoned near Stinking Springs (later Wilcox Springs, New Mexico). The posse killed one of the barricaded men, Charles Bowdre, when he appeared in the doorway. Billy and the three others held out until two days before Christmas when they were starved into surrendering.

Billy was imprisoned that winter of 1881 in Las Vegas, New Mexico, and in Santa Fe. He appealed to Governor Wallace but the general, busy now writing his famous novel *Ben Hur,* and realizing that his governorship would terminate with the inauguration of President James A. Garfield, paid no attention. In the spring Billy was taken to the Spanish-speaking town of Mesilla in the southern part of the state to be tried for his part in the killing of Sheriff Brady. In the little adobe courthouse on the public square dominated by the Catholic church, all the witnesses had to be questioned in Spanish and their answers translated into English for the record. The judge and the community had been on the Murphy side during the "war." Billy the Kid was convicted of murder on April 9, 1881, and four days later was sentenced to be hanged on May 13 in Lincoln. On April 15 he was taken, in a horse-drawn vehicle, on the 150-mile trip to Lincoln, where, on the twenty-first, he was turned over to Sheriff Garrett for safekeeping. His cell in Lincoln was a room on the second floor of a two-story adobe building. This structure, formerly occupied by a store, had recently been remodeled as a makeshift courthouse.

Garrett assigned two deputies to guard the prisoner. But just a week after being jailed, Billy saw his chance in the late afternoon of April 28, 1881. When the handcuff was taken from his left wrist to allow him to eat supper, he felled the one guard on duty with a swinging blow from his loose handcuff, snatched the guard's six-shooter and killed him.

The other guard, who was across the street, heard the shot and raced to the jail. By the time he arrived, Billy had picked up a shotgun, with which he killed the second guard. Still shackled, but armed now with two six-shooters and a Winchester, he hobbled down the jail stairs. At a nearby blacksmith shop he ordered the shackles filed from his ankles and commandeered a horse, which he mounted and rode off.

This sensational break hurt the reputation of Sheriff Garrett, who had been away from town when it happened. To reinstate his reputation, Garrett set out to track down the Kid. On hearing that Billy had a girl at Fort Sumner, an abandoned military post being used by Peter Maxwell as a roadhouse and residence for his ranch workers, Pat Garrett hid near the adobe structure. About midnight he went into Peter Maxwell's bedroom and talked quietly with him. A shadowy youth entered the doorway with a pistol in his hand. Garrett recognized him as Billy the Kid.

Seeing a strange figure in the dark room, Billy asked Maxwell, in Spanish:

"Who is it?"

The sheriff fired two shots, and Billy fell at one end of the fireplace.

Billy the Kid, dressed in a borrowed white shirt much too large for him, was buried in a coffin of plain wood. Ranchmen who had been losing their livestock slept more soundly now that he was gone, but there was no rest for the legends which his career had set in motion, the most notorious being that Billy had killed twenty-one men, not counting Mexicans and Indians, before he was twenty-one years old.

54. *Frontier Feuds*

ACTUALLY, THE FRONTIER feud was a form of lawlessness that involved murder and other major crimes. Yet, in the minds of the feudists, it was something far different. It was a primitive—though, of course, mistaken—means aimed at bringing law of a sort to an area where chaos had prevailed. The clansman who ambushed his enemy and filled him with buckshot thought of himself as an upholder of a higher order.

The typical feud, as C. L. Sonnichsen pointed out in *I'll Die Before I'll Run,* "usually starts when a group of people feel they have been intolerably wronged and take the law into their own hands. This is not lawlessness. It is an appeal to a law that is felt to be a reasonable substitute for legal redress which cannot be obtained—sometimes to a law that is higher or more valid than those on the statute books."

Vengeance, a common motive in the clashes between early settlers and Indians, was evident in many of the quarrels of white frontiersmen. It intensified some of the controversies into bloody vendettas. In thinly populated areas where statutory law was weak, some families or factions felt impelled to seek what they believed to be justice by repaying wrongs in kind. When this brought counteraction from the other side, as usually it did, the feud might become a local war that continued for years.

Regulators Fight Moderators

In Texas, which had more than its share of feuds, one of the bitterest and longest was that of the Regulators and Moderators, or the Shelby County War. It embraced a largely wooded section near the eastern edge of the state and lasted from 1839 through 1844. The trouble had its origin in land frauds, horse stealing, home burnings and other crimes.

The first violence came in the fall of 1840, when a fugitive ruffian, Charles W. Jackson, rode up to Joseph G. Goodbread, who was sitting on a hitching rack in Shelbyville, pointed his rifle at Goodbread, with whom he had had a quarrel, and said he was going to shoot him. Goodbread said he had no ill will against Jackson.

"Besides," he pleaded, "I'm unarmed."

"So much the better!" exclaimed Jackson, as he shot his victim through the heart.

Jackson and some other frontiersmen organized an armed company which they called the Shelby Guards, but which was more generally known as the Regulators. This group of rough, reckless men was ostensibly formed to suppress horse thieving and cattle rustling, but in practice it inflicted terroristic vengeance on persons believed to be enemies of its members. It horsewhipped some, drove others from the county, and killed several. The Regulators also burned houses and, in one instance, crowded into a courtroom and intimidated the judge.

To oppose this high-handed assumption of authority an opposition group, called the Moderators, was formed. The Moderators said they had organized to preserve order and uphold the courts. However, their first aim was to kill Jackson, the leader of the Regulators, which they did by shooting him from ambush.

The Regulators quickly found a new leader in Watt Moorman; and the two bands roved about the country, threatening each other and making occasional depredations. In the fall of 1841, the Regulators, said to number 250, advanced on the town of San Augustine, where the Moderators were camped. A battle seemed imminent but was averted by the recently mustered militia.

Yet terrorism continued, causing some settlers to abandon their farms and discouraging others from coming to the county. "Land is now worth only ten cents an acre in Shelby County, where formerly it was valued at more than twenty times that sum," said the San Augustine, Texas, *Red-Lander* of January 17, 1842, "and the tide of emigration has completely turned from that county, which is shunned as another Sodom."

The feud spread into adjoining counties and became so serious that pitched battles were fought in the summer of 1844. At that point, General Sam Houston, president of the Republic of Texas, decided to interfere. He sent militiamen into the area and went there himself. Sitting on a pile of firewood and whittling a sliver of pine, he listened to local leaders, then issued a proclamation, dispersing both warring factions. Thus the tragic conflict that had taken the lives of about fifty persons came to a close.

Sutton-Taylor Feud

A few decades later, other bitter feuds broke out in the Texas cow country to the west.

The conflict between the Sutton and Taylor families, an outgrowth of disputes over long-horn cattle, began in 1866 and lasted about fifteen years. In the summer of 1866 a party of farmers and ranchmen, led by young William Sutton, set out from DeWitt County, looking for horse thieves. They arrested several men, including Charles Taylor, a fugitive. Taylor made a dash for freedom, but was shot dead.

His murder deepened the antagonism between the Sutton and Taylor families. A few months later, Buck Taylor saw Bill Sutton in a Clinton saloon and threatened to shoot him. Sutton drew faster, killing Taylor and one of his friends, Dick Chisholm. Before long two more Taylors "bit the dust" and Sutton received a bullet wound while sitting in a saloon in Cuero.

In August, 1870, Sutton partisans captured two Kelly brothers, farmers allied with the Taylors, and killed both of them on the flimsy pretext that they were trying to escape. In 1873, two of the Sutton faction were ambushed and killed by Taylor men. A few days later Wes Hardin and Jim Taylor found another foe of the Taylors, Jack Helm, working in a country blacksmith shop.

"You're the man I'm after," shouted Jim, shooting Helm dead before he could reach his gun. The killers rode off unmolested.

In spite of a peace treaty signed later that year, sporadic killings continued. Bill Sutton decided to quit the country. At Indianola he and his wife boarded a ship for New Orleans. But Jim and Bill Taylor followed them up the gangplank and shot Sutton and his friend, Gabe Slaughter, dead.

Late in 1876, after an unusually shocking pair of murders, Texas Rangers, under Lieutenant Lee Hall, were sent into the area. On a rainy night, Hall found most of the Sutton faction at a wedding dance in a country home. Stepping into the doorway, he announced, "I want seven men," and named them.

"How many men you got?" asked one of the feudists.

"Seventeen, counting myself," answered Hall.

"Well, we've got seventy. I guess we'll have to fight it out."

"That's the talk," said Hall. "I'll give you three minutes to get the women and children out of the way." But by that time the fight had faded out of the feudists, and Hall's men disarmed them. Later, with some of the most active feudists cooling off in jail, the conflict subsided.

Horrell-Higgins Feud

Almost as bloody was the Horrell-Higgins feud, which broke out in Central Texas in 1873. It started with cattle rustling near the frontier town of Lampasas, northwest of Austin. There the pastures were not yet fenced. Scrub oaks and cedars made it hard to discover prowlers. The Horrell ranchmen were suspected, and when the sheriff was killed trying to arrest one of them, a squad of state policemen was sent to Lampasas "to clean out the Horrell boys."

In the Gem Saloon on the public square the policemen found the suspected Horrells with some of their friends. The captain spoke to Bill Bowen:

"I see you're wearing a pistol. I arrest you."

Then the shooting began. When the smoke cleared, four of the eight policemen were dead or dying and Mart Horrell was wounded. He was jailed at Georgetown, until friends broke in and freed him. To avoid further difficulties, he and his brothers gathered their herds and trailed them to New Mexico, but they soon ran into trouble there and came back to Texas.

Two of the Horrell faction were tried and cleared of killing the policemen; but the Higgins family, former neighbors and friends, accused them of tampering with their stock. Fiery Pink Higgins announced that, if this continued, he would kill every one of the Horrells. Soon afterward, in January, 1877, he shot and killed Merritt Horrell in a back room of the Gem.

In June someone broke into the courthouse at night and stole all the records on pending criminal cases. Three days later the two factions fought a gun battle for several hours in the Lampasas streets. An innocent bystander was killed while trying to get out of the way, and one of Pink Higgins' friends was wounded.

Late in July the Texas Rangers began action. Sergeant N. O. Reynolds, with a small detachment, set out for the Horrell ranch and reached it during the night. Just before dawn, the Rangers tiptoed into the room where the Horrells and their friends were sleeping. They captured and disarmed them without a fight. Meanwhile other Rangers rounded up the Higgins clan. After long discussions with the Rangers, members of both factions signed a peace pact that, unlike most similar agreements, was strictly observed.

Mason County War

While the Horrell and Higgins factions were still shooting at each other, another cattle feud, known as the Mason County War, or the Hoodoo War, erupted in the rolling ranges two counties to the southwest. Thrifty Mason County settlers, many of them of German ancestry, complained about the stealing of their cattle and blamed outlaws from surrounding counties. Major John B. Jones, head of the Texas Rangers, visited the area in 1874. He found the people aroused over cattle rustling but was unable to make any arrests.

Early in 1875, Sheriff John Clark arrested five men on charges of cow theft and locked them in the jail at Mason. At night a crowd of masked men gathered in front of the jail and demanded that the prisoners be released to them. After the sheriff went for help, the crowd battered the jail door.

"Keep away if you don't want to get shot," the leaders yelled at anyone who threatened to interfere.

When the door fell in, the band took out the alleged rustlers and headed south with them, toward Fredericksburg.

The sheriff led a posse in pursuit but caught up with the vigilantes too late. One prisoner had escaped, one had been shot to death, and three were already strung up—though one of them was cut down in time to save his life.

Two months later, Tim Williamson, a reputable stockman, was arrested on a charge of cattle theft. He made bond, and when John Worley, deputy sheriff, was taking him to court, a party of masked, armed men approached. The deputy, instead of trying to protect his prisoner, shot Williamson's horse, leaving him unmounted as well as unarmed. In a few minutes the defendant lay dying.

This action incensed Williamson's many friends, especially Scott Cooley, a former Ranger, who had worked for Williamson. Before long, Cooley and his friends killed two of the men who had taken Williamson from the non-resisting deputy. They also killed John Worley and took his scalp.

In the next few months, rival armed bands roamed the county and the death toll mounted to fifteen. After the Texas Rangers were called in, some of the feudists were caught and later sent to prison. Others left the state, and Cooley went to another county, where friends protected him. After two years of turmoil, in which men slept with pistols under their pillows, Mason County again became a peaceful cattle range.

Arizona's Pleasant Valley Feud

One of the West's longest and bloodiest feuds took place in Arizona's Tonto Basin, or Pleasant Valley, where cattle ranges were protected on the north by the towering Mogollons. This was the vendetta between the Graham and Tewksbury families and their partisans.

Both families had reached Arizona by way of California. John D. Tewksbury, from Boston, had joined the gold rush and married an Indian woman in California. He had three

Left: *Edwin Tewksbury, leader of Tewksbury clan in the Pleasant Valley War.* Right: *Thomas H. Graham, leader of the Graham faction in the Pleasant Valley War.*

FORREST COLLECTION, ARIZONA PIONEERS' HISTORICAL SOCIETY

sons born there—Edwin, John and James. After his wife died, he went to Arizona, married a woman of English birth and, about 1880, built a cabin on Cherry Creek.

The Graham brothers, Tom and John, had grown up on an Iowa farm and migrated to California. Late in 1882 they settled in Pleasant Valley, Arizona, and built a cabin about ten miles northwest of John Tewksbury's. Later their younger half-brother, William, came to live with them. Sometimes the Tewksbury sons and the Graham brothers worked for neighboring ranchmen, including James Stinson.

Both families had good reputations at first. But, in the fall of 1884, while the younger Tewksburys and the Grahams were working on the Stinson ranch, men of each family were accused of combining to steal Stinson cattle and quarreling over their loot. Although court charges against them were dismissed, the stealing seemed to continue, as did the quarreling between the two suspected families. In 1886, a Stinson foreman accused Ed Tewksbury of stealing horses. Ed shot and wounded him.

In the fall of that year, the Daggs brothers, sheepmen to the north of Pleasant Valley, lacked feed to winter their flocks. The cattlemen in the valley wanted no sheep overstocking their range. Although it was public domain they combined, pronounced the valley "cow country" and warned sheepmen to stay away. The Daggs brothers decided to defy the cattlemen and winter there. To protect their flocks against possible trouble they engaged the Tewksburys and entered the forbidden territory.

This action enraged the Grahams and other cowmen, even though the sheep were grazing on public land. Tom Graham held back the cattle raisers from immediately slaughtering the flocks and herders, but when bullets fired close to the sheepmen at their campfires failed to scare them away, the Grahams began killing the sheep at night. They shot some and drove others into creeks or over bluffs. Early in 1887, a Navajo herder was killed and beheaded.

That spring the Daggs brothers lost so many sheep that they withdrew their herds from the valley, but the feud between the two factions continued. In July the father of the Blevans brothers, who were on the Graham side, disappeared. On August 10, one of the sons, Hampton, rode out with seven friends looking for the missing man. When they stopped in front of a cabin on the Middleton ranch, then occupied by the Tewksbury brothers, a gun battle broke out. As Jim Tewksbury's Winchester blazed from the doorway, Blevans and one of his friends fell dead and several others in the party were wounded.

After the fight the Tewksbury brothers fled to a fortified house in the mountains, but the Grahams followed and besieged them. Jim Tewksbury killed one of the attacking cow hands; and soon afterward Billy Graham, twenty-two, while riding on a lonely trail, was ambushed and killed by a sheepman.

On September 2, after the Tewksburys had reoccupied their cabin, the surviving Grahams and their partisans surrounded the place. They found John Tewksbury and Will Jacobs outside, looking for horses. Andy Blevans shot them both and left their bodies on the ground in front of the house while those inside held off the invaders.

The battle lasted for hours, with many bullets shot ineffectively from each side. Finally after hogs came up to the two bodies and began rooting at them, the cabin door opened. The besiegers heard a woman scream:

"I can't stand it! I must bury them. They'll have to kill me to stop me."

It was Mrs. John Tewksbury, with a shovel in her hand. White-faced but defiant, she risked sudden death and walked straight to the bodies, drove off the hogs, dug shallow graves and buried her husband and his friend. As she worked, the guns were silent. The only sound was the wailing of her baby in the cabin.

As soon as Mrs. Tewksbury returned to the cabin, the shooting started again, but without much effect. Late in the afternoon a posse appeared and the besiegers fled.

Two days later, Andy Blevans was in Holbrook, boasting in a saloon that he had killed Tewksbury and Jacobs. That afternoon the new sheriff of Apache County, Commodore Perry Owens, rode into town on other business. He learned that Blevans was in the home of his stepmother, with three other armed men.

Showing courage far beyond that of many more publicized frontier officers, Owens, carrying a Winchester, went into the house and ordered Blevans to surrender. When the killer refused and began shooting, Owens coolly put his rifle into action. A minute later, Andy and two of the other outlaws lay dying, and the fourth was wounded. The sheriff, without a scratch, was lauded by the coroner's jury and local citizens.

Later that month, Harry Middleton of the Graham faction was killed, and a posse took the lives of John Graham and Charles Blevans. Tom was the only one left of the three Graham brothers. Of the six Blevans men, five were dead and one was in jail. Yet the feud went on. Al Rose, a friend of Graham's, was shot from ambush. In 1888 three men not even engaged in the vendetta were hanged by Tewksbury partisans.

Jim Tewksbury, the deadliest gunman of his family, died of tuberculosis late that year. George Newton, a friend of the Tewksburys, disappeared in 1891. In 1892, Tom Graham was killed by two horsemen while driving along a road with a load of grain. The two were arrested, but one of them, John Rhodes was freed. The other, Ed Tewksbury, was tried. Found guilty in his first trial, Tewksbury obtained a second, in which the jury disagreed. He died in 1904 of tuberculosis. One more killing, that of a cow hand in Reno Pass, ended the feud which had taken more than a score of lives and terrorized for years many families in Pleasant Valley.

55. *Range Wars*

Sheepmen vs. Cattlemen

RIVALRY FOR WATER and grass on the public lands of the West led to many conflicts in which stockmen took the law into their own hands. The sharpest and most lasting of such conflicts were between cattlemen and sheepmen. This clash of interests, which had played only a minor part in Arizona's Graham-Tewksbury feud, was in many sections the cause of bitter range wars.

Even though the government owned most of the pastures in dispute, cowmen regarded sheepmen as intruders. They were not going to be "sheeped out" or have the flocks devour the grass and pollute the streams. The cowboy, usually well mounted, looked down on the sheepherder, who usually traveled on foot, on a burro or in a wagon. The herder was regarded as "lower down than a thief," and the mutton he raised was viewed with contempt.

Cattlemen tried to bolster their position by charging that sheep killed the grass by nibbling it too close and trampling the roots with their sharp hoofs. They pointed out that the odor which sheep left on the grass and in watering places was distasteful to horses and cattle. Sheepman replied that, under good management, sheep and cattle could be grazed indefinitely on the same pastures, but cowmen were not convinced.

Many bands of cowmen, outraged at the intrusion of the flocks on ranges they claimed, terrorized the herders and killed or drove off the sheep. Their methods included clubbing, shooting, dynamiting, poisoning, burning and stampeding the sheep over cliffs, sometimes called rimrocking. Sheep owners and herders were ordered to leave the ranges, and occasionally some were killed.

The herder, usually alone, had little chance to defend himself or his flock when a mounted band of armed cowmen swooped down on his camp in the middle of the night. Often he could do no more than look on helplessly as the raiders slaughtered many of the woollies and scattered others.

Such raids were numerous in Texas, although not as disastrous as in some other sections. In Brown County, Charles Hanna, who had brought the first sheep there in 1869, went out to his rock corral one morning and found that all 300 had had their throats cut. In the San Saba hills a decade later, cowmen set a dog on Peter Bertrand's sheep and ordered him to leave. When Bertrand refused to go, they raided his pen at night, shooting some of the woollies. Also in San Saba County, night riders in 1880 shot many of the Ramsay brothers' 1,300 sheep and slit the throats of others.

Three years later, cowmen ordered several sheep raisers to leave Brown County after burning their homes and pens and firing on their flocks. One who moved two counties northwest ran into similar trouble there. Raiders rode into his camp at night, fired into his herd and cut the throats of some that they could catch.

This same year, cattlemen ordered other sheepmen to leave Hamilton County, and when they refused to go, raiders killed or maimed many animals in one flock and scattered the others. Near Laredo, a Mexican herder was killed in 1884 after he ignored an order to leave.

New Mexican sheepmen had similar troubles. In 1884, five cowmen killed all 700 of the sheep that Arcadio Sais was grazing on the Carrizozo range. The next year, in Lincoln County raiders fired on a herder who had refused to move.

In Arizona, D. A. Sanford's herders were fired on. In the San Francisco Mountain country in 1884, cowmen rounded up more than a hundred wild horses. They strapped cowbells to the necks of some and tied rawhides to the tails of others. Then, yelling and firing their guns, they drove the horses into ten bands of woollies, 25,000 in all, that had been bedded down for the night. With the terrified sheep running in all directions, many were killed or injured. It took a week to gather and separate the others. In the same year, on the Little Colorado range, cowmen drove more than 4,000 sheep into the river, causing hundreds to die in the quicksands.

Colorado cowmen were equally intolerant of sheep, even though in 1869 their territory

Joe Slade kills Jules Reni. Pen and ink by Charles M. Russell.

was said to have twice as many woollies as cattle. In 1874, night raiders entered the corral of John T. Collier and killed all his imported Merino rams, worth $1,000 each. In Bent County in the same year, Jeremiah Booth found 234 of his graded Cotswolds poisoned by men who ordered him to leave within ten days.

Other Colorado sheepmen found their woollies shot or driven off, their herders beaten, their cabins and corrals burned. In Garfield County in 1894, raiders killed 3,800 sheep by stampeding them over a bluff into Parachute Creek after wounding one of the herders. Later, in the same county, only one crippled sheep survived the slaughter of a flock of about 1,500.

Similar troubles plagued sheepmen farther north. In Idaho in 1896, two herders encamped in the Shoshone Basin were shot to death and their flocks scattered. In Montana four years later, eleven cowmen killed R. R. Selway's whole band of 3,000 woollies. In Wyoming, raiders killed nearly 12,000 sheep in a single night. In other instances, they drove flocks over precipices or scattered poison on the ranges. A report from Tie Siding said that raiders set fire to the wool of Charles Herbert's 2,600 sheep, killing most of them.

In Wyoming, after the turn of the century, night raiders became bolder. Near Thermopolis, in 1902, they shot and killed a flockmaster. In the central part of the state that same year they slaughtered several thousand sheep and the herders. In 1904, near Kirby Creek, they shot and killed a sheepman without warning.

Sheepmen in eastern Oregon were having similar tribulations. In raids from 1899 to 1903, thousands of their sheep were killed. In 1904 alone, 6,000 were slaughtered in three counties. Early in that year, more than 2,500 were shot or clubbed to death by five masked men near Christmas Lake. A month later, nine raiders killed more than 2,200 from a flock of 2,700. In 1905 the secretary of the Crook County Sheep Shooters Association boasted that his organization had killed 8,000 to 10,000 woollies during the preceding season and predicted a higher record in the year ahead. Late in 1906 an allotment of the public grazing lands virtually ended this Oregon trouble.

In Wyoming the strife continued. In the summer of 1905, ten masked men rode into a camp on Shell Creek, in the Big Horn Basin, where Louis A. Gantz had 7,000 sheep. They shot or clubbed to death about 4,000 of them, destroyed the wagons and provisions, and tied two dogs to the wagons to be burned to death. Gantz, who lost about $40,000 from this attack, knew better than to prosecute the raiders in a Wyoming court.

There were dynamitings and other sheep killings in Wyoming in 1907. In the spring of the following year, cowmen raided a camp on leased land in the Shoshone Indian Reservation, where Robert Meigh and two herders had a flock belonging to J. W. Blake of Lander. With a volley of shots at about midnight, the attackers drove off the sheepmen, chopped and overturned the wagons, and killed or crippled 350 of the woollies.

On an April night in 1909, five sheepmen were sleeping in their camp on the north side of Spring Creek, in the Big Horn Basin. They had about 5,000 sheep. A score of armed and masked raiders galloped into the camp and killed three of the herders. They poured kerosene on the wagons and burned them, killed several dogs and some of the sheep.

Next day Sheriff Felix Alston hastened out with a posse. He noticed that the tracks of one of the attackers showed a boot heel run over on one side. This led to the arrest of Herbert Brink, who was among those who came to view the bodies. Brink and six others were indicted. Four of them confessed. A court sentenced Brink to be hanged, but his penalty was commuted to life imprisonment.

Serious raids continued well into the twentieth century, but some of the cowmen were learning that they could profit by raising some sheep along with their cattle. The sheep improved the sod with their hoofs, and their droppings fertilized the grass. They also ate some of the grass and shoots that the cattle could not reach and certain weeds that the bovines spurned. Many cattle raisers began tolerating a flock of sheep as a "mortgage raiser" and as a hedge against low beef prices.

Fence Cutters' War

Texas cowmen, although they did not resort to as much violence against sheepmen as did those of some other western states, had a bang-up range clash of their own in 1883. This was the Fence-Cutters' War that marked the transition of the state's vast pastures from open range to fenced ranches.

Texas had relatively few fences before the invention of barbed wire. The reason was that it didn't have, in the grasslands of its western region, enough wood or rock for building them. Fences of smooth wire didn't hold the stock well; and hedges of Osage orange, or *bois d'arc,* were too tedious to plant, grow and trim.

During the 1870's barbed wire began coming into Texas. At first some stockmen ridiculed the newfangled fencing, but the far-sighted ones appreciated the advantage of controlling their own pastures. They began buying land with good grass and water and fencing it. In 1882 the Frying Pan Ranch, in the Panhandle, spent $39,000 erecting a four-wire fence around a pasture of 250,000 acres.

However, not all cowmen had the vision or the money to buy and fence ranches. Many of the smaller ones continued to graze their herds on what was left of the open range, most of it still owned by the state. As they saw fences enclosing choice pastures along streams, they became alarmed. The fencing made it harder for them to find enough grass and, in dry spells, water for their herds.

The plight of the farmers and small stockmen was made infinitely worse by the severe drought of 1883. The grass withered and turned brown. The earth cracked. Creeks dried up, and water holes that had supported large herds shrank to muddy ooze. In some sections, prairie fires added to the disaster.

Some of the open-range cowmen moved farther west, but fences stopped them there, too. Enraged at finding no range for their cattle, which were gaunt now and bawling for water, these small cowmen joined with the homesteaders in protesting that fences extended across public roads prevented people from riding to school or church and impeded the delivery of mail. One settler, E. S. Graham, said that some ranchmen invited trouble "by fencing large bodies of land that did not belong to them and by trampling on the rights of the public."

The growing resistance of the landless cowmen to fencing was backed by the Texas Greenback Party, which regarded barbed wire as a symbol of monopoly. The fencers, it complained, were trying to turn the farmers and small stockmen into serfs.

To the stockmen whose cattle suffered, barbed wire appeared to be an instrument of the devil. They sent letters and telegrams to members of the legislature and to the governor. They held public protest meetings. Finally, when no action resulted from their complaints, many of them decided that the only thing to do was to cut the offending fences.

These desperate cattlemen formed small, secret bands, with passwords and spies. Sometimes these bands had such names as Owls, Javelinas or Blue Devils. Posting guards for protection, they began destroying fences that blocked roads or enclosed other people's land. Usually they did their snipping at night, but in some places they worked during the day. As the drought became worse, some of the cutters destroyed not only unlawful fences but also those that enclosed land legitimately owned by the fencers.

In Tom Green County, night workers cut nineteen miles of fence on the ranch of L. B. Harris. The Fort Worth *Gazette* reported that they piled a carload of Harris' wire on a stack of cedar posts and lighted a $6,000 fire. On the coastal plains, other cutters snipped and ruined three miles of wire fence with which Abel H. ("Shanghai") Pierce had enclosed one of his gigantic pastures.

Sometimes the cutters left notes of warning. On Tehuacana Creek, nine miles southwest of Waco, reported the Galveston *News,* night workers destroyed the fence of a 700-acre privately owned ranch and burned some of the pasture. Then, referring to a pond that had been built on private property, they left a penciled note that read:

> You are ordered not to fence in the Jones tank, as it is a public tank and is the only water there is for stock on this range. Until people can have time to build tanks and catch water, this should not be fenced. No good man will undertake to watch this fence, for the Owls will catch him. There is no more grass on this range than the stock can eat this year.

With most politicians cautiously silent, Texas newspapers denounced the cutters, and ranchmen whose fences had been taken down held indignation meetings. The Law and Order Association of Tom Green County and several similar organizations tried to stop the cutting by offering rewards for incriminating evidence, but few convictions resulted. In some places, defensive gunfire routed the bands of cutters.

With fence cutting reported in more than half the Texas counties, many ranchmen began finding warning notes. On a fence near Castroville a card with a bullet hole said: "If you don't make gates, we will make them for you." A stockman in Hamilton County found a picture of a coffin and a declaration that the cutters would risk their lives for free grass and free water. The Albany, Texas, *Star* told of a coffin nailed to one of the posts of a cut fence. In Coleman County a sheepman found a coffin on his porch, with the words: "This will be your end if you keep fencing." Cutters in Live Oak County dug a grave, dangled a rope in it, and left a note that said: "This will be your fate if you rebuild this fence."

Before many weeks, the work of fence cutters began to be noticed as far away as Chicago. Horace B. Starkweather, a Texas sheepman in Coleman County, had his fences cut twice and two thousand cedar posts burned. When he went to Chicago to borrow money, he found headlines in the papers there:

HELL BREAKS LOOSE IN TEXAS!
Wire Cutters Destroy
500 Miles of Fence
In Coleman County

Unable to obtain a loan, Starkweather hurried home, where he found so much turmoil that he sold his ranch.

In a few places, fences across roads or around land not owned or leased by the fencers were removed by agreement, and the snipping in those sections ended. But in most neighborhoods, feeling was too strong to allow negotiation. Newspapers estimated losses from fence cutting at a million dollars in Brown County and twenty million for the state. Tax valuations, said the Fort Worth *Gazette,* fell more than thirty million as a result of the range war. Some settlers moved out, and many prospective ones feared to come.

At last, on October 15, Governor John Ireland, who preferred to dodge the issue, called a special session of the legislature, to meet on January 8, 1884. Its purpose was "to find a remedy for wanton destruction of fences, to provide a more efficient system of highways, and to amend the law providing for enclosing school lands."

After weeks of argument, the lawmakers set penalties of one to five years in prison for cutting a fence and two to five years for maliciously burning a pasture. They made it a misdemeanor to fence public lands knowingly or to enclose the property of another without his consent. Unlawful fences were required to be taken down within six months. A gate every three miles was required for fences that crossed public roads.

The new law lessened the fence troubles, although some thought the unlawful fencers escaped too easily considering the much heavier penalties against cutters. Yet sporadic troubles continued for a decade, especially during droughts. Navarro County had so much snipping in 1888 that local officers called on the Texas Rangers. Two disguised Rangers, Sergeant

Ira Aten and Jim King, drove into the troubled area in an old farm wagon pulled by a horse and a mule. They found jobs picking cotton, and in the evening King sometimes played his fiddle. By keeping their ears open, the Rangers soon learned who the cutters were. Aten began making bombs to place in the fences. His boss ordered him to desist, but rumors of the bombs quickly stopped the snipping.

Minor outbreaks of fence cutting appeared in most of the other plains states. In Wyoming in 1883, a court ordered a big cattle company to quit fencing public lands and to remove the fences it had built around eleven sections. Three years later a territorial governor there was removed from office because of his unlawful fencing. But in Texas the sale of barbed wire was resumed on a larger scale, and fencing soon ended the era of the open range.

Big Cowmen vs. Little Cowmen: Johnson County War

Of all the violent clashes among western stockmen, the most spectacular and most publicized was the Wyoming cattlemen's war, also known as the Johnson County invasion. This conflict, which erupted in the spring of 1892, was the culmination of bad feeling that had been building up for several years. On one side were the big Wyoming cattlemen, who had come in early and without authority claimed much of the best land. On the other side were the small stockmen and farmers who arrived later and obtained free land under the homestead acts.

The cattle barons resented having small fry homestead their vast grasslands and tried to tag all of them as rustlers, even though most of them were honest. Conversely, the newcomers, whether small stockmen or grangers, resented the big operators, whom they viewed as monopolists. They accused the wealthy cattlemen of having acquired the best pastures and streams by trickery, of poisoning water holes, of allowing their stock to trample crops, of stealing calves from the small herds.

The rift had been made worse by several acts of violence beginning in the summer of 1889. That year ten cattlemen seized two homesteaders who lived on adjoining claims. They were James Averill, a justice of the peace who ran a small store and saloon but had no cattle, and Ella ("Cattle Kate") Watson, who owned a few young cattle. The cattlemen accused the two of stealing and ordered them to leave the region. When they refused, they were hanged, without trial, from a pine in Spring Canyon.

Two years later Tom Waggoner, a thrifty homesteader with a reputation for honesty, was taken from his home near Newcastle and left dangling from the limb of a cottonwood several miles away. A few months later, two armed cattlemen tried to kill Ross Gilbertson and Nathan D. Champion as they slept in a cabin, but Champion, a cow hand from Texas, awoke and fired at them.

In November, 1891, Orley E. ("Ranger") Jones, a young broncobuster for the C Y Ranch, was driving home from Buffalo in a buckboard. As he crossed Big Muddy Creek, an assassin hiding under the bridge shot and killed him. A few days later John A. Tisdale, who had ridden for Theodore Roosevelt, was driving from Buffalo to his ranch on Powder River with groceries for his family and Christmas toys for the children. As he crossed a small stream, he was ambushed and killed.

These killings aroused the people of Johnson County, but no one was punished for any of them. Meanwhile, in Cheyenne the big stockmen were preparing an expedition to invade Johnson County, wipe out the rustlers and put fear into the hearts of all small cowmen and grangers. As their leader they chose Major Frank Wolcott, a ranchman and former army officer, who had come from Kentucky.

Wolcott sent Tom Smith to Texas, where he recruited more than a score of mercenary gunmen to bolster the force. The cattlemen chartered a special train in Denver and loaded it with horses and supplies. It arrived in Cheyenne on the afternoon of April 5, 1892. There it took on more passengers and supplies such as army tents, bedding, rifles, ammunition, dynamite and strychnine. A suspicious onlooker tried to telegraph Sheriff W. G. ("Red") Angus of Johnson County, but the wires had been cut. He mailed a note instead.

The invaders, being backed by men of wealth and prominence, told Acting Governor Amos W. Barber their plans. He apparently approved because the adjutant general of the Wyoming National Guard instructed all units to obey no orders to assemble unless received from state headquarters. This nullified the state's constitutional provision which permitted sheriffs to call them out. The invaders, sure of their questionable rights, took along two war correspondents, one from the Cheyenne *Sun* and the other from the Chicago *Herald*.

After an overnight train trip to the outskirts of Casper, the invaders unloaded their horses and equipment, including three Studebaker wagons for bedding and supplies. With the horses saddled, the party rode north and spent the night at a friendly ranch on the South Fork of Powder River. There Mike Shonsey, a "big outfit" foreman who had ridden in from the north, reported that two of the men they wanted, Nick Ray (sometimes spelled Rae) and Nathan D. Champion were at Nolan's K C Ranch, fourteen miles farther north.

A little after daybreak on April 9, the invaders reached and surrounded the three-room cabin where the two men were staying. When two trappers who had spent the night there went out for water, the cattlemen captured them and learned that Ray and Champion were in the cabin.

A few minutes later, Nick Ray stepped out of the house and was met with shots from a dozen Winchesters. Falling with a bullet in his head, he tried to crawl back but was downed by another shot. Then Nate Champion darted out and dragged Ray in with one hand while firing his pistol with the other.

During the hours that followed, Champion held off his attackers, comforted the dying Nick, and with pencil and paper wrote about the uneven siege as it progressed. "Me and Nick was getting breakfast when the attack took place," he started. Later in the morning he told of Nick's death, and wrote that the invaders had chased travelers who happened to come down the road. He further recorded that the attackers "have just got through shelling the house like hail" and had set it afire by pushing against it a blazing wagon that they had loaded with hay and pitch pine. Champion's final words were, "Goodbye, boys, if I never see you again."

As flames raced through the rooms, Champion rushed out with his Winchester. After a few steps he stumbled and fell—his body riddled with twenty-eight bullets.

A traveler who had been chased, galloped on to Buffalo and informed Sheriff Angus. The sheriff had already received the warning mailed from Cheyenne. After being refused help by the National Guard and the army unit of nearby Fort McKinney, he and several deputies started south to the K C Ranch.

When the invaders learned that the people of Buffalo were aroused and were preparing to defend their town, they decided to stop at the T A Ranch on Crazy Woman Creek, owned by Dr. Harris, a big cattleman in sympathy with the expedition. His large house was built of solid hewed logs. His barn was of ample size and Wolcott found a pile of heavy timbers which he and his men used to make a barricade.

In Buffalo, meanwhile, excitement was rising by the hour. Robert Foote, owner of the biggest store there, invited citizens to take the guns and other equipment they needed, without charge. On his black stallion he rode up and down the main street, calling for recruits.

Forty-nine men started out from Buffalo. Their leader was Arapahoe S. Brown, a homesteader who ran a small flour and feed mill. The next day, Sheriff Angus returned from his mission and followed Brown with forty more men. At the T A Ranch the citizens from in and around Buffalo dug rifle pits, besieged the invaders and captured their wagons. In two days, Sheriff Angus had a force of more than two hundred and fifty men. They put the captured dynamite on a load of hay and prepared to push it against the ranchhouse.

But before this plan could be carried out, the invaders from Cheyenne sent out a plea for help. At night a cowboy whom they had captured on their way north slipped out through the picket lines and, from Hathaway's Crossing, sent a telegram to the governor, who immediately sent frantic wires to both of Wyoming's senators, as well as to President Benjamin Harrison and Brigadier General John R. Brooke of Omaha. The senators routed the President from his bed and persuaded him to order the War Department to send the aid sought. From Fort McKinney, Colonel James J. Van Horn, with three troops of cavalry, arrived at the T A Ranch just in time to save the besieged men from the threat of fire and dynamite. By the time he rescued the invaders, they were surrounded by 320 angry homesteaders and Buffalo townsmen.

Two days later, elaborate funeral services for Nate Champion and Nick Ray were held in Buffalo. Great banks of flowers were arranged in a vacant store building. Women filled all the seats available, while men stood outside. A Baptist minister prayed for justice, and a Methodist eulogized the two slain men as law-abiding citizens. Five hundred mourners marched to the cemetery. Jack Flagg led the horses of Ray and Champion, with empty saddles.

From the T A Ranch the prisoners were escorted by cavalrymen to Fort Fetterman, then taken by special train to Fort D. A. Russell, near Cheyenne. Although supposedly confined, they were able to spend most of their time in Cheyenne. Their lawyers, with threats and with checks that later turned out to be worthless, induced the two star witnesses for the prosecution—the two trappers—to leave the state.

Indignant homesteaders held meetings in Buffalo, Glenrock and Casper to protest the unlawful invasion. But when the invaders came to trial on January 21, 1893, minus the Texans, who had gone home, the court proceedings were a farce. One of the spectators, John Clay, a cattle baron who had been in Scotland during the raid, later remembered watching Judge Richard R. Scott on the bench. Clay pronounced him "slow, solemn, impartial, a little embarrassed, knowing that the trial was a mere puppet show." When no witnesses appeared against the defendants, the charge was dismissed.

Later some of the big cattlemen claimed that the invasion had succeeded because it discouraged cattle rustling. But the homesteading farmers and small stockmen had a more convincing claim to victory. They won the 1892 election and established their rights. As Mrs. D. F. Baber wrote in *The Longest Rope,* "The Johnson County cattle war marks the dividing line between the old West, under the rule of the big cattle kings, and the new West of the pioneer homesteader."

56. *Necktie Parties*

IN MANY A mining camp and cattle range, vigilantes did more to drive out desperadoes than did elected officials. The committees of vigilance were formed because there was no other effective action against crime. The vigilance committees of the West differed from the lynchers of the South in that, instead of circumventing the law, they enforced it. They had a large hand in making the frontier West safe for settlement and in clearing the way for statutory law. They saved many frontier communities from anarchy and bridged the gap between lawlessness and the formal administration of justice that came later.

Frontiersmen who found a horse thief or two dangling from the limb of a tree did not automatically conclude that justice had been violated. Action by the vigilance committee not only was swifter and surer than that of some of the feeble courts but often was fairer. Proceedings of these committees were informal—more so in some instances than in others. But the committees were organized only after conditions had become desperate, and the men they punished were usually those whose guilt was clear beyond doubt.

California Vigilance Committees

Many of the vigilance activities were an outgrowth of the miners' courts that sprang up in the California camps following the discovery of gold. One camp, Dry Diggings, had its name changed to Hangtown after miners had hanged three bandits from branches of a tree near the center of the camp. The name stuck until a later change converted it to Placerville.

In California during the era of the gold rush, the Spanish system of administering a town government with a so-called *alcalde*—a combined mayor and judge—proved ineffective. The miners had to set up their own courts to settle disputes over claims, punish thieves and put dangerous gunmen out of the way. Since the camps had no jails, the most common penalties were banishment, whipping and hanging.

Those who saw the miners' courts in action respected them for their vigor and their fairness. Bayard Taylor, world traveler and author, spent six months in the mining areas in 1849, and he wrote that the decisions of the informal courts were carried out faithfully and that the just penalties deterred crime. The Sacramento *Transcript* said that, in the camps, "this is the only sure means of administering justice."

California's vigilance activities, which began in the mining camps, flowered in the mushroom city of San Francisco. This port, which had had few more than eight hundred people when gold was discovered, quickly became a sprawling and almost lawless metropolis. With the miners and adventurers came a large influx of pickpockets, thugs, highwaymen, and other desperadoes. Soon San Francisco had a vast underworld that included many released prisoners from Australia.

The Australian ruffians, called Sydney Coves or Sydney Ducks, lived in tents and shacks at Clark's Point or Sydney Town, on the fringe of the city. Many existed by robbing miners in the streets at night or stabbing men in saloons and gambling halls and then picking their pockets. They were accused of setting fires that destroyed parts of the city. More than a hundred murders occurred in a few months and many citizens feared to go out at night. Often the desperadoes who were arrested had to be released because no one dared testify against them.

In the spring of 1851, Sam Brannan, with other businessmen, formed a committee of vigilance to protect life and property in the city. This was a formal organization with a constitution and bylaws signed by about two hundred men, including some of the most prominent in the city.

The committee, whose membership was not secret, gave notice through the newspapers that it would take direct action to punish criminals. It called attention to the laxity and corruption of public officials, the insecurity of jails, and the quibbling and technicalities of lawyers. The members announced that they would meet in emergency session whenever they heard two strokes on one of the fire-station bells, repeated at intervals of one minute.

With ink barely dry on their signatures, they were summoned to a night session to try John Jenkins, an Australian with a criminal record, who had been caught stealing a safe. Jenkins was convicted on indisputable evidence and punished before a street crowd by hanging, which was the statutory penalty for grand larceny at that time. San Francisco newspapers approved.

The committee's next action was to deport some thugs to Australia. It also refused landing permits to others on incoming ships. In July the committee tried James Stuart, who had been banished from England to Australia and who in California had a record as a horse thief, a burglar, and the murderer of a merchant in a mining camp. Stuart was hanged on the Market Street wharf as men in the crowd bared their heads and ships in the harbor raised their flags and fired their cannons.

The governor issued a perfunctory objection to the hangings, which was ignored. A judge asked a grand jury to indict the committee members, but the jury, which included members of and sympathizers with the committee, refused.

Next the committee apprehended two other ruffians, Sam Whittaker, an ex-convict from Australia, and Robert McKenzie, an Englishman who had come from New Orleans. Both were sentenced by the committee to be hanged. Before their execution, however, the sheriff took these prisoners from the vigilantes and placed them in the city jail.

On the following Sunday, when all prisoners came out of their cells for divine services, the vigilantes invaded the jail, recaptured the two men, forced them into a carriage and whipped down the street to the committee rooms. A crowd followed the galloping hoofs. Sam Brannan appeared at an open window and announced that both men had confessed to serious crimes. The two were hanged from the beams projecting above the committee rooms on Battery Street.

This double hanging caused some of the Sydney Coves and other desperadoes to leave San Francisco. It also spurred city and county officials into more vigorous action against crime. As a result, the committee gradually became less active and was discontinued early in 1853.

More criminals kept coming in, however. Not only did crime become prevalent again but the city government seemed to depend on criminal votes to stay in power. In the spring of 1855 the *San Francisco Herald* demanded a return of the "good old days of the vigilance committee."

In November, Italian-born Charles Cora, who was a notorious gambler and ballot-box stuffer, shot and killed an unarmed man, General William H. Richardson, outside the Cosmopolitan Saloon. Cora was taken to jail, but his mistress, a prostitute, hired able lawyers, and at his trial the jury disagreed. Newspapers protested, claiming that the delay in justice was due to corruption, a "rigged" court and bribed jurors. Some called for a reorganization of the vigilance committee. Meanwhile, Cora remained in jail.

The next disturbance came in May, 1856. The editor of the *Bulletin* dared state that James P. Casey, a city supervisor and machine politician, had been an inmate of Sing Sing Prison, New York. Although this fact had been admitted by Casey and reported in the papers, the *Bulletin* editor had been more outspoken than others in his attacks on San Francisco's corrupt city administration. Casey, feeling perhaps that he had administration backing, shot and killed the editor as he walked home through a fog.

That night great crowds milled through downtown San Francisco's streets. Some filled the corridors of the jail where Casey was lodged, while others climbed on the roof. The city was alive with rumors that the 1851 committee of vigilance would be revived.

These rumors proved true. Several who had been members of that committee drafted one of their number to reorganize it. He was William T. Coleman, a successful merchant and a civic leader. Citizens were called to meet in a vacant hall the next evening to form the committee, whose membership reached 5,500 in two days.

On Sunday, May 18, Charles Doane, chief marshal of the committee, rode a white horse at the head of 500 marching vigilantes with rifles and bayonets. Stopping in front of the jail, they pointed a cannon at the hoosegow and threatened to destroy it unless the sheriff surrendered both Cora and Casey within five minutes. As the gunner waved his fuse, the sheriff ordered the door opened. Coleman and another vigilante entered and brought out the two murderers. The prisoners were taken to the vigilante court as the mayor and the governor watched helplessly from a hotel roof.

Two days later the defendants received as dignified a trial as the legal one Cora had received earlier. Both men were condemned to hang. They were dropped from hinged wooden platforms extended from windows of the committee's second-story quarters.

The committee remained active for three months, increasing its membership to more than eight thousand. But, although on July 29 it hanged two murderers, Joseph Hetherington and Philander Brace, it did not have much other work beyond giving ruffians one-way tickets on outbound ships. Murders, which had numbered more than a hundred during the six months prior to the committee's formation, practically ceased. In fact there were only two during the three month jurisdiction of this vigilance committee.

On adjourning its activities, August 18, 1856—though it was not formally disbanded until November 3, 1859—the leaders disclaimed any desire for public office. "It is seldom," noted the London *Times*, "that self constituted authorities retire with grace and dignity, but it is due to the vigilance committee to say that they have done so."

By that time, elected officials were able to enforce laws against crime more vigorously than had been the case earlier. One incentive was the knowledge that, if they became lax, another committee might be formed. Three years after the 1856 committee had disbanded, a visitor in San Francisco asked a resident what had become of the vigilantes. The answer came quickly:

"Toll the bell, sir, and you shall see."

Montana's Plummer Gang

People's courts and committees of vigilance became almost as common and as effective in other mining sections of the West as they had been in California. This was especially true in southwestern Montana, which had a mining boom in the 1860's. There and in neighboring Idaho, cutthroats, highwaymen and horse thieves frequently dangled from trees.

In the early 1860's the biggest gang of desperadoes in the area was led by Henry Plummer, an adventurer who had gone from the East to California in 1852. After taking part in stagecoach robberies there and killing two men, he went to Idaho in 1861 and formed a band of robbers. The next year he built two roadhouses, or "shebangs," on the trails, where his men relieved travelers of gold dust and other valuables.

Plummer had spies in Lewiston and elsewhere who kept him posted on the movements of miners and other travelers. But in the fall of that year, after vigilantes had hanged three of his men, he moved to the Montana mining town of Bannack, where he hoped his reputation would not follow him. There, early in 1863, he killed an associate, Jack Cleveland, who knew too much about his past. He failed to kill the unpopular sheriff but chased him out of town and was elected to fill his office.

Plummer had reached his late twenties now and was highly respected for his bravery. As sheriff of Beaverhead County he became the chief law-enforcing officer of the only organized county in Montana Territory, but instead of stamping out the growing lawlessness, he connived with the worst ruffians in Bannack and organized a gang of more than a hundred highway robbers. These men called themselves the Innocents and identified each other by looping their neckties with a special sailor's knot.

As sheriff, Plummer could learn about shipments of gold which his stagecoach robbers promptly appropriated. He also knew about prominent miners who were taking out large sums of money. To these gentry he gave, with his compliments, brightly colored scarfs or mufflers for the trip, and thus marked them for robbery—and often death if there was any chance of their identifying their assailants.

Some of Plummer's men became wealthy, acquiring ranches and stocking them with stolen horses. The deputies he chose to help him were all criminals, with the exception of one man named Dillingham, an educated young fellow from Philadelphia, who made the mistake of warning a wealthy traveler that he was to be ambushed. Plummer's men killed Dillingham, but Plummer was still sufficiently respected to prevent their arrest. Bad as all this seemed, many people favored the corrupt administration. Saloonkeepers, professional gamblers, dance-hall operators and the hangers-on of such establishments profited from the criminals' lavish spending. Plummer, himself, became bolder and took part personally in some highway robberies, making the excuse, when he rode out of town, that he must look for horse thieves or examine the ore in some mine. He felt so sure of himself in this double game that he applied for the position of United States Deputy Marshal and requested leading citizens to give him letters of recommendation.

A few people, however, were beginning to suspect their sheriff. Henry Tilden, when robbed on the road from Horse Prairie to Bannack in November, 1863, recognized Plummer among the armed horsemen who held him up. That same day Tilden's uncle, Colonel Wilbur F. Sanders, decided to follow the sheriff when he and some of his men rode out of town. Although not present at the holdup, he learned many suspicious things about the sheriff's actions. However, at Thanksgiving, he and his wife accepted an invitation to dine with Plummer. Incidentally, this was the first national Thanksgiving proclaimed by Lincoln.

A few days later, one of Plummer's men, handsome, educated George Ives, who was becoming wealthy in the robbing business, killed a man for a span of mules and the large sum of money in his pockets. Winter had come now, with cold weather and falling snow, but an outraged mob of miners arrested Ives and after a three-day trial outdoors beside a roaring campfire in the main street of Nevada City, they hanged him from a ridgepole leaned against and projecting over the log wall of an unfinished building.

The same mob then organized a vigilance committee. Miners in Virginia City, Bannack and other mining towns formed similar committees, all pledged to secrecy, law observance and loyalty to one another. This boded no good for Plummer, and his situation took a turn for the worse early in January, 1864, when vigilantes caught and hanged two of his henchmen, Erastus ("Red") Yager and George Brown. Yager's detailed confession implicated Plummer and his deputies, explaining how they operated.

Other evidence against Plummer came to light now, and full exposure seemed imminent. Then on January 10, the vigilantes saw saddled horses belonging to the sheriff and his deputies being led into town. Evidently Plummer planned to escape. The vigilantes decided to act. Quickly they arrested the sheriff and two of his accomplices, Ned Ray and Buck Stinson. An arctic gale whistled through the dreary town but the vigilantes were unperturbed as they hanged the three men from a gallows which Sheriff Plummer had erected for others.

Next day the Bannack committee hanged two more men, one of them with a clothes-line rope over a pole. A few days later, across the mountains at Virginia City, citizens hanged five Plummer desperadoes at one time, before an audience of several thousand. The executioners threw five ropes across a beam of a new building not yet roofed. The ropes went taut when the packing boxes on which the doomed men stood were kicked out from under them.

Later a spectator asked John X. Beidler, who had adjusted the nooses, "When you put

One rope . . . two ends. Work of Montana vigilantes at Helena, 1870.

the rope about that poor fellow's neck, didn't you feel for him?"

"Yes," Beidler answered. "I felt for his left ear."

That night many of the remaining desperadoes left the Montana mining towns for safer regions, but enough were left to stretch vigilante ropes for several more weeks. By the evening of February 3, after six weeks of operation, the several committees had hanged twenty-two of the worst villains. They also had banished a few and frightened away many others. During the remainder of the year the vigilantes found fewer victims, but they kept their ropes handy and used them on several occasions.

The most noted thief with whom they dealt was Joseph A. Slade, a former division head of the Overland Stage Company. After he had terrorized Virginia City, the local committee dangled him from the cross-beam of a beef scaffold.

By 1865, vigilante activity had subsided in Montana and statutory law became more effective. However, informal executions still took place occasionally. In 1870 more than a thousand citizens gathered in the courthouse square in Helena for the trial of two thugs in a people's court. After a jury found the pair guilty, they were strung from a big cotton-wood on the courthouse grounds.

By that time, Montana committees had hanged at least sixty lawbreakers, and they took care of several more in the next fifteen years. The people there, N. P. Langford recalled in his book, *Vigilante Days and Ways,* "had perfect confidence in the code of the vigilantes, and many of them scouted the idea of there being any better law for their protection." They knew that the penalties, although stern, were just and necessary.

Vigilance Committees in Kansas and the Black Hills

Elsewhere in the mountain region and in the Great Plains, vigilante activities were frequent, although less formally organized than in California and Montana. Men in the Black Hills during the gold rush knew how to tie a noose about the neck of a horse thief or a stagecoach robber. Nebraskans used lariat ropes on those who stole cattle and horses, and in 1875 along the Platte River near Sidney, they let sway in a coulee a thief who had killed a cattleman. About nine years later, vigilantes in the upper Elkhorn country were said to have executed eleven horse thieves.

Kansas had a large number of vigilante hangings. The Kansas State Historical Society has found evidence of 206 between 1856 and 1932, but probably it missed some. Horse stealing was responsible for 93 and murder for 37. Little is known about some of these early executions. In 1864 the Lawrence *Tribune* reported tersely, "A gentleman from Franklin County said eleven horses were stolen, six men arrested, two shot, two hanged, and two dismissed. At Rising Sun, four stock thieves were dropped from the same limb, and a few days later two more joined them."

Widespread horse thieving in Kansas in the early 1870's led to the formation of vigilante groups in several communities. In the spring of 1870, after a large band of horse thieves had trailed 250 stolen mules to Texas, citizens of Winfield organized and began detective work. In the fall, they surrounded four agents of the thieves in a house at a crossing of the Walnut River near Douglass. Three who refused to surrender were shot. The other was strung from a nearby tree.

A few weeks later about seventy-five vigilantes captured four stock thieves near Douglass and hanged them in the woods near Olmstead's mill. When they published the names of other members of the band, several left the county. Near Cherokee, an assassin who had killed a cattleman was caught by witnesses to the crime and strung from the nearest tree.

Caldwell, just above the point where the Chisholm Trail entered Kansas, had vigilante executions in 1872 and 1874. Similar work was found by committees in Ellsworth, Dodge City and other cow towns. In 1884 citizens in Medicine Lodge put to death four men from

Caldwell who tried to hold up their bank and had killed its president. Two of the four were the Caldwell marshal and his assistant.

Up the Rope in Texas

Early Texas, which attracted a large sprinkling of desperadoes along with its decent, upright pioneers, also had many informal executions. In 1841, during the period of the republic, citizens living near the Nueces River caught a notorious horse thief. Later his body was found on the prairie, pierced with five rifle balls. After the Civil War, when outlawry became worse, vigilante activity increased. At Richmond, in 1869, citizens hanged a horse thief from the iron bridge being built across the Brazos River. In Denton, the *Monitor* reported that horse stealing there had become unpopular: "Horse thieves have been strung to limbs whenever caught, and cow thieves have not been slighted."

Other Texas towns took similar steps. At Denison, in 1874, vigilantes caught a horse thief one night and let him swing from a tree west of the slaughterhouse. In nearby Preston a few weeks later, citizens fought a gun battle with horse thieves, killing one and wounding another. In the Texas sheep country that year, vigilantes executed five Mexicans who had killed a ranchman and his wife.

In Grayson County, in 1877, cowmen strung three rustlers from a limb near Goose Pond. They left a card with the bodies: "Cattle Thieves' Doom." Later that year, three horse thieves were hanged in Red River County.

Texas' most active and effective vigilance committee was organized at Fort Griffin. This frontier town on the Clear Fork of the Brazos River, west of Fort Worth, was on the western cattle trail and served as the principal outfitting point and hide market for buffalo hunters. Its saloons, gambling rooms, dance halls and bordellos made it one of the wildest towns on the frontier.

Since Fort Griffin's wild boys were not above stealing a horse now and then, a jury selected from them could hardly be expected to convict a horse thief. Men of property protected themselves by forming a vigilance committee early in 1876. In April they caught a man stealing a horse and left him hanging from a pecan tree. Below, they placed a pick and shovel for anyone who might want to dig his grave. "So far, so good," wrote the correspondent of the Dallas *Herald*. "As long as the committee strings up the right parties, it has the well wishes of every lover of tranquillity."

Later that month the committee fought a gun battle with a gang of horse thieves who had been disguising themselves as Indians to fool their victims. The citizens shot two and hanged three. On the fifth body they pinned a card: "Horse Thief No. 5 that killed and scalped that boy for Indian sign. Shall horse thieves rule the country? He will have company soon." In the next two months, the Fort Griffin night riders strung up three more horse thieves.

Those executions led to an exodus of most of the stock thieves from the area, but two years later the Fort Griffin vigilantes had to act again. John M. Larn, a fugitive, had arrived in Fort Griffin about 1870. He found a job as a cow hand on a ranch and later married the daughter of his boss. He was elected sheriff of Shackelford County, taking office in April, 1876.

As sheriff, Larn was satisfactory at first, but he came under suspicion soon after he contracted to provide the military garrison at the fort with three beeves a day. Neighbors noticed that they lost three fat steers a day, while Larn lost none from his herd. As a result, Larn resigned in March, 1877, but cattle continued to disappear. The situation became worse when two of the cow hands who worked for Larn vanished without explanation.

Ranchmen and farmers who lived near Larn began to keep a close watch on him. One nester discovered that the hides of stolen cattle, with telltale brands, had been dumped into a deep water hole of the Clear Fork near Larn's slaughter pen. He fished some of them out with grappling hooks and reported what he found. For his inquisitiveness he was shot and wounded by Larn and his partner.

Sheriff William Cruger, who had succeeded Larn, was handed a warrant for the arrest of his predecessor. He gathered a posse and rode off at night to the Larn ranch near Camp Cooper. The posse captured Larn in his cowpen without a fight and took him to the flimsy jail in Albany. To prevent escape, the sheriff had a blacksmith rivet shackles to the prisoner's legs and posted a guard at the jail.

But these precautions did not satisfy the Fort Griffin vigilantes, especially after they heard that confederates of Larn planned to free him. Quickly they saddled their horses, put on their slickers and bandanas, and picked up their Winchesters. Riding fifteen miles south to Albany, they arrived just before midnight on June 23, 1877. Overpowering the jail guards, they ended Larn's career with a volley of rifle shots. In a little more than a year they had rid the county of nearly a score of stock thieves.

Stretching Hemp in New Mexico and Arizona

Elsewhere in the frontier West, vigilante action was equally common. In New Mexico, in 1872, citizens executed two outlaws who had killed a Fort Union cavalry sergeant. In 1883 Albuquerque vigilantes, lacking a convenient tree or lamppost, built a scaffold for an outlaw by using a pile of ties on a railway flatcar.

In Arizona, vigilantes were at work in Yuma as early as 1866. Phoenix had a necktie party in 1873, when citizens dangled a Mexican from a tree for stealing a widow's cow. Four years later they killed a desperado who had shot a man through the window of a dance hall. In 1879, a Phoenix committee took charge of a bum who had knifed to death a saloonkeeper and a man who had killed a ranchman. Soon both were swaying from the limb of a cottonwood.

Bill Breakenridge, then a deputy sheriff, recalled that one of the bad men was merely strangled at first, without having his neck broken. The other, as a team started pulling the wagon from under the plank on which he stood, jumped into the air for a quick snap. "He knows just how to do it," remarked one man in the crowd. "He must have been hanged before."

Other Arizona towns also took the law in their own hands. In 1873 Tucson citizens tied four nooses to the same beam and used them for brutal killers. In 1877 Hackberry and Safford witnessed vigilante executions. In 1881 Saint Johns leaders put two murderers out of the way. The next year Globe citizens caught a pair who had killed a stagecoach express messenger and a doctor. As a church bell tolled the death knell, the two outlaws stretched hemp from a nearby sycamore.

Early in 1884 Bisbee and Tombstone citizens took charge of John Heath, leader of a gang that had robbed a Bisbee store and shot up the town, killing three citizens. They left him dangling from a telegraph pole. The next year Holbrook vigilantes weighted two ropes with a pair of killers.

Hangings in Nevada and Colorado

In Nevada, where highwaymen were active, Egan, Hamilton, Treasure City and other towns organized protective associations with written rules. Aurora formed one in 1864 after about thirty citizens had lost their lives by violence in three years. The vigilantes caught four of the outlaws, built a scaffold in front of the armory and placed four nooses. When the governor heard what was going on and wired an inquiry, the United States marshal replied, "Everything quiet in Aurora. Four men to be hanged in fifteen minutes." Then, as a crowd watched, the four stretched rope. At Dayton, Carson, Virginia City, and elsewhere, vigilance committees remained at work for a decade or longer.

In Colorado, outlaws often were sent to the next world in economy-sized packages. Near Sheridan a committee strung four desperadoes from a railroad bridge. On the Denver and Cheyenne road to the north, seven bandits were dropped from another trestle. Denver miners formed a people's court in 1859 and hanged from a cottonwood a prospector who had killed another for his gold. The next year the same court strung up four killers. The most remembered was James Gordon, who had killed a man for refusing to drink with him at a bar. His hanging was witnessed by several thousand, whom the mounted Jefferson Rangers kept in order.

Most of the Colorado mining camps organized people's courts in the 1860's. One historian noted that such courts "were about the only ones thoroughly respected and obeyed." Their proceedings were open and orderly, he said. "They approached the dignity of a regularly constituted tribunal. The prisoner had counsel and could call witnesses if the latter were within reach."

Wyoming and Idaho Follow the Fashion

As railroad building brought desperadoes into Wyoming, citizens there found use for many ropes. Several bandits and killers were set swinging in and around Cheyenne and Laramie in 1868. Where trees were not available, a telegraph pole served for a scaffold. That was the case with the stringing up of Dutch Charley at Carbon and George Parrot ("Big Nose George") at Rawlins.

Idaho also attracted horse thieves, stagecoach robbers and killers who had to be eradicated. Vigilance committees at Payette and Boise did this with dispatch. The most notorious man strung up by the Boise group was David Updyke, leader of a desperado gang, who had been able to win an election for sheriff of Ada County. With Updyke and several of his men out of the way, the Idaho crime wave subsided.

57. *Reach of the Law*

Texas Rangers

IN SOME PARTS of the frontier the transition from vigilante justice to statutory law was accelerated by the activities of mounted rangers or state policemen. Often they were effective where local officials were unable to keep order or feared to act.

The Texas Rangers were the most lasting and most noted organization of this type. On a frontier beset by Comanche scalpers, Mexican cattle thieves and white desperadoes, the Texas Rangers earned a reputation that made them known around the world. John S. Ford, historian of the fall of the Alamo, said that the Texas Ranger could "ride like a Mexican, trail like an Indian, shoot like a Tennessean, and fight like a devil."

The Rangers were established in the early days of Texas settlement. In 1823, colonists appealed to the Spanish governor for protection against Indian raids. He ordered the recruiting of a sergeant and fourteen men, to be stationed at the mouth of the Colorado River. Poorly equipped and unpaid, they nevertheless protected the homes of many settlers. Later that year, Stephen F. Austin hired ten Rangers at his own expense.

A corps of Texas Rangers was more firmly organized in 1835, on the eve of the Texas revolution. Each man provided his own horse, saddle and blankets, and was paid $1.25 a day. In the brief war of independence, the Rangers kept the Indians pacified. During the decade of the Texas Republic, they clashed often with the redskins, making the new Colt revolvers famous. The Rangers, having no uniforms, dressed in buckskin, corduroy or khaki, with leather boots and wide-brimmed felt hats.

In the early years of Texas statehood, the Rangers proved more effective than green federal soldiers for policing the frontier. "Give us one thousand Rangers," Sam Houston shouted in the Senate in 1858, "and we will be responsible for the defense of our frontier. Texas does not want regular troops. Withdraw them if you please."

One of the most capable Ranger captains was L. H. McNelly, in command of a force sent to put down cattle rustling and other banditry along the Mexican border. McNelly, a Civil War veteran, had his hands full. One November morning in 1875 he received a telegram saying that Mexican raiders had crossed the Rio Grande near Las Cuevas with a herd of stolen Texas cattle and were now on the ranch of a notorious cow thief, Juan Flores.

Ordering his thirty men to follow, McNelly hurried to the crossing alone. There he found three troops of United States cavalrymen who had seen the Mexicans drive about 250 longhorns across the river on the preceding evening. His tired Rangers arrived before sundown, and McNelly wanted to lead the combined force across the river at once, but the army officers refused to let their men go, even though they had orders to follow cattle rustlers across the border.

At one o'clock the next morning, McNelly and his Rangers, without the soldiers, started across the Rio Grande on foot. The river was too boggy for horses. After killing four pickets at a ranch on the way, they marched to Las Cuevas Ranch, arriving at dawn.

There the thirty Texans faced several hundred Mexican troops. Dropping below the river bank, they held off repeated attacks by the Mexican soldiers. During the day, thirty American soldiers crossed the river to help, but they insisted on returning to Texas in the evening. After dark, the Mexican commander sent a flag of truce and ordered McNelly to take his Rangers back to their own country. The Texan refused to do so until the thieves and stolen cattle were surrendered.

Thus the Rangers spent a second night in Mexico, and next morning, without help from the American soldiers, they faced the troops again with such determination that the Mexicans dared not molest them. In the evening Captain McNelly told their officers to deliver the stolen cattle and the thieves within an hour or he would attack. Some parleying followed; then the Mexicans sent sixty-five of the longhorns and explained that the thieves had all escaped except one who was killed while running away. These cattle were said to be the first stolen animals ever returned across the Rio Grande.

Horse thieves continued to draw the Rangers' attention, even into the 1890's. Late in 1896 a band of outlaws with a hideout in the Glass Mountains of southwestern Texas was stealing horses from nearby ranches. Captain John R. Hughes and two other Rangers went after them. With the officers were an expert trailer and several ranchmen. The party tracked the thieves to their mountain hideout and charged them on horseback.

"We ran our horses to the top of the mountain," reported Captain Hughes, "when the fight was so hot that we dismounted. Here W. C. Combs got a bullet through his left ear. We drove them off the mountain top to the side, where two of them were killed." The attackers recaptured five stolen horses and made such an impression on the bandits, who escaped, that they did not return.

Among the popular officers of this fighting outfit was Captain W. J. McDonald, better known as Captain Bill. In 1895 McDonald was sent to Dallas to prevent a local promoter from holding a prize fight in violation of a recently passed state law.

When the Ranger captain stepped off the train alone, the mayor was perplexed. "Where are the others?" he asked.

"Hell! ain't I enough?" McDonald answered. "There ain't but one fight, is there?"

Frontier Sheriffs and Marshals

Long before the era of Captain Hughes and Captain McDonald, most communities in the West had marshals and sheriffs capable of keeping order without outside help. Nearly all the local officers were courageous, quiet men whose names seldom appeared in the headlines. But a few, either because they had a flair for publicity or because they served in famous frontier towns, established lasting reputations.

Arizonans look back admiringly to long haired Sheriff Commodore P. Owens of Apache County, who singlehandedly faced four of the state's worst outlaws. In one minute's time he left three of them dying and the other wounded. People in New Mexico remember Sheriff

*Court scene depicts preliminary trial of an outlaw on the American frontier.
Painting by John Mulvaney, 1876.*

Pat Garrett of Lincoln County, who captured Billy the Kid.

Texas had outstanding local peace officers. Dallas recalls Marshal Junius ("June") Peak, who kept order so well in the frontier era that he seldom needed his gun. Fort Worth had as marshal in the same period T. I. ("Long Hair Jim") Courtright. Jim was a tall fellow with a bushy mustache and plenty of nerve. He wore two six-shooters in his belt and was quick on the draw.

Jim was ready to crack down on a horse thief or a killer, but he didn't bother gamblers or dance-hall girls. He allowed his policemen to loaf at the casinos and variety shows and sometimes took time out himself for a bit of gambling or a game of pool. On Saturday nights Jim and his two policemen had to work overtime when visiting cowboys were likely to shoot up the town. Sometimes the officers had to crowd twenty-five to thirty exuberant punchers into the two cells and dungeon of the town's log jail.

Austin was less fortunate in having as marshal a widely known gambler and pistoleer, Ben Thompson. After serving a prison term in Texas for a killing, Thompson had gone north and become a professional gambler in the booming towns of Abilene, Ellsworth, Wichita, Dodge City and Leadville. On his return to Austin, he opened a gambling house of his own. Popular with the roistering element, he decided to run for marshal and, after one defeat, was elected.

Although Thompson's reputation as a gunman cowed some of those who might have made trouble, Ben neglected his duties for drinking, gambling and quarreling. His term as marshal was cut short soon after he killed Jack Harris, the owner of a San Antonio gambling house. Acquitted for this act, Thompson celebrated with wild drinking and shooting sprees. Early in 1884 he took part in a gun fight in a San Antonio variety theater and was killed.

Tom Smith

Several Kansas cow towns produced the West's best-known frontier marshals. Of these, by far the most courageous was the one who had the shortest career, Thomas James Smith, the marshal of Abilene during its boom days as the original terminus of the Chisholm Trail.

Tom Smith, more than any other, exemplified western fiction writer William MacLeod Raine's description of frontier peace officers: "They usually were quiet men. They served fearlessly and with inadequate reward. Their resort to the six-shooter was always in reluctant self-defense."

Early in the cattle season of 1870, Abilene had tried several marshals, but no one had lasted more than a few weeks. Finally, on June 4, the town trustees hired Tom Smith, a husky Irishman who had grown up in New York and been a successful marshal in Wyoming. His pay was $150 a month. One of his jobs was to enforce the ban on carrying firearms. Notices of this edict had been posted in public places, but cowhands from Texas had shot them full of holes.

On Smith's first Saturday night in Abilene, a town rowdy, known as Big Hank, decided to show up the new marshal. With his six-shooter in his belt, Hank swaggered up to Smith and began to taunt him. "Are you the man who thinks he is going to run this town?" he asked.

"I've been hired as marshal," replied the officer. "I'm going to keep order and enforce the law."

"What are you goin' to do about that gun ordinance?" the bully inquired.

"I'm going to see that it's obeyed—and I'll trouble you to hand me your pistol now."

With an oath, Big Hank refused. Smith sprang forward and felled him with a single blow on the jaw. Then he took the ruffian's gun and ordered him to leave town at once—and permanently. Hank slipped out quickly, glad to escape the jibes of the street crowd.

The new marshal's first action impressed those who saw it, and news of what had happened spread to the cow camps on the prairies. In one camp on a branch of Chapman Creek, a braggart called Wyoming Frank bet that he could go into Abilene and wear his six-shooter. He rode in on Sunday morning and had a few drinks before Smith appeared. When Frank saw the marshal walking down the middle of the street, he went out and tried to engage him in a quarrel.

Smith's only answer was a request for the bully's gun, which was refused. Smith, with steel in his eye, advanced toward Frank. The ruffian backed away, sidling through the swinging doors of a saloon where a crowd had gathered to see what might happen.

Smith followed him inside and when Frank again refused to hand over his gun, the marshal pounced on him. With two swift blows, Smith knocked him to the floor, then took the gun and gave Frank five minutes to leave Abilene.

This action so astonished the men in the saloon that, for a moment, they stood speechless. Then the saloonkeeper handed Smith his gun and said, "That was the nerviest act I ever saw. You did your duty, and the coward got what he deserved. Here's my gun. I reckon I'll not need it as long as you're marshal."

Others came forward, offering their six-shooters. The marshal told them to leave the pistols with the bartender until they were ready to go back to their camps.

Smith, who often rode up and down the streets on his gray horse, Silverheels, kept order so well that the town trustees raised his pay to $225 a month and gave him an assistant. He stayed on the job, without wasting any time drinking or gambling; and he found no need to kill anyone, but with peace restored and the cowboys gone until next year's drive, his job was discontinued.

In the fall Tom Smith was appointed a deputy United States marshal for Abilene's federal judicial district, and the local sheriff, unable to arrest a defiant homesteader named Andrew McConnell, appealed to the new federal officer. McConnell lived in a dugout on Chapman Creek about ten miles northeast of town. In self-defense he had killed a neighbor who drove cattle across his cornfield and tried to shoot him.

Tom Smith, with one deputy, rode up to McConnell's dugout on November 2, 1870, and announced that he had a warrant for the occupant's arrest. McConnell, who had a neighbor with him, instantly shot the marshal with his Winchester. Seriously wounded, Smith fired back at the homesteader, piercing his hand. The frightened deputy ran away and Smith, left alone, grappled with McConnell. As they fought, the neighbor struck Smith on the head with his gun, then picked up an ax and chopped his head almost completely off.

Two days later, Abilene gave the marshal the town's biggest funeral, and in 1904, a monument proclaimed him a "fearless hero of frontier days who, in cowboy chaos, established the supremacy of law."

Wild Bill Hickok

During the winter after Tom Smith's death, Abilene had no marshal, but for the 1871 shipping season, which turned out to be Abilene's biggest and last for Texas longhorns, James B. Hickok was hired. Abilene paid the new marshal $150 a month and a fourth of the fines.

Hickok, better known as Wild Bill, had grown up in Illinois, and at eighteen he went to Kansas and later to other parts of the West. He served as a constable, a teamster on the Santa Fe Trail and a stagecoach driver. In the Civil War he was a federal scout and guerrilla fighter. After the war he fought

Wild Bill Hickok.

KANSAS STATE HISTORICAL SOCIETY

Indians and had been a scout for Lieutenant Colonel George A. Custer. He also served a short term as marshal of Hays City, a wild frontier town west of Abilene.

Hickok was a handsome six-footer with a droopy mustache and brown hair curling on his shoulders. In Abilene, Wild Bill usually put aside his buckskin suit for more citified clothes. Sometimes he wore a Prince Albert coat, checkered pants and an embroidered silk vest. His boots had cowboy heels and patent-leather tops. His hat was a dark felt with a broad brim. He always wore a pair of pistols, even when he slept.

Hickok was an expert marksman and sometimes gave demonstrations of his skill. But in Abilene, instead of patrolling the streets as Tom Smith had done, he spent most of his time at the long bar in the Alamo Saloon, or gambling at the round tables in the rear. He had two, and for a while three, policemen to help him. Benefiting from the work that Smith had done a year earlier, from the help of his staff and from his reputation as a pistoleer, Wild Bill kept fairly good order in Abilene without much effort.

His only serious trouble came at the close of the shipping season, after most of the Texans had left and when the others were preparing to ride south. On the night of October 5, some of the remaining cowboys were roistering in the streets and at the bars. Marshal Hickok warned them to keep within bounds, but they became wilder and more hilarious.

When the marshal heard a shot fired outside the Alamo Saloon, he rushed out and found that the offender was Phil Coe, a professional gambler with whom he had quarreled over a girl. Standing only eight feet apart, the two men fired at each other. Coe put a hole in Wild Bill's coat, but the marshal gave the gambler a shot in the stomach, from which he died three days later. As Coe fell, Hickok saw in the darkness another man with a pistol in his hand. He fired two bullets into the man's head, killing him instantly. Then Bill discovered that the man he had slain was a friend of his, a special policeman hired by the Novelty Theater.

Hickok stayed on in Abilene, with little to do, until December 12, 1871, when the city council dismissed him, saying that "the city is no longer in need of his services." Later Wild Bill served another term as marshal at Hays City and toured the country with the theatrical company of William F. ("Buffalo Bill") Cody. On August 2, 1876, while playing poker in a Deadwood saloon, he was shot in the back of the head and killed by a stranger named Jack McCall whose only motive seemed to be that he wanted to kill a famous gunman. McCall was hanged by order of a federal court after a lynch court exonerated him.

Bat Masterson

Another Kansas frontier peace officer whose reputation has been expanded by fiction writers was William Barclay ("Bat") Masterson. Bat, like Wild Bill, grew up in Illinois. At eighteen he went to Kansas, where he became a railroad subcontractor, a buffalo hunter and a scout. He was one of the defenders of the Adobe Walls trading post when Indians attacked it in 1874.

In Dodge City, where trade in cattle was replacing that in buffalo hides, Bat lived by his wits as a gambler. In June, 1877, he got into a street fight with City Marshal Larry Deger,

Bat Masterson.   *Wyatt Earp.*

was severely beaten over the head by Deger, thrown into jail, and fined twenty-five dollars and costs. In the November elections he beat Deger for sheriff by three votes.

Bat was an even more dandified man than Wild Bill. He wore a stylish suit, usually with a pearl-gray bowler and a diamond stickpin. Sometimes he carried a cane, but his hand never was far from his pistol. A gunman of quick draw and sure aim, he kept the cow town in fairly good order during his two-year term. Defeated for re-election in 1879, he moved to Tombstone, Arizona. In 1902 Bat Masterson went to New York and became a sports writer for the *Morning Telegraph.* In 1905 Theodore Roosevelt appointed him a deputy United States marshal, but Masterson resigned after two years to resume his newspaper work. He died at his desk in 1921.

Wyatt Earp

Of lesser repute in real life was that darling of later-day television—tall, mustached Wyatt Earp. Also born in Illinois, though reared in Iowa, young Earp learned about the West as a stagecoach driver, a railroad construction worker and a buffalo hunter. In 1875 he obtained a job as a policeman in Wichita, Kansas. His one year on the force was undistinguished, and after taking part in a street brawl he was fined and dismissed. The city commission withheld his pay until he turned in all money he had collected, then invoked the vagrancy ordinance against him.

During the next month Earp showed up in Dodge City, where he became assistant city marshal. Expert at poker and fast with his guns, he helped to keep visiting trail drivers in hand. However, within a year he quit to join the Deadwood gold rush—as a gunman, not a prospector. In the summer of 1877 he was back in Dodge City long enough to get into a brawl with a dance-hall girl, for which he paid a small fine. He went next to Texas but returned to Dodge City in time to be rehired as assistant marshal in May, 1878.

Earp quit his post again in September, 1879, and left for Las Vegas, New Mexico. He planned to start a stagecoach line in the Southwest but changed his mind and went on to Tombstone, Arizona, which was in the midst of a silver-mining boom. He arrived there in December. After riding stagecoaches for a short time as a messenger for Wells Fargo, he was appointed a deputy sheriff.

A few months later, Wyatt quit as deputy to become a guard protecting the town's biggest gambling house, the Oriental. He received a one-fourth interest in the business, which sometimes brought him $1,000 a week. In the fall of 1880, Wyatt's brother Virgil was appointed marshal to fill a vacancy, but he did not run for election in the following January.

In 1881, horse thieving, stagecoach robbing and the killing of Mexican smugglers became so common in and around Tombstone that citizens formed a safety committee which forced the marshal to resign and put Virgil Earp in his place. Virgil had as deputies his brothers Wyatt and Morgan Earp and John H. ("Doc") Holliday, a derelict dentist more proficient with a six-shooter than with a dental drill.

In October the Earps had trouble with a band of cowboys from Sulphur Springs Valley, some of whom had been accused of rustling cattle. After Virgil had pistol-whipped one of the punchers and Wyatt had done the same to another, the visitors and their friends made the round of the saloons, boasting that they would wipe out the Earps.

The showdown came that afternoon at the O K Corral when the cowboys went to get their horses. The marshal, walking to the corral with his deputies, said he was determined to arrest the troublemakers, but when they met, it was Wyatt—not the marshal—who called on them to surrender. The cowboys reached for their guns and shooting began on both sides. When the smoke cleared, three of the cowboys lay dead. Virgil and Morgan Earp were wounded.

Later, a court freed the Earps on the ground that they were acting in the line of duty. But the judge said that Marshal Virgil Earp was "injudicious and censurable" for calling on Wyatt and Holliday to help arrest men with whom they had been quarreling.

The O K Corral fight hurt the Earps's reputations. They became increasingly unpopular in Tombstone, where many regarded them as murderers. Before long, Virgil, no longer marshal, was shot in the back and wounded. Morgan was shot and killed while playing billiards. Wyatt, accused of murder, left in search of a safer climate.

Seth Bullock, Bill Tilghman, Chris Madsen, et al.

Elsewhere on the frontier, some local officers, still undiscovered by Hollywood, made better records than Wyatt Earp, Bat Masterson, Ben Thompson or Wild Bill Hickok. In the Black Hills of Dakota Territory, two Deadwood sheriffs, Seth Bullock and his successor, A. M. Willard, captured or drove away many outlaws. In Wyoming a federal deputy, Nathaniel K. Boswell, rode out from Laramie and singlehandedly caught two horse thieves, had them put handcuffs on each other, and then brought them back.

Mining-boom towns in Colorado often produced officers whose courage outmatched that of the desperadoes they tamed. In Leadville, roughshod Martin Duggan rid the town of bandits. In Denver, Dave Cook tracked down many a horse thief and killer. As an army detective, beginning in 1863, he outsmarted a gang of robbers and recovered more than $10,000 worth of loot. As marshal, 1866–69, and as sheriff, 1869–73, he made life in Denver risky for villains.

The Indian Territory, a paradise for outlaws of several races, had many officers who risked their lives to establish order. One of them was William Tilghman, a tall, dark-haired fellow with keen, gray-blue eyes. Bill had grown up in Kansas and at sixteen left home to become a buffalo hunter and an Indian fighter. At Dodge City, where he was a deputy sheriff for four years and marshal for three, he captured many desperadoes and became known as a fearless officer.

Opening of the Territory for settlement brought a great influx of settlers and more outlaws to be tamed. Bill Tilghman became a deputy United States marshal there in 1891. Later he was the first marshal in the wild town of Perry. In turn he held other posts, among them that of police chief in Oklahoma City. For thirty-five years he was a familiar and popular figure in Oklahoma's plains and hills, risking his life many times. He was an expert shot but never killed anyone he could take alive.

Early in 1895, Tilghman was on the trail of William Doolin, head of a gang of bank and train robbers. Unwittingly the officer entered a dark dugout where the bandits were hiding. Although he could not see the outlaws, they had him covered with their guns.

Fortunately, Doolin refused to allow his men to shoot. "Tilghman's too good a man to shoot in the back," he said. Thus Tilghman escaped, but he kept on Doolin's trail and a year later overtook him in a health resort, where he had gone to take hot baths for rheumatism.

Tilghman, disguised as a preacher, saw Doolin in the hotel lobby reading a newspaper. Whipping out his pistol, he ordered the bandit to throw up his hands. Doolin sprang up and tried to reach his gun, but Tilghman held his arm and told him he would have to shoot unless he surrendered. The outlaw then gave up and let Tilghman take his six-shooter. Doolin was jailed but soon escaped. Later he was killed in a gun battle with another officer. Tilghman, himself, was killed in 1924 when serving as marshal of Cromwell, a lawless oil town.

An Oklahoma contemporary of Tilghman's, less publicized but equally fearless, was Chris Madsen. For a quarter-century he patrolled some of the country's most dangerous outlaw country and brought in many of its toughest desperadoes.

Born and reared in Denmark, Chris had served in the Danish Army and had fought against the Germans. Then he joined the French Foreign Legion for five years. As a legionnaire he campaigned in Algeria and fought in the Battle of Sedan during the Franco-Prussian War.

Eager to fight Indians, Madsen landed in New York in January, 1876, a month before he was twenty-five. He enlisted in the army and was sent to Fort Hays, Kansas. For fifteen years he served in the West, his last enlistment period expiring early in 1891, when he was stationed in Oklahoma. At that time a new United States marshal was looking for a good deputy. Army officers recommended Madsen. The pay was much larger than a soldier received so he took the job.

One of Madsen's early duties was to help set up a court in the wild, lawless Neutral Strip, the later-day Oklahoma Panhandle. His part in the enterprise was to escort two wagon-loads of prisoners on a 191-mile journey over the primitive trail from El Reno to Beaver City. The judge went along in a third wagon containing the judicial bench, the witness stand and other equipment.

The prisoners were chained together, and armed guards rode horseback beside the wagons. When the strange caravan arrived in frontier Beaver City, Madsen found the jail there already overflowing. He had to leave his charges chained to the wagon wheels. The only place for holding court was a vacant room above a saloon. Madsen and the judge had to sleep on cots in the improvised courtroom because the hotel was full.

The first night, as the two officials lay on their cots, toughs in the saloon below began shooting through the ceiling. Chris put on his boots and went down to the crowded bar-room, where three men were boasting of their gunplay. After another round of drinks, they decided to shoot some more flyspecks off the ceiling.

As the first drew his six-shooter, Chris seized his hand and jerked the gun away. The second rowdy charged Chris, who felled him with the pistol butt. The third came on, with gun drawn, but Chris shot the weapon out of his hand.

"One false move and I'll shoot the flyspecks off you," he said, marching the three men out to chain them to his wagons.

There was no more shooting that night, but townsmen warned Chris to leave town. Some of the arrested men's friends were coming to avenge their humiliation. Trouble would follow. Marshal Madsen "allowed" he would stay, and when two suspicious strangers rode up to the hitch rack and dismounted, Madsen told them, "You two get back on your horses and get out of town as fast as you can."

The hardened pair hesitated, so Madsen added, "Is it you go now, or do I have to kill you?"

A crowd of curious onlookers saw the humbled bullies swing into their saddles and silently ride off. Chris had no more trouble in Beaver City.

Later Madsen, singlehandedly in some cases, captured many of the Southwest's most desperate outlaws, among them Red Odem, a Texan wanted for fifteen murders. Odem fled to Oklahoma where he became deputy sheriff and felt safe until he heard that a requisition had been issued for his arrest. An ordinary warrant issued in one state could not be served in a neighboring territory. Odem fled to the hills and threatened to kill anyone who dared follow him.

Madsen learned that Odem was hiding on a ranch. After dark he overtook the fugitive there, shoved a rifle against his back and ordered him to throw up his hands. His hands went up. Odem died, later, in a Texas jail.

In 1898, soon after the death of his wife, Madsen enlisted in Teddy Roosevelt's Rough Riders, and served as regimental quartermaster. He became marshal for Oklahoma in 1911, but resigned five years later, when the Wilson administration wanted his job filled by a Democrat. Early in 1944 he died, aged ninety-two.

Informal Courts

Some early courts presided over by justices of the peace in the West were as informal as vigilance committee hearings. On the Texas plains a story is told about a justice called "Old Necessity" because he knew no law. The only book on his bench was a mail-order catalog bound in sheepskin. Before each verdict, he put on his spectacles and opened the volume at random. At the conclusion of one case, after a quick look, he announced:

"I fine you $4.88."

The defendant, who had pleaded guilty to a misdemeanor, jumped up to protest. But his lawyer yanked him back in his seat.

"Be thankful," he said, "that he opened it at pants instead of at pianos."

William B. Almond, a former peanut peddler, who was appointed as a judge in San Francisco late in 1849, charged an ounce of gold dust for every motion and postponement. Sitting with his chair tipped back and his feet planted high, he allowed no long speeches. When a case bored him, he might rise from his chair and announce:

"The court's dry. The court's adjourned. Let's take a drink."

Drinking was common in some of the early courts. Once, at Placerville, the trial of a miner charged with assault began before a justice of the peace at eleven o'clock at night. Recesses were taken every few minutes for drinks at a nearby bar. At daybreak, according to the report of a local historian, "a drunken lawyer addressed a drunken jury on behalf of a drunken prosecutor. A drunken judge having delivered an inebriated charge, a fuddled verdict of acquittal was delivered."

Even after more formal courts were set up, the influence of the earlier miners' courts and vigilance committees sometimes made itself felt. In Oregon, after the miners at Jacksonville had elected an *alcalde,* a miner who thought the *alcalde* had made an unjust decision against him appealed to the assembly of miners. In a Sunday mass meeting, the miners retried the case. They reversed the *alcalde's* decision, and their verdict stuck.

Many a frontier judge found it wise to arm himself in court. At Douglas, Wyoming, in 1886, a justice of the peace, Virginia-born Charles E. Clay, was threatened by the gambler friends of a dance-hall bouncer he had sentenced to jail for beating a cowboy.

"You've got to suspend that jail sentence," said one. "If you don't, we'll tar and feather you and ride you out of town on a rail."

Clay, without answering, walked back of the bench and took out a pistol containing a double charge of powder and shot. The gun, he said, "will always be here to make that sentence good."

Equally brusque was an earlier Texas judge, Robert M. Williamson. In 1837, Williamson was sent to the backwoods of Shelby County to set up the first district court there. Some residents with spotty records made it plain that they wanted no court. When Williamson sat behind a dry-goods box to start proceedings, one ruffian told him that the citizens had resolved that no court should be held.

The judge asked by what legal authority such a decision was made. The objector whipped out a bowie knife from his belt and slammed it on the improvised bench.

"This, sir," he snarled, "is the law of Shelby County."

The judge, just as quickly, drew a long-barreled pistol and placed it beside the knife. "If that is the law of Shelby County," he declared, "this is the constitution that overrules your law."

Judge Roy Bean

Of all the justices of the peace in the frontier West, the most publicized was Roy Bean, who held court in a rickety saloon in the arid chaparral country of southwestern Texas. Bean, of Kentucky birth, had been a trader in Mexico until settling at San Antonio. In the early 1880's the Southern Pacific began building westward from the town, and Merchant Bean followed the construction camps to sell food, cigars and liquor to the workers.

Bean had little book learning, but his beard and his dignified appearance led some to bring their disputes to him for decision. Before long, with the nearest court nearly two hundred miles away, even the Texas Rangers began bringing prisoners to him for judgment. Late in 1882 the Rangers obtained his appointment as a justice of the peace.

When the rail line was completed, Roy Bean settled at a dusty village named Langtry, near the Rio Grande and at the eastern edge of the mountainous Big Bend area. In 1884 his status as justice of the peace was continued by an election. He obtained a blank book in which he wrote his "statoots," along with his poker rules.

With no jail at hand, Bean kept prisoners chained to a nearby mesquite tree and let them sleep in the open, with gunnysacks for pillows. Trials regularly opened and closed with drinks at his bar, and any long session probably would be interrupted with recesses for quenching thirst.

Once an Irishman was brought before him on a charge of having killed a Chinese railroad worker. Some of the defendant's husky friends came along and made it plain to Bean

Judge Roy Bean's bar and court.

PHOTO BY WAYNE GARD

that a wrong decision would lead to the boycotting or wrecking of his bar. Faced with this threat, the justice gravely thumbed through his law book and announced that he found no statute against the killing of a Chinaman. The drinks, he quickly added, would be on the Irishman.

Bean lived comfortably from his sale of beer and from his fines, which he pocketed. Even a dead man was not immune from being fined. When the body of Pat O'Brien, killed by falling from a high bridge, was brought before Bean, the judge found that the dead man had a six-shooter and forty dollars. Quickly he confiscated the gun and fined the dead man forty dollars for carrying a concealed weapon.

Frontier Jails and Courthouses

In the slow transition from unlettered justice of the peace to more formal courts, lack of secure jails was a serious drawback. There could be no punishment if the defendant broke out of jail and escaped before brought to trial.

Reports of escapes from frail jails were common in frontier newspapers. At Yerba Buena (which became San Francisco after Commodore John Sloat captured it in 1846 during the Mexican War) a hungry prisoner appeared one morning before the *alcalde,* carrying on his back the door of the hoosegow, to which he was chained, and demanding his breakfast. Later San Francisco used a dismantled brig as a jail. Los Angeles had prisoners chained to a log in an old adobe house. At Monroeville—a cluster of houses soon to disappear in California's then Colusa, later Glenn, County—lawbreakers were locked in an iron cage placed in the shade of a tree.

In Colorado, on one occasion, the sheriff of Gilpin County arrested a pair of suspected horse thieves and held them for trial the next morning. As he had no jail, he took the prisoners to his home and handcuffed them to the post of a bed and let them sleep on the floor. But his wife, who was confined to the bed with a young baby, objected to this arrangement so strenuously that in the morning the sheriff rounded up enough Central City loafers to build a small stone jail.

On the Great Plains, where both stone and timber were scarce, the housing of prisoners was a problem. Often culprits were chained to a tree or placed in a dry cistern. A Kansas officer chained a drunk to a telephone pole. In Texas a Ranger fastened one to the nearest windmill. Elsewhere lawbreakers were housed in a livery stable, a law office or a milk room.

Most of the early jails were so frail that it was easy to dig out or break a hole through the roof. A Texas sheriff explained that his jail was "unsafe and insufficient to detain prisoners with security and safety and could easily be broken open, either by prisoners or by persons without."

One of the frequent pleas of frontier newspaper editors was for secure jails. At Jacksboro, Texas, the *Frontier Echo* demanded a jail "that will securely hold all evildoers who may be put in it, one from which prisoners cannot escape without complicity of the keeper." At O'Neill, Nebraska, the local editor said: "The crying need of O'Neill is a safe place to put the many drunken wretches that disgrace our streets at night. Let us have a jail at any cost."

Almost as great a handicap as the lack of jails was the lack of a safe place for keeping court records. Often the first courthouse was a log cabin or part of a building used for other purposes. It was easily robbed or burned by persons awaiting trial who wanted to destroy the indictments against them. In Texas in the 1870's, courthouse after courthouse was burned by such arsonists.

Some of the early courts in the West were extremely casual in procedure. A visiting Englishman found a Galveston judge resting his feet on his desk and chewing a quid while the lawyers, "ready of speech and loads of references, from Magna Charta upwards," smoked, chewed and whittled. Later, in Guthrie, Oklahoma, according to Colonel Zach Miller in Fred Gipson's *Fabulous Empire,* the official crier at the federal court used to open the proceedings by shouting, "Hear ye! Hear ye! Now all you mully-grubs in the back of the courtroom keep your traps shut and give these swell guys up in front a chance to talk!"

Yet, gradually, serious judges brought formality and dignity into the courthouse. They banned tipsy lawyers and required everyone to leave his six-shooters outside. A few even required jurors to wear coats. Some circuit judges showed unusual energy in riding horseback or driving a buggy many miles from one court to another. In many communities, court sessions came to be social events that attracted farm families who had come to town for marketing.

The Hanging Judge

Federal judges, free from local politics, were especially influential in making courts effective on the frontier. Outstanding was Isaac Charles Parker, known as the Hanging Judge. His court at Fort Smith, Arkansas, had jurisdiction over the wild Indian Territory, where outlaws of several races terrorized large sections of country, robbing and killing with little concern for the law.

Ohio-born Parker had been a Missouri judge and congressman. When he assumed his duties at Fort Smith in 1875, he was, at thirty-six, the youngest man on the federal bench. He took his new duties seriously. In his first court term, he tried ninety-one criminals. Of eighteen murder cases, fifteen ended in conviction. Of eight killers sentenced to be hanged, one was killed while trying to escape and another had his sentence commuted to life in prison, and the other six were hanged in public on September 3, as several thousand watched.

Most people approved of the new judge. "The certainty of punishment is the only sure preventive of crime," said Fort Smith's *Western Independent,* "and the administration of the laws by Judge Parker has made him a terror to all evildoers in the Indian country."

During the twenty-one years in which he presided over the court, Judge Parker lost sixty-five deputy marshals, killed while trying to perform their duties. He tried more than thirteen thousand persons, more than nine thousand of whom were convicted. Of 344 convicted of crimes that carried the death penalty, he sentenced 172 to be hanged. Some escaped the noose by dying in jail or by obtaining commutation or presidential reprieve, but 88 swung from the gallows outside his jail.

By the time of Judge Parker's death, late in 1896, most of the West had been tamed. Feuds, range wars and vigilante hangings were less common. Such primitive means of attaining justice had given way to the application of statutory law through the courts. Except for sporadic outbreaks, the West had become almost as law-abiding as the rest of the country.

PART SIX

KENNEDY GALLERIES, NEW YORK

"The Bucker and the Buckeroo"
by Charles M. Russell

Cowboys and Horses of the American West

by Ramon F. Adams

Harper's Weekly, 1885

On a hot trail. Engraving, after drawing by T. de Thulstrup.

58. *The Cowboy*

"A COWBOY IS a man with guts an' a hoss." This description has a certain crudity but it holds a world of truth.

Since the dawn of creation men of all nations have driven cattle, but the drover remained a nonentity until the opening of the West. It was here that the American cowboy emerged as a distinct character—later to be fictionized in novels, exploited in moving pictures and glamorized on television screens—and despite the impact of social revolution, spaceships and satellites, he retains his popularity. In teeming cities, youngsters who have never seen a cow and seldom a horse proudly buckle on their "six-guns," adjust their cowboy hats and sally forth to round up the alley cats. Impassive Arabs, chattering Javanese, sedate Hindoos, people over the entire globe, crowd movie houses to become engrossed in the adventures of bowlegged riders in "ten-gallon" hats.

Why this universal appeal? Perhaps because the cowboy had a personal dignity which he was ever ready to defend. He had a brusque sense of humor, and with it courage and the capacity to endure hardship without complaint. He displayed a taciturnity born of loneliness, yet his tough mask would crack on occasion to display unexpected softness of heart. He was reckless, generous, loyal. Usually unlettered, and not always a paragon of virtue, the cowboy nevertheless represents a universal summation of what a MAN should be.

The modern American cowboy originated in Texas, but Mexican *vaqueros* were herding cattle south of the Rio Grande long before the earliest Texan choused wild longhorns out of the *brasado*. (The word *brasado* is archaic Spanish for *abrasado,* or burned up. In parts of Texas brush grew so rankly that it had to be burned continually to encourage the grass.) The Texas cowboy adopted much of the *vaquero's* equipment—big-horned saddle, spade bit, rawhide rope—and many of his expressions—*remuda* (spare horse), lariat *(la reata),* even hoosegow *(juzgado),* in which he sometimes awakened after excessive libation.

Then came the Texas revolution and the bloody Alamo, which stirred in Texans a fierce hatred of all things Mexican. The long rope and the Mexican custom of "dallying" (a technique used in roping cattle) disappeared, replaced by a short rope tied fast to the horn. Out went spade and ring bits, replaced by grazing bits. Even the Spanish rig was ousted by the double-rigged saddle. But expressions borrowed from the *vaquero* the Texan kept and corrupted to suit his needs.

It is interesting to note that in California, once wholly Spanish and a land of vast ranchos that had never felt the scourging whip of Santa Anna or wept at the slaughter of the Alamo, the Spanish bit, the long rope and the "dally" were not replaced.

It was during the period following the Civil War that the cowboy came into his greatest glory. Two things had awakened the world to the dangers and picturesqueness of his career. One was the great profit to be made on the so-called Long Drive from Texas to northern ranges. The other was the skill with which contemporary writers portrayed the cowboys.

Various trails were used. Each was from twelve to fifteen hundred miles in length and usually terminated at a Kansas trail town. The most famous was the Chisholm Trail. To go north with a herd on the Chisholm Trail was the ambition of every Texas ranch-raised boy.

Only the best rangemen were hired for the Long Drive through hundreds of miles of wilderness. The work was hard and dangerous, calling for courage, skill and endurance. A trail crew usually consisted of the trail boss, his assistant or *secundo,* the cook, the wrangler, nighthawk and enough men to control the herd—one puncher to every two hundred and fifty to three hundred cattle.

A herd moved slowly, ten to fifteen miles a day, grazing en route. Customarily it consisted of twenty-five hundred to three thousand cattle. At the head of the column, a "lead" or "point" man rode on each side. Spaced behind them were the "swing" riders, followed by the "flank" riders. In the rear, the "drag" riders urged on weak, lazy and footsore animals which dropped behind.

The perils of the Long Drive were innumerable. Hostile Indians were always liable to steal horses and cattle. Raging rivers took their toll. Sometimes vast herds of buffalo would threaten to engulf a herd. Stampeding was commonplace, since longhorns would panic for any reason or no reason. Drought, cloudbursts and vicious hailstorms tormented the riders. Marauding white renegades added to the trail boss's worries.

The roundup. Engraving, after drawing by Frederic Remington.

Century Magazine, 1888

Century Magazine, 1888

Trailing cattle. Engraving, after drawing by Frederic Remington.

None of these droving hazards was altogether new to the business. Coronado had moved a herd of cattle over a much longer trail more than three hundred years earlier. Other big herds had been moved out of Mexico into Texas and Louisiana during the eighteenth and early nineteenth centuries. After Texas won its independence from Mexico in 1836, Texas cowboys habitually trailed herds to Kansas, central Missouri and at least once all the way to St. Louis. In the 1850's, after the gold rush to California, herds of beef were driven from Texas to the "diggin's," over a much longer and more hazardous trail with long spans of desert and with far more dangerous Indians than were found on the Long Drive. Russell, Majors and Waddell's forty thousand freighting oxen of that decade were Texas steers which had been trailed north to the neighborhood of Kansas City. After the Civil War began, Texas cowboys delivered herds to the Confederacy, some dodging Federal gunboats to cross the Mississippi—a feat of swimming much greater than any herd would experience on the Red, the Canadian or the Cimarron rivers of the Long Drive. Yet none of these early cattle-drives attracted much attention. For Texans, droving had become a way of life, like whaling for a Nantucketer.

But after the Civil War everything suddenly changed! Texas beef cattle could be driven north again, over the old route, into Missouri and southeast Kansas—the Shawnee Trail, it was called—and to steamboat ports in Louisiana. Herds clogged the roads, broke farmers' fences, destroyed crops and meadows. Irate farmers ordered the Texans to go back, threatened them with flogging, strung up one or two and held them aloft until they promised to leave the country.

At about this time, when surplus cattle were crowding Texas ranges and there was no easy market for them, an Illinois cattle-buyer in Lincoln's home town of Springfield had an idea that solved the problem and led directly to the great day of the cowboy.

Joseph McCoy was a big operator who shipped hogs, sheep and cattle by carloads. Railroads were being built across the Plains, racing for the Pacific, and while their owners were apt to listen to good customers like McCoy, they considered him a dreamer when he suggested that they build stockyards on their lines west of the settlements. A dreamer, however, with a $2,500,000 checking account in a Springfield bank deserved more than casual attention, and finally the Kansas Pacific Railroads agreed to give him a siding if he would build the yards.

McCoy traveled west to look over the field. He selected a site in central Kansas at the frontier village of Abilene. The Plains were ocean-flat here, and a route southward across Indian territory to Texas had been used for some years by a mixed blood Indian trader named Jesse Chisholm. The ruts cut by his wagons in the prairie sod could be traced in many places. Joe McCoy began building his yards and sent word for Texas drovers to come on!

Some thirty-five thousand cattle arrived in the fall of 1867, double that number in 1868, and by 1871 a million and a half cattle had been loaded at Abilene. Joseph McCoy was richer than ever, and as other railroads reached westward, new loading pens were built.

Of all the shipping points, Dodge City became the most notorious. Here lawlessness met its match against tough frontier marshals who went all the way in enforcing the law. Dodge City was at the end of what was known as the Western Trail. Perhaps the greatest disadvantage of this new trail was its proximity to dangerous Indian country. It skirted the Texas Panhandle where Comanche and Kiowa Indians could still escape from soldiers on the waterless Llano Estacado. To evade the redskins Charles Goodnight and Oliver Loving established a third trail which circled south and west of the dreaded flats and then headed north up the Pecos River to Colorado. They put the first herd through on this trail in 1866, even though its roundabout route required keeping the cattle for a longer time in the hot deserts as summer advanced.

The Goodnight-Loving Trail followed the old Butterfield stage road west from Texas to the Pecos in New Mexico. Cowboys had to drive one stretch of more than a hundred miles without sufficient water for the cattle, pushing the herd continuously without rest. Usually, by the second day the steers were stumbling along, half-crazed with thirst, thickened tongues hanging out, bodies shrunken. The punchers, choked by dust, exhausted by never-ending hours in the saddle and continuously hazing the reluctant beasts, were in little better shape. On the third day, when the lead steers caught a whiff of the cooling waters of the Pecos River ahead, there was always the risk that the drought-stricken cattle would panic and trample each other in a frantic stampede for water. This is how one trail boss described the drive:

> . . . another day of sizzling heat. The cattle became feverish, unmanageable. . . . The lead cattle turned back, wandering aimlessly in any direction. The rear overtook the lead and the cattle lost all semblance to a trail herd. . . . The cattle congregated into a mass of unmanageable animals, milling and lowing in their fever and thirst. . . . No sooner was the milling stopped than they would surge hither and yon. . . . They finally turned back and the utmost efforts of every man failed to stop them. . . . We threw our ropes in their faces, and when that failed, we shot them, but in defiance of smoke and lead they walked sullenly toward the line of horsemen in their front. . . . Six-guns were fired so close as to singe their hair, yet they disregarded this and every other device to turn them. In some cases they walked against our horses, and we realized that the herd was going blind.

Trailing a herd had never been a job for pantywaists, but now the new financial element gave the job great glamour and attracted the attention of the civilized world. A beef steer costing five to ten dollars in Texas fetched three or four times that much on the northern market. The simplest kind of arithmetic showed that a trail herd of three thousand would profit the owner magnificently. Texans who had been cattle-poor found themselves well-to-do. Speculators bought their cattle by hundreds and doubled and tripled their money in three or four months. The profits attracted eastern bankers, British lords, investors everywhere. Cattle was big business now, and cattle-driving suddenly became a popular subject of conversation at social gatherings in New York City.

Some four million cattle were trailed to northern railroads, and many more went on to stock northern ranches during the Long Drive period. And yet, the Lone Star State had as many, and much better, cattle than before the drives began.

As the railroads pushed farther west across the Plains, more cowtowns came into being—Newton, Wichita, Caldwell, Hays City, Ogallala, Cheyenne. Each was wide open, more a settlement than a town. Each was populated by gamblers, harpies, sporting women and other parasites whose sole function was to prey on railroad construction crews and cowboys who had delivered their herds and been paid off.

Newspaper writers, never lacking for adjectives, painted lurid pictures of the lawlessness and depravity of these drovers. Unfortunately, though, the writers saw only one—the least pleasing—side of the cowboy's character.

Many of these young men were scarcely out of their teens. On the Long Drive, they were cut off from civilization for three to four months. Day after day, they had breathed trail dust, been drenched by rain, stopped stampedes by riding madly across dangerous ground often riddled with prairie dog holes. They had swum rivers guiding panicky longhorns. They had battled thunder and lightning and endured drought. And no matter how demanding

Cattle drifting before the storm. Engraving, after drawing by Frederic Remington.

Century Magazine, 1888

the day, each rider had to spend two hours on guard every night, circling the herd in opposite directions. Often, with a "spooky" herd, riders became so "techy" from continuous strain that the only safe way to awaken them when they snatched a brief nap was to throw a pebble; if aroused by a hand they were liable to grab their guns in a reflex action. Was it any wonder, then, that when they finally delivered their herds at trail's end and had money in their pockets, they would go on a wild spree?

Actually, most of their celebrating was harmless. They "yipped" and whooped, rode their wiry little cow ponies along the rude plankwalks, downed too much "rotgut," and were slickered out of every cent of their hard-earned pay by crooked gamblers and painted women. There was some gunplay, some drunken brawls, some flaring tempers, but the picture drawn by newspapermen was vastly exaggerated.

Let's follow a newly paid-off puncher with $100—three or four months' pay—burning a hole in his pocket. First he visits a barber, has a tangle of beard removed and his hair cut. Then he drops into a dry goods store and buys himself a new outfit. Now he is ready to celebrate. The saloon men, the gamblers, the pimps, are all waiting to filch his hard-earned pay. The bartender sets out a bottle of cheap frontier whiskey, "two bits a throw." A little heady after a few drinks, the puncher heads for the poker table, where a flashy gambler is waiting with his marked cards. Our puncher watches the dealer's pile of chips grow and his own melt away. Convinced he is being robbed, he can't prove it. Finally, pockets empty, he pulls away from the table, mounts his pony, races up and down the street and blazes a few indignant shots at the stars. Then, with a yell, he spurs the pony and gallops out of town, heading for the security of his cow camp. And yet, because of this type of conduct, he became known to the Easterner as a bloodthirsty demon, reckless and rowdy, weighted down with guns and itching to use them.

An authentic picture would have made far less interesting newspaper copy. But so thoroughly was this image implanted in the public mind that the trail hand, even a half-century later, was regarded as a semisavage.

Granted, there were affrays, bloody ones. In Newton, Kansas, in July, 1871, Hugh Anderson, a young trail boss, shot one McClusky, night policeman, in Tuttle's Place, avenging McClusky's killing of a friend. Other guns opened up, someone hurled a chair at the lights, orange flashes of flame split the gloom. When the brawl was over, nine men lay dead or dying, among them Anderson. Ghastly, yes, but those were pioneer days, rough-and-ready days, and the six-gun a very potent persuader.

Actually, for every day he spent in town, the average cowboy spent months on the lonely range. His job was working cattle, and his life anything but the exciting round of pleasure and thrills usually depicted. It is hard to find glamour in rising at 4:00 A.M., picking maggots from stinking sores around a cow's horns, yanking steers from bog holes, sweating through fiery summer days and freezing in winter blizzards.

Hardship, isolation and danger were the substance of the cowboy's life, and they developed his sterner qualities to a high degree. Weaklings were quickly weeded out. One coward could endanger the lives of an entire outfit.

It is interesting to review the characteristics of the typical cowboy. No one was more generous, with time or money. He would share anything with a fellow rider. Loyalty to the

A row in a cattle town. Engraving, after drawing by Frederic Remington.

"iron," or brand, was universal. Concern for the cattle, the property of his outfit, came first, and he shrugged off any consideration of risk to his own life or limb.

High in his code was square dealing. His word was his bond. In early Texas days, deals were made, cattle bought and sold, herds changed hands, on a mere say-so. Nothing was put on paper. A man's word was enough.

Generally, punchers were clannish. Their work made them so. Soft-spoken and reserved with strangers, they had the reputation of being taciturn and reticent by nature, which they actually were not. There was no more boisterous, sky-larking, hard-swearing bunch than a party of cowboys around a campfire or in the bunkhouse.

The puncher would tackle any job, providing it could be done from the back of a horse. He would even "snake in" the firewood, dropping a loop over a fallen branch and hauling it behind him, or open a gate from the saddle.

He was independent and perhaps irresponsible. With no domestic worries and no worthwhile possessions outside a gun and a horse, he was apt to be "fiddle-footed." When he tired of a certain vicinity, he simply drew his time, saddled up and departed for points unknown.

As we have pointed out, the cowboy was strictly a horseman. He refused to walk, even for a short distance. Actually, with bowed legs, high heels, glove-fitting boots to which were attached long-shanked spurs with big rowels that often dragged the ground when he walked, he was not equipped to be afoot.

When seeking a job, he was careful to ascertain that there would be no such chores as feeding, digging postholes, cutting stove wood or milking cows. He had a deeply ingrained pride in his calling; he regarded himself as a cavalier, not a laborer.

Milking cows was particularly abhorrent, as a ranch boss learned when he poked his head into the bunkhouse, where eight punchers were lounging after the day's work, and urgently requested a volunteer for the milking chore. Blank-faced, the punchers eyed him, and not a man stirred. The harried boss had to do the job himself.

On another ranch, the hog man ducked out. A puncher was ordered to handle the chore. He promptly quit! In rapid succession three more riders followed suit rather than handle what they considered a menial job. At that point, the irate boss realized he was in danger of losing his entire crew. Yes, he slopped the hogs himself!

Those punchers would have fought prairies fires, stopped dangerous stampedes, ridden all day without a bite, "laid out" all night without a bed, stood guard in rain or sleet, without a murmur. They did not complain about long hours, flood, drought, heat or cold, dust or blizzard, if they could work while mounted. The only footwork they regarded as honorable was roping a mount in the corral or branding. The puncher had his pride.

Another cowboy characteristic was his laconic and often forceful expression. Of one puncher who had encountered a succession of mishaps, a pard said: "For a man who's gone through so many close shaves I don't see how he ever saved his whiskers."

One who narrowly escaped death "had been near enough to hell to smell smoke." When a man vomited he "aired his paunch." Something fragile "wouldn't hold no more than a cobweb would a cow."

Such expressions as "peaceful as a church," "calm as a toad in the sun," "slick as calves' slobbers," "techy as a teased snake," "welcome as a polecat at a picnic," "salty as Lot's wife," "sad as a bloodhound's eye," to pick a few from hundreds, painted vivid, compelling pictures.

A curious custom of the puncher was to ignore a man's surname. Nicknames were the

The midday meal. Engraving, after drawing by Frederic Remington.

Century Magazine, 1888

invariable rule. Within a few days after a tenderfoot or a new man joined an outfit, a nickname—usually descriptive—was tacked onto him, and forever after he was known by no other. A redhead was sure to be dubbed "Red," "Brick," "Sunset" or if a Mormon "the Pink Angel." Freckles might inspire "Speck," "Pinto" or "Paint." Every outfit had its "Slim," "Shorty," "Windy," "Baldy," "Squatty," and "Horseface." "Gloomy" looked on the dark side of life; "Sudden" was impulsive; "Lippy" or "Wagon Tongue" liked to talk; "Brazos," "Cheyenne," "Tucson," "Pecos" are obvious. There were a host of others, such as Swivel-eye, Wild Cat, Holy Father, Kidney Foot, Never Sweat, Bean-Belly, Bones, Jawbone, Suicide, Cranky.

Whatever label his pards decided to affix, the victim was stuck with it. He might have been christened Reginald J. Waterhouse, but he was "Stinky" to them.

Crude and unlettered as he may have been—many had difficulty tracing their names on the back of their pay checks—the oldtime cowboy stands out as a unique American type, the man on a horse, blunt, outspoken, warmhearted, courageous and heroic.

59. *Cowboy Equipment*

Guns

ACTUALLY, THE TYPICAL cowboy did very little shooting. From a practical standpoint, cartridges cost money and his pay was around a dollar a day. Certainly, he packed a gun and, like every other item of his equipment, it had a purpose: self-defense.

It was a common saying that "King Colt rodded the range." The West was wild. Law officers were few and mainly confined to the towns. Renegades were everywhere; lurking savages and rustlers were often more dangerous than rattlesnakes.

In addition, a gun was useful to dispatch a pony when it broke a leg, to turn stampeding cattle, kill a rattlesnake or, with three spaced shots, signal for help.

It was not surprising that bereft of the familiar feel of a "hawg leg" bumping his thigh, the cowboy felt "real naked." And, where almost every man carried "five beans in the wheel," arguments could terminate in gunsmoke.

The cowboy has often been confused with the professional gunman, usually a renegade. These characters lived by virtue of their gun speed. They were not averse to "heisting" a stage or holding up a bank. They would hire out as "gun hands" during a range war. Their trigger fingers were "itchy" and they were "cat-eyed," for they never knew when some other aspiring gunman or avenging foe might blast a hole in them for sheer "glory" or plain hatred. They were the "lobos" of the range country and inevitably, sooner or later, they were concrete proof of the Biblical proverb (Matthew 26:52): "They that take the sword shall perish with the sword."

The average puncher could never approach the professional gunman's skill because that entailed ceaseless hours of practice until the "draw" became a conditioned reflex, literally as fast as lightning.

The puncher spoke of his gun as his "artillery," though it was also referred to as "cutter," "hardware," "blue-lightnin'," "smoke-wagon," "equalizer," "lead-pusher," or any one of a dozen other slang terms. Shotguns, called "scatter guns," were held in contempt, although frontier marshals occasionally used them effectively. Bartenders, too, usually kept one, sawed off, within reach behind the bar to cool off hotheaded patrons.

A bullet was referred to as a "blue whistler" or a "lead plum." Its victim was "bedded down," "sent to Heaven to hunt for a harp," or "he went to hell on a shutter."

If considerably perforated he was "so full of holes he wouldn't float in brine." If wounded, he was carried "to the sawbones to have the lead mined out."

The truth was, however, that the cowboy used his gun only when necessity dictated. On the rare occasions when he visited town he craved to do no more than "wash the trail dust out of his throat" and trade a little friendly talk with kindred souls in the shaded sanctuary of a saloon.

Saddles

When a puncher died he was said to have "sacked his saddle." And few punchers would part with their saddles until the inevitable day came when they "shook hands with Saint Peter."

DRAWING BY JO MORA

A down-on-his-luck puncher might be compelled to sell his gun to obtain the where-withal to eat. Circumstances might even force him to dispose of his pony, but he would stick to his saddle to the bitter end. When a man "sold his saddle" he was financially or morally in the depths. It was his work bench, his pride and his throne. Without it he felt degraded.

Many a puncher would put a year's wages into a saddle and its decorations. With usage, like his Stetson, it gradually accommodated itself to his anatomy until it was as comfortable as an old armchair. He referred to it as "hull," "kak," "tree," "wood" and "gelding smacker." The smooth English-type saddle, for which he had the utmost contempt, was a "hog skin," "kidney pad," "pimple," "pancake" or "postage stamp."

Possibly the first saddles seen in North America were those used by the helmeted Spanish cavalrymen who followed Cortez. Mexican herders added a horn, to which a rope could be tied, and so evolved the stock saddle. In Texas and in California the original Mexican saddle was improved in both quality and comfort until it differed from its forebear as much as a Model T differs from a Cadillac.

The stock saddle was made primarily for utility. It was heavy, weighing usually from thirty to forty pounds. It was comfortable. Many a trail hand, dead on his feet from ceaseless riding, slept in the saddle while his cattle-wise horse faithfully circled the herd. It was ideally suited for its purpose: roping and holding stock.

As time passed, styles in saddles changed. In the early seventies they were short, shallow and clumsy, had a large flat horn, called a "dinner plate."

During the early eighties, the "apple horn" appeared. This horn was almost round and about the size of a small apple. The seat of the saddle was deeper and the stirrups narrower.

The foundation of any saddle was its tree, the wooden frame which the leather covered. Various makers modified the shape of the tree and each new design took a name of its own. There were three parts to the tree: the front, or fork, to which the horn fastened; the cantle, or back rest; the two side-bars connecting fork and cantle. Heavy wooden screws and glue fastened these parts together, but because screws could come loose from rough usage, as few as possible were used. Instead, green, or wet, rawhide was laced over the entire tree. This shrunk as it dried, binding the parts securely together.

There were no copyrights on early-day saddles, and many were copied, particularly if they were of popular design. The Ellenburg was duplicated by many makers; it eventually became the "association" or "contest" saddle, compulsory at all large rodeos. Saddle makers developed other styles known as the "Visalia," "Brazos," "California," "Nelson" and "Cheyenne."

A saddle's gullet was the curved portion of the underside of the fork. Gullets became longer in direct ratio to the swell and height of the horn. The original idea of the swell fork came from a roll of blankets tied just behind the fork to make it harder for the horse to unseat its rider. The early-day cowboy did not have these swells on his saddle. He rode a straight fork.

The cantle, or raised back rest, varied in width, height and slope according to the owner's wish or the custom of the section in which he worked. Ropers and riders in flat country preferred a low cantle, because it was easier to mount and dismount. The rodeo rider liked a low, full cantle, too. Riders in mountainous country chose a high cantle, because it was easier on the rider when his horse scrambled up steep slopes.

Between the fork and cantle were the two side-bars which formed the seat. A strip of galvanized iron, called the "strainer," was arched over them. This strengthened the frame and prevented the seat from sinking or breaking down. The proper length of the seat for each individual depended upon his height and weight, and whether he wanted a tight-fitting saddle or a roomy one. Much of his riding comfort depended upon the fit of the seat.

The horn, from a working viewpoint, was perhaps the most important part of a saddle, for no roping could be done without it. A rider also used it to assist in mounting, and it could save a man from being crushed when his horse threw itself backward too quickly for him to slip out of the saddle. On the other hand, though, the horn has been known to pierce the rider's body, killing him.

The "apple horn" was made of metal. Some had leather covers. Ropers usually preferred leather because it was less slippery when they coiled a rope around it. Saddle makers used various slopes of horn, according to the rider's preference. Horn heads had various pitches, too. A roper might want a horn shaped differently from the type the average rider preferred.

The Mexican saddle used very little leather and was regarded as a creation mostly made of wood. The first improvement on this led eventually to the American "Mother Hubbard," which consisted of little more than stirrup leathers and a tree covered with an almost square piece of leather which had a hole for the horn and a slit for the cantle, making a covering similar to the pony express rider's *mochila*—a padlike pouch in which he carried letters so that they would not be in a thick lump that pounded the back of a galloping horse. The cover, or housing, on an early-day stock saddle eventually became an integral part of later saddles.

Many of the saddle's leathers were called "jockeys." The leather on top of the skirt, fitting closely around the fork, was the "front jockey." The uppermost broad leathers, forming the top of the skirt, joining behind the cantle, were the "back" or "rear jockeys." The "seat jockey" was the flat plate overlaying the stirrup leathers where the latter issued from the seat of the saddle. This was also called the *sudadero*, a Spanish word meaning "handkerchief for wiping the sweat" or "sweat pad." This term was often incorrectly applied to the *rozadura*, or chafe preventer, a vertical wide leather shield sewed to the back of the stirrup leather.

The Spanish word *anquera*, a covering for the *anca* or hindquarters of a horse, was used by Americans to designate the broad piece of leather sewed at the base of the cantle when there was no rear jockey.

A tree entirely covered by leather embossed with a fancy design was called a "full-stamped" saddle. Such artistic craftsmanship was not solely to satisfy the rider's ego. The rough indentations, because of friction between the leather and the rider's smooth pants, allowed him to sit tight in the saddle without the tiresome cramping of his legs which might result from riding a fractious horse with a smooth saddle.

In different sections of the cattle country men rode different types of saddles. When the skirt was short and rounded, it was called a "California skirt." This made a saddle lighter but a blanket was apt to slip from under it and such saddles served best on "corona pads"—pads with thick, rolled edges. The "Texas skirt" was long and square, a design better suited for holding a folded blanket in place. The "rigging" of a saddle referred to the broad straps attached to the tree and the "rigging rings" to which the *latigo* connected. These iron rings, placed under the housing on both sides of the saddle, were also called "tree" or "saddle rings."

The style of the saddle took its name from the position of the rings in relation to the cinch.

Saddles with one cinch were "center-fire," "single-rigged," "single-fire," "single-barreled" and "California rigged"; those with two cinches, "rim-fire," "rimmies," "double-rigged," "double-fire" and "double-barreled." A "three-quarter" rigged saddle had a cinch halfway between the position of the center-fire cinch and the front girth of a "rimmie." "Seven-eighths" and "five-eighths" rigs took their names according to location.

The rigging—center-fire, three-quarter, double-rigged, etc.—determined how well the saddle would stay in place on a horse, and none proved perfect. A horse's girth is smaller just behind his forelegs than around his middle, where a center-fire saddle pinched. Thus, a rim-fire was more apt to stay in place when ridden in level country, but a "bad actor" has been known to buck such a saddle right over his head.

A single-cinch saddle also had the bad habit of flying up behind, the cantle hitting the rider's back, when a taut rope yanked the horn. In the mountains, when a cowboy rode down-hill, a center-fire usually slipped too far front on a horse's withers.

A double-cinch saddle solved these problems, but it was heavier, took almost twice as long to put on a horse, and a rider's spur was apt to catch in the flank cinch.

The cinch, from the Spanish *cincha,* meaning girth, was a broad, short band made of woven horsehair, canvas or cordage. Each end of the cinch had a metal "cinch ring." These were attached by *latigos* to the "saddle rings," thus binding the saddle to the horse's back. The *latigo,* literally a whiplash, was a long strip, preferably of soft chrome leather, which was passed successively through the cinch and saddle rings, and knotted like a four-in-hand neck-tie. This took time, and many cowboys used a little metal contraption known as the Tacka-berry buckle. Rodeo contestants in relay races often used an elastic cinch with a hook. This was fast, but it would gall a horse on a long ride.

Foot supports on a saddle were the stirrups, usually made of wood, sometimes bound in brass or rawhide, but often all iron or brass. The wide, wooden stirrups of the early days were called "dog-house stirrups," "ox-bows" or "ox-yokes" and were usually made of hickory, bent into shape and bolted together at the top. Clumsy in appearance, they were strong enough to protect a rider's foot if his horse fell on it. With improvement in saddle design, stirrups became narrower, making it easier to mount and dismount. The Visalia stirrup was a favorite. With flaring sides and a flat bottom, it had a tread wide enough for a man to put his weight on the ball of his foot with comfort.

"Hobbled stirrups" were those connected with a strap or rope under the horse's belly. These furnished an anchorage when riding a bucking horse, but were held in contempt by real riders and barred at rodeos. They were dangerous, practically tying a rider to the saddle, trapping him if the horse fell.

The *tapadera,* from Spanish *tapar*—to cover—was a wedge-shaped piece of leather which covered the stirrup in front and at both sides, but was open in the rear. Literally "toe fenders," they were made of heavy cowhide, occasionally reinforced by a wooden frame, and were useful in brush country to protect a rider's feet. They also prevented the foot from slipping through the stirrup. They were given distinctive names to describe their shape or cut. "Bulldogs" were short, "monkey-noses" had short, upturned fronts, and "eagle-bills" were long with a hook in front. Stirrups without *tapaderas* were called "open stirrups."

Bridles

The bridle, or "headstall," was the headgear of the horse, composed of "crown-piece," "brow-band," "throat-latch" and, on either side, a "cheek-piece." Bit and reins completed the ensemble.

The cowboy inherited his first bits from the Mexicans, who, in turn, had copied earlier Spanish and Moorish types. These ancient horsemen cared little for the comfort of their mounts, and some of their bits could be extremely cruel when misused.

Americans soon learned that the most effective function of a bit was to suggest physical pain rather than to cause it. Severe, punishing bits were unnecessary. A horse seldom gave of its best when in pain, and rare was the cowboy who used a bit cruelly.

When turning to the right, for example, he did not jerk the horse's mouth by the right rein, but merely moved his bridle hand a couple of inches to the right, bringing the left rein against the horse's neck. A trained cow pony responded instantly.

There were three basic types of bit—the bar, snaffle and curb. All designs fell into one of these categories, or were combinations thereof.

The simplest bit was the straight or slightly curved round rod, called a bar bit. Like most bits, it had a ring at each end to which the reins were attached. Bar bits were more suitable for driving teams than for cow horses. With a bar bit a strong man could pull a running horse to a stop, but the bit was not severe enough to halt the animal in one sliding jump, as was often necessary for a cow horse so he could make a quick turn.

The snaffle bit was a bar bit made in two pieces, connected with interlocking eyes at the middle. Some called it a "broken bit" or "limber bit." A "chain bit" belonged in this classification, since it was made from a small piece of chain. Some cowmen preferred the "chain bit" for young horses, keeping it in position with a jaw strap between the bridle rings. However, it was never widely adopted.

The curb, or grazing, bit had an upward port, or curb, in the center of the mouthpiece and was perhaps the most popular bit in the cattle country. A good cowboy saw that the port, or raise, did not bruise the roof of his horse's mouth. He made sure that it fitted snugly without wrinkling the corners of his mount's lips, or was not so loose that it rattled against the animal's teeth.

Another popular bit was the "half-breed." This had a narrow, wicket-shaped hump in the middle of the mouth-bar within which a roller was fixed, or a vertical wheel with a broad, corrugated rim. This was no bit for a beginner, as it could be cruel in inexperienced hands.

The roller was called a "cricket" because it made a chirping noise with which the animal amused himself with his tongue, also creating music which the cowboy loved to hear. Often these rollers were of copper and dubbed "tasters." They had a flavor which seemed to please the horse, and made him accept the bit in his mouth more readily. Some claimed that the "cricket" kept a horse from getting thirsty, in the same way that a pebble quenched a man's thirst. Others complained that a horse might get so interested playing with the "cricket" that he forgot what he was doing and neglected his work.

The spade bit—more severe than the half-breed—had a piece shaped like a broad screw-

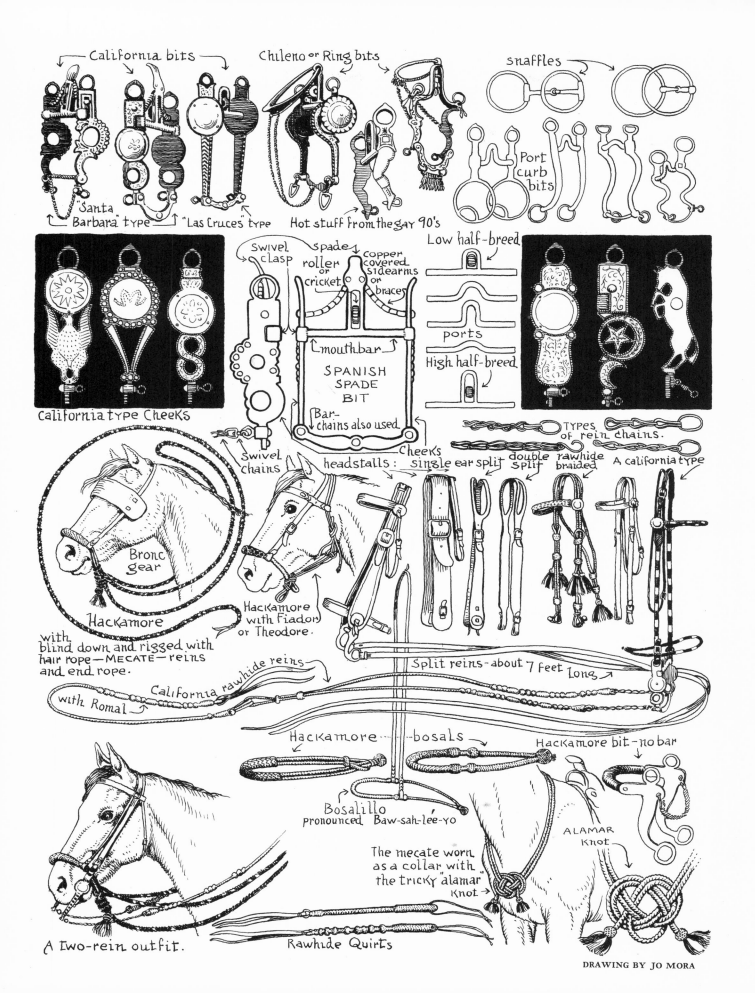

California bits

Chileno or Ring bits

snaffles

"Santa Barbara" type

"Las Cruces" type

Hot stuff from the gay 90's

Port curb bits

California type Cheeks

Swivel clasp

spade roller or cricket

copper covered sidearms or braces

Low half-breed

mouthbar

SPANISH SPADE BIT

Bar-chains also used

ports

High half-breed

Swivel chains

Cheeks

headstalls: single ear

split

double split

rawhide braided

A california type

TYPES of rein chains.

Bronc gear

Hackamore

with blind down and rigged with hair rope—MECATE—reins and end rope.

Hackamore with Fiador or Theodore.

Split reins—about 7 feet long

California rawhide reins

with Romal

Hackamore ·····bosals

Hackamore bit—no bar

Bosalillo pronounced Baw-sah-lée-yo

The mecate worn as a collar with the tricky "alamar" knot

ALAMAR Knot

A two-rein outfit.

Rawhide Quirts

DRAWING BY JO MORA

driver on the mouth-bar. This was three or four inches in length, bent backward at the top. The most sensitive spot in a horse's mouth is the roof, and when the spade touched this spot the animal was aware of its possibilities. Most spades had a roller, and some had two wires closely strung with short copper tubes, or tasters, extending on either side of the spade to the cheek-pieces.

The ring bit included a metal circle around the mount's lower jaw and a whole set of hardware on his tongue. This was the cruelest bit ever put into a horse's mouth and was capable of breaking its jaws. A cowboy who used such a bit would fast be cold-shouldered off the range. It has practically disappeared, except in Mexico.

Reins were the lines running from the bit rings to the rider's hand. They were made of leather, rawhide or horsehair, and were used to guide or control the horse. Some cowboys used reins of flat leather, usually buckled to the bit rings. Others used braided rawhide attached to the bit rings by bridle chains—short pieces of chain connecting the reins with the bit rings. Many fancied these chains because they kept the reins dry when a horse drank. They also prevented him from chewing the reins.

When the reins were not tied together they were called "open reins." Each was usually about seven feet long. "Open reins" were preferred by most cowhands. Among other things, they helped prevent runaways. If a horse fell, or the rider was thrown, such reins would trail on the ground. The horse would step on them, jerk his own head and stop.

A cow pony was so trained that when its rider dismounted and simply dropped the reins, he was "tied to the ground." However, many old cow horses became wise enough to hold their heads to one side and walk away without stepping on the trailing reins.

Reins tied together at the ends or made entirely in one piece, were called "tied," "closed" or "California reins."

These were often made of braided rawhide and worked into a *ramal,* which served as a whip or quirt. Most cowboys disliked them. When tied reins were left over the saddle horn, a horse could not get down his head to graze, but this did not prevent him from walking off. If tied reins were stripped over his head and dropped to the ground, he was apt to step in the loop, get tangled and injure himself.

The *ramal,* as has been indicated, served as a whip but, unlike a whip, it had the advantage of never getting lost, never dropping from a careless rider's hand.

The true quirt—from the Spanish *cuerda*—was a much heavier whip. Made of flexible leather braided on a short stock, never more than a foot long, it had a lash of two to four heavy, loose thongs. The stock was often filled with lead, to strike down a rearing horse which threatened to fall backward. A loop extending from the stock furnished an attachment for the rider's wrist, or the saddle horn. For ordinary riding the cowman seldom carried a quirt, and never on his wrist while roping.

The Hackamore

Horsebreakers, especially west of the Rockies, rarely used a bridle. Instead, they trained horses with hackamores, from the Spanish *jaquima,* or halter. This took more time, but cowmen claimed that hackamores made better cow horses.

A hackamore consisted of a headpiece, something like a bridle, with a *bozal,* or rawhide noseband, in place of a bit. The word is Spanish for "muzzle" or "headstall." Horsebreakers used the *bozal* in two ways. It either rested at the tender crest of the nasal bones, or was placed above the nostrils where it could cut off the animal's breath. This latter method was used only with exceptionally wild or vicious horses. The *bozal* was held in place by soft leather cheek-bands which passed over the horse's head. The back part of the *bozal,* under the horse's jaw, entered a knob of plaited rawhide called the heel. An assembly of heavy, twisted horsehair ropes connected with two complicated knots, passed from the heel over the horse's neck just back of the ears. Young cowboys spent hours learning how to tie the two hackamore knots and felt great pride when they mastered the task.

On this apparently crude headstall there was a horsehair throat-latch, called the *fiador.* This was tied with a sailor's sheet knot—one of those hitches which becomes tighter the harder it is pulled, yet can always be undone easily by reversing the tension.

At the heel knot, a horsehair *mecate* was attached. This served as a lead rope which pulled directly on the back of the horse's neck. The *mecate* could also be looped over the saddle and used as reins. In the Northwest it was known as a "McCarty."

The hackamore had great advantages over any other type of headstall. Serving as both halter and bridle, it proved superior to each. Once placed on the head of an unbroken horse, the animal could eat and drink comfortably without its removal. There was no daily battle to get a bit in and out of its mouth, no head jerking to keep from having ears pulled through a headstall, yet by pressing the *bozal* on the tender nose and, if necessary, shutting off his wind, an unbroken horse could be taught to stop and turn as quickly as could be done with a bit. Furthermore, the animal's mouth was never made to bleed, its jaw broken or tongue cut to ribbons, as sometimes occurred with a spade bit.

When a horse was led, the hackamore served better than a halter, for the reason that the *mecate* pulled directly on the hair rope that encircled the horse's neck. A bronc in an ordinary halter could pull back, and jerk until the buckle to his head-strap snapped, thus freeing him. With a hackamore there was no buckle where the strain came. A frantic horse could pull and shake, but the heavy twisted rope around his ears would hold. The harder he pulled the more it hurt the tender skin at the base of his skull.

Some horsebreakers using a hackamore blindfolded the horse with a *tapaojos* when saddling or mounting. This was a strip of leather about three inches wide. Fastened to the headstall, like a brow-band, it could be slid down over both eyes.

A hackamore man who loved horses was never in a hurry to put a bit in the mouth of the bronc he was breaking. Often he began by inserting a large smooth ring into the animal's mouth. This ring encircled the horse's lower jaw and the *mecate* was attached to it at the heel knot. Thus the horse learned slowly, and without getting frightened, that the pressure of the reins, the pinch of the *bozal* and the pull on the bit all meant the same thing and that none of them hurt him if he responded instantly.

Boots

A cowboy might spend lavishly when he bought a hat, but he really "spread himself" where boots were concerned. Price was no object. Boots were often "custom-mades," the cowboy with pride having little use for the ready-made variety.

These boots had vamps of the finest quality of pliable, thin leather. They fitted tightly around the instep. The legs, of finest kid, were loose and came to the knee. Boots with flapping "pull on" straps at the tops were called "mule ears."

Features of a pair of riding boots included high tops, high heels, sharp toes, thin soles and fancy stitching—and there was a reason for each.

The high tops prevented brush and gravel from working into the boot, and their looseness allowed the air to circulate and prevented sweating. Later, the "peewee," a short and dressier boot with less weight, became stylish, but the cowman shunned low-topped boots. When riding, he pressed his heels downward, and the top of a low boot soon worked below the bottom of his pants in the rear. This created a funnel to trap gravel and twigs that the horse kicked up. With high-topped boots there was no space to act as a "ketch-all," and, too,

DRAWING BY JO MORA

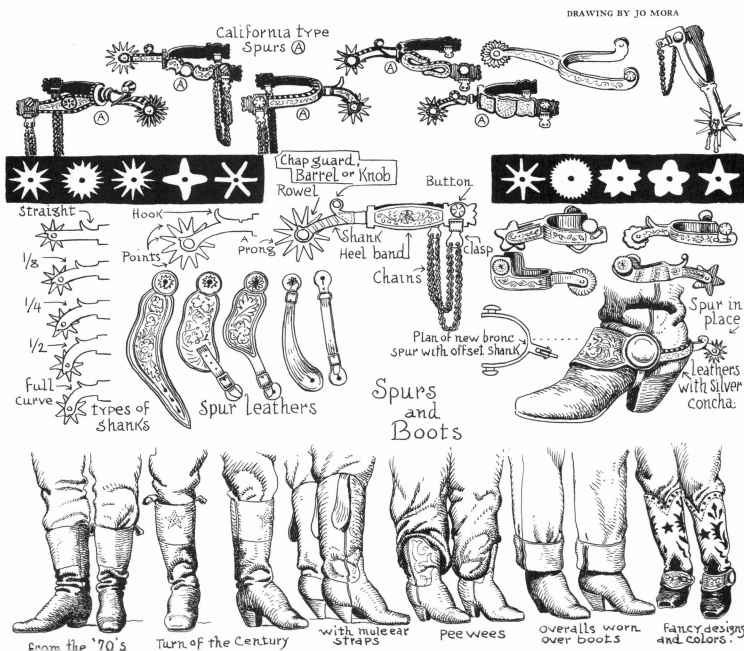

California type Spurs Ⓐ

Chap guard, Barrel or Knob
Rowel
Button
Shank
Heel band
Chains
clasp

straight
Hook
Points
A Prong

1/8
1/4
1/2
Full curve
types of shanks

Spur Leathers

Plan of new bronc spur with offset shank

Spurs and Boots

Spur in place

Leathers with Silver concha

from the '70's   Turn of the Century   with mule ear straps   Pee wees   overalls worn over boots   Fancy designs and colors they could be worn inside or outside the pant legs. High tops were also a protection against stirrup leathers, bumps and brush.

High heels were an important factor. They kept the rider's foot from slipping through the stirrup and hanging; they let him dig in when roping on foot and gave a secure footing in all ground work. There were many times when he could not afford to slip when handling a plunging bronc.

The heels were not only high, but narrow, set under the foot and sloped from behind. With the heel under his foot, the rider's stirrup was held securely under the arch. This gave the cowboy a firm, but easy long-legged seat. Riding was less tiring than when the weight was on the toes or ball of the foot. This narrow, undersloped heel could also prevent a thrown rider from being "hung up"—hanging from the stirrup by one foot—and dragged to death.

With a western saddle, a thrown rider might carry the long stirrup over the seat and, if he fell with his back to the horse, a square boot heel would tend to hold him to the side of the frantic animal. A heel with an underslope would permit him to slip to the ground.

The cowboy wanted the toes of his boots to be pointed, because sharp toes made it easier to pick up the near stirrup on a wheeling or prancing horse, as well as to find the right-hand stirrup after he hit the saddle.

A thin sole let the feel of the stirrup come through; a soft vamp gave more comfort.

Fancy stitching was not just for decoration. It had practical value. Stitching stiffened the leather so that the tops would not break down and become sloppy; it prevented wrinkling at the ankles where the boot contacted the stirrups; it preserved the tops and kept them together when the leather wore thin.

Stitching, too, served another purpose. A cowboy took pride in having small feet. He wanted his boots to fit tightly and appear as though his feet had been poured into them. The fancy toe-stitching made his foot look shorter. Toe stitching also made the boot more comfortable by keeping the lining close to the outside leather.

Ideally fitted for work in the saddle, the cowboy's boots were plainly not made for walking. In fact, so used they were crippling. But no cowboy ever planned to walk.

Spurs

To a city-bred man the cowboy's jingling spur rowels might appear to be pure affectation, but the spurs to which they were attached were a very necessary part of his equipment. Not that the cowboy didn't relish the jingle. Indeed, he often fastened little pear-shaped pendants to the axle of the spur rowel, called "danglers" or "jingle-bobs." Their sole function was to jingle-jangle.

Spurs were known variously as "hooks," "guthooks," "galves," "grappling irons," "can openers" and "pet-makers." An inferior spur was a "tin belly," the huge Mexican spurs, "Chihuahuas."

A cowhand did not buckle on a pair of spurs until he had filed the sharp rowels to make them blunt. Sharp rowels made a horse nervous and he would not give of his best. Spurs were used to signal quick action, not for cruel gigging. Sometimes a motion of the leg was all that was necessary, and usually a mere touch was all a well-trained cow horse needed.

Big-roweled spurs were usually preferred. The larger the rowel the more points it had and those many points did not dig so deeply into a horse's flanks as the few points on a small rowel.

Popular styles of spur were the "gooseneck" with "Texas-star rowel"; the "flower rowel," shaped like the petals of a daisy; and the "sunset rowel," a large spur with many points set close together and giving a minimum of punishment.

The spurs were kept in place on the foot by a broad, crescent-shaped shield of leather laid over the instep. Sometimes twin chains also passed under the boot in front of the heel to anchor the spurs, but if well-balanced these were unnecessary.

Cowboy spurs were usually made in one of three patterns: the upturned, straight or drop shank. These styles might carry any one of a dozen types and sizes of rowels. Spurs with drop shanks often permitted a big rowel to drag when a rider stood on the ground, but when he mounted they gave him a firm hold under a horse's belly. The straight or upturned shank never gave a rider this tong-grip on a horse but proved much more practical when a man dismounted to lead his horse.

The "buck hook" was a blunt-nosed, uncurved piece added to the frame of the spur and used to hook into the cinch or into the side of a bucking horse. The shank of most spurs turned downward to allow this hook to catch without interference by rowels.

Sombreros

A cowboy's hat had to be of best quality to stand up under hard usage, and it had many uses in addition to covering his head.

Often called *sombrero,* from the Spanish, it was variously known as "hair-case," "conk-cover," "lid" or "war bonnet." A certain Philadelphia hat-maker, because of the quality and durability of his product, corralled the cow country hat trade to such an extent that head-pieces on the range became universally known as "Stetsons" or "John B's."

Different styles of hat were worn in various sections of the country. On the Mexican border the true *sombrero*—steeple-crowned, saucer-brimmed, with a shaggy plush surface— was often seen, though some riders along the border wore the huge straw hats associated with Mexican peons. Generally in the Southwest wide brims were needed for shade. In the Northwest a higher crown and narrower brim served better. Texas brush riders wore a style all their own. A wise puncher could tell the state or territory from which a man hailed by the size and shape of his hat.

Most cowhands creased the crown of their hats to conform with local custom, but they might leave it untouched or flatten it on top. A crown with four creases on each side was said to keep the head cooler in hot country; in rainy weather a front crease made a better watershed.

The color of a man's hat was a matter of personal choice, though dove-gray and light brown were the favorites. Most riders decorated theirs with a band, as both ornament and a means of adjusting the fit to their heads. This band might be a leather strap decorated with silver *conchas,* a hand-woven horsehair band, a string of Indian beads or a rattlesnake skin.

Buckskin thongs dangling from the underside of a hat were called "bonnet strings,"

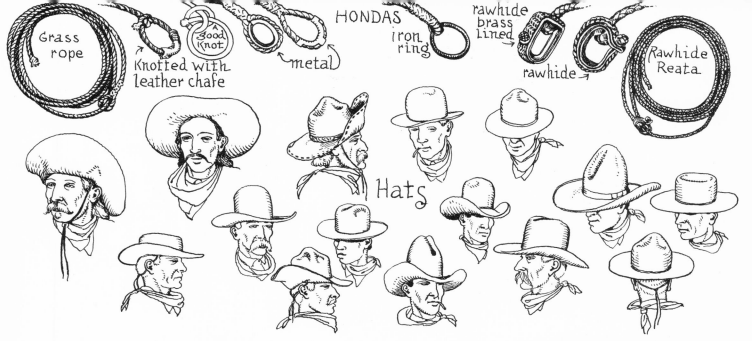

DRAWING BY JO MORA

perhaps a corruption of the Spanish *barbiquejo*. They were run through a bead or ring under the rider's chin and anchored the hat during a fast ride or windstorm.

When riding a bucking horse the cowboy used his hat as a wire walker uses a balancing pole. When he was on foot in a branding pen, if some old mother cow came charging in to rescue her offspring from the sizzling iron, a big hat came in handy to throw in the old girl's face, gaining time to straddle a fence.

The wide brim shaded a rider's eyes from the burning sun; in rainy weather it served as an umbrella; bent into a trough, it made a drinking cup; pulled down and tied over the ears, it gave protection from frostbite. It fanned campfires into life and was even used as a pail to carry water and douse the embers. A rustler used his hat to "wave round" an approaching puncher, signaling that a detour was advisable if the intruder wished to stay healthy. Grass fires have been beaten out by big-brimmed hats. The trail boss signaled with his hat, thus avoiding long rides to talk personally with his men.

By dint of long use, hats became sweat-stained, disreputable in appearance, were kneaded into diverse shapes, but, like wine, their vintage improved with age, and their beauty, in the owner's eye, never faded.

Chaparreras

A conspicuous part of the cowboy's costume were his chaps, derived from the Spanish *chaparreras*. Another corruption was *chaparejos*. These were the leather overalls that shielded his legs from thorny brush. Chaps were essential in the *brasado* country—southern Texas—where hundreds of square miles of range were thickly clothed with prickly pear, almost impenetrable thickets of mesquite and a dozen other thorny growths. Without them, a cowboy's pants and legs would have been speedily ripped into shreds.

In addition to fending off brush and cactus, chaps might protect a rider's legs from injury when he was thrown or when a horse fell on him, pushed him against a fence or attempted to bite him.

Movies to the contrary, the cowboy shed his chaps when he dismounted for ground work because they were hot, cumbersome and uncomfortable to walk in. When he rode to town, he left his chaps in the bunkhouse.

There were several styles of chaps, all developed from the *armitas,* a kind of loose riding apron, which was tied around the waist and knees with thongs. The name is derived from *arma,* Spanish for defensive weapon or shield. The *arma* of the early-day *vaquero* was made of cowhides fastened together beneath the neck of the horse to protect his breast as well as the legs of the rider. When this was reduced in size to cover only the horseman's legs, the name was changed to the Spanish diminutive, *armitas.*

With the passing of the old-time Spanish range customs in the West, *armitas* were replaced by the snugger-fitting *chaparreras.* The first of these to be developed in Texas were "shotgun chaps," so called because the outside seams were sewed together all the way down the leg, which gave some resemblance to the twin barrels of a shotgun. These usually carried a leather fringe down the sides and were pulled over the boots.

On the northern ranges chaps were often made from the skins of goat, bear and other animals, worn hair-side out. Called "hair pants," they were warmer in winter, but in snow or rain they became heavy and soggy, were uncomfortable and smelled to high heaven.

Then "batwing" chaps were developed. These were made of leather, with wide, flapping wings. They immediately became popular, because they snapped on, and a cowboy did not have to pull off his spurs to shed them. A type developed later in Wyoming was called the "Cheyenne leg" or "Cheyenne cut." The wing was narrow and straight, the underpart of the leg being cut back to the knees, with no snaps below that point.

The Texas brush hand wore plain chaps without flapping wings or ornaments. The less surface he gave the brush to grab, the better.

There were other kinds of chaps, but the average cowboy had little use for them. One was the "rodeo chap" used by the professional rodeo rider. Strong enough to protect a rider's legs from chute fences, bull horns and hoofs, the rodeo chap included fancy inland decorations and monograms designed to gratify the wearer's egotistical showmanship. Still others, made for display only, known as "parade chaps," were useless for anything but looks. The man wearing shabby chaps was the real cowboy—he had no use for fancy rigging.

Slicker and Wampus

The old-time cowboy was never without that old "fish," a yellow oilskin slicker rolled and tied behind the cantle of his saddle. Manufacturers made a special pommel-slicker full enough to cover the horn and wide enough in the rear to go over the cantle when a man was in the saddle. A green horse often shied at the sight of his own master wearing this brilliant rustling garment, and was difficult to mount. Modern cowboys seldom carry these waterproofs, but the old-timer was never without one.

The cowboy seldom wore a coat. Not only did it restrict his freedom of action but the horn worked its way under the front buttons and pulled them off. A vest, however, "filled the bill." It was comfortable; when unbuttoned it was cool; buttoned, it was a shield against cold winds. Most important, its pockets were just right for storage purposes—they carried a sack of Bull Durham, book of papers and matches, also the "book." These "books," distributed by commission firms at stockyards and shipping points, were made to fit into a vest pocket. In them a cowboy would record his "time," brands he had seen or wanted to remember, and other memoranda.

In the Texas brush country, where thorn scrub could scratch the shirt off a rider, cowboys wore heavy duck vests or boleros, with sleeves. Similar jackets in the Northwest were sometimes made of denim, as coarse as Levi Straus overalls. Others were of lighter, cooler cotton twill. Called a wampus, or wamus, a jumper was essential in cedar country where a branch was sure to split a shirt from collar to belt the first time a rider lay flat on his horse to dart under a low tree.

Neckerchiefs

A useful part of the cowboy's costume was his neckerchief, or "wipes" as he called it. Neckerchiefs were usually red or blue, like the old bandana of the South, or black silk which did not show the dirt. The rodeo rider of modern days goes in for bright colors. Rangemen usually wished to avoid colors which attracted attention. An inconspicuous rider was more apt to catch a rustler.

Usually the cowboy wore his neck scarf draped loosely over his chest with the knot in the back. If the sun shone on his back he reversed the scarf to protect his neck. When riding in the drag of a herd he pulled it up over mouth and nose to keep out the dust. In winter he might pull it over his eyes to prevent snow blindness or to protect his face from icy winds and stinging sleet. He could also use it to tie down his hat, to serve as an ear muff in cold weather, or to keep his head cool on a blazing summer day by wearing it, wet, under his hat.

When he washed his face in the morning, an ever-ready towel was hanging from his neck. In his work he had this handy mop to wipe the sweat off his face. He could use it for holding the handle of a hot branding iron, for a blindfold on a snaky horse, or as a "pigging string," that is, as a string for tying a roped animal by all four feet the way a hog is tied. Likewise the neckerchief could be used as a makeshift hobble for his horse, a tourniquet a sling for a broken arm, or a bandage.

Bedrolls

The cowboy's bed was usually a waterproof tarp enclosing a couple of quilts, or "soogans." These "soogans," of which there were usually two, were heavy cotton or wool batting quilted between covers of patched pants, coats and overcoats. The bed might also contain a blanket or two. The whole thing was easily "spooled"—rolled up and lashed—to be thrown into a wagon bed or lashed on a pack pony. It was known also as a "lay," "hot roll," "velvet couch," "shakedown," "crumb incubator" or "flea-trap."

Into the cowboy's bed went his "war sack," his life savings. It was his safety deposit box, and a man caught prowling through another's bedroll was looking for a fight.

When in bed on the roundup, if it rained, a cowboy pulled up the canvas flaps and remained as dry and snug "as a bug in a rug." The tarp also kept out snow, sleet and wind. Sometimes, when the cowboy awoke to find the weather freezing outside, he dressed à la

Pullman berth without quitting his warm blankets.

On the trail, or on roundup, the first thing a cowhand did after rising was to roll his bed and lash it. Then he took it over to the wagon and dumped it where it would be handy for loading. To leave it unrolled was a serious breach of etiquette, and a cowboy who did so might learn at the next camp that the bed wagon had arrived without his bed.

60. *The Cowboy's Work*

The Daily Round

NOT ONLY DID the cowboy need to be a good rider and roper, but he was expected to be proficient in many other duties incident to the raising of cattle. His assignment may have been as fence rider (inspect and repair fences), bog rider (yank out bogged-down cattle in swampy terrain), line rider (patrol a boundary line) or wrangler (handle horses). On occasion, blacksmithing, doctoring cattle, fighting fire, combating rustlers and poisoning wolves came within his sphere.

Usually he was known as a cowhand, or simply "hand," although he may have been referred to as a "saddle stiff," "cowpoke," "waddy," "leather pounder," "ranahan" or "saddle-warmer." In the brush country he was a "brush popper," "brush whacker" or "limb skinner." In the Northwest, "buckeroo"; on the southern border, "vaquero." More universally he was called a "cowpuncher."

Originally, a "cowpuncher" was one actively engaged in the shipment of cattle. To urge beef up the loading chute into a railway car he used a "prod," a pole about six feet long, with an iron spike at one end. Thus the designation "cowpuncher." Eventually the term came to mean cowboys in general and was shortened to plain "puncher."

Prior to the manufacture of barbed wire in 1874, there was no practical way of fencing the vast treeless plains. The cost of hauling wood from the East was prohibitive. So the job of keeping cattle within the bounds of the ranch belonged to the line rider. Cowmen maintained line camps along the borders of their range where one or two cowboys who could stand loneliness and their own cooking were quartered. Their job was to keep the boss's cattle on his graze and foreign cattle off it. In addition, they drove stock away from patches of loco weed and out of alkaline surface tanks, both of which poisoned them. In winter cowboys often had to chop watering holes through the ice. Weak animals that fell and could not get up had to be lifted by their tails—tailed up—until their feet were under them again. During storms cattle had to be driven into rough country where the hills and gulches protected them from icy blasts.

Outriders rode anywhere, although their duties were much the same as those of the line rider. The outrider watched the condition of the grass and water, as well as checking on the physical condition of the cattle. If cattle were overgrazing certain sections, he hazed them to new grass.

The cowboy had to be prepared to handle any emergency. If he found a cow which had lost her calf, he would rope her, tie her down and milk her, to keep her udder from spoiling. Sometimes he came across one that had been bitten by a rattler, or another whose nose was full of porcupine quills. A twitching hide and a peculiar odor told him that a cow was suffering from screw worms, which he would doctor.

Always he watched for tracks of livestock, scavengers or strange riders. Each told him a story as plainly as if it had been printed in a book. He might follow a wolf to its den and set out poison, or rope and pull out a cow mired in a bog hole. Perhaps he found an overgrown calf still nursing an emaciated mother. He blabbed the calf—clipped on its nose a thin board six by eight inches in size which prevented suckling but allowed grazing—in order that the mother would gain strength and survive the winter.

After barbed wire was strung across the range the line rider became a fence rider. Armed with combination pliers, wire cutter and hammer, plus a coil of wire, he started his patrol at daylight, riding ten or fifteen miles along the fence, watching for breaks. Lightning could destroy whole panels, and heavy rain could wash out a corner "dead man" or deepen a gully, permitting cattle to walk away. Bulls fighting from opposite sides of the fence would snap wires. Careless men left gates open. A fence rider was always busy.

Perhaps the most unpopular job was riding bog. In the spring, when cattle were weak from poor winter feed, swarms of heel flies tortured them. The cattle sought relief in bog holes, where they could stand in deep mud. Often, in their weakened condition, they bogged down and were trapped. For this reason, "bog riders" patrolled the miry sections to pull cattle to dry ground.

The bog rider needed a stout horse, a strong rope and unlimited perseverance. Usually two worked together, for the task was too strenuous for one man.

One roped the bogged cow. The other waded into the gumbo with a short-handled shovel and began to dig the cow's feet out. As he worked he had to keep his own feet moving in order to avoid bogging down himself. While he dug, his partner yanked on the rope until, eventually, the cow was extracted, usually too exhausted to move. When she showed signs of life, she was tailed up and, invariably, after gaining sufficient strength, showed her gratitude by charging the men who saved her.

Many rivers had quicksand bottoms, and western quicksand had peculiar properties. The tiny grains were flat and stuck together tenaciously. A man or beast could usually walk across quicksand, provided he kept going. But if he paused, he sank and found himself encased in sand as solid as concrete. Pulling upward increased the tension. The more a victim fought for freedom, the deeper he sank. A cow invariably struggled and sank to her belly. To rescue her, the cowboy often pulled off his pants and boots in order that the treacherous sand might not clutch and hold him, too. Bare-legged, he approached the cow and began "tromping" the sand which held her front legs. This forced the water between the tiny flat particles, which could only be separated by lateral flushing. As the sand softened, he pulled the cow's legs out, one at a time. Working fast, he next tried to loosen her hind legs before the front ones became bogged again. With the front legs free and the hind legs loosened, he slipped a rope around the cow's horns and tied it to the horn of his saddle. Then the cow horse went into action and hauled the victim out.

Roping

For the cowhand, roping ability was a "must," but few really mastered the art. Essentials for good roping were an ability to judge distance and a perfect sense of timing. Calculating the speed of a running steer and that of his horse, the roper had to judge the amount of rope to span the distance between them. Top ropers seemed to know by intuition the proper time to throw and place the loop under the cow's feet at the split second they came off the ground. Even with this intuition, the roper needed constant practice to coordinate his judgment of time and distance.

There were many kinds of loops, each with its own name and function. Some ropers used a small "dog loop," while others favored a large "Blocker loop," which turned over just before reaching its mark. This loop was named for John Blocker, a famous Texas cattleman.

The size and manner of throwing a loop depended upon what was to be caught and whether the roper was on foot or in the saddle.

On roundups the top roper of an outfit was usually chosen to catch each man's horse in the improvised rope corral. He used a fast loop, one strictly for a head catch, called the "hooleyann." This, instead of settling like a hoop over the marked animal's head, flipped into place at the last moment, making it harder even for the wisest horse to dodge it.

During branding season it was the roper's job to heel the calves from horseback and drag them to the branding fire. He quietly walked his pony among the calves and their mothers and threw his rope with a quick cast which did not disturb the herd. This was very different from rodeo calf roping, where calves were chased and wrestled down for a hogtie. On the open range where cattle could run, a "heel catch" was difficult. Calves scampering after their

Roping in a horse-corral. Engraving, after drawing by Frederic Remington.

Century Magazine, 1888

mothers usually had to be roped around the neck—an easier target than a pair of flying heels.

The roper whirled his lariat above his head when roping a large animal from horseback on the run. This kept the loop open and gave momentum for a long cast. The beginner usually whirled his arm off, but the expert whirled very little. The whirl was never used for roping in a corral, as it would excite the animals.

To rope and throw grown cattle, two men usually worked together. One roped the horns and held the animal, while the second man threw his loop around the heels. Then the two men rode in opposite directions stretching out the animal. A horn catch was better than a neck catch for stretching out a "critter" because it did not choke the animal and gave more leverage for throwing it on its side.

The most spectacular of all throws was called "going over the hump." With this catch a man on horseback could topple a full-grown steer. The trick was to cast a Blocker loop in such a way that it curled over a running steer's back and circled down just above the ground, where on the next bound both front feet would be thrust through it. Caught in this manner, the animal would somersault and lie breathless and prostrate.

When making this catch it was important to throw "over the hump" or withers, and snare the feet on the off-side. A near-side catch, although easier, gave a direct pull on the rope-horse, which sometimes upset him. "Over the hump," the direct pull and shock came against the steer's own body. Expert ropers enjoyed demonstrating their skill with this throw. Ranchers disapproved, because the violent roll-over sometimes crippled valuable beef.

Two methods were used to attach the lasso (from the Spanish *el lazo*—rope or snare) or lariat (Spanish *la reata*—rope) to the saddle horn. One was called the "dally," the other the "tie." The term "dally" came from the Spanish *dar la vuelta* (to give it a turn). American cowboys corrupted this to "dolly welter," which was soon shortened to "dally."

A dally-man took an encircling hitch around the saddle horn with the rope after the catch was made. The loose end was held in the roper's hand so that he could let it slip in case of emergency, or take it up shorter. This required a longer rope than that required by the tie-man, who made his throw after the rope had been tied to the horn.

For generations the argument as to the respective merits of tying and dallying has raged. As a rule, cowhands east of the Rockies were tie-men, while those west of the mountains dallied. Texans—tie men—would claim that they were no quitters. When they roped anything they figured to hang on to it. The Californian, a dally-man, could release a critter if it proved too much to handle. Another argument against dallying was the danger to a man's hand. When wrapping around the horn, fingers have been caught and snapped off when a big steer hit the other end of the rope.

The rope, dubbed by the cowboy his "line," "string," "hemp," "manila," "whale line," "lass rope," "catgut," "twine" or "hard-twist," was made of various materials. West of the Rockies, the sixty-foot rawhide reata was favored. In Texas, a thirty-five foot length of "manila" supplanted the rawhide. The Mexican "maguey" was made from the fiber of the century plant. It was a good rope, but too stiff for many ropers. A "hair rope" was never used as a *reata*. It kinked too easily and was too light to throw.

Rope lengths varied from twenty-five feet to sixty feet, the short rope being favored for

Harper's Weekly, 1883

The cowboys of Colorado—lassoing and branding calves. Drawing by W. A. Rogers.

steer-roping, calf-roping and corral work, and the longer rope for outside work. Thickness ran from three-eighths to seven-sixteenths of an inch.

Until they were stretched or suppled, ropes were too stiff. Once rendered supple a rope flowed with a hissing sound through the *hondo* (loop) and was said to "sing." When wet the best lariat became stiff as wire and could not be thrown.

Branding

Branding was a sweaty, dusty business. The bawling of indignant mothers mingled with the frightening blatting of calves; perspiration made rivulets down dust-coated riders' faces; red-hot irons sizzled on hides; horns rattled, dust fogged, loops sang.

But branding was an essential chore because the brand was the mark of ownership. Each rancher had his own brand, registered in the official "brand book." When an animal was sold, the new owner placed his band upon it. To prove the transfer was legitimate, the original owner "vented" (Spanish *venta*—sale) his own brand usually by burning a bar across it, thus executing a primitive bill of sale.

Brands took every conceivable form, the object being to obtain one that could not be easily worked over or altered. A brand might be any one of an endless combination of numbers, letters or monograms. Some unusual brands were: Walking R, Cut and Slash, Rocking H, Lazy Y, Forked Lightning, Drag 7, Hobbled O, Seven-up, Man in the Moon, Crazy Three, Window Sash, Currycomb, Scab 8. One outfit simply burned a straight line the length of the cow.

When framed, a brand was "boxed."

The ear cut, added to the brand to facilitate identification on the range, might be a "jinglebob," "jug handle," "swallow fork," "oversplit," "crop," "half-crop," "under-bit"—to name a few.

To impress the brand, a red-hot iron, fashioned in the shape desired, was used. Such a brand was known as a "set brand" or "stamp brand."

For branding on the range, the "running iron" was utilized. This was a straight poker or rod curved at one end, and was much in favor with rustlers, or cattle thieves—so much so that, in the seventies, Texas passed a law against its use. When a stranger was caught on the range with a running iron in his possession, chances were that a "necktie party" was imminent.

Today, because of the value of hides, there is usually only a single brand upon an animal. But in the old days each transfer of ownership meant additional brands until the cow's hide might be so thoroughly etched that it "looked like a brand book." Cattlemen in the gigantic area of Texas had so many identical brands it became necessary to add a "county brand"—a separate letter on the animal's neck. This showed the county in which this particular brand belonged to a certain man.

With the opening of the cattle trails from Texas to northern markets, a new branding problem arose. The animals in a trail herd, having been purchased from many owners, carried many brands. In fact, the same brand might be on cattle in two different trail herds when the owner of each had made purchases from the same ranchman. In case of a stampede or mixup between two herds of this kind it became impossible to determine the ownership of many animals. To prevent this a special "road brand," peculiar to each trail herd, was placed on the left side behind the shoulder of each one of them.

When calves were branded, two "ketch hands" usually rode into the herd to do the roping. Two "flankers" stood by the fire, ready to catch the calf. If heel-roped, it was already down, and easily stretched and held for branding. If neck-roped, it was toppled. The brander, or "iron man" yelled, "Hot iron!" The "iron tender," who heated the branding irons, came up at a trot from the fire with an iron glowing cherry-red.

While the brand was being burned on the prone calf's side, "butchers," or "knife men," cut the proper earmarks and sometimes dewlaps or wattles if the owner also used them for identification. The earmarks were especially important because a brand was sometimes hard to see on the range, but animals always turned their ears toward an approaching rider and their earmark was plainly visible. In addition to this mutilation, if the calf being branded was a male it was castrated and thus became a steer. Last came the "doctors," or "medicine men." With their pots of disinfectant, they smeared the wounds. Later on, there was also a "needle man" who quickly gave inoculations for blackleg and other diseases.

The whole process was somewhat gory, and when the calf scrambled up it usually slung its head and splattered everyone nearby with blood.

Frequently the mother came charging in. Then everyone was busy—dodging. It was every man for himself and the devil take the hindmost.

During branding season, the "tally man" was the only one with an easy job. He was usually an older man or one not physically fit for heavier work. When a roper dragged in a calf he shouted the brand on its mother. The tally man echoed this call and recorded it in his smudged book. On this count depended the owner's estimate of the season's profit.

Branding was no job for a weakling. There were perilous moments in the branding pen. The air was full of wood smoke, animal odors and dust, with never a dull moment for the sweaty, blood-splattered cowboys.

Breaking half-wild range mustangs into useful cow horses was a job usually handled by a specialist—the bronc rider, also known as "bronc peeler," "broncobuster," "bronc twister," "bronc snapper," "flash rider," "bull bat" or one of a dozen other cognomens.

Big outfits had their own "busters," but the small ranch usually hired a "contract buster" who broke horses at so much a head.

"Broncobusters" were in a class by themselves. Two important qualifications were necessary—nerve and self-assurance. If the buster ever became afraid of a horse, the animal knew it before he did, and came out on top.

The ways of a bucking horse were devious. No two animals bucked alike. A "high roller" leaped high into the air when bucking; a "weaver" had a peculiar weaving motion and his feet never struck the ground at the same time; the "pioneer bucker" bucked in circles and figure eights; the "sunfisher" twisted his body in midair until a rider expected him to fall on his side; the "spinner" went up and whirled backward; the "blind bucker" charged at and through anything; the "pile driver" humped his back and came down with all four legs as stiff as ramrods.

Just as no two horses bucked alike, no two busters broke horses alike. Most of the horse-breakers took great pride in their work, and it was an honor to be pointed out as the rider of a rough string. These riders did their best to make good cow horses and not spoil them, for no rancher wanted spoiled horses. A good buster used patience and took his time. The "twister" who took jobs at so much a head used rough methods and hurried the breaking process. For this reason, ranchers who wanted good cow horses put busters on the regular payroll.

Every cow outfit of any size had its own rough string. This was made up of broncs, young horses, old outlaws and spoiled horses that the average cowhand could not or would not ride. The professional broncobusters who hired out to such outfits were mainly young men. They had to be, because when they reached their thirties they could no longer take the punishment.

Usually the best breaking age for a range horse was between three and a half and four years old. Some ranchers liked to break their mounts at three, when the ponies had barely got their growth and were shedding the last of their colt teeth. These horses would then be turned

A dispute over a brand. Pen and ink by Frederic Remington.

Century Magazine, 1888

out to rest, harden and mature. When five years old they would be caught again and put at hard work for the rest of their lives.

"There was never a horse that couldn't be rode, there was never a rider who couldn't be throw'd," so one of the essential things a bronc rider had to learn was how to fall. He learned to kick free of the stirrups, to go limp and hit the ground rolling. He always knew he was leaving a jump or two before he actually went.

A buster was not ashamed of being thrown by a good bucker, but he always did his best to stay on, because horses that consistently threw their riders were apt to become outlaws. No matter what a buster's build, long or short, light or heavy, he had to be made of rawhide.

A horse's intelligence and gentleness developed in proportion to the extent of his contact with an understanding man. In the old days, when horses were caught, saddled, ridden and turned loose again without other handling, it was to be expected that many of a horse's good qualities had no opportunity to develop. Rough treatment by a brutal buster made bad horses. To know horses—how to care for them, keep them in good shape and, at the same time, get the most work out of them—was the real test of a good broncobuster, not his ability to wear a big hat and spurs, and "scratch the hell out of anything that wore hair."

61. *Horses*

Breeds

EARLY TEXAS HORSES were Spanish mustangs, small, but tough and wiry. When ranches were established in the Northwest, Texas cow horses went up the trails and soon were crossed with Clydesdale, Percheron, Morgan and other breeds. This resulted in larger, heavier horses that lacked the nimbleness of a good cow horse.

However, a small Texas horse that could carry a man on the Plains was not big and strong enough to carry him up and down the rough mountains of the Northwest. In Oregon, breeders used Clydesdale sires on small mares to produce heavy horses that in many cases were awkward and earned the name of "Oregon Bigfoots." In Montana and the Dakotas where Percheron sires were used, the issue were called "Percheron Puddin' Foots."

Oregon horsemen also produced the Appaloosa, an oddly colored blue roan with dark spots on its rump. Originally developed by the Nez Percé Indians, this breed had good size and endurance but never became popular as a cow horse. In too many cases the breeding stock was selected for color rather than for the horse's ability to do cow work.

Californians took pride in their palominos, whose coats glowed like newly minted gold. Several efforts were made to fix this color as a breed characteristic, but all failed. The beautiful color seemed to be the result of a cross between two basic pigments—sorrel and bay. So by the law of averages a breeder could never be sure that all the offspring of two palominos would inherit both the basic pigments and thus have the color desired. A certain percentage always seemed to inherit too much of one basic pigment or too much of the other.

The paint, calico or pinto, was a favorite of the Indians but failed to meet favor as a cow

A bucking bronco. Engraving, after drawing by Frederic Remington.

horse. Most cowmen preferred mounts of solid colors—browns, bays or sorrels. Duns, or zebra duns, were thought to possess unusual endurance.

The Quarter Horse, most popular cowboy mount in the mid-twentieth century, was unknown in early days. A sire named Janus, with Quarter Horse characteristics, was reported in colonial Virginia in 1752. In the 1850's two stallions—Steel Dust from Illinois and Shilo from Tennessee—possessed outstanding ability to run a quarter-mile in record time. These animals and their get were subjects of conversation in cow camps for decades, but little is really known about them. No record of colts by either has been preserved, but for generations Texas horse dealers clinched a sale by declaring "He's a Steel Dust."

In 1940 an official registry of Quarter Horses was begun, with many pedigrees going back in an uncertain way to one or both of the two famous sires.

Often a top cowhand judged a ranch by its horses and accepted or rejected an offer of a job accordingly. Allot him a good string of horses and he would endure almost any hardship. But if the horses were inferior he would soon drift to another ranch.

The number of horses allotted to each cowboy as his string varied according to the size of the ranch, nature of the terrain and work to be done. Generally, he received from seven to ten. This would include morning horses, afternoon horses, a good rope horse, a cutting horse and, in the trail days, a night horse and a good river horse. Each man usually had several half-broken horses which were used on short rides and gradually broken.

The Remuda

Since every cowboy had a string of horses and could ride only one at a time, the remainder were called the *remuda*. The word was pronounced "remootha" in the Southwest, but most Texas cowmen merely spoke of the "hosses." Northwestern ranchers called the *remuda* a "cavvy," short for the Spanish *caballada*—a horse herd. The expression "saddle band" was also commonly used.

On some ranches, at the beginning of the season, a "choosin' match" was held for the horses. The foreman had first pick. Next came the older hands. Finally, the new hands, in order of hiring, chose theirs.

Each man's string of horses was his responsibility. Taking a horse from him was the same as asking him to quit. A newly hired cowboy was allotted a string. He was told nothing about them and he asked no questions. Information was taken as an offense, implying lack of confidence in the newcomer's knowledge of horses.

Any cowhand who rode or interfered with another's horse was asking for trouble. If a rider quit, or was fired, the horses in his string were not used until another rider took his place.

The boss not only counted the *remuda* every day to check up on the wrangler, but also watched each rider to see how he handled his mounts. If he saw some animals developing "set fasts" from a back-eating saddle, or noticed too many spur marks, the puncher was invited to saddle his private mount and drift.

Most cowboys loved their horses and treated them well. The hardest experience a trail hand ever underwent was to ride his string up the trail and have the boss sell them with the cattle at delivery.

Century Magazine, 1888

Bronco busters saddling. Pen and ink by Frederic Remington.

Most *remudas* contained only geldings. These made the best cow horses, for stallions fought and disturbed a peaceful *remuda*. Mares were apt to be bunch quitters, too temperamental under the saddle and a constantly disturbing element.

In the fall, when the work was done, a few mounts were held on the ranch. These were fed grain to keep them strong, but most of the horses were turned out to winter on the range, to rest and heal their scars. Before turning them loose, the boss checked their ages, condition, feet.

Out on winter range the horses grew long coats of hair, but their look of well-being was deceptive. They were really weak and when driven up in the spring had to be fed hay before they could be ridden for any length of time.

Every horse in the *remuda* had its name, and every horse was well known to any cowhand who had been on the payroll long. Some of the names were printable, others not. A few samples: Sassy Sam, Few Brains, Old Guts, Leapin' Lena, Dough Gut, Panther, Widow Maker, Rambler, Stockings, Sunfisher, Bullet, Churn Head, Cannon Ball. The name was usually descriptive.

Because roundup work was hard on horses, they were changed three times each twenty-four hours. According to the duty the cowboy was to perform, he switched from circle horse to cutting horse, rope horse to night horse.

Despite what the fiction writers say, the cowboy usually called his horse a horse, or cow horse, and not a "cow pony."

A good horse possessed strength, sure-footedness and an eye for the trail. Above all, he needed good sense. He inherited the gift of keeping one eye for the cow ahead and one for the trail. If he fell, he would be eliminated, for nothing on the range injured as many men as falling horses. And nothing else was more feared by the cowhand, except being dragged.

Western horses had an individuality and a self-reliance not often found in horses raised in confinement. It was not necessary to guide them around treacherous holes or to look out for stones and other obstacles. When led to a strange watering place they satisfied themselves that the bank was not boggy, and before they trusted their weight to the mud they would test it, first with one foot and then another.

There was as much difference in horses as there was in cowboys. Though one horse might look very much like another, each had its individuality. Top horses were as scarce as top hands, but seldom was a top hand found without a top horse.

Types

The pride of every puncher was his horse. He spent more time in the saddle than he did on his feet, and often his life was dependent on the intelligence and reliability of his mount. Deprived of a horse he was at a total loss; there was no greater disgrace than for a cowboy to be "fired" and compelled to leave a ranch on foot.

When cowboys gathered around a campfire, or congregated anywhere, talk invariably, sooner or later, turned to horses. A cowboy's stories of the skill, understanding and ability of mounts he had ridden were liable to approach fantasy, yet he would solemnly swear that they were "gospel truth."

In cowboy vocabulary there were many types of horses. The "mustang" (Spanish— *mesteño*) was a wild horse. In Oregon it was called a "cayuse," after the Cayuse tribe of Indians. "Bronco" (Spanish—*broncho*), also, was a wild or semiwild horse. The word was often contracted to "bronc."

A wild mare was a "mockey." A "cow horse" was one experienced in cattle work. "Stock horses" were brood mares and colts. Young horses, colts and fillies were sometimes called *potros.* "Work horses" were used in harness. A *manada* was a band of mares with a stallion. "Fuzz-tails," or "fuzzies," were range horses. "Willow-tails" were horses, usually mares, with long, loose, coarse tails; conversely, a horse whose tail had very little hair was a "rattail." A trained cow horse with demonstrated skill in cutting and roping was a "top" horse. Most horses were good only for "day-herding" and "riding circle." Horses with little intelligence were "churn-heads," "jug-heads" or "crock-heads." A "cutting horse" was one trained to separate and drive from a herd the cattle indicated by its rider. Another high-type horse was the "rope horse," as was the "night horse"—an animal which understood herding cattle in the dark. Good night horses, along with cutting and roping horses, were treasures beyond price.

A "spoiled horse" was a man-made outlaw, spoiled in breaking. A bad horse was referred to as a "salty bronc," and was "snuffy," "spooky" or "snaky."

A broken-down horse was a "plug." He could be "shad-bellied," "slab-sided," "crowbait" or "buzzard bait." Bloated on grass, a horse was "grass-bellied," "wind-bellied," "whey-bellied" or "pot-gutted."

The question of whether the qualities of a horse could be told by his color will probably never be settled. A white horse, "chalk white," was likely to suffer from weakness as the result of inbreeding, usually pink-eyed the glare of sun on snow blinded it; a "pinto," while hardy,

In with the horse herd. Engraving, after drawing by Frederic Remington.

never attained great size; black horses were said to suffer from heat; bays were regarded as the most vicious; chestnuts, tenderest of skin.

One thing was sure, when a cowboy was discussing his favorite mount it was "so gentle y'u could stake it to a hairpin," it was the fastest "that ever looked through a bridle," and "it could turn on a quarter and give you fifteen cents change."

Cutting Horses

The top-ranking horse in any outfit was one highly trained for cutting-out cattle. The coveted title of "cutting horse" came only after years of training and experience, and the cowboy who could boast of such a horse in his string was the envy of his comrades.

When a good cutting horse began his work he was made to understand which animal was to be cut from the herd for sale or any other reason. Horse and rider quietly urged the animal to the edge of the herd and here the cutting horse proved his worth. A sudden dash was necessary to frighten the animal out of the herd, and quick turns must be made to keep it from getting back. The cow was sure to duck and dodge, trying desperately to rejoin the herd. A well-trained horse anticipated every move and possessed the speed and action necessary to spin and turn faster than the cow. It took an expert horseman to sit a good cutter. A green rider landed in the dirt.

One of the chief qualities of a cutting horse was his ability to work on a loose rein. Many horses became so proficient that they could cut without a bridle. Rarely did a good cutter need any cuing. If the rider did give any help it was done with words, leg action or a slight movement of the rein.

Rope Horses

Another important mount in cattle work was the rope horse. The best roper, no matter how expert he might be, owed much of his success to the training of the animal he rode. It was much more dangerous to rope from horseback than on foot. A cow could always be turned loose when roping on foot, but when a roped steer and a horse got tangled in a mix-up the man did not have much chance to leave the party. Yet roping from horseback was necessary, even in a corral, for grown cattle would attack a man on foot.

When the roper loosened the looped thong, or "nigger catcher," or unbuckled the strap that held his coiled rope below the base of the horn and shook out the loop, the first-class roping horse knew what was expected of him and watched for the animal to be caught. Like a bullet he would race to the side of the cow selected, never past her, and there he would maintain position until the rider cast his loop. If the throw missed, the horse would drop behind, but if the rope settled properly, he displayed his training. A side pull might jerk down both horse and rider, so the horse always faced the roped animal. A touch on the side of the neck with the reins caused him to whirl instantly toward the catch. At the slightest pressure of the bit he sat back, hind feet well under him, forefeet braced out in front, to receive the shock.

A good rope horse never allowed the rope an inch of slack to wind him up and never allowed the roped animal to get a side run on him. Through experience he knew that such blunders would have dire consequences. The instant the roped animal fell, a good horse would pull against the rope and keep it taut. This prevented the cow from getting up. Even if the rider dismounted and left the horse alone, he would maintain that pull on the rope.

Night Horses

Certain mounts in the *remuda* were known as night horses. The old-time cowhand selected them with care. The attributes he looked for were gentleness, sure-footedness, dependability, keen eyesight and a sense of direction.

A night horse's ability to detect an animal in the dark was uncanny. He could see a single cow straying from the herd at night and turn her back without guidance. He could find his way back to the wagon in the darkest night. Many a cowboy, dozing in the saddle as he jogged around the sleeping herd during his two-hour watch, has been aroused by the mount between his knees making a sudden start to "head" some cow that was escaping.

A seasoned night horse was likely to know within a few minutes when the two-hour watch terminated, and he would convey his knowledge to the rider by pulling on the bit and shaking his head. It was said that some night horses could be depended upon as certainly as reading the stars.

It was the horse, not the rider, who had to know what to do during a stampede at night when thunder and lightning boomed and crackled over a frightened herd. The rider, racing along a flank of the surging, horn-clacking torrent of cattle, gave his horse its head and depended upon the animal to see him through. At these times, a sure-footed night horse was worth its weight in gold.

On nights when bad weather threatened and the bedded cattle were nervous, the night horses belonging to off-duty riders stood saddled and tied to the wagon, where they were instantly available to stop a stampede. But in good weather, unless an outfit was shorthanded and the herd they were handling was still jumpy from having stampeded recently, each man unsaddled his night horse and picketed him where the grass was good so that the dependable animal could get all the rest and feed possible.

Swimming Horses

In the old trail days there were many rivers to cross on the Long Drive. A herd starting from San Antonio and heading for Abilene, Kansas, over the Chisholm Trail had to cross the Red, the Cimarron, the Canadian, the Arkansas, or any one of half a dozen other rivers up to a mile wide. Spooky longhorns did not often take kindly to water. The cowboys swam alongside the serpentine column of heavily breathing brutes, guiding the leaders. Great care

Cutting out a steer. Engraving, after drawing by Frederic Remington.

Century Magazine, 1888

had to be taken to prevent the swimming beasts from turning and beginning to mill, for this could quickly change the herd into a confused, frantic mob, in which many would drown while the few survivors crawled out of the water on both banks, many miles downstream.

Again, much depended upon the horse. The steady night horse was a necessity, as was the "smart" cutting horse, but the river horse that enjoyed swimming and knew what to do in swift, deep water, was in a class by himself.

Such horses had a special fitness for river work, for swimming alone, for leading or driving a herd through the water, for anything that had to be done when water was high or deep or dangerous. They seemed to understand a river and know where the water was of swimming depth, where the bottom was firm and safe and where it was treacherous. Besides being strong, a good river horse needed to be gentle.

Some horses swam high in the water and men could remain on their backs. Others swam low and the rider had to slip out of the saddle, keeping one arm across the horse's withers. Guiding a swimming horse was risky business. Splashing a little water on the side of his face would turn him, but care had to be taken not to turn him too much because a swimming horse could be upset easily. To use the reins was even more dangerous. With the usual curb bit, a swimming horse could easily be pulled over backward, and when he came up the best horse was liable to get excited and lose his head. Then he would start pawing the water in a desperate effort to climb out. If he saw his rider, the unlucky puncher was almost sure to be pawed under. Every rider knew that the graves of trail hands decorated the banks of every river on the Long Trail.

62. *Mavericks*

"MAVERICKS" WERE UNBRANDED animals of unknown ownership. Hence, in the early days, it was a case of "finders keepers." An ambitious puncher could build up his modest herd by slapping his brand on any maverick that came his way. In fact, it is said that many riders who later became prosperous and respected ranchers made their starts in this dubious fashion. The big outfits resented seeing any man appropriate calves belonging to their cows as soon as they were weaned. They resented it still more when these interlopers killed one of their cows that had a big unbranded calf and then claimed it as a maverick. Yet the temptation to indulge in such practices became so great that many big outfits denied employment to any puncher who had cattle of his own. In addition, several attempts, none too successful, were made to limit the appropriation of mavericks to the users of the range on which they were found.

Many and varied stories have been told regarding the origin of the word "maverick." The authenticated story associates the name with Samuel A. Maverick, a citizen of San Antonio, and one of the signers of the Texas Declaration of Independence. As a lawyer, not a cattleman, he took over a bunch of cattle for a debt before the Civil War and placed them in charge of a Negro on the San Antonio River. The Negro failed to brand the increase of the herd and allowed the cows to wander far and wide. In 1855, Maverick sold the entire outfit to Toutant de Beauregard, a thrifty man who instigated a systematic roundup. Whenever Beauregard's riders found an unbranded animal, they claimed it to be a Maverick, impressed Beauregard's brand upon it and drove it in. The increase in the original herd was said to be remarkable. Ultimately, the term came to embrace all unbranded cattle.

63. *The Roundup*

IN THE OLD WEST, roundups were held twice a year—in the spring and in the fall. The range was open to anybody who had cattle, and the owners cooperated in these two big annual events. The spring roundup was held for the purpose of branding calves. At the fall roundup—in reality, the ranchers' harvest—beef were gathered for shipment. This was the time when cattle were turned into the cash necessary for continuing the business. Calves born since the spring roundup were also branded on this "fall ride."

One of the bigger outfits usually provided wagons and supplies for these two annual events. Every ranchman attended personally or sent a cowboy. Each man brought his own bedroll and a string of some ten horses. These remounts were put in charge of a wrangler who accompanied the wagons. An experienced cowman—usually a foreman for one of the big outfits—was selected to be "roundup captain" or "wagon boss." Once chosen, his word was law, and the owners of other ranches as well as all the cowboys took orders from him without question. At the end of the roundup all expenses—wages for cook and wranglers and cost of groceries—were prorated among the cattle owners, each paying according to the number of his cattle on the range which had been worked.

To determine the exact number of cattle a man owned was always difficult. A ranchman's account books showed how many he had turned out on the range, but as these animals soon became half-wild, his loss by theft or death had to be estimated. A roundup might gather a thousand cattle in a day. These cattle carried many brands, but they were all mixed together, so that it was impossible to know how many belonged to each ranchman. The cattle could not be separated for a count, since there were no pens or pastures in which they could be held. The best estimate of the number of cows a man owned was made in the spring when a "tally man" kept count of each calf. Presumably a man owned 10 to 15 per cent more cows than calves, but this was only a guess. Yet in spite of the uncertainty of this method of counting, herds were often sold "by book count" as there was no other way of estimating the number.

Barbed-wire fences, which enabled owners to keep their cattle in separate pastures, ended the need for roundups. The system, in its picturesque and exciting form, originated in Texas, but because the land there was owned by the state instead of the federal government and soon went under fence in private hands, the old-fashioned roundup disappeared from that state before it did on the public domain of the Northwest.

While the roundup system lasted, stockmen often organized associations which specified the dates when roundups would be held. In some instances the association even went so far as to decide who could ride with the roundup and who could not. Men suspected of being dishonest were ruled out. This amounted to putting them out of business, because a cattle owner unable to gather his beef and brand his calves could not last long. Small ranchmen often complained that they were barred from the roundup not on account of dishonesty but because the big outfits did not want the little herds to be eating all the grass. Disagreements of this kind were often the basis of range wars. Eventually the small men—the nesters, as homesteaders were called—cut up the open range with so many fences that an open roundup became impossible.

64. *A Day with the Roundup*

THE WORKDAY ON a roundup began with the buzz of the cook's alarm clock before the first streak of dawn. In the dark, he lighted his lantern, built a fresh fire on the previous night's white ashes and hung the five-gallon coffeepot on a pothook suspended from the potrack—an iron bar between two uprights extending the length of a shallow ditch built for the cooking fire.

An unwritten law of the range prohibited any man from complaining about another's cooking, but if meals were not ready on time hell would pop. Knowing this, every roundup cook worked under pressure. As soon as the fire blazed along his trench he set the heavy Dutch ovens and their lids where they would heat. Into each oven he dropped a hunk of beef tallow. Next he began slicing big steaks of meat, and "building" his biscuits—usually with sour dough and soda—in a big dough pan on the chuck wagon's endgate, built to let down like a table. Immediately above it was a cupboard holding tinware or agateware cups and plates, "reloading tools" (knives, forks and spoons), salt, sugar, "java" (Arbuckle's XXX was commonly used), dishrags, towels, soap, etc.

After the beefsteaks were salted, the cook slipped them into a hot Dutch oven. He then pinched biscuits off one end of the newly made loaf of dough, rounded each one between his palms, dipped it in melted tallow and plumped it into a bread oven. When the bottom was filled, he set the lid in place and shoveled hot coals around and over it. As the first batch baked, he prepared a second.

In the meantime, the nighthawk, who had been herding horses out on the flats, would begin gathering his *remuda*. By this time, camp was stirring. The men were rising from their tarpaulin-wrapped beds on the ground, unrolling the trousers they had used as pillows, thrusting their legs into them, pulling on their boots and rolling their beds into neat spools ready for the wagons.

When the sky was paling milky-white, the cook would shout: "Come and get it, before I throw it out!"

The first men to reach the wash basins scrubbed their hands and faces; the others drew water from the cook's barrel into cups and poured it into one another's hands. Here and

Century Magazine, 1888

In a stampede. Engraving, after drawing by Frederic Remington.

there an independent cowboy would hold a cup of water between his knees, slosh it into his cupped hands and give his face a refreshing douse.

Next, a common towel was passed around—soon wet. A comb for those who did not carry the pocket variety also circulated.

Each man helped himself to plate, cup and tools. Then they lined up along the potrack, speared a steak from one Dutch oven and a biscuit from another. Sizzling hot tallow made good "sopping" for the bread. Sometimes there would be a kettle of stewed apricots, cooked the previous day. Their plates filled, the cowhands sat on the ground, cross-legged, tailor-fashion and ate.

As each man finished, he flipped the dregs from his coffee onto the ground and dropped his dirty dishes in the "roundup pan"—a big dishpan set out for the purpose. To neglect placing dishes in this pan was a cardinal sin.

When the *remuda*—the saddle horses—dashed up, the men who had finished eating improvised a corral by stretching ropes from hand to hand and forming a rough square. Such an enclosure might seem flimsy for penning spirited horses, and a tenderfoot might wonder why the animals did not run against the ropes and jerk them from the men's hands. This seldom happened. The horses were schooled to respect a rope. If one did run over or under the stretched rope, he set the stage for his own downfall. A roper would overtake the truant and rope him by the forefeet. This meant a nasty fall, or even a broken neck, but even that was preferred to a horse with the habit of running through *remuda* ropes.

One or two of the best ropers would catch horses from the *remuda*. Too many flying ropes would stampede even the best-trained horses. Most of the cowboys stood with their bridles in their hands and told the roper which horse they wanted. The roper flipped an accurate loop past a dozen tossing heads, and over as many backs, to land around the neck of the animal desired. If the roper missed, the horse might dodge, twist and turn to escape a second throw. Eventually, though, the loop found its mark, and the snared horse came out meekly.

As each man's horse was caught, he bridled it and led it to his saddle. Some horses shied when the blanket was placed on their back. Most, however, stood patiently, although many protested with a nip of the teeth toward the rider when the cinch tightened. If the freshly saddled horse stood with a hump in his back, indicating a desire to buck, he would be led a few paces before mounting. Often some young prankster's horse became uncorked and bucked through the crowd, even across the cook-fire, scattering kettles and equipment. The cook's language was usually unprintable, but this rough fun was part of life on the roundup.

By sunup all were mounted and the *remuda* was driven out to graze under the guardianship of the "wrangler," as the day herder is called. The cowboys, in a column of two's, galloped off to "ride circle."

In the lead, the boss rode with the man he considered best acquainted with the particular part of the range being worked. Every mile or two the column stopped. Two men were detached with orders to gather all the cattle they could find and start them toward the day's bunch ground. So the column gradually dissolved.

Back at the wagons, as soon as the riders left, the cook washed dishes and the nighthawk dried them. Together the two tossed bedrolls into the bed wagon, slammed shut the endgate over the chuck wagon cupboard, wrapped the sooty Dutch ovens in burlap sacks and stowed them away with the potrack. The teams were harnessed, four horses to each wagon, and they headed for the next selected camping site where the cattle being gathered would be bunched. The cook led with the chuck wagon. The nighthawk followed with the bed wagon. The wrangler, with the *remuda*, brought up the rear. On the way, they tossed dry wood on board to be used for the dinner fire.

At the new camp the teams were unhooked. If sufficient wood had not been picked up, the wrangler and nighthawk dragged in a few dry logs at the end of their lariats. The cook dug a trench for his fire, set up his potrack, put on the coffeepot and began preparing dinner.

Now, at last, the nighthawk had time to rest. He usually crawled into the shade under the wagon and fell asleep, his head on someone else's bedroll. With his job he had no use for a bed.

Far out on the horizon encircling the wagons pillars of dust disclosed where cattle were moving. The dust clouds converged slowly on the wagons like wheel spokes to a hub. Before long the cattle themselves could be seen, long strings of them coming in to the bunch ground. By noon the animals were rounded up several hundred yards from the wagons in one seething bedlam of bellowing cows, bawling calves, rumbling hoofs and clacking horns. Bulls that had been separated on the plains met one another and fought furiously. Battles between these beasts were dangerous to the onlooker; for when the loser admitted defeat he turned and ran with blind desperation, bowling over everything in his path.

As soon as the cattle settled down, the boss designated two men to guard the herd and ordered the rest in for dinner. This was the signal for the younger men, still high-spirited after six or seven hours in the saddle, to race for the wagons, testing the speed on their mounts.

Riders unsaddled, let their tired horses roll and then join the nearby *remuda*. Now the cowboys would "grab a root and hog down" their dinners. The nighthawk crawled out from under the wagon to eat and joke with them.

Before the meal was over, the wrangler brought in the *remuda,* and it was corralled once more by stretched ropes. This time "cutting horses" were called for. With these, the real work of the day began—calf branding or cutting out beef for shipment. As a rule, only three

Among the cowboys—betting on the bullfight. Drawing by W. A. Rogers.

Harper's Weekly, 1880

or four men did the cutting while the rest remained on the herd's edge holding the animals together. Too many "cutters" would needlessly disturb the cattle, separate calves from their mothers and make the bunch harder to hold.

There were no pens or corrals on the open range, so the beef selected were driven into the "cut," a small group of animals held separately. Beef animals, being fat, were usually the most rollicking critters in the herd. They would run and buck and were difficult to hold in a small bunch by themselves. So the usual way to start a "cut" was with a decoy of sedate cows. Fat steers would stay with them instead of racing back to the big herd.

When enough beef had been cut into these decoys to make a true "cut herd," the cows were separated and driven back.

While this work proceeded, the nighthawk took a second nap and the cook enjoyed his first leisure of the day—if washing dishes, dragging in wood and filling water kegs could be called leisure.

Moreover, a good roundup cook changed the monotonous diet by preparing soup and stews which were eaten with relish despite their unprintable names. A really imaginative cook occasionally stirred up pastries with dried fruit (the most popular was plum duff) or put up some beans to soak, though on the high plains beans were "out" as it took too long for them to cook.

The cutting or branding on the bunch ground finished, the herd was pointed away from the direction to be rounded up the following day. With wild shouts and whirling ropes they were given a scare that started them on the run. Then the riders returned to the wagons, unloaded their beds, selected suitable sleeping spots and unrolled the tarps.

This was the time of day to kill a beef. A small animal was usually selected—a two-year-old heifer or fat, dry cow served best. The boss asked a good shot to do the job. If the marksman's shot was true, the animal collapsed—stone dead. Several cowboys ran in, bled her and began skinning. Flies and yellow jackets usually gathered as the men worked but disappeared with the setting sun. Finally, the naked carcass was halved with the cook's ax. Each half was hung from an erected wagon tongue, where the meat chilled during the night, and was ready to be eaten in the morning. During the heat of the day the meat was wrapped in tarpaulins. The cook's bed provided extra good insulation. At night the beef was hung out again to chill.

Before dark the *remuda* was driven in for the third time. Night horses were roped, then picketed out or tied to the bed wagon. The wrangler turned the *remuda* over to the night-hawk, who trotted off behind the freed animals for his lonely vigil.

On clear evenings the roundup hands would generally rest for an hour after eating. Stories of fights, bucking contests and chases after wild cattle were told. Contrary to TV programs, a guitar seldom, if ever, appeared. These instruments were too big and fragile to be taken on the roundup. Occasionally someone brought along an accordion, but a mouth organ or jew's-harp was more common. Each man in the circle was called on to play, sing or recite a piece. Then the riders stumbled off to beds under the stars, but never for a full night's rest. Two at a time, they were called to take their place at guarding the herd.

The stars paled and the cook's clock would again raucously salute the dawn. Another day—another dollar!

65. *Famous Ranches and Ranchmen*

"At SADDLE-UP TIME he passed in his checks with a quirt on his wrist and his belly full of black coffee." This would be a fitting epitaph for some of the grim old cattlemen who owned and operated big western ranches. Another epitaph, equally fitting, might be: "No one ever left his home cold or hungry."

Many of the old-time rangemen made their money by hard knocks, hard riding and good luck. They understood cattle and how to handle them. With endless toil and close figuring, they built large herds that in some cases were fiddled away by the ranchman's son and the first dance-hall girl he met.

However, it would be a mistake to believe these examples were typical of all ranchmen. Theodore Roosevelt was a cattleman in South Dakota for sixteen years, running hundreds of head—and losing $23,000 on an $82,000 investment before he sold out in 1899. Compared to others, he paid a cheap price for the experience.

Dozens of other "gentlemen" adventurers tried their hands at ranching. An expansive, good-looking promoter named Alexander H. Swan, who was well-acquainted in Europe and never did anything by halves, raised $3,000,000 in Great Britain for the purchase of a ranch with headquarters on the Chugwater, fifty miles north of Cheyenne, Wyoming. He held title to less than ten square miles, although he had made a small down payment on an additional thirty-eight square miles of railroad land along the Union Pacific. With these holdings, which he had never seen except on a map, he turned loose 120,000 cattle on the public domain stretching from the Union Pacific tracks north to the Platte River, and from Ogallala, Nebraska, west to Fort Steele, Wyoming, a range of from 19,000 to 20,000 square miles. "Free grass," he told investors, "think of it, absolutely free, gentlemen!"

The hard winter of 1886–87 practically wiped out the Swan herd. When spring came that year a man could ride day after day without ever losing sight of a bloating carcass. The bankrupt Swan Company was reorganized in 1888 by John Clay, the fox-hunting son of a well-to-do Scots farmer. He had grazed cattle in the old country, possessed a gift for banking and a weakness for literature. He enjoyed writing and liked to quote poetry as he rode across the rolling plains. A few neighboring critics laughingly remembered that although John Clay came out of Scotland, nothing—not even success—took Scotland out of John Clay. His mother, they said, packed a lunch for him when he boarded the ship in Glasgow, and he still had some of it when he arrived in Cheyenne.

Homesteaders soon began taking up claims on the Swan range, and John Clay realized that his grassland empire was doomed. Although he sympathized with the big cattlemen who fought "nesters" in the Johnson County War, he did not join them. Instead he established a commission firm in the Chicago stockyards, loaned money to some of the small ranchers

Harper's Weekly, 1888

Thanksgiving at the ranch. Engraving, after drawing by Frederic Remington.

who were destroying him and, in addition to collecting good interest on his loans, realized nice commissions for selling their beef.

In 1924 he liquidated the Swan outfit. Living in a magnificent Chicago home, the eighty-year-old man wrote that there were only two places in the world where he really cared to be—in the Cheviot Hills of Scotland or "along Chugwater's brimming tide."

Homesteaders in the Southwest did not inevitably nibble away the big ranches, as they did farther north. Down there ranchmen held title to their grazing lands and were not dependent on the public domain. In New Mexico, Arizona and California great Spanish grants had been given to graziers. In Texas the open country belonged to the state, not the nation, and could be disposed of as the legislature thought fit.

Of all the Texas ranches the most extraordinary was the XIT, with 3,050,000 acres along the western border of the Panhandle. This property was roughly two hundred miles long and averaged twenty-seven miles in width. It was owned by four Chicagoans who, according to the understatement of neighbors, eventually learned to tell the difference between a horse and a cow. Their acquisition of this acreage is unique in ranch history.

In the late 1870's Texas wanted to erect the finest capitol in the nation and had no money to pay for it. The administration offered to deed a gigantic block of Panhandle land to anyone who would build it according to their specifications. Four Chicagoans who had never seen the Panhandle accepted the proposition. Three of them were rich. One was Amos Babcock, a big wheel in Illinois Republican politics who liked to consider himself a maker of Presidents. Another was Charles B. Farwell, a Republican member of Congress who aspired to be a Senator, and then a President. His brother, John V. Farwell, was Chicago's Merchant Prince who gave Marshall Field his start. The fourth member of the partnership, Abner Taylor, was a practical builder rather than a capitalist. He supervised the construction of the capitol built at Austin according to the specifications at an estimated cost of $3,000,000.

The partners had little trouble complying with their contract. Texas got its capitol, but the four speculators had considerable trouble getting their money back from the 3,050,000 acres of land they received in payment. The original plan was to parcel out the newly acquired grasslands to farmers, but when advertising failed to attract buyers, the owners decided, in 1885, to remedy their bargain by pouring more good money after the bad. They spent $7,000,000 on "bob-wire" to fence their empty empire, stocked it with 150,000 cattle and employed B. H. ("Bar-B-Q") Campbell to run the outfit which they called the XIT.

Campbell was a small, wiry man, with considerable experience raising livestock in Illinois. He knew cows but he did not know cowboys—or how to handle either on the range. One of his first acts was to distribute a manual of ranch rules. All employees were prohibited from carrying six-shooters, playing cards or indulging in any form of gambling. They were warned that they must never kick a horse, beat it over the head with a quirt, or spur it in front of the saddle. "Company horses" must never be raced or used to chase buffalo, antelope or wild horses. Most remarkable of all, ranch hands were directed never to kill strays or mavericks for beef. "The XIT Ranch will eat XIT beef or go without," this order stated specifically.

In a country where it was considered poker to eat a neighbor's beef and even brand his weaned calf if you saw it first, Bar-B-Q Campbell's rules were treated with hilarious contempt. Some said, "He's too honest for this country." Others complained that he was crooked at heart—but smooth. Nothing was ever proved against him, but several known cow-thieves were on his payroll. This may well have been due to innocent ignorance, but one thing is certain: The XIT Ranch never made a penny and the four owners never got so much as a porterhouse steak from it.

In 1901 they decided to liquidate. Times had changed. Artesian water had been found and farmers were now eager to pay good prices for the land. After sixteen bad years the owners sold out in small tracts which netted them a total profit far beyond their original dreams.

Another famous ranch, the JA, was also on the Panhandle. It was much smaller, running only 100,000 cattle on 1,335,000 acres. Like the XIT, it had been financed by outside or eastern capitalists. The manager and part-owner, Charles Goodnight, was famous for preserving the buffalo and for the Goodnight-Loving Trail. Born in Illinois in 1838, he had gone to Texas with his parents when he was seven years old. Charlie climbed to success the hard way. Taking to guns and horses as naturally as he did to grits, he fought Indians and served in the Texas Rangers. By leasing a herd of cattle, he became a cowman in his own right, and eventually owned ranches in Texas, New Mexico and Colorado. His genius for finding new ranges and stocking them became proverbial. According to one story, some cowboys, at the turn of the century, were discussing Admiral Peary's efforts to reach the North Pole. One puncher asked, "What does Peary want to go there for? What does he think he'll find?"

"You know damn well what he'll find," another replied. "He'll find Uncle Charles Good-night there with a herd of cows."

In middle age, Charlie was a 200-pound bull of a man. He had bowlegs, penetrating eyes and an aggressive head which hung low, like a buffalo's, between rounded shoulders. With strangers he was gruff and irritable, never got along well with neighbors, did not want them anyway, and could not speak without swearing. He believed that the dinner table was a place to eat, not to talk. When the plate of hot bread was too far away for him to spear a bun with his fork he might bark, "Pass the sonsabitchin' biscuits," but that was all. Yet, with all his profanity, he professed to be a religious man and used his money to build two churches. When asked what church he belonged to he said, "I don't know, but it's a goddamned good one."

He believed frugality to be one of the secrets of success, said that he watched every penny and never let the cook throw out the back door what he brought in the front. Cowboys used to scatter nails along the path to the bunkhouse for the fun of watching the elderly man stoop to pick up every one of them. However, with all his frugality, he spent $25,000 to establish Goodnight College, and gambled a fortune on experimental breeding of black Angus cattle with buffalo to produce cattaloes.

Always quick-tempered, he stormed at photographers who tried to snap his picture. Once a reporter went to the ranch for an interview. He found Goodnight fixing a gate and approached him breezily with, "Colonel [a complimentary title] Goodnight, Brown's my name."

Charlie Goodnight straightened up, turned around and roared, "What in hell can I do about it? I didn't name you."

Uncle Charlie survived for ninety-three years, riding over the hill to the land of no return in 1929. Solid and dependable as the Rockies, and explosive as a thunderstorm at timberline, Charles Goodnight was truly the rangeland's Grand Old Man.

An equally successful but much less picturesque cattleman operated the famous Matador Ranch with its breeding grounds in Texas and fattening ranges in Montana. This outfit, a British syndicate established in 1879, showed unusually steady profits, paying stockholders 15 per cent on their investments over a period of thirty years. Such unprecedented performance was due to the shrewd management of Murdo Mackenzie, a wealthy, middle-class Britisher who quickly mastered western range problems. Like Charlie Goodnight and Bar-B-Q Campbell, he prohibited drinking and gambling on the ranch. A pioneer at heart, he resigned in 1911 to take over the management of a big property in Brazil.

All the above-mentioned ranches were owned by companies or partnerships. The largest single cattle owner in the Old West seems to have been John S. Chisum (1824–84)—no relation to Jesse Chisholm for whom the trail was named. The records of John's early life and business affairs reveal little except that he rode to great wealth in shirtsleeves under a scorching sun, with spurs on his heels and the straight brim of a wide hat pushed low over his eyes. He was born in Tennessee and had no schooling, but he did have an extraordinary memory for numbers and prices. When he was thirteen years old he came with his family to Texas, at the time when that state had just won its independence from Mexico. Thirty years later, with 10,000 cattle, he moved west to New Mexico as one of the first American cattlemen to settle permanently in that Spanish-speaking land. By 1873, from 60,000 to 100,000 cattle were wearing his Long Rail brand and jinglebob.

John Chisum became indirectly involved in the Lincoln County War and at a later date helped elect the sheriff, Pat Garrett, who killed Billy the Kid. When Chisum died, still semi-literate, he was worth half a million dollars.

Of all the West's great cattle spreads, the King Ranch is the most famous, the largest, and has had the most remarkable record for pyramiding profits. The founder, Richard King, at the age of eleven, stowed away on a vessel out of New York. Practically nothing more is known about his youth except that his parents were poor Irish immigrants who apprenticed him to a jeweler. Growing to manhood on southern steamboats, he became a pilot and part-owner of a small steamboat line which held a monopoly on the lower Rio Grande. A picture of him at this time shows a determined face with sloping forehead, snub nose, straight aggressive mouth and keen eyes—a face with the strength and stubbornness of a man who could be depended on in a rough-and-tumble fight. He liked his liquor and when drinking enjoyed using his fists.

At the close of the Mexican War, Richard King purchased a part-interest—all his life he bought part-interests—in a small ranch on Santa Gertrudis Creek, some forty-five miles south-west of Corpus Christi. The property lacked everything usually wanted for a successful cattle outfit. It was located in hot country, tick-infested and monotonously flat. Mesquite and other thorn bushes, higher than a horseman's head, covered the land in a thicket so dense that a steer could seldom be seen more than fifty yards away. Prickly pears grew to enormous size, their round, bristly pads as large as dinner plates. The tasajia and other succulents carried

"Driving to the Roundup." Engraving, after drawing by Frederic Remington.
Century Magazine, 1888

spines that penetrated a rider's leather clothing. Up in San Antonio people said you could always recognize a Flying W (King's brand) rider because he was either rubbing the cactus scratches on his legs or pulling out a thorn. King Ranch mosquitoes were reported to be as big as yearling steers.

During the Civil War this small, unattractive holding assumed new importance. Union war vessels blockaded the mouth of the Rio Grande to stop shipments of cotton to Europe and thus starve the Confederacy. The King Ranch became a depot from which precious bales could be smuggled into Mexico for shipment from blockade-free Matamoros. The dense jungle of chaparral also served as a secure hiding place for Richard King when Union patrols sought to arrest him.

By war's end King had accumulated sufficient ready cash to take full advantage of the great profits to be made in the Long Drive from Texas to the northern railroads. He sent cattle from his own thorny ranges and also bought thousands of head in other parts of Texas to be driven north. More of a businessman than a cowboy, he never rode with the trail herds and usually made partnership deals with the drovers, sharing the profits and thus cutting his own overhead. Often he traveled north to be present at the final stockyard deliveries and division of the profits. Sometimes he had as many as four herds—more than 10,000 cattle—on the trail at one time. While the Long Drive continued he netted $50,000 annually, and reinvested much of it in land and more cattle.

During these years of affluence Richard King allowed his beard to grow. He wore a wide-brimmed black hat like a Confederate cavalryman's, and a broadcloth frock coat. A gold chain across his wrinkled vest was attached to a watch, big as a sour-dough biscuit. He walked with a slight limp acquired in an accident during his steamboat days. Notoriously free with his money in barrooms, he often set up drinks for the house and tossed around tips with western extravagance, but when the spree had ended he recorded the expense with his usual meticulousness. At his death in 1885, he owned over 600,000 acres.

Once, during the height of Richard King's successes, he was badly beaten in a lawsuit, and he immediately employed the victorious attorney. This young man, Robert Kleberg, married King's nineteen-year-old daughter, and on her father's death he assumed the administration of the estate. For the next three generations a Kleberg ran the ranch. Under this family's management the acreage more than doubled, artesian water was brought to the surface, blow torches burned the spines off cactus to make them edible for cattle, and bulldozers cleared off the worst thickets. When a railroad penetrated the vast holding, loading pens—all for King cattle—were built, miles apart along the tracks, thus eliminating long drives under a sultry sun. Cowboys used to complain that in wet weather alligators sometimes crawled into the loading chutes and frightened the cattle, but cowboys like to stretch the blanket.

In 1912, when the period covered by this book ends, the Klebergs were experimenting with their first introduction of Brahman blood into shorthorn cattle, hoping to produce a superior beef animal which was immune to tick fever. This led directly to the establishment of a new cattle breed called the Santa Gertrudis. Half a century later, the annual shipments of King cattle alone often grossed $5,000,000. The King Ranch had become big business with branches in Pennsylvania, Arizona and Australia to supply a world market.

PART SEVEN

"Smoking-up" by Charles M. Russell

Guns of the American West

by Robert Easton

"The Pony of the Northern Rockies." Engraving, after drawing by Frederic Remington.

66. *The Spanish Explorers' Guns*

Cortez brought thirteen guns with him to conquer a new world. He knew the tremendous advantage over his environment that the gun gave him. And the Spanish conquistadors that followed him, to explore and settle much of what is now the American West, continued to use the gun as their chief tool of conquest.

The first Spaniards carried a primitive type of firearm called a matchlock. Matchlocks were of two kinds, a heavy 15- to 20-pound musket and a lighter 8- to 10-pound arquebus. Both consisted essentially of a smoothbored iron tube and a gunlock or firing mechanism in which a charge of powder was ignited by a slow match of wicking or cord. Hence the term "matchlock." The match was clamped in a device called the serpentine, which, when the match was lighted, performed much the same function as a modern gun's hammer. Squeezing the trigger forced the serpentine downward, brought the burning match in touch with the priming powder held in a small metal pan fixed near the butt-end of the barrel, resulting in a spurt of fire flashing through the touchhole and igniting the main charge inside the barrel. The arquebus or harquebus, as it was also called, and the musket were both loaded from the muzzle. A quantity of black powder and a lead ball of from .66 to .80 caliber (that is, from .66 of an inch to .80 of an inch in diameter) were dropped down the barrel. A wad of tow or paper was then tamped down on top of them with a ramrod. This seated the ball firmly against the powder and compressed the force of the explosion when the gun was fired. Both arquebus and musket were fired from the shoulder, usually with the help of a forked rest in the case of the musket. They had an effective range of perhaps a hundred yards, though "three hundred paces" was sometimes claimed.

Besides the thirteen arquebusiers (or musketeers, the terms are loosely used) who were with Cortez when he landed in Mexico, there were thirty-two crossbowmen. The crossbow embodied three features that became standard in firearms. They were stock, trigger, and hook or hammer. The hook or hammer instead of striking released the bowstring which fired the projectile called a bolt or quarrel. These were barbed and often poisoned. They created painful wounds, could pierce armor or light fortifications and were loudly criticized by knights, kings and clergy as unfair, much as nuclear weapons are protested by some people today. Coronado, however, took crossbowmen with him as well as arquebusiers when he went through the Southwest in search of the Seven Cities of Cíbola and found Kansas. Pope Innocent III had banned the crossbow as too inhuman a weapon for use among Christians, but it was sanctioned against the aborigines of Kansas, Texas, and other heathen.

The arquebus and musket were undependable weapons. Rain and wind dampened or blew out powder and match. The touchhole and barrel fouled, resulting in misfire or explosion. Nevertheless for nearly a century the matchlock was the weapon of the invader of the West. Its effect on the natives was devastating; the sound and smoke alone were enough to terrify them. It was clear evidence of superior power.

The conquistadors were never partial to the wheel lock, the successor to the matchlock, though both Coronado and Oñate included them in the armament of their expeditions into New Mexico. The wheel lock's firing mechanism consisted chiefly of a rough wheel which spun against a flint, to create sparks that ignited the powder in the pan, the wheel being motivated by an internal spring which often got out of order. Gunsmiths and spare springs were rare in the New World. Something simpler and sturdier was needed.

The great step forward came about 1625 in the form of the flintlock in which a flint, held in a vise-like arm called a cock, struck a bar of rough steel called the battery and sprayed sparks in the pan, the pan being provided with a lid which "kept your powder dry" until fired. The Spanish-developed flintlock called the "miquelet" had a heavy outside mainspring, easily repaired, a cock with adaptable jaws that could hold the varied-sized flints that a man might pick up in the field and a safety catch to prevent accidental discharge. The cock could be set —that is cocked—in advance of firing, and the cocking compressed the mainspring which, when the trigger was pulled, drove the cock forward against the steel. The flintlock was more dependable, easier to operate, cheaper to manufacture than matchlock or wheel lock.

Spaniards also carried huge unwieldy flintlock pistols. Some were worn on a hook attached to a man's sash. Other such "hand cannon" were carried in holsters.

These early firearms not only paved the way for the winning of the West but became our first sporting weapons, bringing down game as well as humans.

67. *Lewis and Clark Guns*

THE UNITED STATES as a nation did not enter the western picture with its firearms much before 1803 when Lewis and Clark assembled their expedition near St. Louis. Most of the men of the party, being soldiers, carried the standard U. S. infantry weapons, a smoothbore flintlock musket, Model 1795, made at the new U. S. Armory, Springfield, Massachusetts. It was a .69 caliber patterned after the French model of 1763, had a 44¾-inch barrel and weighed 7⅞ pounds, with an over-all length of 5 feet. However, some of Lewis and Clark's men carried a new-model flintlock army rifle. The barrel of this weapon was not smooth inside; it was grooved or, as the gunsmiths said, "rifled," so that a ball fired through it would spin and thus hold its course with greater accuracy and range. This type of shoulder arm was called a "rifle," a term that had come into use following the development of the first rifles in Austria and Germany in the sixteenth and seventeenth centuries.

The new army weapon, or U. S. Flintlock Rifle Model 1803, was .54 caliber, the diameter of the interior of the barrel being measured between the "lands," or uncut portions, and not between the "grooves," or cut portions. The rifled barrel was 33 inches long.

The Army's Model 1803 rifle was superior to the 1795 musket, but although it could kill men at three hundred yards, Lewis and Clark found it inadequate for grizzly bears. Grizzlies could absorb from three to twenty balls before succumbing, as Lewis found out when he wounded one that continued to charge, first him, then his companion, for seventy or eighty yards, not giving either of them time to reload their guns.

Among other weapons Lewis and Clark carried was an English-made rapid-firing air gun which operated on the same principle as a present-day boy's air rifle. A spring compressed an air chamber. Three or four ball-shaped bullets could be dropped into it in succession and fired on the strength of a single pumping, by repeated pullings of the trigger. European gunmakers had high hopes for the air gun in the late eighteenth century, but it never became popular except with poachers, its quiet pop attracting much less attention from gamekeepers than a flintlock's roar.

Lewis and Clark also carried blunderbusses—short-barreled muskets with bell-shaped muzzles that spit large scattershot. These were the traditional "coach guns" of European and American stagecoaches, as well as weapons for cavalry or dragoons. The expedition's armament probably included a few long-barreled, smoothbored fowling pieces for shooting birdshot. Last but not least was the swivel gun or small cannon mounted on their keelboat, similar to those regularly carried on Missouri River boats of the period. These were large bell-mouthed muskets of about 1.50 caliber mounted on a Y-shaped support resembling an oar lock, which fitted into a hole in the front or the side of the boat and could be rotated. The tubes were fixed in the mouth of the "Y" by a pin, which allowed them to be depressed or elevated. It is an interesting fact that similar cannon were mounted on the walls of frontier forts and that artillery of various types played a leading role in the conquest of the West, being carried on expeditions by such explorers as Frémont and being a regular component of traders' caravans on the Santa Fe Trail and elsewhere.

When Lewis and Clark were in doubt as to the impression they were making on the natives, they would fire their cannon, or down a high-flying duck with a lucky shot from a flintlock rifle (as Clark did), or fire a burst with the air gun. Indians were so impressed by these performances, as well as by the personalities of Lewis and Clark, that they offered little resistance, and there were only a few overt clashes during the entire trip across roughly half the continent and back again. The land was ripe for the taking and the superior technology lay in the hands of the invader.

68. *Mountain Men's Guns*

Kentucky Rifles

PROBABLY SOME MEMBERS of the Lewis and Clark party carried the Kentucky rifle, a weapon already well-known on the American frontier. A more appropriate name for it would be the "Pennsylvania rifle," because the first rifles of this type were made as early as 1719 by German and Swiss craftsmen settled in the vicinity of Lancaster and Reading, Pennsylvania.

First called simply the "long rifle," the name "Kentucky" was attached after the exploits of Daniel Boone and other Kentuckians gained literary fame.

The Kentucky came about for a simple reason: frontiersmen wanted a straight-shooting weapon that could be readily carried, would not consume too much precious powder and lead, yet would bring down game or humans at advantageous range.

Many problems confronted local gunsmiths in trying to satisfy these demands. Though rifles had been made for two hundred years, they were difficult to manufacture. Accurate cutting of the lands and grooves required high skill. The tight fit of the ball in the barrel, essential if the ball was to "take" the grooves and spin accurately to the target on firing, made loading slow and difficult. Sometimes ramrods snapped when forcing down the ball. More often the ball was pounded out of shape by blows of the ramrod and did not fly truly when fired. Also, most early rifles were short-barreled, designed for use at a short range, and a long-range gun was what the frontiersmen needed.

Necessity created solutions. Gunsmiths lengthened the barrel to give longer burning time to the powder charge (a powder charge does not "burn" instantaneously; the explosion continues as the bullet goes down the barrel) and thus greater velocity, accuracy and range to the bullet. They reduced the size of the bore to make the gun lighter in weight and this reduced the amount of powder and lead the gunner must carry. Most important of all, somebody thought of the idea of using a ball small enough to go down the barrel without being forced and of wrapping it in a greased leather or linen "patch" before loading. This patch was usually about the size of a silver dollar and was often carried in a "patch box" with a hinged brass cover attached or carved into the right side of the gun's butt.

To load a Kentucky a man placed the butt on the ground, poured out a recognized quantity of coarse black powder from a horn or flask into his hand, perhaps till it reached a certain well-known wrinkle in the crease of his palm, let the powder drain down the muzzle, wrapped a ball in a patch and started it into the barrel with his thumb, then pushed it on down with his ramrod. The patch served to fit the ball into the lands and grooves, forcing it, when fired, to take the rifling and spin toward the mark. In addition, the patch helped confine the propellant gases from the explosion to the seat of the bullet, where the full kick of the charge should strike.

A major advantage of the Kentucky was its long barrel. Hitting a mark depends on the shooter's ability to hold the front and rear of his gun barrel in line with the target. If the barrel is short, he has difficulty noticing a slight divergence which will send a bullet far from a target a hundred or more yards away. With a long barrel any angle of divergence is much more evident, and greater accuracy is possible.

The early Kentuckies were huge unwieldy things, often as large as .60 caliber, with clumsy, thick stocks. But by the time of the American Revolution they had been modified to light, graceful weapons weighing about 8 pounds, with a bore of about .40 caliber in a barrel as much as four feet long. The stock of native maple was occasionally inlaid with brass or silver ornaments. It extended the full length of the barrel and housed the ramrod.

The Kentucky's effective range was at least 400 yards—much greater than other shoulder arms of the period. At 300 yards 50 per cent accuracy on human targets could be expected. The muzzle velocity (speed of the projectile as it leaves the muzzle) depended on the powder charge and barrel length. It sometimes reached 2,000 feet per second, about two-thirds the equivalent of a modern high-powered rifle.

Kentuckies distinguished themselves in Indian fighting, in the Revolution and again in the War of 1812 when Andrew Jackson's men, largely armed with them, disabled 2,000 British in a matter of minutes at the Battle of New Orleans. The first American traders, trappers, explorers to penetrate the Great Plains and Rocky Mountains—such men as John Colter—and army personnel who wanted a more effective weapon than that issued by the military services, carried Kentuckies or modifications of them.

Percussion Ignition: The Hawken

One drawback of the classic Kentucky was that it proved too long and too fragile to be conveniently carried on horseback across the long reaches of the West; another was that it was underpowered for killing grizzly, elk and buffalo. The result was a modification, suited to the new environment, called the Plains rifle. This had a shorter barrel and a larger bore. A famous type of Plains rifle was made in the 1820's, '30's and '40's by the Hawken family of St. Louis, among the first gunmakers to set up shop in the West. The Hawken had a thirty-four-inch barrel (as opposed to forty-four inches for the average Kentucky), took a .50 caliber ball (instead of the average Kentucky's .40 to .45), and was strong enough to hold the extraheavy charges of black powder required for big game, something the Kentucky was not always able to do.

Moreover, the Hawken was fired by the new "percussion system" of ignition, which consisted of a metal cap containing an explosive set on the end of a tube called a "nipple"; when the cap was struck by the hammer, fire flashed down the tube and ignited the main powder charge in the barrel, speeding the ball on its way. The Hawken had an effective range of 350 yards and was a favorite with mountain men until the arrival of breechloaders. Both Kit Carson and Jim Bridger owned them. Hawkens were probably used by Mike Fink and Carpenter in their Homeric tests of nerves when they undertook to shoot whiskey cups off each other's heads during monkeyshines at mountain men's rendezvous.

The percussion system of ignition was a great step forward. Dampness, fouling, hang-fire and misfire had been constant problems. Even the best flintlocks, including Kentuckies, fired only about three-quarters of the time. For a gun to "flash in the pan" without firing became so common that the expression was applied to men who talked big and did little. The percussion system eliminated at one stroke the clumsy flint and steel, the flashpan and attendant difficulties. It also paved the way for the metallic cartridge, which in turn made repeating rifles possible.

Problems in Muzzle Loading: Cartridges

The cartridge was slow in developing. As early as the seventeenth century, powder of measured quantity was being packaged in containers of paper, linen or foil called cartridges. These were usually carried in boxes at the belt and were commonly used by soldiers and western frontiersmen. Often balls were attached to the ends of these cartridges. The tradi-

This Hawken rifle once belonged to Jim Bridger. Sturdy, hard-hitting Hawkens were a favorite with westerners of the 1830's.

PHOTO BY JORUD PHOTO SHOP, HELENA, FROM HISTORICAL SOCIETY OF MONTANA COLLECTION

tional method of loading a gun with them was to tear or bite off the end, pour a little of the powder in the pan if the weapon was a flintlock, and the rest down the barrel, drop in the ball together with the paper and ram all home. This expedited firing and made carrying of powder and ball more convenient, though it did not render completely obsolete the traditional powder horn and bullet pouch.

Even with these improvements and with the addition of the percussion system, to fire three shots a minute from a muzzle-loader required fast shooting. The average, if carefully aimed, was about one shot per minute. Another drawback to muzzle-loaders was the difficulty of loading when lying down, not to mention on horseback, and if a man stood up or halted his mount he became an easy target for the enemy. On horseback, true, he might seat the ball by hitting the butt on his saddle or on the ground, but this required a hard blow and certainly was awkward. Furthermore, sparks remaining from the last shot might ignite the next charge he poured in and blow him to kingdom come.

In hunting, as in battle, a man acts under the pressure of excitement. Guns, especially army guns, should be almost foolproof. Soldiers do strange things in combat. For example: after the battle of Gettysburg, some 37,000 guns were collected on the battlefield and sent to Washington, D.C. Of these, 24,000 were found to be fully loaded and 6,000 had from three to ten loads in the barrel. In other words, many soldiers were so excited they rammed load after load down the muzzles of their guns without firing a shot.

Clearly what was needed for both sporting and military use was a foolproof, rapid-firing weapon that loaded from the breech—the end of the barrel opposite the muzzle. Such a firearm had been the dream of shooters and gunmakers for centuries. Various breech-loading weapons, including a cannon, had been developed but none was successful.

69. *The Coming of Breechloaders and Repeaters*

The Hall Rifle

JOHN H. HALL, a Maine Yankee, produced the first breech-loading firearm in the United States. It was patented in 1811 and was a flintlock rifle, .52 caliber, weighing ten pounds. A hinged breechblock (the metal block which closes the rear of the bore against the force of the charge) contained the chamber (the part of the gun that holds the charge or, in the case of modern weapons, the cartridge). In loading, the front end of the block was lifted by releasing a spring, and the charge was inserted. The block then locked back into the barrel.

The Army accepted Hall's flintlock rifle in 1819. In 1833 a smoothbore carbine (short-barreled) version was issued to the First Regiment of U.S. Dragoons (First Cavalry). The

The Hall Flintlock Rifle was the first successful U. S. breechloader. Shown here with breech open for insertion of the charge, the Hall was accepted by the Army in 1819.

PHOTO BY DON O'NEIL FROM WILLIAM R. WILLIAMSON COLLECTION

barrel was twenty-six inches long. This first cavalry breechloader was also the first Army gun to use the percussion ignition system. Later it was made in a rifled version.

One of the remarkable features of Hall percussion models was that the breechblock, which contained all the gun's working parts, could be removed and used as a pistol if desired. Hall breech-loading carbines and rifles were used in the Mexican War and passed into the West in the hands of mountain men and traders as well as soldiers. The federal government also issued several thousand Halls to state militias, and some of these guns found their way West.

The Hall patent, however, failed to solve the problem which plagued breechloaders from the beginning. The seam between chamber and barrel was not sufficiently tight. Flame tended to spurt from the joint, and there was consequent reduction in velocity because of explosive gas leakage. There were also difficulties with the breech catch. And so the weapon was produced only in limited quantity by the U.S. Armory at Harpers Ferry, and the surplus, sold at bargain prices, made profitable items in the Indian trade.

The Sharps

Christian Sharps, who had worked on the Hall patent at Harpers Ferry Armory, developed the first successful breechloader. Sharps moved to Cincinnati where in 1848 he patented a system that became famous throughout the West when incorporated in the Sharps Breechloading Percussion Single-shot Carbine.

This revolutionary weapon—short-barreled and ideal for western use—employed a linen- or paper-wrapped cartridge with ball attached, though it would take loose ball and powder also. In loading with a cartridge, the trigger guard acted as a lever which lowered the breechblock and exposed the chamber. The cartridge was then inserted. Returning the breechblock to closed position sheared off the end of the cartridge and exposed the powder, so that when the trigger was pulled and the percussion cap exploded, ignition of the powder took place and the gun fired. A skilled shooter could deliver four or five shots a minute in this fashion.

In a variety of calibers from .36 to .52, Sharps breech-loading carbines and rifles were reasonably accurate at long ranges—enthusiasts even claimed up to 1,000 yards but most Easterners had trouble judging distances in the clear atmosphere of the West. However that may be, it is certain that during the 1850's the Sharps became the most popular shoulder arm in the West. It proved superior for hunting buffalo or humans. It was carried in covered wagons on the Oregon and California trails, and it played a leading role in the bloody pro- and antislavery fighting in Kansas that preceded the Civil War. John Brown and his fellow abolitionists carried Sharps rifles. They were called "Beecher's Bibles" because Henry Ward Beecher, the renowned antislavery preacher of Boston, was said to have sent a shipment of them to Brown in Kansas in crates labeled "Bibles." Beecher supposedly said that one Sharps would be more persuasive in the slavery conflict than one hundred Bibles. At any rate, John Brown's men were armed with these famous breech loaders when they attacked the U.S. Armory at Harpers Ferry, Virginia, in 1859, an incident that got Brown hanged and set Union soldiers singing:

Sharps Buffalo Rifle. Never before photographed, this typical Sharps .45 caliber breechloading, single-shot rifle belonged to Buffalo Jones. After gun was cocked by thumbing back hammer, rear trigger, if pulled, "set" front trigger, making it a "hair" trigger for greater accuracy.

PHOTO BY CONARD STUDIO FROM FINNEY COUNTY, KANSAS, HISTORICAL SOCIETY COLLECTION

John Brown's body lies a-mouldering
  in the grave,
His soul goes marching on.

(Confederate soldiers admitted ten years later that this song created more apprehensive terror in Southern ranks than all the cannon Grant and Lincoln could muster.)

So the Sharps enjoyed immense popularity even though it never succeeded in remedying the defects common to breechloaders since the original Hall. Gas escaped at the breech. Parts fouled. Bullets lost velocity and accuracy.

Samuel Colt

Many inventors and manufacturers puzzled over the best way to produce a satisfactory quick-loading, rapid-firing, breech-loading weapon. Among these was Samuel Colt. Born in Hartford, Connecticut, July 19, 1814, to a poor family, Colt was indentured to a farmer; but having other ideas for a career he joined the crew of a sailing ship bound for India via London. During the voyage, perhaps in London, his innate mechanical genius was aroused by sight of an early type of revolving-cylinder pistol. He promptly whittled a better model out of wood. When he got back to Hartford he persuaded a well-known gunsmith, Anson Chase, to make two prototype revolving-cylinder guns based on his wood model. One was a pistol, one a rifle. Colt took them to the United States Patent Office where he was advised to file a claim and make better examples.

It took him three years to make the additional models, during which period he financed himself as "Dr. Coult of New York, London and Calcutta," lecturing on any subject from flying machines to submarines, chiefly to attract an audience. The precocious young man finally obtained a patent in 1836—not for the idea of the revolving cylinder, but for the idea of a revolving cylinder that locked in place behind the barrel by action of the hammer as the gun was cocked.

We will see in detail later what happened to Colt's revolving-cylinder pistol. As for his rifle, it contained six, seven or eight chambers that could be fired before the piece needed reloading. It was made in various calibers from .34 to .69. Kit Carson owned one of these and recommended it to the explorer John C. Frémont. Colt rifles were also used by some United States troops in Florida during the later stages of the Seminole War (1835–42) but were found wanting. The Army felt that its regular troops were not bright enough to master such complicated arms. Furthermore gas escaped from the breech as with other breechloaders, and sometimes all chambers in the cylinder accidentally fired at once, blowing off a shooter's left hand not to mention the waste of powder and ball. Despite his contribution to the solution of the problem of the rapid-firing breech-loading firearm, Samuel Colt went broke.

Nevertheless, the notion of the revolving cylinder attracted favorable attention and several inventors tried versions of their own. A nine-shot Cochran rifle, in which the cylinder revolved about a vertical axis (like a revolving turret) was carried by Josiah Gregg, the author-trader, when he made his overland wagon trip to Santa Fe in 1844. Indeed the 1840's and 1850's saw a great variety of old, new and experimental guns, and it was generally conceded that the gun of the future would be a breech-loading repeater as soon as someone worked out a method of stopping that troublesome gas leakage. The solution was near at hand, and with it came a revolution in all firearms.

Metallic Cartridges

As we have seen, linen- or paper- or even foil-wrapped cartridges had been in use for some time, but they did nothing to prevent blowback from the chamber. Nor did the percussion ignition system place the primer close enough to the charge to ensure maximum dependability against misfire. The answer came in the 1850's in the form of a metallic cartridge. This sealed the barrel against blowback and placed the primer in direct proximity to the charge.

This new cartridge consisted of a case of thin copper alloy, containing both charge and primer, as well as bullet affixed at the end. The explosion of the charge expanded the cartridge case sufficiently to seal the barrel against blowback, and the nearness of primer to charge reduced the possibility of misfire. There were additional assets of safety, mobility, durability.

The soft metal rim-fire cartridge was certainly an improvement over those made of waxed paper or cloth, but it was not entirely satisfactory, especially for heavy charges. A rim-fire casing had to be thin enough to crush under the hammer's blow and thus detonate the priming compound. A casing heavy enough to withstand a big load might not crush under this blow and the gun might misfire. In addition, even when the rim metal was light enough to be crushed the detonating compound was not always spread around it in sufficient quantities to assure an explosion.

To remedy these defects a center-fire cartridge was developed for big-caliber guns and came into general use shortly after the Civil War. This was made of a brass much heavier than the alloy used for the old rim-fires. Too heavy to be crushed by the hammer and detonated in the old manner, the new cartridge carried the detonating compound in a small cup located in the center of its base, where the firing pin was sure to strike.

A center-fire cartridge was more expensive to manufacture than a rim-fire, which is still used for cheap .22 shells, but westerners wanted the increased power in the heavier cartridge and were willing to pay for it. They even excused their extravagance by saying that the heavier brass cartridges could be reloaded.

The first to produce a successful metallic cartridge in the United States was the team of Horace Smith and Samuel B. Wesson, soon to be famous in gun annals as "Smith & Wesson," but others followed them in quick succession.

The Spencer

The metallic cartridge made possible the repeating rifle, and foremost among these was the Spencer, the first successful breech-loading magazine rifle.

Abraham Lincoln test fired a seven-shot Spencer rifle similar to this. The Spencer proved underpowered for long ranges and big game.

PHOTO BY DON O'NEIL FROM ROBERT T. BENSON COLLECTION

Christopher M. Spencer, another of the inventive Yankees who contributed so much to gun development, obtained a patent in 1860 for a repeating rifle and carbine in which the breechblock was operated by the trigger guard acting as a lever, much as in the Sharps breechloader, a principle employed by lever-action rifles ever since. The lever, swinging down, opened the breech, ejected a spent cartridge, and brought a new load into the barrel from a tubular magazine contained in the butt. Though it had to be manually cocked, the seven-shot Spencer was an immense advance. It could be fired seven times in ten seconds or, with reloading, fourteen times in one minute, far faster than anything yet invented. Despite a tendency for its cartridges to explode in the magazine, where they were lined up one after another and a jar of the butt might set them off, it was adopted by the Army and mass-produced for Civil War use.

Before and during hostilities, Spencers like Sharps went West, to stand or fall on their merits. The West, with its variety of terrains and climates, its game large and small, its constant warfare—private and public—provided an ideal testing ground for firearms. Gunmakers coped with problems by producing new and improved models. Thus the West helped develop the gun almost as much as the gun developed the West.

The Henry

Another famous repeating rifle was the Henry. This was invented by another creative New Englander, B. Tyler Henry, who in 1858 had developed a metallic rim-fire cartridge and in 1860 obtained a patent for a rifle to fire it. He called the new shoulder arm the Henry Lever-Action Cartridge Magazine Rifle, and developed it in association with a New Haven shirtmaker named Oliver F. Winchester, under circumstances that bear repeating.

Nobody thought that a historic step was being taken in the 1850's when Winchester purchased an interest in the Volcanic Repeating Arms Company, least of all Winchester. He knew next to nothing about guns. He was a carpenter turned textile manufacturer. But he knew value, whether in men or in shirts, and he thought he saw something worthwhile in gun production and munitions making as well as in the talented group of young men working for the Volcanic Arms Company. He was right.

The young men included the gifted Horace Smith, Samuel B. Wesson and B. Tyler Henry, all of whom were working on the Lewis Jennings patent for a repeating rifle. Jennings, now almost forgotten, had devised one of the earliest repeating shoulder arms, one that embodied features such as the tubular magazine, which appeared on many rifles thereafter.

The Jennings repeater failed largely for lack of a suitable cartridge. It fired a complicated contraption consisting of a hollow bullet with a propellant in its base, the whole ignited by a percussion cap. Smith, Wesson and Henry improved the Jennings rifle, using Winchester's and others' capital, and produced the so-called Volcanic repeating rifles and pistols. However, Volcanic products failed for the same reason the Jennings rifle had failed: lack of a suitable cartridge. The firm went into receivership. Oliver Winchester organized a company to take over its assets and installed B. Tyler Henry as superintendent of a new firm known as the New Haven Repeating Arms Company.

This Henry rifle of 1860 has a special factory engraved receiver and typical tubular magazine extending full length of barrel.

Thus began the memorable association between the gifted inventor, Henry, and the gifted businessman, Winchester. Henry's first task was to devise the metallic cartridge already mentioned. In honor of his achievement, all rim-fire cartridges manufactured by the Winchester company thereafter bore an "H" stamped on their bases—a little "H" that even to this day every American boy with his first rifle notices on the bottom of .22 cartridges.

The original Henry was a .44 caliber weapon that looked a good deal like a modern lever-action Winchester except that the frame, or so-called receiver, at the breech was made of shiny golden brass. A fifteen-shot tubular magazine was located underneath a twenty-four-inch barrel. The total weight was nine and a half pounds.

The Henry was the first rifle in which a simple motion of the lever extracted the fired cartridge, cocked the hammer, reloaded the gun and closed the breech. It differed from the Spencer chiefly in the lever-cocking feature, in having the magazine under the barrel and in being able to deliver with a single reloading thirty shots a minute. The Henry, as we will see later, led to the Winchester, a name which became synonymous with "rifle" in the West.

70. *Indian Guns*

THE INDIAN DESPERATELY wanted the white man's superior weapon, the gun, in order to compete more successfully in the contest for survival. White traders began furnishing Indians with guns certainly as early as the seventeenth century. These were undoubtedly matchlocks, flintlocks, muskets and pistols. In Canada the Hudson's Bay Company devised a special firearm for the Indians known as the "trade gun." By 1800 this weapon was a lightweight (five- to six-pound), short-barreled (thirty-four- to forty-two-inch), cheaply constructed musket, .66 caliber or thereabouts, with a large trigger guard so that it could be fired with a glove or mitten on the finger, indicative of the fact that most trade guns were designed for use in cold climates where furs were good.

The "trade gun" almost invariably had a serpent-like brass figure, known as "the dragon ornament," on the left side-plate, and often there was also a seated fox in a decorative circle elsewhere on the gun. This dragon ornament appeared on Indian guns well into the nineteenth century. It seems to have originated hundreds of years earlier in Europe. A dragonhead adorned the mouths of small blunderbusses carried by seventeenth-century cavalrymen. Soldiers equipped with such weapons were called "dragoneers," literally those who wielded the dragon. The name was soon shortened to the modern "dragoon."

The distribution of "Hudson's Bay guns" or "fusees" was so extensive that Lewis and Clark found them in the hands of Indians on the upper Missouri and at the mouth of the Columbia. Lewis' comments about the feeble "pop" these guns made when fired indicate that the Indians were using an economical charge of costly and hard-to-get powder.

After the American Revolution both the American government and private firms entered the business of trading guns to Indians. Both turned first to British suppliers, but by the early 1800's they were patronizing American manufacturers as well, specifying in either

This 1855 Sharps rifle appears exactly as it was found in a Sioux Indian grave in North Dakota in 1909. Indians often buried guns with their dead.

PHOTO BY DICK SMITH

case that the dragon ornament appear on guns purchased. Muskets of the now conventional pattern were manufactured by Joseph Henry of Philadelphia (not to be confused with B. Tyler Henry, inventor of the Henry rifle), H. E. Leman of Lancaster, Pennsylvania, and many others. The cost was about seven dollars per musket. These guns were distributed by government trading posts on the frontier. When this so-called government factory system was discontinued in the 1820's for private enterprise, guns continued to be sold by such trading companies as the Missouri Fur Company, John Jacob Astor's American Fur Company, the "French Company" and even by such small fry as Louis Vasquez and Jim Bridger. The retail price to the Indian in the 1840's was from twenty-four to twenty-eight dollars.

Meanwhile Canadian fur companies could buy trade guns in Europe for from three to four dollars, so there is little wonder that a large smuggling business developed across the international boundary. After 1849 when the Indian Bureau was administered by the newly created Department of the Interior, guns were given to the Indians as part of treaty stipulations.

Trade Rifles

Trade rifles—as distinct from trade muskets—were a strictly United States development that paralleled the production and distribution of the trade smoothbore. The trade rifle, originally a flintlock, was about .52 caliber and had a relatively short barrel, which in turn was apt to be shortened still further by the western Indian who wanted a weapon to carry on his horse. (He had also shortened his trade muskets, deliberately or by necessity after they burst, as they often did through misloading or other cause.)

The trade rifle was in fact a less expensive version of the Plains rifle already mentioned. It was usually well made, thoroughly tested by the government or trading companies, and produced by a number of native manufacturers, including some of those mentioned in connection with the trade musket and Kentucky rifle. Trade rifles were sold by the manufacturer for about twelve dollars each—considerably higher than the seven-dollar musket—and the cost to the Indians was undoubtedly several times more.

Though the trade rifle was a more accurate and a longer-ranged weapon than the musket, many Indians preferred the musket. It was less expensive, could kill a buffalo at the close range characteristic of the horseback method of hunting, was easier to load, and shot almost any kind of bullet. The Indian, like the western soldier and trapper and settler, poured his own lead in molds carried in his pack.

Other Indian Guns

Trade rifles and muskets were not the only firearms reaching the western Indian. From the beginning, many types of arms came into his hands in various ways, by capture, trade, smuggling, gift. For example, when the Pueblos revolted and drove the Spanish out of New Mexico (1680–93), some three hundred "hackbusses"—by which probably was meant flintlocks as well as harquebuses—were reported as captured by the Indians. American Horse, a Cheyenne, said that wagon trains passing up the South Platte River between 1858 and

1865 were largely armed with Sharps military rifles and carbines, and his people got many in trade and also some cap-and-ball six-shooters. The Cheyenne warriors got their first Spencer repeating rifles in the 1860's by derailing a handcar in Nebraska. In 1862 Bear Ribs, a Sioux chief, had a double-barreled shotgun he got from God knows where. Both North and South enlisted Indian regiments in the Civil War, and these red-skinned G.I.'s retained many of their weapons after discharge, as was customary. Some of the guns used by the Sioux in the Dakota campaigns against United States soldiers were identified as those given them by the Indian Peace Commission at the conclusion of the Fort Rice treaty signed in 1868. Furthermore, "good" or "reservation" Indians—the warlike Sioux included—were issued guns, ostensibly to kill buffalo, even during the period of the Indian Wars. So the trade guns were only part of the picture, and an impressive case can be made for the fact that the Indians were "well armed with guns," sometimes better armed than soldiers.

Regardless of the quality of the Indians' guns, their method of using them was important. To an Indian, war was a personal matter, an event for personal aggrandizement. With a Sioux it was more important to count coups than to kill an enemy. Stanley Vestal, author and student of Indian lore, records that after the first World War Sioux veterans, who were members of the American Legion, applied for admission to their tribal order of Old Warriors. They were refused on grounds that the mere killing of a man with a rifle was not sufficient qualification for a warrior.

Does this mean that some Indian tribes paid little attention to the technique of shooting or to whether or not a weapon was a repeater or a single shot, a rifle or a smoothbore? To some degree this was the case, especially before wide contact with the white man in battle

"When Sioux and Blackfeet Meet." Painting by Charles M. Russell.

taught the Indian new concepts of using the gun. Frontiersmen like William T. Hamilton, Uncle Dick Wooton and Buffalo Jones—Zane Grey's "Last of the Plainsmen"—belittled Indian marksmanship. General Nelson A. Miles praised the shooting ability of the Nez Percés. But, as he had conquered them, he may have been unconsciously complimenting his own men. All seem to agree that an Indian's performance on horseback with a gun was remarkable. He could fire and reload his muzzle-loader at full gallop, shooting over the back and under the neck of his horse. Holding two or more balls at a time in his mouth he spit them into his gun's muzzle after first sloshing in an estimated charge of powder from his powder horn. In this manner a dozen warriors could send a hail of fire into a wagon train or soldiers' entrenchment.

Perhaps the reason Indians were often poor marksmen was due to a scarcity of ammunition for practicing. There is a record of an Indian trading a buffalo robe for three cartridges. At such a price every shot was a rich man's luxury, and the number of bow-and-arrow Indians in most fights indicates that there were relatively no more rich Indians than there were rich whites. In spite of the cost, however, Indians at times displayed excellent shooting ability. As snipers they baffled United States troops in the Modoc War of 1873, as did Joseph's Nez Percés. In several skirmishes the Sioux and Cheyenne outshot the soldiers, so it would be a mistake to completely condemn the red man's marksmanship.

The Custer Fight

If guns in the hands of Indians ever achieved a great victory it was on June 25, 1876, when Custer made his last stand on the Little Big Horn. Experts differ, but the best estimates seem to be that out of approximately 3,000 warriors engaged in the fight, only half, or about 1,500, had guns, and of these another half, or about 750, had repeating rifles. Yet those 750 repeating rifles represented overwhelming firepower, in both quality and quantity. Regardless of the tactics of the battle, Custer's men were outgunned. More than 250 dead United States soldiers yielded their Springfield single-shot carbines and Colt revolvers to the victors, in all some 592 rifles and pistols, further increasing the Indians' already superior armament. Yet the fact remains that half the braves assembled for this battle carried only bows and arrows.

A number of "bona fide Indian guns" used in the Custer fight have been offered for sale. Many are fakes but some are reasonably well authenticated. These include a muzzle-loading musket with British proofmarks; a percussion rifle, .41 caliber, made by J. Henry and Son; a .58 caliber percussion rifle marked "S. Hawken, St. Louis"; and a percussion rifle of .50 caliber marked "H. E. Leman, Lancaster, Pa." The list shows what a motley variety of arms, many of them quite old, had come into Indian hands. There were also single-shot carbines including a .44 Wesson, a Sharps .52, and an Eli Whitney .58—the inventor of the cotton gin being also a gunmaker. The supposition is that some of these were dropped on the field of battle as the Indian possessed himself of a superior weapon from a dead soldier.

After the Custer fight the Indian cause declined, till the end came at the Battle of Wounded Knee, South Dakota, in 1890. At Wounded Knee the Sioux handled their Winchesters ably, but it was the roar of the U. S. artillery—Hotchkiss guns firing two-pound

1873 Springfield .45-70 carbine. U. S. troopers, including Custer's men, used this single-shot weapon in Indian campaigns in the West.

explosive shells—that dominated the field and spelled an end to the gun as an effective weapon in the hands of the Indian. The conquest was over. The murders were over. It is perhaps no coincidence that the American frontier is considered by many to have ceased to exist in 1890, the year of the Battle of Wounded Knee, the last year for all practical purposes when wild, free Indians carried guns on the Plains.

71. *U. S. Army Guns*

THE FIRST ARMY muskets—the old smoothbores of 1795—went west with Lewis and Clark, as we have seen. For over half a century there was little change in this arm. In 1842 it was converted from flintlock to percussion, but otherwise it continued to be much the same old smoothbore right down to the Civil War. As the basic infantry weapon it was taken to practically every military post in the West. It helped subdue the frontier. It helped fight the Mexican War and thereby add all of that country west of the Rocky Mountain Divide and south of Oregon—what is generally called the Far West—to the union. If any one gun won the West, it was the sturdy old workhorse U.S. Musket Model 1795. In all some 850,000 were produced between 1798 and 1848.

The First Rifles

Not that the Army didn't believe in rifles. After the performance of the Kentucky in the Revolutionary War, the rifle could not be ignored. But it was viewed by the military as a special arm for limited sharpshooting or scouting functions. Rifle battalions were organized in the U.S. Army as early as 1792, and in the 1820's infantry regiments often had "light" companies armed with U.S. Flintlock Rifles, successors to the Model 1803 which Lewis and Clark's men carried. The military escort which accompanied Santa Fe traders in 1829 included one company armed with rifles; but most military formations were still of the mass type, with engagements at close range, so the Army in general continued to equip most of its units with the simpler, cheaper muskets.

Flintlock rifles were converted to the percussion system in 1841, just a year before the Model 1795 muskets were changed, and as such earned the name of "Mississippi rifles" when Jefferson Davis' Mississippi Regiment used them with such good effect at Buena Vista in 1847. They were, incidentally, the last service rifles to fire a round ball.

A new projectile was being developed. It was called the Minié ball and was the invention of Captain C. E. Minié of the French Army and James H. Burton, Assistant Master Armorer at Harpers Ferry, Virginia. Instead of being round it was roughly cylindrical in a shape later associated with bullets.

The importance of the Minié ball to the rifle was the fact that it did away with the old "patch" in which round balls had to be wrapped in order to make them fit the barrel. A Minié ball—not a ball at all—was smaller than the gun's rifling so could be dropped down the barrel. It had a hollow base plugged with an iron stopper. The explosion of the charge drove the plug forward expanding the lead of the bullet until it "took" the grooves of the rifling. Burton discovered that the iron plug was unnecessary and that the "take" would occur with the use of the hollow base alone.

With the Minié ball a rifle could be loaded as quickly and easily as a musket. All the shooter needed to do after pouring in his powder was to drop the Minié ball on top of it. From now on all newly designed military shoulder arms would be rifles.

Two such arms, one called a "rifle," one a "rifle musket," were adopted in 1855 for use with the new Minié ball. The difference between the two was a matter of barrel length. Both were .58 caliber. One had a barrel five feet long while the barrel of the other extended a mere fifty inches. The long-barreled "rifle musket" became the chief infantry weapon of the Civil War, and the shorter-barreled model was little used. About two million of the long "rifle muskets" were produced before the war was over, far more than any other arm employed, and these were carried into the West by foot soldiers stationed there as well as by soldiers discharged after the war.

U. S. Repeating Rifles

The Civil War was the great developer of weapons. Lincoln himself took a hand and the results were quickly apparent. The breechloader, for example, had been a recognized, but seldom used, military arm since 1819. Some Hall rifles and carbines were still in use at the time of the Civil War, but Lincoln insisted that a sluggish War Department equip a regiment of sharpshooters with the newer and better Sharps breech-loading rifle.

Some say the term "sharpshooter" derives from this 1st Regiment of U. S. Sharpshooters. But the word was in use long before, deriving from the German *scharfschütz,* and first appeared in English print about 1802 to describe a group of straight-shooting Tyrolians in the Austrian Army. The federal government purchased 80,000 Sharps rifles and carbines before the war was over. However, the breechloaders were never completely satisfactory chiefly because of the gas leakage at the breech-chamber joint. It was the metallic cartridge and repeating rifle that the Civil War brought into its own.

Lincoln was personally responsible for the Army's adoption of the seven-shot Spencer. He test-fired it and whittled an improvised sight for it. Some 94,000 Spencer carbines and 12,000 rifles were produced for the Union Army. Cavalrymen liked these repeaters but laughed at the noise which newfangled metal shells made when carried in the regulation tin-lined cartridge boxes designed for the old wax-paper cartridges. "When a horse trots it sounds like hail on a tin roof, don't it?"

Lincoln also encouraged adoption of the Henry rifle, which, as we have seen, was already in production when hostilities started, but the Army's high brass considered it too complicated and unproven. However, some two thousand Henrys were purchased by the War Department, and two regiments of Sherman's "bummers" carried them during his march across Georgia. Southern writers referred to the Henry as "that damned Yankee rifle that is loaded on Sunday and fired all week."

Samuel Colt had gotten back into the repeating-rifle picture in 1855 with an eight-shot, revolving-cylinder model. It was experimented with by units and individuals in both the Federal and Confederate armies. As the war progressed, the demand for new and better guns was keen. Individuals and detachments often provided their own Spencers, Sharps, Henrys and Colts in preference to government-issue arms. Of all the repeaters the Spencer proved the most popular, far outselling Henrys and Colts. It was also the lowest-priced to the taxpayer, costing the government twenty-five dollars each, as compared to thirty-seven dollars for the Henry and forty-four dollars for the Colt.

Military arms produced or used by Confederates during the war and passing west with its troops and civilians were substantially the same as those of the North: Springfields, Sharps, Henrys, Colts, regulation muskets and rifles. In addition, the South as well as North purchased a quantity of foreign arms, and these exotic models, such as the British Enfield and the Prussian needle rifle, found their way to the plains and mountains when the struggle ended.

The Allin Conversion

In 1865 a new rifle was adopted by the U.S. Army, one that in various forms was to be used for a long time. It was called the Springfield Model 1865 or the "Allin Conversion," after its inventor E. S. Allin, Master Armorer at the Springfield Armory. He devised a scheme whereby the huge surplus of muzzle-loading rifles remaining after the war could be converted to take cartridges. The barrels were sawed off at the breech end so that a cartridge could be inserted. A rising breechblock sealed it in place.

These first Springfield Model '65's were .58 caliber. Later the caliber was reduced to .50 and finally to .45, to become, in conjunction with a powder charge of 70 grains, the long-enduring Springfield .45–70. This arm was to be standard for infantry, and as a carbine for cavalry, until Spanish-American War days. Despite what happened at the Custer fight, despite the fact that the repeater was clearly here to stay, the Army refused to budge from the single-shot Springfield for twenty-five years. The only substantial gesture made during that period toward adopting a new rifle was the Hotchkiss, or U. S. Magazine Rifle Model 1878, the first bolt-action service magazine rifle. It was a .45 caliber with a five-shot magazine in the butt. A few thousand were manufactured by the Winchester Company under army contract before the Hotchkiss was deemed inadequate. Not many found their way West. The .45–70 single-shot Springfield that let Custer down at the Little Big Horn (many of them were found with expanded cartridge cases stuck in their chambers as result of the heating from rapid fire) continued to be the issue weapon.

The Krag

In November 1890 the Army finally convened a testing board to select a new service rifle that would be a repeater and have a much longer range than the old Springfield .45–70.

Smokeless powder would be a determining factor in the new gun. It burned more slowly than black powder, therefore the force of its explosion increased even more drastically as the bullet sped down the barrel, thus achieving greater velocity. A newly developed heat-

The .30-40 Krag. Many Krags are still in use in the West.

PHOTO BY DON O'NEIL FROM ROBERT T. BENSON COLLECTION

"The First Shot." Engraving, after drawing by Frederic Remington.

treated, low-carbon steel for barrels could withstand this high pressure, so that the new gun, instead of being heavier, could be lighter in weight. Velocity and range were increased still further by making the caliber of the bullet one-third smaller and changing the straight metal cartridge to a "bottleneck," thus compressing the charge and increasing its power—a device that would be used extensively on sporting rifles of the future.

The result of all these considerations was the U.S. Magazine Rifle Model 1892, known as the Krag-Jörgensen after its Norwegian inventors. It was substantially the same weapon used in the Danish and other Scandinavian armies. Through modified several times the U.S. Krag remained .30 caliber, center-fire, with a total length of forty-nine inches and weight of about nine and one-half pounds. The stock extended nearly the full length of the barrel as was customary with military rifles. This feature distinguished them from sporting arms and was designed to protect the soldier's hands when the barrel grew hot from rapid firing. It also gave him a heavier weapon to use as a club or in bayoneting.

The Krag had a unique side-constructed, box magazine, the right face of which could be swung out and down to act as loading gate. The cartridge employed, known as the .30–40 Krag or Caliber .30 U.S. Army, was our first smokeless service cartridge. It fired a hard, cupronickel jacketed bullet, considered more humane than the lead Minié ball and its lead successors, all of which mushroomed on impact. However, United States soldiers during the vicious fighting of the 1902 Philippine Insurrection often filed crosses in the ends of the new pencil-shaped bullets to achieve mushrooming effect on the hated Moros, and their favorite war song contained the lines:

> While beneath the Starry Flag
> We'll civilize them with a Krag.

This gun was strong and reliable. Great emphasis had been placed on its ability to act as either a repeater or single-shot rifle. The latter was considered important when the gun was to be handled by privates who were considered low in intelligence. It should be remembered that this rifle was designed for the post–Civil War Army, which had a large percentage of foreign immigrants and semiliterate Americans who were willing to soldier for fifteen dollars a month while the United States boomed with growing prosperity.

The repeating mechanism of the Krag was simple but so slow it proved a real disadvantage in battle. Each cartridge had to be put, one at a time, in the gun's box magazine. Westerners—Roosevelt's Rough Riders and others—at the Battle of San Juan Hill during the Spanish-American War found the Krag sadly lacking in firepower when pitted against the Spaniards' 7 mm. Mausers. These German-designed rifles were loaded with clips containing five cartridges. Thus a Spaniard on the firing line could reload five times faster than an American. This helps explain why 700 Spaniards racked up more than 1,400 American casualties before being overwhelmed.

The Springfield

The "Springfield," or U.S. Rifle Caliber .30 Model 1903, was the result of unpleasant experiences in the Spanish-American War. It was unabashedly a copy of the clip-fed, bolt-action Mauser. In fact the United States purchased the manufacturing rights from the Mauser Company. After early modifications, the weapon's length was fixed at 43 1/5 inches, its barrel at 24 inches, its weight at 8 3/5 pounds. It fired a clip of five cartridges. At first these were rimless with a 220-grain bullet propelled by 43 grains of smokeless powder (a grain being a unit of weight based on the weight of a grain of wheat), but in 1906 the bullet was given a sharper point and reduced in weight to 150 grains, and powder was increased to 49 grains, resulting in an increase of muzzle velocity to 2,700 feet per second. This is the cartridge that became famous as the .30–06, the "06" representing the year of its adoption.

The "Springfield" remained substantially unchanged through two world wars, more than redeeming any shortcomings of its rather infamous predecessors, the Springfield .45–70 and Krag-Jörgensen. Embodying the strength and conviction which came from the winning of the West, plus the wisdom of chastening Spanish-American War experiences, the sturdy Springfield with its .30–06 cartridge was aimed forward with the United States toward a new destiny of world power.

Army Pistols

The first official U.S. military pistol appeared in 1799. Like the first army shoulder arm it was copied from a French model. Made by Simeon North of Berlin, Connecticut, it was a smoothbore flintlock with an eight-and-a-half inch, round barrel, .69 caliber, walnut grip, and weighed three pounds four ounces. North made about 2,000 and sold them for six dollars each. A hundred and fifty years later they were rare collectors' items bringing upward of $2,400.

Between 1799 and the Civil War, the United States services developed their pistols through government armories as well as private firms. A number were single-shot flintlock models both smoothbore and rifled. Most of them resembled North's original model, with eight- to eleven-inch barrels though the caliber was gradually reduced to about .55. The first government-made pistol, the U.S. Model 1806, was produced at Harpers Ferry. Also called the Model 1805 and Model 1807 it was a .54-caliber sixteen-inch weapon weighing two-and-a-half pounds. Another pistol made by Simeon North at this time bore the inscription "U.S. Pistol Model 1808, S. North Navy." This gun with its .64 caliber was the first to bear the "Navy" label.

The first U.S. percussion ignition pistol, a single-shot smoothbore like its predecessors, appeared in 1842. This was followed in 1843 by a rifled version. The 2nd U.S. Dragoons carried these rifled pistols in March, 1846, when they rode into disputed territory south of the Nueces River in Texas, clashed with Mexican patrols, and started the Mexican War.

And this brings us to a famous Colt, the U.S. Army Model 1847—not to be confused with the 1836 which we will discuss later on or with subsequent Colts used by civilians. The Army, while considering multishot rifles, had also considered adopting multishot hand guns, but rejected them as too complicated, dangerous and newfangled. Young Sam Colt, as has been said, went broke producing revolving-cylinder rifles and pistols, which the Army failed to accept. Now the Army put him back in business with an order straight from a battlefield.

Some of Colt's early revolving-cylinder rifles and pistols had been purchased by the Republic of Texas soon after it declared its independence from Mexico in 1836. The weapons were part of the armament of the Texas Navy but eventually the pistols were turned over to the Texas Rangers. In 1846, units of these Rangers were attached to the United States forces which marched to the Rio Grande during the Mexican War. The Rangers' effective use of their Colt "Navy" pistols so impressed General Zachary Taylor that he dispatched Ranger Captain Sam Walker to Washington with orders to buy Colt revolvers.

Walker and Colt got together and the result was the U. S. Repeating Pistol Model 1847, or "Walker Colt," a .44 caliber, rifled, percussion six-shooter, nine inches long, weighing four pounds. One thousand Walker Colts were ordered by the U.S. War Department. They were manufactured at Eli Whitney's factory in Whitneyville near New Haven, Connecticut. (Colt didn't even have a factory. Some say he didn't even have a model gun to base the Walker on, but made up the design from memory with Walker's help.) A second order, also for a thousand, resulted in the 1848 Model Dragoon Colt, produced at the new Colt factory at Hartford. Sam Walker and Zach Taylor had put Sam Colt in business in a big way, and stage drivers, express guards and other Westerners with heavy shooting to do began using the big new heavy Colts, as the Texas Rangers and Army were doing.

The terms "Navy" and "Colt Navy" were soon used for any big pistol. Surely the oddity of pistols for the Republic of Texas' Navy being carried by dry-land Rangers hundreds of miles from the seacoast must have tickled the westerners' fancy. Perhaps, the name alone carried satiric appeal in the arid reaches of the Great Plains. At any rate "Navy" was a good word to add to a pistol.

In 1851 came an officially designated Colt Navy revolver; in 1860 a lighter Army model; and in 1861 a still lighter Navy. Lincoln thought so highly of the Colt Army 1860 Model that he gave a gold-and-silver inlaid pair to Charles XV, the liberal and popular King of Sweden and Norway who was friendly to the Union cause.

A host of other pistols besides Colts were used by the Army and Navy before and during the Civil War. The most popular calibers were .36 and .44 with smaller sizes for pocket weapons. This wide variety of hand guns continued to be produced after the Civil War—the best known was Colt's first center-fire cartridge revolver, the .45 Colt Army of 1873, also called the Peacemaker and the Frontier Model, described later. This famous six-shooter was the cowboys' and gunfighters' pistol and was carried by both military and civilian personnel. Custer's officers and men were armed with them.

In 1878 the Army adopted a Colt .45, known as the Double-Action Army or Frontier Double-Action or Omnipotent. "Double-action" meant that if the trigger was released after firing and then given a long, or double, pull it would recock the hammer and fire the gun again. Presumably this double pull recocked the hammer faster than the thumb could do on single-action pistols, which had to be manually cocked for each shot.

Good marksmen complained that it was impossible to hold steadily on a target while making the long pull necessary to recock a double-action weapon. However, the Army's first such gun was followed by a variety of double-action models in the 1890's and early 1900's, in .32, .38, .38 special and .41 calibers. Smith & Wesson and Remington also made pistols in various calibers that were used by the Army.

The .45 caliber models among these various military revolvers were always fairly effective man-stoppers, but the .38's and smaller calibers led by default to a new-style army pistol when they proved woefully unable to stop beserk Moros during the Philippine Insurrection. The Moros, warlike Mohammedans, would work themselves into a murderous religious ecstasy, perhaps with the aid of drugs, bind the vulnerable parts of their bodies tightly with *kogan,* the long native grass, thus deadening their nerves, then grabbing a creese they would charge down the thatched-hut street carving unbelievers. A .38 slug wouldn't stop them. True they might die in a minute or two from the effects of three or four such slugs, but meantime they might do a lot of damage. Even an undrugged Moro was hard to stop, so murderous were his intentions. The result was the army .45 automatic Colt. This struck a blow of 414 foot-pounds (equal to dropping 414 pounds one foot), and knocked a man over even when hit in the arm or leg. The muzzle energy of the old .38 Smith & Wesson, by contrast, was only 172 foot-pounds—sufficient to kill in a vital spot but not to fell instantly.

The Army's .45 automatic pistol appeared first in 1905 and was refined into the Model 1911 Colt, still in use half a century later. It utilized powder gases to achieve semiautomatic action, an idea patented by John Browning, the famous inventor and gun designer.

Few if any Colt 1911's saw action in the West. With the Springfield '03 they were pointed forward with the United States toward a new and different world.

72. *Civilian Pistols*

As WE HAVE seen, the first pistols were matchlocks. They had huge bores, .60 and .70 caliber, like the contemporary muskets and harquebuses. They were in fact thought of as hand cannon. None of these came into the New World, so far as has been recorded, but certainly the next model pistol did, the wheel lock, which the early Spanish explorers carried. The wheel lock's successor, the flintlock pistol, was common throughout the West from the seventeenth century on. Some were made with a hook, as has been explained, to hang on a man's sash.

The very first pistols—the weapon may take its name from the town of Pistoia in Italy where it was supposedly invented—had short heavy barrels and heavy, clumsy butts nearly at right angles to the barrel, with huge balls or caps on the end of the butts. Then the butts straightened out and grew and the pistol became almost a carbine, till the notion of a hand gun took hold again, and the butts shrank and curled into the grip with which we are familiar today. Large bores continued to be the fashion. The "horse" pistol common on the western frontier of the 1790's was a flintlock with a barrel ten inches long, caliber .65. This was the type that went into the Missouri country before and after Lewis and Clark, and showed up everywhere in traders' camps from Taos to the Columbia River.

Kentucky Models

Many of these early flintlock pistols came from England and Germany, but there was a native American type too, the Kentucky Pistol, a cut-down version of the famous rifle, made by many of the same Pennsylvania craftsmen.

Kentucky pistols usually had a full stock of wood, extending the length of the barrel. They ranged in caliber from about .35 to .55 and averaged fifteen inches in over-all length. Most were smoothbored, some were rifled, thus setting a new style in pistols. Mountain men carried Kentucky pistols as well as the various military models already mentioned, often changing them to percussion in the field. There is a record of the fur-trading explorer, Jedediah Smith, making some such conversion of his firearms at Mission San José in California in 1827.

Dueling Pistols

Dueling was essentially a Southern pastime though practiced in the North and West, too. Experienced mountain men like Jedediah Smith carried dueling pistols as sidearms, not because they expected to get into duels, but because such pistols were the best obtainable in the 1820's and 1830's. Smith was wearing two of them when Comanche ambushed and killed him on the Santa Fe Trail in 1831. These were reported to be of fancy English make, each with a little ramrod under an octagonal barrel that was half stocked with wood.

Typical dueling pistols were matched smoothbore single-shot flintlocks .55 to .70 caliber, exquisitely tooled and balanced, often with "hair" triggers that would move with a slight touch. They usually came packaged in sets of two in an expensive case.

Many army and navy officers carried dueling pistols as sidearms. Most of these were made in England or France, but native American firms such as the Deringer company in Philadelphia began to specialize in them.

The pistol was eminently the personal weapon, the final defense against forces that threatened life, honor, property. This was especially true in the West.

Group of representative derringers commonly used in the Old West as "hide-out" guns or guns secreted on the person. These are in various calibers from .22 to .41.

PHOTO BY DON O'NEIL FROM ROBERT T. BENSON COLLECTION

Colts and Allens

Two men raced neck and neck to capture the burgeoning popular pistol market of the 1830's and 1840's. They were Ethan Allen (no relation to the Revolutionary War hero) and Samuel Colt, who had gone broke making revolving rifles and been put back in business by the Mexican War pistol. Both were endeavoring to produce a pistol which would, in contrast to big flintlocks and fancy dueling pistols, be available to every man. Both Allen and Colt employed the newly developing percussion system to achieve their goals. Both had a multishot weapon in mind, but here their paths separated. Allen went the route of the multibarreled gun, an old idea that had never yet proved feasible. Colt took the new route of the revolver.

Allen produced, in 1837, what was to become the best-selling "pepperbox," a small pocket pistol consisting of a cluster of barrels, usually six, revolving on a single axis in front of a single hammer. As the trigger was pulled each barrel in turn came before the hammer and was fired. Thus the pepperbox was one of the first double-action pistols—much earlier than the Colt Army of 1878 previously described. Allen pepperboxes could be slipped into pocket or purse or drawer or up a sleeve. They far outsold Colts and any other variety of small firearms in the 1830's and early '40's. But they were big and clumsy, especially those of large caliber. You simply couldn't cluster a group of .45 caliber barrels and have anything less than absurdity. Furthermore they were inaccurate. You might aim at a tree and hit "the nigh mule," as Mark Twain recorded in *Roughing It,* when he described a passenger in an overland stage who practiced shooting at a tree with a pepperbox as the stage rolled along. Pepperboxes also had the annoying habit of discharging all barrels at once, if sparks from one charge ignited the others. And they lacked wallop and range, two things men needed in the wide-open spaces of the West. Nevertheless thousands of pepperboxes, largely made by Allen and his associates, went West with emigrants and gold rushers, saw service for and against the vigilantes in San Francisco and many another booming town, as well as in many a duel, assassination, gambling squabble and fancy-house brawl. Pepperboxes could be purchased for as little as ten dollars compared to upward of twenty-five dollars for an early Colt. They were the first common man's gun.

What did Colt offer that eventually enabled him to beat Allen and all the rest of the pistol producers? A better idea, chiefly. Plus the luck of Samuel Colt. We have seen how

METROPOLITAN MUSEUM OF ART, NEW YORK

FROM *The Gun and Its Development* BY W. W. GREENER,
CASSELL AND CO., LTD.

Left to Right: *1836 Paterson Colt Revolver, .40 caliber; the pepperbox, everyman's hand gun in the 1840's; 1836 "Texas" Paterson Colt, .34 caliber.*

the young inventor patented the principle of the revolving cylinder that locked in place with the barrel as the gun was cocked. Each chamber in this cylinder, like each barrel in the pepperbox, must be loaded separately with powder and ball. Also like the pepperbox, caps were placed on nipples behind each load, and every one was fired in turn, as the cap came under the hammer: But with the Colt, instead of all the barrels revolving, only the loaded chambers swung around between the hammer and a single barrel.

Imperfect as early models were, Colt's principle was sound. It enabled him to eventually build a pistol big enough to do heavy work in the West or any other place, yet small enough to be carried on a belt. For city use he would build even smaller, lighter models.

The 1836 Colt

The 1836 Colt or Paterson Colt, as it was also called, was born in the throes of competition and desperate finances in a corner of an abandoned silk factory in Paterson, New Jersey. The very first is supposed to have been a .34 caliber, rifled five-shooter with a four-and-a-half-inch octagon barrel. Some say all these Paterson-made Colts were five-shooters, others claim some were six-shot. Certainly all of them were odd-looking weapons with concealed triggers that dropped into view when the gun was cocked. As there was no visible trigger there was no need for a trigger guard. And to load the pistol it had to be separated into three pieces while the loads were rammed into the chambsrs.

Colt divided his new pistols into three classes for purposes of production: pocket pistols, belt pistols and holster pistols—the last evidently for a saddle. Pocket pistols were as a rule .28, .31 or .34 caliber; belt pistols .31 or .34; holster pistols .36. Barrel lengths varied from two and a half inches for some of the pocket pistols to twelve inches for some of the holster models. Most holster pistols had seven-and-a-half- or nine-inch barrels. All Paterson Colts were single action; in other words they had to be manually cocked for every shot.

At first Colt could not compete with the pepperbox. He found little market for his new weapon. A few were purchased by individual contingents of United States troops and militia; and others, as we have seen, went to Texas for the new republic's Navy.

In 1839, still operating at Paterson, Colt produced an improved model pistol. Some historians say that Sam Walker had come East for the Texas government before Zach Taylor sent for him in 1846, and that he suggested many of the improvements contained in the 1839 Model. Whether or not this is so, the new pistol was much better. It had a grip that came more naturally to the hand, allowing a steadier hold, and internal springs that were more simply made. Best of all a man did not have to remove the cylinder to load it. Instead a hinged ramrod under the barrel did the trick. This 1839 Model is often called the "Original Walker" or the "First Walker" or the "Paterson Walker," to distinguish it from the 1847 "Walker Colt" of Mexican War days. It has caused more controversy among gun collectors than any other single pistol. Adding to the intensity of the argument is the fact that collectors pay $1,900 to $3,800 for Paterson Colts while Walker Colts of the later vintage, being rarer still, bring from $2,500 to $5,500.

Whatever the truth about Walker's earlier visits, Sam Colt went bankrupt in 1842 and it *was* a visit from Walker that put him back in business at the time of the Mexican War, he meanwhile keeping his name before the public with such ingenious inventions as a mine for submarine harbor defense which so impressed Congress that it voted $20,000 for further development.

Colt was a gifted promoter. And with the Walker Colt of 1847, he was off and running. At his Hartford plant he made not only the heavy, 4½-pound army models, but lighter or "Baby" Dragoons, and then in 1849 went all out to capture the popular market from Allen and other pepperbox makers with the .31-caliber pocket pistol, one of the most popular and long-selling models Colt ever produced. It was primarily a city man's and traveler's gun, ideal also for storekeeper and bank clerk, and many went West with the emigrants and gold rushers.

The '49 Colt, however, did not suit the needs of the noncity westerner for a hand gun of power and range that could be readily carried. Colt's Navy Model of 1851 and Army Model of 1860, both service weapons discussed under "Army Pistols," moved toward that goal by combining heavy caliber with reduced weight. No less an authority than Wild Bill Hickok adopted the "Navy" Colt.

"Armys" and "Navys" were a standard sidearm out West till the advent of cartridge revolvers after the Civil War. And there was another hard-hitting but lightweight and readily carried Colt coming onto the market, the so-called New Model Police Pistol of 1862. It was caliber .36, five-shot, weighed only one and five-eighths pounds, and it kept the Army and Navy models company as sidearms for Union and Confederate soldiers, and westerners generally, besides being an effective tool for law-enforcement officers East and West. Some say these Colts were the first to bear the distinctive Colt trademark of a horse rampant with two spears converging on his shoulder. Such people maintain that Samuel Colt, the one-time runaway apprentice who had become rich, authorized the emblem because it was the coat of arms of his Coult—sometimes spelled Coilt—ancestors in Scotland. Others say that the emblem appeared on Colt arms, first in a circle then alone, some time after 1873, and therefore could not have been authorized by Colt, who died in 1862. In any event, the Colt "horse" on the side of a pistol grip became as important to western purchasers as the "dragon" on trade guns had been to Indians.

The impact of Colt revolvers on the West was nothing short of revolutionary. Up through the 1820's and '30's Indians had often shown their disdain for the white man's hand gun as well as his shoulder arms by raiding within sight of frontier posts. However, with the advent of the Colt revolver, this situation began to change. By 1839 the traveler and writer Josiah Gregg recorded Colt firearms being carried on the Santa Fe Trail, and in 1841 Kit Carson and party, defending a Santa Fe traders' caravan with Colt Paterson eight-shot cylinder rifles and five- and six-shot Paterson revolvers, killed or wounded more than 100 Kiowa and Comanche with loss of but one man. The Indians were appalled by weapons that seemingly never needed to be reloaded. Once again the white man's superior gods had spoken.

John C. Frémont lent official status to the Colt by reporting, after his pathfinding journey of 1842 through the Far West, that Carson slept with a pair of Colts at half-cock by his head and a Colt's rifle under the blanket beside him.

Even more telling in favor of the new revolving arms was the episode of 1844 when Colonel John Hays and fifteen Texas Rangers, armed with Colt revolvers, fought eighty

Comanche, killing forty-two of them. This fight received widespread publicity. The Colt legend was growing. What was more, the balance of power in the West had certainly changed.

Remington and Smith & Wesson

One should not think of Samuel Colt as being pressed only by Ethan Allen in providing the ideal personal weapon for the West. A man named Eliphalet Remington was also making pistols of many types, and good ones. By 1860 Remington offered a line of popular pocket revolvers and moved into the western market with a big .36 and .44. These differed from Colts chiefly in the solid frame over the top of the cylinder, which added strength and gave a continuous sighting groove.

Meanwhile Smith & Wesson had pioneered the development of metallic cartridges for pistols and were ready to manufacture something really revolutionary, the first cartridge revolver, when Colt's original patent covering the revolving cylinder expired in 1857. "S. & W." had purchased the Rollin White patent for boring the cylinder all the way through so that a cartridge could be inserted in the back.

White had offered the method to Colt, but Colt, not thinking in terms of metallic cartridges, had turned it down. Consequently Smith and Wesson had a monopoly on cartridge revolvers. They began with a seven-shot .22, added a .32 and .44, many of which were carried as sidearms by Civil War soldiers and all of which showed up in the West. Buffalo Bill owned a Smith & Wesson .44; so did Texas Jack Omohundro, the famous scout and associate of Bill's in the Wild West Show. The S. & W. used a center-fire cartridge with 25 grains of powder and a 218-grain bullet and, being the only cartridge pistol available, was in a fair way to capture the western market.

Then in 1869 the Rollin White patent expired and Colt and other firms jumped into the cartridge-revolver field quickly. First, Colt came out with the Richards conversion of 1871, which cut off the rear from the cylinder of percussion Colts and allowed them to use rim-fire metallic cartridges. Shortly thereafter, Colt appeared with an entirely new line of cartridge revolvers including the famous Peacemaker or Frontier.

Frankie's Little Forty-four

Another famous pistol of the mid-1800's was the derringer, derived from Deringer, surname of a famous gun-making family. In 1825 Henry Deringer, Jr. had converted his fine flintlock dueling pistols to percussion ignition. He was one of the first to make percussion hand guns. Now he cut down his dueling pistol to everyman's size, hoping to compete with Colt and others for the expanding popular market. Like his dueling pistols, the new weapon used percussion ignition. Like them, it was single-shot. Deringer didn't try to compete with Colt and Allen by making a multishot weapon. He concentrated on small size and big wallop. The result was the .44 caliber Deringer, as fine a thing as any little man ever carried to cut a big man down. If it spoke once, at the standard range of ten to twenty feet, that was generally all that was required. A .44 Deringer used at even shorter range became everlastingly famous, or infamous, by being the weapon used by John Wilkes Booth to assassinate Abraham Lincoln.

Deringers were often ordered in pairs like dueling pistols and were used for dueling. Gradually the name ceased being specific and became generic, applying to the whole species of pocket pistols of heavy caliber, and was misspelled "derringer." Colt later made a widely popular derringer. So did Remington and Smith & Wesson. The derringer is accepted by most authorities as being the weapon with which Frankie shot Johnny in the famous popular ballad.

Derringers went West in many a man's pocket, sleeve or traveling bag. According to one account there were 405 killings reported (one wonders how many were not reported) in California in 1855, derringers figuring in many of them. Much the same was true in Colorado, Montana, New Mexico and other gold-rush and mining centers. Around the table and over the bar, when the going got rough the little gun with the big voice was a mighty handy friend to have. Most popular of all derringers was probably the .41 caliber Remington, favorite of the gambler and con man. Anywhere within fifty feet it was likely to be deadly. Remington made over 150,000 of them before they were discontinued.

The idea of personal safety based on the personal weapon of last resort was not confined to males. Many a lady, shady and otherwise, of the mid-nineteenth century found it advisable to carry a tiny Remington Vest Pocket .22 in stocking, bosom or reticule for final reference in case disaster to life, limb, honor or property threatened. When you see or read of the heroine backed into a corner of the hotel bedroom, drawing her gun as a last desperate measure, it is probably the tiny .22 made by Remington or "S. & W." that she holds in her trembling but determined hand.

The Peacemaker Disturbs the Peace

A new era opened with the Colt Peacemaker of 1873. This renowned weapon did more toward the winning of the West than any other pistol. It was patented in 1871 and 1872 and is variously called the "Model 1872," "the 1873 Colt" (because it was issued in 1873), the "Frontier Model" (after the region in which it was to become famous) and the "Colt Army," because the Army bought 8,000 on first order and followed with a second order nearly as large.

The Peacemaker was chambered for a number of different calibers and was made in a variety of barrel lengths. Its great advantage over the earlier cartridge Colt was the fact that it took center-fire cartridges. These, being of heavier metal, could carry more powder and were less likely to misfire. The regular model was .45, single-action, six-shot, barrel seven-and-a-half inches long, weight two pounds five ounces. The original stocks were of walnut, the frame and hammer case-hardened, the finish blued. Nickel or silver plate could be had at extra cost. The gun was strongly and simply built, had an effective range of at least 100 yards, and would stand up under the hard knocks of the frontier, including being "wrapped" around a man's head in what was called "pistol whipping" or "buffaloing," a favorite pastime of frontier peace officers who wished to stop somewhere short of murder in preserving the peace.

The Peacemaker was pre-eminently the weapon of the outdoor westerner—cowboy, gun-

A) *.44 caliber Remington New Model Army pistol;* B) *Colt .45 Peacemaker;* C) *Colt Dragoon Pistol;* D) *.36 Caliber Colt Navy Model 1851;* E) *"Colt Frontier Six Shooter .44-40";* F) *.44 Caliber Colt Richards-Mason Conversion;* G) *.44 Caliber Colt Army Model 1860;* H) *.45 Caliber Smith & Wesson Schofield revolver;* I) *Colt Double-Action .38.*

man, ranch owner, hunter. This gun established the name "six-shooter" for a western man's gun. A list of famous owners of the Frontier .45 would fill this book—nearly. Besides Wyatt Earp, there were Bill Hickok, Bat Masterson, Sam Bass, Ben Thompson and Pat Garrett, to name a few. Garrett is said by Lucian Cary to have had the Peacemaker of Wild Bill Hickok in his hand when he killed Billy the Kid on the night of July 13, 1881, in Pete Maxwell's dark bedroom at Fort Sumner, New Mexico. As Cary tells it, when Jack McCall killed Hickok at Deadwood in 1876, one of two guns Hickok was wearing passed to his sister at Oberlin, Kansas, who gave it to Garrett, a friend of the family. Garrett, the story goes, wore it in memory of Hickok. When Garrett retired he gave it to an Oklahoma City firearms collector named Fred Sutton from whom it has passed from one collector to another, always a much-sought-after item.

Other gun authorities question this story; some say Wild Bill Hickok was wearing a Smith & Wesson .32 when Jack McCall killed him.

The Fast Draw

The era ushered in by the Peacemaker is sometimes called the gunfighting era or the romantic era or the cowboys-and-Indians era of the West. It is the period so much seen, and so often distorted, in movies and television shows, in magazines and books. Speaking in terms of gun technology, it was the era in which the cartridge revolver came into its own in the West.

It was commonly said: "God created men; Colonel Colt made them equal." A resident of El Paso wrote in those days, "I would as soon go out into the street without my pants as without my Colt." With six-guns a recognized article of dress and acknowledged arbiters of disputes, the weapon that spoke first had the best argument, so men developed what was called the "fast draw," and marvelous stories have been preserved about the speed with which a gun-slinger went into action.

Some authorities believe that modern gun experts, with their specially designed holsters and handy, lightweight, but hard-hitting revolvers, would beat the old-timers all hollow on the draw as well as the amount of lead accurately placed. This is difficult to determine because there were no readily available methods for clocking early-day gunfighters at the moment blood was being spilled, but their speed has been estimated at from 1/10 to 1/20 of a second. Under peaceful, noncombat conditions, a modern expert, Dee Woolem, has drawn and fired in 12/100 of a second. Another modern expert, Ed McGivern, has fired all five rounds of his revolver into a target the size of his hand in 2/5 of a second.

The fact that he fired only five rounds brings up some of the hokum that occasionally creeps into the accounts of early gunfighters. Allegedly the typical combat six-shooter carried five loaded shells, and the hammer rested on a sixth empty one. It was said that this was done to prevent an accidental blow on the hammer from discharging the cartridge. However, a Colt Frontier model had a safety notch which held the uncocked hammer back from the cartridge. It was said, truthfully, that by striking the gun's hammer forcefully with a tool-hammer this notch would be sheared and thus allow the gun's hammer to hit the cartridge and explode it.

However, I know of no instance in the movies, TV or actual life of anybody in a western

"A Fight in the Street." Pen and ink by Frederic Remington.

saloon going around with a tool-hammer striking the guns in men's holsters. Of course, it is possible that a gun might fall a sufficient distance and hit a sufficiently hard object to shear off the safety notch and discharge the weapon. But again, of all the places on a gun that might be struck when it fell, how often would the end of the hammer be the place?

There was a chance, yes, as there was with all firearms, but it is odd that a western gunman, a man who presumably took chances in life, would take such meticulous care to avoid a danger that seems so remote. Then too, if a man really feared that a blow on the end of his gun's hammer would shear off the safety, he could, by pulling the trigger as he cocked the weapon, let down the hammer halfway between the two cylinders where no possible blow would ignite a cartridge.

The whole truth of the matter seems to be that the reason for carrying a gun's hammer on an empty cylinder was one of habit or of fashion. Perhaps some gunman set the style, or more likely some journalist who wrote about gunmen said that they carried their weapons in this manner, so others did likewise. Let us never forget that western frontiersmen—cowboys, hunters, trappers, freighters—unconsciously, perhaps, modeled themselves after their literary counterparts. Even the toughest Indian scouts or professional killers like Tom Horn read dime novels avidly or associated with those who did. Certainly it was fashionable for young ranchmen and cowboys at the turn of the century to clump along board sidewalks of a western town in high-heeled boots, hats pulled low over their eyes, and guns in conspicuous evidence. Yet, it might be a great mistake to consider them less truculent and dangerous because they pictured themselves Frederic Remington characters or the heroes of some dime novel.

The correct way for a gunfighter to carry, cock and draw his six-shooter was described in detail by Wyatt Earp to his biographer, Stuart M. Lake. These directions have been amplified by an old-timer who told me that the left thumb was better than the right one for working back the hammer "because the left hand knows less than the right to begin with and so has less to unlearn when it comes to shooting"—an excellent rule surely for other things besides gunfighting.

As for "fanning," Wyatt Earp had little respect for that method of rapid fire achieved by filing off, or holding back, the trigger and brushing the hammer continuously with the left hand. He said that in all his life as a peace officer, he knew of no gunfighter who did not hold this and shooting from the hip in contempt. He said the same about the practice of cutting a notch in the handle of a gun for every man killed with it. Writers of "westerns" like to claim that this was common practice. Earp said that he knew positively that it was not done by such noted peace officers as Hickok, Bill Tilghman, Pat Saghrue, Bat Masterson and Charlie Bassett.

Much has recently been written about the inaccurate shooting of old-time gunfighters. At the famous Battle of the O. K. Corral in Tombstone, Arizona, in which Earp himself participated, between thirty and forty shots were required to kill three men—at close range, sometimes as close as six feet. However, the contents of many cemeteries attest to the reasonable efficiency of western gunplay. Earp thought Hickok unsurpassed as a marksman, citing his ability to drive a cork through a bottle. Bat Masterson, no slouch with a gun himself, thought Wyatt Earp unsurpassed when it came to the draw-and-shoot against a man who could shoot back.

The Buntline Special

For a number of years after 1876 Earp used a Colt presented him by Ned Buntline, the dime novelist and publicizer of Buffalo Bill. Much has been written about this so-called Buntline Special, and there is much disagreement concerning it. Some say that Buntline ordered the Colt factory to make five special .45 Frontier models with extra-long barrels and detachable rifle stocks, which he presented to prominent western peace officers. Others say these extra-long barreled weapons were exhibited by the company at the Centennial Exposition in Philadelphia in 1876; Buntline saw them there and, having an eye for publicity, ordered five for his presentations. Authorities also disagree on the barrel lengths of Buntline Specials but agree that most of the recipients found them too long and cut down the barrels. This may account for the conflicting descriptions. Wyatt Earp's biographer, Stuart Lake, says that Wyatt told him that the barrel of his Buntline Special was twelve inches long, that he did not cut it down and found it satisfactory for a quick draw. Wyatt's gun is also said to have had a detachable walnut stock on which NED was carved. However, both these details are contradicted by the factory records which show Specials to have been made in ten- and sixteen-inch lengths, with skeleton steel stocks. Whether or not Wyatt's memory, or that of his biographer, slipped concerning these details cannot now be proved, for Wyatt's gun is somewhere at the bottom of the Bering Sea. A friend of his lost it overboard during a storm when Wyatt was a saloon operator in Nome.

There were, however, other Colts than Buntlines and Peacemakers. The double-action .38 Lightning and .41 Thunderer came along in 1877. Billy the Kid used a .41 "self-cocker," as Pat Garrett described it. John Wesley Hardin, alleged killer of forty men, carried an old cap-and-ball .44 Colt stuffed under his shirt as late as 1877 when Texas Rangers arrested him at Pensacola Junction, Florida. Then, too, there were Bisley Model Colts, substantially the same as the Peacemakers but with special trigger and grip designed for target shooting, and there was a new Colt Navy, double-action, in 1889. Theodore Roosevelt killed a Spaniard with one during the Cuban fighting in '98.

Of course there were other makes besides Colts. Remington, as well as Smith & Wesson, made .45 six-shooters considered by many to be as good, or better, but they never achieved the Colt's popularity. The Peacemaker legend had grown too big. Although Sam Colt, aged forty-eight, died eleven years before the Peacemaker made him famous, his name lived on in a manner that dominated the West and the whole United States, surpassing the fondest dreams of frowsy little "Dr. Coult," who had supported himself between patents by lecturing on submarines and laughing gas, and who died a millionaire.

In 1878 the Colt company chambered his Peacemaker to take the .44–40 cartridge used by a new Winchester rifle which was becoming the West's most popular shoulder arm. This made the Colt's triumph near complete.

A little detail of the big Colt's mechanism which helped endear it to westerners had not been planned by the designers. This was the gate behind the cylinder where cartridges were slipped in. It swung out like a stubby little finger when opened. Cowboys riding into town after a summer's work soon learned a new use for this protuberance. When the stockhand sat down in the Four Ace Beer Hall or the Bucket of Blood for a friendly little game of cards, he found it convenient to thrust a six-shooter in the waistband of his Levis. The little reloading gate, if left open, prevented the gun from slipping down into his pants. It was part of the costume, part of the code. Last summer, maybe, he had sat by a roundup campfire singing about the stockman's hero:

> Oh his clothes war kie-ney reckless
> At the cowboy's Christmas ball.

Now he was identifying himself with the tradition—but, of course, would not admit it.

Another feature of the Peacemaker kept it in supreme favor. Its big .45 slug with that terrific wallop appealed to cowboys, just as it did to soldiers who wanted to stop Moros in the Philippines. The Colt company manufactured a .32 New Police pistol in 1895 and an improved Police Positive .32 and .38 in 1905. Both of these guns were small enough to carry in the pocket of a cowboy's chaps where they would not beat the hip off a rider when he galloped, but neither captured the cowboy's fancy. They were not big enough. A rider would explain that if a man was "throwed" and his foot hung in the stirrup, he needed a gun that would knock down his horse, whether it killed the brute or not, and thus set the foot free. Probably not one cowboy in a hundred ever got caught in such a situation, and if he did the chance of pulling a gun before the horse kicked or dragged him to death was slim, but this reason was often given to justify the .45.

It should be noted, too, that when the hammer on this famous Colt was drawn back it clicked four times, spelling its own name, people said: C-O-L-T.

The grand old gun continued to hold sway above all others right down to the automatics of the early 1900's. Some have likened it to the rapier and its age to the age of chivalry. Others say it was simply a step downward in man's descent to techniques of mass murder. Eugene Manlove Rhodes, cowhand, author and eyewitness to the era in question, says that gunfighters (whom he calls "gunmen") should be equated with the swordsmen of an earlier era and given a dash of nobility. He cites the personal risk taken by both swordsman and gunman, the romantic gallantry attaching to both; Rhodes does not defend the gunman as good but simply mentions him as a feature of the times, like the longhorned steer and the mustang.

The fact remains that the pistol, the personal weapon, played a substantial role in subduing the West and reached the zenith of its popularity there. It may be significant that the range killer, Tom Horn, escaping from a Cheyenne jail in 1903, was recaptured partly because he could not operate the semiautomatic German Luger he had wrested from one of his jailers. The point isn't that there weren't foreign pistols in the West before. The point is that the Old West of the six-shooter was dead—as dead as Tom Horn, cowboy, Indian fighter, bad man, user of the Peacemaker, was soon to be.

73. *Civilian Rifles and Shotguns*

THE FIRST SPORTING guns in the West—firearms used for nonmilitary purposes—were the matchlocks, wheel locks and flintlocks of the Spanish explorers and settlers. These brought down deer, elk, bear, lion, buffalo. From them developed a tradition of civilian firearm use that reached its climax in the period following the Civil War.

After the war a new mass market developed for shoulder arms as it already had for pistols. The American who had purchased the pistol in quantity for self-defense now began to purchase rifles and shotguns in quantity for sport. Not that self-defense was omitted entirely, but it played an increasingly smaller part. There was the added factor of utility. The westerner could use his sporting weapon to kill game for the table and to keep down wolves and coyotes, as well as to defend his life and property. Firearms were part of his everyday life.

The Winchester

The brass-framed lever-action Henry rifle, developed by B. Tyler Henry and Oliver F. Winchester, proved popular, as has been seen, after its appearance in 1860, but its mechanism was complicated and the tubular magazine had to be loaded from the muzzle end. This was done by compressing a spring by means of a thumb lug. The lug worked up and down in an

1886 Winchester carbine, commonly called the "Yellow Boy" because of its shiny yellow brass frame, was a favorite with westerners generally. It was easily carried on a saddle and easily loaded through the side gate in its revolver.

PHOTO BY DON O'NEIL FROM ROBERT T. BENSON COLLECTION

open slot extending the entire length of the magazine. Dust and foreign matter lodged in the slot, dirtying cartridges and causing stoppage. Nevertheless the Henry became a favorite civilian arm. It was easy to pack on a saddle and, above all, its fifteen shots represented tremendous firepower.

In 1866, the year after the Civil War ended, Winchester and Henry remedied some of the faults of their 1860 model with the first true Winchester. It was produced at New Haven under the firm's new name of The Winchester Repeating Arms Company. The Winchester Model 1866 had a side-loading gate in a brass frame, thus doing away with the objectionable slot in the magazine. The gun also had a less complicated action, but it continued to use the .44 rim-fire cartridge with 28 grains of powder—not a heavy enough load for the long distances and big game of the West, but as heavy as the thin-shelled rim-fire cartridge could safely hold. This first true Winchester was a trim, easily carried, multishot weapon eagerly accepted by frontiersmen, Indians and the general outdoor public. It gave Winchester a good start on the postwar civilian market. But it, too, had defects—and serious competition.

First among its competitors was the Spencer, by far the most popular repeating rifle used in the Civil War. Christopher Spencer, its inventor, was a talented young man. He lacked two gifts, however: Oliver Winchester's business ability and a rifle that had range and shocking power sufficient for western needs. The seven-shot Spencer was even more underpowered than the Winchester for long range and big game. Though larger in caliber—.50 and .54 against the Winchester .44—it had a lower velocity and a shorter range. Furthermore it packed less than half as many cartridges as the Winchester '66.

When the Spencer firm failed in 1869, Oliver Winchester was on hand to purchase the plant. The onetime carpenter and shirtmaker was now on his way to fame and fortune, riding the crest of the new industrialism and the new civilian market in guns. He had hoped for big military orders, but these were not forthcoming. Perhaps this was a blessing in disguise. It forced Winchester to scratch hard in the civilian field, which in the end proved more rewarding.

The Winchester Model 1873

Winchester saw that his 1866 rifle had two outstanding assets: its capacity to fire rapidly and its ease of handling, but its bullet lacked impact and range. He took steps to correct these deficiencies. The result was a famous weapon that has been called, with so many others, "the gun that won the West"—the illustrious Winchester .44–40 or Model 1873. In 12-shot, 20-inch-barrel carbine, and 15-shot, 24-inch-barrel rifle, this fine all-purpose model won its way into the hearts of westerners until the word "Winchester" became synonymous for rifle from the Plains to the Pacific. A Denver newspaper correspondent once reported, so the story goes, that during a strike at a Remington factory the loyal employees came to work with "their trusty Winchesters"—a phrase so natural no one questioned it.

The 1873 Winchester was stronger, simpler, lighter in weight than the '66. But its greatest improvement was its center-fire cartridge, which contained 40 grains of powder, representing a substantial increase in range and shocking power over the old rim-fire load of only 28 grains.

Another advantage of the Winchester '73, or .44–40, was its caliber. We have noted that

The Model 1873 Winchester rifle caliber .44-40, the first Winchester to employ the powerful and dependable center-fire cartridge.

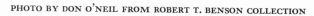

Colt's Peacemaker revolver was rechambered in 1878 for the .44 Winchester rifle cartridge. From then on a man needed to carry only one kind of ammunition for his pistol and rifle. This represented a real saving where weight—on the person or in the pack—was a critical factor. It also represented a safety factor. More than one man, when forced to abandon a swimming horse, had been unable to save himself because two or three heavy cartridge belts dragged him under.

At any rate the Model '73, with its handy counterpart the Colt, is said to have killed more game, more Indians and more U.S. soldiers than any other firearm. A dubious claim to fame, but apparently entirely true.

Buffalo Bill Cody owned half a dozen '73's. He wrote the Winchester Company in 1875 from Fort McPherson, Nebraska, that he had tried nearly every kind of gun made in the United States for hunting and Indian fighting and found the '73 the best. He added, by way of additional proof, that an Indian would give more for it than for any other gun. Cody closed by saying he had shot a grizzly in the Black Hills with his trusty '73, bringing it down with eleven shots.

PHOTO BY DON O'NEIL FROM ROBERT T. BENSON COLLECTION

The .50-110 Express Model 1886, Winchester's entry in the race for the larger caliber rifles needed for the big game of the West. It appeared too late for the buffalo, but took its toll of elk and remaining grizzly.

PHOTO BY DICK SMITH

Durable, portable, economical, versatile, the Winchester .30-30 became the favorite all-purpose gun for ranchers and western-ers generally. This original Model 1894 has been used on a California cattle ranch for sixty years and has brought down game ranging in size from rabbits to wild bulls.

The Remington

Popular as the Winchester Model '73 proved to be, it was not just what the West wanted. Witness Cody's eleven shots on one bear. A more powerful and reliable rifle was needed for such big game as grizzly and buffalo. Even elk, moose and deer at ranges beyond two hundred yards were reasonably safe.

Leading the field against the Winchester line was the Remington Rolling-block .50, a single-shot rifle firing a cartridge with 70 grains of black powder compared to the Model '73's 40. This Remington was more accurate and had half again the range of the '73. The rolling-block consisted of a mechanism at the breech end of the barrel which rotated about a heavy pin driven at right angles through the receiver of the rifle. To load, a man thumbed back the hammer to full cock, swung (or "rolled") the breechlock back, thus exposing the breech. This operation also extracted the expended cartridge. A cartridge could now be inserted in the chamber and the breechblock flipped forward into place behind it. A firing pin penetrated the block and transmitted the hammer's blow to the cartridge.

General Custer received a Rolling-block .50 from the Remington Company in 1872 and found that he preferred it to his Winchester. In '74 he bagged a grizzly with it in the Black Hills. This Remington appears to be the one which he carried into battle on the Little Big Horn and which passed into Indian hands. Custer wrote an endorsement of it to the Remington Company, saying that the forty-one antelope he had killed with it were hit at distances averaging 250 yards. At the same time he was joking with his brother Tom for using a Winchester '73 that was "remarkably accurate up to one hundred yards, and not so beyond that distance."

Such commendation from one of the leading figures in the West did Remington products no harm. As with Buffalo Bill's endorsement of the Winchester, one senses a behind-the-scenes competition between gun manufacturers for testimonial letters. Gun making was becoming big business and big business needed big advertising.

The very popular Remington .50 had been available in various versions since 1866, first as a rim-fire, now as a center-fire, but always as single shot. Best known in America as a sporting arm, it was popular elsewhere as a military weapon. Remingtons were used as service arms from Egypt to Sweden and were sold in great quantities in Prussia and France. Some historians say that if there had been a war in Europe during the mid-1870's it would have been fought largely with Remington rifles.

COURTESY OF REMINGTON ARMS CO., INC.

Remington Rolling-block .50 was a favorite with western big game hunters. The Rolling-block Rifle was manufactured by Remington from 1867 to 1890 in various calibers from .22 to .58 and was also known as The Remington Buffalo Gun and Remington Sporting Rifle No. 1.

Buffalo Guns

Buffalo rifles were almost a special category of big-bore weapon, and here again the big firms clashed competitively. Buffaloes were a major item on the western scene and in the national economy of the 1870's. Commercial buffalo hunting was reaching its climax. Two hundred thousand hides were marketed in Fort Worth in a single day. Good though the Winchester '73 was as an all-purpose saddle gun, it did not satisfy the buffalo hunters' demand for a heavy-hitting long-range weapon.

True, buffaloes could be killed from horseback at short range as had been done for years, and no doubt Buffalo Bill actually did kill thousands this way with his Springfield Model 1866 military rifle. But far more practical in the commercial hunter's view was the dismounted method commonly employed. By this procedure the hunter would try to slip up to within two hundred yards of a comparatively small bunch of twenty to sixty buffaloes, a fragment of some large herd. Hoping to shoot them all down in what was called "a stand," he would aim first at the leader, usually a cow. If she dropped, the bunch might run a hundred yards or so and a new leader would take charge. A second shot would be aimed at this animal, and if a third buffalo now took the lead it too would be dropped. The remaining buffaloes often "stood" bewildered, while the hunter killed them all.

What was needed for this type of work was a heavy long-range weapon, and Oliver Winchester's competitors were satisfying the need.

Remington's Rolling-block single shot, chambered for a .44–90 cartridge with a heavy 400-grain bullet, was called by its makers, The Buffalo Gun. "Brazos Bob" McRae, an early Texas hunter, is described as killing fifty-four buffaloes with fifty-four shots with his Remington Buffalo Gun. Another Remington saga tells how Nelson Story and thirty cowhands, who took one of the first Texas cattle herds to Montana, fought their way through hostile Sioux with their .50 caliber Remingtons and reached the vicinity of Gallatin with the loss of only one man. Winchester offered nothing that could compete with the Remington when it came to power, range and accuracy.

Eli Whitney, Jr., was another who offered stiff competition. He obtained manufacturing rights to the Laidley and Emery breech-loading patents and developed a weapon similar to the Rolling-block .50, the Laidley-Whitney .44, .45 and .50 caliber single-shot breechloader. It became a real competitor in the buffalo gun field. Another was the Ballard which, like the Laidley-Whitney, is almost forgotten but was a famous weapon in its time. To own a Ballard in the 1860's, '70's and '80's was to own as fine a rifle as any in the world. Ballards came in a variety of calibers from .22 to .56, all single shot. As .45–70's they were very popular with buffalo hunters. Theodore Roosevelt owned one. After the firm failed in 1875 Ballards were made by John M. Marlin under the name of Ballard-Marlins, or Marlin-Ballards.

The Marlin firm became a competitor under its own name after 1881, producing Marlin rifles in various calibers, beginning with a .45–70 model.

The Sharps

But the toughest competition for Winchester and Remington, at least where buffaloes were concerned, came from the Sharps. Of all the heavy-bore single-shot breech-loading rifles in the West, the Sharps was by far the most popular with buffalo hunters. We have already seen that the early breech-loading Sharps and its linen cartridge achieved fame for rapid firing prior to the Civil War. These guns gave Sharps a good name in the West long before Winchesters and Remingtons appeared. To hold its place in the business race after the war, the Sharps company, in 1869, modified some 30,000 percussion carbines to take the new metallic cartridges. The result was a .50 caliber center-fire breechloader sometimes called the "Big Fifty," but collectors restrict this name to the later Sharps .50–95 or .50–100.

At the same time the company brought out a sporting rifle to take .40–75 or .40–70 cartridges. This same model Sharps of 1869 was later chambered for .44–70 and .50–70 loads. In .45 caliber firing a 550-grain bullet with a 120-grain powder charge, the Sharps had more

"At Close Quarters." Painting by Charles M. Russell.

shocking power than the Remington Buffalo Gun. It was said to kill dependably at 1,000 yards.

However, marksmen, like fishermen, are not noted for veracity. At 1,000 yards a buffalo appears smaller than the bead-sight on a rifle, so it practically disappears when aimed at. In addition, before accepting the alleged long-distance performance of this early-day 550-bullet in its .45–120 cartridge, it should be noted that careful measurements of the modern 405-grain bullet in a .45–70 shell show that it drops eighty-four inches in the first 300 yards, and a 510-grain bullet in a .458 Winchester backed by superspeed magnum powder drops thirty-three inches in the same distance. Therefore, it seems more than probable that the 550-grain bullet of the old black powder buffalo gun would drop a truly great distance at 1,000 yards. Actually the mathematical formula for falling projectiles indicates that, with no wind resistance, the bullet would fall over sixty-two feet.

In short, a marksman shooting at a buffalo almost three fifths of a mile away would have to use rare judgment in aiming more than 62 feet above a mark he could not see. So the man who tells about regular game shots at 1,000 yards is probably indulging in what westerners like to call "stretching the blanket." Ned Buntline, who was something of a crack shot in his time, said that a hunter should use rock salt instead of lead for such long shots, and thus preserve the meat until he got to it.

Regardless of these conclusions the Sharps .45 and .50–140–700 were reckoned great guns on the Plains—although they must have kicked like an army mule. Another favorite was the Sharps Creedmoor (or Creedmore) of .44 caliber, named for the shooting grounds on Long Island where international matches were held. Buffalo hunters like J. Wright Mooar and Charles J. ("Buffalo") Jones swore by them. Sportsmen like Theodore Roosevelt kept a Sharps .40–90 for long-range work.

Yet the Sharps firm made one fatal error. It banked too confidently on the success of its seemingly invincible single-shot arm in a day when the repeating rifle's popularity was clearly ascending. With the passing of the buffalo the Sharps firm closed its doors.

The Race for the Big Bores

To stay in the running with the big gun needed for big game, Winchester brought out its Model 1876. This was called the "Centennial" because it was marketed in the United States' one-hundredth anniversary year. It was chambered for a variety of big charges, one of the most popular being the .45 caliber using 75 grains of black powder to propel a 350-grain bullet. The '76 was big enough to stop a buffalo or grizzly, yet handy enough to be carried on a saddle, and it was in the main stream of gun progress that was making the magazine rifle clearly superior to the single-shot breechloader. Ranchers and cattlemen like Theodore Roosevelt, then running cows on his spread at Medora in the Dakota Bad Lands, enthusiastically adopted the Model '76. Roosevelt wrote that he preferred it to his Sharps .45–120 or his double-barreled English express—a firearm so heavy that special gunbearers carried it for sportsmen in Africa. "I now use it [the Winchester '76] almost exclusively, having killed every kind of game with it, from a grizzly to a bighorn." He also hunted men with it, taking it along on a chase after horse thieves, and there is a famous photograph of him in western garb holding a half-magazine '76 at high port.

The Centennial model put Winchester back in the big-bore race. Incidentally this gun was adopted in carbine form by the Northwest Mounted Police and carried by them until 1914.

In 1878 Winchester brought out its Hotchkiss bolt-action, already mentioned as a military arm, and Remington replied in 1880 with its bolt-action Keene. The Keene was chambered for .44–40 and more powerful loads, the Hotchkiss for .45–70. Bolt-actions served better for these big charges, but the bolt's thick, heavy mechanism chafed the underside of a rider's knee when carried on his saddle, and westerners in the 1880's were not yet ready for bolt-action models, which in time became stronger and simpler than lever-action rifles. Instead, the race continued for guns of familiar pattern possessing heavier striking power and greater range.

The next gun to make a name for itself in the race for the big bores was the Winchester Model '86, designed by John Moses Browning. It retained the lever-action of the Centennial Model in a smoother, faster and stronger form. These guns were manufactured in .50–110, .45–90, .45–70 and lower calibers down to .38–56. The biggest bores were plainly for America's biggest game. Both the .50–110 and the .45–90 kicked like bay steers. As for the .45–70, it was too small. This writer knew a man who shot two buffaloes with it. The first, hit in the heart when standing, ran a hundred yards before collapsing stone dead. The other was shot running and the first bullet punctured lungs, guts and lodged in the shoulder. Two more were necessary to kill the buffalo, the last a neck shot as the wounded animal charged.

Obviously a more powerful gun was needed for such game. Remington offered a new bolt-action repeater built for extra-heavy loads, but again hunters failed to buy many of them.

Smokeless Powder

Bigger cartridges firing bigger bullets in heavier guns had reached the point of diminishing returns, when Alfred Nobel produced the first practical smokeless powder in Sweden in 1888. The new powder burned at a slower, more even rate than black powder and built a constantly increasing pressure behind the bullet. Thus smaller powder charges and smaller bullets fired in lighter gun barrels could achieve greater shocking power and range than the old big-bores using huge charges of black powder. Stronger and lighter steels for gun barrels also came into the picture. Practically all newly designed American sporting rifles became lighter in weight after DuPont produced the first smokeless powder in the United States in 1893.

With the new powder in mind, Browning designed for Winchester a .30–30 rifle and carbine (note the reduced caliber and powder charge). This was the lever-action Model 1894—the first smokeless-powder Winchester—and it became the most popular sporting rifle in history, replacing the '73 as standard for deer hunters, ranchers and outdoor people generally. Over two million Winchester .30–30's were sold in the next half-century. My own stands in the corner of the room as this is written. Purchased in 1899 at Golcher's, a famous sporting goods store on Market Street, San Francisco, for all-purpose use on a Spanish land-grant rancho in southern California, it has killed bobcat, coyote, fox, rabbit, rattlesnake and squirrel, as well as deer. It stands forty-four inches over-all, has an octagon barrel twenty-six inches long with a full-length eight-shot tubular magazine and buckhorn rear sight. It has been packed hundreds of miles on the saddle, used as combination walking stick and machete up and down shaly, brush-covered hillsides, and has never let its bearer down.

One of the great advantages in owning a .30–30 was the knowledge that the man in the next camp probably owned one also. Thus the cowboy who ran out of "catridges" could usually "borrey" some from the first rider he met. The name ".30–30" like the name "Winchester," became synonymous for rifle. No course in sociology was needed to understand what the Mexican *insurrectos* on the Texas border in 1911 meant when they chanted:

> Compañeros of the plow,
>   Tired, starved and dirty,
> There's but one road to travel now,
>   So grab your .30–30!

Having expressed these sentiments the dark-skinned riders in their enormous hats saw nothing inconsistent in swinging .45–90's, .45–70's and military Mausers across the flat horns of their saddles and jogging off to fight for God and Francisco Madero.

Yet with all its popularity, the .30–30 was an inferior weapon. True, it was sturdy and flat for carrying under a man's leg on a saddle. This and the fact that it was the first smoke-less-powder Winchester accounted for its wide sale, and although it has probably killed more deer than any other gun, the man who wanted to be sure of meat on the table sought something with a bigger, deadlier bullet.

New Styles in Cartridges

Winchester's big .32–40, produced contemporarily with the .30–30 in 1894, had the required shocking power. Its 165-grain bullet with a soft-lead expanding nose had noticeably more knock-down shocking power on big game than the .30–30's 150-grain projectile. Like the .30–30, the heavier .32–40 held up well at a hundred yards. But for a long shot of 300 yards a .30–30 bullet dropped 27.2 inches while the heavier .32–40 dropped more than twice that distance. Obviously there was a need for a long-range cartridge with the flat trajectory (the curve of the projectile in flight) of the .30–30 and the shocking power of the bigger .32–40. This was accomplished by changing the shape of the .32–40 cartridge—by giving it the bottleneck of the .30–30 and Army Krag, thus concentrating the force of the same powder explosion and expelling the bullet with more than two and a half times the foot-pounds of energy. With this ingenious change, a 170-grain bullet with its terrific slugging power held up to within less than four inches of the lighter .30–30 at 300 yards. And a variation of only four inches on the side of an elk or deer seldom prevents a hunter from eating liver for supper.

The new version of the .32–40 Model '94 which was chambered for this bottleneck cartridge was called the .32 Special and it soon became the second most popular gun in the West, favored by hunters, while the .30–30 continued to be the all-round cowboy rifle. Roosevelt and others took both these guns to Africa where the .32 Special killed almost every type of big game, including lion and rhino; the .30–30 also gave a good account of itself. The deadly shocking power of these small-bore high-powered rifles was further increased by the use of soft-nosed bullets which mushroomed into much larger calibers when they hit. One of the most famous was the Hoxie bullet, which spread out on contact like a star, tearing a hole bigger than the old .50 and .60 caliber weapons had done.

Among the new firms capitalizing on the new principle of higher velocity and greater impact was the Savage Arms Company. Their deservedly renowned .303 was first made in 1895. It had a six-shot magazine of rotary type and a twenty-six-inch barrel and was also made in carbine style. The action was unique. Sleek-looking and hammerless, it operated with a lever under a closed solid-breech receiver and side ejector. The total weight was about seven pounds. Many sportsmen consider the Savage the finest of the lever-action rifles, ideal for deer and smaller game.

These newer and finer guns did not eliminate the older arms altogether. Obsolete, "black-powder" Springfield .45–70's continued to be used all over the West, and as has been said, Mexican *insurrectos* carried old Winchester .45–90's as late as 1911 during the Madero Revolution and Pancho Villa forays. Bolt-action Mausers captured from Mexican regulars made their appearance on both sides of the border in those days. As for the Krag .30–40's, when they were sold cheaply as army surplus a number of them passed into western sheep camps where they were used as alarm guns by herders to frighten off marauding wolves and coyotes. A shot in the air after dark was often sufficient to do the job. These "Long Toms," as they were called, proved clumsy for a herder to strap on his saddle. The butt and muzzle were so far apart a rider dared not turn his horse, lest the animal hit his head on one end of the gun or his hips on the other. Camp-movers even found "Long Toms" awkward to pack on burros, although some packers learned to use the long barrel as a twist for tightening the rope on a diamond hitch when it worked loose—an ignoble use, surely, for the once-proud Krag that had stormed San Juan Hill.

The .30–06

And now the .30–06—most famous of them all with men who know guns. The first sporting models of this primarily military weapon appear to have been made in 1910 in Los Angeles for Stewart Edward White, the western author and big-game hunter, to take to Africa. Winchester had already made the lever-action Model '95 in .405 caliber, and some '95's were chambered for the .30–06 government cartridge. Roosevelt took two .405's to Africa where they performed well. But it was the .30–06 bolt-action, patterned after the Army Springfield '03, that was to catch on for western hunting.

Using a variety of bullets from 110 to 220 grain, it could take care of anything on the North American continent, including grizzly.

"The Fugitive." Engraving, after drawing by Frederic Remington.

CLARENCE P. HORNUNG COLLECTION

White found that in Africa it bettered any rifle he had yet used. In *The Land of Foot-prints,* an account of his African trip, he noted that the specially made "Army Springfield, model 1903, to take the 1906 cartridge" had remarkably flat trajectory and killing power. "The Springfield," he wrote, "dropped nearly half the animals dead with one shot; a most unusual record, as every sportsman will recognize."

His experience demonstrated the all-round superiority of the .30–06, and practically every major firm, following the path Stewart Edward White had pioneered, eventually manufactured .30–06 rifles. Few weapons have proved more popular. Remington furnished its .30–06 with a bolt handle that did not protrude as objectionably as on most bolt-action models and could therefore be carried more comfortably in a saddle holster. This writer's Remington has knocked down the 1,500-pound wild bulls of the Sisquoc River with one shot, and they have stayed down. Incidentally one of these animals was so tough-skulled that a Colt Frontier .44 emptied into its forehead at a range of three feet—while it was down but not out—failed to penetrate the bone. After the .30–06 gave the quietus, I picked the flattened .44 slugs with my fingers from the hide of the bull's forehead.

Yet the hard-hitting .30–06 proved equally satisfactory for antelope and deer. The secret of its versatility lay in the variety of cartridges available for it. A 150-grain deer bullet dropped only fifteen inches in 300 yards. The same bullet in a .30–30 dropped twenty-six inches. If a hunter met a grizzly or a bull moose all he had to do was to slip in a cartridge carrying a 220-grain bullet. This was big enough for anything that walked, and at 300 yards it still dropped less than the lighter .30–30 or the .32 Special. But these heavy bullets kicked. If a man was careless, his thumb on the stock might hit his nose a blood-letting blow.

The tremendous velocity of the .30–06 cartridge was all the force that a bullet could stand. The 220 projectile would plow through dense cover and hit a smashing blow. But the light 150 bullet might fly to pieces if it hit a twig before reaching the mark. A friend of mine once fired at a running antelope. The bullet hit the top of a sagebrush, shattered, and a fragment killed another antelope. He has switched to the 180-grain bullet even for antelope. True, the 180 bullet drops over two inches more at 300 yards, but that is seldom enough to be critical.

The .30–06 is typical of those rifles deriving from the last decade of the nineteenth century and the first decade of the twentieth that have remained in use to this day in substantially their original form. The peep sight (usually a Lyman) came into use in the early 1900's. Being located on the stock it added twelve to sixteen inches to the distance between front and rear sights, thus serving to the shooter's advantage much as the extra length of the Kentucky rifle had done, but without adding the extra cumbersomeness. The telescope sight would come into common use later, but to all intents and purposes the gun itself could not be improved upon. It could do everything it had to do. The West was won. All that mattered now was to enjoy it— and to do well by it.

Pump Guns

The repeating rifles described so far have been either lever- or bolt-actions operated by the shooter's right or trigger hand. With both these mechanisms, the marksman was apt to lower the gun from his cheek between shots and thus lose precious time. An attempt to correct this disadvantage was made with a new model in which the rifle's front grip, the one under the barrel held by the left hand, could be slipped back and forth to eject the spent cartridge, place a new one in the chamber and cock the hammer all with one movement.

These slide-action rifles, generally .22 or .32 caliber, enabled a man to hold his gun on the target and pump shot after shot at it with great rapidity. The action proved unusually efficient for a man who needed a free right arm to encircle a branch when shooting out of a tree. But who does much shooting out of a tree? Oddly enough javelina hunters in the brush country of south Texas often climbed into live oaks so that they could look down into spiny cactus jungles. The little wild pigs ran in droves, and a fast man with a pump gun could sometimes knock down two or three as they trotted under him, their tusks clicking like castanets.

However, pump guns were never generally popular in the West, except possibly the small caliber ones as ranch "house guns." In a saddle scabbard the slide-action was dangerous. A horse's trot might work the slide back and forth and set the gun to repeating. But the ammunition was cheap, and a man who liked to shoot could afford to ping away all day at rabbits, chipmunks or birds around the corral. A good marksman might even shoot the heads off sage hens as they stalked solemnly down to spring or windmill, necks erect as tenpins.

Double-barreled Death

Sometimes in reading about the gunfighting era one gets the impression that Wyatt Earp and his contemporaries spent most of their time walking around with double-barreled shotguns, either blowing each other to pieces or threatening to. Certainly, the shotgun came West long before the Civil War, and some, as we have seen, were owned by Indians. However, shotguns were never popular in the early days. Until gentlemen ranchers brought them West they were mostly a defensive weapon for use at close range against humans. Such guns frequently had the ends of the barrels sawed off. They were used by guards on overland stages, by lookouts in gambling halls and by killers out to get an enemy. Those carried by Wells Fargo guards were English-made, mainly 10-gauge. Later these guards carried Winchesters, cut down either by the factory or by a hacksaw in private hands. As late as 1894 one of the latter was carried by Jim McConnell, the guard riding the four-horse stagecoach which crossed the foothills between Milton and Sonora in the California gold country. McConnell sat inconspicuously inside on the rear seat, the 10-gauge across his knees.

The gauge of a shotgun is reckoned differently than the caliber of a rifle. Instead of being the diameter of the bore measured in fractions of an inch, a shotgun's gauge is determined as follows: a 12-gauge gun is one in which a lead ball the size of the bore weighs one-twelfth of a pound, or in other words, twelve balls the size of the bore weigh a pound; a 10-gauge is one in which ten of the balls that fit it weigh a pound; and so forth. The lower gauges—8, 6, etc.—therefore indicate increasingly larger bores.

Examples of big-bore shotguns used commercially in the West reached their climax in the San Francisco Bay area of the '80's and '90's, when professional duck hunters supplying

"In a Cañon of the Coeur d'Alene." Engraving, after drawing by Frederic Remington.

markets and fancy restaurants blasted flocks in the Suisun marshes and Sacramento delta. At ranges up to one hundred yards they sometimes killed fifty and sixty at a shot.

However, around cow camps and on "real" ranches a shotgun was considered "sissy"— the city man's gun used to kill birds. But as the West became pacified and game grew scarcer, shotgun shooting both as a sport and as a source of food became popular. Roosevelt, ranching in the Dakotas, owned two double-barreled shotguns, one a 10-gauge choke-bore made by Thomas of Chicago which he used for ducks and geese.

The choke of a gun refers to the amount the barrel is constricted at the muzzle to prevent the shot from scattering. A barrel that is full choke will deliver 65 to 75 per cent of the pellets in the load in a thirty-inch circle at forty yards. For the heavy, waterproof plumage of ducks and geese Roosevelt would need such a concentration of shot to penetrate the feathers in killing quantity and bring down the game.

Roosevelt also had a 16-gauge hammerless, made especially for him by Kennedy of St. Paul, which he used for grouse and plover. This undoubtedly had a modified choke in one barrel, which means that only 45 to 55 per cent of the shot from that barrel will be delivered in the thirty-inch circle. The remainder, or approximately half of the load, will scatter outside the circle in quantities that may still be sufficient to kill light-feathered birds. In other words a marksman shooting a gun with a modified choke does not need to aim so accurately to make a hit because his shot scatters more widely, though not in such deadly quantities. Grouse, plover, quail and doves, all small birds easy to kill, are erratic fliers, apt to swerve, dart and tumble. Even the best shooter needs this wider spread of shot to fill his game bag.

Most double-barreled guns are made with one barrel full choke and one modified, so the shooter can use his judgment and fire the suitable one when the game is flushed—the modified for a quick close shot, the full choke for long range.

Few cowhands and dirt ranchmen could afford Roosevelt's custom-made guns, but as the shotgun's popularity grew mass-produced guns became available. Among the first commercial models to be brought West by sportsmen was the Winchester 1877, a lever-action designed by Browning. It fired five shots of the then-new ready-loaded ammunition in the later-familiar half-paper shells. Browning followed this in 1893 with the first Winchester pump—redesigned in 1897 and built in 12- and 16-gauges. Browning also designed the Remington automatic of 1905, a self-loader, delivering five shots as fast as a shooter could pull the trigger. These guns eventually supplanted in popularity such time-honored double-barreled shotguns as the L. C. Smith, Parker and Ithaca produced in the 1890's and early 1900's, but the change was slow, much slower than with rifles. As has been said, most double-barreled shotguns were never utilitarian. They were the "gentleman's gun," had been since the seventeenth century, and gentlemen's sports—like fox hunting for example—are hard to change. When the period of this book ends in 1912 the best makes of the double-barreled shotguns still reigned supreme.

Stunt Shots and After

With the shotgun and civilian sporting rifle, the gun in the West ceased to be a thing of daily utility and became an instrument of recreation, or stunt performance. Such famous early figures as Bill Hickok, who appeared one year on the stage with Buffalo Bill, pioneered the stunt field, breaking up several scenes by shooting too near the other actors' feet with live ammunition.

Buffalo Bill himself lent stature to stunt shooting after he opened his Wild West Show by banging at glass balls and other objects with special .44–40 cartridges partially loaded with No. 7½ chilled shot—thus breaking the balls without shooting holes in members of the audience or in the roof of Madison Square Garden where he often performed.

Among the female sureshots in Buffalo Bill's show, Little Annie Oakley, the sweetest thing this side of Boot Hill, captivated audiences by extinguishing cigarettes held in the mouth of her husband, Frank Butler.

Another famous exhibition shooter was W. F. ("Doc") Carver, a one-time dentist and for a while an associate of Buffalo Bill's in the Wild West show, later proprietor of a rival show. Using a .22 rifle, Carver set what he claimed was a world's record by breaking 59,340 of 60,000 glass balls tossed in the air. However he was badly outclassed in 1907 when a Texan, Adolph Topperwein, in ten days' firing with a .22 automatic at 72,500 wooden blocks, two-and-a-half inches square, tossed thirty feet into the air from a point twenty-five feet in front of him, missed only 9.

As with fast-draw artists, arguments rage as to how these latter-day crack shots would stack up against old-timers when the chips were down—and in the question probably lies the answer. The chips can never be down again. Not in the same way. Times have changed. We cannot go back to the O. K. Corral or that moment in Ellsworth when Wyatt Earp walked out alone across the square to meet Ben Thompson. Pete Maxwell's darkened room at Fort Sumner, where Billy the Kid died at the hands of Pat Garrett, will not return, nor will Billy Dixon's long shot at Adobe Walls.

The West has been won. New issues are with us. At Los Alamos, New Mexico, near where Coronado passed with his first matchlocks and wheel locks, there has been an atomic blast. The intercontinental ballistic missile is the new big gun of the West.

"An Old-Time Mountain Man With His Ponies." Pen and ink by Frederic Remington.

CLARENCE P. HORNUNG COLLECTION

PART EIGHT

KENNEDY GALLERIES, NEW YORK

"Monarch of the Plains" by Henry M. Shrady

Wild Life of the American West

by Natt N. Dodge

Big Game

Carnivores—Flesh-Eaters
  of the West

Rodents—The Small Gnawers
  with the Big Teeth

Birds of the West

Crawlers in the Western Sands

Buffalo herd at watering place.

74. *Big Game*

TRAVELERS WHO CROSSED the Missouri into the West soon found themselves in a world different from the rest of North America. Before them lay the Great Plains, a short-grass country stretching endlessly to the horizon. It was a strange new world, a vast, featureless domain inhabited by mammals and birds unlike those in the East. Here were the pronghorns which protected themselves by staying in the center of great flats where an enemy could not creep up on them. Here were the buffalo, so big and in such vast herds that they feared nothing and grazed boldly in plain view. Here were the jackrabbits that survived on account of their great speed, the prairie wolves or coyotes that disliked the eastern forests, and the villages of prairie dogs. The grouse on the Plains were larger than their woodland cousins, and did not roost in trees. The owls of this region had burrows in the earth for their homes.

The pioneers who had crossed from the Atlantic to the Missouri were woodsmen, accustomed to conquering a wilderness with their axes. But at the edge of the Plains, both ax and axman became obsolete. From this point on, a pioneer had to become a plainsman or perish.

The bold spirits who ventured into this vacuum under the big sky did not realize that they were climbing, but every mile they advanced across the deceptively level plains took them four feet higher above sea level. And with the increase in elevation they felt an increase in energy and a stimulating, sharp, champagne dryness in the air.

At the hundredth meridian, in western Kansas, the Rockies—still well over two hundred miles away—peeped above the horizon. Their snow-clad summits looked like clouds in the western sky. The Rocky Mountains were not like the Appalachians. They were gigantic fangs of granite snapping at the clouds, not tired old blue ridges worn down by the ages to puffy gums. Unlike the eastern mountains, the Rockies' shoulders were black with evergreens, somber and brooding throughout the year. Only a few patches of cottonwood, aspens and box elders changed color with the seasons. These forests and the lush green meadows among the trees were the favorite home of the antlered clan, the bears and the cougars. The best beaver fur was taken in icy mountain streams.

West of the mountains lay still another area—one of great brittle deserts covering most of Arizona and Nevada and parts of Utah, Oregon, California and Idaho. Out there few rains eroded the hills, and they stood in sharp-edged forms called buttes and mesas. All desert plants were drought-resistant and they all carried spines. Only specialized animal life could survive here, yet it did so in considerable numbers. This was the land of the horned toad and the lizard, the scorpion and the tarantula. Prongbucks that could travel long distances to water ventured into this country; so did the desert bighorn. A long and lanky black-tailed jackrabbit thrived here. Kit foxes, hawks, eagles and vultures preyed on this desert life.

Still farther west, beyond the deserts, rose the snow-capped Sierra Nevadas in California— the highest mountains in the Far West. Just below them lay Death Valley, a desert sink lower than the level of the sea. West of the Sierra stretched California's great Central Valley, and beyond it the Coast Range stood like a wall against the pounding Pacific surf. Wild life here was radically different from that of the deserts. The roach-backed grizzly, dwarf elk and sea otter were peculiar to the Pacific territories, so they never assumed the importance of other animals in the story of the West. Furthermore, because white men came into this part of the West on ships and brought their supplies with them, wild game was less important to their existence here.

However, in most of the West wild life was essential to the pioneers. The first explorers sought beaver for their high-priced fur. Buffalo were depended on for food by early-day trappers and the covered-wagon emigrants, as well as by Plains Indians. Elk and deer became the meat commonly eaten by the first settlers—so common, indeed, that a host would apologize for serving it to a guest. But the importance of wild life as food eventually became subordinate to its appeal to sportsmen, eastern sightseers and nature lovers. By 1912, the established stockmen were dismayed to discover that big-game hunters and summer tourists were beginning to bring more money into the West than did the cattle and sheep which had been considered the backbone of the country's economy.

Buffalo—Wild Cattle of the Plains

The North American buffalo, or bison, was our nation's largest game animal. Most gregarious of all wild cattle, the bulls, cows and calves grazed together throughout the year.

The genus *Bison* has been an inhabitant of North America for at least twenty-two centuries. The modern species became the economic mainstay of the Plains Indians, providing a dependable source of food, clothing and shelter. Even the buffalo's dried dung—called buffalo chips—served as the only fuel on the treeless Plains. And an excellent fuel it was; the finely ground-up grass glued together with juices of digestion and dropped in flat plates ignited easily when dry and burned with little smoke.

Although the original range of the big ruminants extended from Canada to Mexico and from Oregon to Georgia, the "short-grass" prairies of the Great Plains west of the Missouri and east of the Rockies was their principal range, providing both summer and winter grazing for immense numbers of these animals. Ernest Thompson Seton, famous naturalist and pioneer conservationist, estimated that, before the arrival of Europeans, sixty million bison roamed the continent. Except for a subspecies—the relatively few wood bison of central Canada south of Great Slave Lake—all the rest have been considered identical, although J. D. Figgins, while director of the Colorado Museum of Natural History, discovered that bison had two distinct types of horns. This led him to conclude that they may have descended from two distinct ancestors. The smaller, darker buffalo of the mountain parks of the Rockies have also been recognized by some scientists as a distinct race. All, however, seem to interbreed.

A bison family group with new-born calf.

An immense beast, the bison bull stood five and a half to six feet high at the shoulders and weighed 1,800 to 2,200 pounds. The smaller cows weighed about 1,000 pounds less. During the winters the animals were covered with long, shaggy brown hair with a dense, woolly undercoat. When warm weather came, they shed their coats in big or feltlike wads until their hindquarters were practically nude. They then became targets for innumerable biting flies and mosquitoes from which they desperately sought relief. One popular method was to find marshy spots where they could roll and wallow in the mud, plastering themselves with wet clay which, when it dried, helped in the shedding process and was an effective protection from insects. Buffalo wallows remained in many places throughout the Great Plains almost a century after they had been used.

These old wallows were often the source of practical jokes on tenderfeet. As we have seen, buffalo chips were the best source of fuel on the Plains, and one of the first chores at every new encampment was to collect baskets full of them for the supper fire. If the camp happened to be near an old buffalo wallow where the monsters had come out dripping mud from their woolly coats, the surrounding country would be covered with counterfeit buffalo chips which greenhorns picked up avidly only to be laughed out of camp when they trudged in with their loads.

Fully as permanent as the buffalo wallows were the "rubbing places" where the shaggy beasts had sought to relieve itching caused by loose hair and insect bites. The irritated animals often debarked trees and polished solid rock until it became smooth and round. Again and again they pushed over the poles of the first telegraph lines, and continued to use them as scratching posts even when protected by clusters of bristling spikes.

After the calving season, April through June, the vast herds of bison wandered contentedly over the prairies in bands of eight or ten to a hundred or more, the tawny calves frolicking together as they followed their mothers to creeks and water holes. With the start of the breeding or "running" season in August, the animals became restless, fights between bulls became more frequent and intense, and the wandering groups and bands merged into enormous, traveling herds "whose passing shook the earth and whose constant bellowing made sleep at night impossible."

Authorities disagree as to whether bison in the native state were monagamous or polygamous, and whether bulls or cows were leaders of the herds. There is evidence that in some groups a bull of strong personality was herd boss, whereas the majority of bands were led by a cow. In describing a buffalo stampede, the naturalist Victor Cahalane wrote: "The signal to run is almost always given by a female, whereupon all of the animals gallop off as a unit."

Buffalo stampedes were not unusual and were greatly feared by prairie travelers who might find themselves directly in the path of thousands of snorting, charging monsters. Cahalane wrote: "A stampeding herd of buffalo is an irresistible force. When thoroughly frightened, the animals may run for miles in a blind, unheeding, compact mass. It seems that no obstacle, alive or inanimate, will stop them. The thunder of hoofs shakes the ground, and the rush of galloping bodies sounds like Niagara." Indians took advantage of this tendency to stampede blindly, by purposely startling herds and directing them toward cliffs over which the leaders were forced by the pressure of the mass of rushing bodies behind them. Animals not killed by the fall were easily dispatched by the hunters.

This characteristic of traveling in great herds with eager followers pushing the leaders to their deaths was repeatedly displayed along rivers in the spring. Accustomed all winter to crossing and recrossing ice-bound streams, the herds continued to venture out on the frozen surfaces after they were weakened by a spring thaw. No longer able to support the immense weight, the ice would give way. Hundreds of the heavy animals dropped into the surging water and hundreds more were pushed in by the oncoming masses behind. Such catastrophes were welcomed by the Indians for the meat kept well in the icy water and the women pounced on every carcass which lodged along the river banks.

In summer, quicksands took their toll of buffalo. The stubborn determination to push ahead on a straight course caused the leaders to bog down and be trampled by those behind—which in turn soon became engulfed in the same quicksands.

Many writers have concluded that buffalo made great seasonal migrations from Canada to Texas and back again. It is true that the deep buffalo trails which emigrant wagons bumped across lay in a north and south direction. However, plains streams run from west to east, so wild animals would naturally come to water from the north or south. There is no proof that the buffalo herds did more than wander randomly from local summer and winter ranges. Plenty of early records describe buffalo in Montana during the winter. This alone should discredit the stories about wholesale migrations.

Bison often fed in a restricted area for several days, then the entire herd moved five or ten miles in as many hours, snatching only a mouthful here and there before settling down to steady grazing. They customarily took a rest, lying down to chew their cuds for four or five hours during the middle of the day, and usually bedded down an hour or two after sunset, each calf beside its mother, with the bulls toward the edges of the herd. A bedground might be used for several nights in succession or might be abandoned after one sleep.

Buffalo were much more sedentary in winter. Well protected from low temperatures by their shaggy coats, and accustomed to pawing away snow to get at the cured prairie grasses, the hardy animals usually came through the winter in good condition. However, blizzards undoubtedly took the lives of many, sometimes wiping out entire herds, as was the case in the Dakotas in the winter of 1880–81. Other "blizzard winters" which took heavy toll of the big ruminants were those of 1855–56 and 1871–72.

Wolves were a more serious threat to bison in winter than during other seasons. Every band had its following of the grim gray predators which picked off the young, the wounded and the stragglers weakened by illness, age, parasites or malnutrition. Even under the compulsion of extreme hunger, wolves would hesitate to attack a healthy, vigorous adult whose sharp horns and smashing hoofs were sure death to a persistent enemy.

Two-Gun White Calf, the Indian whose profile used to appear on the five-cent piece, said that he saw a bear hide on top of a bank and strike a buffalo cow that walked below. This may have been so, but when the Indian added that the cow's mate hunted down the bear and disemboweled it on his sharp horns, some listeners questioned the entire account. Indians liked to tell stories that tourists wanted to hear.

Prairie fires were a direct menace to the buffalo herds. Not only did they destroy the food grasses but they singed the animals' shaggy hair, burning their skins and scorching their

William Cody, better known as "Buffalo Bill," as a western frontiersman and in later life.

"Buffalo Drive" shows Sioux Indians stampeding buffalo over cliff to secure food and robes for the winter. Painting by William R. Leigh.

eyeballs. Blind buffalo were frequently found accompanying herds; their quickened senses of hearing and smell and their increased alertness enabled them to detect approaching danger and warn the rest of the band. Normal bison had notably poor eyesight which often made them appear stupid. A hunter only partially concealed behind rocks or brush might shoot down several before being detected, but the bison's lack of sharp vision was counterbalanced by exceptionally keen senses of hearing and smell.

Before the arrival of the white man with his horses and guns, Indians had difficulty in killing enough buffalo to provide meat for food and hides for tepees, garments and robes. When the snow was deep, Indians on snowshoes had a distinct advantage, but such occasions were rare and the Indian hunter afoot had to exercise extreme skill in order to get close enough to one of the big beasts to kill it with spear or bow and arrow. Early reports state that certain tribes used the "surround" method, whereby a large number of hunters formed a cordon around a small herd of buffalo and by running around and around the animals, started them milling in a circle. Thus the Indians were able to get within killing distance of those on the outside of the encircling herd.

When Plains Indians acquired the white man's horse in the early 1700's their ability to kill buffalo increased greatly. A good buffalo pony could outrun the fleetest bison, and that animal's peculiar habit of following an undeviating course enabled a horseman to ride beside the racing beast and kill it. A range steer or cow would turn away from a rider, but not a buffalo once its mind was made up. Bernard De Voto, historian of the West, stated in his book, *Across the Wide Missouri*: "When Indians coursed buffalo they used the lance or arrow. One arrow was enough if properly placed, and it was frequently driven clear through the beast so that it slid along the plain on the further side."

During the first half of the ninteenth century Plains Indians with their horses and guns began killing buffalo in large numbers. The artist, George Catlin, reported that as early as 1832 from 150,000 to 200,000 robes were being offered traders by the Indians. In 1835, John C. Frémont, the Pathfinder, reported that buffalo herds on the western slope of the northern Rockies had been seriously reduced. After 1840 when the last trappers' rendezvous was held, some mountain men and many Indians turned from beaver trapping to buffalo hunting. Permanent posts became necessary to store the bulky hides until they were sent east by boat or wagon train. In 1842, Frémont found distress among the Indians along the Platte due to a buffalo shortage, but in 1868 buffalo were still sufficiently numerous for William F. Cody to agree to supply buffalo meat to construction crews of the Kansas Pacific Railroad. During a period of eighteen months he is said to have killed 4,280 bison, and thus earned the nickname of "Buffalo Bill."

When the Union Pacific Railroad reached Cheyenne, Wyoming, it had split the buffalo country in two, forming a dividing line between the "south herd" and the "north herd." Following construction of the Santa Fe Railroad across Kansas in 1871, "skin hunters" began the slaughter of the south herd. Hides sold for $1.25, tongues fetched $.25 each, and hindquarters went on the market at $0.1 per pound. From 1870 to 1875, Dodge City was the buffalo market place of the world, and by 1880 only a few scattered bison bands remained in the southland.

Plains Indians bitterly opposed the slaughter as well as the white men's intrusion on their domain. Realizing that their existence depended upon buffalo, the western Sioux fought white hunters and succeeded in closing the Bozeman Trail, which crossed their best buffalo range. In 1880 the Northern Pacific Railroad opened a way into the heartland of the north herd, and by 1885 hide hunters had slaughtered all but a few small bands between the Missouri and the Yellowstone.

William T. Hornaday, naturalist of the National Museum, estimated that in 1887, of the millions of buffalo in the West a decade before, only 1,091 remained on the North American continent, and half of these were a wild remnant somewhere in Canada near Great Slave Lake. Two hundred had been saved in Yellowstone National Park. In private hands the largest herd, numbering under a hundred, was owned by S. L. Bedson in Manitoba. The next largest owner was "Buffalo" (Charles J.) Jones. Buffalo Bill's herd ranked third in size. Charles Allard, of the Flathead Indian Reservation in Montana, had thirty-five. Rancher Charles Goodnight had thirteen in Texas. The Santa Fe Railroad maintained ten as a tourist attraction. Fred Dupree, of the Cheyenne Agency, kept nine in Dakota Territory. Four were held in Rapid City, and fourteen others were owned here and there, singly or in pairs. Some twenty-seven could be found in five American zoos. Two more were on exhibition in England, two in Germany, one in India. The total number in captivity amounted to 256, with 216 of them being kept for breeding purposes. This small number, with careful propagation, saved the species and within a generation the excess had to be killed periodically.

Frank Gilbert Roe, in his book *The North American Buffalo* wrote:

> The presence of this animal deeply affected the civilization of the North American continent—perhaps more vitally than has ever been the case with any other single species in its indigenous environment in any portion of the globe. It constituted the almost sole source of subsistence of entire nations of aboriginal people. It is the only known creature which has ever thronged in such prodigious hosts a geographical range. Its near extermination at the hand of man is a shameful episode in American history.

And it should be added that the bison's reclamation is one of the finest examples of what can be done with judicious conservation.

Deer—Principal Big Game of the West

Dr. Ira N. Gabrielson, when he was president of the Wildlife Management Institute, wrote, "Of the larger game animals on this continent, the deer is the most adaptable, most widely distributed, most heavily hunted, best loved, and among the most misunderstood." With the possible exception of bison and beaver, deer had more to do with the exploration and development of the West than any other native animal. They provided pioneers with a dependable and seemingly inexhaustible source of food and clothing. It has been estimated that forty to fifty million deer roamed this continent in primitive times.

Deer bones and bone implements found in ancient pueblo ruins illustrate the importance of this animal to prehistoric Indians. Their women were skilled in converting deer hides into leggings, moccasins, tunics and dresses, often decorating them with beads, shells,

Male mule deer near Devil's Tower, Wyoming.

elk teeth and porcupine quills. They used deer sinew for thread. Indian-tanned buckskin was milk-white and soft as velvet, making attractive gowns for brown-faced girls with their long braids of black hair. For men buckskin shirts had drawbacks. When wet, they stretched, sometimes as long as a dress, then dried stiff as paper. Indians prevented this by smoking the white skin with willow bark that changed the color to a dull yellow, but kept the softness and added a pleasant fragrance—the "Indian smell"—which, once sampled, is hard to forget.

Red hunters used antler tips to flake flint for arrow and spear points. They dried venison into "jerky" which kept indefinitely, could be chewed raw or soaked into an edible meat stew. In fact primitive Americans used every part of the deer except its calls, even imitating them in ceremonial rites.

In addition to stalking and shooting deer with bows and arrows, Indians ambushed them at salt licks and trapped them by digging pitfalls on their runways. Early writers reported deer drives with the population of an entire Indian village forming a skirmish line through the woods to herd the deer before them into a previously prepared enclosure.

Pioneers used deer fat in making soap and candles. Buckskin was made into breeches, jackets and moccasins—the latter not fully satisfactory according to a report from the Lewis and Clark expedition which complained that prickly pear spines penetrated them.

As settlements grew, market hunting developed. During the last half of the nineteenth century, thousands of deer were killed for their meat and hides, the latter bringing from fifty cents to one dollar each. In 1874, on the Pacific Coast, 3,000 were slaughtered during five months in an area of less than two hundred miles. The meat went on the market at four cents per pound. Market hunters extirpated the animals from much of their original range. In some states restrictive game laws were enacted in the 1880's, but it was the passage of the Lacey Act in 1900, regulating interstate commerce in game animals, that ended the reign of the market hunter and saved the deer.

Three species of deer, including the subspecies of each, inhabit the West. The small (up to 230 pounds) whitetail deer are widely scattered throughout the hilly, deciduous woodlands in all the states except Nevada and Utah. In Arizona their range is limited, and in California they can be found only in the extreme northeast corner. They are easily recognized by their large tails, white on the underside, which they erect when alarmed. The flash warns others and serves as a guiding beacon in flight. This species is called "flag-tail" in the Southwest. Antlers of the whitetail are small and pronged rather than multiforked.

The blacktail of the West Coast is considered by some to be a new species of mule deer in the making. With a maximum weight of about 300 pounds and a relatively small rack of antlers, its most noticeable characteristic is its black tail which is considerably smaller than a whitetail's and is not "flagged" when running.

The true mule deer, named for its ears, ranges from the highest mountains through the foothills to the hottest deserts. It is easily identified by its great size (up to 400 pounds), large ears, wide rack of forked antlers, and extensive white rump patch with small, black-tipped tail.

Generally considered browsing animals, deer eat a wide variety of foods depending largely upon what is seasonally available. In spring they eagerly seek the fresh growth of succulent grasses. In summer, herbaceous plants, mushrooms and the new growth of shrubs provide ample variety. In the fall they begin nibbling manzanita, sagebrush, mountain mahogany and cliff rose. Deer also relish acorns and other mast such as pinyon nuts, mesquite beans and various pods and seeds.

Winter imposes a serious diet restriction. On southern deserts deer crunch cactus fruits. In northern forests they browse such low-growing evergreens as kinnikinnick, Oregon grape and buckbrush until covered with snow. They eat fallen leaves to some extent. Green pine needles, juniper and Douglas fir form an important part of their winter menu. In northern latitudes where the snow becomes deep they band together in "yards" with mutually tramped-out trails to reach food. This is a critical season for young animals which are not tall enough to reach the food still available to the adults.

The deer of the high mountains in lower latitudes move each spring and fall to summer and winter ranges. Although they normally graze in small bands, often less than ten, they have some way of agreeing upon the night to emigrate. Thus a horseman may ride across the snow under bare quaking aspens one fall afternoon and see no deer tracks. Retracing his steps in the morning, he may find the snow tramped out by hundreds of hoofs as though a band of sheep had passed, but in reality the deer went by in dozens and dozens of small groups.

In late October and early December the bucks range widely in search of mates. Although they do not round up and guard harems, they usually mate with several females and, when following a particular doe, resent the intrusion of other males. This sometimes leads to violent battles. The clashes are usually brief, the larger and stronger animal soon establishing dominance. When equally matched, bucks may push, feint, spar and jab until exhausted. Occasionally their antlers became firmly locked and both animals face a lingering death by starvation.

Aggressive and domineering when fully antlered, bucks make a ludicrous appearance in late February or March when they begin to shed their antlers. One invariably falls off before the other and this lopsided arrangement forces the buck to run with his head on one side. By the last of March both antlers are gone and as spring approaches new ones bulge up from the tops of the bucks' heads. These protuberances are full of blood, covered with "velvet" and very tender. During the summer, as the antlers grow, a buck is careful how he runs through the brush lest he bruise the sensitive, growing horn.

Deer are blessed with an acute sense of smell, keen hearing and a peculiar eyesight which is unable to identify a motionless object but reacts instantly to the slightest movement. Thus a hunter, if "downwind" and walking quietly across grass, may approach within shooting range of a deer in the open if he drops to the ground every time the deer switches its tail— a sure sign the grazing animal is going to raise its head and look around.

Once alarmed, whitetails race away like horses. Mule deer invariably bound off with curious stiff-legged jumps, all four feet striking the ground simultaneously. This odd gait is peculiarly effective in down timber or on steep brushy hillsides. Mule deer normally cover twelve to sixteen feet at a jump. They have been known to go over eight-and-a-half-foot fences and to bound horizontally thirty feet. At top speed they have been clocked at twenty to thirty-five miles per hour—a rate which they can maintain only for short distances. In their native habitat of brush and woodland they are adept at keeping out of sight, easily eluding hunters whom they have seen or heard.

A deer's winter coat of blue-gray usually grows in September. Each hair is an air-filled tube affording excellent insulation, and great buoyancy in water. Deer in their winter coats swim with their backs well above the surface. In summer, wearing their "red" or tan pelage, they swim low with only their heads appearing. From mid-June to mid-July spotted fawns are born after a gestation period of approximately two hundred days. Twins are common and occasionally triplets appear. Their mother usually hides them separately, some little distance apart, but located where she can keep her eye on each. A prostrate animal gives off little scent, and the fawns are relatively safe unless stumbled upon by a hungry carnivore. A prowling coyote or bobcat is no match for a watchful mother. She will strike at him with her sharp hoofs and chase him out of the neighborhood. If found by a man a fawn lies perfectly still, but if he puts a finger in the fawn's mouth the little fellow will suck it and then toddle off after him while the doe, invisible in a thicket, bleats a protest.

Before the white man with his traps and guns nearly exterminated the wolves, they preyed heavily on deer of all ages. The black bear, which has held its own with man, continues to take some fawns and probably catches a few injured or otherwise disabled adults. Deer are also plagued by a number of parasites which periodically kill many of them. Every year some hunters are bound to come in with a deer which looks all right but proves unfit to eat. The animal was undoubtedly sick but this was not apparent at a shooting distance.

It is generally conceded that the deer's principal enemy is the cougar, or mountain lion. Each of these big cats is credited with a potential victim every week. Suffice it to say that in regions where mountain lions have been eliminated, deer populations have grown enormously, sometimes to a point where harvesting by hunting has failed to check the increase, and hundreds of deer have starved to death after consuming all the edible vegetation.

Deer are so widely distributed and have become so accustomed to humans, especially in national parks, monuments and wild-life preserves where they are protected, that nearly everyone has seen and enjoyed their beauty. In common with the coyote they have developed a remarkable ability to live in close proximity to man, even when hunted, and this antlered native American should continue indefinitely to grace our nation's hills and woodlands.

Pronghorn—Phantom of the Plains

How fast can an antelope run? Scientists do not agree. Arthur Einarsen, of the Oregon Cooperative Wildlife Research Unit, in his book, *The Pronghorn Antelope,* reported racing several small bands on the dry, hard bed of Spanish Lake. One big buck which ran beside his car at fifty miles an hour suddenly increased its pace and, as the speedometer registered sixty-one miles per hour, dashed across his course to continue the race on the other side of the car.

Pronghorn antelope group near North Platte River, Wyoming.

AMERICAN MUSEUM OF NATURAL HISTORY, NEW YORK

Such high speeds are, of course, possible only for short spurts, but the pronghorns' easy gait of twenty to thirty miles per hour makes their daily range greater than that of slower-moving big game. The *Journal of Mammalogy* reports that a careful observer, Carlyle Carr, clocked a band of pronghorns paralleling a roadway outside Rincon, New Mexico, that averaged thirty miles per hour for seven miles.

The pronghorn has no close relatives. Neither a sheep, deer, goat nor true antelope, it has some characteristics of each, but is a distinct and entirely different species. An estimated forty to fifty million of these dainty little creatures mingled with the vast herds of bison when Coronado led the first Europeans into the Southwest in 1540. Unrestricted slaughter, competition with domestic livestock, and a rapidly expanding agriculture reduced them by 1908 to an estimated 17,000. Less than half a century later, under complete protection, they had increased to 200,000 with limited hunting permitted in several states.

Though comparatively small, pronghorns appear larger than they are because of their long legs. An average buck weighs a little over a hundred pounds. The body color is a rich, reddish tan with white belly and white blotches on the chest, neck and head. The nose, horns and hoofs are jet black. This contrast of colors provides excellent camouflage, and when patches of snow are on the ground a large herd, even at a relatively short distance, is practically invisible.

The pronghorns' long legs, built for speed, enable the animals to forage in concealing stands of sagebrush, saltbush and rabbit brush, and yet keep watch over the surrounding plains. Their eyes, which are larger than those of a horse, are so placed as to have an especially wide angle of vision, and therefore little escapes them. The horns, present in both sexes, grow much larger in the male. They are hooked like the horns of a chamois but have an additional forward-extending prong which gives the animal its name. The sheath of the horn is shed annually, usually at the close of the rutting season in early December, leaving a short permanent core. Thus an occasional hunter late in the season, shooting what he believes to be a record head, may ride up and find with dismay that his fallen quarry has little stubby horns, the sheaths having dropped off as the buck fell. After shedding, the bucks grow new sheaths which are complete in July and ready for the sparring matches between the males as the breeding season approaches.

Perhaps the most spectacular feature of the pronghorn's anatomy is the erectile hairs on its white rump patch. When disturbed or frightened, the animal raises these hairs to form a shining rosette extending fully three inches beyond the normal contour of the hips. When done in bright sunlight the resulting flash, like a heliograph signal, may be seen for miles. All other antelope grazing in the vicinity respond in kind so that within seconds an alarm has been spread far and wide.

Because of its keen vision, fantastic speed and remarkable endurance the pronghorn can outdistance its enemies. Indians occasionally stalked them successfully, shot them from blinds built of stones near water holes or, when a herd was reported in the vicinity of an encampment, used the surround and stampede method. Frequently the entire population of the village joined the chase. Horsemen encircled the herd and, assisted by others afoot, gradually decreased the size of the circle while the frantic animals rushed from one side to the other, their timidity preventing them from bolting between the riders. Eventually their nervous fear and continuous motion wore them down until they could be slaughtered, even with primitive weapons.

As the West was settled, market hunters began slaughtering antelope. Thousands of these beautiful creatures roamed the plains of the San Joaquin Valley in California. As late as the 1870's their meat became the commonest and cheapest flesh in the nearby city markets.

In addition to being shot by market hunters, occasionally deep snows covered the prong-bucks' natural forage, causing the little runners to starve to death. Drifts also reduced their lifesaving speed, making them an easy prey for wolves and coyotes. In a weakened condition, herds became subject to diseases which killed thousands. In Montana, a long-time hunter and guide reported that the fearful winter of 1893 killed at least four-fifths of the antelope in his area. Yet with remarkable vitality these dainty little animals have always staged a comeback.

Although a pronghorn can easily outdistance a lone wolf or coyote, the sagacious predators hunted in groups and, by taking turns, could finally exhaust and drag down an individual found away from the herd. To meet the menace of wolves, pronghorns mingled with bison capable of fighting them off, and it is possible that the rapid depletion of the antelope at the same time as the buffalo may have been more than coincidence.

Not migratory in the true sense, pronghorns drift from one range to another as the result of weather conditions, the drying up of water holes, molestation and other causes. Certain open areas, dotted with clumps of low brush, are particularly suited for kidding grounds, and the pronghorns seek semi-isolation there to give birth to their young. This event usually takes place in May in the North and as early as March in Texas. Single births are frequent, but twins are the rule, the mother dropping them several hundred feet apart, then grazing nonchalantly nearby where she can keep a watchful eye on both locations.

Well hidden among clumps of brush, the kids, weighing from four to six pounds each, lie quietly until the mother comes to feed them. The first few days of a pronghorn kid's life are fraught with danger, but the mother's alertness usually enables her to spot a coyote or bobcat before it can sneak dangerously close to her kid's hiding place. She may try to lure the predator away and, if the ruse fails, may rush to attack. There are records of several antelope, and even of lone mothers, attacking and driving off these animals. They butt with their short horns and strike at the intruder with their front feet, attempting to slash the dodging marauder with the sharp edges of their hoofs. Theodore Roosevelt wrote: "A doe will fight most gallantly for her fawn and is an overmatch for a coyote, but can do little against a large wolf."

By its sixth day of life—some say earlier—a young pronghorn can run twenty miles an hour, fast enough to elude most pursuers. With its mother it joins the main band and, during June and July, the family life of the herd is orderly and relaxed. By mid-August—earlier in the South—restlessness is noticeable among the adult males. Soon the bucks attempt to drive selected does into personal flocks or harems, guarding them from other bucks with a ferocity mounting almost to mania. Fights between bucks are a common occurrence, occasionally continuing to the death. Within a month the rutting season is over. Does born in May breed the second September, and the gestation period is approximately eight months.

Along with the pronghorns' peculiar proclivity to race and cross in front of a fast-moving traveler, they have an impelling curiosity which causes them to investigate anything strange that moves. This characteristic was exploited by Indians and later by pioneer hunters who assumed weird poses and, while hidden, waved pieces of cloth to attract the curious, but wary, animals within shooting range. A hunter, lying flat on his stomach in concealing brush, could sometimes get a shot by bending one knee and waving his foot. The pronghorns that saw it would often venture timidly forward closer and closer, stopping many times. Finally with a whirring bark they would wheel away and race over the horizon but the hunter should wait patiently, for the dainty little creatures were apt to reappear at some other point of the compass and repeat the performance, coming a little closer to the mysterious waving object. Finally their inquisitiveness would entice them within short range. The hunter could now rise up and get a good running shot as the antelope raced away. Running like race horses, with a smooth even gait, they made the easiest of running shots, but no running shot is easy; and according to some hunters an antelope can run so fast its feet, at full speed, blur like the wings of a hummingbird in flight.

Normally the pronghorn is a browsing animal, preferring such shrubby plants as sagebrush, rabbit brush, saltbush and snowberry. They prefer to live on open flats where they can be seen and also see an approaching enemy. On deserts they endure long periods without water, obtaining essential moisture from the vegetation they eat, including such succulents as the pads of prickly-pear cactus.

Under the protection of state and federal laws, the species has exhibited an amazing ability to coexist with humans. Fences, especially those of woven wire surrounding sheep ranges, restrict their movements, as pronghorns are unable or unwilling to leap over even a low fence. However, they are adept at crawling under barbed wire and, if the strands are loose, these "four-legged birds" will actually fold back their forelegs and plunge through between the wires. Many ranchers enjoy the presence of these beautiful animals on their ranges where they mingle with cattle and horses much as they once did with the bison that roamed the open plains.

Bighorn—Royalty of the Rocks

Bighorn, commonly known as "mountain sheep," never wander far from rocky terrain. They are equally at home on the highest icy peaks and in the deepest desert canyons. Their sure-footed ability to clamber up and down almost perpendicular cliffs and across rough, treacherous slopes enables them to escape from coyotes, wolves and mountain lions. When frightened in open, alpine meadows, bands dash up the nearest heights. Thus hunters try always to be above their feeding grounds where the game, if disturbed, is apt to come up within shooting distance.

Keen eyesight and a miraculous agility in rugged country have always been the bighorns' chief means of protection. If cornered, however, they stand and fight. A valiant ewe with her sharp horns is no mean adversary when defending her lamb from a four-footed enemy or even an air-borne eagle.

The little ones are usually born on the summer feeding grounds in May and June, earlier in the snowless, barren mountains of the Southwest. Twins are uncommon. When the babies

Pair of bighorn sheep.

have toddled around for one or two weeks, their mothers lead them to the herd, which at this season consists of from twenty to forty (up to seventy-five) yearlings, barren ewes and bachelor rams aged one to three. The mature rams with their imposing corkscrew horns travel by themselves in bands of six to ten, usually joining the main herds in September.

By mid-November, earlier in the Southwest, the rutting season is in full swing. Bighorn rams are the most promiscuous of all native big game animals and rarely acquire and guard harems as do most wild ruminants. In fact three or more rams may be found in the same herd of ewes. Although as bachelors they have run together contentedly all summer, now they fight periodically—showing off, no doubt, before the girls, because the vanquished is seldom hurt seriously and he usually remains in the herd.

The fights are battles royal which would have delighted knights of old. The challengers back away from each other, sometimes as far as fifty feet. They both rear and start toward each other on their hind feet, drop to all fours and with lowered heads come together like pile drivers. Again and again the two massive battering rams back off and smash together, horn to horn. Weight and endurance count. Finally one gives up and runs away—but usually only to the far side of the herd, leaving the nearby ewes to the victor.

With the coming of the fierce winter storms, bands of mountain bighorn make their way gradually to lower elevations where snow does not accumulate to great depths and where windswept ridges expose abundant grass. Bighorn often seek shelter in caves and in protected coves at the base of cliffs. In the Southwest such caves also provide protection from the intense heat of the summer sun.

Indians hunted bighorn for their flesh and hides. They converted rams' horns into spoons and ladles and used them to back wooden bows. The Pima and Papago of southern Arizona, who depended heavily on bighorn for meat, ceremoniously built up huge piles of their horns in the belief that this might propitiate evil spirits and ensure favorable weather. Members of the Lewis and Clark expedition of 1804–6 found bighorn ranging the river bluffs as far east as the junction of the Missouri and Yellowstone, where they became an easy prey for Plains Indians. Ernest Thompson Seton, popular naturalist, reported that in his western travels he saw heads of mountain sheep permanently embedded in the wood of growing trees. He surmised that Blackfeet or Shoshoni had placed them there as markers.

Under the protection of state and federal laws since the turn of the century, mountain sheep have increased in number but not with the rapidity of other wild ruminants. The settlement of open country between the rugged bighorn ranges has separated the wild bands and encouraged inbreeding which may have weakened the species' resistance to epidemics. Scabies, lungworm and pneumonia have all taken their toll, and poachers have persistently risked arrest to kill a record head. In summer domestic sheep graze some of the bighorns' best native pastures, eating grass which might support their wild cousins in the winter. These accumulating liabilities have been balanced by conservationists and state fish and game departments which have supplied feed to hungry bands and injected new blood into herds through the introduction of rams trapped in other herds. This program of conservation seems to be succeeding to such an extent that Cleveland Grant, lecturer and photographer for the Audubon Society, has reported a noticeable increase in the number of bighorn on ranges where they were becoming scarce.

Mountain Goat—Courageous Climber of the Crags

Unlike the mountain sheep, the white mountain goat has maintained approximately the same range and the same population (about 15,000 in the United States) since the earliest recorded history. This distinction is unique among big game animals of the West. At home on the high peaks of the Bitter Roots, the Rockies and the Cascades, this bearded steeplejack lives far above the grazing grounds of domestic livestock, hence has not suffered from their competition. His musky flesh and small horns make him unattractive for meat or trophy.

The mountain goats' high, isolated haunts prevented early-day travelers from seeing them. Indians showed Lewis and Clark the white shaggy hides and black spike-horns of goats they had killed, and the explorers believed them to be from wild sheep. Actually these animals are neither sheep nor goat, being more closely related to chamois. Built with high shoulders and low-slung heads, like bison, they are the color of the snow except for black nostrils, lips, horns and hoofs. Thick underwear of dense, fine wool covered with an overcoat of long shaggy hair protects them from the intense cold. During fierce blizzards or storms of long duration most bands seek temporary shelter in caves.

The kids, usually singles but occasionally twins, are born in May and are active within a few hours. If unmolested, nannies with kids stay alone or in a small family group for a few weeks in a relatively small feeding area. Later in the summer they form bands which, with the males, contain fifteen or twenty head.

Although few four-legged predators penetrate to the chilly heights, the kids are never entirely free from enterprising bobcats, coyotes, wolverines, grizzly bears and cougars. However, among the cliffs and crags, the sure-footed, agile goats, including the youngsters, can usually avoid any pursuer except the golden eagle, which constitutes the greatest danger for young kids.

The slender jet horns of the mountain goat, though only nine or ten inches long, are as sharp and effective as rapiers. A coyote is no match for an aroused mother, and there is at least one record of a male goat killing a grizzly bear. Although some authorities insist that mountain goats are monogamous, they indulge in a definite rutting season each November, during which the billies become pugnacious and occasionally engage in deadly battles. The rivals walk stiff-legged around each other, often rising on their hind legs to spar awkwardly but with determination. A successful thrust in the belly with dagger-like horns may result in peritonitis, a not uncommon cause of death.

A New York hunter, B. T. Van Nostrand, reported watching two billies fight until the vanquished was bleeding around the neck, had one flank badly torn, and a loop of his intestines almost dragged on the ground. Owen Wister, whose novels and short stories did so much to popularize the West, noticed on a hunting trip that mountain goats and bighorn never grazed together on the same mountain. After some study he came to the conclusion that bighorn feared the goats. In a fair fight the three-hundred-pound battering ram was no match for an agile billie which —standing on its hind legs awaiting the charge—dodged like a matador and struck down from above with those deadly black horns.

The Rocky Mountain goat deliberately chooses to live in the land of glaciers and eternal snow. His greatest foe has always been the snowslide, which is particularly dangerous during spring thaws. Unannounced and remorselessly swift, this thundering demon of goatland sometimes wipes out entire bands which cannot escape from its path. Able to cope with most enemies, the sturdy, even-tempered, resourceful and sure-footed dweller in the heights has no defense against the avalanche.

Rocky Mountain goat group.

AMERICAN MUSEUM OF NATURAL HISTORY, NEW YORK

Elk—Wapiti of the Rockies

Every autumn in the Rocky Mountains a high-pitched "bugling" rings across the sun-splashed aspen groves and fir-fringed meadows. This whistling sound comes from bull elk challenging one another to fight for mastery of their harems. The clashing of antlers and the grunts of heavy-breathing stags as they push, shove and jab during the battles are as much a part of every fall in the high country as the turning of the aspens from green to gold. The combatants, if evenly matched, may spar until one or the other is killed but this rarely happens. Instead the weaker animal, feeling himself being overpowered, runs away.

A bull elk, or wapiti, is the sultan of all American deer. During the breeding season (mid-September to late October) he gathers and defends a seraglio of from twelve to as many as sixty cows. Within this period he fights continually with other herd masters that attempt to lure away his cows or even take his entire harem.

With the end of the breeding period, the bull-dominated bands gradually merge, growing larger and larger. These herds slowly work their way downward from the higher watersheds in a well-defined migration toward the wide intermountain valleys to winter where grassy meadows and sagebrush flats accumulate less snow. During this mass movement, the animals are particularly vulnerable to hunters.

Elk originally ranged far out on the buffalo plains. Visible for miles and easily run down on horseback, they were soon exterminated everywhere except in the high mountains. Indians prized their hides for tepee covers which were lighter to carry than those made from bison skins. An elk horn, with the tines sawed off, made a good stock for a warrior's whip. The estimated ten million elk that ranged much of the northern two-thirds of the United States in primitive times was reduced by 1895 to less than 100,000, located principally in the northern Rockies, with scattered bands of Roosevelt elk on the Olympic Peninsula of Washington and a remnant of the small Tule elk of the Sierra Nevada bordering California's San Joaquin Valley. A third subspecies, the Merriam elk of the Southwest, was exterminated before records of their size were obtained, but they are believed to have been larger than the Rocky Mountain animals.

Many elk were killed for their meat and hides, but the most serious slaughter resulted from the demand for bull elks' canine teeth, or tusks, for ornaments. Other thousands died of starvation when their winter range was homesteaded and the wild grass was cut to feed livestock. Survivors lurked around the fenced haystacks after dark. A bull's antlers had three prongs on the end, much like a pitchfork. He soon learned to reach over a stack-yard fence and with a twist of his neck pitch out great flakes of hay, destroying a small stack in a single night. Farmers killed such animals as pests. When game laws prevented this slaughter, states reimbursed farmers for the elks' damages, and in some cases bought hay in advance, paying to have it scattered for the elk during the worst winter months.

By mid-March of each year the bulls begin to drop their antlers and, except for their larger size, look much like the cows. Spring touches the northern valleys by mid-April, and with the gradual greening of the hillsides, the winter-weakened survivors start the slow return to their summer pastures, feeding as they go. At this time the first newly born calves

Wapiti family group shows bull starting to bugle, northern Colorado.

appear and, after a few days in hiding to gain strength, join with their mothers on the gradual trek to the mountains. By mid-June or early July the herds are well scattered in the high country; bulls, yearlings and calfless cows having already spread over the summer ranges.

Although mountain lions, grizzly bears, wolves and even coyotes kill some adult elk, particularly old or injured individuals, the newborn calves are their coveted prey, especially in the spring before rodents have come out of hibernation. Cow elk drive off coyotes, and frequently a number will "gang up" to repel a wolf or mountain lion, but irate mothers are no match for a grizzly. When this huge beast appears, a distraught cow's only defense is to play sick or crippled and decoy the killer from her calf's hiding place.

During the summer, bulls remain by themselves, solitary or in small groups, feeding and resting to build their strength and their growing antlers for the violence of the rutting season to come. Magnificent animals, the Rocky Mountain and Roosevelt elk bulls weigh an average of 700 pounds, and individuals of 1,100 pounds have been recorded. Early settlers sometimes tell about a giant bull they have killed which had antlers so long that when the head was cut off and stood upside down on the ground, a six foot man could walk under the arch formed by the horns. "Yes, Siree! and without stooping." However that may be, taxidermists often distort the elk heads they mount by spreading the antlers at least four inches. This makes the whole head appear more majestic.

Serious as life must be for all wild animals which are constantly hunted, most of them enjoy their lighter moments, and elk are no exception. Calves frolic, play tag, and follow-the-leader. They butt and spar, and enjoy splashing in lakes and shallow streams. One curious amusement of the adults is called the "circle dance" and has been reported by several observers who were attracted to a column of dust which appeared something like those stirred up by whirlwinds. H. W. Skinner, a big game hunter from Chicago, wrote in August, 1890, "I found that it was caused by a band of elk, numbering 12 to 20, who seemed to be trotting quite rapidly, with occasional awkward gallops, in a circle about 30 feet in diameter. My impression is that they were all bulls."

Elk were fast trotters. This was their favorite gait, but when frightened or in deep snow they galloped. Hunters who have chased them on horseback claim that when a trotting elk broke into a gallop his speed was not so fast. This may be so. Certainly, elk had a reputation for being able to out-trot a horse. In Rock Springs, Wyoming, a man named Pat Whalen raised an elk calf and trained it to work in harness. This was in the horse and buggy days when men prided themselves on having the fastest trotters in town. Pat liked to hitch up his elk, come out of a side street just behind some famous trotting horse and overtake it. The trotter, hearing spinning wheels at its rear, would do its best but the elk always overtook it. The worst part of the race occurred when the elk came abreast of the blinders on his competitor's bridle, where the horse could see what was beating it. Invariably the horse broke its own trot and ran away in terror or disgust. The town fathers had to pass a special ordinance prohibiting Pat from driving his elk in town.

The Mighty Moose

The largest of the antlered animals of the West is the moose. They are found only in Montana, Wyoming and Idaho. Relatively few pioneers saw them, due to the fact that moose are semi-aquatic animals that never live in the open flats frequented by overland travelers. The giant horselike beast is readily recognized by the dewlap, a bell-like appendage beneath the throats of both sexes, and by the bulls' broadly palmate antlers, sometimes with a near six-foot spread. A big male may stand seven and a half feet high at the shoulders and weigh from 900 to 1,800 pounds. The western range of these grotesque monsters has remained much the same since the first written records, but their bones and antlers have been found in mountain meadows surrounded by quaking aspen trees as far south as Colorado.

Unlike the male elk, a bull moose collects no harem but remains with one cow for eight to ten days during the four- to eight-week breeding season (mid-October to late November), then sets out in search of another mate. During this period a bull may travel many miles, following the enticing calls of unattached cows and battling with other males he considers rivals. Hunters, by imitating a cow's call, are able to draw bulls into shooting range.

Throughout the rest of the year, family groups of moose stay within a relatively small territory, usually headquartering in a swampy valley and browsing on the surrounding hillsides. In winter, when the snow is deep, their wandering is still further restricted and they seek a sheltered area or "yard" where food is abundant and through which they trample a network of pathways while browsing. Old bulls often yard together.

During the winter, moose browse many of the evergreens, but in summer they find an abundance of deciduous trees and shrubs, eat grasses and sedges, and even wade far out into shallow lakes, submerging their heads to graze on the bottom.

Authorities agree that moose have poor eyesight but phenomenally keen hearing. They

A pair of bull moose in combat.

disagree, however, as to the acuteness of their sense of smell in detecting an enemy. Once alarmed, the big creatures are able to move silently through the woods and disappear without snapping a twig or moving a branch.

Calving takes place in late May or June, the bay, nonspotted youngsters (twins are not unusual) staying with the mother for an entire year. All members of the family frequent shallow lakes and streams which they sometimes enter to escape flies and to eat aquatic plants. Their long, stilt legs carry them safely through mudholes or quicksands.

Throughout the summer, while the cow is raising her young and the outcast yearlings are learning about the motherless world, the big bulls are lazing about growing new sets of antlers which sprout in May and harden to maturity when the velvet is rubbed off in August. Their tempers seem to develop with their shovel-like antlers, and it is not unusual for a bull to put a bear, or a man, up a tree. During the breeding season a bull moose is especially cantankerous and has few friends among the other animals of the woods. But in the winter, after shedding his antlers, he becomes mild-mannered and tolerant. At that season he welcomes the attentions of Canada jays, or "moose birds," which frequent the "yards," possibly to pick parasites from the coats of the big animals and to feast on the grubs exposed by the moose in rooting among fallen tree trunks in their search for mosses and other winter greenery.

Little Pig of the Big Southwest

The smallest of all the hoofed animals of the West are the peccary, or javelinas (hav-ah-LEEN-ahs) as they are called. These little pigs are gregarious, traveling in bands of from four to forty made up of all sizes and both sexes. Although notably short-tempered and with ugly dispositions, members of the herd get along with a minimum of squabbling. If captured when young, peccary make interesting and playful but untrustworthy pets.

Once on a warm December afternoon in Arizona Theodore Knipe, of the State Department of Game and Fish, watched for nearly an hour while a band of sixteen peccary, or muskhogs, took their usual afternoon siesta under a paloverde tree. They were, according to Knipe, "lined up head to tail with one red pigling wedged in between two adults. As the shade shifted, the end pig would get up and move to the head of the row to keep in the shade."

The collared peccary ranges from central Texas to southwestern Arizona. Formerly these piglike animals could be found as far north and east as the Red River in Arkansas. Between 1850 and the 1880's they were greatly reduced in numbers by hunters, many of them soldiers stationed at various military posts. In Texas, according to Theodore Roosevelt—

> . . . these little wild hogs were not much molested until 1886 and abounded in the dense chaparral along the lower Rio Grande. In that year it was suddenly discovered that their hides had a market value, being worth four bits—that is, half a dollar—apiece; and many Mexicans and not a few shiftless Texans went into the business of hunting them. As a result, they were speedily exterminated in many localities where they had formerly been numerous.

Only distantly related to the domestic pig, the peccary is hoglike in appearance with a large head, small eyes, long snout, thick neck, and body covered with coarse black and gray bristlelike hair. Adults range from twenty to twenty-eight inches high at the shoulder, thirty-four to forty inches in length, and weigh forty to forty-five pounds. The grizzled coat is set off by a light-colored stripe circling the body from the withers to the breast. When the bristles are erected, this collar almost doubles the apparent size of the head. Thus a peccary, standing at bay with only his head visible at the mouth of a cave or cactus tangle, looks like a truly formidable antagonist, especially when he bares his sharp scimitar-shaped tusks.

Perhaps the most distinctive physical feature of the peccary is the musk gland with its opening superficially resembling a navel located in the small of the back about eight inches above the knobby, almost rudimentary tail. Since peccary have poor eyesight and only moderate hearing, a keen sense of smell helps keep the herd together and enables the young to find and follow their mothers.

The staple year-around food of peccary is cactus, principally the prickly pear. In springtime they graze on a variety of herbs and continually root for underground tubers, bulbs and rhizomes. Another favorite food is the core of agaves (ah-GAH-vees) or century plants. Acorns and pinyon nuts provide a welcome change in diet.

Javelinas are rarely found in open deserts or grasslands, since they hesitate to leave the protection afforded by low-growing shrubs and rock-lined washes. They frequently retreat into caves or abandoned mine tunnels, leaving a guard at the entrance. Although more than a match for a coyote, a single peccary is sometimes separated from the band and killed by three or four of them working as a team. When deer are scarce, mountain lions may turn to peccary for food. Another possible enemy is the rattlesnake, which abounds on some javelina ranges. The giant diamondbacks, when poised to strike, loom higher than a peccary's head. Ernest Thompson Seton reported an instance when the discovery of a rattler

. . . brought the whole drove of peccaries to the spot. The peccaries stood with their backs highly arched and their feet drawn together like so many angry cats, threatening and uttering shrill grunts. Then one of them rose suddenly into the air, and with his four hoofs held close together, pounced down upon the coiled body of the snake. Another followed, and another, and another. After a short while the snake lay still, crushed beneath their feet. The whole squad then seized it in their teeth and tore it to pieces.

Many early-day reports credited peccary with ferocious attacks upon men, sometimes forcing them to climb trees to escape the tusks of a bristling herd. Later investigations indicate that such encounters were relatively rare, members of the band usually scattering in fright when disturbed. However, twentieth-century hunters who surprise a herd continue to squeal like a wounded pig, hoping to lure back some belligerent member. A few may return to lurk out of sight in nearby chaparral and snap their teeth menacingly, but they never show themselves unless routed out by dogs.

Because peccary are restricted to a relatively small region of the West, they rate high as an attraction for tourists interested in wild life, for ranchmen who relish wild meat and for hunters seeking an odd trophy to hang on the wall.

75. Carnivores—Flesh-Eaters of the West

Grizzly Bear—Hermit of the Hills

THE SEVERAL SPECIES of grizzly bears are the largest carnivores on earth. In pioneer times they ranged over the western half of North America from central Mexico to the northwestern tip of Alaska. King of bears, the grizzly was also monarch of the wilderness, fearing no creature. Living alone, his life was normally peaceful and uneventful, but when aroused to fury he became a terrible monster of destruction.

Although four or five well-armed Indians might attack a grizzly under favorable conditions, they killed relatively few. It was not until the white man with his firearms invaded the West that the grizzly finally recognized a conqueror.

Some grizzlies were much more given to a meat diet than others. These found sheep and cattle easier prey than bison and elk, and became a serious menace to stockmen, thus giving all grizzlies such a bad name that in the 1880's several states placed bounties on them. Hunting grizzlies soon became profitable and their numbers were rapidly reduced. The first to be exterminated were those which ranged on the high, rolling plains. By 1910, only a few of the great bears remained (outside of the national parks where they were protected), and these were in isolated locations, deep in the mountains. Though easily recognized by their huge size, humped shoulders, big heads with dished faces, and long, gray-to-buffy fur often sprinkled with white hairs which gave them a grizzled appearance and the name "silver tip," grizzlies were seldom encountered. The survivors had developed a shyness that kept the once numerous species well hidden.

AMERICAN MUSEUM OF NATURAL HISTORY, NEW YORK

Male grizzly.

A grizzly bear can find sustenance in a wide variety of environments. Being omniverous, he is not dependent solely upon meat for food and eats many kinds of vegetation including grass. He is especially fond of berries, stripping them from the bushes—leaves, twigs and all. He tears up large patches of ground in his search for succulent roots, and patiently turns over rocks as he hunts for insects. Nuts, honey, snakes, frogs, fish, birds, eggs, mice, ground squirrels, marmots—almost all edibles that he can harvest or catch are included in his diet. His enormous size and great strength enable him to kill and carry off a full-grown elk or steer, and for an animal of such bulk he is fleet of foot and has extraordinary endurance. An average-size grizzly weighs about 1,000 pounds and can maintain a running speed of twenty-five miles per hour for a considerable distance. Individuals weighing 1,600 pounds are on record.

Like some other carnivores, a grizzly bear stores excess food for future consumption. Whereas the well-fed cougar covers with leaves and brush the kill to which he expects to return, the grizzly covers his with sod and soil. This not only protects the carcass from flies and sun but, more important—since grizzlies are notorious carrion eaters—serves as a warning to all comers that this is the property of the mighty hermit of the hills, so beware!

When grizzlies were numerous, it was not unusual to find several of them feeding together, usually before 9:00 A.M. and after 4:00 P.M. One observer wrote, "I have seen as many as nine grizzlies in one berry patch and five fishing in one riffle of a salmon stream. They not only came and went singly but, while there, gave no outward sign of recognition or even of mutual consciousness."

Except during the mating season, adult grizzlies are supreme individualists who prefer a solitary life and pay little attention to others of their kind. Black bears give the grizzly a wide berth. If several blacks are interrupted in their feeding by a crotchety grizzly, the smaller bruins scatter in all directions, sometimes climbing trees for safety, leaving the plunder in the undisputed possession of the invader. Claws of the grizzly are too long to hook into tree bark, hence the big bears are unable to climb trees.

Summer is the mating season of grizzly bears. Pairs travel together for a month or more. Following a gestation period of approximately six months, the cubs (normally two, sometimes three or one) are born, usually in January while the mother is hibernating. For such a large adult, the cubs are very small, weighing only about one and a half pounds. Their eyes open on the ninth or tenth day after birth. The winter den in which they are born is customarily located on the side of a ridge or hill where the snow drifts deep, thereby blanketing the sleeping occupant from the intense outside cold. Cubs are suckled as long as the mother remains in the winter den, and begin to eat solid food soon after entering the "outside" world in the spring. Male grizzlies usually come out much earlier than the females and prowl among the snow drifts on lofty mountainsides in March. They also "den up" at a later date in the fall, and do not hibernate until deep snow has covered all their food.

Hibernation is peculiar to bears in the Northwest, not to those in the South where food is available the year around. With the coming of deep snow at high elevations many animals migrate to lower levels. Nature has saved the bear from these long trips by equipping his body so he can lie dormant in a snug den for months on end, all his functions at a low ebb. Hunters who have crawled back into a sleeping bear's den have found the occupant "dead to the world." But not always. At least one man who tried this was crushed to death as the frantic monster charged past him seeking to get out.

Grizzly bear cubs may stay with their mother for a year and a half, sometimes longer, although there is some doubt that they occupy her den the second winter. The cubs grow more slowly than those of black bears and require eight to ten years to reach full size and weight. In captivity they have lived more than twenty-five years.

Grizzlies are unbelievably strong. They have been known to break the neck of a full-grown steer with a single blow of that wickedly hooked paw. A ranger at one of our national forests reported following a grizzly track along an old road. At one place the foresters had erected a tall, sheet-iron box for fire-fighting tools. It was painted bright red. This evidently annoyed the bear and as he passed the box he swatted it, smashing in the whole metal side. In the same forest a sheepherder reported seeing a grizzly meet a lamb on the trail and with one downward slap flatten out the little creature as though a steam-roller had gone over it.

How dangerous is the grizzly to man? There are a number of cases on record of men being terribly mauled by the big bears, and a number have been killed. Theodore Roosevelt in his *Hunting Trips on the Prairie* tells about a neighbor of his on the Little Missouri who walked along a brushy stream bed and stumbled suddenly on a grizzly which with one blow crushed his skull like an egg shell. Roosevelt knew of another man who wounded a grizzly in the Big Horn Mountains. The animal charged past him and without stopping struck a side blow. It almost missed the hunter but not quite. One of those claw hooks tore out the man's collarbone and snapped through three or four ribs. He died that night.

There is also the case of the two cavalrymen at Fort Wingate, New Mexico, in 1872, who pursued a grizzly, wounding it with their Spencer rifles. The bear turned, struck down one man's horse and killed the rider. His companion dismounted to come to his rescue. The bear killed him too. Californians tell a story about a cowboy who roped a bear and attempted to drag the creature to death. But the bear stood up on his hind legs and began pulling in on the rope, hand over hand. The cowboy lost his horse, but managed to save his own life.

Normally, however, the grizzly is content to let man alone if left alone. The explorer Major Stephen H. Long wrote in 1820: "Notwithstanding the formidable character of this bear, we have not used any precaution against their attacks and, although they have been several times prowling about us at night, they have not evidenced any disposition to attack us."

If suddenly startled or wounded, grizzlies are likely to charge viciously. At such times they can be extremely dangerous, and at no time is it safe to molest them. In those of our national parks where there are grizzlies, signs warn visitors always to make a noise as they move along the trails. If a bear hears them coming he will move away, but if they should surprise him he might attack.

Black Bear—Comedian of the Wilds

Enos Mills, the noted naturalist of Estes Park, Colorado, called the black bear, "Happy Hooligan of the woods," and said he had seen them romping with coyotes. He reported that bears even tried, unsuccessfully, to make playmates out of stupid porcupines. "On one occasion," wrote Mills, "the bear leaped into an empty barrel and then overturned it on the steep slope. Away downhill rolled the barrel, at a lively pace, with the bear inside. Thrusting out his forepaws, he guided the course of the barrel and controlled its speed." Bear cubs are notoriously playful and, like small boys, thrive on praise and invent new antics in response to applause.

More than any other western mammal, the black bear resembles man. It climbs trees when frightened, whimpers and sobs when hurt, and when it wants a better view or wishes to wrestle with a rival, it stands upright on its hind legs.

The name "black" bear is a misnomer, but to differentiate it from the grizzly it might be called "short-clawed" bear. Actually, "black" bears may be brown, yellow or cinnamon. A very black mother sometimes has a blond, a brunet and a cinnamon in the same litter. Incidentally, most bear cubs are twins, but occasionally litters contain triplets or single births.

In primitive times Indians hunted black bears for food, used their big skins for warm bedding and made ornaments and decorations from their claws. However, they considered the bear as a powerful spirit and sought to assuage its anger. Among the Navajo anyone who killed a bear had to carry out various cleansing ceremonies to appease the animal's spirit.

A good day's bear hunt near Mount Shasta, Illustrated London News, 1888.

Although principally an animal of the forests and woodlands, the black bear also frequents mountain meadows and brushy hillsides. Its diet includes everything from grass, berries, nuts, honey, roots, rodents and insects to carrion, sheep and hogs. As occasional raiders of pigsties, bears gained the enmity of early-day settlers, who found them easy to catch by placing a comb of honey in a log pen with a steel trap at the entrance.

Like the grizzly, the black bear is essentially a solitary creature, except during the mating season in June and also when family groups of grown cubs travel with their mothers. Each individual ranges as widely as his need for food requires, which may take him over a territory ten or fifteen miles in length. In his travels he follows much the same routes, soon developing definite pathways. At points along these trails he marks certain trees by rearing up on his hind legs, reaching to his fullest extent and scratching the bark with claws and teeth. The significance of these "bear trees" remains a mystery. They may present a challenge to other bears or mark the locality of the occupant's home territory.

If sufficiently fat, a black bear begins to fast some time before entering his winter den, usually in November, where he hibernates for four or five months. During the first few weeks his sleep is natural and he is easily aroused, but as winter progresses his stupor becomes deeper, respiration and circulation are retarded, and it becomes impossible to awaken him to full consciousness. In northern climes, most bears come out of hibernation in March or early April.

Black bear cubs are born in January while the mother is hibernating. Weighing less than one pound at birth, they grow rapidly although their eyes remain closed for about forty days. By the time they are two months old the mother is ready to come out of the winter den, but she leaves the cubs behind for several weeks. Finally, when the snow melts sufficiently for them to find solid food, she brings them out for a period of rigorous training which continues until they are a year and a half old.

Most black bears are timid and inoffensive but under some conditions they lose their fear of man. If molested or teased they may use their great strength to maul or even kill their tormentors. When wounded, cornered, or if their cubs are threatened, bears will usually fight fiercely. A full-grown bear weighing from 300 to 500 pounds can disable a man with one blow of its paw, or injure him severely with claws and teeth.

Black bears sometimes fight among themselves over food, during the mating season or just to find out which is the superior bear. Cubs may also cause fights between mothers. When fighting, bears do not "hug" as is sometimes assumed. Instead they bite, slap and claw. Their battles are usually brief and not serious, although they have been known to continue until one participant was killed. Blacks are cannibalistic and apparently relish the flesh of their own kind as much as deer or elk meat.

It seems doubtful that a lone cougar would attack a black bear unless the latter was sick or wounded. Nevertheless there are numerous records of black bears killed by cougars, as well as by grizzlies and also by porcupines. Carcasses of bears have been found, their faces and mouths so full of quills that they were unable to eat.

Reports on the shipments of black bear hides during the last quarter of the nineteenth century indicate that approximately 30,000 of the animals were killed every year—a total of 750,000. It is little wonder that by 1910 very few remained in a wild state outside the national parks of the Rockies, Cascades, Sierra Nevada and other mountain reservations. Nevertheless the species managed to adapt itself to an expanding civilization. With keen senses of hearing and smell, the sly, wary, good-natured clown of the woods not only survived but increased amazingly in spite of an open hunting season, high-powered rifles and packs of trailing dogs. By the middle of the twentieth century black bears had established themselves in what seemed to be a permanent population throughout most of the forested areas of the West, even venturing at times into metropolitan regions.

The Gray Wolf—Freebooter of the Wild

When bison covered the prairies of western North America like a vast brown blanket, the immense herds were followed by hundreds of great gray wolves that preyed on the old, the injured and the weak. During the epoch of the hide hunters and the tongue takers, the wolves followed the buffalo killers, gorging themselves on the abandoned carcasses.

As the herds dwindled under relentless slaughter, wolves found it difficult to subsist on deer, antelope, rabbits, rodents and other prairie dwellers. It is not surprising that they turned for food to the cattle, sheep and horses which replaced buffalo on western ranges. Ranchers promptly instituted a vigorous war against them, using every lethal device then known. By 1910, only a few hardy and cunning pairs were left to kill livestock on the open plains, or subsist on deer and bighorn sheep deep in the nation's isolated back country. Canada and Alaska contained the largest remnants of the two million wolves which once ranged over almost the entire North American continent in Colonial times (according to estimates by Ernest Thompson Seton).

During the early days, before Europeans with their firearms invaded the West, wolves showed little fear of man. They sometimes entered Indian villages at night and fought with the dogs, which may have been hybrid wolves themselves. Certainly wolves and coyotes do not interbreed, but Vilhjalmur Stefansson, an expert on arctic wolves, believed that wolves and dogs did interbreed, although he was not sure. Most sled-dog men in the North affirm his belief. It is true, also, that Indians occasionally captured wolf pups and raised them as dogs.

Rabid wolves occasionally invaded Indian camps in daytime, snapping at the people, their dogs and horses. Any person who later showed signs of rabies was bound with buffalo-hide thongs to prevent him from injuring himself and others.

Indians prized wolf skins for robes and wolf tails for trimmings. In bow-and-arrow times, Plains Indians dressed in wolf skins and crept up within striking distance of a buffalo without disturbing the quarry. Some writers have claimed that the Indians buried their dead in trees and on scaffolds to prevent wolves from digging up the bodies, but many Indians say that the odd burials were to make it easier for the dead to go to the spirit world.

In the middle and later 1800's, a wolf hunter, or wolfer, would shoot a buffalo and, while poisoning the meat with strychnine, might find himself encircled by ten or more wolves waiting for him to complete the job and go away. Returning the following day, he would pick up stiffened bodies near the scattered buffalo bones. Poisoning not only killed many wolves but also made serious inroads on the populations of foxes and skunks along with hawks, eagles, magpies and ravens. The wolves which survived this constant warfare with hunters became cautious, wary and timid, shunning any meeting with humans. They

Timber wolves.

AMERICAN MUSEUM OF NATURAL HISTORY, NEW YORK

kept well out of rifle range and learned to avoid traps and detect meat poisoned by hunters.

In winter when snow piles deep over the land, most wild creatures hibernate, and in the early days wolves sometimes became maddened with hunger. This was the traditional season for the "wolf at the door," the time when a lone camper saw a circle of menacing eyes surrounding his fire, and when sleigh parties in Russia were pursued by wolf packs. However, Stefansson, after a great deal of careful investigation, came to the conclusion that wolves do not run in packs—except in literature and in folklore—nor do they prey on humans. He quoted David Mills, of the National Association of Fur Industries, as authority for the statement that scientific inquiry has never authenticated an attack on sleighs in Russia by wolves. In Washington, the Biological Survey for many years investigated every published account of people said to have been attacked or killed by wolf packs in the United States and Canada. Without a single exception, all proved to be purely imaginary.

On the other hand, some men with experience maintain stoutly that wolves do run in packs, that they personally have seen them. Skeptics reply that these "packs" may be two parents and their maturing pups—never totaling more than a dozen, unless two families happened to pounce on the same quarry at the same time. Recent studies in Isle Royale National Park report a "pack" of seventeen members.

Wolves did become famous for their teamwork when bringing down animals too large or too swift for one to handle alone. A certain howl or "muster call" was said to gather the scattered members of the family together for an attack in force. A big moose, bull elk or buffalo would be surrounded and as he turned, slashing with his horns at the swarming enemies, a wolf in the rear would snap in two the great tendon at the back of the animal's hock. Thus "hamstrung" and rendered immobile, the wolves made short work of him, tearing open his flanks and cutting his jugular vein.

Even the swift antelope was sometimes fair game for wolves. If they found a lone prongbuck they could not outrun it, but they might chase it in relays until the victim was exhausted. Wolves have been known to establish an ambush, one or two driving the prey to the location where others lay in wait.

Range cattle were relatively easy prey for wolves, which sometimes killed several in a single night. It was not uncommon to see a big steer with his tail snipped off by a "lobo" which probably struck for the flank, hoping to disembowel his prey, but missed. One New Mexico cowman, at about the turn of the century, figured on an annual loss by wolves of approximately 10 per cent.

Wolves are cannibalistic, and sometimes when one member of a family pack was shot, the others would turn and tear it to pieces. Each pair and its family hunted in its own territory, following a circular "runway," or travel route, which might be as much as 100 miles in circumference.

Standing 30 inches high at the shoulder and measuring six feet from nose tip to tail tip, a big male might weigh 125 pounds or more, with 100 pounds a fair average. The females are considerably smaller. Their extreme strength and the power of their jaws enable wolves to accomplish unbelievable feats. Lassoed wolves have severed a half-inch Manila rope with one clip of the jaws. A six-month-old pup is known to have dragged a trap fastened to a 100-pound weight more than a quarter of a mile. A female wolf carried

Century MAGAZINE, 1888

Broncos attacked by timber wolf pack. Engraving, after drawing by Frederic Remington.

and dragged a 52-pound steer head for a mile and a half at a pace faster than a man on foot could follow her. Theodore Roosevelt, in writing about a horse that he saw attacked by a wolf, stated, "with a few savage snaps the wolf hamstrung and partially disemboweled it."

Authorities generally agree that wolves are monogamous, pairing for life. The breeding season extends from late January to early March, and five to twelve pups are born approximately nine weeks later. The den was usually a natural cave or a burrow on a south-facing slope in badlands or foothill country. As the pups grew and thrived, both parents brought food to the den for them. So strong was the parental attachment that they would, in their anxiety, when the pups were disturbed, come close enough to an intruder to be shot. In fact, the usually wary and gun-shy wolf was most vulnerable during denning time. Ranchers, bounty hunters and the later, government predator-control men took advantage of this Achilles heel to clean out entire families of the big, gray freebooters.

Small wolf pups were subject to capture by eagles as they played about the entrance of their den. They were also subject to tapeworms, ticks and other parasites. Dog distemper, when brought to North America from Europe, played havoc among wolves, as it did with coyotes and Indian dogs, but nothing destroyed the wolves as effectively as the white man's guns, traps and poisons.

As the big "loafers" or "lobos" became scarce in many communities, often one lone animal became notorious for its ability to outwit hunters and its record of kills. Among these famous outlaws was the huge Roosevelt wolf of Medora, South Dakota, which between 1894 and 1902 killed thousands of dollars worth of cattle. It showed contempt for dogs, traps, poisoned baits and the many men who tried to shoot it. When finally killed in 1902, he was found to weigh 168 pounds, a monster of his kind. There was also "The White Wolf of Cheyenne," a great marauder; the "Custer Wolf" near Custer, South Dakota, with a $500 bounty placed on his head; "Old Three Toes" and her pack that killed innumerable calves and sheep near Thatcher, Colorado; and "Sycan," a white wolf of southern Oregon that caused losses of $15,000 worth of livestock.

The record of destruction left by cattle-killing wolves justified the following comment by Joseph Neal, veteran stockman of Meeker, Colorado: "The history of the gray wolf in the West became a chronicle of the struggle between the wolf and the livestock industry, with failure or success of the industry depending on the outcome." The industry won, and today the big gray wolf of the West is little more than a memory—but a memory of one of the strongest, most intelligent, most intrepid animals that mankind has found it necessary to combat.

Coyote—Little Wild Dog of the Plains

The story is told of an easterner who, on reaching his western destination, waxed eloquent about the prairie dogs he had seen on the trip. His description, however, fitted coyotes. When this was explained he admitted ignorance, but since he had seen them on the prairies and they resembled dogs, he assumed that they must be the prairie dogs he had heard about.

Certainly the coyote does resemble a small, gray collie dog. He is also called brush wolf and prairie wolf, and is a close relative of the big, gray buffalo wolves that roamed the Great Plains. Weighing from eighteen to forty pounds with a shoulder height of twenty-three to twenty-six inches, the coyote appears much larger in winter because of its coat of long, coarse fur.

Unlike most other native animals found throughout the West, coyotes have actually extended their range while being hunted, trapped, poisoned and otherwise persecuted by mankind. The smart little prairie wolves have long been the most destructive of American predators. They kill domestic poultry, every kind of small livestock, and the young of larger kinds. Actually, only about 20 per cent of their diet is domestic livestock. They live chiefly on wild creatures and under certain conditions have committed serious depredations, even among big game animals,

Coyotes prey principally on rabbits, prairie dogs, mice, gophers and ground squirrels. They also eat snakes, lizards, toads, songbirds, fruits and nuts, birds' eggs, grasshoppers, and beetles, with rabbits and carrion their chief bill of fare. They do not hesitate to cannibalize their own kind when the opportunity presents itself.

In addition to man, the little prairie wolf has many enemies including bears, mountain lions, bobcats, and wolves, although coyotes have been known to follow them at a safe distance and take advantage of their kills. Coyotes and badgers are sometimes seen hunting together, and coyotes often traveled with buffalo herds, ready to pounce upon any rodents stirred up by the hoofs of the big ruminants.

Like their larger relatives, the gray wolves, coyotes produce volumes of vocal music, particularly during the night and just before sunrise. Their yapping and howling has long been a trademark of the western wildlands. Also, like gray wolves, coyotes use small caves or dig burrows for dens, both the father and the mother killing and bringing home food for the growing whelps which number, usually, from five to seven. Litters of ten to twelve are not uncommon, and as many as seventeen have been recorded. Pups are born in April following a gestation period of sixty to sixty-three days. When they are eight to ten weeks old the family leaves the den and roves about, remaining together until fall when the pups are full grown and able to fend for themselves.

Coyotes, as a rule, do not mate for life, although a pair may remain mated for several years. There are known cases on record of apparent polygamy with two litters of pups in the same den at the same time.

It was not until the middle of the nineteenth century, when the beaver population was being rapidly depleted, that much attention was paid to coyote skins. By 1860 the "wolfers" found a growing demand for prairie wolf pelts for which they received from $.75 to $1.50 each. The price increased tenfold in the next half century, but the coyote held his own. Winter, not man, became his greatest enemy because the rodents on which he lives hibernate. At this season, too, mange may be fatal, as it ruins the animal's coat and leaves him unprotected from the cold. Other parasites, including tapeworms, fleas, ticks, and lice, make his life unpleasant and sometimes downright unbearable. Coyotes, like wolves, are also subject to distemper and rabies. In nearly all instances where coyotes have attacked man, the animal was found to be rabid.

The coyote is one of the outstanding examples of an animal that has adapted itself to advancing civilization. "No other carnivore," wrote Ira N. Gabrielson, president of the Wildlife Management Institute, "has been more intimately associated with the romantic history of the western plains, and none has been more heavily persecuted by man than the little wild dog of the sagebrush and buffalo grass. The night song of the coyote is as much a part of the West—and of America itself—as the Grand Canyon or the Great Plains." And it promises to be as lasting!

Foxes—Smallest of the Wild Dogs

"Smart as a fox," when applied to a human is a long-standing tribute to the West's craftiest animal. There are three species: the red, the gray, and the desert kit, or swift fox—smallest of the three.

Not much larger than a house-cat with immense ears and a long, bushy tail, the buffy-gray kit fox, although shy, is much less suspicious than its relatives and is easily trapped or poisoned. Its principal food consists of kangaroo rats and cottontail rabbits which it hunts at night. It also includes in its diet other nocturnal rodents along with insects, cactus fruits, lizards, ground-dwelling birds and birds' eggs.

When alarmed, the little desert fox runs close to the ground, seeming to float along effortlessly at great speed for short distances—hence the name of "swift." If closely followed, it zigzags or changes its course, baffling its pursuer until it can dodge into a burrow, a thicket or crevice among the rocks.

Unless very hungry, the kit fox carries its food to its den, which is usually located in the sandy bank of a desert wash. Here with its mate the fox dines at leisure. In February five to seven pups are born. After they are old enough to eat meat, both father and mother hunt and bring food to them. When big enough to venture into the world of sagebrush and cactus their lessons begin.

The gray fox is the only member of the dog family that regularly climbs trees, sometimes escaping pursuit by leaping up among the branches, jumping from limb to limb, and then hiding quietly among the foliage. At other times it may seek an arboreal roost for a nap. In the foothills of the Sierra Nevada in California, one gray fox mother made her nest of leaves and shredded bark in a large hollow limb twenty-five feet up in an oak tree.

Usually shy and retiring, gray foxes sometimes become bold when not molested and at times, in the evening, come to the kitchen door of a dogless ranch to look for scraps. Although the gray fox prefers meat, it also eats vegetables, nuts and fruits. Rodents make up much of its diet augmented by ground-nesting birds, reptiles, insects and carrion. It is especially fond of eggs, and preys on domestic poultry but not to the extent that its red cousin does.

Unlike the gray fox, which is an animal of the brushlands, cactus thickets and rocky hillsides, the red fox prefers mixed farmlands and woodlots and the high, green meadows near timberline. In the farming country it adapts itself to frequent contact with humans, raiding their poultry houses and tantalizing their dogs. Since a fox weighs only eight to ten pounds, it has little chance in a fight with a large dog, but it seems to enjoy matching wits with hounds and usually is skillful enough to evade them in a chase.

Rodents constitute the chief food of the red fox, and it is so fond of mice that "still hunters" imitate the squeak of a mouse to entice reynard within shooting distance. The red fox also eats turtles and their eggs, insects, fruits, berries, frogs, even earthworms. When food is abundant he caches some of it for possible future consumption. In winter his diet is restricted to such small animals as do not hibernate and to fruits which can be reached beneath the snow.

Red foxes do not mate for life, but pairs remain together until they have raised their litter. The four to nine pups born in March or April are brought their food and instructed in the ways of life by both parents until fall, when they are abandoned and must take care of themselves.

Foxes seem to be particularly susceptible to rabies, which periodically becomes epidemic when fox populations increase and disappears when their numbers have been reduced. A rabid fox loses all sense of fear and, in the last stages of the disease, travels about snapping at dogs, cattle, people and even inanimate objects.

A red fox is not always red. There are three other color phases: black, silver, and brownish yellow or "cross," a name applied because of a broad black band of underfur down the back and across the shoulders. All four colors may be represented among members of a single litter.

Fox skins have been in demand since early in the nineteenth century, and the demand for them became so great by the 1900's that a fur farming boom began, but the pelts of the wild animals were generally considered the best and they brought the highest prices.

In spite of traps, dogs, guns.and poison baits, red and gray foxes, like coyotes and deer, have held their own regardless of civilization. Intelligent, crafty and full of tricks, they have learned to circumvent the white man's wiles and to turn encroaching farms to their own uses. Only the big-eared kit fox of the Southwest has failed to meet the challenge of changing times and has gradually decreased in numbers as mankind expanded his activities in the desert.

Cougar—Tawny Killer of the Canyons

Held in awe by prehistoric Indians and hounded wherever found by ranchers and professional hunters, the cougar (puma, panther or mountain lion) is exceeded in size in the western hemisphere by only one other cat, the jaguar of Central and South America. In pioneer days cougars were found from seashore to mountaintops throughout the entire United States, but by 1900 they had been killed out or greatly reduced in numbers except in the Rocky Mountains and in New Mexico, Arizona and west Texas. Weighing from 100 to 150 pounds or more, and measuring more than seven feet from its nose to the tip of its long, heavy tail, the tawny (sometimes gray), short-haired puma was a hated killer of deer, elk and bighorn sheep as well as domestic sheep, goats and horses.

Preferring high and rough terrain, the mountain lion nevertheless roamed the prairies, hunting along the forested watercourses and roaming the wooded, rocky hills. It was rarely seen on the open grasslands except when crossing from one range of hills to another. An extensive wanderer, the big cat might cover as much as twenty-five miles in a single night. Doing much of its hunting during the hours of darkness, it relied on both sight and scent while following a circular route or "travelway" which required from fifteen to eighteen days to encompass. When food became scarce in this area the lion established a new route in more productive territory.

Mountain lions subsist principally on deer where those animals are abundant, each cat killing one deer a week on the average. This menu may be supplemented by any other prey available, ranging from moose to mice. Cougars have been seen catching and eating grasshoppers, and are known to consume rabbits, beavers, raccoons, peccary, coyotes, even skunks and porcupines. They are particularly fond of horse meat, preferring young colts. Trappers have reported that their snares were robbed of foxes and bobcats by mountain lions, and there are a few records of cougars eating their own kind.

Having gorged on a fresh kill, the big cat covers it with leaves and sticks, usually returning to finish the meal a few days later. Females with kittens hunt in the vicinity of the den bringing home items that the young can devour. As the kittens get big enough to travel, the mother may take them to a nearby kill but hustles them back to the den after they have fed.

Four or five toms sometimes fight over a female in heat, yowling and caterwauling much like domestic cats but, of course, many times louder and more terrifying. Settlers, hearing these screams in the night, reported that they sounded like the shrill cry of a frightened woman. Some even added the preposterous conjecture that the cats were trying to entice a man into the forest and kill him. Theodore Roosevelt heard a lion cry on one of his hunting trips and wrote: "although a silent beast, yet at times, especially during the breeding season, the males utter a wild scream, and the females also cry and call."

Following a gestation period of ninety-six days, from one to four kittens are born, at any time of year, in a den or lair usually located in a cave among the rocks, beneath an uprooted tree, or other nook or thicket protected from the weather. The kittens are spotted like leopards. After two weeks their eyes open. Three or four weeks later they are weaned but usually stay with their mother learning how to hunt and kill until fully grown, sometimes until two years old.

A mother cougar will fight viciously to defend her young, and animals hard-pressed by hounds often turn and fight the dogs, yet the big cats are normally so shy and elusive that they are not often seen. This shrinking characteristic was not forced on them by white men because records of the Lewis and Clark expedition of 1804–6 state that the puma "is very seldom found and when found [is] so wary it is difficult to reach him with a musket."

In spite of its apparent timidity the cougar has a high degree of curiosity and campers sometimes find in the morning the tracks of a cougar that passed close to their beds during the night. At times cougars will also follow a man for miles, keeping on his trail but out of sight. Although making no move to attack, the action is suspicious and the man who discovers by the tracks that he has been followed remembers the incident with a mixture of relief and apprehension.

For an animal so powerful and so easily capable of killing a man, it is surprising that dependable records of unprovoked attacks by cougars are extremely rare. In several cases the individual attacked had already been injured and was bleeding, the smell of fresh blood being more than the lion could resist. In other cases the attacking cougar was believed to be rabid or too old to kill its natural prey.

Mountain lion, or puma, in its rocky lair.

AMERICAN MUSEUM OF NATURAL HISTORY, NEW YORK

A cougar usually kills a deer by creeping close to it behind a rock or fallen tree. When within forty or fifty feet the lion springs forward and in one or two bounds pounces on its victim's side or back, the claws of all four feet hooking into the deer's flesh while the lion's powerful teeth crush its spine at the base of the skull. Trappers who have watched a cougar make a kill in winter on the snow say that it acted much like a house-cat stalking a bird or mouse. Before making the first great leap the lion tested its footing like a sprinter, rocking gently on its hind legs, the long tail nervously sweeping an arc in the snow.

Many people have wondered how a cougar, having killed a deer, manages to carry the large animal away to a hiding place, usually under the low branches of a tree, where it is eaten at leisure. Tracks in the snow show plainly enough where the deer and lion went down in a heap during the kill, but from this matted patch in the snow only the lion's tracks lead to the place of concealment. Obviously the deer could not have been dragged there. The explanation is simple. The cougar carried the deer, which probably weighed as much as he did, across his own back and, holding it with his teeth, walked away. The deer's feet and antlers may have trailed on the ground but not the body.

In regions where pumas killed much domestic livestock, bounty payments for the animals were generally paid during the nineteenth century. Poisoning, trapping with catnip oil for bait, and trailing with dogs were all used successfully to destroy them. Elimination of the big cats in some localities led to such a rapid increase in the deer herds that they became a nuisance. For centuries cougars had kept deer in equilibrium, preventing overpopulation by killing the slow, the stupid and the sick, thus leaving the finest to propagate future generations.

Bobcat—The Big Pussy with the Short Tail

To say that a man can "whip his weight in wildcats" is the highest tribute that can be paid his fighting ability. Yet the wildcat is normally shy and retiring. When cornered, however, he suddenly becomes dynamite, biting and clawing viciously. In single combat he is more than a match for a big dog and on numerous occasions has successfully fought off several at once.

The wildcat, commonly called bobcat in the West on account of its stubby tail, resembles in many ways an immense, gray-brown, spotted house-cat. Weighing from fifteen to twenty-five pounds it measures thirty to thirty-eight inches from the tip of its blunt nose to the end of its bobbed tail. In primitive times it was common over all of the United States, and throughout most of the West. The big, furry cat held its own in spite of the efforts of farmers, ranchers and trappers to destroy it.

The bobcat hunts by night and is rarely seen in full daylight, although it is often abroad early in the morning and soon after sunset. Rabbits, rodents of all kinds, ground-nesting birds and their eggs, fawns, even porcupines, carrion, domestic sheep and poultry constitute its all-meat diet. It prefers open woodlands with dense thickets and rocky outcroppings blanketed with chaparral. Although quite able to climb, it hunts on the ground and rarely takes to a tree unless closely pursued.

Bobcats range within home territories which vary in size according to the abundance of food, but are usually five or six square miles in extent. The cat hunts by sight rather than by scent, wandering here and there, crossing its own trail many times and constantly keeping a sharp lookout for anything edible. Once prey is sighted, the stealthy cat creeps silently toward it. When within distance, it crouches, tenses its muscles for the spring and with a great bound—sometimes seven or eight feet—pounces upon the unsuspecting victim. During the mating season, from late January to early March, the animals cover a much larger territory than their hunting ranges, possibly an area as much as twenty or twenty-five miles in diameter.

Usually in April, the female bobcat makes her nest, which she lines with moss or dried leaves, among the rocks, beneath a thicket-protected overhanging ledge or in a hollow tree. The two to four kittens are quite helpless at first, but their eyes open on the ninth day. There are no records to indicate that the male accepts any family responsibilities whatever, leaving the rearing and training of the kittens entirely to their mother, who weans them in June. By early autumn each kitten weighs five or six pounds and is able to shift for itself. Young bobcats usually remain together through the first winter, but older cats live and hunt alone.

During the mating season bobcats squall and yowl and make the night hideous with their varied repertory of astounding range and volume. Throughout the rest of the year they are generally silent but when trapped or cornered they growl, snarl and hiss ferociously.

Because the bobcat occasionally varies its rodent diet with venison, quail, lamb, or turkey, it has been called a "varmint," and has been trapped and shot without mercy. Bounties were offered for its scalp as early as 1727, and several states still paid for them at the beginning of the twentieth century. Pelts have long been in demand for men's coat collars and for women's jackets. Bobcat flesh is reported excellent by hunters who have eaten it.

The ubiquitous bobcat compensates for his destruction of domestic animals and game by killing hundreds of rodents which would otherwise destroy farm crops. Like the fox and coyote, he has now become recognized as a useful element in the balance of nature.

Wolverine—Largest of the Weasels

"Picture a weasel—that small atom of insensate courage, that symbol of slaughter, sleeplessness, and tireless, incredible activity—picture that scrap of demoniac fury, multiply that mite some 50 times, and you have the likeness of the wolverine." So wrote Ernest Thompson Seton in describing that "little tough guy," the skunk-bear, carcajou or wolverine. Although it is the largest of the weasels, the Indian Devil, as it is sometimes called, is the smallest of the big-time predators. Standing only twelve inches high, this squat, short-legged fighter with the big growl is between three and four feet in over-all length and weighs only twenty-five to thirty-five pounds.

This hard character is feared by beasts of prey many times its size, for its raw courage is no less than its amazing strength. There are numerous eyewitness records of black bears, coyotes, even mountain lions abandoning their kills at the snarling advance of a wolverine. Somewhat resembling a small, long-haired, buffy-yellow to dark brown bear, the wolverine has two lighter colored stripes along the sides of the back, a coarse, bushy tail and a nauseating musky odor like that of the skunk. An animal of snowy Canada, it originally ranged the northern tier of states, the Sierra Nevada and the Rocky Mountains as far south as northern New Mexico.

Almost wholly carnivorous and remaining active throughout the entire winter, the wolverine feeds on any meat that it can catch or steal. Rabbits, ground squirrels, fish, frogs, birds, marmots, mice and other small animals make up its diet. When such large herbivores as deer and bighorn have bogged down in deep snow, the wolverine has been known to leap upon their backs and sever the spinal cord.

Wary and solitary, the wolverine keeps out of sight but knows that where man is, there too is food. Its well-known habit of following a woodsman as he tends his trap line, stealing both bait and trapped animals, has earned him the everlasting hatred of trappers. He sometimes steals the traps, too, and hides them. Wolverines often break into cabins and eat or carry off all meat, as well as tear up and smear with their foul musk everything they consider inedible.

The home den for the female may be in a cave, an enlargement of a ready-made burrow or a cleft among the rocks. Following a gestation period of about ninety days, the two to four young are born in June. They remain with their mother as a family until fall. The mother, a fearless and determined fighter, will promptly and ferociously attack anything, including man, that molests them.

Chief enemy of the wolverine, other than man, is the porcupine, which, in sacrificing its life often proves to be a fatal meal. The quills puncture the wolverine's intestines causing death within a week or ten days.

Too coarse and bulky to be made into garments, the fur of the wolverine is highly prized as a trim for parka hoods because the moisture in human breath does not freeze on it. During the eighty-five years between 1821 and 1906, the Hudson's Bay Company collected 101,426 wolverine skins. Never abundant anywhere in the United States, the skunk-bear has been exterminated by continued trapping in most of the West; in fact, by the mid-twentieth century only a few remained in the Rockies and Sierra Nevada.

Ernest Thompson Seton, fascinated by the wolverine's personality, called him "a tremendous character," and regretted that "it cannot be a question of many years before the wise and valiant wolverine is known only by musty skins and dusty records."

76. Rodents—The Small Gnawers with the Big Teeth

Nature's Engineer

OF ALL THE creatures in the West the one that did more than any other to hasten exploration and open up the silent places was the beaver. He has a body shapeless as a sack of grain and weighs from thirty to sixty pounds. A peculiar property of his fur gives the beaver great commercial value and caused his near extermination. Beaver fur has coarse guard hairs over an undercoat of brown velvet. The fibers of this undercoat are barbed in a manner which makes them hold together tenaciously when matted into felt.

Early in the nineteenth century a good beaver hat became the mark of a gentlemen, and eager traders risked their lives and their capital to get the fur. In the 1820's a beaver pelt was usually worth about five dollars, and by the mid-1830's its value had increased to six dollars. When stretched in a hoop the pelt was as round as a wagon wheel with a diameter of about three feet. According to legend, a fur trader would stand a rifle on the ground and any Indian who wished to buy it had to pile up beaver skins until the stack was as high as the gun. Like most legends, this is an exaggeration, for it would take at least forty beaver pelts— worth a total of $200 to $240—to make a pile as tall as a rifle. This could amount to a profit of some 6,000 to 7,000 per cent on the cost of a three- to four-dollar trade gun. Such capital gains are fantastic, of course. However, it is true that traders often marked up the sales price of their goods at least 1,000 per cent, which seems large but not exorbitant in view of the trader's transportation costs and the danger of being scalped, robbed or lost in the wilderness.

By 1840 beaver had become so scarce that the big fur companies which had been organized to buy them shifted their trade to buffalo hides. Sixty years later beaver were practically extinct in the West. Only a few remained in the remote swamps of the Pacific Northwest and in isolated meadows high in the interior valleys of the Rocky Mountains.

Although some lakes and ponds with an abundance of willow, alder, cottonwood or aspen trees fringing their shores were natural haunts for beaver, most beaver built their own ponds. Thus they created an environment in which they soon multiplied rapidly when protected by game laws.

A beaver matures when two years old. His mother, who expects a new litter every spring, drives him from the lodge at this age and henceforth he must make his own living. His home pond is probably full of other mothers, fathers and yearlings. There are insufficient trees around the shore to provide food for all of them, so the young male starts up or down stream. He swims when he can, or waddles across the shallows. It is springtime in the Rockies, marsh marigolds nod on the swampy banks, new aspen leaves are uncurling overhead. Occasionally, where rock slides or log jams block the way, the young beaver must detour.

Agile and graceful in the water, he is awkward on land. His front legs are short, with small paws that scarcely lift his heavy body off the ground. His huge, webbed hind feet, powerful for swimming, are clumsy on rough ground. His broad, black, hairless tail, ten inches long and six wide, serves excellently as both oar and rudder in the water. On land it has no purpose except as a chair when he sits erect to gnaw a tree trunk. It is never used as a spade or trowel, though this is a popular belief.

The young beaver, on his overland detours, may be pounced upon by a wandering wolverine, mountain lion, lynx, wolf or possibly even an eagle. If not molested, he may follow the stream for several days. Probably he passes several beaver ponds where he is unwelcome, but he eventually finds a suitable location for a home. Plenty of building ma-

Group of beavers building a dam.

terials are at hand in the form of willow and aspen trees; a fallen log on one side of the stream provides a secure anchor post for a dam; and a small swampy swale a short distance upstream provides adequate space for flooding.

Dam building requires a beaver to cut a great deal of brush and many poles. His most important tools are four orange-yellow, self-sharpening, wood-cutting teeth. With these, a pair of beaver can fell a three-inch sapling in three minutes, but they require about an hour to down a six-inch tree. With one night's work they can fell a cottonwood a foot in diameter. A beaver, working alone, has been clocked cutting off a four-inch hardwood: he completed the job in fifteen minutes.

Contrary to popular belief, beavers do not cut trees so that they always fall into their ponds. Actually beavers are unable to control the direction of the fall. In fact, trees sometimes fall on a beaver, killing him. However, as pond-side trees generally lean toward the water, they often fall in that direction.

With the first tree down, the lone beaver cuts off the branches and begins building his dam by sinking them in the bed of the stream. To hold them in place he brings rocks, walking on his hind feet and holding a stone in his forearms pressed against his shoulder or under his chin. He carries mud in the same manner. As the summer advances the dam of sticks, brush, rocks and poles grows higher and longer because the stream has spread out of its bed and around the ends of the starting dam. The small pond he has created makes his task much easier, for he now can float materials down to the damsite. Having cut most of the smaller trees along the shores of the stream, he has developed several muddy trails, and if there is a high bank it is sure to have a beaver-slide which, when in use, is kept wet and slippery.

Finishing touches to the dam include carrying quantities of mud to the tangled network of brush and sticks, plugging the many leaks with leaves, sod, parts of water plants, clumps of grass and other debris. How much of this busy work is instinctive and how much engineering skill is open to argument. Beaver in captivity behind a concrete dam will carry mud and sticks to patch holes that do not exist.

By the time of the first frost a new beaver dam must be sufficiently watertight to form a sizable pond. With winter approaching, the young pioneer concentrates all his energy on collecting tree trunks and branches. He weighs these down underwater with rocks. The tender inner bark will provide him with food during the coming winter when ice prevents him from foraging outside.

This first year the young beaver has no time to build a lodge. Instead he selects a bank of the pond which rises several feet above the water. Working well beneath the surface, the young beaver tunnels into the bank, gradually pushing upward until he is above the level of the pond. Here he excavates a den about three feet in diameter and two feet high. In the domed ceiling he makes a small opening to admit air from the ground surface above. In this chamber he will spend most of the winter, protected from the cold and storms of the outside world, with easy access by means of the sloping tunnel to the deeper water of the pond where his food is stored.

Spring comes! Again Webfoot wanders away, this time in search of a mate. According to Indian tradition if he goes back to his old home, the family—consisting now of papa, mama, the yearlings and a new set of babies—make a slave of him insisting that he do woman's work. However this may be, certainly most of the young bachelor beavers return to their newly made ponds with young females. Together, they start to build a lodge. Selecting a shallowly submerged shelf at the edge of deep water, the two beavers construct a small island of poles and sticks. This foundation rises four or five inches above the high-water level of the pond. They then begin to build walls to form a rough oval. On the deep-water side, two slide-hole doorways are left in the floor. After they have built the walls to a height of about two feet, they begin to slope them inward until the walls merge as a dome-shaped roof. More and more sticks are dragged up onto the structure until the lodge looks like a great pile of sticks and peeled poles thoroughly embedded in mud. The former Chief Biologist of the National Park Service, Victor Cahalane, reports that in large colonies a number of family lodges may be built close together, and eventually the accumulation of poles and sticks makes one huge pile as much as seven feet high and thirty-five feet in diameter. Cahalane also reported a beaver dam in the Jefferson River, of Montana, which was 2,140 feet long.

In a one-family structure, the space inside is usually four or five feet across and as much as three feet high. John Colter, of the Lewis and Clark expedition, is said to have made a miraculous escape from closely pursuing Blackfeet in 1809 by diving into a beaver pond and crawling into a beaver lodge through its underwater entrance while the puzzled Indians searched the shores of the pond and the surrounding woods without success. However, the best evidence indicates that he hid in the Jefferson River under a pile of drift-logs which may have resembled a beaver house.

Beavers usually mate during the winter, and the young are born a little less than four months later. Just before the happy event the father leaves the family lodge and takes up bachelor quarters in his bank den. He thus temporarily becomes a "bank beaver." Under some conditions, particularly in deep or swift streams which beavers cannot dam or in the Southwest where winters are mild, they do not build lodges but live entirely in bank dens, often connected with a labyrinth of tunnels and burrows.

Before the young are born, all of the two-year-old children are driven out of the family lodge, leaving the mother with only her yearling brood. When born, the three to five kits each weigh, on the average, less than one pound. They grow rapidly and apparently need no swimming lessons. When about three weeks old, they wander from the home lodge, playing water tag and other games with other youngsters of the colony, or cut down small saplings in imitation of their elders.

Beavers of both sexes have a pair of musk glands called castors, located in the rear of the abdomen, which are especially active during the mating season. These were once believed to have medicinal value and brought trappers as much as twenty dollars per pound. In later years the musk, called "castoreum," was used extensively by trappers to attract beavers to their sets.

An important part of a professional trapper's skill was to know the habits of beavers, to recognize fresh sign and to decide accurately where to place traps. The standard New-house double-spring beaver trap with five feet of chain weighed about five pounds. Its general design did not change for three hundred years. A dozen or fifteen traps were about all one man wanted to carry, although some trappers had a "string" of twenty-five. The best place to make a set was where beavers habitually climbed out of the water onto the bank. To find these places a man usually waded upstream. Thus the human scent, which frightens beavers, floated away from him. Finding a beaver trail in the grass, the trapper drove a stake solidly in the stream bottom. He attached the chain to this and set his trap, preferably on a rock five or six inches below the surface. He would often take two willow wands three or four feet long and place them on the water like the letter V, the point being at the beaver trail. These were to act as wings which would guide a swimming beaver to the exact spot where, when he put down his feet to climb out, he would step in the trap. A skilled trapper claimed he could place these wands so accurately that he could determine which foot his victim would place in the trap. The beaver, as soon as caught, invariably dived into deep water. It was important to fix the chain on the stake so the animal could not surface and climb out on the bank, for if he did the beaver was sure to twist off his trapped foot and escape.

When all was set the trapper splashed water over the bank to wash away all man-scent. Then he dropped a little castoreum in the trail. Next morning he walked boldly along the bank, hoping to see in the sluggish current the drowned beaver waving his flat tail at him.

The carcass, when dragged out of the water, was skinned at once. The trapper saved only the pelt, castors and sometimes the tail, which was considered a delicacy when broiled, after the scaly skin had been charred off.

At the rendezvous beaver pelts were pressed into bales by handmade devices of logs and rocks. Each bale weighed from ninety to a hundred pounds, and two were considered a standard load for a horse. In this form they made the fifteen-hundred-mile trip to market in St. Louis.

Before the coming of the white man, Indians hunted beavers with bow and arrow. A favorite method was to tear a hole in the dam and ambush the beavers that came to repair it. Another Indian method was to block the underwater tunnels entering a beaver lodge, then chop through the roof and pull out the ungainly beasts. Perhaps the most heartless Indian method of catching beavers was to drown them under the ice in winter. By this method the Indian walked out on the frozen beaver dam, located the store-pile of sticks being used for winter food and fenced it by driving down poles through the ice. He would then remove one pole thus making a gate by which a beaver could enter. At this gap he placed a willow wand which would wave as the beaver passed in. His work completed the Indian wrapped himself snugly in his blanket on shore and waited.

In due time some member of the beaver family came to the store to fetch a stick on which all could dine in the comfort of the lodge. He would swim around the palisade, find the entrance and go in. The Indian, seeing the willow wand wave would hurry to the spot, drive a pole in the gap, and wait.

A beaver can hold its breath from five to ten minutes. Nature has given it peculiarly elastic veins which stretch and thus hold back blood from the lungs when they contain no fresh air. With this life preserver, the trapped beaver would swim once around his prison and, finding no exit, stop where he came in and wait until he drowned.

The Indian invariably found the dead beaver here, hauled it out on the ice, reset the willow wand and renewed his watch. Sooner or later another beaver came from the lodge to get food for the family or to learn why the first had failed to return. This one was trapped like his predecessor, and slowly one by one the entire family was caught. In all there might be eight to twelve beavers in the lodge—worth a tidy sum to any aborigine.

Primitive Indians believed the beaver and the white man to be two of the most intelligent of all creatures—good reason, indeed, for taking pride in being able to kill either one!

Porcupine—Quilled Denizen of the Forests

Most wild animals attack an enemy head first, biting, striking with their forefeet, butting with their heads. The porcupine acts in reverse, attacking with his other end, slapping with his quill-armed tail. Few animals are foolish enough to face this menacing bundle of needle-pointed darts, and those that do long rue the day.

Contrary to popular belief, porcupines do not throw their quills. The slender, pithy shafts, one to four inches long, are held loosely beneath porky's skin. Occasionally one or more may shake free and fly through the air from the animal's rapidly agitated tail. Because of their barbed tips, the quills easily become fixed in the skin of an assailant and work their way painfully into the flesh, sometimes into the body cavity. Frantic efforts to paw them loose only drive them deeper.

When the porcupine is relaxed, his more than 30,000 quills are hidden among much longer, yellow-tipped hairs of the animal's coat. Quill-bases are loosely seated in a layer of muscle just beneath the skin so that, at a moment's notice, porky can erect the entire armament. Only his face, feet and belly are not quilled, and his hunched position of defense keeps these parts protected.

Excepting beavers, porcupines are the largest of the rodents and may measure thirty to thirty-five inches in length and weigh from fifteen to thirty pounds. The western species are found from Arizona to Alaska, usually in timbered country, although they seem quite at home in brushy canyons. In summer they feed on flowers, catkins and leaves of trees and shrubs, also on grass and herbs. In winter, they find protected dens among rocks and ledges, rarely wandering farther from them than to a nearby feeding tree where they climb to a convenient branch and eat the inner bark, twigs and some coniferous foliage. They are especially fond of mistletoe. A porcupine may remain in one tree for several weeks, even in zero weather, in preference to returning to his den over snow-covered terrain. Salt is a great attraction to porcupines, which makes them nuisances around camps where they come, usually at night, and gnaw anything and everything with a salty flavor. An ax handle is a delicacy which may be ruined at one sitting.

Guided principally by the senses of smell and hearing, porcupines have poor eyesight and may pass quite close to a person who remains motionless. They express little fear of man or, in fact, of any animal, relying implicitly on the protection afforded by their armament of quills. In pioneer times, the fisher (relative of the skunk and wolverine) was their principal enemy. Some mountain lions and bobcats have learned to reach under and flip over a bristling porky, ripping open the unprotected underparts.

Porcupines breed in the fall, and after a gestation period of 209 days, the single youngster (rarely twins) weighing about a pound—larger than a newborn bear cub—appears in April or May. It begins to eat green food within a week, but may not be completely weaned for several months. Although adult porcupines are stolid and unsocial, the young are as playful as puppies, grunting and whining with evident enjoyment as they romp. In localities where suitable rock outcroppings are scarce, a number of adults may den in adjoining crevices, but they travel alone except in the mating season. During that period they communicate by chattering their teeth, whining, grunting, and moaning—sounds quite unlike anything porcupines might be expected to make.

Indians in the Southwest have long treated porcupines as semideities. In the North, Crow Indians fashioned combs from dried porcupine tails. Sioux women learned to soften the quills' deadly barbs by holding them in their mouths; then, after dying and flattening them, they worked the quills into effective designs on their buckskin clothes. Some tribes considered "porky" a dependable, if inadequate, source of food.

A porcupine is easily killed with a club. There was once an unwritten law which protected them as possible food for an unarmed man lost in the woods. This attitude changed somewhat with the expansion of the lumber industry. Porcupines damage and sometimes kill trees, so a campaign to reduce their numbers was started. Oddly enough, they have been difficult to poison because the tannic acid in their tree-bark diet makes them partially immune to strychnine. Care, of course, has been taken by the United States Fish and Wildlife Service to prevent the extermination of these grotesque creatures, and it seems likely that some of them will remain indefinitely in our woodlands.

The Rabbit—Everybody's Dinner

Of all wild creatures none provides as dependable a food supply for as many beasts, from snakes to grizzly bears, as the group popularly called rabbits. Strictly speaking, the term "rabbit" in the West should be applied only to the ubiquitous cottontail, the brush rabbit of the Pacific Coast, and, possibly, the pigmy rabbit of eastern Oregon and Idaho. Others, including jackrabbits and snowshoe rabbits, are actually hares, not rabbits.

Smaller than the domestic rabbit, the gray to buffy little cottontail weighs from two to two-and-a-half pounds. It is easily recognized by the powderpuff tail, like a fluffy patch of cotton pinned to its posterior, which bobs and flashes through the underbrush as the little animal dashes away.

At home throughout most of the United States from the hot, dry deserts, prairie wood-lands and farm lot fencerows to sagebrush flats and mountain meadows, the cottontails eat nearly every kind of grass, succulent herb or flowering plant including growing crops and curing hay. In winter when leafy vegetation is unavailable, they subsist on shoots, sprouts, berries, dry grass, buds and bark of shrubs and trees. Cottontails do not dig for roots and bulbs, nor do they feed on insects or other animals, being almost entirely vegetarian.

Big game of the small boy, the cottontail is hunted by man as well as by hawks, skunks, minks, weasels, foxes, coyotes, bears, mountain lions, domestic cats and dogs. Its chance of living to reach its first birthday is about one in twenty, yet it is so prolific and so adaptable to many environments that there has been little over-all reduction in its numbers since pioneer times.

Ill-equipped to defend itself, the cottontail trusts to its speed, ability to dodge in zigzag flight and promptness in reaching the protective cover of brush piles, dense growth of shrubs or cactus thickets to escape pursuit. Any crevice among the rocks, abandoned burrow or other hiding place is acceptable in time of danger. Even in preparing a nest for its young, the cottontail does not dig its own burrow but often remodels that left by some other ani-mal, or lines with leaves, grass and fur a pocket among rocks or between the spreading roots of a tree.

The pigmy rabbit of the Northwest brushlands is the only one that habitually digs and lives in underground burrows. The brush rabbit of the coast has much the same habits as the cottontail, eating the same food and dodging the same enemies.

Group of jackrabbits in underbrush.

AMERICAN MUSEUM OF NATURAL HISTORY, NEW YORK

Promiscuous in its breeding practices and with a gestation period of only one month, a female cottontail may have three, four or even five families in one season, and each family may number from one to eight babies which are quite helpless at birth. If the young are molested or the nest disturbed, the mother cottontail may move them all to another location, carrying them one at a time in her mouth to the new nest and covering them with leaves and with fur pulled from her own abdomen.

When approximately one week old, young cottontails are well clothed in gray fur and their eyes are open. Brush rabbits require ten or eleven days to reach this stage of development.

Most young cottontails find a home within a mile of their birthplace and, once settled, live out their lives in a territory of fifteen to twenty acres, the extent varying with the type of terrain and abundance of food and cover. Adult males roam more widely and do not defend a specific territory, but a female trespassing on the feeding grounds of a mother with young is in for a fight. In combat, the cottontail can lash out vigorously with its hind feet which, equipped with sharp toe nails, are highly effective weapons.

Rabbits are host to a great variety of parasites including ticks, fleas, mites, warble-fly larvae, tapeworms and roundworms, most of which weaken, and if abundant may kill, the animals. Tularemia is a rabbit ailment which is highly lethal to cottontails as well as to hares and to certain rodents. Humans may contract the disease by handling infected animals or by eating rabbit meat that has not been thoroughly cooked. No one should ever handle or even touch a cottontail, jackrabbit, or rodent that has died a natural death or that looks or acts sick.

Mr. Bigears, the Jackrabbit

Three kinds of jackrabbits—originally called jackass rabbits on account of their ears—may be found in the West: the whitetail of the northern plains, the blacktail, and the "antelope jackrabbit" of the Southwest. The last is a variety of the blacktail, with a white rump-patch of erectile hairs. All three are lean and rangy with long, powerful hind legs. They weigh from four to eight pounds and lope conspicuously across the prairies, long ears erect and delicately attuned, like radio antennae, to catch the slightest sound of danger. While running they have an odd habit of making an occasional vertical leap, or sky-hop, to look around. When resting during the middle of the day, they retire to previously prepared pockets or body-fitting "forms" usually beneath a shrub or clump of grass where, comfortably crouched with their big ears flat on their backs, they blend inconspicuously with their surroundings. If one is discovered, he explodes from his form bounding away with great leaps which can take him at a maximum speed of thirty-five to forty miles per hour—enough to outdistance any fox or coyote, which must resort to strategy to capture the big hares. Jackrabbits, themselves, resort to strategy to escape greyhounds. They do this by running in a large circle so they can act as relays. The dogs, which run by sight alone, never seem to notice the change and dash past the spent runner if it crouches in a clump of weeds.

Jackrabbit populations fluctuate in cycles, averaging about seven years in length. During one peak it was estimated that there were 20,000,000 jacks in the eastern half of Oregon.

Under such conditions, farmers and ranchers have been forced to resort to drastic measures for protection of their crops, using poison baits and organized hunts. Forming long lines, human "beaters" have rounded up and driven into enclosures as many as 20,000 jackrabbits in a single "drive" in California's San Joaquin Valley.

Farmers have noticed that a marked increase in the rabbit population usually follows a campaign to eradicate coyotes from a range. This increase might well reach explosion proportions were it not for the foxes, hawks, eagles and even snakes which remain to prey constantly on old and young alike.

The mating season for jackrabbits is long, lasting from January to September in the Southland and from early spring until midsummer in the North. Much sparring, and sometimes violent fights, occur between males, which stand on their hind legs punching like boxers and striking with their muscular hind legs. Their powerful feet, armed with heavy claws, can inflict a serious and sometimes fatal injury.

Young jackrabbits are born in well-hidden nests which they leave when only a week old, and are independent of maternal care when less than a month of age. In blacktail families there are usually only two or three young while the more prolific whitetails average four. All jackrabbits differ from cottontails by being fully furred, eyes open and lower incisor teeth developed when they are born. Only their ears are disproportionately small, but these grow fast.

Wintering is not a serious problem for jackrabbits on the southern ranges, but can be rugged in the North where deep snow covers the grasslands. To escape the bitter winds, whitetailed jacks claw tunnels for three or four feet into the drifts. They also put on a white coat of fur which blends with their surroundings—a characteristic shared with the arctic hare of the Far North and the varying hare or snowshoe rabbit of the western mountains.

The Varying Hare—Master of Camouflage

Common in Canada and Alaska, the varying hare, or snowshoe rabbit, is found in the West only in the "parks" of the higher mountains. It can travel over the ground or snow at thirty miles an hour, and it can dodge and zigzag at full speed. This dexterity is made possible by the animal's large feet, with long widespread toes covered with coarse hair which allows it to skim over a crusted surface or across soft snow without sinking into it.

Another notable characteristic of the snowshoe is its change of pelage from brown in summer to white in winter and back to brown in spring. Thus it matches its surroundings the year around. A middle-sized hare (four to five pounds) the varying hare is strictly vegetarian, feeding on succulent herbs and grasses in summer, buds, twigs and bark—as high as it can reach—in winter.

Snowshoe rabbits use their large hind feet for "thumping" or signaling, a performance practiced more or less by all wild hares and rabbits. Not social in the usual sense, varying hares do not defend home territory, and in heavily populated feeding areas often develop and use a network of community trails which are especially noticeable in winter.

Varying hares are subject to cyclic fluctuations in population like others of their kind. When they are numerous the big owls, bobcats, foxes, coyotes and weasels live well. Near human habitations, house-cats catch their share of young snowshoes. These ups and downs in numbers are usually unnoticed because the species' range in the West is limited.

Pika—Little Chief Hare of the Rockslides

The pika, or cony, is one of the few mammals which spends its life at timberline in the rockslides of the West's mightiest mountains. Even more unusual, the Little Chief does not hibernate but remains active throughout the year. In summer this tiny rock rabbit, resembling a middle-sized, buffy-gray guinea pig, spends much of its time gathering grasses, leaves and herbs which it stacks in the sunshine to dry before carrying this "hay" down through the twisting passageways among the rocks to its storehouse. At that time of year conies need fear only hawks, eagles, and the occasional bobcat, red fox or coyote that ventures high in the mountains.

During the long winter months conies scurry about their business in the heart of the talus, subsisting on the hay harvested the previous summer. Well protected now by the deep snow, their only enemy is the slim weasel, which can thread its way through the intricate labyrinth among the rocks and boulders. However, fleas, tapeworms and other parasites do cause the little rabbits some annoyance.

The most noticeable characteristic of the pika is its shrill squeak or bleat, which may be a signal of alarm. Sharp, clear, lonely, the sound is always associated with towering peaks, rock slides, melting snowbanks, spring marigolds bobbing in the thin, chill alpine air, water tinkling into icy pools which reflect the blue brilliance of the sky. In these surroundings the cony's short, shrill bark has a ventriloquistic quality which makes its producer difficult to locate as he hides within the shadowy entrance to his rocky home or sits hunched like a big, tailless, Roman-nosed mouse among the boulders.

Little is known about the pika's family life. Three or four young are probably born during any month from May to September, for the little ones have been seen in varying ages. But no man has as yet found the home of these tiny timberline hares, though it is known to be deep in the heart of the jumble of broken rocks below the highest cliffs.

Prairie Dog—Mound Builder of the Grasslands

Imagine, if you can, underground cities with five billion inhabitants scattered from central Texas and western Arizona to northwestern Montana. This was the way prairie dogs lived when the first white men went west.

Two major groups of prairie dogs, each with several species, are recognized: the black-tailed "dogs" of the high plains and the whitetailed barkers of the mesas and mountain meadows above 6,000 feet. These animals, of course, are not dogs, but are large (two to three pounds), fat, pot-bellied, reddish brown ground squirrels. Their alarm call, a high-pitched "yek, yek, yek" that sounds much like the yapping of a small dog, has given them the popular name "prairie dog." They were originally and much more accurately called "prairie marmots."

Largest of the grassland rodents (porcupines and beavers are animals of woodlands and streams), the prairie dog has a number of smaller relatives. Among the most common of these is the amazing jumper, the dainty and delicate kangaroo rat, a nocturnal creature especially active on moonlight nights. A diurnal cousin is the thirteen-striped ground squirrel, usually called the picket-pin gopher, because he stands as erect and slim as a stake. Practical jokers on the range used to point to one of them and tell a tenderfoot to "tether your horse to that picket-pin." A really green man might actually lead his

AMERICAN MUSEUM OF NATURAL HISTORY, NEW YORK

Prairie dogs.

horse toward the marmot which as he approached invariably greeted him with what sounded like a chattering laugh, then disappeared. But that was not all! Another picket-pin was sure to stand a hundred or so feet beyond. The confused tenderfoot would wonder if he had made a mistake and repeat the performance, much to the delight of the seasoned plainsmen watching from camp.

Picket-pin gophers and prairie dogs are both sun worshipers. Neither comes out of its burrow at night, and frequently they even stay underground during the daytime if the weather is cloudy or stormy.

Prairie dogs dig elaborate subterranean homes, each opening to the upper world in the crater-like center of a large mound which they build to prevent flood waters from entering the burrow. From this protected entrance the burrow plunges almost vertically for ten to fourteen feet, then it connects with a horizontal tunnel that may extend ten to forty feet with a number of side niches or "bedrooms." Sometimes several of the vertical "plunge holes" are interconnected with a network of horizontal tubes.

Timid and defenseless, the prairie dog stakes his life upon the protection afforded by his burrow, and he rarely strays more than 100 feet from its funnel-like entrance. Next to laying on fat for winter, watching for an enemy is his chief business in life. To assure an unobstructed view he snips off every plant within his feeding territory tall enough to prevent him from seeing in all directions when he sits up on his haunches, a position he assumes much of the time between short shifts of grazing. The mound surrounding his burrow entrance serves as a watchtower to which he hastens as fast as his short legs will carry him when he hears the "yek, yek, yek" of alarm from any of the many other "dogs" in the vicinity, several of which are constantly on the lookout. If an enemy is sighted, all of the alerted prairie dogs standing upright on their mounds set up a chorus of barks. When approached, they plunge with a flick of their tails into their burrows, their muffled voices rising sporadically from below.

Hawks, eagles, wolves, coyotes, bobcats, foxes and badgers all enjoy eating plump prairie dogs. The black-footed ferret, a large member of the weasel family, subsists almost entirely on them. Bull snakes and rattlesnakes feed on the young and also use the burrows to escape from the winter cold, hibernating well below the frost line. Burrowing owls inhabit these same tunnels, sometimes eating young prairie dogs and having their own eggs or young swallowed by snakes.

Prairie dogs themselves do not hibernate, and on balmy winter days they often come out of their burrows to enjoy the warm sunshine, even when there is snow on the ground. Having stored no plants during the summer when forage was abundant, they must endure many weeks without food, apparently living on the body fat they have accumulated. They also get along well without water, but have been seen drinking from puddles after a rain. Scientists who have excavated their burrows found them to be bone dry inside.

About 98 per cent of a prairie dog's food is vegetable matter, including alfalfa, grains and garden crops. They eat some insects, chiefly cutworms, grasshoppers and beetles.

Prairie dogs mate but once each year, usually during April or May. The gestation period is approximately thirty days, the young being born in a nest in one of the niches of the burrow's underground tunnel system in May or June. When the two to eight young are about seven weeks old they find their way to the burrow mouth and soon begin their training. This consists principally of learning to eat vegetation and to be on the lookout for enemies. Soon after weaning her young, the mother leaves them in the hole and moves to an abandoned burrow or excavates a new one of her own. For some time the pups stay in and around the natal "diggins" but, as they become more independent, leave home one at a time, each taking possession of an abandoned burrow, repairing its interior runways and outside mound. With luck and continued watchfulness a prairie dog may live for as long as eight years.

In primitive times a considerable array of meat eaters found the widespread prairie dog cities a dependable if somewhat skimpy source of year-around food. Plains Indians considered fat prairie dog a welcome variation from a constant diet of buffalo meat. The alert rodents provided excellent targets to challenge the marksmanship of Indian boys learning the rudiments of stalking game with bow and arrow.

When the homesteader came with his livestock, his guns and traps, he immediately declared war on wolves, coyotes, foxes and bobcats. Prairie dogs, relieved of their major enemies, increased by leaps and bounds. Not only did they eat the range grasses which settlers and ranchers needed for their sheep and cattle, but they spread rapidly into cultivated fields where they riddled irrigation ditches and destroyed the crops. By 1880 ranchers realized that the rodents were putting them out of business. Guns and traps made no impression on the millions, and the tide did not turn until the United States Biological Survey began using poisoned grain and lethal gas.

By 1900 the teeming prairie dog population of the plains had been brought under control, but these rodents are as incompatible with farming as buffalo are with cattle, or wolves with sheep. Undoubtedly the roly-poly, barking marmot of the prairies and his pursuing shadow, the black-footed ferret, are destined for eventual extinction except in National Parks and Monuments.

"Pack Rat"—Trader in the Dark

That any animal should collect curios is difficult to believe, but the wood rat has such a mania for carrying things to his home that he has earned the popular name of "pack rat." Moreover, when "packing" something home, if he sees an object more to his fancy, he will drop what he is carrying to pick it up. A prospector who carelessly leaves his false teeth on the chair at his bedside may find a cactus joint there in the morning. A spoon left on the table may be replaced by a rusty can opener or bit of broken china. This habit causes some people to call him the "trade rat."

The wood rat is a really beautiful creature about the size of the common rat. He is fawn-colored with creamy white underparts, a bushy tail, big bright eyes, long gray and black whiskers. Campers who move into a deserted cabin for the night often find him looking down at them from between the roof poles.

The wood rat is found throughout the West from sea level to above 9,000 feet in the mountains. He prefers rocky terrain, often making his home in crevices or small caves. In the desert he selects thickets of cholla (CHOH-yah) cactus, and builds his home beneath the densest growth.

The wood rat's nest is a globular mass, six to ten inches in diameter, made of fine grass, shredded bark and other soft, warm materials. It is surrounded by a rainproof, intricately tangled assortment of sticks, twigs, bark, cactus joints, animal droppings, rocks and other strange materials through which the rat has made travelways. This protective structure is usually four or five feet in diameter, and one or two feet high, but may be considerably larger. The owner is continually adding to the pile which, like a beaver dam, is never finished to its owner's satisfaction. These nests are sometimes built beneath the floors of cabins, tent-house frames, and in mine structures, where the furry tenant makes a nuisance of himself for the human residents by scurrying noisily around inside the buildings at night.

Wood rats are nocturnal, remaining within the protection of their trash-pile homes during the day. Even at home they do not escape all of their many enemies, for snakes sometimes are able to get through the tangle of sticks and cactus joints. Hawks, owls, skunks, ringtails, coyotes, bobcats and badgers like nothing better than a tender wood rat and are ready to pounce on him whenever he leaves the protection of home. Indians considered wood rat meat a delicacy as did Spanish-American pioneers throughout the Southwest.

In general, wood rats live alone in their jackstraw palaces. The males begin to search for the homes of females in January and, if acceptable, take up temporary residence. The young, usually two in a brood, arrive in March. There may be as many as three broods a year, the latest being born in September.

Eating almost any vegetation found within the feeding radius of their homes, wood rats prefer nuts, seeds and berries. They are fond of mushrooms and, under severe conditions, gnaw the bark from trees and shrubs. Since they remain active all winter, in climes where much snow accumulates, they stockpile enough food to tide them over. Indians of the Southwest mesa lands took advantage of this habit, finding it much easier to rob the rats' nests of stored pinyon nuts than to gather the small seeds from beneath the trees.

77. *Birds of the West*

Mountain men, explorers, pioneer settlers and other early-day adventurers throughout the West saw many unfamiliar species of birds. Most travelers were too occupied with more important matters to pay much attention to them, but a few expeditions were accompanied by naturalists who recorded the wild creatures and gave names to some of them. The Lewis and Clark expedition brought back to Washington records of many previously unknown species, two of which—the Lewis woodpecker and Clark nutcracker—were named in honor of the leaders of the expedition.

Clark's Nutcracker

Conspicuous in their black, white and gray plumage, the noisy Clark's nutcrackers are birds of the forested mountain heights where they feed on insects and seeds of the pine trees. They descend to lower elevations in winter, finding an abundance of pinyon nuts and other food on the mesas and foothills. Egg-laying begins in February and March with an incubation period of eighteen days. Nutcrackers are bold and aggressive, frequenting camps where they pick up any bits of food left uncovered. Trappers found them useful in cleaning fat and flesh from pelts hung up to cure, but the birds made nuisances of themselves by following the trapper as he tended his pelt line, and stealing baits from the freshly set traps.

Whisky Jack

The real "camp robber" is the robin-sized, drab gray, short-billed Rocky Mountain jay, or whisky jack, which seems to wait at likely campsites, and boldly swoops down in silent flight from an overhanging branch to snatch food from the frying pan or even out of the hand. No other bird is so bold. He will carry off matches or cigarettes, and peck to pieces candles and soap. He comes silently from the deep woods, bringing his family and neighbors to settle on a freshly killed deer while it is being cleaned, even alighting on the hunter's shoulders and head as he works. This strange bird nests in late winter and may incubate when temperatures are far below zero.

Water Ouzel

Another bird recorded by pioneer travelers which seems to thrive in cold weather is the water ouzel or dipper. Slate gray and chunky, this wrenlike water lover haunts the swift currents of mountain streams, builds its nest in the spray of a rapid or waterfall, and calmly walks about on the bottom of foam-covered pools to pick up small fish, aquatic insects and

484

their larvae. Bobbing to the surface like a cork, it swims easily to shore or to a boulder in mid-stream where it stands dipping and nodding. Ouzels spend the winter in the same surroundings, though usually at a lower elevation where the rushing stream is not locked by ice. Zero weather fails to quiet their cheerful singing or restrict their search for food beneath the surface of frigid water.

Magpie

The magpie is probably the most strikingly noticeable of all western birds, because of its large size, brilliant black-and-white plumage, long tail and vociferous cry. Lewis and Clark saw this bird first on the Missouri River and noted the fact in their journals. Magpies frequent all the wooded streams on the plains and in the foothills. They build massive nests of sticks in cottonwood trees, in willows or other brush. These bold marauders raid the nests of mourning doves, meadow larks and other ground nesting birds. They eat crickets, grasshoppers, mice and ground squirrels. Several of them, with a great deal of raucous squawking, sometimes "gang up" on a young rabbit and with repeated attacks cripple and eventually kill it. Magpies also congregate in large numbers about the bodies of dead animals to join ravens, eagles, vultures, and coyotes in a feast of carrion.

AMERICAN MUSEUM OF NATURAL HISTORY, NEW YORK

Yellow-billed magpie group.

Sage Hens

Sage hens, the largest of the grouse, weigh up to eight pounds. In pioneer days they were found in abundance throughout the sagebrush lands of the West, and became an important item of food for travelers and settlers. Mottled grayish brown plumage provides concealing coloration for these birds as they feed in small flocks among the shrubs on grasshoppers, ants and other insects and on the aromatic leaves, buds and flowers of sagebrush. Except for man, coyotes are their principal enemies, especially while nesting. Cowboys have sport with the young birds. When learning to fly, a young sage hen will explode out of a clump of brush and roar away for fifty to a hundred yards, then drop exhausted. A horseman may race after the bird and sometimes pick it up from the ground before it regains its breath, but to do so he must have a fast horse and be an excellent rider.

During the mating and nesting period in April and May, sage cocks gather in small bands on "booming grounds" where they stalk about with tails erect and spread and the air sacs of their necks and breasts greatly distended. Each performance of this strutting "dance" is concluded by expulsion of air with a variety of chuckling, cackling and rumbling sounds.

Mountain Grouse

Open meadows and dense forests bordering alpine streams provide the favored habitat for the mountain grouse, of which there are several species. Feeding on berries, insects, seeds and, in winter, on the needles of coniferous trees, these game birds spend most of their time in small family flocks on the ground. When disturbed they hide among the shrubby forest understory or explode noisily into the trees. Hunters have learned that by first shooting those on the lower branches, the ones above are usually not alarmed and most of the group can be bagged. This habit has earned mountain grouse the name of "fool hen."

AMERICAN MUSEUM OF NATURAL HISTORY, NEW YORK

Prairie hens.

Prairie Chicken

The sage grouse's spectacular courtship ritual is exceeded only by the performances of the lesser prairie chicken, or pinnated grouse, a bird of the Great Plains and grasslands. From a dozen to twenty or more of the male birds assemble in the early morning on traditional "booming grounds" where they erect the feathers of their necks and tails, inflate the orange-colored air sacs on each side of their necks and, dragging the ground with stiffened wings, go through ecstatic antics of dancing, strutting and parading while stamping their feet to the accompaniment of cooing, cackling and hooting. Sparring and fighting among participants often interrupt the strange performance.

Homesteaders used the birds for food, and market hunters later killed and shipped thousands to eastern markets. This slaughter reduced the once tremendous flocks of prairie chickens to a few remnants in Texas, Oklahoma, Kansas, eastern Colorado and New Mexico.

Road Runner

The grotesque road runner, or *paisano* (Spanish for native, or fellow countryman), has long been recognized as the clown of the Southwest. He has a rascally, devil-may-care appearance. His plumage resembles a shepherd's plaid jacket, his long, strong beak and erectable crest resemble a locomotive engineer's bill-cap, and his long, expressive tail adds the finishing touch to his comical appearance. He has an odd habit of running and hiding instead of taking flight. In the days of horse travel, these desert birds seemed to delight in racing ahead of a wagon, stagecoach or other vehicle, keeping well in front of the horses. Tiring of this sport, a *paisano* would dash to the side of the road and assume an erect posture as though seeking applause when the vehicle passed.

Although the road runner occasionally robs nests of other birds, it feeds principally upon grasshoppers, beetles, mice and other small rodents and insects. It also consumes lizards and snakes, including rattlers. However, there is no truth to the widespread story that the road runner has a special antipathy toward rattlesnakes and that, before killing one, it builds a hedge of cactus joints about its victim to prevent its escape.

The road runner builds its nest, usually in April, in the center of a thick clump of bushes or in the low forks of a mesquite tree. The eggs are laid at intervals of several days, so it is not unusual to find eggs and partly feathered young in the nest at the same time.

Burrowing Owl

Well known to horsemen and covered-wagon travelers of the nineteenth century were the small, long-legged, round-headed burrowing owls which often watched curiously from prairie dog mounds as the dusty caravans rumbled past. If an observer rode around it, the owl would turn its head, always facing the intruder. This led to odd stories and a belief that by continuing to circle the owl, it could be made to wring its own neck. As a matter of fact the bird, at intervals, made a quick about face, although the movement was faster than human eyes could detect. When the rider approached closer, the owl crouched as if to take flight but instead, dodged into the nearby burrow's mouth.

Unlike most night birds, burrowing owls see well and hunt in broad daylight as well as after dark, catching grasshoppers, rats, mice, lizards and small snakes. They use abandoned burrows of prairie dogs and other rodents as their homes, nesting in their depths. The young do not venture far from the burrow entrance until they can fly.

Bald and Golden Eagles

Eagles are among the largest and most powerful of western flesh-eating birds, exceeded only by the giant condor of California. With a length of about three feet and a wingspread of six to seven feet, an eagle can lift prey weighing up to twelve pounds, but can fly away with only about eight pounds. The adult golden eagle is predominantly dark brown with a golden wash on the head and upper neck, and is white at the base of the tail. These features distinguish it from the bald eagle which has a conspicuously white head and tail. When young the two birds look much alike, both being over-all brownish black. The young golden eagle has white patches under the wings and a white tail with a black border which becomes wider as the bird matures. Full adult plumage is not acquired until the eagles are three years old.

The tail feathers of the golden eagle were much in demand by Sioux Indians for war bonnets. The young bird's white feathers with the black tips were most valuable, and each

American bald eagle.

year as the bird matured and the tip became larger the value decreased. Other Indians used eagle feathers for religious ceremonies. Pueblo Indians captured eagles alive and kept them caged, a living source of feathers and down which they dyed bright colors and carried on dancing sticks.

Eagles build bulky nests lined with grass on ledges or in tall trees, returning to the same nesting site each spring and adding more sticks to the old nest. The females usually lay two eggs, sometimes one or three, which require four weeks to hatch. The young remain in the nest for about two months.

Whereas bald eagles are fish eaters, hence are usually found near water, goldens prey on jackrabbits, prairie dogs, ground squirrels and other small mammals, grouse, wild turkeys, waterfowl and occasionally on fawns and antelope kids. They also kill snakes, including rattlers, and feed on carrion. Trappers waged war on them because they not only robbed traps but damaged the pelts of coyotes killed by poison.

Whooping Crane and Condor

Two western birds received unusual newspaper notoriety in the middle of the twentieth century because their extinction seemed imminent. Both were rare during the pioneer period covered by this book, but neither received much notice then, probably because neither was prized for food. Most conspicuous of the two was the whooping crane, the other the gigantic California condor—not to be confused with the condor of the Andes which is a different species.

The whooping crane stands five feet tall—higher than any other North American bird. With brilliant red faces and white plumage, these birds are conspicuous when seen in coastal Texas stalking on stilt legs among palmettos beneath the streamers of mournful gray moss hanging from the skeletons of half-dead cypress trees, or when flying in V-formation against the blue sky and bluer Gulf of Mexico.

By 1962 only thirty-two of these cranes had survived, and their ultimate extinction seems imminent. Their natural reproduction is slow. The females lay but two eggs a year and bird

488

watchers count with care the number of young that live. With complete protection this modest increase might preserve the species but whooping cranes are difficult to protect. Each spring and fall they migrate, flying across the full length of the Great Plains from their nesting area in the semi-arctic muskeg of Wood Buffalo Park, Alberta, Canada, to the palmettos, brackish waters, and sun-drenched sand bars of the Aransas National Wildlife Refuge which has been set aside for them northeast of Corpus Christi, Texas. In both their northern and southern refuges they are relatively safe, but on the 2,300-mile flights in each direction, danger lurks at every place they stop to feed and rest. Hunters who know and appreciate these beautiful birds are careful not to molest them, but in some communities an unprincipled man or thoughtless boy with his first rifle may shoot the conspicuous white birds. Even more threatening to the species is the chance that some of the diseases common to wild life may wipe them out.

AMERICAN MUSEUM OF NATURAL HISTORY, NEW YORK

Adult male whooping crane. Painting by John J. Audubon.

The California condors' hope for survival is little better, though these birds seem to be holding their own. However, the fifty or sixty living condors are certainly a small number to be relied upon for the preservation of the species. In the days of the Spanish dons, when cattle were raised for their hides alone, skinned carcasses were left on the open range. Condors feasted on them and flourished, but modern ranchmen do not leave a dead animal in the field. Instead they call the nearest rendering plant to truck it away, and the condors go hungry unless they can find a dead deer, which the greedy birds will devour in a few minutes, leaving only hide and bones. Deer, however, fail to solve the condors' food problem. They usually die on brushy hillsides or in deep gulches where a condor with his nine- to ten-foot wingspread has difficulty landing, and much more difficulty getting back into the sky. The huge bird requires an unobstructed runway of twenty yards or more to become air-borne, and this is hard to find in the mountains. On the ground a condor is slow, clumsy and can easily be caught by a man.

As with the whooping crane, the condor's natural reproduction barely compensates for the natural loss. Although individuals have been known to live for forty years, the condor's average life is estimated to about fifteen. They mate for life and the female lays but one egg every two years. These are often infertile, due to inbreeding it is thought. The young, if raised, are fed by their parents for a year and do not mate until five years old.

In a desperate effort to save this apparently vanishing species the government has set aside 53,000 acres of rocky, inhospitable mountain peaks where the only remnant of these birds build their nests—if dusting out a hollow on a rocky ledge may be called a nest. This reserve, some forty miles east of Santa Barbara, California, is patrolled by a mounted ranger who keeps out all trespassers. But even with such protection the condor's ultimate fate is uncertain. However, while they survive, the sight of these magnificent birds, soaring in the sky, circling, zooming, floating hour after hour without an apparent flap of wings, is a delight to nature lovers, and a constant wonder to designers of airplanes, who have attempted for years to duplicate the secrets of a condor's flight.

Buffalo Bird

One other bird deserves mention although not exclusively a western species. The cowbird, common throughout most of the United States, was called a "buffalo bird" on the Great Plains. Flocks of them lived among the bison, perching on their backs and walking in the dust kicked up by their cloven hoofs. Some people believed that buffalo birds nested in their hosts' woolly coats and the curly hair between their horns. The idea probably originated from the fact that small birds on the treeless plains did occasionally nest in a dead bison's tangled mane. However, buffalo birds never did this because they do not build nests. Instead, they are bold, promiscuous tramps, gregarious by nature, with no sense of domesticity. When the female lays an egg, she does so in another bird's nest, and leaves the work and worry of raising the youngster to an innocent foster parent. This imposition is accepted without noticeable protest, even when the growing intruder gets more than a fair share of the food which the mother bird brings, grows faster than the legitimate babies and sometimes crowds them out of the nest.

78. Crawlers in the Western Sands

The Horned Toad That Isn't a Toad

THE LITTLE, FLAT-BODIED, grotesquely spined, short-tailed horned toads discovered by early western travelers were true oddities of the reptile world, more like miniature dinosaurs than present-day creatures. Technically not toads, although so called because of their toad-shaped bodies, some fourteen species of these small (two to six inches long) lizards were encountered throughout the plains and deserts from Canada to Mexico. Sandy flats and rocky mesas are their usual homes, but they have been found at elevations up to 9,500 feet in arid mountain ranges of the Southwest.

Horned toads are most active during the warmest parts of the day, sometimes seeking shelter from the sun in the shade of a shrub or rock. Temperatures below 70 degrees Fahrenheit are too low for them to carry on normal activities. Generally gray in color with irregular blotches of other shades ranging from yellow to black, the little creatures blend so completely with their backgrounds that they usually escape notice unless they move. Some species have the ability to modify their colors to match the shade of soil or sand surrounding them. When dusk comes, they burrow into the warm sand, burying themselves up to the top of the head.

Ants constitute the principal food of horned toads, which capture them with a quick outthrust of the thick, viscid tongue. The diet also includes beetles, grasshoppers, crickets and butterflies. Since most insects contain abundant body juices, horned toads require little other moisture, but do lap drops of rain from the edges of leaves.

AMERICAN MUSEUM OF NATURAL HISTORY, NEW YORK

Horned lizards.

As soon as the summer heat has passed, usually in September or October, hornies go underground and remain in hibernation without food or moisture until April or May. Mating takes place soon after emergence in the spring, and in late May or June females of a number of species lay from twenty to thirty-five tough-skinned eggs, burying them in loose soil or sand. The eggs hatch in about six weeks. Eggs of other species hatch within a few hours, and females of some species give birth to living young.

Because of their rough, scaly bodies and the sharp, thornlike horns or spines which are especially long and robust around the back of the head and prominent at the base of the tail and along the body fringes, horned toads make poor tidbits for flesh-eating animals. Occasionally a dead snake is found with the spikes of a swallowed horned toad protruding through its skin, ample evidence that the snake exercised poor judgment in attempting to make a meal of the thorny reptile.

In addition to their armament of spines and an ability to remain out of sight, horned toads have other methods of defense. When attacked or irritated, they often face a tormentor with open mouth, hiss audibly and puff up their bodies. However, lacking teeth, a horned toad's bite is a weak and harmless pinch. The reptile's most striking means of defense is its peculiar ability to eject from a corner of its eye a fine stream of blood to a distance of several feet. This unexpected and unorthodox action usually disconcerts a potential enemy long enough to enable the little reptile to scuttle into cover.

There is no basis in fact to the often-repeated stories about horned toads, sealed in building cornerstones, being found alive and active many years later. Although these small lizards survive in a dormant state for several months without food or water, they must have air, and their maximum life span under the most favorable conditions is only about eight years.

Hopi Indians of northern Arizona, who attributed supernatural characteristics to many native animals, credited the horned toad with healing powers and the ability to bring many children to couples who solicited its favor. The little lizards are easy to capture, are generally docile, contented in captivity and make interesting and amusing pets. However, they should be kept only a short time and returned promptly to their native habitat.

Swifts—Scaly Saurians of the Sun

All of the little lizards known as "swifts" are insect eaters, including in their diets mites, spiders and scorpions. Grasshoppers, moths and other large insects are grasped firmly in the lizard's mouth and then beaten back and forth against the ground before being swallowed.

Swifts, in turn, are items in the menus of a variety of animals including coyotes, skunks, snakes and some of the larger predatory lizards. Such birds as the road runner, shrike, magpie, sparrow hawk and others are confirmed lizard eaters. In addition to the swifts' agility and quickness in dodging into burrow entrances, crevices among the rocks and beneath shrubs or cactus pads, they have a unique and highly effective method of defense. A swift's tail is so constructed that it fractures easily at the middle of one of the vertebrae. The surprised attacker often finds himself holding a small bit of posterior appendage while his intended victim has made a successful escape. The swift soon regenerates a new tail which is usually shorter and more finely scaled than the original. A lizard occasionally will regenerate a twin growth, thereby giving the tail stump a forked tip. Tail regeneration does not restore vertebrae; instead, a cartilaginous rod replaces them.

The majority of swifts are oviparous, covering their eggs, which number from four to thirteen depending upon the species, with sand, soil or forest duff. Some of the spiny swifts give birth to living young. Juveniles have disproportionately large heads and long legs which grow less rapidly than the body until the lizards reach adult size.

As do the majority of lizards, swifts depend upon the sun to provide body heat and are most active when temperatures are favorable. At night and during the cold season they go underground, remaining until the sun again brings adequate warmth to their bodies. On cool or cloudy days and in the early morning and late afternoon, they are often seen basking on rocks or other exposed locations to absorb as much heat as possible.

Summer heat in the Southwest deserts often reaches such high temperatures that people say, "It's so hot even the lizards have to pack little sticks to rest on while they blow on their toes." This overstatement has some basis in fact. Swifts cannot survive a body temperature above 104 degrees Fahrenheit, and deserts often get hotter than that. On such days they make only short forays into the open, alternating with cooling-off periods in shallow burrows, in rock crevices or in the shade of vegetation. They do most

Common swifts or fence lizards.

of their feeding during the morning when they can dart about in the bright but not too hot sunshine. Thus the swift's life is governed by the sun, and without its warmth the little lizards become inactive and inert.

Gila Monster—Beaded Lizard of the Desert

Many misconceptions regarding the Gila (HEE-lah) monster have become established in western folklore. Among these are stories that it spits venom and uses its tongue as a sting, that its breath is deadly, that it has no anus and that regurgitated fecal matter is the source of its poison, that it springs upon its prey and that vapors from its dead body can poison anyone closely approaching it.

Any relatively rare, poisonous creature usually acquires a sinister reputation, and the Gila monster of the desert regions of the Southwest is no exception. Largest of all lizards in the United States, Gilas occasionally attain a length of two feet, although the average is about nineteen inches. The Gila monster is the only poisonous lizard native to the United States.

Heavy-bodied, short-legged and covered with beadlike tubercles in place of scales, the black-and-coral Gila monster is readily recognized although rarely encountered. Restricted to the hot, dry deserts of Arizona, Utah, Nevada and New Mexico, it is usually found in rocky terrain at elevations between 1,500 and 4,000 feet. The heart of its range is the Gila River Valley of southern Arizona, hence its name.

Unlike the rattlesnake, the Gila monster has no tubular fangs for injecting poison, nor is it able to strike. If disturbed or teased it snaps viciously with quick turns of its neck. Its wide, black mouth is equipped with sharp, slightly hooked teeth, and its jaws are massive

Gila monster near Tucson, Arizona.

AMERICAN MUSEUM OF NATURAL HISTORY, NEW YORK

and strong. Lower teeth are grooved, forming channels for the venom from poison glands in the underjaw to mix with saliva and become absorbed into wounds from the bite. Once a Gila monster gets a firm hold on an object, it retains its grip with bulldog tenacity. The jaws must be cut or pried apart in order to free the victim. Effects of the poison on humans differ in no important respect from those of venomous snakes, and first aid treatment is much the same. Fortunately the animal is rarely capable of injecting enough poison to cause death. It is immune to its own poison.

Nocturnal during the heat of summer, Gila monsters may be abroad during the day in cool, cloudy or rainy weather. In common with other reptiles, the temperature of a Gila's body depends on the atmosphere. He cannot survive prolonged heat above 104 degrees or cold below 40 degrees, and is most active and seemingly most comfortable when temperatures are in the eighties. During the winter, Gila monsters remain dormant in protected burrows or beneath rocks, living for months, without eating, on the reservoir of fat stored in the clublike tail.

Food of the beaded lizards consists principally of small mammals, lizards, eggs and young of ground-nesting birds and the eggs of other reptiles. Gila monsters are fond of water and apparently enjoy lying partly immersed. They seek locations where there is damp sand, an important requirement for incubation of the large, oval eggs. These may be as much as two and one-half inches in length and are covered with a tough, membranous shell. In July or August, the female lays from five to as many as thirteen in a hole scooped three to five inches deep in moist sand in a sunny location. They hatch in twenty-eight to thirty days.

Because of its relatively poor eyesight and apparent lack of hearing, the Gila monster depends to a large extent in its search for food on its sense of smell. The flat, protrusible, forked tongue is an important olfactory organ and does much to keep the lizard informed about other creatures in its immediate surroundings.

Actually the Gila monster is an extremely interesting desert reptile worthy of respect and protection. It fills a specific niche and plays a definite role, albeit a minor one, in desert ecology. Except for an occasional young Gila being captured and carried off by one of the large hawks or owls, it apparently has no important enemies. Its gravest danger comes from the gradual reduction of its desert home to make room for cotton fields and real estate developments.

Rattlesnakes—Terror of the Prairies

Of all the western snakes, the best known are the rattlers. Many people are violently afraid of them. However, much of this fear is unnecessary, for these poisonous reptiles' sinister reputation is only partly deserved. In general, they are peaceable and nonaggressive, avoiding conflict with mankind whenever possible. Their bite is poisonous but they normally give fair warning before striking and a person usually has time to get out of the way. Moreover, a rattlesnake bite, although dangerous, is not necessarily deadly, and in parts of Arizona where rattlers are unusually numerous, they cause less than one death a year. This is a small fatality record when compared to the number killed by Rocky Mountain fever which is transmitted through wood tick bites.

Some of the hair-raising stories about rattlesnakes date back to exaggerated reports of pioneer days or campfire yarns invented especially to hoax gullible immigrants. Many travelers were told that a rattlesnake bite was one of the greatest dangers to be encountered in the western wilds, and that the strike of a full-grown rattlesnake was always fatal, sometimes within three or four minutes, that even an ax handle or wheel spoke when bitten by a diamondback would swell up big as a man's arm.

Some Indian tribes believed that rattlesnakes were gifted with supernatural powers, and therefore they treated them with anxious reverence. Many tribes maintained a taboo against killing them, apparently fearing vengeance from the dead snake's relatives. The famous Hopi snake dance has long been a prayer for rain, with the snakes, some of them rattlers, being sent forth as emissaries to serpent deities believed to control the water supply. Some tribes, however, ate rattlesnakes when hard-pressed for food or in connection with certain religious ceremonies.

The diamondback of the Southwest is considered among the most dangerous. The desert sidewinder, so named for its looping motion of travel, is quite rare. Being drab, gray and indistinguishable from the sand in which it lives, riders often pass one without seeing it.

Rattler attacking buffalo.

The prairie rattler—the most widely distributed—is found throughout the Great Plains and the Rocky Mountain states from western Montana to central Texas. Other species are found in the Pacific Coast states.

Rattlesnakes vary greatly in size and appearance. Some species grow three to four times longer than others and have a body weight fifty times greater. The largest authenticated Sonoran desert sidewinder measured slightly less than two feet in length, whereas the longest western diamondback stretched the tape to six feet, eleven inches. Diamondbacks up to fifteen pounds in weight have been recorded.

Rattlesnakes evidently have little eye for color, in fact experiments have shown that they have very poor eyesight. Neither do they have ears, but they are extremely sensitive to vibrations, especially those transmitted to their bodies through the ground. They are therefore quick to detect the footfalls of an approaching animal. Their sense of smell is unusually keen and is conducted through the delicate, forked tongue which is almost continually flicking in and out, testing the air, when the snake is alert or excited.

On each side of a rattlesnake's face, between the eye and the nostril, is a small but deep pit which has given the group of snakes exhibiting this feature the name "pit vipers." The pit is inordinately sensitive to any deviation in heat from that of the surrounding atmosphere, and enables the snake to detect the approach of any warm-blooded animal and to strike it accurately with its fangs. This remarkable sense organ is of special value in the dark. On hot summer days rattlesnakes remain under cover when the sun is in the sky, but go abroad to hunt at night.

The rattlesnake's remarkable poison-injecting apparatus is primarily a means of capturing its prey, not a weapon of attack. Unable to travel faster than a maximum three-miles per hour and ill-equipped to catch or hold its prey or to kill it by squeezing as the constrictors do, the rattlesnake lies in wait beside a rabbit run or near the entrance to a ground squirrel burrow. When an unsuspecting victim approaches, the snake pulls back its head and lunges forward, with the two erected, tubular fangs protruding ahead of the upper jaw. These pierce the flesh of the victim, and inject a dose of poison appropriate to the size of the prey which runs a few steps, staggers and falls.

This method of killing its prey is graphically portrayed by Raymond Ditmars, Curator of Reptiles of the New York Zoological Park, in his *Reptiles of the World* (published by Macmillan). The author, on a hunting trip, was riding one night along a path, and he described the ensuing events with the following words:

> As the feet of the mules sank noiselessly in the sand, our nerves were set a-quiver by a series of piercing squeals. Then came an advancing thrashing through the undergrowth and across the beam of the guiding lantern sped a rabbit, evidently pursued by some nocturnal creature.
>
> "Queer," muttered the guide, "mighty queer. A rabbit don't holler unless something's got hold of him."
>
> We stopped to listen. While the frightened animal had crossed the sandy trail and dashed into the heavy growth on the opposite side, it had not gone far, for there was silence. Suddenly from the direction whence it had disappeared came an irregular rustling

of the leaves. Through the brush nothing could be seen. The guide looked at me squarely. His face had assumed a solemn expression.

"What's the matter?" was my query.

"That rabbit's kicking his last," he answered. "I know the noise they make in the leaves when they're done for. I've shot plenty."

"Kicking his last? Why, what on earth—" but an idea had dawned on the author.

"Diamond-back," was the guide's slow answer.

The mention of that word brings a thrill when in such surroundings. One of the deadly snakes was prowling near by. It was a stab from its long fangs that had killed the rabbit. Would the creature follow the trail of the prey and cross the path?

We waited long and patiently, starting at every sound, but the serpent failed to appear. At length we started on our hunt. The return was uneventful until we arrived at the scene of the rabbit episode, where curiosity compelled a stop. The guide had dismounted and was examining the trail with the small lantern which proved so handy in night journeys. He appeared excited and there was just reason.

Across the fine sand of the trail was seen the path of a snake. Straight as the course of a wheel it led from where the fated "cottontail" had sped across the open, thence into the thicket whence the rabbit had dashed to be overcome by the poison. From the direct course of the serpent's path we at once recognized it to be that of a rattlesnake, and, from its width of fully three inches, a Diamond-back of great size. Nor was this the only discovery. A little distance on was another path of a snake, wider and more deeply imprinted in the sand.

And so we realized that after we had gone on, the slayer of the rabbit had crossed the trail, devoured its prey and with heavy body dragged the scaly length back into the thicket and away . . . to hide.

Many times as we afterward passed that spot we searched for the monster, and without success.

As Ditmars explains, a rattler, having killed its prey, crawls leisurely to the carcass. Here the snake grasps the still warm body by the nose, and begins the slow process of ingestion. A rattler's easily dislocated lower jaw and distensible throat enables it to swallow an animal with as large a diameter as itself. An adult rattlesnake requires a full meal about once every ten days in the spring, once every three weeks in summer and once every two weeks in the fall. Where water is available, rattlers drink occasionally, especially when preparing to shed their skins, but in desert areas where water is lacking, they obtain most of their moisture from the body juices of their prey.

Rattlesnakes also use their highly effective poison mechanism as a means of defense. If stepped upon, injured or in fear of attack, the rattlesnake promptly goes on the warpath. Its fighting or striking pose is a series of body kinks, with the rattles vibrating rapidly, and the head raised toward the enemy. In striking, the forepart of the body lunges forward, the snake opening its mouth to the fullest extent with the down-curved fangs protruding. Stabbing into flesh, the weight of the snake's body holds the fangs embedded while muscular pressure on the poison sacs forces venom through the tubular fangs into the wounds. As soon as the fangs tear loose, the snake quickly resumes its fighting stance and is ready to strike again, its rattles buzzing a high-pitched warning. When angered to a frenzy, a rattlesnake is capable of striking a distance of approximately three-fourths the length of its own body. Under normal stimulus, it rarely hits a target more than half its body length distant.

The rattle itself, at the extreme tip of the tail, is composed of a series of hollow, horny segments which, when the snake vibrates its tail rapidly (20 to 90 cycles per second depending upon the prevailing temperature), clash against one another at numerous places. The chain of chitinous segments may be long or short, depending on the age of the snake and whether several of the rattles have accidentally been broken off. A segment is added each time the snake sheds its skin, which may be several times each summer season. The popular myth that there are as many segments in a snake's rattle as the reptile is years of age is entirely without basis in fact.

Temperature is an extremely important factor, not only in the speed with which the snake is able to vibrate its rattles, but in all its other activities as well. Since a rattlesnake has no body temperature, the serpent's activity varies in direct proportion to the climate. The warmer the atmosphere the faster it can move. Rattlers are at their best between 80 and 90 degrees Fahrenheit. Uncomfortable at 100 degrees they are killed by even a short exposure to a temperature of 113 degrees or more. At the other end of the scale, they are unable to flex their muscles at temperatures below 35 or 40 degrees F., and normally seek underground protection when daytime temperatures remain below 60 to 65 degrees.

The underground retreats, or hibernation "dens," often become refuges for as many as 250 snakes congregating from a widespread summer range. In cold climates, where temperatures remain far below freezing, snakes seek caverns and crevices which extend well below the frost line. In the plains where there are no rocky outcrops with underground fissures, rattlesnakes are forced to use mammal burrows, especially those of gregarious prairie dogs. They may come out to bask in the sun on warm days in late fall or early spring, but return underground until the cold season has passed. During the hibernation period, which may last four or five months, rattlesnakes do not eat; instead, they live on the fat acquired during the previous summer. Thus they come out of hibernation more or less emaciated. After leaving the winter dens, rattlesnakes gradually spread out over the surrounding territory, each to its individual summer range.

No vegetable food is consumed by rattlesnakes. They subsist largely on such small rodents as mice, rats, gophers, chipmunks, ground squirrels and the young of larger mammals. Adults of the bigger species of snakes are able to swallow full-grown rabbits and prairie dogs. Ground-nesting birds, lizards and occasionally frogs and toads vary the diet. Because of their food habits, rattlesnakes, like coyotes, foxes and other snakes, are of considerable benefit to stockmen and farmers whose grasslands and crops are threatened by large populations of small mammals.

Horses and cattle on the open range have long been subject to rattlesnake bites. Most livestock are bitten on the head while grazing or smelling a snake encountered in the grass or beneath a low shrub. Heads of bitten horses and cattle swell enormously, but the animals usually recover. Hogs and sheep have been considered immune, probably because the thick wool of sheep prevents the fangs from reaching the flesh while the thick layer of fat on a

Timber rattlesnakes, male and female.

hog has kept the venom from entering the blood stream. Farm dogs, attempting to kill rattle-snakes, have frequently been bitten, sometimes with fatal results.

Although some snakes lay eggs, rattlesnakes are among those that give birth to living young. In the South, breeding takes place annually in the spring soon after the snakes come out of hibernation, and the young are born from late August to early October. Farther north, where the season of activity and growth is much shorter, young are born only in alternate years, with breeding in the fall and births in midsummer. Development of the embryos, like other bodily functions, becomes slower during periods of low temperatures and dormancy, so that the normal gestation period of approximately 155 days is considerably lengthened by hibernation.

Mankind, of course, has long been the chief destroyer of rattlesnakes, but other animals kill them for food or because of fear. Badgers are probably the only mammals that kill rattle-snakes for amusement. Deer, pronghorn antelope, peccary and other herbivores jump or stamp on them with their sharp hooves. Eagles, hawks and road runners include them as a minor item of their diets.

Rattlesnakes have long had commercial value, which has lured adventurous men to capture or kill them. Trade in live rattlesnakes is an old business, dating back into the seventeenth century. In addition to their value for zoos and reptile "shows," they are prized for the production of antivenin. Rattlesnake oil was much in demand at one time, and snake skins have had periods of popularity. The only serious use of rattlesnakes for food has been on an emergency basis during the early period of cross-prairie travel. Rattlesnakes were easily killed, even by people weakened from starvation, and sometimes provided the only food available. The flesh has been reported to be quite palatable, although only a small amount is found, even on a large snake.

In making their seasonal mass pilgrimages between their summer ranges and their winter hibernation dens, rattlesnakes are sometimes encountered in considerable numbers, all travel-in the same direction. This has given rise to the erroneous theory that rattlesnakes migrate. Also, in some localities, rattlesnakes become more numerous in some years than in others. This may be due to cycles of abundance, so noticeable among rabbits. However, there is no evidence to support this and rattlesnakes seem to be immune to devastating disease epidemics which have been the cause of great reductions in populations of rabbits and some of the rodents.

Knowledge of rattlesnake populations has never been adequate. Unquestionably there has been, through the years since pioneer days, a gradual reduction in numbers, but the various species throughout the West have survived in the face of advancing civilization and concentrated use of the land. Secretive, shy and retiring, rattlesnakes remain in hiding much of the time and, even when in the open, are readily overlooked because of their coloring which blends effectively with the surroundings. Here, then, is a native denizen of the West that should be considered with respect, treated with caution and eliminated only from the pathways traveled by man.

Tarantulas and Scorpions

In addition to rattlesnakes and Gila monsters, two other poisonous creatures had a bad reputation in the pioneer West. One was the tarantula, the other the scorpion. Both belong to the group of eight-legged animals called arachnids. Scorpions are yellow, brown or greenish flat-bodied creatures, from one to five inches long with a pair of strong pincer-like claws at the front end. The poison gland and sting is located at the tip of the tail. Of the forty species in the United States, only two, both in southern Arizona and adjoining portions of neighboring states and Mexico, may be deadly to small children. Stings of the other United States species are painful but not dangerous.

Although most numerous in the hot deserts of the Southwest, scorpions are found throughout the entire West, where they are active during the warm months. Their food consists of soft-bodied insects and spiders which they hunt at night. They are cannibalistic to some extent. During the day they hide in moist places under logs or stones and beneath loose bark on trees and stumps. Some species burrow into loose, moist earth or sand. Campers occasionally find them hiding in bedding, and wise travelers in pioneer times shook out their shoes and coats before putting them on.

Scorpions do not lay eggs, for the young—sometimes as many as sixty—are born fully developed. They cling to the mother's back for the first few days, leaving one at a time to start independent lives. Scorpions are completely nonsocial, are practically always found singly, and can survive for as long as six months without food or water.

The new residual insecticides such as DDT, chlordane, lindane, dieldrin, etc., especially in combination, are effective in eradicating scorpions if applied to infested buildings. No chemical has yet been found that will act as an effective repellent.

Tarantulas, of which there are about thirty species in the United States, are the largest American spiders, some with a body length of two inches and a leg span of five. Due to their formidable, hairy appearance they have acquired the undeserved reputation of being dangerous and, in pioneer days, were considered by easterners as being one of the major hazards of a trip through the Southwest. Although the bite is painful and mildly poisonous, the venom is not toxic to humans. The big spiders are not aggressive, biting in defense only when provoked. Stories that they spring from hiding upon an unwary person are entirely without foundation.

American tarantulas are ground dwellers, living in web-lined holes, usually on south-facing slopes from which they emerge to hunt insects, their chief source of food. They also eat other spiders, and are not averse to attacking a small mouse, toad or lizard. Some species are nocturnal. Females remain in the same locality, often in the same nest hole, their entire lives, which may be as long as sixteen years. Males, during late summer and fall, wander widely in search of mates. These were the ones usually seen and reported by nineteenth-century travelers and pioneers.

Of the 300 to 600 spiderlings that hatch from egg cocoons guarded by female tarantulas within their burrows, only half a dozen may survive the ten years required to reach maturity. Rodents, snakes, lizards and many species of birds include tarantulas in their diets. The principal enemy of the big arachnids is the "tarantula hawk," a large wasp that paralyzes the tarantula with its sting and lays its egg on the living but helpless spider whose body provides ample food for the wasp's larva after the egg hatches.

Scorpion and tarantula.

AMERICAN MUSEUM OF NATURAL HISTORY, NEW YORK

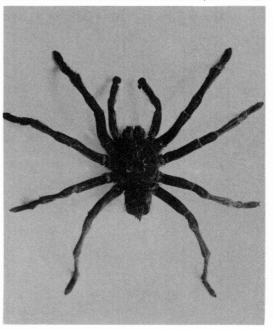

PART NINE

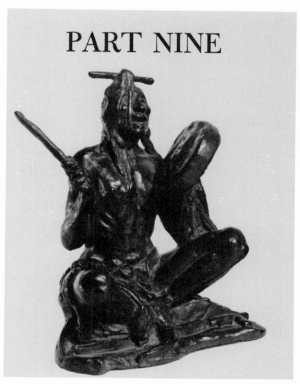

"The Medicine Man" by Charles M. Russell

A Sampler of Western Folklore and Songs

by B. A. Botkin

"I took ye for an injun." Pen and ink by Frederic Remington.

79. *Preface*

Folklore, according to Martha Warren Beckwith, is "human fantasy as it appears in popular sources." Without folklore there would be no image of the West as it exists today in the minds of Americans and the people of other countries. And without the impact of the West on the popular imagination American folklore would be lacking in some of its most characteristically American heroes, themes and motifs.

People from everywhere settled the West, bringing with them the songs, stories, beliefs, customs and sayings of many regions and many lands. In the broad sense, western folklore includes all folklore found in the West, regardless of place of origin. This sampler presents a selection of Anglo-American songs and stories growing out of the western movement.

Those who went West in search of God's country usually found that "God's country isn't in the country; it is in the mind." But the dream of finding it inspired both mythmakers and believers, good storytellers and good listeners.

80. *Indians and White Men*

In the west the white man encountered the Indian's mythology—the only true mythology produced on this continent—which, in spite of occasional borrowings and intrusions of Biblical legends and fairy tales, remained the Indian's own, separate and distinct from European-American tradition. Yet, as a character in the white man's stories, the Indian became a part of western folklore.

Meanwhile, in his own inventions the white man imitated Indian legends, and Catholic legend and ceremonial influenced the Indian in the Spanish Southwest. After his conquest and conversion by the Spanish, the Pueblo Indian adopted the saints as part of his mythology and ritualism alongside his own animal, plant and supernatural spirits. The dualism is illustrated by the rain ceremony. This involves the carrying of the image of the patron saint on his fiesta day to the fields to see how dry they are and how much they need rain. On the return from the fields there is a ceremonial dance, with a rain chant.

The following story illustrates the difficulty of converting Indians to Christianity. In the San Juan pueblo, almost three hundred years after Oñate had established his colony there, the people were still only nominally Christianized, and they had their faith badly shaken when they invoked the power of the Christ Child to break a terrible drouth.

. . . The growing corn of the Indians began to turn yellow and dry, and the water in the river became too low to be led by the irrigation ditches to the new fields which the Indians had made on the higher bank across the river when they gave up their old fields to the Spaniards. Formerly, had such a situation as this arisen, these Indians would have had a great rain-making ceremonial dance and called on their old gods to send them rain. Now, with implicit faith in the magic of the powerful gods of their new friends, the chiefs of the clans went to the padre at the mission church and asked him to lend them the blessed image of the child Jesus. The padre inquired of them why they wished the image, and the chief of the corn clan answered: "We wish to carry the child Jesus around the cornfields, so that he can see in what bad condition they now are, and maybe he will have pity on us and send the rain."

The padre agreed that the Christ child might go, and the Indians carried it with ceremony over all their fields, chanting and pleading with the little image for rain. Then they returned it to the padre at the mission and went home to await results.

Now as sometimes happens in New Mexico in summer, a great cloudburst rose over the Jemez Mountains and swept up the Rio Grande valley. It deluged the Indian fields and beat the corn to the ground, and worse still, hail followed the rain and completed utterly the destruction of the crops.

When the Indians saw what had happened they were very much cast down, for corn was their main staple of diet. That evening the chiefs held a council and early the next morning they again presented themselves before the padre and this time asked that he lend them the image of Mother Mary. The padre was surprised and inquired the reason for the request. The chiefs hesitated, but on his refusing to lend them the image without explanation, one chief said: "Padre, we wish to carry the Mother Mary around the fields this morning, so that she can see for herself what a mess her naughty little boy has made of our cornfields."

The Indians of San Juan say to this day that if you will look at the image of Saint Mary in the old mission church there, you can still see on her cheeks traces of the tears she shed from pity when she saw their ruined cornfields.

Ever since that time the San Juan Indians have had respect for the Christian gods, but they appeal to their own tribal nature gods when they want rain for their growing corn. Then they dress in the ceremonial costumes as in ancient times and paint themselves with ceremonial colors, and carrying sprigs of green spruce they form in long lines and shake gourd rattles filled with seeds, to simulate the rain falling to the green corn leaves. So they dance from sunrise to sunset to bring down the rain, while nearby a large drum made of a hollowed cottonwood log, covered with rawhide, is beaten to imitate the thunder, and a chorus sings the ancient incantations.

Frank G. Applegate, Indian Stories from the Pueblos *(Philadelphia: J. B. Lippincott Co., 1929), pp. 45-48.*

From Spanish California comes the eighteenth-century tale of the Governor's glass eye, a story of the conflict between Christianity and magic and the resultant weakening of the Indian's acquired faith.

. . . It happened that Governor Hermenegildo [Salvatierra of the Presidio of Monterey] had one of his eyes shot out by an Indian arrow and went eyeless. But after Pegleg Scudder, of the schooner "General Court," had visited the port of Monterey in 1797, the Governor was miraculously furnished with another eye, which was an amazement to the Indians as well as to many of the citizens. The Indians would come over from Mission San Carlos by twos and threes and wait about the Governor's Palace till they had a glimpse of him, and they observed that the eye did not move as he looked at them, and they were afraid. It was said that the new eye was an evil eye, so that they grew shy of being looked at by it. So it came about, rather than that should happen, that they would, if they had business with the Governor, do anything he asked them so they might the sooner get quit of him and the baleful look of his unmoving eye. They were the more alarmed by it because the Padre at the Mission had told them that it was a miraculous eye which had come to the Governor as an answer to prayer, so that it grew upon them that there was evil in the glance of it. Also that there was evil in its effect on the Governor, who, by reason of their fear of him, grew more and more overbearing and harsh and was greatly hated on that account.

Now there was an Indian at San Carlos named Tonito who had special reason to dread the eye, because he supposed that it caught him in more than one piece of mischief which he thought otherwise could not have been detected. So it came into Tonito's head that he could not do better for himself and the rest of the Indians than to put an end to the miraculous eye by destroying it.

Having determined upon this course, he crept away from the Mission in the night and came to the Governor's house, and in the dead of the dark he came into the Governor's bedroom. He came with a light for the purpose of seeing the eye to make sure of it, and behold there was the eye wide open and staring at him. So fearful this sight was, Tonito screamed aloud, so that the Governor rose up in his bed and the guard came running. The guard made at Tonito, who struggled mightily, and in the scrimmage someone hit the Governor's eye with a fist, at which he cried out, and the next day the eye was seen to have disappeared.

Well, then, said the Indians, between fear and satisfaction, let him pray it back again. The Padre preached to them about the iniquity of making protest against the miraculous and prescribed a penance for them, but it was observed that the Governor was greatly humiliated by the loss of his eye, and grew humble and returned to his old manner, so that it began to be believed that the eye really had been evil. Therefore they left off the penance, and he that had a member missing learned to be content without it. It was said by my grandfather that from that time forth there were no more miracles performed at the Presidio of Monterey.

Mary Austin, One-Smoke Stories *(Boston: Houghton Mifflin Co., 1934), pp. 30-33.*

In the white man's legends, tales and anecdotes, the Indian appears in the roles of the Noble Savage or the Red Devil, the Simple or Cunning Child of Nature. Pseudo-Indian legends of the origin of place names are a relic of the days when Indians and white men gave aboriginal names to American places, and Americans sought in the Indian's legendary past the basis for an American epic. A favorite theme of the place name legend is the tragic love of a beautiful Indian maiden for a brave of another tribe.

A typical example of this Noble Red Man tradition is the Nebraska legend of Weeping Water, a town in Cass County situated on the creek for which it is named. The French called the creek "L'Eau qui Pleure," from a confusion of its Omaha with its Oto name— Nigahoe, "rustling water," with Nihoage, "weeping water." According to local tradition, an Oto warrior fell in love with the daughter of the Omaha chief. Rejected by her father, the warrior abducted her while she was bathing with her companions in a lake near the village. "Pursuit," writes Lilian L. Fitzpatrick in *Nebraska Place-Names,* "immediately followed with disastrous results, for all of the pursuers [in some versions the pursued as well] were killed in the fight. When the women came upon the dead warriors, they wept so long that their tears formed the Weeping Water."

President Lincoln is credited with making an amusing addition to the lore of Weeping Water when some visitors who had just returned from a western tour referred to a Nebraska stream with an Indian name meaning "weeping water." Said Mr. Lincoln: "As 'laughing water,' according to Longfellow, is 'Minnehaha,' this evidently should be 'Minneboohoo.' "

A facetious place name story involving a pun is illustrated by the following apocryphal account of the naming of Naponee in Franklin County, Nebraska (actually named for a town in Canada).

An old Indian, who was hunting for his runaway pony, was stopped by a party of travellers who wished to know the name of the settlement they saw in the distance. The Indian, who did not understand many words of English, thought they were asking him where his pony was, so he answered "No pony." The settlers, thinking the old Indian was naming the village, called it Naponee from that time on.

Nebraska Folklore Pamphlets, No. 14, Place Name Stories *(Lincoln: Nebraska Writer's Project, 1938), p. 8.*

In another type of place name legend, the name is explained by an atrocity story similar to those found in popular collections of Indian horrors (*Indian Horrors* was the lurid title of a book by the Reverend Henry Davenport Northrop published in 1891) and in sensational narratives of white captivity such as the Reverend R. B. Stratton's *Captivity of the Oatman Girls,* published in 1857.

Typical of the genre is the Nebraska tale of how Rawhide Creek got its name.

Inevitably fantastic tales sprouted along the great migration trail, with the inevitable atrocity stories, sometimes told to entertain and shock, sometimes by those who feared that settlement would kill what was left of the fur trade, or those who wanted the Indian destroyed to free the land, as had happened all the way from Plymouth Rock to the West. Out of these tales came such names as Rawhide Creek, which was on maps, at one time or another, all the way from the Alleghenies to the Pacific mountains.

There were several versions of the Nebraska rawhide story spread over perhaps fifteen years of time, all with the inconsistencies and anachronisms that betrayed alien origins. The general locale of several of these was the north bend of the Platte River, one near

"The Pony War-Dance." Wash drawing by Frederic Remington.

the present Rawhide Creek, not far from Pahuk Point. Simplified, these stories tell of a party of perhaps a hundred Iowans who struck straight westward "through the Great Desert of Nebraska." The party included a reckless young man around twenty-two who claimed that one of his relatives—the stories differ on the degree of relationship—was killed by some eastern Indians. Now that he was going out into the wilderness, he swore he would avenge his relative by killing the first Indian he saw. One day while the party was crossing a little stream they passed an Indian woman and a girl about twelve sitting on a log weaving rush baskets. The man drew his pistol and, before anyone could stop him, fired at the woman. She fell, and the girl fled silently into the brush. There was anger and concern over such recklessness. Scouts were sent along the strung-out party to warn them of a threatened attack, but hours passed and nothing happened. That night the camp of the overlanders was suddenly surrounded by Pawnee warriors threatening a general massacre if the murderer was not delivered to them at once. Far outnumbered and surrounded, with the dark empty wilderness all around, the party decided to let the Indian girl and three or four braves come to the campfires to pick out the man. The girl pointed to the young braggart, and although he cried to be saved, he was dragged away to the bank of the stream, stripped of clothing and bound to a tree. Then, while the rest of the party had to see this done, listen to his screams, the Indians skinned him alive, taking off pieces here and there, but carefully at first, so he wouldn't die too fast; at last growing impatient, they cut loose bigger strips and ripped them off, until the man was only bare quivering flesh. Then they scalped him.

According to one story, the young man's relatives received no letters, heard no news of him, for years. Finally they inquired of a member of the party and were told of the skinning with much detail that couldn't possibly have been seen in the night. There was no mention of a burial spot because it seems the party hadn't even rescued the body. One version of this rawhide story has a warrior killed instead of a woman. Another says a man named Rhines, a silversmith from Wisconsin, headed west in the gold rush, and shot a young Pawnee woman out of a group of morning visitors. He was tied to a wagon wheel and skinned alive.

Altogether these stories, in any form, were proper ones to tell timid stay-at-homes.

Mari Sandoz, Love Song to the Plains (New York: Harper & Row, Copyright © 1961 by Mari Sandoz), pp. 103-105. Reprinted by permission of the publishers.

In a third type of story the Indian appears more as an individual and a human being than as a romantic stereotype or monster. This is the realistic anecdote of Indian-white relations and attitudes in which the white man is seen laughing outwardly at the Indian and the latter laughing inwardly at the white man. As a reflection of what each race thinks of the other, colored by misunderstanding and prejudice, these anecdotes belong to the folklore of both groups. As an expression of the callous humor of the West, where hoaxes and tricks are a natural outlet for distrust and dislike of the out-group on the part of the in-group, Indian anecdotes also belong to social history.

To enhance the humor and realism of the anecdote as a true or true-to-life story illustrating a trait of an individual or group, the Indian anecdote employs "Indian talk" much as "greenhorn" stories use dialect. The tradition of "pidgin Indian" and picturesque or comic Indian English goes back to eighteenth-century New England. One of the earliest examples is contained in a warrant directed to his Indian constable and deputy by an Indian justice of the peace named Hihoudi or High Howder:

Me *High Howder,* yu constable, yu deputy, best way yu look um Jeremiah Wicket, strong yu take um, fast yu hold um, quick yu bring um before me.

George Lyman Kittredge, The Old Farmer and His Almanack (Boston: William Ware & Co., 1904), p. 333.

Monosyllabic and reticent Indian talk in its most simplified form became a convention of western humorous writing and the dime novel. Albert D. Richardson reports this three-line colloquy with a Delaware Indian in Kansas in 1858, in which the author lapses into Indian talk ("umph" being his equivalent for the usual "Ugh"):

He.—Umph. How?
I.—How? Wet weather.
He.—Umph. Much wet.

Albert D. Richardson, Beyond the Mississippi (Hartford: American Publishing Co., 1867), p. 95.

One of the ancestors of western Indian talk is Chinook, the *lingua franca* of the Indians and early fur traders and settlers of Oregon and Washington. The following is an attempt to render in broken English the "most jerky and broken Chinook" of a ragged, root-digging Klickitat's harangue delivered in a "naso-guttural choke":

What you white man want get 'em here? Why him no stay Boston country? Me stay my country; no ask you come here. Too much soldier man go all around everywhere. Too much make pop-gun. Him say kill bird, kill bear—sometime him kill Indian. Soldier man too much shut eye, open eye at squaw. Squaw no like; s'pose squaw like, Indian man no like nohow. Me no understand white man. Plenty good thing him country; plenty blanket; plenty gun; plenty powder; plenty horse. Indian country plenty nothing. No good Weenas give you horse. No good Loolowcan go Dalles. Bad Indian there. Smallpox there. Very much all bad. Me no like white man nohow. S'pose go way, me like. Me think all same pretty fine good. You big chief, got plenty thing. Indian poor, no got nothing. Howdydo? Howdydo? Want swap coat? Want swap horse? S'pose give Indian plenty thing. Much good. Much very big good great chief white man!

> *Theodore Winthrop*, The Canoe and the Saddle (*Boston: Ticknor & Fields, 1863*), *pp. 199-200.*

In his autobiography, George W. Conover cites a written example of the Indian's "heroic effort at the use of English as he had learned it." In the following letter addressed to Mr. Conover back in 1891, when he had a considerable herd of cattle, a Kiowa chief named "Stomblaing" Bear shows "a great deal of concentration of mind on the main subject":

Anadarko Indian Territory,
     Indian Agency,
          July 2nd, 1891.
Dear Sir:

All your friends thay ask you for some cow to kill. they chief ask you for a cow they are much of you because they said you are good men they said, all they Kiowa round they this agency they ask you for one cow, they chief asked you for it Kiowa chief they asked for a cow. all friends Kiowa chief they said you are a honest man in world they said and they know you very much they think about a great deal about and they asked you to day all you friend Kiowa chief for a cow. we are very hungry to day.

they are a good men they said if you please, from
                         you friend
                         Stomblaing bear,
he they man asked you for cow and also this friends they asked you for cow.
                                             [Signatures of eleven Kiowa chiefs]
We are all sing here for all they Kiowa Chief, we asked you for cow. Give us one of you cow.

"Well they got the cow," concludes Conover.

> *George W. Conover*, Sixty Years in Southwest Oklahoma (*Anadarko, Okla.,*
> *Published by the author, 1927*), *pp. 124-125*

In the following anecdotes the Indian is seen parrying the white man's questions or giving him a piece of his mind.

In 1893, when the United States government reclaimed and put on sale half the Sioux reservation in South Dakota, a grizzled old Sioux was asked for his opinion and aired his grievances in broken English as follows:

All same old story.... White men come, build chu-chu [railroad] through reservation. White men yawpy-yawpy [talk]. Say: "Good Indian, good Indian; we want land. We give muz-es-kow [money]; liliota muz-es-kow [plenty money]." Indian say, "Yes." What Indian get? Wah-nee-che [nothing]. Some day white man want move Indian. White men yawpy-yawpy: "Good Indian, good Indian; give good Indian liliota muz-es-kow." What Indian get? Wah-nee-che. Some day white man want half big reservation. He come Indian. Yawpy-yawpy: "Good Indian; we give Indian liliota muz-es-kow." Indian heap fool. He say, "Yes." What Indian get? Wah-nee-che. All same old story. "Good Indian, good Indian." Get nothing.

Julian Ralph, Our Great West *(New York: Harper & Brothers, 1893), p. 165.*

White man smart, Indian smarter when he plays dumb. Such is the implication of this story about an Indian who is being questioned by a prospector concerning his lost horse.

"You know much," he said to Indian George. "You hear anything about my horse?"
"What horse?"
"Pete."
"Oh, Pete horse. Black horse, white foot?"
"That's right."
"Got crooked tail?"
"That's him."
"Got blaze on face?"
"That's the horse."
Indian George appeared plunged in thought.
"Got wild eye?" he asked finally.
"Yes, a bad eye. Where is he?"
George shook his head.
"Dunno. I no see 'um."

George Haven Putnam, Death Valley and Its Country *(New York: Duell, Sloan and Pearce, 1946), p. 73.*

In this tale a squaw gets back at an inquisitive white woman who talks Indian-talk to her.

When the Montana Union connected Butte with the Northern Pacific at Garrison in 1883, the junction platform quickly became a rendezvous for neighboring Indians, begging or selling baskets and bead-work to travelers changing trains. On one occasion a squaw, with a solemn-faced papoose strapped to her back, attracted the attention of a woman traveling to Butte for the first time. The woman was interested in the baby, which appeared to be of lighter complexion than most papooses. She addressed the mother on the subject, speaking patronizingly in what she supposed to be the vernacular of the Indians. "Him full-blooded Injun?" she asked, pointing to the child. "No," the squaw answered after a moment, her eyes expressionless, "him part Injun, part Injuneer."

C. B. Glasscock, The War of the Copper Kings *(Indianapolis: The Bobbs-Merrill Co., Copyright 1935 by C. B. Glasscock; 1962, by Mrs. Marion T. Glasscock), pp. 77-78. Reprinted by permission of the publishers.*

In his naive or quizzical comments on white ways the Indian displays a cryptic irony. Here are some examples:

The Indians despise the huge campfires of the white men. They say, "Make small fire, can get close to it; big fire keep you away, no good."

Wallis Nash, Oregon: There and Back in 1877 *(London: Macmillan & Co., 1878), p. 32.*

Not long ago a young churchman, who was overzealous and somewhat flip in his manner, went to Washakie [Chief of the Shoshoni] and asked him if he could not work among his people and teach them about God. Washakie eyed the young man from head to foot, and then asked him, "Young man, are you sure you know God yourself?"

Joseph A. Breckons, "Washakie, Chief of the Shoshones," in Collections of the Wyoming Historical Society, *I, 1879, p. 90.*

Because the Indian talks little and is sometimes slow to answer is no sign of dullness. It is only that he considers it improper to show haste. Once a missionary preached a long sermon to some full-bloods. He told of the fall of Adam, the coming of Christ to atone for man's sins, His miracles, etc.

At last he finished and an Indian rose to thank him. This is what he said: "What you have told us is good. It is a bad idea to eat apples. They should be made into cider. Then the cider should be allowed to stand a while. It is better so. We thank you for coming so far to tell us these things that you have heard from your mother."

"Indian Legends and Traditions," in Sturm's Statehood Magazine *(Tulsa), II (1906), p. 86.*

Once when Quanah Parker, the white-haired Comanche chief, had, on a very hot day, just taken a drink of ice water, a bystander, a white man, remarked, "White man pretty smart, ain't he?"

"Yes," Quanah replied, "white man smarter than God."

"Oh, no, not smarter than God. Why do you think so?" returned the white man.

"Why," said Quanah, "God, he make ice in the winter time, white man he make um summer time all same." The white man made no reply.

"Indian Legends and Traditions," in Sturm's Statehood Magazine *(Tulsa), II (1906), p. 86.*

*A mountain hunter. Pen and ink
by Frederic Remington.*

Century MAGAZINE, 1888

81· *Mountain Men*

Wᴿɪᴛɪɴɢ ᴏꜰ ᴛʜᴇ American tall tale in *Farthest Frontier,* Sidney Warren states: "A particular brand was developed on the frontier, originated by the fur trappers, influenced by the Indian legends, brought by the various national groups." Whether or not the trappers actually originated the tall tale of frontier adventure, they were among its earliest practitioners in the West and gave it a distinctive coloring of grim humor and weird fantasy that may have had some relation to the Indians'. Aboriginal mythology with its grotesque transformations and confusion of animals and men, in monsters, giants and animal tricksters, rubbed off on the "white Indians," some of the more mystical of whom may well have found the Indians' primitive beliefs and superstitions peculiarly congenial to their own wild flights of imagination.

One of these was William Sherley ("Old Bill") Williams, erstwhile Baptist preacher and missionary to the Osage. Somewhere in his solitary wanderings "Old Bill" had picked up strange, distorted notions of the transmigration of souls and the kind of animal he was to become on his death. "Uncle Dick" Wootton recalled the following story about "Old Bill":

> One night when there were a dozen or more of us together in camp—that was when he was growing quite old—he told us, with as great an air of solemnity as though he had been preaching his own funeral, that when he ceased to be "Bill" Williams, he was to become a buck elk, and would make his home in the very neighborhood where we were then encamped. He had pictured out, in his own mind, what kind of a looking elk he would be, and described to us certain peculiarities which he should have, which would enable us to distinguish him from other elks, and cautioned us not to shoot an elk of that description, should we ever run across one after his death.

Howard Louis Conard, "Uncle Dick" Wootton (Chicago: W. E. Dibble & Co., 1890), pp. 201-202.

"Old Bill's" elk story, if not mere hallucination, smacks of a hoax and suggests the hoaxing tall tales that were the real folk tales of the trapper. Told for the entertainment of fellow trappers around the campfire or to trick greenhorns, these whoppers reduced to absurdity

512

trappers' hairbreadth escapes from Indians, their other exciting adventures and their observations of the freaks and wonders of nature.

The master yarn-spinner among mountain men was James ("Old Gabe") Bridger. To discourage the questions of curious pilgrims whom he guided across the plains or who stopped at his trading post at Fort Bridger, Wyoming, "Old Gabe" spun his outlandish yarns with the same eye for detail that made him such an expert pathfinder. In fact, his reputation as a windjammer all but eclipsed his fame as scout and guide. The following yarn might almost be a burlesque of Colter's escape from the Blackfeet:

"You must have had some curious adventures with, and hairbreadth escapes from, the Indians during your long life among them," observed one of a party of a dozen or more, who had been relentlessly plying him with questions.

"Yes, I've had a few," he responded reflectively, "an' I never to my dyin' day shall forget one in perticlar."

The crowd manifested an eager desire to hear the story. I will not undertake to give his words, but no story was ever more graphically told, and no throng of listeners ever followed a story's detail with more intense interest. He was on horseback and alone. He had been suddenly surprised by a party of six Indians, and putting spurs to his horse sought to escape. The Indians, mounted on fleet ponies, quickly followed in pursuit. His only weapon was a six-shooter. The moment the leading Indian came within shooting distance, he turned in his saddle and gave him a shot. His shot always meant a dead Indian. In this way he picked off five of the Indians, but the last one kept up the pursuit relentlessly and refused to be shaken off.

"We wus nearin' the edge of a deep an' wide gorge," said Bridger. "No horse could leap over that awful chasm, an' a fall to the bottom meant sartin death. I turned my horse suddint an' the Injun wus upon me. We both fired to once, an' both horses wus killed. We now engaged in a han'-to-han' conflict with butcher knives. He wus a powerful Injun—tallest I ever see. It wus a long an' fierce struggle. One moment I hed the best of it, an' the next the odds wus agin me. Finally—"

Here Bridger paused as if to get breath.

"How did it end?" at length asked one of his breathless listeners, anxiously.

"The Injun killed me," he replied with slow deliberation. The climax freed him from further questioning by that party.

Capt. J. Lee Humfreyville, Twenty Years Among Our Hostile Indians
(New York: Hunter & Co., 2nd edition, 1903), p. 465.

Perhaps the best known of trapper's tall tales is Moses ("Black") Harris' story of the "putrefied forest." Trapper, guide, raconteur and "liar" like Bridger, Harris was dining in a tavern at Liberty, Missouri, when he told the yarn to a lady who inquired about his travels:

"Well, Mister Harris, trappers are great travlers, and you goes over a sight of ground in your perishinations, I'll be bound to say."

"A sight, marm. . . . I've seen a putrefied forest."

"La, Mister Harris, a what?"

"A putrefied forest, marm, as sure as my rifle's got hindsights, and *she* shoots center. I was out on the Black Hills, Bill Sublette knows the time—the year it rained fire—and everybody knows when that was. If thar wasn't cold doins about that time, this child wouldn't say so. The snow was about fifty foot deep, and the bufler lay dead on the ground like bees after a beein'; not whar we was tho', for thar was no bufler, and no meat, and me and my band had been livin' on our moccasins (leastwise the parflesh) for six weeks; and poor doins that feedin' is, marm, as you'll never know. One day we crossed a 'cañon' and over a 'divide,' and got into a peraira, whar was green grass, and green trees, and green leaves on the trees, and birds singing in the green leaves, and this in Febrary, wagh! Our animals was like to die when they see the green grass, and we all sung out, 'hurraw for summer doins.'

" 'Hyar goes for meat,' says I, and I jest ups old Ginger at one of them singing birds, and down come the crittur elegant; its darned head spinning away from the body, but never stops singing, and when I takes up the meat, I finds it stone, wagh! 'Hyar's damp powder and no fire to dry it,' I says, quite skeared.

" 'Fire be dogged!' says old Rube. 'Hyar's a hos as'll make fire come'; and with that he takes his ax and lets drive at a cotton wood. Schr-u-k—goes the ax agin the tree, and out comes a bit of the blade as big as my hand. We looks at the animals, and thar they stood shaking over the grass, which I'm dog-gone if it wasn't stone, too. Young Sublette comes up, and he'd been clerking down to the fort on Platte, so he know'd something. He looks and looks, and scrapes the trees with his butcher knife, and snaps the grass like pipe stems, and breaks the leaves a-snappin' like Californy shells.

" 'What's all this, boy?' I asks.

" 'Putrefactions,' says he, looking smart, 'putrefactions. . . .' "

George F. Ruxton, Life in the Far West *(Edinburgh: W. Blackwood & Sons, 1849), pp. 14-18.*

The petrifications in Yellowstone Park figure in a similar yarn by Jim Bridger, who probably visited the park region as early as 1830. For comparison with the Black Harris tale here is Bridger's account of the geological marvels of Specimen Ridge:

According to his account there exists in the Park country a mountain which was once cursed by a great medicine man of the Crow nation. Everything upon the mountain at the time of this dire event became instantly petrified and has remained so ever since. All forms of life are standing about in stone where they were suddenly caught by the petrifying influences, even as the inhabitants of ancient Pompeii were surprised by the ashes of Vesuvius. Sage brush, grass, prairie fowl, antelope, elk, and bears may there be seen as perfect as in actual life. Even flowers are blooming in colors of crystal, and birds soar with wings spread in motionless flight, while the air floats with music and perfumes siliceous, and the sun and the moon shine with petrified light!

Hiram Martin Chittenden, The Yellowstone National Park *(Cincinnati: The Robert Clarke Co., 1905), pp. 50-51.*

Another and even wilder petrification story, said by Chittenden to be the "work of some later interpolator," has been attributed to Bridger.

> . . . Bridger, one evening after a long day's ride, was approaching a familiar camping place in this region of petrifications but from a direction not before taken. Quite unexpectedly he came upon a narrow, deep precipitous chasm which completely blocked his way. Exhausted as both he and his horse were with their long march, he was completely disheartened at this obstacle, to pass which might cause him several hours of strenuous exertion and carry him far into the night.
>
> Riding up to the brink to reconnoiter he found that he could not stop his horse, which kept moving right along as if by its own momentum out over the edge of the precipice, straight on at a steady gait and on a level line, as if supported by an invisible bridge. Almost before he realized it he was safe on the other side, and in his desired camp. His utter amazement at this miracle soon abated when he remembered the strange character of the country he was in, and he concluded that this chasm was simply a place where the attraction of gravitation was petrified.

Hiram Martin Chittenden, Yellowstone National Park. *Revised by Eleanor Chittenden Cress and Isabelle F. Story. (Stanford: Stanford University Press, 1940), p. 45n.*

Ironically, the two white men who contributed so much to our early knowledge of the Yellowstone region—John Colter and Jim Bridger—were ridiculed as prevaricators. These two trappers were among the earliest to explore the area. Colter, who had been a hunter for Lewis and Clark, visited the area in 1807 or 1808. He missed the geysers and colorful hot pots but found hot springs above Cody, Wyoming. These appear on the official Lewis and Clark map of the expedition as "Hot Spring" and "Brimstone." But as Washington Irving notes in *The Adventures of Captain Bonneville,* Yellowstone's "gloomy terrors, its hidden fires, smoking pits, noxious steams, and the all-pervading 'smell of brimstone' . . . received, and has ever since retained among trappers, the name of 'Colter's Hell.'" And, as "Colter's Hell," the wonders of Yellowstone were for a long time considered a joke.

In the same way, when Jim Bridger tried to tell the truth about the geysers and hot springs of the Firehole Valley, his descriptions were ridiculed as "Old Jim Bridger's lies." In an article in *Contributions to the Historical Society of Montana* in 1900, William S. Brackett wrote: "Disgusted at his unmerited treatment, he retaliated, as so many other old mountain men have done, by stuffing his 'tenderfoot' listeners with the most preposterous stories his imagination could conjure up."

Ultimately "Jim Bridger's Lies" became the title of a column in the weekly paper, *Ned Buntline's Own,* published by Ned Buntline (E. Z. C. Judson), the dime novelist and promoter of Buffalo Bill, who "ghosted" stories of "Old Gabe's" hairbreadth escapes.

As an example of the thin line that separates fact from fantasy, there is Bridger's tale of the "fireless cooker," on the west shore of Yellowstone Lake, where a fisherman could catch a trout and boil it on the hook. Chittenden explains the facts as follows:

> Somewhere along the shore an immense boiling spring discharges its overflow directly into the lake. The specific gravity of the water is less than that of the lake, owing

probably to the expansive action of heat, and it floats in a stratum three or four feet thick upon the cold water underneath. When Bridger was in need of fish it was to this place that he went. Through the hot upper stratum he let fall his bait to the subjacent habitable zone, and having hooked his victim, cooked him *on the way out!*

Hiram Martin Chittenden, The Yellowstone National Park *(Cincinnati: The Robert Clarke Co., 1905), p. 50.*

In like manner Bridger's famous yarn of the "Glass Mountain," still repeated by park rangers to curious visitors, was inspired by the black volcanic glass of the Obsidian Cliff on the road between Mammoth Hot Springs and the Norris Geyser Basin.

"Its discovery by Bridger," writes Chittenden, "was the result of one of his hunting trips, and it happened in this wise."

Coming one day in sight of a magnificent elk, he took careful aim at the unsuspecting animal and fired. To his great amazement, the elk not only was not wounded, but seemed not even to have heard the report of the rifle. Bridger drew considerably nearer and gave the elk the benefit of his most deliberate aim; but with the same result as before. A third and a fourth effort met with a similar fate. Utterly exasperated, he seized his rifle by the barrel, resolved to use it as a club since it had failed as a firearm. He rushed madly toward the elk, but suddenly crashed into an immovable vertical wall which proved to be a mountain of perfectly transparent glass, on the farther side of which, still in peaceful security, the elk was quietly grazing. Stranger still, the mountain was not only of pure glass, but was a perfect telescopic lens, and, whereas the elk seemed but a few hundred yards off, it was in reality twenty-five miles away!

Hiram Martin Chittenden, The Yellowstone National Park *(Cincinnati: The Robert Clarke Co., 1905), pp. 48-49.*

Throughout western folklore runs the leitmotif of tricking the Indian, not only to get out of a tight place but also as a way of asserting the white man's superiority. Many of the classic frontier tales deal with clever ruses which prove the hunter, trapper and Indian fighter to be more than a match for the Indian's cunning in the wilderness struggle for survival. One such story, for example, tells how trapper and trader Thomas ("Broken Hand") Fitzpatrick once took advantage of the Indian's ignorance concerning firearms.

[He] had one day got separated from his companions and was pursuing his game alone in the wilderness; and, as ill luck would have it, he was seen by a war party of Indians, who immediately prepared to give chase. There was not the smallest chance of escape for him; but the young hunter made a feint of turning away, in order, if possible, to gain time. He happened to know that these savages, who as yet were little acquainted with the use of firearms, had several times, when they had taken white hunters prisoners, put the muzzles of their rifles close to their breasts, and fired them by way of experiment to see what would come of it. He therefore thought it prudent to extract the bullet from his, and then continued his flight. The Indians followed, and very soon overtook him; and then they disarmed him and tied him to a tree. One of the warriors, who it appeared understood how to pull a trigger, then seized the rifle, placed himself a few paces in front of the owner of it, took aim at his breast, and fired; but when the Indians looked eagerly through the smoke towards where Fitzpatrick stood they saw he was safe and sound in his place, and he quietly took out of his pocket the bullet he had previously placed there, and tossed it to his enemies who were all amazement. They declared he had arrested the bullet in its flight, was an invulnerable and wonderful conjuror, and what was more, that some great misfortune would most likely befall the tribe if they did not set him free immediately, and they therefore cut his bonds and made off as fast as possible, leaving Fitzpatrick to go where he pleased.

Henry Hupfeld, ed., Encyclopaedia of Wit and Wisdom *(Philadelphia: David McKay, 1897), pp. 951-952.*

As a protection against Indian arrows trappers sometimes made crude armor out of buckskin which they believed could be toughened by soaking. Indian fighters also used shields made out of buffalo bull hide. J. Frank Dobie's story of "Bigfoot Wallace and the Hickory Nuts," which he heard from Captain Dan Smith, who heard it more than once from Bigfoot, tells of an even cruder and more incredible armor contrived by the Texas Ranger, scout and Indian fighter, William A. ("Bigfoot") Wallace. During the "Comanche moon," a frontier term for the time of the full moon when the Comanche were on the rampage, "Bigfoot" was following the trail of some Comanche who had stolen all of his horses—except a gray mare named White Bean, on which he started out.

It was hickory nut time and the trees and the ground were thick with nuts. He was wearing roomy buckskin breeches and shirt, and with some buckskin strings he tied his sleeves about his wrists and the bottoms of his breeches about his ankles. Then he stuffed his shirt and breeches with nuts "until he was padded out bigger than Santa Claus." He even filled his hat half full of hickory nuts as a helmet. When he caught up with the Comanche—forty-two of them by actual count—he faced them with his long-barreled, muzzle-loading rifle, Sweet Lips, ready for action. When they saw him standing there all swollen like a super-natural giant, they halted; then, apparently recognizing him, they attacked, yelling and shooting.

Every time a bowstring twanged, an arrow hit a hickory nut, split it, and then fell to the ground. Bigfoot said the arrows got stacked up so high in front of him that he stepped up on the pile and stood three inches taller. . . . The hickory nuts were getting shelled faster than a Missouri mule could bite the grains off an ear of corn.

Finally, all the Indians concentrated on a rear assault. By gravy, he said, those arrows kept jamming the hickory nuts in under his knee joints until he got so tickled he had to bust out laughing. Then he whirled around, and just as he did the last Indian shot the last arrow in the last quiver of the whole band.

Well, sir, when they saw that their ammunition was all gone and that, though not an arrow had missed, the enormous target was still unharmed, they acted as if a bolt of lightning had struck the ground in front of them. For about a minute they stood with their eyes rolling and their tongues hanging out. Then all at once they stampeded like a herd of longhorn steers jumping up off the bedground. They made a beeline for the Rio Grande, seventy miles away. They didn't even give the horses a look.

"I stood there in my tracks," Bigfoot said, "as still and solemn as a cigar Indian, until the devils were clean out of sight. Then I untied the strings around my wrists and ankles, and the hickory nuts just rolled out. If there was a peck of them there were two bushels, and you can kick me to death with grasshopper legs if a single, solitary hickory nut in the whole passel hadn't been split open.

"I thought what a pity it was to lose all those hickory nuts when they were so good at fattening hogs. I walked back to White Bean hid there in the brush and got on her and rode up to the battleground. Then I tied up the coltskin the Indians had peeled off (one of my colts that they had killed and cooked) and filled it with hickory nuts until it looked like a Mexican's goatskin full of pulque. I loaded it on White Bean and got home before dark with all my horses, except the et colt.

"I guess this was the most remarkable experience I ever had with Indians."

J. Frank Dobie, Tales of Old-Time Texas (Boston: Little, Brown & Co., Copyright 1928, 1930, 1931, 1943, 1955, by J. Frank Dobie), pp. 48, 50. Reprinted by permission of the publishers.

Life in the wilderness unfitted many mountain men for civilization. A number of stories deal with their inability to adjust to city ways and manner of dress. Once, in New Mexico, as Nolie Mumey relates in *The Life of Jim Baker, 1818–1898*, the famous trapper discarded his leggings, moccasins and other mountain gear for a store-bought outfit. Said Captain Randolph B. Marcy, the explorer, who was visiting him, "You're so metamorphosed, I hardly knew you!"

"I don't know what you call it," said Jim, "but confound these store-bought boots. They choke my feet like hell!"

It was not long before he was seen walking along the street in bare feet, boots in hand, and soon he was back in his old outfit.

"I'll never wear any more store-bought clo'es," he vowed, "or act like a gentleman again."

Baker's ignorance of the use of the cuspidor is the subject of another anecdote—an old joke told about many backwoods and frontier characters.

On one of Baker's visits to Denver, while seated in one of the hotels chewing tobacco, he spat on the carpet. A Negro porter who happened to see him moved the cuspidor to the spot where he had expectorated, whereupon Jim turned his head and spat in the opposite direction. The porter again moved the cuspidor to that side. Jim, not heeding this, spat again on the carpet.

Finally the porter made several attempts to place it within the range of his amber spray, and having been unsuccessful, he placed the brass receptacle directly in front of him. Old Jim looked down and replied in his rather droll way, "You know, by G—, if you keep movin' that thing around I'm li'ble to spit in it."

Nolie Mumey, The Life of Jim Baker, 1818-1898 (Denver: The World Press, 1931), pp. 172-173.

How thin a line separated Baker's uncouthness from callousness (another frontier trait) is illustrated by the following incidents:

He told me of [a] time he was with an Indian camp on Cherry Creek, where Denver now is, when they were attacked by soldiers and prospectors. He said Cherry Creek was so high they had to swim it to get away. He had a papoose then and took the papoose on his horse and swam across with it and said the squaw drowned.

I told him he should have saved the squaw, "Oh, well," he said "there's lots of squaws."

When he was trapping near Freezeout Mountains in the year 1874, he was up in the mountains with a party shooting bears. He and his partner wounded one. The bear came down the hill right towards them. His partner, who had on buckskin pants, tried to climb a dry quaking aspen tree (which is very slippery). He kept sliding down but finally got up to the limbs. Here he got his arm over a knot in the tree and hung. Baker said he ran to a green pine and climbed up it. The bear came and laid down by the tree and died. His partner called to him. "Can't you shoot him?" "No," said Baker, "he's lying there watching me." "Kill him if you can, 'cause I can't hang on here much longer," shouted the partner. "Well," said Baker, "I thought I'd let him hang on there long enough, so finally said, 'You might as well come down because he's dead.' Say, he slipped his arm off that knot and came down like he was shot and gave me a good cussing for not telling him before that he was dead."

"Recollections of Taylor Pennock," Annals of Wyoming, VI (1929), pp. 219-220.

In his eccentricities and pranks, which he often carried to the point of cruelty and even crime, the trapper expressed not only his defiance of social conventions but also his aversion to civilization, especially of the eastern brand. If he seemed like a barbarian to the people in the settlements, they seemed like snobs and fools to him. This conflict between the frontiersman and civilization is best illustrated by the storyteller and joker Joseph L. Meek, mountain man who became one of the founders of Oregon. What is perhaps his most famous remark was made at the expense of two snobbish army officers who were visiting the fort at Vancouver.

As our friend Meek was sure to be found wherever there was anything novel or exciting transpiring, so he was sure to fall in with visitors so distinguished as these, and as ready to answer their questions as they were to ask them. The conversation chanced one day to run upon the changes that had taken place in the country since the earliest settlement by the Americans, and Meek, who felt an honest pride in them, was expatiating at some length, to the ill-concealed amusement of the young officers, who probably saw nothing to admire in the rude improvements of the Oregon pioneers.

"Mr. Meek," said one of them, "if you have been so long in the country and have witnessed such wonderful transformations, doubtless you may have observed equally great ones in nature; in the rivers and mountains, for instance?"

Meek gave a lightning glance at the speaker, who had so mistaken his respondent.

"I reckon I have," said he slowly.

Then waving his hand gracefully toward the majestic Mt. Hood, towering thousands of feet above the summit of the Cascade range, and white with everlasting snows: "When *I* came to this country, Mount Hood was *a hole in the ground!*"

Mrs. Frances Fuller Victor, The River of the West (Hartford: Columbian Book Co., 1870), p. 366.

(Compare the Colorado equivalent, "When Pike's Peak was a hole in the ground.")

82. *Songs of the Forty-Niners*

THE THEME SONG of the California gold rush was "Oh! Susanna," in the miners' folk adaptation of Foster's original song. Because of its lilting banjo tune, made famous by Christy's minstrels, "Oh, Susanna" lent itself to parody. Much imitated was that of the men of the bark *Eliza*, which left Salem, Massachusetts, for California on November 23, 1848. Here are the first and last stanzas with chorus:

I came from Salem City
  With my washbowl on my knee,
I'm going to California,
  The gold dust for to see.
It rained all night the day I left,
  The weather it was dry,
The sun so hot I froze to death,
  Oh, brothers, don't you cry.

Chorus:

Oh! California,
  That's the land for me,
I'm going to Sacramento
  With my washbowl on my knee.

I soon shall be in Francisco,
  And then I'll look around,
And when I see the gold lumps there,
  I'll pick them off the ground.

I'll scrape the mountains clean,
  I'll drain the rivers dry,
A pocket full of rocks bring home,
  So, brothers, don't you cry.

Octavius Thorndike Howe, Argonauts of '49 *(Cambridge: Harvard University Press, 1923), pp. 78-79.*

A later California production that has rivaled "Oh, Susanna" is the sophisticated mock-sentimental ballad, "Clementine," a favorite of the Bohemians of San Francisco toward the end of the century.

Meanwhile, the Overland Trail was producing its own humorous, hard-hitting songs that made light of the trials, hardships and perils of crossing the plains. The best known is "Sweet Betsey from Pike," sung to the tune of "Villikins and His Dinah." Not the least of the troubles that afflicted Betsey and her lover Ike, as depicted in the following stanzas, were love troubles, which culminated in marriage and divorce when they reached Placerville (originally named Hangtown after a triple hanging).

Sweet Betsey From Pike

520

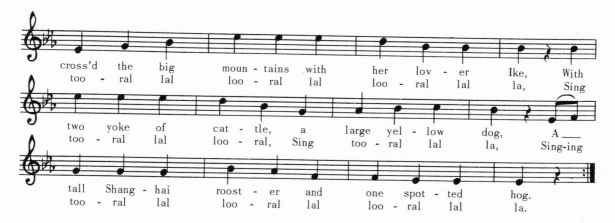

cross'd the big moun-tains with her lov-er Ike, With
too - ral lal loo - ral lal loo - ral lal la, Sing

two yoke of cat-tle, a large yel-low dog, A___
too - ral lal loo - ral, Sing too - ral lal la, Sing-ing

tall Shang-hai roost-er and one spot-ted hog.
too - ral lal loo - ral lal loo - ral lal la.

2. One evening quite early they camped on the Platte,
'Twas near by the road on a green shady flat,
Where Betsey, sore-footed, lay down to repose—
With wonder Ike gazed on that Pike County rose.

3. Their wagons broke down with a terrible crash,
And out on the prairie rolled all kinds of trash;
A few little baby clothes done up with care—
'Twas rather suspicious, though all on the *square*.

4. The shanghai ran off, and their cattle all died;
That morning the last piece of bacon was fried;
Poor Ike was discouraged, and Betsey got mad,
The dog drooped his tail and looked wondrously sad.

5. They stopped at Salt Lake to inquire the way,
When Brigham declared that Sweet Betsey should stay;
But Betsey got frightened and ran like a deer,
While Brigham stood pawing the ground like a steer.

6. They soon reached the desert, where Betsey gave out,
And down in the sand she lay rolling about;
While Ike, half-distracted, looked on with surprise,
Saying, "Betsey, get up, you'll get sand in your eyes."

7. Sweet Betsey got up in a great deal of pain,
Declared she'd go back to Pike County again;
But Ike gave a sigh and they fondly embraced,
And they traveled along with his arm round her waist.

8. They suddenly stopped on a very high hill,
With wonder looked down upon old Placerville;
Ike sighed when he said, and he cast his eyes down:
"Sweet Betsey, my darling, we've got to Hangtown."

9. Long Ike and sweet Betsey attended a dance;
Ike wore a pair of his Pike County pants;
Sweet Betsey was covered with ribbons and rings;
Says Ike, "You're an angel, but where are your wings?"

10. A miner said, "Betsey, will you dance with me?"
"I will that, old hoss, if you don't make too free;
But don't dance me hard; do you want to know why?
Dog on you! I'm chock full of strong alkali!"

11. This Pike County couple got married of course,
And Ike became jealous—obtained a divorce;
Sweet Betsey, well satisfied, said with a shout,
"Good-bye, you big lummox, I'm glad you've backed out!"

Text: John A. Stone, Put's Golden Songster *(San Francisco: D. E. Appleton & Co., 1858) p. 50. Tune recorded and transcribed by Sidney Robertson as sung by John McCready of Groveland, California.*

In his preface to *Put's Original California Songster* (1854) "Old Put," ex-miner, composer, collector and singer, whose real name was John A. Stone wrote: "Ever since the time of his crossing the Plains, in the memorable year of '50, he has been in the habit of noting down a few of the leading items of his experience, and clothing them in the garb of humorous though not irreverent verse."

Like Sweet Betsey, Joe Bowers, hero of another comic-sentimental song of the gold rush, hailed from Pike County, Missouri, celebrated as the home of the first immigrants to California. A stock comic figure in gold rush songs and stories, the "Pike" or Pike County Man, as he was called whether he came from Missouri, Arkansas, southern Illinois or eastern Kentucky, typified the "poor white" or "Anglo-Saxon relapsed into semi-barbarism." Bayard Taylor describes him as "long, lathy, and sallow," addicted to drinking, expectorating tobacco juice and the "shakes."

Joe Bowers

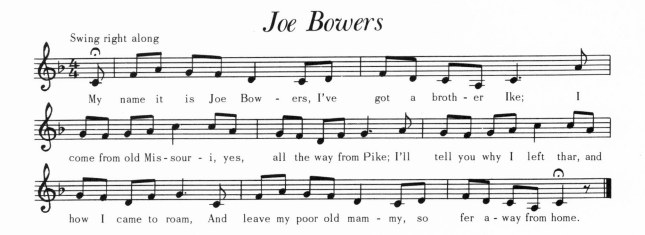

Swing right along

My name it is Joe Bow - ers, I've got a broth - er Ike; I
come from old Mis-sour - i, yes, all the way from Pike; I'll tell you why I left thar, and
how I came to roam, And leave my poor old mam - my, so fer a - way from home.

2. I used to love a gal thar, they call'd her Sally Black.
I axed her for to marry me, she said it was a whack.
Says she to me, "Joe Bowers, before we hitch for life,
You'd orter have a little home to keep your little wife."

3. Says I, "My dearest Sally, oh Sally, for your sake,
I'll go to Californy, and try to raise a stake."
Says she to me, "Joe Bowers, oh, you're the chap to win,
Give me a buss to seal the bargain," and she threw a douzen in!

4. I shall ne'er forget my feelin's when I bid adieu to all.
Sally cotched me round the neck, then I began to bawl.
When I sot in, they all commenced—you ne'er did hear the like,
How they all took on and cried, the day I left old Pike.

5. When I got to this 'ere country, I hadn't nary red.
I had such wolfish feelin's I wish'd myself 'most dead;
But the thoughts of my dear Sally soon made them feelin's git,
And whispered hopes to Bowers—Lord, I wish I had 'em yit!

6. At length I went to minin', put in my biggest licks,
Come down upon the boulders jist like a thousand bricks.
I worked both late and airly, in rain, and sun, and snow,
But I was working for my Sally, so 'twas all the same to Joe.

7. I made a very lucky strike, as the gold itself did tell,
And saved it for my Sally, the gal I loved so well.
I saved it for my Sally, that I might pour it at her feet,
That she might kiss and hug me, and call me something sweet.

8. But one day I got a letter from my dear, kind brother, Ike—
It come from old Missouri, sent all the way from Pike.
It brought me the gol-darn'dest news as ever you did hear—
My heart is almost bustin', so, pray, excuse this tear.

9. It said my Sal was fickle, that her love for me had fled;
That she'd married with a butcher, whose har was orful red!
It tole me more than that—oh! it's enough to make one swar,
It said Sally had a baby, and the baby had red har!

10. Now, I've told you all I could tell, about this sad affair,
'Bout Sally marryin' the butcher, and the butcher had red har.
Whether 'twas a boy or gal child, the letter never said,
It only said its cussed har was inclined to be a red!

Text: Johnson's Original Comic Songs *(San Francisco: D. E. Appleton & Co., second ed., 1860). Tune recorded and transcribed by Sidney Robertson as sung by Ben Strong of Cassville, Missouri.*

"Sweet Betsey from Pike" and "Joe Bowers" are typical folk songs of the Overland Trail. If the songs of the gold rush proper show the influence of print (newspapers, broadsides, songsters) and the marks of "literary" (especially stage) rather than "folk" origin, it is because of the high degree of literacy among the gold-seekers, as attested by their diaries and journals, and the speed with which, in that "fast country," history passed into song. All ranks and conditions of men were caught up by gold fever; and their common traits—ignorance of the West and mass hysteria—made them a rich subject for topical song, burlesque and parody, with an abundance of familiar and singable tunes ready at hand in the minstrel and popular songs of the day. Singing was one of the chief amusements of the overland journey, and songs of the mining camps quickly circulated along the trails, carried by immigrants and traveling singers. In the mining camps and towns themselves, theaters, dance halls and saloons featured the songs, as performed by singing groups and troupes.

The fickleness of Joe Bowers' Sally was of a piece with the forty-niner's other misfortunes. In fact, the hard luck that pursued him while en route to the gold fields as well as following his arrival has been immortalized in the popular expression of the time, "seeing the elephant." This was the title both of a song published in *Put's Original California Songster,* sung to the minstrel tune, "De Boatman Dance," and of a musical show put together by Dr. D. G. Robinson, which opened at the Phoenix Theatre in San Francisco on March 23, 1850.

The expression has been traced to the circus, where the elephant was the principal attraction and where, having seen the elephant, one had seen everything. Thus the phrase acquired the ironic and cynical connotation, according to Carl I. Wheat, "that one had experienced the ultimate possibilities of a situation, had passed through a most difficult experience, or had experienced hard luck in a manner seemingly inevitable."

One stanza in "Seeing the Elephant," a song relating the trials and tribulations of crossing the plains, establishes the fact that "coming around the Horn" was another way of seeing him.

> When the elephant I had seen,
> I'm damn'd if I thought I was green;
> And others say, both night and morn,
> They saw him coming round the Horn.

John A. Stone, Put's Original California Songster *(San Francisco: D. E. Appleton & Co., 1854), p. 19.*

To substantiate the fact, here is the song, "Coming Around the Horn," sung to the minstrel tune, "Dearest Mae":

Coming Around the Horn

Oh, I re-mem-ber well the lies they used to tell, Of
gold so bright, it hurt the sight, and made the min-ers yell.

2. We left old New York City, with the weather very thick,
   The second way we puked up boats, oh, wasn't we all sea-sick!
   I swallowed pork tied to a string, which made a dreadful shout,
   I felt it strike the bottom, but I could not pull it out.

3. We all were owners in the ship, and soon began to growl,
   Because we hadn't ham and eggs, and now and then a fowl;
   We told the captain what to do, as him we had to pay,
   The captain swore that he was boss, and we should him obey.

4. We lived like hogs, penned up to fat, our vessel was so small,
   We had a "duff" but once a month, and twice a day a squall;
   A meeting now and then was held, which kicked up quite a stink,
   The captain damned us fore and aft, and wished the box would sink.

5. Off Cape Horn, where we lay becalmed, kind Providence seemed to frown,
   We had to stand up night and day, none of us dared sit down;
   For some had half a dozen boils, 'twas awful, sure's you're born,
   But some would try it on the sly, and got pricked by the Horn.

6. We stopped at Valparaiso, where the women are so loose,
   And all got drunk as usual, got shoved in the Calaboose;
   Our ragged, rotten sails were patched, the ship made ready for sea,
   But every man, except the cook, was up town on a spree.

7. We sobered off, set sail again, on short allowance, of course,
   With water thick as castor oil, and stinking beef much worse;
   We had the scurvy and the itch, and any amount of lice,
   The medicine chest went overboard, with bluemass, cards and dice.

8. We arrived at San Francisco, and all went to the mines,
   We left an agent back to sell our goods of various kinds;
   A friend wrote up to let us know our gent, Mr. Gates,
   Had sold the ship and cargo, sent the money to the States.

John A. Stone, Put's Original California Songster *(San Francisco: D. E. Appleton & Co., 1854), p. 37.*

Typical both of "seeing the elephant" and of the graphic doggerel reportage in which the gold rush songs excel is "Arrival of the Greenhorn," sung to the tune of "Jeanette and Jeanot." This follows the overland journey from departure to arrival.

Arrival of the Greenhorn

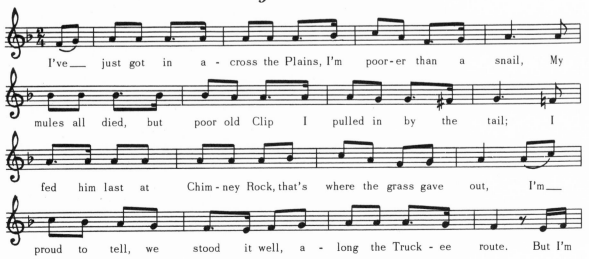

I've— just got in a-cross the Plains, I'm poor-er than a snail, My
mules all died, but poor old Clip I pulled in by the tail; I
fed him last at Chim-ney Rock, that's where the grass gave out, I'm—
proud to tell, we stood it well, a-long the Truck-ee route. But I'm

ver - y weak and lean, though I start - ed plump and fat How I

wish I had the gold ma-chine, I left back on the Platte! And a

pair of strip - ed bed - tick pants, my Sal - ly made for me To___

wear while dig - ging af - ter gold, and when I left says she "Here,___

take the laud' - num with you Sam, to check the di - a - ree."

2. When I left Missouri river, with my California rig,
I had a shovel, pick and pan, and tools they used to dig;
My mules gave out along the Platte, where they got alkalied,
And I sick with the "di-a-ree," my laudanum by my side.
When I reached the little Blue, I'd one boot and a shoe,
Which I thought by greasing once or twice, would last me nearly through;
I had needles, thread and pills, which my mammy did prescribe,
And a flint-lock musket full, to shoot the Digger tribe,
But I left them all on Goose Creek where I freely did imbibe.

3. I joined in with a train from Pike, at Independence Rock,
The Indians came in that night, stampeded all their stock;
They laughed at me, said, "Go-a-foot," but soon they stopped their fun,
For my old mule was left behind so poor he could not run.
So I packed my fancy nag, for the rest I could not wait,
And I traveled up Sweet Water, till I came to Devil's Gate;
When my mule gave out in sight of where I started in the morn,
I'd have given all my boots and shoes if I had not been born,
Or I'd rather stripped at New Orleans, to swim around the Horn.

4. I arrived at Salt Lake City, on the 18th of July,
Old Brigham Young was on a "bust," he swore they'd never die;
I went to see the Jordan, with a lady, God forgive her,
She took me to the water's edge, and shoved me in the river;
I crawled out and started on, and I managed very well,
Until I struck the Humboldt, which I thought was nearly hell;
I traveled till I struck the sink where outlet can't be found,
The Lord got through late Saturday night, he'd finished all around,
But would not work on Sunday, so he run it in the ground.

5. The Peyouts [Paiutes] stole what grub I had, they left me not a bite,
And now the devil was to pay—the Desert was in sight;
And as the people passed along, they'd say to me, "You fool,
You'll never get through in the world, unless you leave that mule."
But I pushed, pulled and coaxed, till I finally made a start,
And his bones, they squeaked and rattled so, I thought he'd fall apart;
I killed a buzzard now and then, gave Clip the legs and head.
We crossed the Truckee thirty times, but not a tear was shed,
We crossed the summit, took the trail, that to Nevada led.

6. When I got to Sacramento, I got on a little tight,
I lodged aboard the Prison brig, one-half a day and night;
I vamoosed when I got ashore, went to the Northern mines,
There found the saying very true, "All is not gold that shines."
I dug, packed and chopped, and have drifted night and day,
But I haven't struck a single lead, that would me wages pay.
At home they think we ought to have gold on our cabin shelves,
Wear high-heeled boots, well blacked, instead of rubbers No. twelves;
But let them come and try it, 'till they satisfy themselves.

John A. Stone, Put's Original California Songster (San Francisco: D. E Appleton & Co., 1854), p. 31.

"MANY OF THE Good Luck stories of the placer mining era," wrote Charles Peters in his *Autobiography,* "read like tales from the 'Arabian Nights.' Luck was a word to conjure with. In no other pursuit was the element of chance a more potent factor. . . . 'How's your luck?' became a common form of salutation."

The first lesson the greenhorn learned or should have learned on his arrival in the gold fields was "All is not gold that shines." The hazards of mining and dreams of striking it rich made greenhorns easy prey for tricksters. Salting or planting gold by firing it from shotguns, sowing nuggets, etc., as a prank or a promotion scheme, was one of the oldest of miners' swindles. Robert Welles Ritchie tells how Pike Sellers once salted jack pines with nuggets in order to divert a greenhorn from a rich strike. Such a combination of "a noteworthy swindle, a practical joke, a brilliant hoax" was known in the northern mines as a "whizzer."

One of the earliest Whizzers of the gold diggin's to gain immortality was that one perpetrated by a genius whose name comes down as Pike Sellers—undoubtedly one of the Wild Missouri hellions generically lumped as "Pikes," in the vocabulary of the mines. This Pike had an imagination and a devilishly sly humor which would qualify him today for one of our highly specialized lines of salesmanship.

It was in the spring of '50 when word of the incredible richness of Downie's Flat, away up near the headwaters of Yuba's north fork, swept downstream and set a crowd of wild-eyed boomers hurrying thither. Original discoverers of Downie's Flat were digging a pound of gold a day to the man out of crevices under the rim rock with the point of a butcher knife. Major Downie himself had sifted downstream to Bullard's Bar with $3000 in nuggets, result of three days' work! So rumor exploded.

When the first of the rush commenced to lower themselves hand over hand down the precipitous wall of the gorge to Downie's camp on the forks of white water they were not very cordially received by the ten or a dozen original discoverers who'd spent a hard winter there. It was, in fact, quite true that Downie and his associates had been hitting raw gold out of the bank with butcher knives and iron spoons over several months; and they did not welcome a division of riches.

Then it was that Pike Sellers had his inspiration.

He was working away at the soft dirt of the stream bank one day when he saw one of the boomers, pack on back, crawling precariously down trail. Pike, unseen himself, scrambled up out of the stream bed and commenced furiously prying with his long knife at the bark slabs on a jack-pine. Just as the stranger came up one of the rough shags of bark became loosened. Pike pushed two fingers behind it and withdrew a fat old nugget.

Eyes of the stranger popped. Pike tackled another bark slab without so much as a glance over shoulder at the fascinated onlooker. By a simple trick of legerdemain that hunk yielded a second alluring gold pebble.

"My Gawd!"—from the tenderfoot. "I hearn ye was diggin' the yaller stuff outa cracks in the rocks, but I didn't know she grew on trees."

"Gits lodged thar when th' tree's pushing up through th' soil," indifferently from Pike. "Most of th' nuggets is up higher, but too dam'd much trouble to shin up th' trees. Me, I'm jist satisfied to peck round nigh th' ground."

Under the believing eyes of the newcomer Pike found a couple more nuggets. Then the former whipped out his bowie-knife and started to work on a near-by jack-pine.

"Hold on thar!" commandingly from the Sellers person. "Yo're on my claim. Rule in this camp ev'ry fella's entitled to ten gold bearin' pines; that thar one belongs to me."

The boomer wanted to know in an excited whine where he could stake himself to a tree. Reluctantly Pike Sellers abandoned his work to stride through the forest to where a jack-pine of smaller growth reared.

"Like I said, she's richest nigh th' top. Ye can climb this one 'thout a ladder iffen yo're so minded." Pike showed a commendable interest in seeing the newcomer make his first strike of jack-pine gold. The latter dropped his pack and, bowie in teeth, commenced to shin up the rough trunk.

"Higher up's better," bawled Pike when his protege had come to the first limbs. "Nothin' but flake gold low down mostly."

Up went the avid tenderfoot, before his eyes the vision of a man prying nuggets from beneath tree bark. Pike let him risk his neck until the luckless light-wit was fifty or sixty feet from the ground.

"That's a likely 'nough place to begin on. Only be mighty keerful not to drop any nuggets. I kain't be held responsible fer losses like that."

The searcher after tree gold began to attack the bark with his bowie knife. Pike Sellers sifted back to the stream bed to bring an audience for the farce comedy he had staged. Thereafter "jack-pine gold" became a synonym through all the Northern Mines.

Pike Sellers reaped enduring fame as the father of a Whizzer.

Robert Welles Ritchie, The Hell-Roarin' Forty-Niners (New York: J. H. Sears & Co., 1928), pp. 233-237.

Greenhorns were not the only victims of hoaxers and tricksters. Experienced miners were also taken in. The Comstock Lode was a special haven of roving or strolling bogus miners, who went from camp to camp plying their swindling trade. Dan De Quille (William Wright) explains the fine points of the trick known as "doctoring the tape-line."

This operation is simple enough. All that is to be done is to get hold of the line of the foreman, superintendent, or whoever is likely to measure the work, and cut out a few feet. The line is then neatly sewed together again. In order to succeed in this game it is necessary for those playing it to "doctor" the line a few hours before their work is to be measured—at night, for instance, when they know their work is to be measured the first thing in the morning.

A mining superintendent on the Comstock range one day said to me: "I had my tape-line 'doctored' the other day, and, confound the fellows! they got away with their trick nicely."

"How was that?" I asked.

"Well, I had let a contract to some boys who came along to sink a small shaft to the depth of fifty feet. One morning they told me the shaft was finished, and asked me to go out and measure the work.

"One of the men got into the bucket and was lowered into the shaft, holding the end of the line, which was reeled off as he descended. When he got down he held his end of the line on the bottom of the shaft, and, looking at my end, I found the shaft exactly fifty feet in depth. I paid the men their money and they left. In a day or two I had occasion to measure something—a stick of timber—and was astonished to find it much longer than it looked. Overhauling my tape-line, I found that just six feet had been cut out of it and the two parts neatly sewed together again. I knew then that my shaft was exactly forty-four feet deep, and, I tell you, I never was more ashamed of anything in all my life!"

Dan De Quille (William Wright), The History of the Big Bonanza (Hartford: American Publishing Co., 1876), pp. 332-333.

A local character who became legendary in the early Colorado boom days for the ingenuity with which he bluffed and swindled his way out of bad contracts was the eccentric wag, "Gassy" Thompson. One "Gassy" Thompson story—a favorite of the late Levette J. Davidson, western folklorist and story teller, who told it to me—illustrates how "Gassy's" distaste for manual labor stimulated his inventiveness.

If a mining shaft is left unworked for a while, very likely water will accumulate for maybe several hundred feet. And if the mine is to be operated again, then it has to be pumped out. And if done by hand, this, of course, takes quite a long time and means a lot of backbreaking work. Gassy took a contract to unwater this particular mining shaft [at Central City, near Black Hawk] and then regretted that he had signed up for so much work. He went up to look over the place and found that there was a lot of water in the mine. So he sat down to think. He noticed a stray dog running along, he hurled a rock at it, knocked it over, went over and killed the dog. Then with a brilliant idea back of his actions he dragged it to the mouth of the shaft, found an old hat and coat that had been abandoned nearby, daubed it over with some of the dog's blood. Then he tied a rock around the dog's neck and dropped it in and heard it hit the water and splash and go to the bottom. His next step was to go down to Central City and sort of circulate through the bars, spreading the word that he suspected foul play up at that mine, that there was evidence that there had been a struggle, and blood was around there. He didn't know just what had happened but it looked bad to him. Before long the boys went up to investigate and they found sure enough evidences that aroused their suspicions. So they went back down town and got the sheriff. He in turn organized a posse and they borrowed some pumps from the county commissioners and they went up to that mine. The boys set to with a will and before long they had pumped the shaft dry. Sure enough, they found the body, but it was of the dog. In the meantime, Gassy, of course, had skipped the country. He did come back a little later to collect the wages from the owners of the shaft for the quickest and most efficient job of unwatering a mine that had been done for some time.

Recorded by B. A. Botkin in A Treasury of Western Folklore, *ed. B. A. Botkin (New York: Crown Publishers, 1951), p. 458.*

The ultimate in mining hoaxes is the scheme of the old-timer (more recently, an oil prospector) who goes to heaven and, finding it crowded, starts a rumor of a gold (or oil) strike in hell, only to fall for it himself. The story is also a fable of the prospector's eternal dream of finding gold—a dream which to him is as important as the gold itself. The following version is from Nevada:

Two prospectors died in the fulness of their years, and contrary to their own expectation and that of their friends found themselves in Heaven. A third, unknown to them, came later to the Gate and was admitted by St. Peter with some hesitation.

"What's the trouble?" the newcomer asked. "You let me in but I don't hear any welcoming chorus."

"I have to let you in," said St. Peter. "You've always worked hard for your grub-stakers, and you've worshiped God out under the stars at night, and played fair and haven't told any lies that would do any one any real harm. You are in the Book to be let in, but I must admit that you are not very welcome. I let a couple of prospectors in a while back and they've been a nuisance. They're always tearing up the golden streets."

"Well," said the newcomer, "I'll fix that. You show me these fellers and I'll get rid of 'em for you."

So the newcomer was welcomed and introduced to the others. They greeted him cordially and tried to sell him a claim. When that failed they pointed out adjoining ground that he might locate himself. Presently he was as busy as they, sinking assessment holes. St. Peter appeared, drew the newcomer aside and protested.

"Oh, yes," the prospector agreed. "This is such good ground that I forgot. But I'll keep my word."

And a day or two later the two original prospectors appeared at the Gate and asked to be released. No amount of questioning could get at the reason for their request, but St. Peter, having warned them that once out they couldn't come back, agreed cheerfully to let them go.

All was peace in Heaven for a few days. Then St. Peter came upon the third and remaining prospector, seated in thought upon a heap of golden paving stones.

"You did very well, my good man," he said. "Your friends have gone. How did you arrange it?"

The prospector grinned. "I just let it drop that there was a rich new strike in Hell," he said.

But that wasn't all. And here is the revelation of the prospector spirit. A few days later the remaining prospector approached St. Peter at the Gate.

"I'd like to get out," he said.

"Why? Everything is peaceful and lovely here now since your destructive associates have left. Heaven certainly owes you a debt of thanks. If there is anything we can do to make you happier, you may command me and it will be done."

"Well, I reckon you'd better let me out. I been thinkin' about that new strike in Hell, an' I believe there's something in it. I'd like to get down there ahead of the rush an' stake me a few good claims."

C. B. Glasscock, Gold in Them Hills (Indianapolis: The Bobbs-Merrill Co., Copyright 1932 by C. B. Glasscock; 1959, by Mrs. Marion T. Glasscock), pp. 152-154. Reprinted by permission of the publishers.

Stories of accidental discoveries were a staple of miners' luck. Many a claim or mining camp got its start through a lucky find. W. A. Chalfant, in *Outposts of Civilization,* tells of a miner who wandered off into the hills to get away from a fourth of July celebration at Dogtown, California, and lay down to rest in the shade of a boulder on a slope toward Mono Lake. As he lay face downward, he was seized with a spell of coughing that disturbed the sand and revealed gold. The discovery started a rush that resulted in the founding of Monoville and the virtual abandonment of Dogtown.

In Colorado during the Leadville boom of 1877–79, according to Ernest Ingersoll, in *The Crest of the Continent,* a miner named Scotty died. A man was hired to dig a grave through ten feet of snow and six feet of frozen ground. When the gravedigger did not show up for three days, the boys found that the grave had turned into a mine, which the digger refused to yield, and the prospecting continued while Scotty lay forgotten in a snowbank till April. The claim was known as the Dead Man Claim.

A more common version of the "cemetery find," tells how a discovery interrupted a sermon, much as the announcement of a wreck or the arrival of a large school of fish interrupted sermons in New England coastal towns.

In '49, on Carson Creek, a miner died and his friends arranged to bury him as decently as possible.

A grave was dug near his cabin; his coffin was made with pine boards planed and stained black.

There was no minister on the creek, so a clerical looking miner, who had been nicknamed the "Deacon," and who had a bible and some religious books, was asked to officiate.

The friends of the deceased gathered around the grave in the afternoon. The "Deacon" spoke an eulogy; read from the epistle of St. Paul, and then knelt in prayer. While he prayed, one of the miners, with lowered eyes, who was standing upon some of the dirt thrown out in the digging of the grave, saw a nugget sticking out of the dirt. He stooped and picked it up just as the "Deacon" said Amen. The attention of some of the other miners was attracted to the nugget finder and this caused the "Deacon" to look that way. "What's that?" interjected he. "Gold! Gold! Hold on, boys! Postpone this funeral until we locate our claims." And locate they did. The embryo graveyard proved to be a rich placer. Another grave was dug where ground did not appear to show a "color" and the funeral ceremonies were finished there.

Charles Peters, The Autobiography of Charles Peters *(Sacramento: The La Grave Co., 1915), p. 199.*

From accidental discovery the trail often leads to a lost mine—a trail of mystery, mania, hoax, hardship, failure and death. The pattern is traditional. Ore is discovered under circumstances that make it difficult for the finder to retrace his steps. A party is organized and an attempt is made to locate the original bearings. A series of obstacles—Indians, obliteration of landmarks by storm and flood, loss of memory, death—keep the finder from reaching his goal. With the help of a map, secret information or new clues and finds, the search is continued by others, with similar results, until the will-o'-the-wisp mystery passes into myth. The superstition that the finder of an "excitement" or discovery is usually doomed to an untimely or violent death may account for the aura of tragedy surrounding lost-mine stories.

Typical of the genre is the well-known legend of the Lost Pegleg mine. John G. ("Pegleg") Smith, according to his friend Major Horace Bell in *On the Old West Coast,* was "an artistic old liar . . . the most superlative liar that ever honored California with his presence. . . . Ever since the old man died people have been searching for the Pegleg Mine, but they will never find it . . . because it is a myth, a Pegleg lie. . . ."

Pegleg's memory is fittingly honored by a rock-pile monument erected in 1947 in the Borrego Valley at the foot of Coyote Mountain. Here each year on New Year's Eve is held the desert Liars' Contest. Competitors are required (as visitors are invited) to add to the monument, in accordance with the inscription on the marker:

Let Him Who Seeks Pegleg Smith's Gold
Add 10 Rocks to This Monument.

Here is the story of various attempts to find the Lost Pegleg Mine:

In 1837, nearly a dozen years before gold was found at Sutter's Mill, a trapper and roustabout named John G. Smith, later known as Pegleg, because of an accident that left him with one leg, started from Yuma for Los Angeles. He was in haste to be at his journey's end, and so, instead of keeping to the old trail made by the Spaniards and which followed its meandering way from one uncertain waterhole to another, he attempted a short cut across the desert and over the hills. Somewhere east of Warner's Pass, whence the trail leads down into the Mission grants which now form the orange belt of California, Smith lost his way and to regain his bearings climbed the highest of these low hills.

While reconnoitering he picked up some lumps of black and burned looking ore, thickly sprinkled with yellow particles of varying size, which literally covered the hill. The presence of gold in those regions was not then dreamed of, but attracted by the curious appearance of the rock, which he supposed to be copper, he gathered up a few samples of convenient size and carried them with him to Los Angeles. These Smith

retained until after the discovery of gold in 1848, when accident led to their examination by an expert, who at once pronounced the yellow particles pure gold. Their discoverer, when told of how through ignorance he had missed great wealth, promptly
organized an expedition to relocate the hill so rich in gold. The party, however, at an
early stage of its journey, had all of its stock run off by Indians. This so discouraged
the leader that he gave up the quest in disgust, and his companions had to follow his
example. And the legend runs that before he could contrive the outfitting of another
party, Smith took to his bed and died of brain fever.

In the years that immediately followed many prospectors started out from Yuma
and Los Angeles in a vain search for the lost mine, and the skeletons of some of them
continue to be found to this day. The passage of time, however, brought proof of a sort
that the location of the lost mine was known to at least one native of the region. In the
early sixties of the last century the owner of a large ranch on the edge of the desert had
a number of Mexicans in his employ as riders and herders. One day a rider asked his
employer for money with which to make a trip to Los Angeles. The rancher refused
the request knowing that it was the prelude to a spree, and having moreover pressing
need at the moment for all his hands. Whereupon the Mexican replied:

"All right. I know where there is plenty of gold. I can get all I want."

A few hours later, mounted on a horse borrowed without leave from his employer,
he disappeared into the desert. He returned at the end of three days with a few thousand dollars' worth of burnt black gold of the Pegleg, which he deposited with the
storekeeper at the ranch, and on the proceeds of which he reveled to his heart's content.
Thereafter, whenever his funds ran low he would leave the ranch, and soon return, his
pockets filled with nuggets. Time and again efforts were made to follow him, but at a
certain point his pursuers always lost him. From this point he was invariably absent

Miners of Forty-nine.

only one day, so it was concluded that the Pegleg was less than twelve hours' ride distant from it.

The Mexican did not live long to enjoy his prosperity, being cut to pieces in a knife duel with another Mexican, with whom he had quarreled over a woman of their race. He left on deposit with the ranch storekeeper $4000 in nuggets and coarse gold, but his secret died with him. Although the storekeeper made many efforts to wrest it from the desert all of them proved futile, and in the end he gave up the search. A more tragic quest was that of Tom Carver, a former sheriff of San Bernardino County, who while hunting horse thieves had once met the Mexican in the hills. Carver also sought the Pegleg, taking as a starting point the spot where he had encountered the Mexican. One day he started up a canyon, leaving his single companion to wait for him in a buckboard on the trail. He never came back and although his friends left no stone unturned in efforts to recover his body they never found trace of it.

Yet a third time the Pegleg appears to have been found and lost. Sixty-odd years ago a miner who had crossed the desert several times before arrived in Yuma, and, reluctant to wait for companions, decided to make the trip to Los Angeles alone. He followed the trail on muleback a part of the way, and then concluded, like Smith in an earlier time, to shorten the journey by cutting across country. Soon after leaving the trail he encountered a succession of low hills and steep canyons, of a sort calculated to perplex even a seasoned desert traveler. The miner to make sure of his course rode to the top of one of a little group of hills, and while taking his bearings chanced to glance at the rock on which he was standing. Instantly he discovered that the hill was a mass of broken quartz and free gold.

He did what any other miner would have done under like conditions. He emptied his saddlebags of their contents, refilled them with the last possible pound of the precious metal, and, taking careful note of his surroundings, continued on to Los Angeles. There he fell ill as a result of the hardships he had undergone. The doctor who attended him for many weeks was told of the find in the desert, and in the end given a portion of the ore for his services. The two men were making ready for a journey into the desert, when the miner had a relapse and in a few days was in his grave.

A little later the doctor made a visit to Yuma, and employed Indians to search for the lost mine, but their efforts continued through several seasons yielded no practical results. To a Doubting Thomas ignorant of the country it would seem an easy matter to relocate the Pegleg. There are, however, hundreds of square miles of the desert so broken that often the traveler cannot see fifty yards ahead of him, and to lose one's bearings means to perish from thirst. And so, although the tracks of the Southern Pacific must run close to it, death and disaster stand guard through the years over the hill of gold.

Rufus Rockwell Wilson, Out of the West (New York: The Press of the Pioneers, 1936), pp. 352-355.

When a prospector was not looking for a lost mine, he might be looking for a lost burro—his magic animal helper and comic hindrance. In this connection, here is "Slim" Ludwick's story of his prospector friend who was testifying for the defense in a case before Judge Stratton at Buckhorn.

The lawyer for the defense was tryin' to qualify him as an expert witness, an' asked him how long he'd been a prospector. "Thirty years," he says. Well, pretty soon the prosecutin' attorney gets to cross-examine him.

"How many years have you prospected?" he asks.

" 'Bout five years," says the witness.

"Ah ha!" says the prosecutor, lookin' mean an' successful. "Your Honor, I'd like to have you note that the witness under oath has already said he has been a prospector for thirty years, an' now he says he's prospected five years."

"Wait a minute, wait a minute," says the witness. "I said I'd been a prospector for thirty years, an' I have. I said I'd prospected five years an' I have. Both statements is facts, your Honor. Five years I prospected and the other twenty-five I spent lookin' for my burros. You know how it is, your Honor."

"The witness qualifies as an expert," says the j.p., thereby qualifyin' himself as a judge.

C. B. Glasscock, Gold in Them Hills *(Indianapolis: The Bobbs-Merrill Co., Copyright 1932, by C. B. Glasscock; 1959, by Mrs. Marion T. Glasscock), pp. 19-20.*

The following stories illustrate the way of a prospector with his burros:

The burro, in his native habitat, is a noble beast—not in appearance, not in disposition, not in speed or energy, but in heart, stamina and adaptability. Like the prospector who commands him, the burro may lie and steal, but he persists. He gets there, regardless of all obstacles, as gaunt and hungry and thirsty as his master, but still on his feet.

The true prospector gives him credit not only for a devilish ingenuity in evading work and obtaining food, but for an uncanny intelligence. The old-timer who has lived with and leaned upon the beast for a third of a century can tell a hundred tales of burro wisdom. Charley Higgins, who has made a study of burros over a thousand miles of desert wastes, and in scores of desert camps, tells one of the best.

"It was at the old camp of Tuscarora, back twenty-five or thirty years ago," says Charley. "Tuscarora was what the magazine writers like to call a 'ghost town.' It was sort of ghostly at that. There were a number of old abandoned shacks and cabins, with the doors and windows fallen in. But there was a little excitement there at this time I'm speaking about, and a number of men were working, and prospectors doing location work on new claims. Down in the flat there must have been fifty or sixty burros roaming around, picking up what they could.

"I needed three or four good burros for a trip I was planning and I went to a prospector I knew and offered to buy his string. He was working then, and didn't need 'em. He said all right, and when he finished his shift he went with me down to the flat and we walked around and he pointed out his burros to me. We made a deal, and next morning I went down to cut out these burros. They weren't there. All the rest of the herd was there, calm as usual, but these four were gone.

"So I went back to my friend and told him. He said I must be mistaken. But I knew I wasn't. I knew burros, and I'd have been able to pick out these four in four hundred after he had pointed them out to me, just as you'd be able to pick out a friend in any crowd. Well, finally he went down with me to see about it, and sure enough the other fifty or sixty burros were scattered down in the flat below the old abandoned cabins, but his burros weren't there. We looked at every animal. At last we gave it up, and started back to camp, figuring I'd have to buy some others.

"But just as I passed one of the old abandoned cabins, I caught a glimpse of a gray nose sticking out through a window. I went in, and what do you suppose? Hiding there in that cabin were those four burros I'd bought. And some folks say a burro is dumb."

Perhaps Charley would not want to be put on record as believing that those four burros knew his plan to put them to work, but you are welcome to your conclusions. On the heels of this story he tells another, with a twinkle in his eye.

One prospector, meeting another in a small temporary camp, asked his friend if he were going to the new strike in the Skull Mountains. It was in the early evening when the burros had come into camp for water, and were standing within ear-shot.

"No," said the second prospector, "I don't reckon I'll go." Half an hour later, however, when the burros had strayed away about their business, he drew the newcomer aside. "Sure, I'll jine ye. I was figgerin' on gettin' an early start in the mornin', an' I didn't want them damn burros to know."

C. B. Glasscock, Gold in Them Hills *(Indianapolis: The Bobbs-Merrill Co., Copyright 1932, by C. B. Glasscock; 1959, by Mrs. Marion T. Glasscock), pp. 186-189*

From Colorado come these stories of the miner's burro above and below ground, as told to me by Levette J. Davidson.

The Rocky Mountain burro, or, as he is sometimes called because of his musical voice, "Rocky Mountain canary," was an essential feature of the early days in prospecting, also in working mines even after the mines had gone underground. Many stories are told of the burros that were stubborn or the burros that were faithful or the burros that were intelligent. One I like is concerning the well-trained burro called Old Tom that one prospector trusted implicitly. He used to ride along the gulches going from one good prospect hole to another to work. One day he went to sleep because it was a warm afternoon. It seemed the burro was dozing off too, although it kept on plodding along the path until it came to the edge of a great precipice, and without wakening, the burro went over, and of course, the prospector on top. As they fell, both came to, and the prospector was quick enough to realize that if they landed they'd both be dead! As they were falling—one hundred, two hundred, three hundred, four hundred feet—the prospector had a little chance to think it over. And so when they got about fifty feet from the ground, he called "Whoa!" And Old Tom just through good training didn't do a thing but stop short! And then the prospector just kind of eased himself off and lowered down, and finally he and Old Tom both were there unhurt on the bottom of the canyon. All he had to do then was to mount Old Tom and the two of them proceeded on their way—all because the prospector had properly trained his burro to obey.

Of course not all burros were that well trained. Some of them were stubborn. In one of the mines there was a trammer who found a new burro balking—wouldn't pull the ore car. So, wondering what he'd do next, he reached into his pocket and pulled out a package of chawin' terbacca. And after taking a chaw himself he noticed that his burro wrinkled up its nose and seemed interested. He reached out the package of Beechnut to his burro. The burro took about twenty cents' worth in one big chaw and with a smile on its face set off to work the rest of the day uncomplaining. Well, this trammer had to buy a lot of chawin' terbacca, but he never had any trouble getting work out of that burro.

One time, though, this trammer decided to change jobs, and he went over to a new mine, and was getting along fine when along came the boss from the old mine. He said: "Look here! You've got a right to change your job, if you want to, but you haven't got no right to take over your trammin' tricks. How on earth do you get that burro to work?"

And of course the trammer said: "Well, I'll tell you. 'Tain't no secret now. But I want to advise you. That burro will do anything you ask if you just give him chawin' terbacca. But be sure and get Beechnut! 'Tain't Horseshoe, nor 'tain't Star! It's Beechnut that does it!"

Recorded by B. A. Botkin in A Treasury of Western Folklore, ed. B. A. Botkin (New York: Crown Publishers, 1951), pp. 656-657.

84. "Lords of the Lash"

To BE A good mule skinner or bullwhacker required nerve and skill plus an ornery authority and mastery of cussing equal to the orneriness and cussedness of the team. Picturesque swearing, in fact, became a special folk art. In *The Golden Hoof* Winifred Kupper tells of the Texas sheep-country teamster whose mules had balked at one of the rare pasture gateways of the region. Unaware that a mail hack had stopped behind him with a preacher as lone passenger, the teamster concluded a stream of colorful invective with: "You goddamned sons of hell, you'd make a goddamned preacher cuss." At that point the preacher got out, walked up behind him, and said sympathetically: "Brother, I believe you're right."

The following is a favorite story of General Sherman's on the secret of the bullwhacker's success with army wagon trains.

One of the members of a freighting firm in St. Louis desired to discourage the continual blasphemy of the bullwhackers in their employ. Orders were accordingly issued to their trainmasters to discharge any man that should curse the cattle. The wagonmasters were selected more for their piety than for any extensive knowledge of their duties in the handling of trains. The outfit had not proceeded more than a hundred and fifty miles before it was stuck fast. A messenger was dispatched to the firm with the information that the cattle would not pull a pound unless they were *cursed as usual*. Permission to do this was requested and granted, after which the train proceeded to Salt Lake, to which place good time was made.

Frederick E. Shearer, ed., The Pacific Tourist (New York: J. R. Bowman, 1882-83), p. 57.

Charles Fletcher Lummis records an example of a New Mexico bullwhacker's oration to his oxen ("New Mexico is the native heath of profanity") when the hind wheels of the wagon in which they were crossing an *arroyo* went down in a quicksand.

"Malditos bueyes! Of ill-said sires and dams! [Nothing intentional here.] *Malaia* your faces! Also your souls, bodies, and tails! [Crack!] That your fathers be accursed, and your mothers three times! [Crack!] Jump, then! May condemnation overtake your ears, and your brand-marks *tambien*! [Crack!] The Evil One take away your sisters and brothers, and the cousin of your grandmother! [Crack! Crack!] That the coyotes may eat your uncles and aunts! *Diablos!* [Crack!] Get out of this! Go, sons of sleeping mothers that were too tired to eat! *Como?* [Crack! Crack!] The fool that broke you, would that he had to drive you in *inferno*, with all your cousins and relations by marriage! [Crack!] Ill-said family, that wear out the yoke with nodding in it! Curse your tallow and hoofs! Would that I had a *chicote* of all your hides at once, to give you blows! [Crack!] *Malaia* your ribs and your knee-joints, and any other bones I may forget! Anathema upon your great-great-grandfathers, and everything else that ever wore horns! *Mal—"*

Here I interposed, for I was slowly freezing, and Tircio was just beginning to get interested. Business before pleasure, always; and the first business was to send him for assistance. The last words I caught, as he trudged off to San Mateo through the storm, were:

"—and your dewlaps and livers! And curse everything from here to Albuquerque and back four times! And—"

Then he faded into the night, while I tried to remember his adjectives to keep warm— for there was nothing wherewith to build a fire.

Charles Fletcher Lummis, A Tramp Across the Continent *(New York: Charles Scribner's Sons, 1892), pp. 178-179.*

Like his oath, the driver's rawhide whip, it is said, was the "longest ever known." When wielded by a skilled skinner the popper on the whip, called the "persuader," could be placed on any desired spot on any animal in the train—the belly with a light flick, the hip with a cutting lash, an ear with a convincing sting. For pastime bullwhackers also hit empty cans in mid-air, setting them spinning. According to J. Frank Dobie in *The Ben Lilly Legend*, Ben could "fleck a fly with his whip cracker off an ox twenty or thirty feet away without disturbing a hair of the ox. . . . He would bet ten dollars that he could pop the loosened tops off ten beer bottles without turning over a bottle. . . . He could pop the tune of 'Yankee Doodle' with his whip. He could pop a grapevine as a makeshift whip."

The Pacific Tourist described a contest in which a coin was placed on top of a stick loosely in the ground. If the bullwhacker could knock the coin off without disturbing the stake, it was his; otherwise he lost the value of the coin.

In the same volume we read of another contest.

A bullwhacker, noted for the accuracy with which he throws his lash . . . bet a comrade a pint of whisky that he could cut the cloth on the back of [the other's] pantaloons without touching the skin beneath. The bet was accepted. The individual put himself in position, stooping over to give fair chance. The blow was delivered carefully but in earnest, and thereon ensued the tallest jump ever put on record, the owner [of the whisky] being minus a portion of his skin, as well as a large fragment of his breeches, and the bull-whacker's sorrowful cry, "Thunder, I've lost the whisky!"

Frederick E. Shearer, ed., The Pacific Tourist *(New York: J. R. Bowman, 1882-83), p. 57.*

Profanity, although officially frowned upon, was also part of the stage driver's stock in trade. Here is how one driver got around the company rule against swearing.

On one occasion . . . a driver was hauling a Methodist minister when they came to a bad ford. The stream, swollen by recent rains, had commenced to recede with the result that the steep banks were slippery. The driver had met such situations before. He stopped his stage and said, "Preacher! I want you to get out and walk across that ford." "Why?" the minister asked. "Well," drawled the driver, "Old Ben told me not to cuss these horses, but I know I can't cross the d——d ford unless I do." The minister obligingly got out, and the driver aided by profanity urged the horses across the stream and up the opposite bank.

J. V. Frederick, Ben Holladay, The Stagecoach King *(Glendale, Calif.: The Arthur H. Clark Co., 1949), p. 74. Reprinted by permission of the publishers.*

As the "kings of the road" who carried the mail, stage drivers were used to having their way, especially with slow wagon trains. To bullwhackers who got in their way stage drivers cried impatiently: "Clar the road! Git out of the way thar with your bull-teams!" "And if this was not complied with quickly," recalls James F. Rusling in *Across America,* "they made no hesitation in running into the oxen, and swearing till all was blue. I have a vivid recollection of one instance of the kind when we ran into an ox-team, and the justly exasperated teamster sent us his compliments in the shape of a bullet whizzing through the air as we whirled away again."

The stage driver also had his way with the passengers, toward whom he maintained a professional silence and dignity befitting his status and the requirements of safety. When an especially silent stage driver came in contact with an especially talkative passenger, the result was bound to be something like that described by Edward Hungerford.

John Blake [was a] stage driver—a sort of Beau Brummel in dress, who was a good fellow, and fairly talkative on the ground, but as silent as a clam when on duty.

On one occasion a traveling salesman had secured a seat on the driver's box beside him. After the start had been made and the stage was well under way, the passenger offered John a cigar, but the only response was a shake of the head. A little later, the passenger began to comment on the weather, upon the scenery, upon John's fine horses and the masterly way he handled them. Still no response. Later in the afternoon the passenger thought he would try again to break through the crust of the Sphinx, and asked: "Mr. Blake, what time do we arrive?" John looked at him for a moment and replied: "There is a clock in the office when we get there."

Edward Hungerford, Wells Fargo *(New York: Random House, 1949), p. 68.*

Hank Monk, the most celebrated of stage drivers, was a great joker. His masterpiece was his famous ride with Horace Greeley from Carson City to Placerville in 1859, following which his saying, "Keep your seat, Mr. Greeley, I'll get you through on time," is said to have gained some currency as a California byword. The "baldheaded anecdote" has been related with embellishments by Bayard Taylor, Albert D. Richardson, J. Ross Browne, Artemus Ward and others. Mark Twain claimed that he heard the story over and over again as he rode the stage. It was

"Stage Coach in the Mountains."
Painting by Ernest Tonk.

told to him by drivers, conductors, passengers, tavern landlords, Chinese and vagrant Indians. He heard it in a babel of tongues "flavored with whisky, brandy, beer, cologne, sozodont, tobacco, garlic, onions, grasshoppers."

Here is Major Ben. C. Truman's version of the incident and its aftermath:

Henry Kinkead, once Governor of Nevada, said to me one day in 1881, while we were being driven by Monk from Glenbrook to Carson: "Hank is greatly overrated as a stage driver. I know scores of better ones. But his getting Horace Greeley across the Sierra and down into Placerville 'on time' gave him great notoriety. It was a dreadful drive, and that it didn't kill the old editor was no fault of Monk's. The road was slow and rough and Hank was full of tarantula juice when he left Carson. Hank was thirty-eight years old. In the goodness of Greeley's heart he presented Hank with a gold watch, which he has many times pawned, sold, and managed to get back. But there were so many ridiculous exaggerations and right up and down falsehoods told of that ride that Greeley became very 'tired,' and in reply to a request of Hank, some twenty years ago, for some favor, Horace wrote: 'I would rather see you 10,000 fathoms in hell than ever give you a crust of bread, for you are the only man who ever had the opportunity to place me in a ridiculous light, and you villainously exercised that opportunity, you damned scamp.'"

Major Ben C. Truman, "Knights of the Lash, Old Time Stage Drivers of the West Coast," in Overland Monthly, XXXI, Second Series (1898), p. 24.

85. *Cow Business*

"THE COW BUSINESS," goes the old cowman's saying, "is a damn fine business for men and mules, but it's hell on horses and women." It is also damn fine for storytelling. With plenty of opportunity to observe nature, animal and human, and to spin and swap yarns at "auguring matches" or story-topping sessions—around the campfire, on ranchhouse porches and in the bunkhouse—cowman and cowpuncher alike became skillful narrators of fanciful tall tales and realistic anecdotes, full of authentic and colorful details of range life.

Range tales are also notable for their "cowboy lingo." In his book of that title Ramon F. Adams notes that, despite changes in methods, dress and accouterments, the comboy still "speaks the same language as his earlier brother and he will cling to this lingo as long as men handle cattle." In the following sayings from Adams' *Cowboy Lingo* and his later volume, *Western Words,* the men who made their living working with horses and cattle gave expression to the philosophy of their calling in the speech that sprang from it:

It's the man that's the cowhand, not the outfit he wears.

You can judge a man by the hoss he rides.

Any hoss's tail kin ketch cockleburs.

Polishin' your pants on saddle leather don't make you a rider.

If the saddle creaks, it's not paid for.

Tossin' your rope before buildin' a loop don't ketch the calf.

It's sometimes safer to pull your freight than pull your gun.

Only a fool argues with a skunk, a mule, or a cook.

There ain't no hoss that can't be rode;
There ain't no man that can't be throwed.

Brains in the head saves blisters on the feet.

The bigger the mouth, the better it looks when shut.

Man's the only animal that can be skinned more'n once.

The man that always straddles the fence usually has a sore crotch.

Ramon F. Adams, Western Words *(Norman: University of Oklahoma Press, 1944), passim.*

Y'u never can trust women, fleas, nor tenderfoots.

Ramon F. Adams, Cowboy Lingo *(Boston: Houghton Mifflin Co., 1936), pp. 232, 238.*

"You'd think a puncher growed horns an' was haired over," observes Rawhide Rawlins in Charles Edward Russell's *Trails Plowed Under*. But the cowboy on a spree played up to this popular image of his animal proclivities in his boasting chants and yells, in which the ringtailed roarer or half horse, half alligator of the Davy Crockett and Mike Fink tradition rides again. The following examples given to me by Walter R. Smith of St. Louis, Oklahoma, are variants of Southwest brags heard in the seventies and eighties:

Half horse, half alligator, with a little touch of snapping turtle, clumb a streak of lightning, and slid down a locust tree a hundred feet high, with a wild cat under each arm and never got a scratch. Whoopee-yip-ho!

I come to this country riding a lion, whipping him over the head with a .45 and picking my teeth with a .38 and wearing a .45 on each hip, using a cactus for a piller, whe-ee-e! I'm a two-gun man and a very bad man and won't do to monkey with. Whe-ee-o, I'm a bad man! Whoopee!

Raised in the backwoods, suckled by a polar bear, nine rows of jaw teeth, a double coat of hair, steel ribs, wire intestine, and a barbed wire tail, and I don't give a dang where I drag it. Whoopee-whee-a-ha!

B. A. Botkin, "Tall Talk and Tall Tales of the Southwest," in The New Mexico Candle, Las Vegas, June 28, 1933.

"Late Summer Range." Painting by Ernest Tonk.

GRAND CENTRAL ART GALLERIES, NEW YORK

Among range trickster tales the story of cheating a greenhorn cattle buyer by counting cattle more than once is a staple. As Frank Benton tells the tale, Senator Dorsey had a little herd of cattle in northern New Mexico, which he represented to some glass-eyed Englishmen as a large herd, for sale at twenty-five dollars a head. The Englishmen insisted on counting the herd instead of taking the Senator's books for them. The Senator agreed and went to his foreman, Jack Hill.

"Jack," he said, "I want you to find me a small mountain around which a herd of cattle can be circled several times in one day. This mountain must have a kind of natural stand where men can get a good count on cattle stringing by but where they can't possibly get a view of what is going on outside. Sabe?"

Jack selected a little round mountain with a canyon on one side of it. Here on the bank of the canyon he stationed the Englishmen and their bookkeepers and Senator Dorsey. The Senator had only about 1,000 cattle, and these Jack and the cowboys separated into two bunches out in the hills. Keeping the two herds about a mile apart, they now drove the first herd into the canyon. . . . It was hardly out of sight before the second bunch came stringing along. Meantime cowboys galloped the first herd around back of the mountain and had them coming down the canyon past the Englishmen again for a second count. And they were hardly out of sight before the second division was around the mountain and coming along to be tallied again. Thus the good work went on all morning, the Senator and the Englishmen having only a few minutes to snatch a bite and tap fresh bottles.

At noon Dorsey's foreman told the English party that his men were yet holding an enormous herd back in the hills from which they were cutting off these small bunches of 500 and bringing them along to be tallied. But about three o'clock in the afternoon the cattle began to get thirsty and footsore. Every critter had already traveled thirty miles that day, and lots of them began to drop out and lie down. In one of the herds was an old yellow steer. He was bobtailed, lophorned, and had a game leg. When for the fifteenth time he limped by the crowd that was counting, milord screwed his eyeglass a little tighter on his eye and says:

"There is more bloody, blarsted, lophorned, bobtailed, yellow crippled brutes than anything else, it seems."

Milord's dogrobber speaks up and says, "But, me lord, there's no hanimal like 'im hin the other 'erd."

The Senator overheard this interesting conversation, and, taking the foreman aside, told him when they got that herd on the other side of the mountain again to cut out the old yellow reprobate and not let him come by again. So Jack cut him out and ran him off a ways. But old yellow had got trained to going around that mountain, and the herd wasn't any more than tallied again till here come old Buck, as the cowboys called him, limping down the canyon, the Englishmen staring at him with open mouths and Senator Dorsey looking at old Jack Hill in a reproachful, grieved kind of way. The cowboys ran old Buck off still farther next time, but half an hour afterwards he appeared over a little rise and slowly limped by again.

The Senator now announced that there was only one herd more to count and signalled to Jack to ride around and stop the cowboys. . . . But as the party broke up and started for the ranch, old Buck came by again, looking like he was in a trance. That night the cowboys said the Senator was groaning in his sleep in a frightful way, and when one of them woke him up and asked if he was sick, he told them, while big drops of cold sweat dropped off his face, that he'd had a terrible nightmare. He said that he thought he was yoked up with a yellow, bobtailed, lophorned, lame steer and was being dragged by the animal through a canyon and around a mountain, day after day, in a hot, broiling sun, while crowds of witless Englishmen and jibbering cowboys were looking on. He insisted on saddling up and going back through the moonlight to the mountain to see if old Buck was still there. A cowboy went with him and after they had got to the canyon and waited a while they heard something coming. Sure enough, directly in the bright moonlight they saw old Buck painfully limping along, stopping now and then to rest.

A week later a cowboy reported finding old Buck dead on his well-worn trail. No one ever rides that way on moonlight nights now, for the cowboys have a tradition that during each full moon old Buck's ghost still limps down the canyon.

Frank Benton, Cowboy Life on the Sidetrack *(Denver: The Western Stories Syndicate, 1903), cited in J. Frank Dobie,* A Vaquero of the Brush Country *(Dallas: The Southwest Press, 1929), pp. 165-166.*

The lore of the longhorn has its other sagas of steer heroes and villains. Among the heroes were Old Sancho, the returner, who loved his home in Texas so well that he walked all the way back from Wyoming to Esperanza Creek in Frio County. There was also Old Blue, the lead steer, who led Charles Goodnight's herds up the trail from Pablo Duro to Dodge City. Among the villains were the steers branded Murder and Ruidoso (Noisy), the Ghost Steer of the Pecos.

To summarize what happened before Jack Potter took charge of Ruidoso in 1888: It had all started back in the 1870's when John Chisum of the Jingle Bob Ranch, South Spring, New Mexico, made decoys out of several oversized bull mavericks, branded with the "rail" brand. One of these was found by Bob Ollinger who branded him with the "skull and bones" brand, named him Ruidoso (Noisy) and put a curse on him. There followed a string of tragedies beginning with the Lincoln County Cattle War, in which Ollinger himself was killed by Billy the Kid during the latter's escape from the Lincoln County jail. Among Ruidoso's other victims was Clay Allison, who was thrown from his wagon and broke his neck when Ruidoso scared his mules and started a runaway.

In 1888, when Ruidoso was in his eleventh year, he was declared public property and condemned to be auctioned and sold to the highest bidder along with other strays, according to a law passed by the territorial legislature. At the close of the roundup time, when the herds were being shaped up, all the bosses save Potter refused to handle Ruidoso with their outfits.

After finding out that I was the only trail boss that would volunteer to take old Ruidoso to the shipping point, I went over to the herd and contacted him. I said: "Ruidoso, you old outlaw devil: you might think that I have come over here to give you a big cussin'. Not so. I just want to give you a lecture. You must remember that you have blazed a trail of tragedies west of the Pecos, but now at your age you are supposed to be what you might call a 'has been.' But one thing sure, you cannot hide your identity with all them ugly brands on your hide, including the skull and bones. It looks to me like as if you ever returned to your range you will be in a can labeled 'Corned Beef'; nevertheless your old hide will be placed in the State Historical Museum at Santa Fe, to show posterity those brands which give your career in the bloody Lincoln County War. I do not care how old and ragged you are. Your kind never lose their instinct and knowledge of storms and directions. I think that you will be a valuable asset in piloting my herd across a pathless plains country with watering places far apart, which calls for night drives, and I must admit that I have never trailed at night only under the North Star. Now I'm going to depend on you, and I'll expect you to behave yourself and not start anything."

Ruidoso was a valuable asset and we blazed one of the straightest trails in history to Amarillo.

In making this drive I had the same trouble with my cowboys as I had had on former drives. They would bunch up and tell their grievances to one another. They would say that the old lead steer had the boss coming his way. One of them said: "I'm afraid this drive will wind up like Coronado's expedition, with that damned Indian leading him to the Gran Quivira, or the Seven Cities of the Cibola. I figure it is time for us to take some action in defense of ourselves."

Nevertheless the drive went on without incident and we arrived at Amarillo, a new town built down in a lake bed.

We shaped up our herd and loaded it out with a consignment to the L. A. Allen Livestock Commission Company in Kansas City. I sent a letter along advising them how to handle the proceeds of the Ruidoso steer as he was public property.

When I arrived back at Fort Sumner with my crew, everybody congratulated me on the success of the drive. "But have you heard the news?" they asked. "How could you expect us to hear anything?" I asked them. "You're the first people we have seen since leaving Amarillo."

Well, it seemed that within ten hours after the cattle train pulled out of Amarillo there was a wreck and the cattle and crew were lost, including old Ruidoso. As the version goes now, this was a curse on the new town of Amarillo and the next year its location was moved to the present site.

Nor was that the last heard of Ruidoso. Strange stories were told in the towns and camps of a terrible bellowing in the breaks and on the plains. Old Vicinte Otero of Fort Sumner was supposed to be the first man to see and hear old Ruidoso (or his ghost) after the wreck. It made a terrible impression on him. He would get down on his knees and bellow like old Ruidoso and the boys became convinced that he was connected with the devil.

The ghost of Ruidoso ranged over a wide territory. He was first heard on top of a mountain which lies in sight of Tascosa—a mountain full of tradition and legend called "El Sierrito de La Vera Crus" (little mountain of the Holy Cross).

During the next few years following the train wreck the voice of the Ghost Steer was heard from Monnihan Wells on the staked Plains to Anton Chico on the Pecos.

The climax of this Ghost Steer's career came one night in the neighborhood of Blazer's Mill and the burial ground of such Lincoln County War victims as Buckshot Roberts, Dick Brewer, and Bob Ollinger.

The Mescalero Indians in the vicinity were highly superstitious and had heard of the Ghost of Ruidoso.

Colonel A. J. Fountain had just gotten through investigating some cattle stealing cases with good results and was ready to start back to Las Cruces, from Lincoln County with his young son. An old Mescalero buck stopped them and told them he had heard the Ghost Steer bellow three nights over toward Blazer's Mill and the burial ground, and just the previous night a light flashed over the reservation to the west and in that flash could be seen the images of the Ghost Steer, Bob Ollinger, and Buckshot Roberts. The Colonel laughed at the Indian's warning and went on his way. That was the last time Colonel Fountain and his son were seen alive. The tragedy of their disappearance is still unsolved.

And this brings to an end the strange tale of Ruidoso, Ghost Steer of the Pecos.

Colonel Jack Potter, "Ruidoso, Ghost Steer of the Pecos," in The Cattleman, Fort Worth, Texas, XXXVII (1950), pp. 58, 60-61.

86. *Singing Cowboys*

ONCE IN SAN ANTONIO, recalls Colonel Jack Potter in Floyd Streeter's *The Kaw*, he applied to Ab Blocker for a job. The famous trail boss asked him: "Can you ride a pitching bronc? Can you rope a horse out of the remuda without throwing the loop around your own head? Are you good-natured? In case of a stampede at night, would you drift along in front or circle the cattle to a mill? . . . Just one more question: can you sing?"

As Jack Potter learned to his dismay, the cattle couldn't stand his singing. Every time he went on guard and sang, the cattle would get up and mill around the bed ground. But as soon as Ab Blocker began singing, the cattle commenced to lie down. Potter was fired.

Another old-timer, Edward Charles ("Teddy Blue") Abbott was more successful. He could not only sing but also make up verses—"anything that came into your head." He had a hand in composing the "Ogallaly Song," as he tells in *We Pointed Them North*. This was "just made up as the trail went north by men singing on night guard, with a verse for every river on the trail," starting from the Nueces in Texas and ending with the Yellowstone in Montana. "When I first heard it it only went as far as Ogallaly on the South Platte, which is why I called it the Ogallaly song."

Considering that so few cowboys could sing and that it wasn't the quality of the singing that counted—just the reassuring sound of a familiar voice or even a humming or whistling or yodeling—it is a wonder that cowboy songs are as good as they are. As a matter of fact, most cowboy songs, especially cowboy ballads, were written by known (if forgotten) cowboy poets, to older tunes.

Except as they help to soothe restless cattle or to keep them moving, cowboy songs are not true work songs like sailor's chanteys and Negro gang songs (which keep time to the work and are of the leader-and-chorus instead of solo type). They are more like lumberjack songs—occupational and recreational songs—in which men sing about their work and play and express certain occupational attitudes. Cowboy songs have the freedom, casualness and uncomplicated quality of the cowboy's life. Because the cowboy's subjects are so few and basic, he has mastered them and can handle them simply and sincerely.

As the Chisholm Trail from Texas to Kansas was the classic cattle trail, so the song that takes its name from the trail is the classic trail song. The easy swing of the tune is deceptive considering the cowboy's troubles on the trail—weather, food, boss, pay. The list may be extended by adding stanzas.

The Old Chisholm Trail

2. Oh, a ten-dollar hoss and a forty-dollar saddle,
   And I'm goin' to punchin' Texas cattle.

3. I wake in the mornin' afore daylight
   And afore I sleep the moon shines bright.

4. It's cloudy in the west, a-lookin' like rain,
   And my durned old slicker's in the wagon again.

5. No chaps, no slicker, and it's pourin' down rain,
   And I swear, by gosh, I'll never night-herd again.

6. Feet in the stirrups and seat in the saddle,
   I hung and rattled with them long-horn cattle.

7. The wind commenced to blow, and the rain began to fall,
   Hit looked, by grab, like we was goin' to lose 'em all.

8. I don't give a darn if they never do stop;
   I'll ride as long as an eight-day clock.

9. We rounded 'em up and put 'em on the cars,
   And that was the last of the old Two Bars.

10. Oh, it's bacon and beans most every day,
    I'd as soon be a-eatin' prairie hay.

11. I went to the boss to draw my roll,
    He had it figgered out I was nine dollars in the hole.

12. Goin' back to town to draw my money,
    Goin' back home to see my honey.

13. With my knees in the saddle and my seat in the sky,
    I'll quit punchin' cows in the sweet by and by.

Alan Lomax, Charles Seeger, and Ruth Crawford Seeger, eds., American Songs for American Children
(Chicago: Music Educators National Conference, 1942), pp 8-9.

A dogie is originally "a calf whose mammy has gone off and left it and whose daddy has took up with another cow"; then, loosely, any young animal or even any of the herd that has a claim on the cowboy's affection, as in "Git Along, Little Dogies."

Git Along Little Dogies

2. Some fellows goes up the trail for pleasure,
    But that's where they've got it most awfully wrong,
   For you haven't an idea the trouble they give us,
    As we go a-driving them dogies along.

3. Oh, you'll be soup for Uncle Sam's Injuns,
    "It's beef, heap beef," I hear them cry.
   Git along, git along, you lazy little mavericks,
    You're going to be beef steers by and by.

4. The night's coming on, we'll hold them on the bedground,
    These little dogies that roll on so slow.
   Round up the herd and cut out the strays,
    And roll the little dogies that never rolled before.

Margaret Larkin and Helen Black, Singing Cowboy *(New York: Alfred A. Knopf, 1931), pp. 96-97.*

"The Texas Cowboy" tells of the Texan's gripe against the Montana winter and Montana ways.

2. Montana is too cold for me,
      The winters are too long,
   Before the roundups do begin,
      Your money is all gone.

3. I've worked down in Nebraska,
      Where the grass grows ten feet high,
   And the cattle are such rustlers,
      They seldom ever die.

4. I've worked up in the sand hills,
      And down upon the Platte,
   Where the cowboys are good fellows,
      And the cattle always fat.

5. I've travelled lots of country,
      Nebraska's hills of sand,
   Down through the Indian Nation
      And up the Rio Grande.

6. But the Bad Lands of Montana
      Are the worst I've ever seen,
   The cowboys are all tenderfeet,
      The dogies are all lean.

7. Work in Montana
      Is six months in the year,
   When all your bills are settled,
      There's nothing left for beer.

8. Come all you Texas cowboys,
      And warning take from me,
   And do not go to Montana
      To spend your money free.

Margaret Larkin and Helen Black, eds., Singing Cowboy *(New York: Alfred A. Knopf, 1931), pp. 54-55.*

In "The Horse Wrangler" the tenderfoot has his say if not his way. Also known as "The Tenderfoot," the song is by D. J. O'Malley, of Eau Claire, Wisconsin, who first published it in the Miles City, Montana, *Stock Growers' Journal* of February 3, 1894, under the pseudonym, R. J. Stovall—said to be a friend who "wished to surprise his wife in Denver by blossoming out as a poet."

The Horse Wrangler

cows was done; So when the round - up had be - gun, I tack - led the cat - tle king. Says he: "My fore - man's gone to town; He's in a sa - loon and his name is Brown. If you see him, he'll take you down," Says I, "That's just the thing."—

2. We started for the ranch next day:
   Brown argered me most all the way.
   He said that cow-punching was nothing but play,
   That it was no work at all—
   That all you had to do was ride,
   'Twas only drifting with the tide;
   The son of a gun, oh, how he lied!
   Don't you think he had his gall?

3. He put me in charge of a cavyard,
   And told me not to work too hard,
   That all I had to do was guard
   The horses from getting away;
   I had one hundred and sixty head,
   I sometimes wished that I was dead;
   When one got away, Brown's head turned red,
   And there was the devil to pay.

4. Sometimes one would make a break,
   Across the prairie he would take,
   As if running for a stake—
   It seemed to them but play;
   Sometimes I could not head them all,
   Sometimes my horse would catch a fall
   And I'd shoot on like a cannon ball
   Till the earth came in my way.

5. They saddled me up an old gray hack
   With two set-fasts on his back,
   They padded him down with a gunny sack
   And used my bedding all.
   When I got on he quit the ground,
   Went up in the air and turned around,
   And I came down and busted the ground—
   I got one hell of a fall.

6. They took me up and carried me in
   And rubbed me down with an old stake pin.
   "That's the way they all begin;
   You're doing well," says Brown.
   "And in the morning, if you don't die,
   I'll give you another horse to try."
   "Oh, say, can't I walk?" says I.
   Say he, "Yes, back to town."

7. I've traveled up and I've traveled down,
   I've traveled this country round and round,
   I've lived in city and I've lived in town,
   But I've got this much to say:
   Before you try cow-punching, kiss your wife,
   Take a heavy insurance on your life,
   Then cut your throat with a barlow knife—
   For it's easier done that way.

"The Horse Wrangler," collected, adapted, & arranged by John A. & Alan Lomax.
Copyright 1938, by Ludlow Music, Inc., New York, N. Y. Used by permission.

Sam Bass was the cowboy's favorite Robin Hood and good cowboy gone wrong. In his book, *Sam Bass,* Wayne Gard touches on typical aspects of the outlaw's legend—his innumerable hideouts, his generosity with twenty-dollar gold pieces, his buried riches. His life and legend inspired this ballad:

Sam Bass

Sam Bass was born in In - di - an - a, It was his na - tive

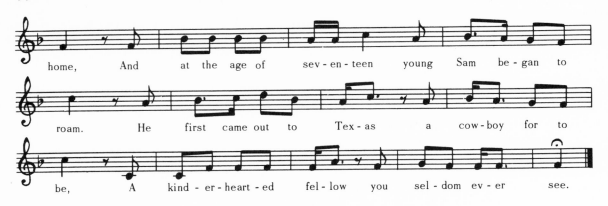

home, And at the age of sev-en-teen young Sam be-gan to

roam. He first came out to Tex-as a cow-boy for to

be, A kind-er-heart-ed fel-low you sel-dom ev-er see.

2. Sam used to deal in race stock, he owned the Denton mare,
He matched her in scrub races and took her to the Fair.
He fairly coined the money and spent it frank and free.
He always drank good whiskey wherever he might be.

3. Sam left where he was working one pretty morning in May,
A-heading for the Black Hills with his cattle and his pay.
Sold out in Custer City and then got on a spree,
A harder set of cowboys oyu seldom ever see.

4. A-riding back to Texas they robbed the U. P. train,
For safety split in couples and started out again.
Joe Collins and his partner were overtaken soon,
With all their hard-earned money they had to meet their doom.

5. Sam made it back to Texas all right side up with care,
Rode into the town of Denton with all his friends to share.
Sam's life was short in Texas; three robberies did he do,
The passenger and Express cars and U. S. Mail Car too.

6. Now Sam he had four partners, all dring, bold, and bad,
There was Richardson and Jackson, Joe Collins and Old Dad.
Four more bold and daring cowboys the Rangers never knew;
They whipped the Texas Rangers and dodged the boys in blue.

7. Sam had another companion called Arkansas for short,
But Thomas Floyd, the Ranger, cut his career quite short.
Oh, Tom is a big six-footer and think's he's mighty fly,
But I can tell you his racket, —he's a deadbeat on the sly.

8. Jim Murphy was arrested and then let out on bail,
He jumped the train for Terrell after breaking Tyler jail.
Old Major Jones stood in with Jim and it was all a stall,
A put-up job to catch poor Sam, before the coming Fall.

9. Sam met his fate at Round Rock, July the twenty-first.
They pierced poor Sam with rifle balls and emptied out his purse.
Poor Sam he is a dead cowboy and six feet under clay,
And Jackson's in the mesquite trying to get away.

10. Jim had borrowed Sam's good gold and didn't want to pay,
His only idea it was to give brave Sam away.
He sold out Sam and Barnes and left their friends to mourn,
Oh, what a scorching Jim will get when Gabriel blows his horn.

11. Perhaps he's got to heaven, there's none of us can say,
But if I'm right in my surmise he's gone the other way.

♪ *Margaret Larkin and Helen Black, eds.,* Singing Cowboy *(New York: Alfred A. Knopf, 1931), pp. 162-164.*

87. *Settlers' Songs*

The Handcart Song

"THE LORD, THROUGH his prophet, says of the poor, 'Let them come on foot, with handcarts or wheelbarrows; let them gird up their loins, and walk through, and nothing shall hinder them.'" These words, from the epistle to the Saints issued by the Mormon Church in 1855, inspired the handcart migration of 1856–60—a saga unique in the annals of the Overland Trail. Unique, too, in western folk song were the handcart songs with which the Mormons cheered themselves on their march. The peculiar circumstances of the handcart journey (including the tragic suffering and fatalities of the fourth and fifth companies which started out in July, 1856, and were overtaken by winter) have given the handcart songs a special folk character, part hymn, part social song, combining religious dedication with pioneer cooperation and cheerfulness.

The best known of the handcart songs is the marching song with the refrain beginning, "Some must push and some must pull." The following version was recorded by Austin and Alta Fife from the singing of L. M. Hilton of Ogden, Utah. Mr. Hilton comments, "It's been a song that every one loved to sing in Utah ever since pioneer days."

Some Must Push and Some Must Pull

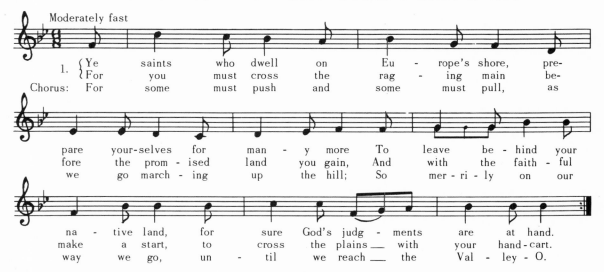

2. The lands that boast of modern light,
   We known are all as dark as night,
   Where poor men toil and want for bread,
   Where peasant hosts are blindly led.
   These lands that boast of liberty
   You ne'er again would wish to see,
   When you from Europe make a start
   To cross the plains with your handcart.

3. As on the road the carts are pulled,
   'Twould very much surprise the world
   To see the old and feeble dame
   Thus lend a hand to pull the same;
   And maidens fair will dance and sing,
   Young men more happy than the king,
   And children, too, will laugh and play,
   Their strength increasing day by day.

4. But some will say, "It is too bad,
   The saints upon the foot to pad,
   And more than that, to pull a load
   As they go marching o'er the road."
   But then we say, "It is the plan
   To gather up the best of men,
   And women, too, for none but they
   Will ever travel in this way."

5. And long before the valley's gained,
   We will be met upon the plain
   With music sweet and friends so dear,
   And fresh supplies our hearts to cheer;
   And then with music and with song,
   How cheerfully we'll march along,
   And thank the day we made a start
   To cross the plains with our handcarts.

6. When you get there among the rest,
   Obedient be and you'll be blessed,
   And in God's chambers be shut in,
   While judgments cleanse the earth from sin;
   For we do know it will be so,
   God's servant spoke it long ago.
   We say it is high time to start
   To cross the plains with our handcarts.

B. A. Botkin, ed., A Treasury of Western Folklore *(New York: Crown Publishers, 1951), pp. 753-754. Transcribed by Ruth Crawford Seeger from record in Archive of Folk Song, Library of Congress, Washington, D. C.*

Railroad Songs

Many Mormons feared that the coming of the railroad would mean the end of their isolation and their religion, but Brigham Young, who saw both the immediate and long-range possibilities, said, "A religion that can't stand a railroad isn't worth its salt." Accordingly, he signed contracts with both the Central Pacific and the Union Pacific. To their grading work in Weber and Echo canyons the Mormons brought their usual zeal and good humor. The following version of "Echo Canyon," sung by L. M. Hilton, Ogden, Utah, in 1946, was recorded by Austin and Alta Fife.

Echo Canyon

2. Now there's Mister Reed, he's a gentleman too,
   He knows very well what we Mormons can do.
   He knows in our work we are faithful and true,
   And if Mormon boys start it, it's bound to go through.

3. Our camp is united, we all labor hard,
   And if we are faithful we'll gain our reward.
   Our leader is wise and a great leader, too,
   And a things he tells us, we're right glad to do.

4. The boys in our camp are light-hearted and gay,
   We work on the railroad ten hours a day.
   We're thinking of fine times we'll have in the fall
   When we'll be with our ladies and go to the ball.

5. We surely must live in a very fast age.
   We've traveled by ox team and then took the stage.
   But when such conveyance is all done away,
   We'll travel in steam cars upon the railway.

6. The great locomotive next season will come
   To gather the saints from their far distant home,
   And bring them to Utah in peace here to stay
   While the judgments of God sweep the wicked away.

B. A. Botkin, ed., A Treasury of Western Folklore (New York: Crown Publishers, 1951), pp. 752-753. Transcribed by Ruth Crawford Seeger from record in Archive of Folk Song, Library of Congress, Washington, D. C.

Of Gentile origin is the comic song, "Zack the Mormon Engineer," as sung by L. M. Hilton, of Ogden, Utah, and recorded by Willard Rhodes.

Zack the Mormon Engineer

Moderate

1. Old Zack, he came to U-tah, way___ back in Seven-ty-three.
A right good Mor-mon gen-tle-man and a bish-op, too, was he.
He drove a lo-co-mo-tive for the D. and R.___ G.
With wo-men he was pop-u-lar as pop-u-lar could be.

Chorus
And when he'd whis-tle, Hoo!___ Hoo!___ Ma-ma'd un-der-stand
That Zack was head-ed home-ward on the Den-ver'n Ri-o Grande.

2. Old Zack, he had a wif-ey in_____ ev-ery rail-road town.
3. Old Zack, he claimed to love his wives and love them all the same,

No mat-ter where he stopped he had a place to lay him down.
But al-ways lit-tle Ma-bel was the one that Zack would name.

And when his train was com-ing, he want-ed her to know,
And as he would pass her, he'd blow his whis-tle loud,

So　　　as　he passed each wif-ey's home　　his　　whis-tle　he　would blow.
And　　when she'd throw a　kiss　to him,　　old　　Zack would look　so　proud.

> 4. Now listen, everybody, because this story's true.
> Old Zack, he had a wife in every town that he passed through.
> They tried to make him transfer on to the old UP,
> But Zack said "No," because his wives were on the D. and
> R. G.

B. A. Botkin and Alvin F. Harlow, eds., A Treasury of Railroad Folklore *(New York: Crown Publishers, 1953), p. 444. From* Mormon Folk Songs, *recorded and notes by Willard Rhodes, Folkways Records, Album No. FP 36 A6 (New York: Folkways Records & Service Corp., 1952).*

The plight of the "boomer" railroad construction worker on the short lines of the pioneer West is described in "Way Out in Idaho."

Way Out in Idaho

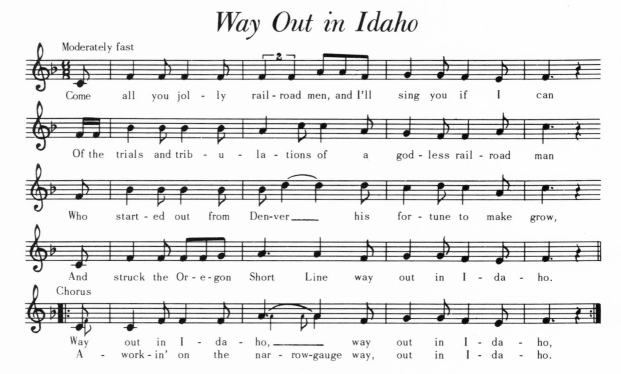

Come　all　you jol-ly　rail-road men, and I'll　sing you if　I　can

Of the　trials and trib-u-la-tions of　a　god-less rail-road　man

Who　start-ed out　from　Den-ver___　his　for-tune to　make　grow,

And　struck the Or-e-gon　Short　Line　way　out　in　I-da-ho.

Chorus

Way　　out in I-da-ho,___　　way　out　in　I-da-ho,
A-work-in' on　the　nar-row-gauge way,　out　in　I-da-ho.

2. I was roaming around in Denver one luckless rainy day
   When Kilpatrick's man, Catcher, stepped up to me and did say,
   I'll lay you down five dollars as quickly as I can
   And you'll hurry up and catch the train, she's starting for Cheyenne."

3. He laid me down five dollars, like many another man,
   And I started for the depot as happy as a clam;
   When I got to Pocatello, my troubles began to grow,
   A-wading through the sagebrush in frost and rain and snow.

4. When I got to American Falls, it was there I met Fat Jack.
   He said he kept a hotel in a dirty canvas shack.
   "We hear you are a stranger and perhaps your funds are low.
   Well, yonder stands my hotel tent, the best in Idaho."

5. I followed my conductor into his hotel tent,
   And for one square and hearty meal I paid him my last cent;
   But Jack's a jolly fellow, and you'll always find him so,
   A-workin' on the narrow-gauge way out in Idaho.

6. They put me to work next morning with a cranky cuss called Bill,
   And they gave me a ten-pound hammer to strike upon a drill.
   They said if I didn't like it I could take my shirt and go,
   And they'd keep my blanket for my board way out in Idaho.

7. It filled my heart with pity as I walked along the track
   To see so many old bummers with their turkeys on their backs.
   They said the work was heavy and the grub they couldn't go.
   Around Kilpatrick's tables way out in Idaho.

8. But now I'm well and happy, down in the harvest camps,
   And there I will continue till I make a few more stamps.
   I'll go down to New Mexico and I'll marry the girl I know,
   And I'll buy me a horse and buggy and go back to Idaho.

Collected, adapted, & arranged by John A. & Alan Lomax. Copyright 1941, by Ludlow Music, Inc., New York, N. Y. Used by permission.

Homesteading Songs

The railroads engaged in active campaigns to attract settlers to the West's open spaces. Homesteaders came by the thousands, invading the cattleman's paradise of free land, grass and water. The cowboy's uncomplimentary name for these immigrants was "nesters." According to John M. Hendrix, as cited in Ramon F. Adams' *Western Words,* "Viewed from some ridge, the early nester's home, as he cleared his little patch of brush and stacked it in a circular form to protect his first feed patch from range cattle, looked like a gigantic bird's nest. . . . The name spread and stuck to every man that settled on the plains to till the soil."

In "The Wyoming Nester," the cowboy says hail and farewell to the "drylander." The first stanza is sometimes used as a chorus.

The Wyoming Nester

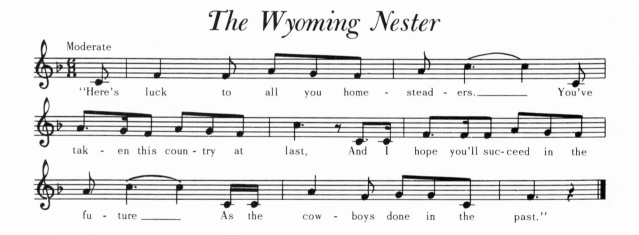

"Here's luck to all you home-stead-ers.____ You've tak-en this coun-try at last, And I hope you'll suc-ceed in the fu-ture ____ As the cow-boys done in the past."

2. "You've homesteaded all of this country,
   Where the slicks and the mavericks did roam;
   You've driven me far from my country,
   Far from my birthplace and home.

3. "The cattle are still getting thinner,
   And the ranches are shorter on men,
   But I've got me a full quart of whisky
   And nearly a full quart of gin.

4. "You have taken up all of the water
   And all of the land that's nearby—"
   And he took a big drink from his bottle
   Of good old '99 rye.

5. He rode far into the evening,
   His limbs at last had grown tired.
   He shifted himself in his saddle,
   And he slowly hung down his head.

6. His saddle he used for a pillow;
   His blanket he used for a bed,
   As he lay himself down for a night's slumber
   These words he to himself then said:

7. "I'm leaving this grand state forever,
   This land and the home of my birth.
   It fills my heart with sorrow,
   But it fills your heart with mirth."

J. Frank Dobie, "More Ballads and Songs of Frontier Folk," in Foller de Drinkin' Gou'd, *edited by J. Frank Dobie (Austin: The Texas Folklore Society, 1928), pp. 175-176.*

The drylander was as much of a gambler as the prospector. As the saying went, "The government bets title to 320 acres against your filing fee that you'll starve before proving up—and the government usually wins." And the gamble proved to be a battle—against drought, searing high winds, cyclones, prairie fires, blizzards, grasshopper plagues and human as well as animal predators.

To the tune of "Beulah Land" the busted sodbusters sang "Dakota Land" (or "Nebraska Land," as the case might be)—the "psalm of a desolate people," according to Carl Sandburg.

Dakota Land

We've reached the land of des-ert sweet, Where noth-ing grows for man to eat, The wind it blows with fev-'rish heat A-cross the plains so hard to beat.

Chorus

O Da-ko-ta land, sweet Da-ko-ta land As on thy fier-y soil I stand, I look a-cross the plains, And won-der why it nev-er rains, Till Ga-briel blows his trum-pet sound, And says the rain's just gone a-round.

2. We've reached the land of hills and stones
   Where all is strewn with buffalo bones.
   O buffalo bones, bleached buffalo bones,
   I seem to hear your sighs and moans.

3. We have no wheat, we have no oats,
   We have no corn to feed our shoats;
   Our chickens are so very poor
   They beg for crumbs outside the door.

4. Our horses are of bronco race;
   Starvation stares them in the face.
   We do not live, we only stay;
   We are too poor to get away.

Carl Sandburg, The American Songbag (*New York: Harcourt, Brace & World, Inc., 1927*), *pp. 280-281.*

In 1904 the Kinkaid Act increased the size of homesteads in western Nebraska to 640 acres. According to Mari Sandoz in *Old Jules* the first Kinkaiders said of the sand-hill country, "The cattlemen should be paid to live in it." Yet at picnics and reunions to the tune of "Maryland, My Maryland," the Kinkaiders sang the praises of their benefactor, Moses P. Kinkaid, and of the garden they hoped to make out of the "new Great American Desert."

Kinkaiders' Song

2. The corn we raise is our delight,
   The melons, too, are out of sight.
   Potatoes grown are extra fine
   And can't be beat in any clime.

3. The peaceful cows in pastures dream
   And furnish us with golden cream,
   So I shall keep my Kinkaid home
   And never far away shall roam.

Chorus 2:

Then let us all with hearts sincere
Thank him for what has brought us here,
And for the homestead law he made,
This noble Moses P. Kinkaid.

Carl Sandburg, The American Songbag *(New York: Harcourt, Brace & World, Inc., 1927), pp. 278-279.*

On the treeless prairie the settler's new home was a "little old sod shanty," as described in this adaptation of Will S. Hays' "The Little Old Log Cabin in the Lane" (1871). Louise Pound attributes the parody to a Nebraskan, Emery Miller, who wrote it while holding down a claim in the Eighties.

Little Old Sod Shanty

Moderately fast

I am look-ing rath-er seed-y now while hold-ing down my claim,

And my vic-tuals are not al-ways served the best;

And the mice play shy-ly round me as I nes-tle down to rest,

In my lit-tle old sod shan-ty in the West.

The hin-ges are of leath-er and the win-dows have no glass,

While the board roof lets the howl-ing bliz-zards in,

And I hear the hun-gry coy-ote as he slinks up through the grass

Round my lit-tle old sod shan-ty on my claim.

2. Yet I rather like the novelty of living in this way,
   Though my bill of fare is always rather tame,
   But I'm happy as a clam on the land of Uncle Sam
   In the little old sod shanty on my claim.
   But when I left my Eastern home, a bachelor so gay,
   To try and win my way to wealth and fame,
   I little thought I'd come down to burning twisted hay
   In the little old sod shanty on my claim.

3. My clothes are plastered o'er with dough, I'm looking like a fright,
   And everything is scattered round the room,
   But I wouldn't give the freedom that I have out in the West
   For the table of the Eastern man's old home.
   Still I wish that some kindhearted girl would pity on me take,
   And relieve me from the mess than I am in;
   The angel how I'd bless her if this her home she'd make
   In the little old sod shanty on my claim.

4. And we would make our fortune on the prairies of the West,

      Just as happy as two lovers we'd remain;

  We'd forget the trials and troubles we endured at the first,

      In the little old sod shanty on my claim.

  And if fate should bless us with now and then an heir,

      To cheer our hearts with honest pride of fame,

  Oh, then we'd be contented for the toil that we had spent

      In the little old sod shanty on our claim.

B. A. Botkin, ed., A Treasury of Western Folklore (New York: Crown Publishers, 1951), pp. 742-743. Sung by Clyde (Slim) Wilson, Springfield, Mo. Recorded by Sidney Robertson. Transcribed by Ruth Crawford Seeger from record in Archive of Folk Song, Library of Congress, Washington, D. C.

A companion to "The Little Old Sod Shanty" is "Starving to Death on a Government Claim," or "The Lane County Bachelor." In the Oklahoma version, "Greer County" takes the place of Lane County, Kansas, and Frank Bolar is replaced by "Tom Hight."

The Lane County Bachelor

2. My clothes they are ragged, my language is rough,
My head is case-hardened, both solid and tough;
The dough it is scattered all over the room
And the floor would get scared at the sight of a broom;
My dishes are dirty and some in the bed
Covered with sorghum and government bread;
But I have a good time, and live at my ease
On common sop-sorghum, old bacon and grease.

Chorus:
But hurrah for Lane County, the land of the West,
Where the farmers and laborers are always at rest,
Where you've nothing to do but sweetly remain,
And starve like a man on your government claim.

3. How happy am I when I crawl into bed,
And a rattlesnake rattles his tail at my head,
And the gay little centipede, void of all fear
Crawls over my pillow and into my ear,
And the nice little bedbug so cheerful and bright,
Keeps me a-scratching full half of the night,
And the gay little flea with toes sharp as a tack
Plays "Why don't you catch me?" all over my back.

Chorus:
But hurrah for Lane County, where blizzards arise,
Where the winds never cease and the flea never dies,
Where the sun is so hot if in it you remain
'Twill burn you quite black on your government claim.

4. How happy am I on my government claim,
Where I've nothing to lose and nothing to gain,
Nothing to eat and nothing to wear,
Nothing from nothing is honest and square.
But here I am stuck, and here I must stay,
My money's all gone and I can't get away;
There's nothing will make a man hard and profane
Like starving to death on a government claim.

Chorus:
Then come to Lane County, there's room for you all,
Where the winds never cease and the rains never fall,
Come join in the chorus and boast of her fame,
While starving to death on your government claim.

5. Now don't get discouraged, ye poor hungry men,
We're all here as free as a pig in a pen;
Just stick to your homestead and battle your fleas,
And pray to your Maker to send you a breeze.
Now a word to claim-holders who are bound for to stay:
You may chew your hard-tack till you're toothless
and gray,
But as for me, I'll no longer remain
And starve like a dog on my government claim.

Chorus:
Farewell to Lane County, farewell to the West,
I'll travel back East to the girl I love best;
I'll stop in Missouri and get me a wife,
And live on corn dodgers the rest of my life.

Carl Sandburg, The American Songbag *(New York: Harcourt, Brace & World, Inc., 1927), pp. 120-122.*

But despite the hardships and disappointments the settlers kept coming. At the opening of Oklahoma Territory at noon, April 22, 1889, covered wagons bore witty and plucky inscriptions reminiscent of Pike's Peak and other rushes. One boomer in particular is reported to have exhibited on his wagon sheet in bold letters the following saga of his successive migrations:

White-capped in Indiany,
Chintz-bugged in Illinoy,
Cicloned in Nebraska,
Prohibited in Kansas,
Oklahoma or bust!

H. H. McConnell, "Five Years a Cavalryman," in Frontier Times, *Bandera, Texas, II (1934), p. 213.*

"A Study From Life." Pen and ink by Frederic Remington.

CLARENCE P. HORNUNG COLLECTION

PART TEN

"The Bug Hunters" by Charles M. Russell

A Gallery of Western Art

Commentary and
Biographical Notes by
Clarence P. Hornung

"Oto Warrior No-Way-Ke-Sug-Ga" by George Bird King Colored Lithograph

Charles Bird King (1785-1862) King, a native of Rhode Island, studied art first in New York and then in London under Benjamin West. He later settled in Washington, D.C., where, encouraged by Thomas McKenny, U.S. Superintendent of Indian Trade, he achieved recognition for his portraits of visiting Indian chieftains. All but three paintings of his collection, an important part of the government's Indian Gallery, were burned in the Smithsonian fire of 1865.

The Art of the American West

WESTERN ART as such is a thing apart from old-time western life. Except for "Custer's Last Fight," which hung in countless saloons, few western pictures circulated on the frontier until livestock commission firms began sending elaborate calendars to their customers. These were often prepared by nationally renowned illustrators who glamorized western life.

But long before that time, eastern artists had been painting for easterners a West that incorporated and fixed the national dream. No hardier band of adventurers ever went into the untamed wilderness than the "brothers of the brush and palette" who accompanied various public and private expeditions to capture pictorially the magnitude and the beauty of the "un-discovered" lands. Those early painters included stalwart pioneers like Samuel Seymour, George Catlin, Carl Bodmer, Alfred Jacob Miller and John Mix Stanley. Theirs was a reportorial craft rather than an art practiced for esthetic or inspirational sustenance. They came to record what they saw and to bring back pictorial evidence for government reports, scientific investigations and narratives of high adventure.

While George Catlin is generally regarded as the first painter of the West whose work has survived, in actual time he was preceded by Samuel Seymour, who traveled with Stephen Long's expedition up the South Platte in 1819-20. Seymour is said to have done about 150 pictures, crudely rendered for the most part, but nonetheless authentic. Though most of his work has disappeared, his fame rests upon his having been the first to provide a view of the Rockies.

From the very beginning Indians became symbols of the West, but for many generations all Indians in pictures looked pretty much alike. By the 1820's, when the United States was reforming its Indian policy, representatives from many tribes were coming to Washington. Portraits of these visitors painted by Charles Bird King became the nucleus of the government's "Indian Gallery," which grew by future acquisitions into a sizable collection that was eventually housed in the Smithsonian Institution. In addition to King's work, the "gallery" acquired paintings by others, including George Catlin and John Mix Stanley, both of whom had seen "wild" Indians. Most of the Indians whose portraits were painted came from the midland forests and southern swamps, not from the faraway and unexplored West; but a few from those distant lands were brought to Washington, and fortunately some portraits of them have been preserved.

The two men who dominate the early documentary western field are George Catlin and Carl Bodmer, both of whom journeyed up the Missouri River, crossing the Great Plains during the 1830's. Catlin, as a young man, made his living painting portraits in Philadelphia. One day he saw a delegation of Indians being conducted to Washington. Their beaded clothes and stately feathers fascinated him, and he resolved to devote his life to painting wild Indians in their western homes. Though he had only limited funds, he traveled on a fur-trader's boat as far up the Missouri as the Yellowstone, where he spent a month at Fort Union painting the red men. His most important works depict the rites and ceremonies of the Mandan, among whom he saw horrors and tortures seldom witnessed by white men. He completed many hundreds of paintings and sketches which he eventually organized into a traveling exhibit that he supplemented with tribal paraphernalia and living models wearing Indian costumes. His exhibitions created the image of the Old West which still exists.

Unlike Catlin, who traveled without subsidy, Carl Bodmer went up the Missouri River in 1833 as a member of a scientific expedition led by a German princeling, Maximilian von Wied-Neuwied. Bodmer's job was to draw with scientific accuracy, but he also incorporated artistry in his work, which was printed in a folio volume of his patron's study entitled *Reise in das innere Nord-Amerika in den Jahren 1832 bis 1834*, later appearing in many English translations of this study. No other work of its kind attained such renown or has been so frequently reproduced as source material. A superb draftsman and accomplished portraitist, Bodmer was outstanding in his vitality and exactitude. His details were precise, minute and exquisite without being labored. His pictures were painted mainly to portray the Indian's accoutrements, his costumes and ornaments; the cut and tie of his moccasins, shirts and leggings; the headdress with its fur, horns and feathers; the ceremonial lance with blade, feathered decorations and dangling scalps; the war paint and body decorations; the tomahawks and war bonnets.

Among the most famous artists of the pre–Civil War period was Alfred Jacob Miller, a talented painter from Baltimore who was employed by the Scottish nobleman, William Drummond Stewart, to accompany him on a western hunting expedition in 1837. Miller came back with sketches and water colors of unusually high quality. From these he painted murals to adorn Sir William's castle in Scotland. He also faithfully copied many of them at twelve dollars each for William T. Walters. The originals remained in the Miller family for almost a century; but by 1860 some ninety of the copies had been delivered to Walters, and it is this fabulous collection that now resides in the Walters Art Gallery in Baltimore. Miller's pictures are important, being the only spot drawings of a trapper rendezvous. He captured the gaiety and excitement of those picturesque gatherings. From him we learn the details of the men's equipment, see the good-looking native women, watch the feasts and dances. Much impressed by Joseph Mallord Turner's water colors, their soft lights and hazy landscapes, Miller used the Turner technique to create the crystal clear atmosphere of the West, and in this he failed completely; but the charm of his drawings and the romance of his subjects' lives make his pictures rank historically with the most valuable western productions.

About mid-century, a generation or so after the Amerindic painters had introduced the public to the wild savages and their primitive ways, a group of landscapists began to gain popularity by depicting the wondrous natural beauty of the West. Gallery showings of their canvases attracted large crowds of visitors who gazed in awe at the scenic splendors of the Sierra Nevada and the Yellowstone. If the viewer could not readily act on Greeley's advice, "Go West, young man," he could at least enjoy vicariously the grandeur displayed in the paintings of Albert Bierstadt, F. E. Church, Thomas Moran and, later, William Keith. The enormity in scale of these painters' works, their panoramic sweep, startled and captivated audiences.

Paintings, galleries and museums, however, were not the only means by which the image of the West was conveyed. Americans of a century ago could be grateful that the art of reproduction and the processes of commercial lithography were perfected and that a dozen firms, most prominent of which was Currier & Ives, spewed out millions of popular pictures at a price well within reach of all. With a full understanding of the popular psychology and merchandising policies to match, this enterprising firm published western prints that catered to our cherished folk symbol. The services of many fine artists were employed where special talents were called for — in landscape, hunting scene, Indian encounter, westward trek or steamboat run. The wide influence of the huge Currier & Ives output upon mass audiences cannot be underestimated, and it is safe to say that it easily outweighed the combined impact of contemporary American painters for several decades following the Civil War.

It was inevitable that the latter half of the nineteenth century, which witnessed such a surge in pioneer settlement in the West, should have found worthy artists to depict the romance of this migration. Skirmishes, ambushes and Indian encounters, the drive by covered wagon or iron horse, the glories and miseries of frontier life, all found their way into visual expression. The painter's field was considerably broadened by the demands of the weeklies, which now bid for illustrators and published genre pictures in each issue, catering to a combined circulation of about a half-million readers. Artists like Winslow Homer, W. M. Cary, T. R. Davis, Paul Frenzeny, Jules Tavernier, Rufus Zogbaum and A. R. Waud appeared regularly in such magazines as *Harper's Weekly* and *Leslie's*. The exigencies of reproducing machine-age art often caused the final result, as interpreted by the wood engraver under pressure of deadlines, to be far removed from the artist's original. But the lack of esthetic fidelity was offset by the fact that these pictures were reaching millions who were remote from direct contact with any art forms.

The closing years of the century saw a growing number of painters who left vital and colorful records of the excitement of the already vanishing West. Among the thousands of easterners who joined the movement were a small group of determined artists and sketch reporters, either on official assignments or on their own. Charles Schreyvogel, for example, limned swashbuckling cavalry charges, kidnappings by Indian renegades, attacks on stockades and sackings of Indian villages. Following the overnight success of "My Bunkie," his pictures attracted huge crowds wherever they were shown. Henry Farny, too, was celebrated both here and abroad for his fine renditions of the western scene with strong emphasis on the role of the Indian. A simple, quiet setting featuring some central theme characterized his most successful canvases including "The Last Vigil," "The Captive" and "Song of the Talking Wire."

But it remained for Frederic Remington and his successor, Charles M. Russell, to epitomize the vanishing West in many of its aspects. The sun-baked cowboy or buckaroo, the ranch hand, the bronco, corral and roundup—countless incidents of rugged life on the Plains were depicted by these artists with their supreme gift of narration. Their deft and unforgettable strokes filled in the canvas that had been prepared by a procession of keen observers for seventy-five years.

The paintings and prints in this capsule gallery of western art are a representative cross section of the ways in which notable artists and printmakers treated the western scene over a period of almost a century. Space has, of course, prevented the inclusion of many fine paintings by dozens of talented artists whose works have long been acclaimed. Those reproduced here have been selected to show the wide variety of viewpoints and techniques which the American West inspired. It is hoped that this gallery in miniature will serve as an introduction to the noted western collections exhibited by many fine museums throughout the nation.

"The Interior of the Hut of a Mandan Chief" by Carl Bodmer   Colored Lithograph

Carl Bodmer (1809-1893) Arriving in this country in 1832 from his native Switzerland during his twenties (the best authorities disagree on his age), Bodmer accompanied the German princeling and accomplished naturalist Maximilian von Wied-Neuwied on his mission to explore the western regions and to report, in a voluminous book about his scientific observations. Bodmer, who was commissioned by von Wied-Neuwied to paint and sketch

what he saw, had already distinguished himself with a Parisian career of more than average promise. The expedition left St. Louis in 1833 and traveled up the Missouri aboard the *Yellowstone* as far as Fort Pierre, where the party changed boats and proceeded on the *Assiniboin* to Fort Clark, the region of the Mandan villages and finally Fort McKenzie, returning to St. Louis in the spring of 1834. The scientific research of both author and

"Buffalo Dance of the Mandan" by Carl Bodmer   Colored Lithograph

artist resulted in a most comprehensive and important work. The *Atlas,* a separate folio containing Bodmer's plates, following the issuance of von Wied-Neuwied's *Travels* in 1839 and 1843, was a significant contribution to American ethnology. The paintings by the gifted and imaginative Bodmer convey in sharp and exquisite detail, as had never been done before or since, the life, habits and customs of various Indian groups. Bodmer was a superb draftsman, a perceptive chronicler and documentary reporter without peer. With photographic clarity and exactitude his detailing covered the most minute observations of Indian trappings, leggings, quills, headdresses, fringes and ornamentation of costumes. It has been said that Bodmer was the first artist to do justice to the West. He returned to France after this epochal trip, living at Barbizon until his death.

"Sketch of the Rockies" by Samuel Seymour   Water Color 7¾ x 13½

Samuel Seymour (1806-— ?) Noted primarily as one of the first artists to journey to the West, Seymour came to this country from England and established himself as a painter and engraver in Philadelphia, being active there as early as 1801. He was chosen to accompany the expedition of Major Stephen H. Long to "explore the country between the Mississippi and the Rocky Mountains . . . and to acquire as thorough and accurate knowledge as may be practicable." Seymour did sketches of the terrain and painted portraits of Indian chieftains in tribal festivities. His view of the Rockies from the River Platte is the first white man's rendering of the scenic wonder of the West. He painted more than 150 pictures, a selection of which appeared in a printed report of the expedition. Seymour's work was done in water color and, while not finished or proficient, furnishes one of the earliest pictorial accounts of the vast country that was soon to attract more accomplished men of the palette and brush. Little more is known of his life except that he exhibited his paintings in Philadelphia in 1832.

568

George Catlin (1796-1872) Catlin, a Pennsylvanian by birth, studied law and practiced briefly before commencing a career as a portrait miniaturist in Philadelphia. He was so intrigued by the sight of a delegation of Indians en route to Washington, D.C., that he decided to devote his life to painting Indians in their natural habitat, a decision that was to keep him busy from that time on. Catlin voyaged up the Missouri from St. Louis in 1832, painting Indian portraits and depicting the daily pursuits of the Indians and the landscapes along the way. He journeyed into the Southwest in 1834 and later visited the upper Mississippi and the Great Lakes. Wherever his travels took him, he was welcomed as a friendly white man who came on a mission easily understood by the Indians. He painted more than five hundred canvases of Indians, Indian life and wild animals, many of which appeared in his two-volume work entitled *Manners, Customs, and Conditions of the North American Indians,* published in 1841. From 1837 to 1857 he took his "Indian Gallery" on a tour of Europe, as well as North and South American cities and towns. Catlin was truly a pioneer artist with a mission: to bring the story of the aborigines to the American people. In this, he succeeded as no other man did.

"Buffalo Hunt, with Wolf-Skin Mask" by George Catlin   Colored Lithograph

"Buffalo Hunt, on Snow-Shoes" by George Catlin   Colored Lithograph

"The Bull Dance" by George Catlin   Oil 16 x 22½

"Smoking the Shield" by George Catlin   Oil 16 x 22½

"The Buffalo Hunt" by John Mix Stanley   Oil 26 x 36

John Mix Stanley (1814-1872) Stanley spent his boyhood at Canandaigua, New York, going later to Detroit. With no formal art training, he began painting portraits and landscapes in 1835, earning a living meanwhile as a sign painter. His restless nature took him to Chicago, Galena, Fort Snelling (where he occupied himself doing Indian portraits), Washington, D.C., New York, Philadelphia and Baltimore. But the lure of the Indian country so attracted him that with another artist he set up a studio in Fort Gibson, Indian Territory, in the fall of 1842. He painted many portraits of Cherokee, Osage, Creek and Chickasaw Indians. After the outbreak of the Mexican War he accompanied soldiers to San Diego and produced a splendid pictorial record of his travels and adventures. His gallery of Indian paintings and portraits was widely exhibited, and he tried repeatedly to interest the government in purchasing his collection. Ironically, while Congress was deliberating over the matter, some two hundred of his paintings were destroyed in the Smithsonian fire of 1865.

"Indians Approaching Fort Benton" by Charles Wimar   Oil 28 x 40

Charles Wimar (1828-1862) At the age of fifteen, Wimar came to this country from Germany to join his family in St. Louis, Missouri. He had had some training at Düsseldorf and preferred painting, but in order to eke out an existence in a rugged frontier town where fur trading dominated the scene, young Wimar decorated wagon panels and did signs for merchants. He was befriended by an old Indian warrior who took him on short trips into the neighboring countryside, where he met the red men who fascinated him so and were to become his subjects. Wimar made several excursions up the Missouri and once sketched six forts on a single page: Forts Berthold, Union, Clark, Pierre Chouteau, Kipp and Benton. Having gathered many sketches and vivid impressions of life on the Plains, Wimar was now determined to record his experience in a number of documentary paintings, typical of which are his "Attack on an Emigrant Train," "Turf House on the Plains," "The Buffalo Hunt" and "The Buffalo Dance." His reputation was now on the ascent, especially in St. Louis, where in 1861 he received an important commission to decorate the rotunda of the courthouse with appropriate scenes. Shortly after completing this work, Wimar died.

"Interior of Fort Laramie" by Alfred Jacob Miller   *Water Color 6 x 9½*

"Sioux Reconnoitring" by Alfred Jacob Miller   Oil 14 x 20

Alfred Jacob Miller (1810-1874) A native of Baltimore, Maryland, Miller showed an early talent for painting. His abilities came to the attention of the wealthy Baltimorean art patron, Robert Gilmore, who in 1833 sponsored Miller's trip to Europe to study in Paris and later in Rome. Back in the United States, he went to New Orleans, where he met Sir William Drummond Stewart, an adventurous Scottish sportsman who was planning a hunting expedition to the Rockies. Stewart engaged Miller to go along, not only to record scenery and incidents of the trip but to do a group of western paintings for his castle in Scotland. On that journey Miller made over one hundred sketches, some mere jottings, others worthy of consideration as more finished works. These copious notes and memoranda were to serve as Miller's basic material over his lifetime. In 1840 he followed Stewart to Scotland, where he rendered many of his sketches into murals to remind the baronet of his days in the American West. After nearly two years abroad doing Indian subjects in addition to portraits, both in Scotland and London, Miller returned home to Baltimore as a journeyman artist, painting portraits and local scenes and making household copies of famous paintings. But only his Indian and western pictures brought him recognition. It was during this period of his life that the munificent William Walters, founder of the Baltimore art gallery of the same name, commissioned him to do copies of many of his earlier sketches to add to his fabulous collection. Miller's contribution was a unique pictorial history of the trappers' lives: lonely encampments in the lush high country; buckskin-clad figures spinning tall tales or dancing around a campfire; the excitement of a buffalo chase; Indian maidens bathing *au naturel*. Two of his pictures of Fort Laramie show details of great historical importance.

"*The Trapper's Bride*" *by Alfred Jacob Miller   Water Color 12 x 9⅜*

"*Landing Charettes*" *by Alfred Jacob Miller   Water Color 9¼ x 15*

"The Lasso" by William Ranney   Oil 36 x 54½

William T. Ranney (1813-1857) Born in Middletown, Connecticut, Ranney spent his youth in North Carolina, returning north later to settle in New York City. It was here that he first received art instruction and began painting portraits at the age of twenty. With the outbreak of the Mexican War he enlisted and was assigned to duty in the Southwest. Fascinated with what he saw of Plains life, he decided to devote his time, after his return to civilian life, to painting and recording episodes of the western scene. When he was elected an associate of the National Academy of Design in 1850 he was one of the few artists making a career as anecdotist, along with William Sidney Mount and Thomas Matteson. While Mount depicted the locale of his beloved Long Island and Matteson specialized in episodes from the early life of New England, Ranney turned to the frontier. He had observed first-hand such settings as he painted in "The Lasso," "The Prairie Fire," "The Pioneers," "The Trappers," "The Caravan on the Prairies" and "The Scouting Party." Ranney's compositions are noted for their simple majesty. His scouts and pioneers display only a trace of the sentimentality featured by so many of the story-telling painters. He died at West Hoboken, New Jersey, leaving in his studio a number of unfinished works which were completed by his friend, Mount.

576

"Sunrise, Yosemite Valley" by Albert Bierstadt   Oil 36½ x 52

Albert Bierstadt (1830-1902) Though he was born in Solingen, Germany, in 1830, Bierstadt was brought as an infant to this country where his parents settled at New Bedford, Massachusetts. His academic studies took him back to Germany, where, at Düsseldorf, he acquired the necessary technical facility for his later career as a painter of grandeur in the Rockies. In 1858, Bierstadt visited the West and from that time on applied himself to the great composite canvases that glorified its titanic beauty. By 1860 he was already exhibiting the results of his appraisal of the western scene and winning acclaim. His pictures, always painstakingly constructed in their topographical features, yet thin and hard in workmanship, sometimes brought as much as $25,000, a fabulous sum for a living artist of those days. Unfortunately, however, the vogue for his work diminished during his lifetime.

577

"Wolf River, Kansas" by Albert Bierstadt   Oil 48 x 38

"In the Teton Range" by Thomas Moran   Oil 20 x 30¼

Thomas Moran   (1837-1926) Of English birth, Moran arrived in America at the age of seven. He studied art in Philadelphia and later in England, being particularly influenced by the work of Turner. Moran was very much attracted by the wild and idyllic beauty of the newly discovered West. A student of nature, he sought to capture breadth of effect without sacrifice of detail and succeeded in this almost impossible endeavor. He once said of his approach: "My general scope is not realistic; all my tendencies are toward idealization. Topography in art is valueless . . . except as it furnishes material from which to construct a picture." Moran's huge "Grand Canyon of the Yellowstone" and his later "Chasm of the Colorado" were bought by Congress for $10,000 apiece. These purchases were said to have so fired the legislative imagination that they were in no small measure responsible for the establishment of our national parks program. Today Moran's work is rare and in great demand.

"Grand Canyon of the Yellowstone" by Thomas Moran   Oil 25 x 19¾

"Wahsatch Mountains" by William Keith   Oil 24 x 36

William Keith (1839-1911) At the age of eleven, Keith came with his mother to New York where he was apprenticed to an engraver. In 1858, he traveled to San Francisco, where he made a precarious living by engraving letterheads, stagecoach posters and labels for wine bottles. His great opportunity came when the new Oregon Navigation & Railroad Company, to attract tourists, employed him to paint scenes of interest along the company's route. Keith viewed the wonders of the Columbia, the dignity of Mounts Hood and Ranier, the gigantic Oregon forests, and he portrayed them in all their native grandeur. As a whole, his type of art has been called an aberration, for he confused the majesty of western landscapes with diverting and often irrelevant details. However, at the beginning of the twentieth century he was rated as one of the leading landscape painters in California.

"Custer's Last Stand" by Frederic Remington   Oil 47 x 64

Frederic Remington (1861-1909) The son of a soldier-newspaperman, Remington was born in Canton, New York, and grew up in nearby Ogdensburg, a vigorous youth, all-round athlete and hunter. He attended military academy at Worcester, Massachusetts, and entered Yale in 1878, where he achieved fame as a member of the football team captained by Walter Camp. His college education came to an end after two years due to his father's death. In 1881 he made a short trip to Montana and on his return he sold *Harper's Weekly* one of his drawings, the first step in a career that was to establish him as a top-flight illustrator. In 1883 he bought a sheep ranch in Kansas, but did not stay there long. A desire to see more of the West and document the vanishing frontier in all its exciting moods dominated his life, drawing him south and west to Texas, Indian Territory, New Mexico and Arizona. His sketchbook soon bulged with drawings of hard-riding cowboys, taciturn mountain men, prospectors, feathered Indians and soldiers on galloping horses. Between trips he re-turned east to make the rounds of the New York publishers. Soon *Harper's* and *Outing* were regular buyers of his work. In 1888 his pictures were hung in the annual exhibition of the American Water Color Society and he won prizes for his paintings in the 63rd Annual National Academy Show. That year he started a series of illustrations for *Century* to accompany articles written by Theodore Roosevelt, published later under the title *Ranch Life and the Hunting Trail*. Both artist and writer scored a huge success with this venture, and it was the start of a warm friendship that lasted until Remington's death. In addition to his illustrations and paintings, he also did some sculpture, beginning with "Bronco Buster," modeled when he was about thirty-three. Many museum experts rate his sculptures above his paintings, and in fact accepted them long before availing themselves of his paintings. Half a century after Remington's death his reputation as an artist of the West and historian of its vanished glory was undiminished and the popularity of his pictures remained as great as ever.

"An Apache Indian" by Frederic Remington   Oil 26 x 36

"Campfire, Big Horn Mountains" by Frederic Remington   Oil 26 x 30

"The Rocky Mountains" by Currier & Ives   Colored Lithograph

Currier & Ives Starting a modest lithograph business in 1835, Nathaniel Currier accidentally stumbled onto the tremendous sales potential of newsworthy pictures in 1840 when he printed a picture showing the wreck of the ship "Lexington." Ten years later he entered into partnership with James Merritt Ives to form the highly successful firm of Currier & Ives. Known as "Printmakers to the American People," the firm in a sixty-year period achieved a total output of over seven thousand prints, pouring forth millions of inexpensive pictures that depicted in color contemporary scenes and events of American life over the last two-thirds of the nineteenth century. With fidelity and endless imagination, punctuated at times, however, with mawkish sentimentality, these pictures paralleled the country's growth and, by keeping a picture-hungry public posted on westward expansion, did more to popu-

"Taking a Backtrack" by Currier & Ives   Colored Lithograph

"Across the Continent" by Currier & Ives   Colored Lithograph

larize the glories and terrors of frontier and pioneer life than the best efforts of our country's finest painters, whose work, after all, was destined to be viewed only by a fortunate few. Emerging quickly as a national institution, the concern employed the services of some of the best talents available: Arthur Fitzwilliam Tait, George Durrie, Fanny Palmer, George Inness, Eastman Johnson, George Catlin, Louis Maurer, Thomas Worth and a host of others. Many of these artists had specialties which made them invaluable to the firm. Well over a hundred Currier & Ives prints covered the western scene, including railroad and river travel, Indian attacks and encounters, hunting and mountain scenes, overland treks, prairie fires and gold-mining scenes. By 1888, the prosperous establishment had introduced finely executed lithographic prints into nearly every American home.

"A Parley" by Currier & Ives   Colored Lithograph

Charles Schreyvogel (1861-1912) Born into a poor family on New York's lower East Side, Schreyvogel had no formal art instruction, but as a youth was apprenticed to art lithographers, working on sketches and stone for calendars, labels and the like. Two wealthy art patrons recognized his great promise and sent him abroad for three years to study in Munich. On his return, he continued working for art lithographers until 1893, when he finally realized his life's ambition with a trip west to Colorado and Arizona, where he spent the summer at a Ute reservation making sketches, clay models, taking photographs and collecting firearms and artifacts —studies that were to serve him well in the years ahead in his Hoboken, New Jersey, studio. Western themes had by now become his primary interest, and he worked assiduously on many paintings and compositions, despite little interest from either the buying public or the publishers. When his painting "My Bunkie" was awarded first prize at the annual National Academy exhibit he achieved overnight fame, and his days of struggle were over. He then busied himself as a historical illustrator, chronicling scenes and events with a sound background of facts gathered from his firsthand studies on western junkets. He was an accomplished horseman and showed a love of horseflesh in every painting. Schreyvogel's canvases always told a stirring story of the West that was gone before his time—troopers in violent encounters with the Sioux or Apache, the fierce charge of a cavalry unit, the wounded soldiers or the thrilling tale of an attempted kidnaping. For a while after Remington's death he was referred to as "America's greatest living interpreter of the Old West."

"In Safe Hands" by Charles Schreyvogel   Oil 25 x 34

"Indian Trading Post" by Frank T. Johnson   Oil 36¼ x 46

Frank Tenney Johnson (1874-1939)

A native of Big Grove, Iowa, Johnson studied at the Art Students League in New York under the well-known artist Robert Henri. He spent his summers in those early years riding the range, coming east for the winter to paint and illustrate the life of the range. The examples of Remington and Russell inspired in him a desire to paint every phase of western life. Most notable are his renderings of riders and rustlers, stampeding cattle and moonlight scenes featuring cowboy life. A critic once said of him: "Johnson's gentler, mellower art celebrates the spacious beauty of the range, its white moonlight, its crimson stained sunsets, the very twilight of the Old West. He painted the West that except in his canvases will never live again." Johnson is represented today in many private and public collections.

"The Stage Drivers" by Edward Borein   Oil 23 x 28

587

Edward Borein (1873-1945) At an early age Ed Borein left home in San Leandro, California, to become a ranch hand and cowboy. By day he learned the skills of ranch life; at night he turned to his sketch pad to record what had interested him most that day. His prolific sketches covered the walls of the bunkhouses on the various ranches where he worked, and when he moved on from one ranch to the next he seldom bothered to take along his random jottings. His wanderings took him as far as Mexico, where he spent two years, and then back to California. Despite his lack of formal art training, he soon turned to oils and became known in the San Francisco Bay region as a painter of western genre. His pictures of men and horses appeared on magazine covers and as story illustrations at a time when Remington and Russell, too, were at the top of their careers. Following the earthquake of 1906 Borein left Oakland for New York, where he learned the art of the etching needle at the Art Students League. The ensuing years found his prints attracting critical acclaim; they were sought by collectors in this country and Europe as well. Besides his vast output of etchings, Borein continued to turn out water colors and oils in his later years, making frequent visits to Montana, Canada and the Indian country of the Southwest. His keen memory made working from models unnecessary, and although his sketchbooks were voluminous he seldom referred to them in developing a finished canvas. Borein rates as one of the foremost painters of the West.

"The Long Throw" by Edward Borein   Etching 7½ x 12

"*Song of the Talking Wire*" *by Henry F. Farny   Oil 22⅟₁₆ x 40*

Henry F. Farny (1847-1916) Born in Alsace-Lorraine, Farny spent his childhood in western Pennsylvania before his family moved on to Cincinnati. This was to become his home, the place where most of his adult years were spent, except for frequent forays into the West. His early apprenticeship included work for a lithographer and for *Harper's Weekly,* a popular periodical that gave him many assignments over the years. In 1881, after several excursions to study in Europe, he decided to concentrate on the western scene. It was a wise move, for he had ample preparation for a career that was to land him in the first ranks and even merit commendation at the hands of the noted artist and critic, Joseph Pennell. Farny's enthusiasm for the West and what it had to offer led him to report that "the plains, the buttes, the whole country and its people are fuller of material for the artist than any country in Europe." In addition to prolific output for such magazines as *Harper's, Scribner's* and the *Century,* he illustrated many books, including the celebrated *McGuffey's Reader.* His preference in subject matter led him to be classified as an "Indian painter"—an outgrowth of a thoroughly sympathetic understanding of the temperament as well as the environment of the aborigines. Farny left a rich group of over a hundred oils, a much greater number of water colors and illustrations and an invaluable contribution to the lore of the American West.

"Cowboy Life" by Charles Russell   Oil 18½ x 24¼

Charles M. Russell (1864-1926) From early childhood, Russell exhibited a strong desire to draw and travel in the Far West. By the time he was sixteen his parents had given up trying to dissuade him from these ambitions, and he left St. Louis for Montana under the guardianship of a sheepman, from whom he soon parted company. Russell had no artistic training at any time, but he was a person of rigid discipline, a characteristic that enabled him to overcome what in another man might be inadequacies. He understood and respected the frontier which he felt was fast disappearing, and he determined to become the Old West's chief graphic chronicler. He hoped that his pencil would immortalize the vanishing "wild" Indian, the chaotic tumult of a buffalo stampede, the vast pageant of prairie schooners and army supply trains, the movement of great herds of longhorns across dusty plains. He had a rare gift for recreating the past and preserving the status quo which manifested itself in every fresh canvas he painted. He drew and painted in cabins, cow camps or saloons, carrying modeling clay in his pocket and fashioning figurines while he talked or listened to random conversations. Most of his important works were done without the aid of models, for his retentive memory could fill in necessary details with extreme accuracy.

"Last of the Herd" by Charles Russell   Oil 30 x 48

"The Signal" by Charles Russell   Oil 18 x 22

"The Lookout" by William Robinson Leigh   Oil 59 x 84

William Robinson Leigh (1866-1955)

On the West Virginia farm where he was born, Leigh started as a boy to draw animals. At twelve he won a hundred-dollar award from W. W. Corcoran of Washington, D.C., for his sketch of a dog. He studied at the Maryland Art Institute in Baltimore and later in Munich, where he became a proficient draftsman, especially skilled in drawing horses. His outdoor illustrations were soon attracting the attention of magazine art directors, and in 1897 *Scribner's* sent him on an assignment to North Dakota. By 1906 Leigh had decided to devote his full energies to depicting western life. He worked on a grand scale, showing the western scene in a broad sweep. His work is notable for its studied composition, gained from a thorough knowledge of his subject, and unsurpassed draftsmanship. Wherever shown, his impressive canvases registered a strong popular appeal. Leigh's studio in later years was located in New York, where he died.

SUGGESTIONS FOR ADDITIONAL READING

The volumes listed below have been selected to supplement the text of *The Book of the American West*. They should not be considered as a bibliography of works used by our authors. Instead, these books have been chosen because of their availability, readability and reliability. In order to give a variety of coverage the list includes personal narratives, specialized studies and general accounts by outstanding western writers of past generations as well as by present-day authorities. Many books equally commendable have been omitted, but readers will certainly be led to them through the pages of the following publications.

Adams, Andy. *The Log of a Cowboy*. Boston and New York: Houghton Mifflin Co., 1927.

Adams, Ramon F. *The Old-Time Cowhand*. New York: Macmillan Co., 1961.

——. *Western Words*. Norman: University of Oklahoma Press, 1944.

Alter, J. Cecil. *James Bridger, Trapper, Frontiersman, Scout and Guide*. Salt Lake City: Shepard Book Co., 1925; rev. ed., 1952; entirely recast as *Jim Bridger*. Norman: University of Oklahoma Press, 1962.

Athearn, Robert G. *William Tecumseh Sherman and the Settlement of the West*. Norman: University of Oklahoma Press, 1956.

Bakeless, John Edwin. *Lewis & Clark, Partners in Discovery*. New York: William Morrow & Co., 1947.

Bancroft, Hubert Howe. *Popular Tribunals*. 2 vols. San Francisco: History Co., 1887.

Beebe, Lucius, and Clegg, Charles. *U.S. West: The Saga of Wells Fargo*. New York: E. P. Dutton, 1949.

Berry, Don. *A Majority of Scoundrels: An Informal History of the Rocky Mountain Fur Company*. New York: Harper & Brothers, 1961.

Boatright, Mody C. *Folk Laughter on the Frontier*. New York: Macmillan Co., 1949.

Bolton, Herbert E. *Coronado, Knight of Pueblos and Plains*. New York: Whittlesey House, 1949.

Botkin, B. A. (ed.). *A Treasury of Western Folklore*. New York: Crown Publishers, Inc., 1951.

Bourke, John G. *On the Border with Crook*. New York: Charles Scribner's Sons, 1891; Columbus, Ohio: Long's College Book Co., 1950.

Cahalane, Victor H. *Mammals of North America*. New York: Macmillan Co., 1947.

Carey, A. Merwyn. *American Firearms Makers*. New York: Thos. Y. Crowell Co., 1953.

Carman, W. Y. *A History of Firearms from Earliest Times to 1914*. London: Routledge & Kegan Paul, Ltd., 1955.

Carson, Christopher. *Kit Carson's Own Story of His Life*, ed. Blanche C. Grant. Taos, New Mexico: printed, not published, 1926; also published as *Kit Carson's Autobiography*, ed. Milo. M. Quaife. Chicago: R. R. Donnelley & Sons Co., 1935.

Cary, Lucian. *The Colt Gun Book*. New York: Arco Publishing Co., Inc., 1961.

——. *The New Lucian Cary on Guns*. New York: Arco Publishing Co., Inc., 1957.

Chapman, Arthur. *The Pony Express*. New York: A. L. Burt Co., 1932.

Chittenden, Hiram Martin. *The American Fur Trade of the Far West*. 3 vols. New York: F. P. Harper, 1902; reprinted, 2 vols. New York: The Press of the Pioneers, 1935.

——. *History of Early Steamboat Navigation on the Missouri River*. New York: F. P. Harper, 1903.

Cleland, Robert Glass. *This Reckless Breed of Men*. New York: Alfred A. Knopf, 1950.

Connelley, William E. *Wild Bill and His Era*. New York: Press of the Pioneers, 1933.

Croy, Homer. *Trigger Marshal: The Story of Chris Madsen*. New York: Duell, Sloan & Pearce, 1958.

Custer, G. A. *My Life on the Plains*. New York: Sheldon & Co., 1874.

Dale, Edward Everett. *The Range Cattle Industry*. Norman: University of Oklahoma Press, 1930.

Dale, Harrison C. *The Ashley-Smith Explorations and the Discovery of a Central Route to the Pacific, 1822–1829*. Cleveland: Arthur H. Clark Co., 1918; rev. ed., Glendale, Calif., 1941.

Dane, G. Ezra, and Dane, Beatrice J. *Ghost Town*. New York: Alfred A. Knopf, 1941.

Davidson, Levette J., and Blake, Forrester (eds.). *Rocky Mountain Tales*. Norman: University of Oklahoma Press, 1947.

Davis, Britton. *The Truth about Geronimo.* New Haven: Yale University Press, 1929.

DeVoto, Bernard. *Across the Wide Missouri.* Cambridge, Mass.: Houghton Mifflin Co., 1947.

Dimsdale, Thomas J. *The Vigilantes of Montana.* Virginia City, Mont. Terr.: D. W. Tilton & Co., 1866; new ed., Norman: University of Oklahoma Press, 1953.

Ditmars, Raymond L. *The Reptiles of North America.* Garden City, N.Y.: Doubleday & Co., 1946.

Dobie, J. Frank. *Apache Gold and Yaqui Silver.* Boston: Little, Brown & Co., 1939.

———. *Coronado's Children.* Dallas: Southwest Press, 1930.

———. *The Longhorns.* Boston: Little, Brown & Co., 1941.

———. *A Vaquero of the Brush Country.* Dallas: Southwest Press, 1929.

Dodge, Natt N. *Poisonous Dwellers of the Desert.* Globe, Ariz.: Southwestern Monuments Association, 1961.

Duffus, R. L. *The Santa Fe Trail.* New York: Longmans, Green and Co., 1930.

Easton, Robert, and Brown, Mackenzie. *Lord of Beasts: The Saga of Buffalo Jones.* Tucson: University of Arizona Press, 1961.

Favour, Alpheus. *Old Bill Williams, Mountain Man.* Chapel Hill: University of North Carolina Press, 1936; new ed., Norman: University of Oklahoma Press, 1962.

Fife, Austin, and Fife, Alta. *Saints of Sage and Saddle.* Bloomington: Indiana University Press, 1956.

Forrest, Earle R. *Arizona's Dark and Bloody Ground.* Caldwell, Ida.: Caxton Printers, 1936.

Fowler, Harlan D. *Camels to California.* Stanford, Calif.: Stanford University Press, 1950.

Gard, Wayne. *The Chisholm Trail.* Norman: University of Oklahoma Press, 1954.

———. *Frontier Justice.* Norman: University of Oklahoma Press, 1949.

———. *Sam Bass.* Boston and New York: Houghton Mifflin Co., 1936.

Ghent, W. J. *The Road to Oregon: A Chronicle of the Great Emigrant Trail.* New York: Tudor Publishing Co., 1934.

Glasscock, C. B. *The War of the Copper Kings.* Indianapolis: Bobbs-Merrill Co., 1935.

Graham, W. A. *The Custer Myth: A Source Book of Custeriana.* Harrisburg, Pa.: Stackpole Co., 1953.

Gregg, Josiah. *Commerce of the Prairies.* 2 vols. New York: H. G. Langley, 1844; many later editions.

Hafen, LeRoy R. *The Overland Mail, 1849–1869.* Cleveland: Arthur H. Clark Co., 1926.

——— and Hafen, Ann W. *Handcarts to Zion.* Glendale, Calif.: Arthur H. Clark Co., 1960.

———. *Old Spanish Trail.* Glendale, Calif.: Arthur H. Clark Co., 1954.

Haley, J. Evetts. *Charles Goodnight, Cowman & Plainsman.* Boston: Houghton Mifflin Co., 1936.

Hammond, George Peter, and Rey, Agapito. *Don Juan de Oñate, Colonizer of New Mexico, 1595–1628.* 2 vols. Albuquerque: University of New Mexico Press, 1953.

Hardin, John Wesley. *The Life of John Wesley Hardin.* Seguin, Texas: Smith & Moore, 1896; new ed., Norman: University of Oklahoma Press, 1961.

Harpending, Asbury. *The Great Diamond Hoax.* San Francisco: John H. Barry Co., 1913

Holbrook, Stewart H. *Holy Old Mackinaw.* New York: Macmillan Co., 1938.

Hulbert, Arthur B. *Forty-Niners: The Chronicle of the California Trail.* Boston: Little, Brown & Co., 1949.

Hyde, George E. *Red Cloud's Folk.* Norman: University of Oklahoma Press, 1937, 1957.

Irving, Washington. *Astoria.* 2 vols. Philadelphia: Carey, Lea & Blanchard, 1836.

Jackson, Joseph Henry. *Bad Company.* New York: Harcourt, Brace & Co., 1949.

Jenkins, Olaf P. (ed.). *The Mother Lode Company.* San Francisco: State of California, Division of Mines, 1948.

Karsner, David. *Silver Dollar.* New York: Covici-Friede, 1932.

Keleher, William A. *Violence in Lincoln County, 1869–1881.* Albuquerque: University of New Mexico Press, 1957.

Klauber, Laurence M. *Rattlesnakes, Their Habits, Life Histories, and Influence on Mankind.* 2 vols. Berkeley and Los Angeles: University of California Press, 1956.

Koller, Larry. *The Fireside Book of Guns.* New York: Simon & Schuster, 1959.

Lavender, David S. *Bent's Fort.* Garden City, N. Y.: Doubleday & Co., 1954.

Lea, Tom. *The King Ranch.* Boston: Little, Brown & Co., 1957.

Lewis, Oscar. *Silver Kings*. New York: Alfred A. Knopf, 1947.

Mercer, Asa Shinn. *The Banditti of the Plains*. Cheyenne: pub. by author, 1894; new ed., Norman: University of Oklahoma Press, 1954.

Morgan, Dale L. *The Great Salt Lake*. Indianapolis: Bobbs-Merrill Co., 1947.

———. *Jedediah Smith and the Opening of the West*. Indianapolis: Bobbs-Merrill Co., 1953.

Murray, Keith A. *The Modocs and Their War*. Norman: University of Oklahoma Press, 1959.

Myers, John M. *The Last Chance, Tombstone's Early Years*. New York: Alfred A. Knopf, 1950.

O'Connor, Richard. *Bat Masterson*. Garden City, N. Y.: Doubleday & Co., 1957.

Parsons, John E., and DuMont, John S. *Firearms in the Custer Battle*. Harrisburg, Pa.: Stackpole Co., 1953.

Peterson, Harold L. *A History of Firearms*. New York: Charles Scribner's Sons, 1961.

Potomac Corral of The Westerners. *Great Western Indian Fights*. Garden City, N. Y.: Doubleday & Co., Inc., 1960.

Pound, Louise. *Nebraska Folklore*. Lincoln: University of Nebraska Press, 1959.

Rascoe, Burton. *Belle Starr, "The Bandit Queen."* New York: Random House, 1941.

Riegel, Robert E. *The Story of the Western Railroads*. New York: Macmillan Co., 1926.

Rister, Carl Coke. *Border Command: General Phil Sheridan in the West*. Norman: University of Oklahoma Press, 1944.

Roe, Frank Gilbert. *The North American Buffalo*. Toronto, Canada: University of Toronto Press, 1951.

Russell, Carl P. *Guns on the Early Frontiers*. Berkeley and Los Angeles: University of California Press, 1957.

Russell, Don. *The Lives and Legends of Buffalo Bill*. Norman: University of Oklahoma Press, 1960.

Seton, Ernest Thompson. *Lives of the Game Animals*. 4 vols. Boston: Charles T. Branford Co., 1953.

Sharpe, Philip B. *The Rifle in America* (2nd ed.). New York: Funk & Wagnalls Company, 1947.

Smith, Grant H. *History of the Comstock Lode*. Reno: Nevada State Bureau of Mines, 1943.

Sonnichsen, C. L. *Roy Bean; Law West of the Pecos*. New York: Macmillan Co., 1943.

Sprague, Marshall. *Money Mountain: The Story of Cripple Creek Gold*. Boston: Little, Brown & Co., 1853.

Stuart, Robert. *The Discovery of the Oregon Trail; Robert Stuart's Narratives of His Overland Trip Eastward from Astoria in 1812–13*, ed. Philip Ashton Rollins. New York: Charles Scribner's Sons, 1935.

Taylor, Walter P. *The Deer of North America*. Harrisburg, Pa.: Stackpole Co., 1956.

Van Name, Willard G. *American Wild Life*. New York: William H. Wise & Co., Inc., 1961.

Vestal, Stanley. *Warpath and Council Fire*. New York: Random House, 1948.

Waters, Frank. *The Earp Brothers of Tombstone*. New York: Clarkson N. Potter, 1960.

Webb, Walter Prescott. *The Texas Rangers*. Boston and New York: Houghton Mifflin Co., 1935.

Wellman, Paul I. *The Indian Wars of the West*. Garden City, N. Y.: Doubleday & Co., Inc., 1954; previously published as *Death on Horseback*, 1947, combining *Death on the Prairie*, 1934, and *Death in the Desert*, 1935.

Wild Animals of North America. Washington, D.C.: National Geographic Society, 1960.

Winther, Oscar Osburn. *The Old Oregon Country: A History of Frontier Trade, Transportation and Travel*. Stanford, California: Stanford University Press, 1950.

———. *Via Western Express & Stagecoach*. Stanford, Calif.: Stanford University Press, 1945.

Young, Stanley P., and Jackson, H. H. T. *The Clever Coyote*. Harrisburg, Pa.: Stackpole Co., 1951.

About the Editor-in-Chief and Authors of
THE BOOK OF THE AMERICAN WEST

EDITOR-IN-CHIEF: **JAY MONAGHAN.** Author of many books on the West, the Civil War and Abraham Lincoln, Mr. Monaghan was editor of the American Trails Series, State Historian of Illinois and is now Consultant for the University of California's Wyles Collection of Lincolniana and Western Americana at Santa Barbara.

RAMON F. ADAMS. A native of Texas, Mr. Adams' special field of interest, since boyhood, has been the language of the cattle country. Author of such books as *Cowboy Lingo, Western Words* and *The Old-Time Cowhand,* he is a contributor to many western magazines and a member of the Texas Institute of Letters.

BENJAMIN A. BOTKIN. Well known as the editor of many popular collections of folklore, among them *A Treasury of American Folklore, A Treasury of Western Folklore* and *Sidewalks of America,* Mr. Botkin was for many years Library of Congress Fellow in Folklore and Chief of the Library's Archive of American Folk Song. He is a past-president of the American-Folklore Society and a contributing editor of *New York Folklore Quarterly.*

NATT NOYES DODGE. Regional Naturalist for the National Park Service with headquarters in Santa Fe, Mr. Dodge has written hundreds of articles for many publications and is the author of several books, including *The American Southwest.*

ROBERT EASTON. Mr. Easton, who was raised in small towns and on ranches, is co-author of *Lord of Beasts: The Saga of Buffalo Jones,* and a contributor to many national magazines. His stories have appeared in numerous anthologies, including *Out West* and *Great Tales of the American West.*

WAYNE GARD. A widely known historian of the frontier West, Mr. Gard is the author of such books as *Sam Bass, Frontier Justice, The Great Buffalo Hunt* and *The Chisholm Trail.* He is a contributor to national magazines, including *American Heritage,* and a Fellow of the Texas State Historical Association.

CLARENCE P. HORNUNG. Art director of this book and author of the text accompanying "A Gallery of Western Art," Mr. Hornung is an illustrator, graphic arts consultant and archivist of western Americana. He is the author of a half dozen books, among them *Wheels Across America.*

OSCAR LEWIS. A native of San Francisco, Mr. Lewis has to date written over thirty books of history or biography on western themes, among them *The Big Four, Silver Kings, California Heritage* and *Sagebrush Casinos.*

DALE MORGAN. An authority on western history in general and on fur trade, exploration and overland emigration in particular, Mr. Morgan has published articles and reviews in numerous historical magazines and has written articles on the West for *Encyclopaedia Britannica* and *Encyclopedia Americana.* His books include *Jedediah Smith and the Opening of the West* and *The West of William Ashley.* He is a Fellow of the Utah State Historical Society, Associate Historical Consultant to the Navajo Tribe and currently Editor of the Bancroft Library, University of California.

DON RUSSELL. Known to many as editor of *The Westerners Brand Book,* Chicago, Mr. Russell is also senior associate editor of *New Standard Encyclopedia.* He is the author of *The Lives and Legends of Buffalo Bill, One Hundred and Three Fights and Scrimmages: The Story of General Reuben F. Bernard* and a contributor to such publications as *Dictionary of American History, Encyclopedia Americana* and numerous historical reviews.

OSCAR OSBURN WINTHER. Professor of History and Associate Dean of the Graduate School at Indiana University, Professor Winther is author or editor of ten books on the West, including *The Great Northwest, The Old Oregon Country, Via Western Express and Stagecoach* and *A Friend of the Mormons.*

608